OXFORD CONSTITUTIONAL THEORY

Series Editors:
Martin Loughlin, John P. McCormick, and Neil Walker

Popular Sovereignty in Early Modern Constitutional Thought

OXFORD CONSTITUTIONAL THEORY

Series Editors:
Martin Loughlin, John P. McCormick, and Neil Walker

Oxford Constitutional Theory has rapidly established itself as the primary point of reference for theoretical reflections on the growing interest in constitutions and constitutional law in domestic, regional and global contexts. The majority of the works published in the series are monographs that advance new understandings of their subject. But the series aims to provide a forum for further innovation in the field by also including well-conceived edited collections that bring a variety of perspectives and disciplinary approaches to bear on specific themes in constitutional thought and by publishing English translations of leading monographs in constitutional theory that have originally been written in languages other than English.

ALSO AVAILABLE IN THE SERIES

The Cultural Defense of Nations A Liberal Theory of Majority Rights
Liav Orgad

The Cosmopolitan Constitution
Alexander Somek

The Structure of Pluralism
Victor M. Muniz-Fraticelli

Constitutional Courts and Deliberative Democracy
Conrado Hübner Mendes

Fault Lines of Globalization Legal Order and the Politics of A-Legality
Hans Lindahl

The Cosmopolitan State
H Patrick Glenn

After Public Law
Edited by Cormac Mac Amhlaigh, Claudio Michelon, and Neil Walker

The Three Branches A Comparative Model of Separation of Powers
Christoph Möllers

The Global Model of Constitutional Rights
Kai Möller

The Twilight of Constitutionalism?
Edited by Petra Dobner and Martin Loughlin

Beyond Constitutionalism The Pluralist Structure of Postnational Law
Nico Krisch

Constituting Economic and Social Rights
Katharine G. Young

Constitutional Referendums The Theory and Practice of Republican Deliberation
Stephen Tierney

Constitutional Fragments Societal Constitutionalism and Globalization
Gunther Teubner

Popular Sovereignty in Early Modern Constitutional Thought

Daniel Lee

University of California, Berkeley

OXFORD
UNIVERSITY PRESS

OXFORD
UNIVERSITY PRESS

Great Clarendon Street, Oxford, OX2 6DP,
United Kingdom

Oxford University Press is a department of the University of Oxford. It furthers the University's objective of excellence in research, scholarship, and education by publishing worldwide. Oxford is a registered trade mark of Oxford University Press in the UK and in certain other countries

Impression: 1

First Edition published in 2016

Published in the United States of America by Oxford University Press
198 Madison Avenue, New York, NY 10016, United States of America

British Library Cataloguing in Publication Data
Data available

Library of Congress Control Number: 2015960856

ISBN 978–0–19–874516–7

Printed and bound by
CPI Group (UK) Ltd, Croydon, CR0 4YY

For Caleb

Acknowledgements

This book began as my dissertation at Princeton, which I originally conceived as a study investigating theories of popular resistance and constitutional change in early modern political thought. In the earliest stages of my graduate studies, I envisioned the dissertation as a study of radical Monarchomach tracts, but I gradually observed that what united them was the shared technical language by which these writers investigated the idea that the people must always be regarded as the sovereign power undergirding institutions of public authority. That language was the juridical science of Roman law, even today perhaps the least studied of the major classical sources shaping modern political, social, and legal thought. Although it was not my original intention to devote my studies to the Roman law tradition, it became the natural consequence of the early choices I made as a graduate student.

For this reason, it is, I think, proper to begin by expressing my gratitude to those who first guided me in making those choices. I give my sincerest thanks first to Philip Pettit, who not only supervised, with the greatest patience and care, the original dissertation from which this book developed, but provided the occasion sparking my interest in the problem of popular sovereignty in the first place, in graduate seminars on the topic of the people and the polity, as well as on Hobbes. His work remains for me, as it does for so many others, an inspirational model of what political theory can be, and I can only hope he will see this book as a small token of thanks for all that he has done for me during my studies and in my career. I also wish to thank Alan Patten, Melissa Lane, and Steve Macedo, for their valuable guidance and generosity, as well as Bill Jordan and Paul Sigmund for originally introducing me to the world of medieval legal history and medieval political thought.

Over the years, I have accumulated many substantial moral debts in preparing this book, and I am deeply grateful to the many friends and colleagues, who have generously given not only their time and expertise in providing valuable advice and feedback on this project, but also encouragement and reassurance when I needed it most: Cliff Ando, Ryan Balot, Ronnie Beiner, Teresa Bejan, Annabel Brett, Joe Canning, Joe Carens, Simone Chambers, Kathleen Davis, Charlie Donahue, Julian Franklin, Ralph Giesey, Kinch Hoekstra, David Johnston, Rebecca Kingston, Peggy Kohn, Laurent Mayali, Ben McKean, Sankar Muthu, Cliff Orwin, Evan Oxman, Tom Poole, Arthur Ripstein, Jon Robinson, Magnus Ryan, Melissa Schwartzberg, Andrew Sepielli, Quentin Skinner, Johann Sommerville, Simon Stern, Benjamin Straumann, Richard Tuck, Nadia Urbinati, and Melissa Williams. I owe, in addition, special thanks to Ken Pennington and David Dyzenhaus who kindly agreed to read through the manuscript and for leading discussion in a tremendously helpful manuscript workshop generously sponsored by the Department of Political Science at the University of Toronto. I have also benefited greatly from the opportunity to present various chapters of this book to seminars and colloquia, and I wish to thank both my hosts and audience members at Cambridge University, Columbia University, European University Institute, London School of Economics, University of Chicago, the Centre for Ethics and Faculty of Law in the University of Toronto, and the University Center for Human Values at Princeton University. I am also sincerely grateful to the superb graduate research assistants at Toronto and Berkeley who have aided me in various ways in the preparation of this study: Jason Aaron Brown, Alexander Kirby, Sibbyl Nickerson, and Mauricio Suchowlansky. Needless to say, I remain entirely responsible for the shortcomings and errors, which are, no doubt, to be found in the following pages.

I could not have written this book without the generous financial support of various institutions, and I am honored to name them here. These include the University Center for Human Values at Princeton University, the Master and Fellows of Trinity College, Cambridge, the Centre for Ethics of the University of Toronto, and the Social Sciences and Humanities Research Council. I am especially grateful to the Columbia Society of Fellows for electing me to the Mellon Fellowship, which enabled me to make use of the outstanding textual resources held in the Columbia University libraries.

For better or worse, scholarship in the history of constitutional thought and legal history has become increasingly dependent upon digitized texts. Having now spent some years navigating through the world of rare books and early printed materials, I am starting to appreciate the lament intoned by past mentors that something truly valuable is lost in studying these texts through the digital medium. For this reason, I must express special thanks to the librarians and curators of various collections who, over the years, have helped me locate and handle the various sources I needed to consult for this study: Consuelo Dutschke of the Rare Books and Manuscripts Library at Columbia University, Sabrina Sondhi of the Special Collections of the Arthur W. Diamond Library at Columbia Law School, P.J. Carefoote of the Thomas P. Fisher Rare Books Library at the University of Toronto, Sandy Paul of the Wren Library at Trinity College, Cambridge, Stephen Ferguson of the Department of Rare Books and Special Collections at Princeton University, and Jennifer Nelson of the Robbins Collection in the Law Library of Boalt Hall, University of California, Berkeley. I am especially grateful to the Robbins Collection for permission to use a reproduction of the *Arbor Iurisdictionum*, or "tree of jurisdictions," from a 1544 edition of Bartolus' *Commentaria* on the *Digestum Vetus* on the cover of this book. In this regard, I feel it is most proper to convey my very special thanks to Tony Grafton who first impressed upon me during my graduate studies the discipline and patience required for this kind of scholarship. I can only hope that this book, even if it ultimately fails to reach the very high standard of scholarship that he has always expected and demanded of me, at least begins to approach it.

I also wish to acknowledge gratefully the editors and publishers of the following publications for granting permission to incorporate the following works into this book.

- "Private Law Models for Public Law Concepts: The Roman Law Theory of *Dominium* and the Monarchomach Doctrine of Popular Sovereignty" in *The Review of Politics* 70 (2008).
- "Office Is a Thing Borrowed: Jean Bodin on the Right of Offices and Seigneurial Government" in *Political Theory* 41 (2013).

- "Roman Law, German Liberties, and the Constitution of the Holy Roman Empire" to Volume I of *Freedom and the Construction of Europe*, edited by Quentin Skinner and Martin Van Gelderen (Cambridge, 2013).
- "Popular Liberty, Princely Government, and the Roman Law in Hugo Grotius's *De Jure Belli ac Pacis*," *Journal of the History of Ideas* 72 (2011).

Finally, I want to thank the outstanding editorial staff at Oxford University Press for their support of this project, as well as the series editors for originally considering my proposal. I am, above all, the extraordinarily fortunate beneficiary of the expert advice and guidance offered by Natasha Flemming and Elinor Shields, and I remain ever grateful for their support.

But I reserve my greatest thanks, and thanks of a different sort, for my family. My wife, Rebecca Wiseman Lee, has heard and read more than her fair share about sovereignty and Roman law, much more than she probably ever cared to hear. Not only has she read substantial parts of the manuscript and provided expert advice on it, she has been a steady source of love and support, especially when I needed it most. I owe her so much more than she can ever know. My son, Caleb Wiseman Lee, was born just three days before Oxford University Press had sent me the readers' reports on the manuscript. My memories of writing and rewriting this book will, as a result, forever remain connected to my memories of becoming a father. Many of the pages that follow were written in the sleepless daze of the pre-dawn hours while stirring and heating countless bottles of formula, holding Caleb in his swaddle, and, on not a few occasions, imploring Caleb to return to sleep. No doubt, I will have, despite my very best effort, made more than a few errors in judgment, for which I take complete responsibility. But as much as raising a child has been, and continues to be, a transformative and humbling experience, so too, I have learned, has been writing a book, and I am thankful to Caleb for teaching me the virtues required for both of these journeys. With hearfelt devotion, I am proud to dedicate this work to my son.

Daniel Lee
Berkeley, California

Contents

List of Abbreviations

Alciato	Andrea Alciato, *Opera Omnia*, 4 Vols. (Basel: Thomas Guarinus, 1582) [*Commentaria in Digesta, seu Pandectas Iuris Civilis* and *Paradoxa Libri VI*]
Azo	Azo, *Summa Azonis Locuples Iuris Civilis Thesaurus* (Venice, 1566); Azo, *Azonis Summa* (Lyon, 1557; reprinted Frankfurt am Main, 1968)
Baldus	Baldus de Ubaldis, *Commentaria*, 9 Vols. (Venice, 1577)
Bartolus	Bartolus of Sassoferrato, *Omnia Quae Extant Opera*, 10 Vols. (Venice, 1590)
C.	*Corpus Iuris Civilis: Codex Iustinianus*, ed. Paul Krueger (Berlin, 1954)
C. [Vulgate]	*Codicis*, ed. Denis Godefroy (Lyon, 1604)
Commonweale	Jean Bodin, *Six Bookes of a Commonweale* [Facsimile reprint of the English translation of Richard Knolles, 1606] ed. Kenneth Douglas McRae (Cambridge: Harvard University Press, 1962)
D. [English]	*The Digest of Justinian*, 4 Vols., trans. Alan Watson (Philadelphia: University of Pennsylvania Press, 1985)
D. [Latin]	*Corpus Iuris Civilis: Iustiniani Digesta*, ed. Theodor Mommsen and Paul Krueger (Berlin: Weidmann, 1870)
D. [Vulgate]	*Digestum Vetus seu Pandectarum Iuris Civilis*, ed. Denis Godefroy (Lyon, 1604) [=D.1.1.1-24.2.11]
D. [Vulgate]	*Infortiatum seu Pandectarum Iuris Civilis*, ed. Denis Godefroy (Lyon, 1604) [=D.24.3.1-38.17.10]
D. [Vulgate]	*Digestum Novum seu Pandectarum Iuris Civilis*, ed. Denis Godefroy (Lyon, 1604) [=D.39.1.1-50.17.211]
De Cive	Thomas Hobbes, *On the Citizen*, ed. Richard Tuck and Michael Silverthorne (Cambridge: Cambridge University Press, 1998)
De Cive 1647	Thomas Hobbes, *Elementa Philosophica de Cive* (Amsterdam: Elzevir, 1647)
De Corpore Politico	Thomas Hobbes, *De Corpore Politico: Or the Elements of Law, Moral and Politick* (London: Printed for J. Martin and J. Ridley, 1650)
De Iure Belli	Hugo Grotius, *De Ivre Belli ac Pacis Libri Tres* (Paris: Nicolaus Buon, 1625)
De Republica	Jean Bodin, *De Republica Libri Six* (Paris: Jacques Du Puys, 1586)
Donellus	Hugues Doneau, in *Opera Omnia*, 12 Vols. (Rome: typis J. Salviucci, 1828) [*Commentaria de Iure Civili*]
Duarenus	François La Douaren, *Francisci Duareni Opera Omnia*, 4 Vols. (Lucca: typis J. Rochii, 1765)

Dumoulin	Charles Dumoulin, *Omnia Quae Extant Opera*, 5 Vols. (Paris: Damian Foucault, 1681) [*Commentaria in Consuetudines Parienses*]
Francogallia	François Hotman, *Francogallia*, ed. Ralph Giesey, trans. J.H.M. Salmon (New York: Cambridge University Press, 1972)
Gaius	*Institutes of Gaius*, ed. Francis de Zulueta (Oxford: Clarendon Press, 1953)
Glossa Ordinaria	[See the Vulgate editions of 'C.,' 'D.,' and 'Inst.']
Inst.	*Institutes of Justinian*, ed. J.B. Moyle (Oxford: Oxford University Press, 1913)
Inst. [Vulgate]	*Institutionum sive Primorum Totius Iurisprudentiae Elementorum*, ed. Denis Godefroy (Lyon, 1604)
Iuris Universi Distributio	Jean Bodin, *Exposé du Droit Universel*, ed. Lucien Jerphagnon, Simone Goyard-Fabre, and René-Marie Rampelberg (Paris: Presses Universitaires de France, 1985)
Leviathan	Thomas Hobbes, *Leviathan*, 3 Vols., ed. Noel Malcolm (Oxford: Clarendon Press, 2012)
Method	Jean Bodin, *Method for the Easy Comprehension of History*, trans. Beatrice Reynolds (New York: Norton, 1945) [Translation of *Methodus ad Facilem Historiarum Cognitionem*]
Methodus	Jean Bodin, *Methodus ad Facilem Historiarum Cognitionem* (Paris: Martin le Jeune, 1566)
Nov.	*Corpus Iuris Civilis: Iustiniani Novellae*, ed. Rudolf Schoell (Berlin: Weidmann, 1954)
Politica	Johannes Althusius, *Politica Methodice Digesta*, ed. Carl Friedrich (Cambridge: Harvard University Press, 1932)
République	Jean Bodin, *Six Livres de la République* (Paris: Jacques Du Puys, 1583)
Vindiciae	*Vindiciae Contra Tyrannos*, ed. and trans. George Garnett (New York: Cambridge University Press, 1994)
Vindiciae 1579	*Vindiciae Contra Tyrannos* (Edinburgh [Basel], 1579)
War and Peace	Hugo Grotius, *The Rights of War and Peace*, ed. Richard Tuck (Indianapolis: Liberty Fund, 2005).

Introduction: Popular Sovereignty, Constitutionalism, and the Civil Law

CONSTITUTIONALISM AND POPULAR SOVEREIGNTY: LIMITED GOVERNMENT AND UNLIMITED AUTHORITY

Few doctrines have become as foundational to modern constitutional theory as the doctrine of popular sovereignty, the notion that the ultimate source of all authority exercised through the public institutions of the state originates in the people. It is a doctrine central to the vision of modern constitutional government articulated by its most influential theorists such as Locke, Montesquieu, Rousseau, Madison, and Sieyès.

Popular sovereignty, however, poses a serious conceptual problem for constitutionalism, and that is because, despite their apparently mutual affinity, the two ideas are fundamentally at odds with each other. Constitutionalism is, after all, a political philosophy of limited government. It is a body of legal and political thought united by the common idea that the exercise of public authority, whether democratic or otherwise, ought to be limited and regulated somehow by impartial law.[1] The nature of these legal limitations are, of course, diverse in form: they might range from institutional "binding devices" such as the separation of powers, use of supermajorities, and judicial review of democratically enacted legislation to the entrenchment of legal rights and the recognition of some scheme of higher legal norms set beyond the scope of the ordinary institutionally circumscribed political activity of democratic majorities.[2] But what all these various features of constitutionalism have in common is the core normative principle that public authority, in all its forms, must somehow be limited and circumscribed within the bounds of law.

[1] Jeremy Waldron doubts that even this basic idea can be considered the unifying core idea of constitutionalism. "Constitutionalism – A Skeptical View," *Contemporary Debates in Political Philosophy*, ed. Thomas Christiano and John Christman (Malden, MA: Wiley-Blackwell, 2009). See, more generally, the essays in Petra Dobner and Martin Loughlin, ed., *The Twilight of Constitutionalism?* (Oxford: Oxford University Press, 2010).

[2] Jon Elster, *Ulysses Unbound: Studies in Rationality, Precommitment, and Constraints* (Cambridge: Cambridge University Press, 2000); Stephen Holmes, "Precommitment and the Paradox of Democracy," *Constitutionalism and Democracy*, ed. Jon Elster and Rune Slagstad (Cambridge: Cambridge University Press, 1988).

Popular sovereignty, by contrast, is fundamentally defined by the concept of *sovereignty*, the essential quality of which is its extralegal and extra-institutional quality. What makes the doctrine of popular sovereignty distinctive is the view that the "sovereign people" hold in reserve, outside the realm of constitutionally bound political activity, what is in effect an extraordinary or extralegal power that is, in theory, unlimited and absolute, superior to all other constituted forms of public authority.[3] It is, needless to say, a controversial—and some commentators suggest, a discredited—juristic theory of public authority, not least because it subjects the validity and rule of law to the unbound will of the popular sovereign, in a manner directly antithetical to the constitutionalist logic of legally limited government.[4]

The problem is this: How is it possible for such a doctrine of *unlimited* and absolute sovereignty to be, without contradiction, deployed in a theory intended to realize a state committed to just the opposite goal, *limited* government? Is it even intelligible to argue, as theorists of popular sovereignty endorse, that *limited* government can only be secured by postulating an *unlimited* form of popular power anterior or exterior to state institutions, precisely what constitutionalism does not allow? At first glance, it does not seem so. And this, one might argue, is because the very idea of popular sovereignty appears to militate directly against the core principle of constitutional limitations on the public authority it is intended to support.[5]

In light of this seemingly unavoidable tension—what has recently been called the "paradox of constitutionalism"—constitutional theorists have offered various strategies aimed at resolving this mutual hostility between the competing ideals of unlimited popular self-rule and constitutionalism.[6] One common solution simply proposes decoupling these two ideals from each other and expunging the doctrine of popular sovereignty altogether from constitutional inquiry, so that the modern project of realizing the constitutional state is treated as entirely independent of populist politics or an extralegal concept of constitution-authoring peoples.[7]

[3] Bonnie Honig, *Emergency Politics: Paradox, Law, Democracy* (Princeton: Princeton University Press, 2009); Andreas Kalyvas, *Democracy and the Politics of the Extraordinary* (Cambridge: Cambridge University Press, 2009); Andreas Kalyvas, "Popular Sovereignty, Democracy, and the Constituent Power," *Constellations* 12 (2005): 223–44. See also, more recently, Martin Loughlin, "The Concept of Constituent Power," *European Journal of Political Theory* 13 (2014): 218–37; Philip Pettit, *On the People's Terms: A Republican Theory and Model of Democracy* (Cambridge: Cambridge University Press, 2012), especially Ch. 5. The doctrine of popular sovereignty has particular importance in recent scholarship in American constitutional jurisprudence, such as Frank Michelman, "Constitutional Authorship by the People," *Notre Dame Law Review* 74 (1999); Akhil Amar, "Consent of the Governed: Constitutional Amendment Outside Article V," *Columbia Law Review* 94 (1994).

[4] Pavlos Eleftheriadis, "Law and Sovereignty," *Law and Philosophy* 29 (2010): 535–69.

[5] David Dyzenhaus, "Constitutionalism in an Old Key: Legality and Constituent Power," *Global Constitutionalism* 1 (2012): 229–60.

[6] Martin Loughlin and Neil Walker, ed., *The Paradox of Constitutionalism: Constituent Power and Constitutional Form* (Oxford: Oxford University Press, 2008).

[7] For a recent example of this strategy, Lars Vinx, "The Incoherence of Strong Popular Sovereignty," *International Journal of Constitutional Law* 11 (2013): 101–24. This decoupling becomes even more urgent

The suggestion is, of course, an old one and is informed, in part, by a deep-seated distrust of unstable popular majorities in settling constitutional questions and, more generally, a skepticism about the feasibility of popular self-rule. The worry here is that popular majorities can easily undo those very legal limitations that make limited government possible, especially those entrenched legal rights that protect unpopular minorities from the democratic tyranny of majorities.[8] If the constitutionalist goal is to limit and regulate the exercise of public authority, why bother at all, then, with such a troublesome notion as popular sovereignty, which can potentially undermine that very goal?

WHY POPULAR SOVEREIGNTY?

One way to answer this challenge might begin simply by conjecturing why a doctrine such as popular sovereignty had to be "invented" in the first place. For, if we understand the antecedent problem, to which popular sovereignty was originally thought to be the solution, we might arrive at a better understanding of its intended function in constitutional thought. The aim of this book is to offer an answer to this challenge. In so doing, I hope to show not only *why* popular sovereignty emerged in the history of constitutional thought but also *how* it was thought to fortify the constitutionalist aim of limiting and regulating public authority.

There is, to be sure, no shortage of accounts purporting to explain the origins of popular sovereignty in these terms.[9] Indeed, this study takes much of

at the level of supra-national global politics, where constitutional norms and institutions develop independently of democratic politics. Martin Loughlin, "What Is Constitutionalisation?" *The Twilight of Constitutionalism?* ed. Petra Dobner and Martin Loughlin (Oxford: Oxford University Press, 2010); Robert Keohane, Stephen Macedo, and Andrew Moravcsik, "Democracy-Enhancing Multilateralism," *International Organization* 63 (2009): 1–31.

[8] Classic statements of this worry in American legal scholarship can be found in the analysis of judicial review in a constitutional democracy: Alexander Bickel, *The Least Dangerous Branch: The Supreme Court at the Bar of Politics* (New Haven: Yale University Press, 1986); John Hart Ely, *Democracy and Distrust: A Theory of Judicial Review* (Cambridge: Harvard University Press, 1981). More recent defenses of the democracy-enhancing function of judicial review have been prompted by the novel theory of "popular constitutionalism," such as from Larry Kramer, *The People Themselves: Popular Constitutionalism and Judicial Review* (New York: Oxford University Press, 2005) and Mark Tushnet, "Popular Constitutionalism as Political Law," *Chicago-Kent Law Review* 81 (2006): 991–1006. These include Erwin Chemerinsky, "In Defense of Judicial Review: The Perils of Popular Constitutionalism," *University of Illinois Law Review* (2004). Related are, Christopher Eisgruber, *Constitutional Self-Government* (Cambridge: Harvard University Press, 2001) and Jeremy Waldron, *Law and Disagreement* (Oxford: Oxford University Press, 1999).

[9] A number of recent examples following this approach include Margaret Canovan, *The People* (Cambridge: Polity, 2005); Matthew Weinert, *Democratic Sovereignty* (New York: UCL Press, 2007); Adam Lupel, *Globalization and Popular Sovereignty: Democracy's Transnational Dilemma* (Oxford: Routledge, 2009); Ethan Putterman, *Rousseau, Law and the Sovereignty of the People* (Cambridge: Cambridge University Press, 2010); Geneviève Nootens, *Popular Sovereignty in the West: Polities, Contention, and Ideas* (London: Routledge, 2013). The doctrine of popular sovereignty has special meaning in the context of antebellum American legal history, where the doctrine, legalized in the Kansas-Nebraska Act, was crafted to protect the right of settlers in federal territories to decide the legality of slavery. Christian Fritz, *American Sovereigns: The People and America's Constitutionalist Tradition* (Cambridge: Cambridge University Press, 2008); Sean Wilentz, *The Rise of American Democracy: Jefferson to Lincoln* (New York: W.W. Norton, 2006); Georgina

its inspiration from this background of scholarship in the history of political thought. So before I lay out the fundamentals of my own argument in this book, let me begin first by outlining what I take to be a conventional view on the origins and purposes of popular sovereignty, which this book tries to recalibrate.

In this conventional narrative, popular sovereignty emerged—or, as one prominent historian of popular sovereignty put it, was "invented"—in early modernity in the constitutional struggles of the seventeenth century, primarily as a doctrine of opposition or resistance.[10] On this view, popular sovereignty emerged as a "criticism of absolutism" and functioned as a "critical tool to limit the power of government."[11] In short, popular *sovereignty* was thought to be nothing other than popular *resistance*.[12] Quite naturally, then, scholars focused their attention almost exclusively on radical popular discourses of rebellion and resistance to tyranny. Popular sovereignty has, as a result, been most often associated with the political thought surrounding radical movements, such as the Dutch Revolt, the English Revolution, the American Revolution, and the French Revolution. This is the case, for example, in Edmund Morgan's influential study on the doctrine, which locates the "invention" of popular sovereignty in England chiefly as a body of polemical thought framed as a radical response to theories of royal absolutism and divine right.

The notion of a sovereign people emerges, on these interpretations, almost as an afterthought, playing the role of the heroic agent of resistance to constrain the domination of the established legal and political order. Popular sovereignty was seen as a corrective *remedy* to perceived abuses of (almost always) royal power by showing that the people held in reserve at all times the capacity to contest and hold the governing authority accountable, an idea encapsulated in John Locke's revolutionary declaration that only "the people shall be judge" of the actions of their government, especially when it exercises a "power beyond right."[13]

Green, *The Majesty of the People: Popular Sovereignty and the Role of the Writer in the 1790s* (Oxford: Oxford University Press, 2014).

[10] Edmund Morgan, *Inventing the People: The Rise of Popular Sovereignty in England and America* (New York: W.W. Norton, 1989).

[11] Lupel, *Globalization and Popular Sovereignty* 15.

[12] Canovan, *The People* 14.

[13] John Locke, *Two Treatises of Government*, ed. Peter Laslett (Cambridge: Cambridge University Press, 1988) 427 [II, §240]. "Power beyond right" [e.g., II, §199] is Locke's operational definition of tyranny in the *Second Treatise*. Other early modern examples of this interpretation of popular sovereignty include George Buchanan, William Reynolds [Rossaeus], and George Lawson. See Francis Oakley, "On the Road from Constance to 1688: The Political Thought of John Major and George Buchanan," *Journal of British Studies* 1 (1962): 1–31; J.H.M. Salmon, "An Alternative Theory of Popular Resistance: Buchanan, Rossaeus, and Locke," *Renaissance and Revolt* (Cambridge: Cambridge University Press, 1987); Julian Franklin, *John Locke and the Theory of Sovereignty: Mixed Monarchy and the Right of Resistance in the Political Thought of the English Revolution* (Cambridge: Cambridge University Press, 1981). Classic accounts of this thesis include J.N. Figgis, *Studies of Political Thought from Gerson to Grotius* (Cambridge: Cambridge University Press, 1907) and Harold Laski, "Political Theory in the Later Middle Ages," *Cambridge Medieval History* (Cambridge: Cambridge University Press, 1911–36) 8:638.

The function of "the people" in these theories of popular sovereignty, such as in Buchanan, Lawson, and Locke, was not so much to *create* or *constitute* a new political order. Rather, it was to provide an Archimedean point to evaluate, from a critical distance removed from the fray of institutionalized politics, the legitimacy of an existing political order and, if necessary, to contest and reconstitute that political order. On this view, popular sovereignty was to be understood almost as "anti-political." The people do not govern directly, but merely create the conditions and the institutions by which others could govern on their behalf. Here, the sovereignty of the people merely lurks in the shadows and in the background, as one scholar has described, like a phantom or "ghostly body politic."[14] The people take no active political role in governing the state, but rather, a "contestatory" role. Popular sovereignty indeed requires them to be *disengaged* from political activity, as the people become silent onlookers subjecting holders of public authority to an unending panoptical surveillance from the outside looking in.

What makes the people, however, the bearers of sovereignty, supreme even over their constituted government, is the trump card they are always presumed to hold in reserve, and that is the extralegal capacity of the people to dissolve the constituted authority, by radical means if necessary. Like a *deus ex machina*, the people appear only at discrete "constitutional moments" when the machinery of the existing legal and political order is in need of repair. Once that task is completed, they return to a state of constitutional hibernation to become, as Richard Tuck described it, a sleeping sovereign.[15]

CONSTITUTIONALISM WITHOUT STATES: MEDIEVAL CONSTITUTIONALISM AND THE PROBLEM OF PLURALISTIC AUTHORITY

This, in brief, is how popular sovereignty has traditionally been reconciled with the constitutional ideal of limited government. The argument envisages the proper constitutional role of "the people" chiefly as an extrainstitutional *limit-imposing* force, acting as an external agent of constitutional contestation, change, and reform—above all, in cases where the exercise of authority degenerates into tyranny. It posits an outer limit on public authority by fixing constitutional boundaries policed directly by the people, rather than indirectly by, say, courts.[16]

[14] Joshua Miller, "The Ghostly Body Politic: The Federalist Papers and Popular Sovereigtny," *Political Theory* 16 (1988): 99–119.

[15] On "constitutional moments" and popular sovereignty, Bruce Ackerman, *We the People*, Vol. 1, *Foundations* (Cambridge: Belknap Press of Harvard University, 1993). On the metaphor of the sleeping sovereign, see Richard Tuck's Seeley Lectures, *The Sleeping Sovereign: The Invention of Modern Democracy* (Cambridge: Cambridge University Press, 2016).

[16] For example, Richard Bellamy, *Political Constitutionalism: A Republican Defence of the Constitutionality of Democracy* (Cambridge: Cambridge University Press, 2007).

It is, of course, a sensible argument for popular sovereignty, if one understands the task of constitutional theory to be one of specifying and imposing *limits* on constituted public authority. But it is often forgotten that constitutional theory, historically, has concerned more than just specifying *limits* on public authority. It concerned the investigation of a more fundamental question that was common to both political philosophy and public law: What *constitutes* public authority, in the first place?[17]

Despite the obvious importance of this question, modern constitutionalism has generally tended to shy away from answering or even acknowledging it, focusing instead on the more practical question of limiting such authority. This shift in focus was possible, I argue, only because there has been, for several centuries now, since at least the Enlightenment, a near-universal acceptance of what the *target* of constitutional limitations must be—that is, the impersonal sovereign nation-state and its institutional structure of a territorially bound public authority. Needless to say, recognition of the sovereign nation-state as the proper target and setting for designing constitutional limitations has transformed much of modern constitutionalism fundamentally into a *state-centered* theory, so much so, that it is practically impossible to treat the topic of constitutionalism without some reference to state authority and state institutions. Constitutionalism is so parasitic on the idea of the state that it has become, in essence, a body of thought concerning the "constitutional state," or what German jurists have traditionally called the *Rechtsstaat*.[18] At least one commentator has suggested that a viable constitutionalism even *requires* a notion of the sovereign state.[19]

There is an important consequence to this recognition of the state in modern constitutional theory. Since public authority is already assumed *ex ante* to be "monopolized" and defined by formal institutions of the state, modern theorists of constitutionalism can conveniently avoid entirely the more elementary question of how public authority is constituted. In the modern age of state-centered politics, there is rarely any need to do so, except in those extraordinary moments of constitutional emergency where the very authority of the state is itself questioned. Since, at most times, the authority of the state could safely be assumed and treated almost as a universal axiom of modern constitutional theorizing, constitutionalism could instead focus entirely on how to *limit* or *control* (whether by ordinary or extraordinary means) an already-existing and antecedently constituted public authority, rather than deal with the more vexing and potentially disruptive task of explaining how such an authority is to be legitimately constituted in the first place.

[17] In this respect, my approach follows the spirit of Martin Loughlin, *Foundations of Public Law* (Oxford: Oxford University Press, 2010) 12 and 231–37 in his understanding of "political right."

[18] Nick Barber, *The Constitutional State* (Oxford: Oxford University Press, 2011).

[19] Jeremy Rabkin, *Law Without Nations: Why Constitutional Government Requires Sovereign States* (Princeton: Princeton University Press, 2005).

A major problem arises, however, when the authority of the state itself is brought into question and when the very legitimacy of the state and its central institutions can no longer be safely assumed. If the state *cannot* be regarded as the site of public authority, who or what is a constitutionalist supposed to bind or limit? This is, incidentally, a question of central importance to the contemporary understanding of the crisis surrounding the modern constitutional state in an age of global politics.[20] Given the numerous new challenges to the traditional authority of the state in an increasingly globalized and pluralistic world, it is no longer feasible to treat constitutionalism solely in terms of domestic limitations on constituted structures of public authority defined within the boundaries of the state.

Constitutional theorists are, thus, faced with a crisis of constitutionalism, precisely because the authority that their theory is supposed to limit is no longer readily visible as a uniform target. With the transformation of the Westphalian sovereign state in the era of global politics and international law, public authority itself has been decentered and dispersed, leading one commentator to describe sovereign orders as nothing more than "organized hypocrisy."[21] We are witnessing, as Neil Walker has put it, the very process of "sovereignty in transition" unfolding what may be described speculatively as a post-modern and post-national politics without sovereignty.[22] In these circumstances, the constitutional doctrine of popular sovereignty seems not only incoherent, by assuming axiomatically the very existence of that which must be explained—that is, public authority organized and expressed in the modern form of the bounded sovereign state. It also seems obsolete and even regressive, by crafting a theory that envisages the agent of resistance and change within the modern constitutional state specifically in terms of a dubious notion of the "people"—or nation, *gens, Volk*—as a homogeneous collective actor, which belies what John Rawls once called the unavoidable modern fact of pluralism.[23]

Despite its growing contemporary relevance in international law and politics, the problem is, by no means, a new one. On the contrary, the question of constituting public authority in the absence of the state was *the* major question of constitutional theory prior to the seventeenth century, disagreement over which yielded not only a steady stream of constitutional and political thought, but, too often, horrifyingly bloody consequences in terms of religious, civil, and even "private" feudal wars. The prime reason for this was that there was no *uniform* concept of the "state" in the pre-modern context.[24] Indeed, the idea

[20] Nico Krisch, *Beyond Constitutionalism* (Oxford: Oxford University Press, 2012).

[21] Stephen Krasner, *Sovereignty: Organized Hypocrisy* (Princeton: Princeton University Press, 1999).

[22] Neil Walker, *Sovereignty in Transition* (Oxford: Hart, 2003). See also Christopher Bickerton, Philip Cunliffe, and Alexander Gourevitch, ed., *Politics without Sovereignty: A Critique of International Relations* (London: UCL Press, 2007); James Martel, "Can There Be Politics Without Sovereignty: Arendt, Derrida and the Question of Sovereign Inevitability," *Law, Culture, and the Humanities* 6 (2010): 153–66.

[23] John Rawls, *Political Liberalism* (New York: Columbia University Press, 1993).

[24] Even the word, "state" (and cognates in other European languages, such as *lo stato, l'état, der Staat*) as a site of public authority is a relatively recent notion in the history of ideas, which, as Quentin Skinner

of public authority itself was actively contested. There was no settled and shared understanding of what legitimate public authority was and how it was constituted.

To be clear, this is not to suggest that there were *no* theories of public authority in pre-modern thought at all. If anything, the problem was just the opposite: there were *too many* theories of public authority in the later medieval and early modern context, none of which commanded uniform obligation or generated universal acceptance.[25] Indeed, this diversity and proliferation of opinions on notions of public authority, much of which lacked the clarity and precision of modern analysis in public law, was precisely the problem: there was no consensus on the structure of public authority and, more importantly, what made it legitimate. Until such a uniform theory of public authority could be settled and recognized in common, set beyond the scope of active contestation, the project of constitutionalism—limiting and regulating the exercise of public authority by law—would have to remain fundamentally incomplete.

Of course, one might ask: "Couldn't theorists simply craft a constitutionalism *without* a notion of the state?" They certainly tried. Indeed, as the eminent historian of constitutional thought, Charles Howard McIlwain, once tried to show (against those who maintained that constitutionalism was a distinctive product of modernity), there was no shortage of constitutional ideas in Classical Antiquity and especially in the Middle Ages, all forged in the absence of the sovereign authority of the state.[26]

The problem was that, despite this apparent flourishing of constitutional ideas, they were actually not all that well suited to the task of limiting authority. Part of the reason for this is that there was no conceptual space in medieval constitutional thought for a robust and stable notion of institutional checks,

has shown, is hardly uniform or uncontested. Part of the difficulty is that the concept signified by "state" was, in the later medieval and early modern context, connected to a variety of related terms in Latin, such as *respublica, regnum, civitas, politeia*, and most significantly, *populus* or *universitas*. Quentin Skinner, "A Genealogy of the Modern State," *Proceedings of the British Academy* 162 (2009) 325–70; Quentin Skinner, "From the State of Princes to the Person of the State," *Vision of Politics*, Vol. 2, *Renaissance Virtues* (Cambridge: Cambridge University Press, 2002).

[25] See, in general, Walter Ullmann, *The Growth of Papal Government in the Middle Ages* (London: Methuen, 1962); Brian Tierney, *Foundations of the Conciliarist Theory: The Contribution of the Medieval Canonists from Gratian to the Great Schism* (Cambridge: Cambridge University Press, 1955); Michael Wilks, *The Problem of Sovereignty in the Later Middle Ages* (Cambridge: Cambridge University Press, 1963); Francis Oakley, *The Political Thought of Pierre d'Ailly: The Voluntarist Tradition* (New Haven: Yale University Press, 1964); Antony Black, *Monarchy and Community: Political Ideas in the Later Conciliar Controversy, 1430-1450* (Cambridge: Cambridge University Press, 1970); Francesco Calasso, *I Glossatori e la Teoria della Sovranità* (Milan: Giuffre, 1951); Walter Ullmann, "The Development of the Medieval Idea of Sovereignty," *English Historical Review* 64 (1949): 1–33; Kenneth Pennington, *The Prince and the Law, 1200–1600* (Berkeley: University of California Press, 1993).

[26] Charles Howard McIlwain, *Constitutionalism Ancient and Modern* (Ithaca: Cornell University Press, 1947). Classic studies of "medieval constitutionalism" include Ewarts Lewis, *Medieval Political Ideas* (New York: A.A. Knopf, 1954); R.W. Carlyle and A.J. Carlyle, *History of Mediaeval Political Theory in the West*, 6 vols. (London: Blackwood and Sons, 1903–38); Otto von Gierke, *Political Theories of the Middle Ages*, trans. F.W. Maitland (Cambridge: Cambridge University Press, 1900); Fritz Kern, *Kingship and Law in the Middle Ages*, trans. S.B. Chrimes (Oxford: Blackwell, 1939).

balances, and safeguards to enforce limitations on authority.[27] Medieval theorists, of course, identified higher law norms which were thought to regulate the conduct of princes, such as natural law, divine law, and fundamental law, as well as general principles of equitable rule such as the *utilitas publica* or, in the case of the Papal monarchy, the *status ecclesiae*.[28] But without a formal mechanism for control in cases where such norms were violated, the best medieval theorists could do was entreat rulers to subject themselves to the law.[29]

But there was a more compelling reason for the difficulties, and ultimate failure, of medieval constitutionalism. Without a notion of the state as the uncontested center of public authority carving out a space for politics, constitutional theorists were faced with a constantly moving target. Indeed, supposing that constitutionalism was a theory of *limiting* authority, the problem here was that it was still not clear who—or what—was supposed to be limited. This was especially problematic in medieval thought, where concepts of authority were commingled together with notions of private right, so much so, that a princely ruler might licitly treat his right to rule as part of his private patrimony. Authority, in medieval legal thought, was in this sense "privatized" or "personalized," treated just as if public power were any other object of private property.

This confused notion of authority presented an unavoidable dilemma for medieval constitutional theorists. Should constitutional limitations target *persons* holding and exercising authority, or should they target the *institutions* empowering persons to exercise such authority? The question raised by this distinction was a critically important one because it carved out two mutually exclusive strategies of constitutional limitation, either as a strategy of limiting *personal* authority or as a strategy of limiting *institutional* authority.[30] Consequently, medieval constitutionalism could be nothing other than pluralistic, and this precisely because authority itself was understood, likewise, to be pluralistic in form. There was no "monopoly" of authority. There could not, therefore, be a uniform grand strategy of constitutional limitations until the antecedent problem of pluralistic authority was first addressed.

[27] There was, of course, a robust and technically sophisticated notion of rule of law and due process in medieval jurisprudence, as numerous studies in medieval legal history have demonstrated, such as Pennington, *Prince and the Law*; James Brundage, *Medieval Origins of the Legal Profession: Canonists, Civilians, and Courts* (Chicago: University of Chicago Press, 2008); Manlio Bellomo, *Common Legal Past of Europe, 1000–1800*, trans. Lydia Cochrane (Washington: Catholic University of America Press, 1995); Brian Tierney, *Religion, Law, and the Growth of Constitutional Thought, 1150–1650* (Cambridge: Cambridge University Press, 1982).

[28] On the *status ecclesiae* and *utilitas publica* and the related term, *status regni*, as normative limits on princely authority, see Pennington, *Prince and the Law* 278, Tierney, *Foundations of the Conciliar Theory* 50–53, 58–59, 194–95, and Gaines Post, *Studies in Medieval Legal Thought: Public Law and the State, 1100–1322* (Princeton: Princeton University Press, 1964) 241–309.

[29] Brian Tierney, "Bracton on Government," *Speculum* 38 (1963).

[30] Quentin Skinner once observed that, in the absence of sovereign states, "what matters most in good government is not the fabric of institutions, but rather the spirit and outlook of the men who run them." *Foundations of Modern Political Thought*, Vol. 1, *The Renaissance* (Cambridge: Cambridge University Press, 1978) 46.

This background of medieval constitutionalism defined what was, certainly by the sixteenth century, seen to be the most urgent task of early modern constitutional thought—indeed, it is against this background that the chief early modern theorists of state and sovereignty, such as Bodin, Grotius, and Pufendorf, begin to disentangle these confused notions of private rights and public powers in order to construct a selfstanding science of public law and sovereign authority.[31] Since it would potentially be a more effective constitutional strategy to target and limit one recognized unitary source of authority, rather than many scattered, plural, conflicting, and even quasi-independent sources of legal authority, it was thought that the optimal strategy would be, as a preliminary conceptual task, to gather these scattered, pluralistic centers of authority (whether feudal, provincial, ecclesiastical, corporatist, or otherwise) and tie them together as members of one system, even before addressing the issue of limiting and controlling authority. In this context, what was urgently needed was not so much a *regulative theory* of public authority, but rather, something more foundational, a *constitutive theory* of public authority.[32]

THE POPULAR CONSTITUTION OF PUBLIC AUTHORITY

The argument of this book is that the doctrine of popular sovereignty was crafted as a *constitutive* theory, the chief task of which was to elucidate, against this medieval background, the *constitution* of public authority in the modern form of the unitary state. In this respect, popular sovereignty was "invented" not so much as a regulative doctrine of opposition or resistance, designed to *limit* or "regulate" some *existing* public authority, but rather as a constitutive doctrine of legitimation, designed to show, in a world without states, what properly *constitutes* such public authority in the first place.[33] On this view, the doctrine of popular sovereignty played a unique role in early modern constitutional theory, by presenting a distinctive solution to the background problem of pluralistic, overlapping, and conflicting sites of authorities, which plagued later medieval legal thought.[34]

As a constitutive concept, sovereignty in all its forms—and, above all, popular sovereignty—was regarded, by its adherents, as intrinsic to, and inseparable from, the concept of the state and its authority.[35] It was, as Jean Bodin would

[31] This is the argument offered, for example, in Loughlin's account of the origins of public law as an autonomous area of "political jurisprudence" or *droit publique*. See *Foundations of Public Law* 58–59.

[32] I borrow from the Kantian distinction between *constitutive* and *regulative* principles. I thank Arthur Ripstein for this suggestion. On the constitutive and regulative distinction, see John Searle, *Speech Acts* (Cambridge: Cambridge University Press, 1969) 33, and John Searle, *The Construction of Social Reality* (New York: Free Press, 1995).

[33] Joel Colon-Rios, "The Legitimacy of the Juridical: Constituent Power, Democracy, and the Limits of Constitutional Reform," *Osgoode Hall Law Journal* 48 (2010): 199–245.

[34] McIlwain, *Constitutionalism Ancient and Modern* 83.

[35] Cp. Loughlin, *Foundations of Public Law* 184. Another common confusion is the distinction drawn between "ruler sovereignty," "state sovereignty," and "popular sovereignty," as for example in Nootens,

describe it in his *Six Livres de la République*, what would become the single most important early modern text on state sovereignty, "the true foundation and hinge whereupon the state of a [commonweale] turneth: whereof all the magistrats, lawes, and ordinances dependeth; and by whose force and power, all colleges, corporations, families, and citisens are brought as it were into one perfect bodie of a Commonweale."[36] Sovereignty was, for them, that which must antecedently be assumed and accepted as an axiom in order for the state, as a unitary system of public authority, to even be possible. It was what made the state different from other forms of human associations, such as the family and legal corporations. To put the same point differently: without sovereignty, there could be no state.

But as foundational as sovereignty was, functioning as a constitutive concept undergirding a theory of state, there was less agreement concerning the observable *form* of sovereignty. Indeed, it was, at least in the initial investigations of the concept, regarded a comparatively less urgent matter. *Who* the sovereign was seems to have mattered far less than the question of *what* the function or purpose of sovereignty actually was. Thus, it was simply assumed that the constitutive function of sovereignty could be carried out, in principle, by a prince, just as it could with equal validity be carried out by a people, provided that the bearer of sovereignty—whether a prince or people or otherwise—were considered as one indivisible entity with a unitary will and personality. So long as this critical *proviso* was observed, sovereignty could be expressed and manifested in any one of numerous possible forms.

This indivisibility *proviso*, however, itself became an independent source of controversy in the analysis of sovereignty because theorists contested the view that the form of sovereignty—often rendered as the *forma imperii*, or even *status reipublicae* in early modern theory—could be left open and indeterminate—what has recently been called "constitutional indifferentism."[37] As we shall see, early modern theorists of sovereignty such as François Hotman and Johannes Althusius, while accepting the basic necessity of sovereignty as a constitutive doctrine of the state, nevertheless rejected the "indifferentist" view. Instead, theoretical debates on sovereignty, especially beginning in the seventeenth century, tied together sovereignty's substance and form, as two sides of the same coin. Both the very idea of indivisibility and the constitutive function of

Popular Sovereignty in the West Ch. 2, 34–5, or Weinert, *Democratic Sovereignty* 2–3. These treatments mistake the genus for the species.

[36] Jean Bodin, *Six Bookes of a Commonweale*, trans. Richard Knolles (London, 1606), ed. Kenneth McRae (Cambridge: Harvard University Press, 1962) 10 [I, 2]. The English word, "commonweale," was Knolles' translation for the French *république* and Latin *respublica*. But given the meaning of the term, it should more properly be translated as "state," as modern translators of Bodin's text into other European languages have done, such as the Italian translation of Margherita Isnardi Parente (*lo stato*) and the German translation of Bernd Wimmer (*der Staat*).

[37] Lars Vinx, "Constitutional Indifferentism and Republican Freedom," *Political Theory* 38 (2010): 809–37.

sovereignty, it was thought, had to entail a certain form of sovereignty. What that form was exactly, of course, was the issue.

The doctrine of popular sovereignty emerged in this early modern context to show that the constitutive function of sovereignty requires that its form must always be, without exception, popular: state sovereignty originates and always remains with the people, even while sovereignty may be exercised, as if through a loan or commission, through an intermediary agent.[38] This was not only because the authority of the state was thought to be *derivative* of popular consent, as was commonly argued, especially in the social-contract tradition and earlier in the medieval legal doctrine of the *quod omnes tangit* ["What touches all ought to be decided by all"].[39] It was, more significantly (and unlike the social-contract tradition), because of the view that the unity of the state—as a collective actor or, as early modern jurists began to regard it, a legally fictive "moral person" [*persona moralis*, or *persona ficta*]—depended entirely upon the anterior unity of the people, rather than the other way around.[40] Statehood, in short, presupposes peoplehood. On this view, the people—and only the people—can legitimately create, or constitute, states and legally empower its public institutions with the right to exercise legitimate authority. And this, in turn, was because of the general principle that the greater [*maior*] is always more powerful [*potior*] than the lesser.[41]

This constitutive doctrine of popular sovereignty became something of an axiom in constitutional theory by the eighteenth century, feeding directly into modern ideas of national self-determination, which require boundaries of states to match and be fixed by the anterior, pre-political boundaries of "nations" or "peoples." But, it was by no means axiomatic prior to the eighteenth century, and that is because it was not at all clear in early modern thought why peoples should be exclusively privileged with the sovereign right of creating and empowering states, as the constitutive doctrine entails. After all, popular sovereignty was certainly not the only doctrine supplying an answer to the question of sovereignty's form. Indeed, a king could conceivably play just the same constitutive role as a people, as a kind of legal *primum movens*, in constituting a unified structure of public authority as a state. There was, at least at

[38] The model of popular sovereignty developed here is similar to what democratic theorists have recently called "delegative democracy." See, for example, G.A. O'Donnell, "Delegative Democracy," *Journal of Democracy* 5 (1994): 55–69.

[39] On the *Quod omnes tangit*, see the classic study of Gaines Post, "A Romano-Canonical Maxim, *Quod Omnes Tangit*, in Bracton," *Traditio* 4 (1946): 197–251.

[40] Hobbes was perhaps the only theorist in the modern social contract tradition to explore this principle of unity. It plays a minimal role in the theories of Locke and Rousseau, and for good reason. Whereas Hobbes utterly rejected as incoherent the view that a people can act by themselves, the latter writers accepted that a people can act as a unitary collective actor with its own collective, or "general," will.

[41] There is an ambiguity in the comparative adjective, "greater" [*maior*], which shapes the nominative form of this term in Latin. Clifford Ando has suggested "greater-ness" [*maiestas*]. *Law, Language, and Empire in the Roman Tradition* (Philadelphia: University of Pennsylvania Press, 2011) 103–07. It could mean "greater" in a quantitative sense, but it could just as easily mean "greater" in a qualitative sense—as Marsilius once exploited in his discussion of the authority of the *maior pars*.

first glance, nothing unique about the concept of the people—or a *demos* or *populus*—to suggest any *prima facie* reason why it should have such a sovereign right, while a prince should not.

Princely sovereignty, as some early modern defenders of monarchy would fiercely argue, even had certain practical advantages over popular sovereignty as a constitutive doctrine, the most important of which was the fact that the attribution of sovereignty to a real living "natural" person—a monarch—obviated altogether the need to rely upon controversial theories of peoplehood and collective agency in order to explain the alleged unity of a sovereign people. Why resort to metaphysically dubious, mystically Parmenidean notions of a "sovereign people" as both a unity and a plurality, when an individual prince might, in his own individual person, directly embody and "represent" the unity of a state as a bearer of actionable rights and obligations? If, as the constitutive doctrine suggests, the unity of the state relies entirely on the unity of the constituter, wouldn't it be more sensible simply to assign that constitutive role to one person rather than to the many?

This line of questioning was central to framing the criticism of popular sovereignty, especially among early modern defenders of monarchy who were deeply skeptical of the conceptual coherence and viability of the notion of a sovereign people, as a collective agent with a uniform set of actionable rights and an unchanging identity extended over time. No less a royalist than Sir Robert Filmer, author of the *Patriarcha*, the work that would eventually become John Locke's target in his *First Treatise of Civil Government*, captured the anti-populist mood of his age when he observed famously that:

> The people...is a thing or body in continuall alteration and change, it never continues one minute the same, being composed of a multitude of parts, whereof divers continually decay and perish, and others renew and succeed in their place...they which are the people this minute, are not the people the next minute.[42]

How could such an unstable, constantly changing body serve as the permanent, unchanging source for the public authority of the state?

The simple answer is that it most likely could not. But that is only true if the "people" can be conceptualized as nothing other than a multitude or aggregate of individuals—or, as writers have variously suggested, a fickle mob, a crowd, a throng, and even a "many-headed monster" [*bellua multorum capitum*]

[42] Robert Filmer, *Observations upon Aristotle's Politiques* [1652] in *Patriarcha and Other Writings*, ed. J.P. Sommerville (New York: Cambridge University Press, 1991) 277. The issue of continuity and change over time in the composition and identity of a people, as an ever-changing collective self, remains an issue in various literatures in democratic and legal theory, such as Jed Rubenfeld, *Freedom and Time: A Theory of Constitutional Self-Government* (New Haven: Yale University Press, 2001) and Paulina Ochoa Espejo, *Time of Popular Sovereignty: Process and the Democratic State* (University Park: Pennsylvania State University Press, 2011). The problem is particularly troublesome in American constitutional jurisprudence in relation to "originalism," since, on this view, the authority and meaning of a constitutional text is entirely dependent upon the sovereign act of a people in late-eighteenth-century America.

and a "madman" [*furiosus*].[43] Indeed, what this early modern criticism of popular sovereignty seems to ignore, perhaps willfully, is that the very word—"people"—had a built-in ambiguity, a "double-signification" once recognized by Hobbes as indicating not only an aggregate of individuals but also a collective agent.[44]

But even if we grant the internal coherence of the notion of a sovereign people as something more than simply a disordered crowd, by application of a juridical casuistry, why might this be the best way to formulate the constitutive doctrine undergirding the unity—or, indeed, the "personality"—of the state?[45] Why ground the state's authority on a theory of *popular* sovereignty, rather than, say, *princely* sovereignty?

The answer is that popular sovereignty represented a considered strategy of risk-avoidance in handling the constitutively necessary, but volatile, notion of sovereignty. Constituting structures of public authority was far too important—and potentially too dangerous—to assign to any individual, especially to a prince. No one person should have such sovereign right entirely. By attributing this authority-creating function to a virtually omnipresent and conceptually fictive "people," rather than to any particular concrete individual, or even aggregate of individuals, the chief architects of the doctrine effectively *depersonalized* the form of sovereignty, detaching it entirely from notions of princely—indeed, personal—rule. Sovereignty, in this way, becomes *impersonal*, belonging not to any person or even group of persons, but to a concept, an idea, some might even say, a fiction, thought to be anterior to, and independent of, the public institutions it creates and invests with authority.

In this respect, then, we might see the original purpose of popular sovereignty as being not so much to show, as a positive argument, to whom sovereignty should belong (whether the prince or the people or someone else), but rather, as a negative argument, to show to whom sovereignty should *not* belong. This negative argument, as we shall see, targeted *inter alia* the controversial idea that sovereign rights actually belonged personally to princes, such that sovereignty could even be treated legally as if it were patrimony or property, falling under the category of what jurists called *dominium*. The origins of

[43] Horace, *Epistles* [I.1.76]; Bodin, *Commonweale* 700 [6.4]. Cp. 200 [2.2], where Bodin, citing Cicero, calls "the rage of the furious and turbulent people" the worst kind of tyranny. The term, "furious," is a reference to the Roman law notion of the *furiosus* ["madman"] who, in the law of guardianship, is in need of a *curator* as guardian.

[44] *De Corpore Politico* 86 [II,2,§11]. Classical languages distinguish between the two concepts, such as in Greek [*demos* and *ochlos*] and Latin [*populus* and *plebs* or *vulgus*]. This last distinction is preserved in the Roman law texts at Inst.1.2.4. On the various meanings of *populus* in medieval legal thought, see J.P. Canning, *Political Thought of Baldus de Ubaldis* (Cambridge: Cambridge University Press, 1987) 185–86.

[45] On the personality of the state, see now David Runciman, *Pluralism and the Personality of the State* (Cambridge: Cambridge University Press, 2005) and, more recently, Ben Holland, "The Moral Person of the State: Emer de Vattel and the Foundations of International Legal Order," *History of European Ideas* 37 (2011): 438–45, and "Natural Law and the Theory of International Society: Otto von Gierke and the Three Traditions of International Theory," *Journal of International Political Theory* 8 (2012): 48–73. The classic study is Gierke's *Das Deutsche Genossenschaftsrecht*.

this criticism, as we shall see, can be traced to the critiques of medieval feudal jurisdiction in the scholarship of sixteenth-century legal humanists, who denied that feudal tenure implicitly conferred corresponding private rights of jurisdiction, a notion that I explore in Chapter 3. But it became something even more radical when jurists, using the analysis of the humanists, turned their attention to the legal rights of kings, including the right to exercise the constitutive higher-order functions of sovereignty. No king, they argued, could claim sovereignty personally as his own, and that is because, according to the argument for an impersonal concept of rulership, sovereignty, by its very nature, simply was not the sort of thing over which any individual, even a king, could assert a personal right of *dominium*. It is indeed a sort of category mistake to treat sovereignty as one's personal property, a thought that would become foundational for modern public law.

In this argument, then, the notion of the sovereign people emerges not only to displace kings from their *regalia*, or *principes* from their *imperium*, but more importantly, to act as a conceptual placeholder for kingship in the modern mind, by playing the constitutional role of the imagined fictive bearer of a depersonalized sovereignty. But how can this actually be said to be a concept of sovereignty? Isn't this depersonalized notion of popular sovereignty, as De Maistre once mocked, really just an absurdity, implying "a sovereign that cannot exercise its sovereignty"?[46]

ROMAN LAW AND THE LEGAL SCIENCE OF SOVEREIGNTY

The burden of showing the coherence and function of popular sovereignty in constitutional theory fell upon the doctrine's chief defenders in early modern thought—that is, jurists. Understanding how they attempted to accomplish this task, however, remains puzzling as ever, and that is because the early analysis of popular sovereignty was framed and interpreted in the only "language" or discursive medium that was thought to be appropriate for investigating such a complex constitutional doctrine. That "language" was the juridical language of the "civil law" [*ius civile*]—that is, Roman law.[47]

Since its rediscovery in eleventh-century Italy, inaugurating what Paul Vinogradoff once described as the "second life of Roman law," the canonical texts of Roman law—the Justinianic codification of Roman law in the "Body of Civil Law," or *Corpus Iuris Civilis*, comprised of the *Code*, the *Digest* (or sometimes the *Pandects*), the *Institutes*, and the *Novels*—provided not only a universal framework for a scientific jurisprudence, as the foundation for Western legal

[46] Joseph De Maistre, "Study on Sovereignty" in *The Generative Principle of Political Constitutions: Studies on Sovereignty, Religion, and Enlightenment*, ed. and trans. Jack Lively (Piscataway, Transaction Publishers, 2012) 93.

[47] The *Digest* defines "civil law" in D.1.1.6 and 1.1.7. Technically, it is the law of any *civitas*, but since, in the Roman law tradition, it deals specifically with the law pertaining to the Roman *civitas*, the term, "civil law" or *ius civile*, is treated as a synonym for Roman law. But, as Gaius indicates in D.1.1.9, any law-governed *civitas* or *populus* has its own civil law that is proper to it [*ius proprium*].

science, but also "the makings of a larger framework of social thought" and even "a firm foundation on which to base the political and social ethics of their day."[48] Roman law was not to be seen simply as a lifeless artifact of an ancient civilization, but as the living source of all timeless legal wisdom. For this reason, Roman law was customarily hailed as "written reason" [*ratio scripta*], the "true philosophy" [*vera philosophia*], and even regarded to be divinely inspired sacred texts, conveying "knowledge of things divine and human," as portrayed, for example, in Canto VI, of Dante's *Paradisio*.[49] The Roman law texts functioned as a general "learned law" of reference and, alongside canon and feudal law, acquired a privileged status in European legal thought as a *ius commune*, universal to, and shared in common by, all law-governed nations.

Given its profound cultural and intellectual significance, Roman law played a central role in the development of the theory of sovereignty, so much so, that it is not too much to say that sovereignty and Roman law were inextricably tied to each other as mutually supporting.[50] It was indeed an indispensable tool in the early modern project of statecraft by offering a pristine model of what a complete, orderly, and rational legal system might look like. Legal reform and modernization, especially beginning in the "elegant" legal science of sixteenth-century humanist jurists, thus took a decidedly Romanist turn through attempts at the formal reception, incorporation, and assimilation of Roman legal rules in emerging legally unitary national states.[51]

Not everybody welcomed this "Romanizing" of modern legal thought. For a variety of reasons, early modern jurists and political theorists who sought to

[48] Paul Vinogradoff, *Roman Law in Medieval Europe* (Oxford: Clarendon Press, 1929) 13; Donald Kelley, "Civil Science in the Renaissance: Jurisprudence in the French Manner," *History of European Ideas* 2 (1981): 269; Franz Wieacker, *A History of Private Law in Europe*, trans. Tony Weir (Oxford: Clarendon Press, 1995) 69. The term, *Corpus Iuris Civilis*, is the early modern title adopted by Denis Godefroy for his 1583 edition of the Justinianic texts. The medieval version of the *Digest* was divided into three parts, the *Digestum Vetus* (D.1.1-24.2), the *Infortiatum* (D.24.3-38.18), and the *Digestum Novum* (D.39.1-50.17). The *Institutes* and the *Novels* (titled the *Authentica*) were gathered in a separate volume, the *Volumen Parvum*, which also included the central learned text of feudal law, the *Libri Feudorum*.

[49] Donald Kelley, "*Vera Philosophia*: The Philosophical Significance of Renaissance Jurisprudence," *Journal of the History of Philosophy* 14 (1976): 267, citing D.1.1.10.2.

[50] Gerald Strauss, *Law, Resistance and the State: The Opposition to Roman Law in Reformation Germany* (Princeton: Princeton University Press, 1986) 73–4, 97–8; John Gerard Ruggie, "Territoriality and Beyond: Problematizing Modernity in International Relations," *International Organization* 47 (1993): 139–74; Friedrich Kratochwil, "Of Systems, Boundaries, and Territoriality: An Inquiry in the Formation of the State System," *World Politics* 39 (1986): 27–52; Friedrich Kratochwil, "Sovereignty as *Dominium*: Is There a Right of Humanitarian Intervention?" *Beyond Westphalia? State Sovereignty and International Intervention*, ed. Gene Lyons and Michael Mastanduno (Baltimore: Johns Hopkins University Press, 1995); Charles Tilly, "Reflections on the History of European Statemaking," *Formation of National States in Western Europe*, ed. Charles Tilly (Princeton: Princeton University Press, 1975); John Strayer, *On the Medieval Origins of the Modern State* (Princeton: Princeton University Press, 1972) 23–26; Perry Anderson, *Lineages of the Absolutist State* (London: Verso, 1979) 24–29; Ben Holland, "Sovereignty as *Dominium*? Reconstructing the Constructivist Roman Law Thesis," *International Studies Quarterly* 54 (2010): 449–80. For a general survey, see James Sheehan, "The Problem of Sovereignty in European History," *American Historical Review* 111 (2006).

[51] Strauss, *Law, Resistance and the State* 123.

articulate the constitutive foundations of the modern sovereign state derided this historical, even accidental, connection to the Roman law tradition. Roman law was thought to be "absolutist," favoring unlimited princely authority. It was the product of a slaveholding society and a reminder of the ancient legacy of imperial conquest and foreign domination of Rome over free peoples and their local customs.[52] Others criticized the dependence upon Roman law as being like a crutch to assist in building national legal systems and constitutions. There was no good reason why, for example, modern nations should be bound to mimic an ancient legal code when they could just as well craft their own.

It became, therefore, a task of the highest urgency in seventeenth-century legal thought to disentangle the public law concept of sovereignty from its Roman law origins.[53] Writing in 1677, for example, Leibniz—a doctor of civil law in his own right—observed just how unavoidable Roman law had become in articulating his own theory of sovereignty:

> In explaining the concept of sovereignty, I confess I must enter into... a field which is thorny and little cultivated... The reason for this is that, because of a deplorable mania, those who undertake to write on sovereignty have eyes only for what is ancient, of which vestiges scarcely survive... for them, all wisdom appears collected in the tomes of Roman law alone.[54]

The puzzle for us, as it was for Leibniz, is to understand the origins of this "mania." Why was the analysis of sovereignty originally framed in this juridical language of Roman law in the first place?

One reason for this was simply that the historical experience of the Roman Empire provided an attractive classical model of sovereignty that might potentially be imitated and reproduced in modern post-classical states, claiming a similar sort of sovereign or imperial authority—or *imperium*—as Rome. Indeed, among the most famous texts of Roman law were extracts concerning the legal—or indeed, extralegal—authority of the *princeps*, or emperor, whom Roman jurisconsults described as being "unbound by the laws" [*legibus solutus*] and, for that very reason, having the full power of *imperium*, the unlimited discretionary authority to issue commands by decree or edict carrying the fully binding statutory force of law [*legis vigor*].[55] Even more significant were the reasons given in the Roman law texts explaining why the emperor was thought to have such a legally absolute power in the first place. It is only because the Roman people—the *populus Romanus*—conferred their original authority

[52] See, for example, François Hotman's *Antitribonian*, which articulates this early modern humanist opposition to the *Corpus Iuris Civilis*. Tribonian, Hotman's target, was the sixth-century jurist commissioned by Justinian to compile the texts comprising the *Corpus*.

[53] Reinhard Zimmermann, "Foreword," to Franz Wieacker, *A History of Private Law in Europe*, trans. Tony Weir (Oxford: Clarendon Press, 1995) xii. Cp., Loughlin, *Foundations of Public Law* Ch. 2.

[54] Gottfried Wilhelm Leibniz, "Caesarinus Fürstenerius: De Suprematu Principum Germaniae," *Political Writings*, ed. Patrick Riley (Cambridge: Cambridge University Press, 1988) 113.

[55] D.1.3.31, 1.4.1, Inst.1.2.6.

upon the emperor and, thus, empowered him to rule the Empire with full sovereignty. As we shall see, these statements concerning *imperium* had a profound influence on later medieval legal thought, by likening the authority of monarchies, principalities, and even those of independent cities, to the *imperium* of the Roman *princeps*.

But as important as these analogies with Roman public law were, they reveal only a relatively small part of the story.[56] Even though Justinian's codification contained some limited statements concerning the public or constitutional law of the Roman state and its administrative organs, it nevertheless remains the case that Roman law was fundamentally a body of *private* law. It was, as the classical Roman jurist, Gaius, famously declared in his *Institutes*, a system of law ultimately concerning either "persons, things, or actions."[57] Of course, the Romans clearly understood the difference between public and private law: Ulpian, for example, makes this very distinction between public law [*ius publicum*] and private law [*ius privatum*] in his *Institutes*.[58] But as most of the legal rules that would comprise the equivalent of Roman public law remained customary and unwritten, the predominant focus of the Roman law codified by Justinian in the texts of the *Corpus Iuris Civilis* and, consequently, of Western legal science in the tradition of the civil law, was conceived "first and foremost as a private law legal science," touching upon matters such as contracts, property, commercial transactions, and enforcing performance of legal obligations.[59]

Here, then, is the problem. If Roman law was primarily a system of *private* law, then how could it possibly have influenced the development of what was perhaps the central concept of *public* law, the concept of sovereignty? The answer is that Roman law provided a uniform conceptual grammar and vocabulary—a "language"—for framing the analysis of sovereignty in the terms of private law, expressed as actionable rights and obligations.[60] Despite its deafening silence on most matters of public law, the textual authorities comprising Roman law nevertheless offered technically sophisticated treatments on matters of private law concerning jural relations and actionable rights between persons. While these sources were originally intended to apply only to the rights and obligations of *private* persons, enterprising jurists carefully widened the scope of application such that the civil law might function

[56] Wieacker, *History of Private Law* 99–100.

[57] Gaius, *Institutes* 1.8; cited in D.1.5.1.

[58] D.1.1.1.2.

[59] Zimmermann, "Foreword," to Wieacker, *History of Private Law* xii. However, as Francesco Calasso rightly stresses in his classic study on the Glossators, the focus of medieval jurisprudence was not exclusively private law, as the Glossators focused on two central branches of public law, criminal law and procedural law. Francesco Calasso, *I Glossatori e la Teoria della Sovranità*, 2nd ed. (Milan: Dott. A. Giuffrè Editore, 1951) 21.

[60] This was especially important for the emergence of public international law, the rules of which were taken directly from Roman private law. Randall Lesaffer, "Argument from Roman Law in Current International Law: Occupation and Acquisitive Prescription," *European Journal of International Law* 16 (2005).

equivalently as a language in framing the rights and obligations of public persons, the sovereign state and its agents, as well.[61]

That Roman law functioned as a distinct "language" of constitutional theory is, of course, a claim that has attracted much critical attention in the scholarship on the history of political thought and intellectual history. Like Aristotelian philosophy and Scholastic theology in the Middle Ages, the civil law provided, as J.H. Burns once put it, "a common language and methodology for the discussion of critical issues" in political and legal philosophy across ideological cleavages, such that even the most ardent royalists and radical populists could participate in ideologically polarizing debates while sharing a common intellectual commitment to the structure and framework of juridical reasoning.[62] Despite the traditional perception of Roman law as ideologically being aligned with absolutist political thought (no doubt due to its elevation of the *princeps* beyond the boundaries of law), Roman legal ideas were historically deployed not only in defense of absolutism, but in defense of constitutionalism as well.[63] Indeed, arguments from Roman law were even "invoked...by some of the most radical opponents of absolutism in early modern Europe," in order to defend the legality of resistance.[64] As Quentin Skinner has influentially shown in a range of studies, Roman law functioned as a highly versatile ideological tool, even a weapon, to be wielded on the battlefield of ideological conflict. Equally accessible to Catholics and Protestants, royalists and republicans, absolutists and constitutionalists, scholastics and humanists, Roman law became what Peter Stein once described as "a kind of legal supermarket" of ideas.[65]

But there is a danger in viewing Roman law almost exclusively in terms of its function as a discursive medium or language for normative political theory, locked, as Walter Ullmann once put it, inside "the arena of political conflicts."[66] This is because the "civilians"—that is, the practitioners and scholars of the civil law—saw their craft as something more than simply an ideologically bound

[61] William Freegard, *Roman Law and Resistance Right: A Study of Question Three of the Vindiciae Contra Tyrannos* (University of Iowa, Ph.D. Dissertation, 1971) 77–113 on the use of C.2.53(54).4. I am grateful to the late Ralph Giesey for providing me with the typescript of this dissertation.

[62] J.H. Burns, *Lordship, Kingship and Empire: The Idea of Monarchy, 1400-1525* (New York: Oxford University Press, 1992) 7.

[63] This was one of McIlwain's major conclusions in *Constitutionalism Ancient and Modern*. The thesis was developed further by Walter Ullmann, Brian Tierney, and Kenneth Pennington. One of the major sources for this constitutionalist tradition of Roman law was the *Digna vox*, C.1.14.4, which was often seen as the doctrinal antithesis to the *legibus solutus* doctrine, since it declared the emperor to be "bound by the laws" [*legibus alligatus*].

[64] Skinner, *Foundations of Modern Political Thought* 2:124. One important example of the anti-absolutist uses of Roman law concerns resistance to unjust contracts. See for example Cynus of Pistoia on C.1.14.4, which references C.10.1.5, and Baldus de Ubaldis, *Consilium* 3.371. I thank Kenneth Pennington for these references.

[65] Peter Stein, *Roman Law in European History* (New York: Cambridge University Press, 1999) 2.

[66] Walter Ullmann, *Law and Politics in the Middle Ages* (Ithaca: Cornell University Press, 1975) 77.

discursive language game. Civil law was different from politics. It was, as they saw it, a "science"—even a Kuhnian "normal science"—in its own right.[67] Indeed, it was the science of right [*scientia iuris*], or, as even modern German jurists call it, *Rechtswissenschaft*. And as a science, it called for a special kind of analytical reasoning, which jurists recorded in the form of glosses, commentaries, consilia, and treatises on specific points of law.[68] This understanding of the civil law as an autonomous science, insulated from the vicissitudes of politics, helped to cultivate learned law as the exclusive domain of its "priests," the legal profession as a whole.[69] But more important, it reinforced the notion that certain topics or conceptual puzzles ought to be "depoliticized" and properly treated by jurists as a matter of methodical scientific inquiry, rather than as a matter of normative argumentation.

This, as we shall see, was the jurists' attitude even with respect to the issue of public authority, in general, and of sovereignty, in particular. Such matters were far too serious, complex, and divisive to leave to the layperson, or worse (in their eyes), the philosopher. The analysis of the constitutive foundations of public authority became fundamentally a question of legal science, framed in the civilian language of *imperium, iurisdictio*, and *dominium*. And it was in this juridical language that popular sovereignty emerged as the solution.

My task in the chapters to follow is to "decode" or "decipher" this juridical language of Roman legal science as it was deployed by jurists in the civil law tradition, such as Azo, Bartolus, Hotman, Bodin, Althusius, and Grotius, in the analysis and defense of popular sovereignty. In doing so, I hope to show why Roman law was thought to be the appropriate discursive medium for what today might be called "constitutional theory." It provided the necessary conceptual tools to present popular sovereignty as a constitutive doctrine of public authority without having to commit to a potentially controversial normative view on precisely *how* such popular sovereignty ought to be administered or exercised. Civilian jurists demonstrated why popular sovereignty did not necessarily entail democracy, but rather, might even be fully compatible with undemocratic institutional arrangements. What emerges in the constitutional theory of the civilians, then, is something more than simple normative argument, but a grand unified theory of sovereign statehood that uniformly traces the source of all public authority to an original concessive—and fully revocable—act of delegation by a free and independent people.

[67] Ulpian, at D.1.1.1, famously calls law the "art of goodness and fairness" [*ars boni et aequi* and describes, at D.1.1.10.2, "practical wisdom in matters of right" [*iuris prudentia* = "jurisprudence"] to be properly a *scientia*. The medieval *Glossa Ordinaria* on this rubric [on D.1.1.1, *Ius est ars*] specifies that such "art" should properly be understood as a "distinct science" or "knowledge" [*scientia finita*]. On "normal science," see Thomas Kuhn, *The Structure of Scientific Revolutions* (Chicago: University of Chicago Press, 1962).

[68] Jurisprudence was, thus, called the *scientia civilis* or the "civil science." Kelley, "*Vera Philosophia*" 267. See also Bellomo, *Common Legal Past of Europe* 195–202; 163–66; 126–48.

[69] Ulpian describes jurists as "priests of justice" [*sacerdotes iustitiae*] in the opening rubric of the *Digest*, D.1.1.1.

STRUCTURE

The theory of popular sovereignty that was crafted by the Roman law jurists relied on an elementary legal distinction between *right* and *exercise*. The distinction, as I show in the chapters to follow, originates in connection with the law of property which became particularly influential in the humanist legal thought of the sixteenth century: an owner of some object of property—whether land or movables—may have a legal right of ownership over it, even while some other party enjoys the limited exercise or use of that property, such as a usufructuary. Early modern theorists of sovereignty relied on this distinction to frame the analysis of a prince's sovereignty. A prince may formally have the bare legal right of sovereignty over his realm, even while the prince's government—his ministers, magistrates, judges, and other subordinate agents—is delegated the actual exercise of public authority on the prince's behalf. What makes the prince sovereign is that his sovereign right, even over his government, remains firmly secure and actionable at his pleasure.

This analysis, however, was not exclusive to sovereign princes. Even a sovereign people with full right of sovereignty could just as well delegate the exercise of authority to a constituted government. Indeed, such an arrangement of delegated popular sovereignty could, as theorists of republicanism suggest, potentially enhance the efficacy of popular self-rule, by implementing institutional devices to tame and regulate the popular will. But even though sovereignty originates in the people and formally remains with them as a popular legal right, the exercise of popular sovereignty could be mediated and realized through potentially non-democratic institutional means. Just as it is the formal right of a sovereign people to constitute a legally regulated government, subject to a self-legislated constitution, so too is it consistent with that same sovereign right to create an almighty Caesar Augustus, who is unbound from law.

This ambiguity has been the source of much anxiety concerning the understanding of popular sovereignty, especially among constitutional theorists who fear the potentially undemocratic or illiberal consequences of unbridled sovereign constitution-making and legislation by unmediated popular majorities. While it is often thought that this is an anxiety characteristic of modern democracy, I hope to show that it originates and develops out of the tradition of Roman-inspired legal thought.

The first part of the book, consisting of two chapters, begins with a general introduction to the Roman law background concerning theories of popular sovereignty. As lawyers of the civilian tradition were well aware, the Roman Empire was constitutionally established upon a doctrine of popular sovereignty, captured in a legendary statute known as the *lex regia*, or "royal law," whereby the Roman people were said to have "transferred" [*transtulit*] all their authority and power to the emperor. Much of the existing scholarship concerning popular sovereignty and political thought in the Roman law tradition focuses on arguments based on this *lex regia*. Chapter 1 will, therefore, begin by discussing critically the origins and reception of this *lex regia* and discuss some of the major interpretive and conceptual difficulties concerning the idea of popular sovereignty in the Roman legal tradition. Chief among those difficulties was the issue whether the transfer of sovereignty by the Roman people to the emperor ought to be understood as a revocable *concession* or as an irrevocable *alienation* of power. As we shall see, the varieties of legal interpretations concerning the Roman *lex regia*, especially in the law schools of the High Middle Ages, opened a period of careful theoretical reflection, expressed in juridical vocabulary, on how a people can play the constitutive role of public authority on the private law model of delegated exercise. Building on this background, Chapter 2 considers how Roman principles of popular sovereignty came to have a "second life" in a post-Roman world of *de facto* autonomous kingdoms, principalities, and free republics, within the *de iure* universal jurisdiction of Church and Empire. The chapter focuses on how later medieval jurists, especially the great Roman law Commentators, Bartolus and Baldus, introduced an interpretive recalibration of the Roman law texts to enable Roman legal doctrines of sovereignty to apply in a post-Roman world.

The second part of the book considers how proprietary concepts provided the vehicle by which early notions of sovereignty began to be expressed and formulated by jurists, especially in the context of early modern monarchy. Chapter 3 considers the case of sixteenth-century French legal humanists, especially Alciato and Donellus, who assigned the proprietary right of *dominium* over jurisdictional authority exclusively to the king, while treating lesser authorities with delegated power as equivalent to the status of usufructuaries in private law. Chapter 4 then focuses on the criticism and expropriation of these theories as articulated in the Huguenot Monarchomach treatises of the *Francogallia* (1573) and the *Vindiciae Contra Tyrannos* (1579), both of which reject the idea that *dominium* is exclusive to the king. Drawing on a wealth of Roman law arguments, these treatises show instead that *dominium* must always reside in the body of an assembled people, and it is only by an act of delegation that a king exercises authority, almost like a usufructuary, a tutor, or an agent.

With the background developed in the immediately foregoing chapters, the third part of the book focuses on the thought of the most important French jurist and political theorist of sovereignty in the sixteenth century, Jean Bodin. Bodin is almost always portrayed in the history of political thought as the quintessential defender of princely absolutism in French thought, and a predecessor to later absolutists such as Filmer and Hobbes. My goal in these chapters, however, is to resist that conclusion and argue instead that Bodin deserves to be seen as perhaps the most important theorist of popular sovereignty, a conclusion which follows, as I shall show, from his conceptual analysis of sovereignty. Key to this analysis is Bodin's reliance upon Roman law. Chapter 5 investigates his study of Roman law in his first major published work, the *Methodus ad Facilem Historiarum Cognitionem* (1566), as well as his recognition of the shortcomings of legal humanist scholarship in crafting a general theory of state sovereignty. Central to this discussion of sovereignty—or *summum imperium*—was the issue whether such authority could legally be delegated to subordinates. As I show, Bodin supplies a technically sophisticated answer that moves beyond the medieval legal doctrines on delegated jurisdiction and allows sovereignty to be exercised legally by way of delegation. Chapter 6 then traces Bodin's development of these ideas in his most important work of political and legal theory, the *Six Livres de la République* (originally published in French in 1576). Bodin's insistence that even a people can hold the right of sovereignty—the most important classical example of which was the constitution of the Roman Republic—leads him to apply the delegation analysis even in popular states. A sovereign people may constitute a government, whether by offices or commissions, to exercise its authority legally by way of delegation, just as a sovereign prince may likewise constitute a government of ministers and magistrates for exactly the same purpose. Although popular rule was certainly not his preferred form of sovereignty, he acknowledged its validity as a constitutional state form, and his analysis of delegated popular sovereignty provided a model that would uniformly shape the early modern understanding of popular sovereignty as a viable alternative to monarchy.

The fourth and final part of the book traces the varieties of doctrines of popular sovereignty emerging in early modern constitutional thought, based on the Roman law model. Chapter 7 details the theory of popular sovereignty in the *Politica Methodice Digesta* (1603) of Bodin's most important early modern German critic, the jurist and syndic of Emden, Johannes Althusius. Chapter 8 considers how the Dutch jurist, Hugo Grotius, in his *De Iure Belli ac Pacis* (1625) uses Roman law concepts of *libertas* and usufruct to develop a theory of popular sovereignty, even in states which are governed by princes. Finally, Chapter 9 concludes with a study on popular sovereignty in the constitutional thought of Stuart England, with special focus on the legal ideas of the English civilians and their influence on competing ideas of sovereignty and peoplehood during the period of the English Civil War.

1

The Lex Regia: *The Theory of Popular Sovereignty in the Roman Law Tradition*

INTRODUCTION

One of Wagner's early and now rarely staged operas, *Rienzi*, chronicles the rise and fall of the self-styled last Tribune of the Roman People, Cola di Rienzo (1313–1354). In reality, Cola was more of a medieval "demagogue," as J.G.A. Pocock once described him, and even perhaps a "lunatic," who invoked the memory of Roman Republican glory to restrain the insolence and corruption of the Roman nobility, which had, among other acts of treachery, murdered his brother.[1] In justifying his battle against the Roman *ottimati*, Cola revived a basic tenet of the classical constitution of the Roman Republic, that full public authority was permanently and exclusively vested in the Roman people and actionable through the people's tribune against even the highest magistrates.

Cola's theory of Roman popular sovereignty, however, rested on a historical fiction that the medieval commune of *Trecento* Rome followed its Republican constitution in an unbroken line of continuity unchanged over many centuries and originating in the ancient Roman Republic. The significance of this fiction was in Cola's radical conclusion that the sovereignty of the Roman people remained fully intact, though perhaps in a dormant state, waiting to be reawakened by a latter-day tribune as a champion of the Roman people.

What emboldened Cola's resolve to revive Roman popular sovereignty in this medieval setting was a stunning discovery that has traditionally been attributed to him, that is, the discovery of the bronze tablet in the Church of St. John Lateran with the only known inscription of a *lex de imperio*, or "a statute concerning authority," legally conferring the full public authority of the Roman people upon the Roman emperor—in this case, the Emperor Vespasian. The significance of Rienzo's discovery for medieval and early

[1] J.G.A. Pocock, *The Machiavellien Moment* (Princeton: Princeton University Press, 1975) 51; Ferdinand Gregorovius, *History of the City of Rome in the Middle Ages* (Cambridge: Cambridge University Press, 1898) 240. On Rienzo, Ronald Musto, *Apocalypse in Rome: Cola di Rienzo and the Politics of the New Age* (Berkeley: University of California Press, 2003); Amanda Collins, *Greater than Emperor: Cola di Rienzo and the World of Fourteenth-Century Rome* (Ann Arbor: University of Michigan Press, 2002). See also the collection of letters exchanged between Rienzo and Petrarch in *The Revolution of Cola di Rienzo*, ed. Mario Emilio Cosenza, Ronald Musto, 3rd ed. (New York: Italica Press, 1996).

modern constitutional thought can hardly be overstated. This *lex de imperio Vespasiani* was seen as concrete historical evidence not only of the popular foundations of Roman imperial authority, but indeed of the popular foundations of all forms of public authority, whether Roman or otherwise. Medieval jurists in particular treated it as an example of the mysterious *lex regia*, referenced by the classical Roman jurisconsult, Ulpian, who described it as the legal device or instrument by which Roman popular sovereignty was fully alienated and transferred to the Roman Emperor as "lord," or *dominus*, of all the world.

Whether the *lex de imperio* actually can be treated as functionally equivalent to the *lex regia* of classical Roman law was a cause of intense academic controversy, especially among French and Dutch legal humanists, lasting even until the eighteenth century.[2] But its central importance in the juridical interpretation of popular sovereignty makes it the natural starting point for the study of Roman law as a distinctive source of constitutional thought. And so, it is with the *lex regia* that I begin this study.

This chapter will discuss the medieval constitutional arguments emerging from the interpretive schools concerning the *lex regia*. I shall begin with a discussion of the *lex regia* in classical Roman law, where it is referenced in the writings of later Imperial jurists, especially Ulpian, so as to legitimize the law-making capacity of the Roman emperors by tracing its origins to the Roman people. As I shall show, there was actually no single legal act or *lex* in Roman constitutional history, whereby such plenary authority was transferred from *populus* to *princeps*. It was, rather, an ex post facto rationalization or fiction postulated by later jurists to explain the legality of the constitutional transition from Republic to Principate in the first century B.C.E., in terms of popular sovereignty. Having established this classical background, I next consider the medieval reception of the *lex regia* by the Italian jurists of Bologna, the "Glossators" of Roman law. As we shall see, the major interpretive dispute among these Glossators concerned the nature of the conveyance of authority from *populus* to *princeps* described in the *lex regia*. Some of these writers, such as Irnerius and Placentinus, understood this conveyance to be a complete and irrevocable *translatio*, such that the people could no longer be said to have any public authority, once they have delivered it in full to the *princeps*. But in contrast to this "translation theory," other Glossators, most notably Azo, argued that the transfer of authority should properly be understood as a *concessio*, which allows the people a residual capacity to revoke and recover, when necessary, the authority it has delegated to the emperor. In recounting the two interpretive theories of the *lex regia*, I proceed to examine how this debate,

[2] Participants in this scholarly debate included Jean de Coras, François Baudouin, Jacques Cujas, François Hotman, François Connan, Johann Friedrich Gronow [Gronovius], Hubert Van Giffen, Ulrik Huber, and Gerard Noodt. See Fabrizio Lomonaco, *New Studies on Lex Regia: Right, Philology, and Fides Historica in Holland between the 17th and 18th Centuries* (New York: Peter Lang, 2011). On Huber, see also Theo Veen, "Interpretations of Inst.1.2.6, D.1.4.1, and D.1.3.31: Huber's Historical, Juridical and Political-Theoretical Reflections on the *Lex Regia*," *Tijdschrift voor Rechtsgeschiedenis* 53 (1985): 357–77.

as recalled in the *Glossa Ordinaria* of Accursius, promotes a theory of constitutional asymmetry between the *populus* and *princeps* and I explore how the Glossators favoring this view use aspects of Roman law, such as the law of property and the law of delegated jurisdiction, to present what is perhaps the first formal statement of the popular sovereignty doctrine in medieval legal thought. I conclude with a note on the monumental influence of the Glossators on later commentators of the *lex regia*, while also noting its limited scope of application in post-classical jurisprudence, a limitation that ultimately could only be overcome by introducing novel techniques of interpretation, which assimilated Roman law, along with canon and feudal law, as a common legal system [*ius commune*] for all of Western Christendom.

THE *LEX REGIA* IN CLASSICAL ROMAN LAW

The Roman *lex regia* or "royal law" was, in the civil law tradition, the legal device or instrument enacted to effect the transfer of plenary public authority from the Roman people to the Roman emperor. Its purpose was to function not only as a kind of "enabling act" whereby the powers traditionally held by the *populus* in the Republic would thereafter be exercised by the Emperor, or *princeps*, but also as a constitutional "(re)foundation of Rome itself de novo."[3] Commentators on Roman law would be right to rank the *lex regia* as among the most important pieces of Roman legislation, perhaps even as something approximating a constitutional law of the whole Roman Empire. That would certainly be a sensible conclusion—if only such a *lex* had actually existed. But in reality, no such law ever did exist. The *lex regia* was, rather, a fiction, an "ex

[3] Clifford Ando, "The Origins and Import of Republican Constitutionalism," *Cardozo Law Review* 34 (2013) 933. D.1.4.1, Inst.1.2.6, C.1.17.1.7. It is implicit in Gaius, *Institutes* 1.5 and D.1.2.2.11. A *lex regia* may also refer to an ancient law dating from the early Roman Monarchy, such as the body of legislation promulgated by Romulus as described by Dionysius of Halicarnassus in Book II of his *Roman Antiquities*. These *leges regiae*, such as the *lex regia* referenced at D.11.8.2, were enacted by the assembled *comitia* under the presidency of the king and were to be distinguished from a *lex tribunicia* which was enacted by the *comitia* under the presidency of the *tribunus celerum*, which Pomponius's *Enchiridion* (D.1.2.2.15) identifies as a rank second in command after the king. This pattern of early Roman royal legislation involving the king and his *comitia* (described at D. 1.2.2.2) produced a body of law, now lost, called the *ius civile Papirianum*, named after its compiler, Sextus Papirius. Cicero may have had this in mind at *De Republica* 2.17 in his account of the *comitia curiatia*, assembled under the interrex, selecting Tullius Hostilius as the new Roman king. The Dutch humanist Gronovius criticized Coras and Baudouin for confusing these two distinct uses of *lex regia*. See Lomonaco, *New Studies on Lex Regia* 104. See also Alan Watson, "Roman Private Law and the *Leges Regiae*," *Legal Origins and Legal Change* (London: Hambledon Press, 1991). On Pomponius and the constitutional function of the *lex regia*, see also Benjamin Straumann, "The Roman Republic as a Constitutional Order from the Principate to the Renaissance," *Republics and the Classical Past, 1500–1800* (Leiden: Brill, forthcoming), and more generally, Fergus Millar, *The Roman Republic in Political Thought* (Hanover: University Press of New England, 2002) 52. A major early modern source for this constitutionalist reading of the *lex regia* may also be found in Mario Salamonius, *De Principatu* (Paris, 1578), which considers competing interpretations of the transfer of *imperium* from people to *princeps*. See Skinner, *Foundations* 2:132–34; Straumann, "The Roman Republic as a Constitutional Order from the Principate to the Renaissance"; Benjamin Straumann, *Crisis and Constitutionalism: Roman Political Thought from the Fall of the Republic to the Age of Revolution* (Oxford: Oxford University Press, 2016), Ch. 6. See also Mario D'Addio, *L'Idea del Contratto Sociale dai Sofisti all Riforma e il De Principatu di Mario Salamonio* (Milan: Giuffrè, 1954).

post facto juristic construction" or "rationalization" whose existence was postulated by later Imperial jurists—above all, the third-century jurist, Ulpian—to legitimize the authority of the Roman Emperor by tracing the roots of Imperial power to a comitial act of the Roman *populus* to invest *imperium* in Augustus.[4] It was, as Clifford Ando put it, one of many "retrospective efforts by Romans to explain to themselves, within a single framework and using a single language, both the failure of democratic republicanism and its resolution in the pernicious façade of republican monarchy."[5]

To be sure, the hypothesis of a constitutional *lex regia* establishing the Empire was not entirely speculative. Aside from the few mentions of the *lex regia* in the *Corpus*, perhaps the closest approximation to a *lex regia*—and the supposed evidence corroborating its existence in classical law—was the *lex de imperio Vespasiani* of 69 C.E., discovered by Cola di Rienzo, the formal legal act of the ceremonial curiate assembly, or *comitia curiata*, whereby imperial authority, or *imperium*, was formally invested by the Roman people in the Emperor Vespasian.[6] This *lex* seems like a promising candidate for what later jurists would call the *lex regia*. Indeed, early modern commentators, most notably Bodin, specifically identified the *lex regia* with the *lex de imperio Vespasiani*, thus dating the origins of the Principate, not with Augustus in 27 B.C.E., but nearly a century later with Vespasian.[7]

[4] Theodor Mommsen, *Römisches Staatsrecht*, Vol. 2, 3rd ed. (Leipzig: S. Hirzel, 1887) 876–9. J.P. Canning, *Political Thought of Baldus de Ubaldis* (Cambridge: Cambridge University Press, 1987) 25; J.P. Canning, *A History of Medieval Political Thought* (London: Routledge, 2005) 8; David Johnston, "The General Influence of Roman Institutions of State and Public Law," *The Civilian Tradition and Scots Law: Aberdeen Quincentenary Essays*, ed. D.L. Carey Miller and R. Zimmermann (Berlin: Duncker & Humblot, 1997) 91–2; W.W. Buckland, *A Textbook of Roman Law from Augustus to Justinian*, 3rd ed. (Cambridge: Cambridge University Press, 1963) 16. The Dutch humanist jurist, Martin Schoockius, in his *Tractatus de Lege Regia* suggested that the *lex regia* was even "invented" by Tribonian. Lomonaco, *New Studies on Lex Regia* 104, n.78, and 147.

[5] Ando, "Origins and Import" 935.

[6] However, in the *Glossa Ordinaria* on D.1.4.1 [on *lex regia*], Accursius hypothesizes that the *lex regia* refers instead to the *lex Hortensia* of 287 B.C.E. referenced by Pomponius in D.1.2.2.8: the statute which recognized *plebiscita* as valid legal enactments binding on all Roman citizens. The identification of the *lex regia* with the *lex de imperio Vespasiani* was only possible after the discovery of the latter text by Rienzo, a century after Accursius' analysis. The text of the *lex de imperio Vespasiani* can be found in Salvator Riccobono, *Fontes Iuris Romani Antejustiniani*, 3 vols. (Florence: Barbera, 1941) 1:154–6. The form of the *lex* is technically that of a *senatusconsultum*. The classic discussion of this *lex de imperio* in modern classical scholarship is P.A. Brunt, "Lex de Imperio Vespasiani," *Journal of Roman Studies* 67 (1977): 95–116. Gibbon notes Rienzo's "stupendous and laughable" transcription error in this text concerning the emperor's authority "to advance and to move forward the boundary lines of the *pomerium*" [*fines pomerii proferre promouere*]. *Pomerium* [an outer boundary of a city] was mistakenly transcribed as *pomarium* [orchard]. Edward Gibbon, *The History of the Decline and Fall of the Roman Empire*, 4 vols., 5th ed. (New York: Harper, 1887) 4:387 [Ch. 70, n.24].

[7] Bodin, *Commonweale* 98 [1.8]; cp. *Methodus* 177 and *Commonweale* 188–89 [2.1], 244 [2.7], 249 [2.7], which was likely supported by the study by Nicholas de Grouchy on the Roman *comitia*, *De Comitiis Romanorum* (Paris, 1555). On Grouchy's influence on Bodin, see Richard Tuck, "Hobbes and Democracy," *Rethinking the Foundations of Modern Political Thought*, ed. Annabel Brett, James Tully, and Holly Hamilton-Bleakley (Cambridge: Cambridge University Press, 2006) 182–3, and his forthcoming, *The Sleeping Sovereign*. John Selden suggests this identification of the *lex de imperio Vespasiani* with the *lex regia* was an early modern commonplace endorsed by such French legal humanist authorities as François Hotman, François Connan,

However, several considerations cast doubt upon that theory. One obvious difficulty concerned the description of this *lex* establishing the Empire as a "royal" [*regia*] law. As Vico would observe in his reading of Tacitus, "what kind of wisdom could suggest to designate that law with a word [i.e., *regia* = "royal"] so hateful to the Romans?"[8] Indeed, Augustus, whom Gibbon called "that subtle tyrant," was known to be careful in preserving the façade of Republican forms intact, precisely to keep up the appearance of continuity and avoid the accusation that his exercise of accumulated magisterial powers might be described—and, thus, opposed—as a new Roman monarchy.[9] More likely, the description of such a "royal" law was a later interpolation in the Dominate when, having dispensed with this Republican façade, it was well established that the Empire could properly be described as a monarchy.[10]

More important was the difference in the nature of the grant of authority envisaged by the two different *leges*. Whereas the *lex regia* was understood in the jurists' theory to be a "general mandate of authority containing neither specific limitations on imperial power nor specific exemptions from particular laws," the *lex de imperio* had in practice more precise parameters for its operation.[11] While a *lex de imperio* might, for example, grant specific dispensations from certain legal requirements or formalities or allow specific derogations from the law (the original meaning of the famous phrase, *legibus solutus*, appearing at D.1.3.31), it did not authorize the officeholder to make law, nor did it exempt the officeholder from *all* the laws.[12] In the Republican constitution,

and Pierre Grégoire [Gregorius]. John Selden, *Ioannis Seldeni ad Fletam Dissertatio* [*Ad Fletam*] ed. David Ogg (Cambridge: Cambridge University Press, 1925) 37.

[8] Giambattista Vico, *Universal Right*, trans. Giorgio Pinton and Margaret Diehl (Amsterdam: Rodopi, 2000) 137 [Chapter 160]. Gronovius, observing the improbability that Romans would have accepted a *princeps* with royal power [*potestas regia*], calls Augustus a "hypocrite." Lomonaco, *New Studies on Lex Regia* 109–10. Augustus' strategic decision to eschew the title of *rex, dictator*, or *Romulus* in favor of the more Republican-minded *princeps*—"the first citizen"—to designate his position in the emerging political order indicates the continuing anti-monarchical sentiment, or at least the risk of publicly appearing too sympathetic to monarchy.

[9] Augustus, at *Res Gestae Divi Augusti* 1.6, points out that, on three occasions (19, 18, 11 B.C.E.), he refused the extralegal powers to govern without a colleague offered to him by the and people by way of a *legis datio*. Karl Loewenstein, *The Governance of Rome* (The Hague: Martinus Nijhoff, 1973) 271. Greek commentators, such as Appian and Cassius Dio, however, saw through the façade and did not hesitate to call the Augustan Principate a monarchy. Appian, *Praef.* 14.60; *Civ.* 1.24. Cassius Dio, *Roman History* 53.16–18. See also Clifford Ando, "From Republic to Empire," *The Oxford Handbook of Social Relations in the Roman World*, ed. Michael Peachin (Oxford: Oxford University Press, 2011).

[10] Canning, *History of Medieval Political Thought* 9, suggests the monarchical language could have been a later Byzantine interpolation, but also notes Mommsen's hypothesis that it may simply reflect Ulpian's own Syrian heritage. Mommsen, *Römisches Staatsrecht* 2:876–9, and cp. Francesco Lucrezi, *Leges Super Principem* (Naples: Jovene, 1982) 179–84.

[11] Brian Tierney, "The Prince Is Not Bound by the Laws: Accursius and the Origins of the Modern State," *Comparative Studies in Society and History* 5 (1963): 390.

[12] See also D.32.23, C.6.23.3, Inst.2.17.8[7] for descriptions of the *princeps* as *legibus solutus*; see D.50.16.102 on what it means for a law to be *derogatur* or *abrogatur.* Cp. Buckland, *Text-Book of Roman Law* 15. Cujas, for example, insists that the rule of D.1.3.31 is an exemption of the *princeps* only from the *lex Iulia et Papia Poppaea*. Lomonaco, *New Studies on Lex Regia* 142.

for example, elected magistrates formally received their *imperium* only after the passage in the curiate assembly of a *lex de imperio* conferring such authority. Although it was chiefly a ceremonial act which typically followed election as a matter of course, these *leges de imperio* allowed the transfer of *imperium* to magistrates only on terms so narrowly crafted as never to be construed as an irrevocable investiture of an omnipotent, all-embracing sovereign power over the whole state.[13] Even extraordinary grants of *imperium*, such as the *imperium extra ordinem* or *imperium maius* extended to Pompey in 67 B.C.E., still came with an expiration date attached to the statute granting such proconsular authority, the *lex Gabinia de piratis persequendis*.[14] Above all, the continued usage of the curiate *leges de imperio* into the early Principate to invest *imperium* in the *princeps* as an "agglomeration of separate offices"—and not as a single person—indicates still further just how far apart historical reality was from the idealized *lex regia* imagined by later jurists.[15]

These considerations must rule out equating the *lex regia* exclusively with the *lex de imperio*, and we are left then with the unsettling conclusion that there was, in fact, no *lex regia* except as a fiction or heuristic for the periodization of Roman history invented in the historical imagination of later Imperial jurists. One consequence of profound importance follows from this. Because there never was such a *lex regia*, there can be no single date or moment in Roman constitutional history when the Roman Republic suddenly transformed legally into a different constitutional form, the Principate.[16] One fades gradually and imperceptibly into the other in the stream of constitutional evolution.

What would then be the point of the *lex regia* in Roman legal thought? Two related observations might be suggested. One concerns continuity. The purpose of the *lex regia* is to function as a historical device to connect two otherwise disjointed eras of Roman constitutional history in one continuous narrative. It is what would have to be assumed to treat the Republic and Principate as two historical periods of one and the same state, rather than as two entirely different, successive states punctuated by violent revolution.[17]

[13] Ando, *Law, Language, and Empire in the Roman Tradition* 102.

[14] It is precisely for this reason that Bodin viewed Pompey as holding "absolute" power though not "sovereign" power. *Commonweale* 90 [1.8]; cp. on the *lex Gabinia*, W.R. Loader, "Pompey's Command under the *Lex Gabinia*," *The Classical Review* 54 (1940): 134–6. In the Latin edition of *De Republica* 84 [1.8], Bodin inserts a discussion of the *lex regia*, arguing that the first *princeps* was not sovereign, even though he is absolute, "exempted from every law of his country indefinitely" [*etiamsi omnibus patriae legibus in perpetuo solutus sit*]. This is consistent with his view that the Roman emperors only became truly sovereign beginning with Vespasian.

[15] Ando, *Law, Language, and Empire in the Roman Tradition* 101.

[16] A common theme in classical scholarship is that the major institutional features of Roman imperialism were already well developed long before the *lex Titia* of 43 B.C.E. granting an almost omnicompetent authority first to the Triumvirate of Augustus, Antony, and Lepidus, and finally, Augustus alone. The Augustan Principate operated under the "façade" of *de iure* Republican forms, even while political power was exercised *de facto* as a monarchy.

[17] James Hankins, "Exclusivist Republicanism and the Non-Monarchical Republic," *Political Theory* 38 (2010): 453–4. The influence of Tacitus is palpable.

The other point concerns legitimacy. In explaining why the Republic became an Empire, the *lex regia* offers a normative theory justifying the legality of this transformation. That normative theory was a doctrine of popular sovereignty: The Roman Empire, governed under the supreme authority of the *princeps*, is legitimate *only* because the Roman people had legally established it by a free sovereign act.[18]

Whether such an act should be called popular sovereignty is, however, open to interpretation; in part because it is not yet clear what such a doctrine requires of the people. Can the *lex regia*—assuming it did exist—genuinely be called a constitutional law of popular sovereignty if such a transferal of popular authority to the *princeps* was complete and irrevocable, such that the *populus* divested itself of its original authority? Or did the *populus Romanus* reserve some residual authority for themselves in making the grant via the *lex regia*?

THE GLOSSATORS AND THE *LEX REGIA*: THE TRANSLATION THEORY

Classical Roman law provided no guidance on the proper interpretive position on this question. It didn't need to provide such guidance. Aside from the absence of any such *lex* to interpret (as we have seen above), there was no real constitutional doubt, by the time Ulpian makes reference to the *lex regia* in the third century, that the Roman Emperor held supreme authority as a *rex* in his own right (or *dominus* beginning in the reign of Diocletian), and not behind the Republican constitutional façade of the *princeps* as a super-magistrate exercising authority only by a lawful concessive grant of the Roman people. References to the *populus* as the sole source of princely authority became instead more of a perfunctory afterthought, certainly not intended to be taken seriously as an expression of popular sovereignty in the Roman Imperial context. The story of the Roman people in the *lex regia* was indeed a part of a popular civic mythology, what Gibbon dismissed as nothing but a "fancy" of Ulpian and Tribonian, or as one recent historian has put it, an "old wives' tale" that even Justinian, in his Constitution, *Deo Auctore* in 530 C.E., found it convenient to invoke in announcing his grand legislative project in codifying the texts that would become the *Corpus Iuris Civilis*.[19]

It is only when these Justinianic texts of Roman law were rediscovered and studied outside of their classical context in the universities of medieval Italy, after centuries of dormancy and long after the decline of the Western Roman

[18] There is a more complicated addendum to this theory, owing to the divine source of the Imperial authority in the Constitution, *Deo Auctore*. See Canning, *A History of Medieval Political Thought* 7 and Magnus Ryan, "Political Thought," *Cambridge Companion to Roman Law*, ed. David Johnston (Cambridge: Cambridge University Press, 2015).

[19] Justinian, D. *Constitutio Deo Auctore*, §7. Edward Gibbon, *The History of the Decline and Fall of the Roman Empire*, ed. J.B. Bury (Cambridge: Cambridge University Press, 1898 [2013]) 4:451 [Ch. 44]; Olaf Pedersen, *The First Universities: Studium Generale and the Origins of University Education in Europe* (Cambridge: Cambridge University Press, 1997) 37.

Empire as a genuine political and military force, that the interpretation of the *lex regia* became a real live constitutional question attracting serious theoretical argumentation and reflection.[20] It is here, in the context of medieval legal scholarship that the juridical origins of modern sovereignty doctrines are to be found.

This was the singular achievement of the jurists who, in studying and commenting upon the newly discovered Roman law books in the university of Bologna, revived Western legal science and consequently made possible what Paul Vinogradoff once called the "second life of Roman law."[21] Because of their scholarly practice of inserting technical or explanatory notes and cross-references in the form of marginal "glosses" in the legal texts themselves, these early generations of jurists were called the "Glossators." In reading and glossing these texts, the Glossators saw their primary task as one of exegesis. Their charge was to render these ancient legal texts legible and coherent for a post-Classical readership, a task which often required the careful harmonizing of facially contradictory source texts.[22] Over time, their collected glosses formed a massive body of legal scholarship in its own right, equal in importance to the Roman texts themselves.

The renewed interest in legal science beginning in the eleventh century, however, was not exclusively academic.[23] There was an important political motivation for promoting the study of the Roman law, rooted in the perceived need for a formal statement on the juridical foundations and scope of public authority in the fragmented pluralistic political world of the European Middle Ages.[24] For the Glossators who painstakingly pieced together the doctrines scattered throughout Justinian's texts, the *lex regia* was of paramount importance in this respect. It provided one of the very few instances in all of the *Corpus Iuris Civilis* that commented directly on the legal meaning and status of the term, *princeps*, and more specifically, the constitutional foundations of princely *imperium* in Roman law.[25] To be sure, this was not a priority for the jurists of Roman Antiquity whose focus was almost exclusively on private law.

[20] Although the Justinianic texts were only rediscovered in the eleventh century, other "vulgar" sources of Roman law, such as the *Lex Visigothorum*, remained accessible in the early Middle Ages. On the medieval rediscovery of Roman law, in general, see Stein, *Roman Law in European History* 43–9 and, more generally, Bellomo, *Common Legal Past of Europe*; Ullmann, *Law and Politics in the Middle Ages*; Wieacker, *A History of Private Law in Europe*.

[21] Paul Vinogradoff, *Roman Law in Medieval Europe* (Oxford: Clarendon Press, 1929) 13.

[22] One famous example concerns the *princeps legibus solutus* of D.1.3.31 and the *digna vox* of C.1.14.4, which describes the emperor as subject to the laws. See Tierney, "The Prince Is Not Bound By the Laws" and, more generally, Hermann Kantorowicz and W.W. Buckland, ed., *Studies in the Glossators of the Roman Law* (Cambridge: Cambridge University Press, 1938).

[23] Francesco Calasso, *I Glossatori: E la Teoria della Sovranita*, 2nd ed. (Milan: Guiffré Editore, 1951).

[24] H. Koeppler, "Frederick Barbarossa and the Schools of Bologna," *English Historical Review* 54 (1939): 577–607.

[25] On the Glossators' use of Roman law to develop doctrines of princely authority in general, see Pennington, *Prince and the Law* Chs. 1–3, especially 77–90.

But for the jurists of the Italian Middle Ages, where the rule of princes or *signori* was something of a constitutional norm, it was the major question of public law that needed to be settled, and the Roman law provided the Glossators with the analytical tools to begin investigating it methodically.

At first glance, the doctrine established in the *lex regia* appears simple and straightforward: the Roman *populus* conferred [*conferat*] their original lawmaking authority upon the Roman *princeps* by a general comitial act which thereby established the constitution of the Augustan Principate and legitimized, thereafter, the emperor's lawmaking authority over all Romans.[26] It is *because* of the people's voluntary act of surrender by the *lex regia* that the emperor gets to make law without restriction as it "pleases" [*placuit*] him.[27] But it was not clear, according to the medieval Glossators, what kind of transfer or transaction was entailed by the term, *conferat* (or, in some editions of the medieval *Digestum Vetus*, rendered by a slight conjugation, *contulerit*). What would it mean, legally speaking, for one party to "bestow," "convey," or "confer" [*conferre*] authority upon another party?

Two principal positions emerged among the Glossators in response to this interpretive puzzle in medieval legal thought.[28] On the one hand, the *lex regia* could be understood as a *translatio imperii*—an irrevocable transfer, conveyance, and even alienation of authority—such that the Roman *populus* divested itself completely of its original authority and, thus, retained no residual claim over the authority given to the *princeps*. On the other hand, the *lex regia* could be understood as a mere *concessio*—a temporary or conditional grant of authority—such that princely authority was understood to be a revocable investiture and held and exercised theoretically only by the permissive will of the people.

[26] D.1.4.1; Inst. 2.1.6; C.1.17.1.7. I am grateful to Kenneth Pennington for indicating the locus in the digital facsimile of the *Codex Florentinus* (Florence: Biblioteca Laurenziana).

[27] The meaning of Ulpian's infamous phrase at D.1.4.1, *Quod principi placuit legis habet vigorem* ["What please the prince has the force of law"], relies on a technically narrow meaning of the expression, *placere mihi*, which in classical Roman law simply means, "in my opinion," and was used to indicate a jurist's opinion on a specific matter of law. So, for example, *Papiniano placuit* is rendered, "In Papinian's opinion, this is what the law means." The expression, *Quod principi placuit*, thus, did not originally indicate an arbitrary or discretionary lawmaking will or absolute power of the *princeps*, as it did for post-classical jurists, but simply the judgment of the *princeps* over the opinion of inferior judges. Fritz Schulz, "Bracton on Kingship," *English Historical Review* 60 (1945): 154.

[28] The *loci classici* of the Glossators' treatment of the *lex regia* in the Anglophone scholarship include Carlyle, *A History of Mediaeval Political Theory in the West* Ch. 7; Gierke, *Political Theories of the Middle Ages* 37–46; C.N.S. Woolf, *Bartolus of Sassoferrato: His Position in the History of Medieval Political Thought* (Cambridge: Cambridge University Press, 1913) 35–41; Walter Ullmann, *The Medieval Idea of Law as Represented by Lucas De Penna: A Study in Fourteenth-Century Legal Scholarship* (London: Methuen, 1946) 48–9; Tierney, *Religion, Law, and the Growth of Constitutional Thought* 56–60; Canning, *Political Thought of Baldus de Ubaldis* 55–64. Although the *lex regia* was a common object of study in humanist legal scholarship, perhaps the earliest major modern discussion of the Glossators' scholarship can be found in Friedrich Karl von Savigny, *Geschichte des Römischen Rechts im Mittelalter* (Heidelberg: Mohr, 1834). Francesco Calasso warns of the narrow idealism of such nineteenth-century German Romantic scholarship in *I Glossatori* 18–20. See also Ennio Cortese, *La Norma Giuridica: Spunti Teorici nel Diritto Comune Classico*, 2 vols. (Milan: Giuffrè, 1962).

Adjudicating between these two interpretive poles was a critically important matter, because how one answered the question would have had direct consequences for the Romanist theory of princely authority. Reading the verb, "to convey" [*conferre*], as a *translatio* would have signaled an ideological orientation favoring princely absolutism, since an irrevocable and permanent donation or conveyance of authority—as the word, *translatio*, implied—would undoubtedly empower a *princeps* to exercise a broad set of powers, untethered not only from the will of the people, but, indeed, also from the law itself [*legibus solutus*].[29] This "translation theory" of the *lex regia*—what Walter Ullmann once described as "the majority opinion" of the Glossators—is perhaps one of the major reasons why Roman law rapidly acquired a reputation, especially in early modern Anglophone legal thought, as favoring absolutism.[30]

The first Glossators, who founded the Bolognese school at the beginning of the eleventh century, had developed this opinion in their canonical readings of the *lex regia*. These readings formed the core of the Glossators' teachings on civil law and significantly shaped how later generations assimilated Roman legal doctrines to a post-Roman world. This was particularly important in the case of the *lex regia*. In his gloss on a central passage in the *Digestum Vetus*, Irnerius (c.1050–c.1130), the "Father of the Glossators," explains that the Roman people may have had the power to make and unmake law at one time in Antiquity, but they had fully lost that capacity in his day "because such power has already been transferred [*translata*] to the Emperor." Thus, what the *Digest* says (D.1.3.32) concerning the residual ability of the people to "abrogate" [*abrogentur*] a law simply by the "tacit consent of all the people through desuetude" [*tacito consensu omnium per desuetudinem*] was no longer valid and, thus, should be treated merely as a curious historical artifact of pre-Imperial Rome [*sua tempora*].[31]

Irnerius' position on the *lex regia* as a complete and irrevocable transfer became the standard doctrine for later Glossators. Placentinus (d.1192), who studied at Bologna and later taught civil law at Montpellier, likewise in his *Summa Institutionum* denies any residual lawmaking power in the people because, as he writes, "the people, in transferring [*transferendo*] their public power to the Emperor, reserved nothing for themselves."[32] While the people

[29] Tierney, "Prince Is Not Bound by the Laws" 389. While Adhemar Esmein locates the absolutist interpretation of the *lex regia* in the Glossators in "La maxime Princeps legibus solutus est dans l'ancien droit public français," *Essays in Legal History*, ed. Paul Vinogradoff (Oxford: Oxford University Press, 1913), Fritz Schulz suggests, in "Bracton on Kingship" 136–76, that Justinian's sixth-century compilers were themselves receptive to this view, suggesting that legislative absolutism was not a uniquely medieval doctrine. On the word, *transferre*, and what can and cannot be "transferred" [*translata*], see D.50.17.11; 50.17.54.

[30] Ullmann, *The Medieval Idea of Law* 48–9.

[31] Irnerius on D.1.3.32, quoted in Savigny, *Geschichte des Römischen Rechts im Mittelalter* 4:387 (texts for n.49). Savigny is citing MS.Par.4451. See also Ryan, "Political Thought" 3, n.6. Cp. the canonist doctrine of Gratian, *De Legibus*, D.4, *dictum post c.3*, which cites C.1.14.8, indicating that *leges* certainly can be abrogated by *mores* of the people.

[32] Placentinus, *Summa Institutionum* 1.2, quoted in Carlyle, *History of Mediaeval Political Theory* 2:60, n.2.

may have had the ability to create new customs, the power to make formal written statutes now belonged exclusively to the Emperor by the *lex regia* and could not be overridden or abrogated by the people.[33] Placentinus' contemporary, Rogerius (d. c.1162–66), again recites, in his *Summa,* the substance of the translation theory, stating that "the people transferred [*transtulit*] to him and in him all their power [*potestatem omnem*]."[34] For him, the popular origin of princely authority is simply irrelevant. Since the people have already surrendered all claim to power, it can now only be the Emperor alone, or his authorized designee, who can properly make valid law.

Taken together, the Glossators reading the *lex regia* in favor of the translation theory accepted the basic assumption that all princely authority ultimately originated in the Roman people. But they insisted on distinguishing between two very different ways of understanding the constitutional significance of the popular origins of such authority. While they may willingly accept, as a point of historical fact, that princely authority originated in the Roman people, they were less willing to accept the far more controversial view that, *because* they were the source of the emperor's authority, it can be assumed that the Roman people therefore reserved some residual claim over the powers it had given away. For these Glossators, the outcome of the *lex regia* which constituted the Augustan regime was an irreversible and historically unique act. Just because the people were, historically, the *source* of the emperor's power, it did not follow from that fact alone that the people were entitled to recover it at some later date. The translation theorists insisted that the original sovereignty of the *populus Romanus* can only be understood as a historical curiosity, but nothing more.

One important consequence of the translation theory is that it seems to make popular sovereignty not so much the antithesis of princely absolutism, but rather its original foundation. By co-opting the Republican language of popular sovereignty in this way, these jurists have managed to turn the *lex regia* into a formula that effectively muzzles the popular will while lending popular legitimacy to even the most absolutist arrangements of princely rule. As we shall see, it is a strategic use of popular sovereignty doctrines later to be deployed in exactly the same manner by modern natural rights theorists such as Grotius and Hobbes, and to be rejected, in turn, by Rousseau.

THE GLOSSATORS AND THE *LEX REGIA*: THE CONCESSION THEORY OF AZO

If the translation theory was the majority view of the Glossators on the *lex regia,* it was certainly not the unanimous view. Alongside the interpretation of the *lex regia* as an alienation or *translatio* of popular authority, arose what Walter Ullman described as an influential "minority opinion" which treated

33 Placentinus on C.8.52(53).2, quoted in Ullmann, *Medieval Idea of Law* 49.

34 Rogerius, *Summa Codicis* 1.12, quoted in Carlyle, *History of Mediaeval Political Theory* 2:61, n.1.

the Roman people's conferral of authority as a *concessio.*[35] The position presented a stark contrast to the prevailing view that the *lex regia* was an irrevocable *translatio.* The idea here was that, in the "conferral" of authority by the ancient *lex regia*, the people granted such authority only by way of a limited and fully revocable concessive delegation. It was not a gift, but a loan. The upshot is that the people must have retained some residual or reserve power over the *princeps* who, consequently, is seen to function as a kind of appointed agent acting only on the people's mandate. He remains tethered to the will of the people. The relationship between *populus* and *princeps* is, thus, reversed in the concession theory. Whereas the *princeps* was understood to have supreme authority under the translation theory, it is, in the concession theory, the Roman *populus* which is constitutionally supreme.

This interpretation of the *lex regia* was initially suggested by the Glossator, Joannes Bassianus, but its most important and prominent defender was his pupil, Azo Portius (1150–1230), whom Quentin Skinner singles out not only for having "defended a doctrine of popular sovereignty," but also for having played a central role in the "rediscovery of republican values" in twelfth-century Italy.[36] Also a product of the Bolognese School, Azo developed his theory in his influential *Summa* on Justinian's *Code*—"one of the most popular and frequently cited works"—in direct opposition to the doctrine articulated by Irnerius, Rogerius, and Placentinus.[37] His most famous statement of the concession theory appears in connection with a constitution of Emperor Justinian in the rubric, *De legibus et constitutionibus principum et edictis* [D.1.14(17)], in the *Code.* Here, Justinian considers the question regarding the competence of the emperor to act as an *interpreter* of the law, not just an *author* of law. His answer leaves no doubt that "all interpretations of the laws by the emperor" are "to be held valid and indisputable."[38] This is because the capacity to interpret the laws [*leges interpretari*] is implicit in the capacity "to make laws" [*leges condere*]. And since the capacity to make laws is "conceded exclusively to the emperor alone" [*soli imperatori concessum est*], it follows that the "emperor alone" [*solus imperator*] is as much "author of the laws" as he is "interpreter of the laws" [*tam conditor quam interpres legum*].[39]

This stunning statement of princely authority in the *Code* presented an obvious challenge to Azo's attempt to derive a genuine theory of popular sovereignty out of Roman law. How could the *populus* be understood to be the sovereign and independent source of law in the Empire if the "emperor alone,"

[35] Ullmann, *Medieval Idea of Law* 48. More recently, Ando, *Law, Language, and Empire in the Roman Tradition* 93. Paris, Bibliothèque Nationale de France lat.4450 shows the interlinear glosses on D.1.4.1, which specify that the verb, *conferat*, ought to be understood as *cessit*. I am grateful to Kenneth Pennington for sharing this text.

[36] Quentin Skinner, "The Rediscovery of Republican Values," *Visions of Politics*, Vol. 2 (Cambridge: Cambridge University Press, 2002) 2:14; cp. Ando, *Law, Language, and Empire* 89–9.

[37] Ullmann, *Law and Politics in the Middle Ages* 100.

[38] C.1.14.12.3.

[39] C.1.14.12.5.

as Justinian makes plain in this text, is the exclusive maker and interpreter of all law?

Azo's solution reaches into the heart of the interpretive problem presented by the *lex regia*. He begins in his influential *Summa* on the *Code*, where he lays out his position, in defiance of Justinian and of the earlier Bolognese Glossators who defended the emperor's juridical absolutism: "Law," Azo writes in the *Summa*, "can perhaps be made by the Roman people even today [i.e., twelfth-century Italy]."[40] But he acknowledges the problem presented by the *lex regia*, since "it is said such lawmaking power has been transferred [*translata*] into the *princeps*."[41] The corresponding discussion in Azo's *Lectura* on this rubric, again, highlights this problem, observing that "the Roman people does not have the power of making law [*potestatem legis condendae*] which they once held, but by the *lex regia*, they transferred [*transtulit*] all such right [*ius*] to the emperor."[42]

But what does it mean for the people to have "transferred" lawmaking power to the emperor? Unlike Irnerius, Placentinus, and Rogerius, Azo explains that the proper way to understand this "transfer," signified by the various conjugations of the verb, "*transferre*," in the *Code*, is to think of it specifically as something that has been "conceded" [*concessa*], such that "the people will not have entirely abdicated [*abdicaverit*] their power," but instead will be presumed to have reserved some residual right over those powers which are entrusted to the emperor.[43]

The implication was clear. Whatever is conceded by one party to another can again be revoked or reclaimed by the concessor. So, it follows that, if the *populus Romanus* "conceded" their original power to the emperor, so as to be exercised on mandate as an agent or delegate of the people, the *populus* must also be presumed to have retained in principle the residual capacity to revoke the emperor's power as well. And that is precisely Azo's finding in the *Summa*:

> For even after they [the *populus*] had transferred [*transtulerat*] their power to make laws, they were nevertheless able to revoke [*revocavit*] that transfer at a later stage, as it is reported in [D.1.2.2.3, 1.2.2.14, 1.2.2.24].[44]

So it seems that, even after the transfer of their original authority, the Roman *populus* still retained at least two basic, but very important, legal capacities—(1) the capacity to make valid law via custom, as reported by Julian [at D.1.3.32.1, an analysis previously rejected by Irnerius and Placentinus], and (2) the residual capacity to revoke the emperor's plenary lawmaking power.[45]

[40] Azo, *Azonis Summa* [Lyon, 1557] (Frankfurt am Main, 1968) fol. 7 [on C.1.14, §8]. I defer until the next chapter a discussion of what Glossators mean by the locution, "Roman people today."

[41] Azo, *Summa* fol. 7 [on C.1.14(17), §8].

[42] Azo, *Lectura Azonis et Magni Apparatus ad Singulas Leges Duodecim Librorum Codicis Iustiniani* (Paris, 1581) 44 [on C.1.14(17).12(11), §§49–50, on *Soli Imperatori*]; cp. Ullmann, *Law and Politics* 101, n.1.

[43] Azo, *Summa* fol. 7 [on C.1.14(17), §8]. Cp. Azo, *Lectura* 44 [on C.1.14(17).12,(11) *Soli Imperatori* §§49–52] and the *Lectura* on C.8.52(53).2.

[44] Azo, *Summa* fol. 7 [on C.1.14(17), §8].

[45] Cp. Gratian D.12, c.6.

But how does Azo's theory of popular sovereignty square with Justinian's statement in the *Code*, which declared that only the emperor, and no other, can make and interpret law? Azo accepts that, by the *lex regia*, the *populus* voluntarily divested itself of some lawmaking powers by "conceding" those powers to the emperor. As a result, the people entered a passive state of constitutional dormancy, while the emperor actively governed in their place. They are thus "excluded" from the power to make laws, so long as the emperor held such power.[46] But Azo adds one additional point of monumental importance for the theory of popular sovereignty:

> The people are not excluded [from "the power of making law"], but merely the individual members comprising the body of the people [*singuli de populo*]. In this respect the people are similar to the well-known example of Scipio. Scipio alone [*Solus Scipio*] acted in freeing the whole Roman *civitas*. However, the people was not excluded in this act... Indeed, it is closer to truth to say the people as a whole acted, much more so than any one particular individual separate from the others. Individuals are thus for this reason excluded, but not the people considered as a whole [*universitas sive populus*].[47]

In this way, Azo distinguishes between two fundamentally different ways of understanding the term, *populus*, as it appears in the *lex regia*. One concept of the *populus* views it as a collection of separate individuals [*singuli*]. But the other concept of the *populus* introduces the notion that the people can be regarded as a unified whole, and not simply as an aggregate of individual parts. To give expression to this concept, he applied the medieval term of art, *universitas*, to emphasize its whole and indivisible [*universus*] nature as a unitary entity.[48] This important conceptual distinction between the "people" as a mere collection of *singuli* and the "people" as a whole *universus* famously allows him to specify in what way the *populus* is legally sovereign over the emperor: "Although the emperor is of greater power than any individual member of the populace [*quilibet de populo*], he is not of greater power than the populace as a whole [*totus populus*]," an analysis which Peter Stein has described as "momentous for political theory."[49]

Azo, thus, gives us a profound statement on interpreting the constitutional relationship between *populus* and *princeps* in the *lex regia*. But there is a more general lesson to take away. Not only is the *populus* (taken as *universitas*) supreme over the *princeps*, but the *populus* is indeed supreme over all legally constituted public authorities lawfully exercising jurisdiction, which, for Azo, includes inferior magistrates exercising a jurisdiction of a lesser grade than

[46] D.13.6.5.15. [47] Azo, *Lectura* 44 [on C.1.14(17).12(11), *Soli Imperatori* §§51–2].

[48] On the people as *universitas* represented through its legal *procurator*, see Gierke, *Political Theories of the Middle Ages* 63; Tierney, *Religion, Law, and the Growth of Constitutional Thought* 19–28; Ando, *Law, Language, and Empire in the Roman Tradition* 94–9. Cp. Inst.1.2.4 on *Populi Universi*.

[49] Stein, *Roman Law in European History* 60, citing Azo on C.8.52(53).2.

that of the *princeps*.[50] This is because the source of all such public authority—whether that of the emperor or that of the lowest magistrate—can only be located uniformly in the "consent of the whole community considered as a collectivity [*universitas*]."[51] Like the emperor, then, civil magistrates similarly derive their authority from similar concessive acts, approximating the *lex regia*. The result is that all public power (not just princely power) must originate in the *universitas* of the people, and it is to this popular *universitas* that all public power must ultimately return.

THE *LEX REGIA* AND THE *GLOSSA ORDINARIA*

Like the early Glossators' textual scholarship on other areas of Roman law, these early interpretive debates on the *lex regia* in the school of Bologna produced a standard set of texts summarizing the various arguments and explaining the translation and concession theories. They did so in a way that underscored the Glossators' working assumption that the civil law as a whole was fully consistent, admitting no internal contradictions. But because these doctrines developed only gradually as marginalia, like layers sedimenting haphazardly on the original Roman law text, it became necessary for later Glossators to begin organizing these notes in a more orderly and accessible manner. Early attempts yielded such works as the *Summa Trecensis* and the *Dissensiones Dominorum*, as well as Azo's own *Summa* on the *Code*, which were explanatory texts used by the Glossators to summarize their exegetical strategies in teaching the civil law.

Without doubt the most important of the Glossatorial texts was the *Glossa Ordinaria* to the civil law, compiled by Azo's pupil, the thirteenth-century Bolognese Glossator, Accursius (c.1182–c.1260). Its importance lay not solely in its content, but also in its form of presentation. The *Glossa Ordinaria*—or the "Great Gloss"—was not a standalone work, like a printed book; it was, instead, the presentation of the Roman law with the accompanying glosses comprising exegetical notes and cross references written in the margins of the page surrounding the relevant Roman text, like a modern critical edition of a primary text. With an estimated 100,000 glosses, Accursius' compilation was by far the most ambitious of its time, earning him the title, "Prince of the Glossators."[52] Indeed, because of its magisterial scope and presentation, the Accursian Gloss became the standard reference work in the study and practice of civil law; so much so, that Accursius' text was treated as being equally important as the Justinianic text to which it referred.

It is difficult to understate the significance of Accursius' work for civil law. Manuscript transcriptions as well as *incunabula* of the Roman law always included the *Glossa Ordinaria*, and it was in this standardized form, combining

[50] Myron Piper Gilmore, *Argument from Roman Law in Political Thought, 1200–1600* (Cambridge: Harvard University Press, 1941) 15–27. See Chapter 3 below.

[51] Stein, *Roman Law in European History* 60.

[52] Bellomo, *Common Legal Past of Europe* 172–4.

the Roman text with the full medieval Accursian apparatus, that university law students studied civil law for centuries, well beyond the Middle Ages. Even as late as the sixteenth century, when humanist jurists began to question the value of the glosses, civilians continued to rely on the authority of Accursius in parsing Justinian's original text, a legal practice supported by the publication of Denis Godefroy's standard edition of the *Corpus Iuris Civilis*, which included not only the Justinianic text, but also the *Glossa Ordinaria*.

Despite the later continuing influence of the Accursian Gloss, the actual content of the glosses themselves were largely derivative, dependent on the work of his Bolognese predecessors. This was by design. Accursius envisaged the *Glossa Ordinaria* chiefly as a reference work and as a teaching tool, which gathered together and summarized the various opinions on all topics of the civil law. His primary purpose was merely to catalogue and present a balanced account of the legal dicta the Glossators had taught on specific points of civil law, not to pass judgment on them.

This was the case for Accursius' treatment of the *lex regia* in the *Glossa Ordinaria*. While Accursius presented the case and textual support for both the translation theory and the concession theory, the Great Gloss officially generated no decisive view on what counted as a proper reading of the *lex regia*.[53] Indeed, Accursius' text was facially neutral on the matter, even though Azo's concession theory undoubtedly remained an unorthodox "minority" view among the Glossators as well as for later jurists.

Yet, it is evident, when one looks closely at the web of interconnected texts constituting the glosses on the *lex regia*, that Accursius carefully pieced together a doctrine potentially favorable to the concession theory of popular sovereignty. Though unremarkable by itself and perhaps even unintended by Accursius himself, the presence of this concession analysis on such a prominent stage offered later generations of jurists the analytical resources in the civil law to craft a constitutional doctrine that inverted the juridical relationship between *populus* and *princeps*, locating supremacy in the former rather than the latter.

Accursius' main point of entry for his analysis of the *lex regia* was, unsurprisingly, Ulpian's use of that troublesome verb, *conferre*. Recalling the dispute between the translation theorists and the concession theorists, Accursius suggested that *conferre* [or *contulerit* or *conferat*] in this context should be read as equivalent in meaning to another account of this constitutional rupture in Roman history appearing elsewhere in the *Digestum Vetus*, the moment when a *lex regia* would theoretically have been enacted by the *populus*:

> For whereas in the times of our ancestors supreme power was temporarily entrusted to dictators, and they chose masters of the horse who wielded power in the second degree after the dictator as associates sharing in their burdens for military purposes; so too when governance of the commonwealth [*regimentis rei*

[53] Gierke, *Political Theories of the Middle Age* 150, n.158.

> *publicae*] was transferred to permanent emperors [*ad imperatores perpetuos translatis*], they chose prefects of the praetorian guard, on the analogy of the masters of the horse.[54]

Accursius presents a similar analysis on the *lex regia* in a corresponding passage in the *Institutes*:

> What the Emperor determines has the force of a statute, the people having conferred [*contulerit*; *concessit*] on him all their authority and power by the *lex regia*, which was passed concerning his office and authority.[55]

The gloss on *contulerit*, however, makes clear that *contulerit* should be read as *translatio*:

> "Conferred": That is, the people transferred [*transtulerit*] their authority and power, in such a manner that the people themselves no longer held this right, as at [C.1.17(20).2.21] and [C.1.14(17).12(11)].[56]

Taken together, it would appear that the position of the Great Gloss favored the translation theory, that the people gave up entirely their original *imperium* and transferred it in full, as a *translatio*, to the emperor.[57]

But this would be an incomplete and even superficial conclusion because, in the same gloss, Accursius recognizes that jurists, above all Azo, suggested another way of looking at the issue:

> Others say [*alii dicunt*] nevertheless that the people are still able to make law, and it is said that only the prince [*solum principem*] is able to do this alone—that is, no other individual [*nullus alius solus*], according to Azo.[58]

But even Accursius opens this possibility in his own analysis, and this is because, for him, the word, *translatio*, can have complex meanings in the civil law.

He pursues this hermeneutic line of inquiry, beginning with his relatively short gloss on D.1.11.1 cited above. In that gloss, Accursius clarifies that *translatis* or, more generally, conjugations of the verb, *transferre*, should properly be read according to the analysis he supplies in glosses on two other key instances of *transferre* in the Roman law, one of which appears in the *Code*, and the other appears in another rubric of the *Digest*.[59]

[54] *Glossa Ordinaria* on D.1.4.1 on *Contulerit*, referencing D.1.11.1.pr.

[55] Inst.1.2.6. This text appears to be corrupt, as John Selden observed in his discussion of the *lex regia* in the *Ad Fletam Dissertatio* 25. Godefroy renders the verb in the dependent clause as *contulerit*, as it appears at D.1.4.1, and it is upon this word that Accursius writes his gloss (Denis Godefroy's *Volumen Legum Parvum* (Lyon, 1604)). But modern editions have it slightly differently, such as Krueger or in Eduard Huschke's edition of the *Institutes* (Leipzig, 1868) 5.

[56] *Glossa Ordinaria* on Inst.1.2.6, on *Contulerit*.

[57] Cp. *Glossa Ordinaria* on *Libri Feudorum* 26.1, on *An imperatorem*.

[58] *Glossa Ordinaria* on Inst.1.2.6, on *Contulerit*. Accursius does not mention it, but he is referring to Azo's comments on C.1.14(17).12(11). Here is an example of Accursius' neutrality—he reports, but does not judge which is the better view, a strategy typical of the Glossators.

[59] *Glossa Ordinaria* on D.1.11.1.pr, on *Translatis*.

Accursius' first citation refers to a statement of the Emperor Justinian recorded in the *Code* concerning the authority of the classical jurists (who, from Justinian's sixth-century point of view, would be already more than two centuries old). In commissioning Tribonian to redact the vast sources of Roman law into what would become the texts of the *Corpus Iuris Civilis*, Justinian explains the authority on which he is able to command him to undertake such a massive project of legal reform:

> For as by an ancient law which is designated "royal" [*regia*], all the rights and power of the Roman people were transferred [*translata sunt*] to the Imperial authority.[60]

Accursius observes, in this instance of the *lex regia*, that Justinian explicitly describes the conveyance of authority from people to emperor as a *translatio*. But the gloss on the phrase, *translata sunt*, introduces another critical clarification of meaning, when he writes that, "This is understood to be *concessa*, as in [D.1.21.1]."[61] I will return to this reference in just a moment, but let us consider first Accursius' other citation in his gloss.

In addition to his citation to the *Code*, Accursius supplies another citation in the gloss on D.1.11.1.pr. to a text in an earlier rubric in Book I of the *Digest* concerning the varieties of the sources of Roman law. The relevant text here again invokes Ulpian who, in evaluating the legal force of *senatusconsulta*, states that "there is no doubt that the senate has lawmaking power."[62]

The extensive gloss on this relatively short text is especially remarkable. Accursius asks speculatively "whether the senate today [i.e., of the thirteenth century] is able to make law," likely referring to the reconstituted Roman Senate in the medieval free Commune of Rome.[63] He recalls the analysis of his teacher's teacher, Bassianus, that the senate can certainly exercise public authority but only if the emperor has expressly permitted it [*nisi princeps permiserit*], since, according to the *Code*, only the emperor can make law. The senate's lawmaking capacity is thus presented as a case of an inferior delegated jurisdiction, subordinate to the full omnicompetent jurisdiction of the emperor and exercised only by way of concession.

This was, of course, not the only way to understand the Roman senate's lawmaking power and function. Its authority might just as well be understood as being capable of being acted on independently of the emperor's permissive will, which, as Accursius acknowledges, "others declare" [*alii dicunt*] and endorse.[64] It is true, Accursius observes from the *Code*, that the emperor

[60] C.1.17.1.7. [61] *Glossa Ordinaria* on C.1.17(20).1.7 on *Translata sunt*. [62] D.1.3.9.

[63] *Glossa Ordinaria* on D.1.3.9, *Non ambigitur*. Also note that "senate" becomes a generic term in medieval political theory to refer to any government of "optimates." Gregorovius, *History of the City of Rome in the Middle Ages*. Cp. Bartolus on D.49.15.24.n.6 on the meaning of *Populus Romanus*, Canning, *Political Thought of Baldus* 57, and Constantin Fasolt, *Limits of History* (Chicago: University of Chicago Press, 2004) 169.

[64] Accursius does not specify, but he is most likely referencing the *apparatus* of Azo and Hugolinus, his two major sources for the *Summa*. Bellomo, *Common Legal Past of Europe* 171–72. Observe the similarity of language with the gloss on Inst.1.2.6.

is the only individual who is empowered to make law in the Roman Empire. This legal rule, thus, excludes other individuals from exercising lawmaking power so that no other individual [*nullus alius solus*], other than the emperor, can rightfully make valid law. But remarkably, the rule does *not* exclude other *non*-individuals from exercising lawmaking power, so the senate (as one example of a non-individual, collective entity) can be said to have lawmaking power, which is precisely the opinion articulated in Ulpian's text in the *Digest*.

But the gloss does not end here. Accursius's reasoning exempted the senate from the legal rule reserving legislative competence exclusively for the emperor against all other individuals on the grounds that this rule does not apply to the senate, since it is not an individual but a collective unit—or as Azo put it, a *universitas*. Collective units, like senates, appear to have a valid claim to legislative competence. On this emerging doctrine, however, Accursius does not specify whether it is only the senate that is so privileged in this way, or whether this should be seen as a general rule suggesting that the genus of all collective units—of which the senate is but a species—might potentially be seen as possessing some degree of lawmaking power. Could, say, private corporations or associations make law? Could families make law?

In the present gloss, Accursius does not supply a concrete answer to this conceptual question; he leaves it open for others to parse. But he gives some hints indicating how it might be answered. We know, first of all, that the exemption from the rule was not to be limited to the senate since, as he now intimates in the gloss, even the *populus Romanus*—not just the senate—can be said to have a lawmaking power. So there is a broader lesson to be gleaned from this narrow analysis of the senate's legislative competence. Even more remarkably, Accursius seems to reject entirely the thesis that the senate's power derives from an antecedent concessive grant of the emperor, as suggested previously by Bassianus. Echoing Azo's earlier argument concerning the uniform source of all jurisdictional authority in the people, Accursius' gloss declares that it is not the emperor's lawmaking power that the senate exercises by way of concession. It is, rather, the people's.

Two related points of importance now emerge here. The first concerns the senate. While Accursius may allow, in principle, that collective units—whether senates or peoples—are empowered to make law, they are by no means equally positioned with respect to each other. Indeed, the gloss presents the senate as a lawmaking body, in some sense, *belonging* to the people.[65] Consequently, legislative acts of senatorial bodies, *senatusconsulta*, cannot properly be understood

[65] This interpretation is supported by the description of the senate as belonging to the people, in the phrase, *senatus eius*, in the gloss. The singular pronoun, "*eius*," in this sentence refers to *populus*. *Glossa Ordinaria* on D.1.3.9 on *Non ambigitur*. It is noteworthy that the author chooses to use the singular genitive, rather than the plural genitive, *eorum*. It indicates that the *populus* should be understood as a singular collective, rather than as a plural. On the significance of the singular and plural conceptions of the *populus* in the classical sources, see Ando, *Law, Language, and Empire in the Roman Tradition* 94–99, which discusses the present issue in connection with Cicero and Varro.

as untethered from popular consent, but are instead fundamentally derivative from—and, thus, attributable to—the people.

The second point redeploys this analysis to uncover the source of the emperor's authority. There is, to recapitulate, no doubt that the emperor alone [*solus imperator*], *qua* individual, has the exclusive power to make law, by imperial constitutions, edicts, and rescripts. This is never in question.[66] But what *is* in question is the reason *why* the emperor should have such authority at all. The answer is a familiar one. The only reason why the emperor is the only individual who can make law at all is "because the people transferred [*transtulit*] all their *imperium* to him [*in eum*]."[67]

Accursius has then, in a roundabout route, returned to the *lex regia*, but he has done so in a way that fundamentally displaces the emperor from his traditional position of juridical supremacy and reassigns it instead to the *populus Romanus*. It is, for Accursius, the people from whom senates and emperors derive their respective legal powers. To be sure, this, by itself, is an underwhelming statement of popular sovereignty since, as Placentinus and Rogerius have already observed, demonstrating the historical origins of imperial power in the people does not in any way derogate from the full authority presently enjoyed by the emperor. Something more, therefore, was necessary in the argument to explain how the *populus* could still be juridically supreme, even while accepting fully, without compromise, the validity of the emperor's lawmaking power.

The solution recorded in the gloss accomplishes this by reinterpreting the nature of the transfer of authority from the *populus* to the *princeps* in the *lex regia* in the terms of a concession:

> The Roman people can revoke [*revocare potest*] what it has conceded [*concessit*], like a judge who delegates jurisdiction, since they retained the right of ownership [*proprietas*] over that which they have granted, as at [D.1.21.1].[68]

In the end, then, Accursius concludes again by citing exactly the same passage in his gloss on Justinian's use of *translata sunt* in the *Code*—that is, D.1.21.1.

There are numerous moving parts packed tightly into this statement, so it is worth unpacking each part for inspection. We might begin with the concept of a "concession." It is not very difficult to see the significance of describing the people's transfer of authority as a conditionally limited concession.[69] Since anything that is granted by way of concession can be recovered, it follows that the *populus Romanus*, who "conceded" [*concessit*] their *imperium* to the emperor, can recover it as well. One immediate implication of this concession theory was that the *lex regia* could no longer be thought of simply as an ancient Roman

[66] Magnus Ryan, "Bartolus of Sassoferrato and the Free Cities," *Transactions of the Royal Historical Society*, Sixth Series, 10 (2000): 70.

[67] *Glossa Ordinaria* on D.1.3.9, *Non ambigitur.*

[68] *Glossa Ordinaria* on D.1.3.9, *Non ambigitur.*

[69] C.1.14(17).12(11).3.

relic stuck irretrievably in the classical past with no contemporary relevance. So long as there was a Roman Empire (even a fictive "Holy" Roman Empire), so must there also be a corresponding constitutional *lex* that authorizes or activates this *imperium.*[70] Not only does this finding suggest a major legal hermeneutic shift in the treatment of the *lex regia*, which can now be treated as a valid legal act still theoretically in effect.[71] It also opens up a potentially radical possibility, that a *populus* may theoretically dispossess their *princeps*—or any bearer of *imperium*—of his authority by re-activating and abrogating the very *lex* which transferred such authority to him in the first place.

But there are two additional features of this gloss that have, incidentally, received less attention in the modern scholarship on the *lex regia*, and it is on these features that I bring this chapter to a close. The first is Accursius' direct appeal to the analysis of D.1.21.1 in parsing the legal meaning of a *concessio.* The cited passage is a monumentally important text in the *Digest* originally by Papinian under the rubric concerning "delegated jurisdiction." It concerned a relatively narrow matter of civil procedure—i.e., the capacity of ordinary legally-constituted magistrates (such as praetors, proconsuls, or provincial governors) with jurisdiction held independently "by their own right" [*suo iure*] to delegate some share of their jurisdiction [*iurisdictionem mandare*] over civil disputes to private lay judges [*iudices*] or "arbiters" [*arbitri*] who, in turn, were said to exercise jurisdiction "by the favor of another" [*alieno beneficio*].[72] Accursius' strategy was, evidently, to draw an explicit comparison between the juridical relationship of the *populus* and *princeps* in the *lex regia*, as discussed by Ulpian, and the corresponding homologous relationship between the magistrate with ordinary jurisdiction and the lay judge with delegated jurisdiction. One is a "principal"; the other an "agent."

At first glance, this is not an obvious connection. The *lex regia* concerned the constitutional foundation of the Roman Empire by a transfer of *imperium* and *potestas* from *populus* to *princeps*. Papinian's text, by contrast, concerned a technical matter in the administration of justice in the Empire. Indeed, Papinian's commentary on delegated jurisdiction was more frequently invoked in medieval jurisprudence as a model for the analysis of the relationship between the emperor and his inferior magistrates, rather than the

[70] C.1.14(17).4. The gloss on C.6.23.3, *Lex imperii*, specifies that such a law should be understood to be the *lex regia*.

[71] Since this suggests that the *lex regia* is a kind of "living law" undergirding every instance of *imperium*, it is up to the jurist to determine what legal rule or practice approximates its function. One notable example might be Bracton's thesis that the English Coronation Oath functions as an English *lex regia*. See McIlwain, *Constitutionalism Ancient and Modern* 73–4; Philip Hamburger, *Law and Judicial Duty* (Cambridge: Harvard University Press, 2009) 71–3.

[72] *Suo iure* and *alieno beneficio* appear at D.2.1.5; cp. D.1.16.1, 1.16.5, 1.16.6, 1.16.7, 1.16.13, 1.17.9, 2.1.13, 2.1.16, 2.1.17. There is disagreement among the Romans whether delegation of an ordinary magistrate's *iurisdictio* can also be taken to imply a delegation of that magistrate's *imperium* as well. Paul, unlike Papinian, seems to take the dissenting view that it can. D.1.21.1.1, 1.21.5.1.

relationship between the Roman people and the emperor.[73] So what was the relevant connection?

The critical move was Accursius' suggestion that the emperor, despite all his legal powers, was nevertheless a mere delegate or agent of the people, not unlike the inferior lay judge exercising jurisdiction by mandate.[74] Imperial power is placed [*ponitur*] in trust to be exercised only by way of an agent or trustee created by concessive grant, and it is this fact that makes the emperor nothing more than what Hugolinus called a *procurator* ad hoc, or, as Otto von Gierke once put it, nothing more than a "Republican Magistrate" appointed (and potentially removable) by the people.[75] Indeed, in a gloss on another well-known rubric in the *Digest*, Accursius explicitly indicates that, like a lesser magistrate or a legate, the emperor likewise holds his imperial authority *alieno beneficio*, as a delegate of the Roman people, a reading made plausible only by insisting, as he does in the gloss on Ulpian's *lex regia* text, that *potestatem* should really be read as *iurisdictionem*.[76]

This analysis introduces a very different way of understanding the transfer of authority adumbrated in the *lex regia*. Since the emperor is a kind of delegated agent created by law, he is held to be constrained by the very same normative principles on concessive delegation identified by Papinian in the *Digest*:

> One who has undertaken a delegated jurisdiction [*mandatam iurisdictionem*] has no competence of his own [*proprium nihil habet*] but exercises [*utitur*] the jurisdiction belonging to the one who gave [*qui mandavit*] him his mandate.[77]

The bottom line for Accursius is this: If the *lex regia* is to be read according to the concession theory, it is imperative to read *concessio* in the same way jurisdiction is said to be delegated [*mandata*], as when the magistrate, as a principal, entrusts his jurisdiction to an inferior, as his agent. The result is an asymmetrical relationship which locates supremacy not in the agent, but in the principal—the people.[78]

The asymmetrical character of this relationship between *princeps* and *populus* is underscored by a second related feature of the gloss, which uses the proprietary language of ownership [*proprietas*] to explain the chief reason why the people may revoke the emperor's authority: the authority belongs to them.

[73] Gilmore, *Argument from Roman Law* 27–8. I discuss the usages of this text in Ch. 3.

[74] Cp. Stein, *Roman Law in European History* 59–60, who connects this principle to C.1.14.4.

[75] Hugolinus de Presbyteris, *Distinctiones* §148 cited in Calasso, *I Glossatori* 92–3, and Carlyle, *History of Mediaeval Political Theory in the West* 2:66. Note especially Hugolinus' use of the verb, "*constituit*," to interpret the *lex regia* as a limited conveyance. Gierke, *Political Theories of the Middle Age* 46. On Hugolinus, see Bellomo, *Common Legal Past of Europe* 133; 168–9.

[76] *Glossa Ordinaria* on D.2.1.5, *Alieno Beneficio*. *Glossa Ordinaria* on D.1.4.1, *Potestatem*. For the significance of this reading of *potestas* as *iurisdictio*, see Chapter 3.

[77] D.1.21.1.1 (slightly modified from Watson's translation).

[78] *Glossa Ordinaria* on C.1.14.12 on *Soli Imperatori*. Accursius is clearly relying on Azo's analysis.

The people "own" the prince's authority which, according to this suggestion, is understood to be granted conditionally on a kind of loan for use.

Accursius himself does not directly offer further commentary on this principle in the gloss. But it is not difficult for any student of the civil law to extrapolate what he has in mind. *Proprietas*, in civil law, could be classified in one of two ways. *Plena proprietas* signified the full and absolute right of property over some thing, as well as its factual use. A landowner who directly made use of the estate to which he had lawful title would be regarded as having a *plena proprietas* over it. *Nuda proprietas*, by contrast, signified the legal abstraction of one's bare right of property over some thing, while it is factually in someone else's use.[79] It is the abstract legal title that remains [*remansit*] with the landowner who lets his estate to be used and occupied by a tenant or usufructuary. But the crucial point is that, even an owner who grants away the use of his estate to another, still retains the legal rights constitutive of the *nuda proprietas*. And, most important, the civil law gives an action to that owner to recover the estate that is in another's control.

To say then, as Accursius does, that the *proprietas* over the powers conceded to the emperor "remained" [*remanserit*] with the people, even while the emperor makes use of those powers, suggests that the juridical relationship between the *populus* and *princeps* can be understood in terms of ownership. Like the landowner's residual abstract title to an estate that is currently being used by another, the people similarly reserve a bare legal title approximating the *nuda proprietas*, even while the emperor makes use of the public authority, like a usufructuary. More important, as the bearer of a *nuda proprietas*, the people are entitled in principle to reclaim the property that rightfully belongs to them, just as the landowner may dispossess the usufructuary.

The gloss has nothing more to say on the doctrinal implications of this proprietary theory of popular sovereignty. But Accursius has cleared the pathway for later jurists to explore this alternative and potentially radical way of understanding the popular foundation of the Roman state.

CONCLUSION

The aim of this chapter was to investigate the doctrine of popular sovereignty connected with the Roman *lex regia*, the legendary constitutional act by which the plenary authority of the Roman people was transferred to Augustus at the start of the Principate. As we have seen, the medieval jurists of Bologna who studied and glossed the texts of Roman law, following its recovery in medieval Italy, debated in careful detail whether the conveyance of authority from *populus* to *princeps* through this *lex regia* was an irrevocable *translatio* or a revocable *concessio*. For proponents of the latter "concession" view, such as Azo and Accursius, the Roman people did indeed retain a residual capacity to recover

[79] Thus, D.9.4.18, the usufructuary has an action against the bare owner, if the latter tries to take the slave that is in the usufructuary's use.

the authority it had granted to the emperor by concessive delegation. The Roman people were entitled to do so, according to the concession theorists, because the emperor held authority only as a "delegated jurisdiction," which, despite its use by the emperor, remained fully under the proprietary right of the people as a whole body, or *universitas*.

These early interpretive debates among the Glossators of the Bolognese school, while narrowly academic and almost pedantic at first, indelibly shaped how subsequent generations of jurists would read and understand the constitutional significance and function of the *lex regia*. This was, in large part, because the formal training of later jurists in the civil law involved close study of the legal teachings recorded in these glosses. As a result, a sharp interpretive divide separating translation theorists from concession theorists emerged in Western constitutional jurisprudence, shaping legal and political thought far beyond the cloistered halls of Bologna and, perhaps more important, outside Italy.

While both schools of thought accepted as axiomatic the popular origins of the Roman emperor's authority, it was over the consequences of this shared starting point that the two fundamentally diverged. For those translation theorists who treated the *lex regia* merely as a historically unique event in Roman Antiquity, never again to be reenacted by the *populus Romanus*, the work of the early Glossators provided the resources to craft a doctrine of princely absolutism, which set the Roman *princeps* beyond the scope of popular control or accountability and even absolved him of any legal bond or obligation.[80] This was, as we shall see, the doctrine established by some of the leading jurists on the *lex regia* of the later Middle Ages, including the founders of the post-Glossator school of Commentators—Cynus da Pistoia (c.1270–1336/37), Bartolus of Sassoferrato (1314–1357), and Baldus de Ubaldis (1327–1400)—all of whom recognized the special legal position of the *princeps* in the system of Roman law.[81] The anti-populist overtones of the translation theorists' reading of the *lex regia* would continue to resonate, especially among early modern theorists of princely absolutism, such as Pierre Grégoire and William Barclay, who treated the *lex regia* as an important piece of evidence denying a right of popular sovereignty. And, as we shall see, it will play a critical role in the political thought of Bodin and Hobbes.

Like the translation theory, the concession theory would also find its adherents among later generations of civil lawyers, beginning with one of Accursius' own students. In his *Lectura* on the *Digestum Vetus*, Odofredus de Denariis (d.1265, a pupil and, later, a successor, of Accursius in Bologna) reaffirmed the basic thesis of the concession theory, stating that "the people had the power of making law, which they conceded [*concessit*] to the emperors, but did not

[80] See Ullmann, "The Development of the Medieval Idea of Sovereignty" and Pennington, *The Prince and the Law*. Also useful is the more recent discussion of Fasolt, *Limits of History* Ch. 4.

[81] Cynus da Pistoia on C.1.14.12, §4; Bartolus of Sassoferrato on D.1.3.8, §§5-11, D.49.15.24, §6, C.1.14.11, §§3-4; Baldus de Ubaldis on D.1.2.2, 1.2.11, §§1-2, 1.3.9, C.8.47.2, C.1.14.12.

entirely renounce [*abdicavit*] it."[82] What is perhaps far more significant, however, is that the concession theory found favor in the civil law faculties outside Italy. The French jurist, Jacques de Révigny (c.1230/35–1296), commenting on C.1.14.12, explained for example that, even after the conveyance of *imperium* to the *princeps*, the *populus* was fully "able to make law."[83] Incorporating the analysis of Azo and Accursius, Révigny compares the *lex regia* to the Roman law on delegated jurisdiction:

> Just as one's *iurisdictio* is not renounced in delegating authority to a judge [*in iudice delegante*], the Roman people conceded to the emperor, but did not renounce, the power of *imperium*.[84]

But Révigny went even further in highlighting the radical overtones of the concession theory in the tradition of Azo:

> I believe, if the emperor governs poorly, the people can remove [*revocare*] him... Indeed, the people does not have a superior. It is true that the emperor is the superior over any one individual of the people, but he is not superior over the people as a whole.[85]

Even in England, where civil law had very limited doctrinal influence, the English jurist, Henry de Bracton (c.1210–1268), a student of Azo, had applied the *lex regia* to the law of English kingship, suggesting that the English Coronation Oath functioned as a kind of English *lex regia*, whereby *imperium* passed from the people to the king, but also bound him to the very law—like a "bridle" as Bracton says—by which the people made him king in the first place.[86]

We must remember, however, that all of these theoretical debates were, in the end, interpretive debates about Roman law, not constitutional theory constructed *in abstracto*. It may be true that the Glossators used the *lex regia* to postulate a doctrine of popular sovereignty that located a residual power in the people to make law independently and to recover the balance of public authority, which they had conceded to the emperor. But what must be stressed is that these were not general statements that could properly count as political or constitutional theory—at least, not yet. The Glossators' purpose was narrowly academic, still confined to the Roman texts, and we must be careful in treating a popular sovereignty doctrine emerging out of a concession theory

[82] Odofredus, *Lectura Super Digesto Veteri* (Lyon, 1550) fol. 17 [on D.1.4.1].

[83] Jacques de Révigny, *Lectura Super Codice* (Paris, 1519; facsimile reprinted Bologna: Forni, 1967) fol. 36 [on C.1.14(17).12(11), on *Si imperialis*].

[84] Révigny, *Lectura Super Codice* fol. 36 [on C.1.14(17).12(11)].

[85] Révigny, *Lectura Super Codice* fol. 36 [on C.1.14(17).12(11)]. Ullmann, in *Medieval Idea of Law* 48–9, n.5, incorrectly attributes this text to Belleperche. Révigny follows Azo and Accursius in drawing the comparisons to Scipio and D.1.21.1, but he also adds an additional comparison to Pomponius' *Enchiridion* on the Decemvirate at D.1.2.2.24.

[86] On Bracton's constitutionalism, see Tierney, "Bracton on Government" and, more recently, Cary Nederman, *The Lineages of European Political Thought* (Washington: Catholic University of America Press, 2009) Ch. 6.

chiefly within the context of an antiquarian scholarly exercise in rendering the Roman law intelligible to medieval lawyers. While the Glossators may be said to have traced the origins of sovereignty in the people, their concern was only with *populus Romanus*, not *populi in genere*.

This introduces a major interpretive difficulty for the enterprising jurist hoping to use the civil law to craft a new system of constitutional thought. If the *lex regia* was indeed historically unique to the Roman Empire and restricted only to the case of the *populus Romanus*, it would appear that the Glossators' doctrine of popular sovereignty would have little, if any, relevance for the post-Classical world. It is only the Roman *princeps*—and not just any *princeps*—who is entitled to bear the *imperium*. And it is only from the Roman *populus*—and not just any *populus liber* or *gens*—that such a *princeps* receives his *imperium*.

But for reasons we must begin investigating in the next chapter, the *lex regia* and, more generally, the Roman law gradually became widely available as a model and inspiration for a wide variety of early modern theories of popular sovereignty, influencing not only medieval legal theorists, but philosophers and theologians as well.[87] The reason for this is that Roman law became something more than just a historical artifact of Roman Antiquity. Its revival in the legal curricula of the universities and its application in the courts of later medieval Europe made it rather the centerpiece, alongside canon law, of an emerging legal order, the *ius commune*, functioning as a system of legal rules and principles accessible not only to the Roman people, but to all peoples.[88] In this new legal order, Roman law provided a shared vocabulary and a grammar—indeed, a "language"—to construct the foundations of modern constitutional and political theory. And it is in this juridically-inflected linguistic domain, in which Roman law becomes known as "written reason" [*ratio scripta*], the "true philosophy" [*vera philosophia*], and the universal science of right, where popular sovereignty is no longer the substratum for just the Roman constitutional state, but indeed, for every constitutional state.[89]

[87] See, for example, J.P. Canning, *Ideas of Power in the Late Middle Ages, 1296–1417* (Cambridge: Cambridge University Press, 2014) 126, n.50 citing Ockham, *Breviloquium de Principatu Tyrannico* 3, §14.

[88] Brundage, *Medieval Origins of the Legal Profession*. The *ius commune* consisted of civil law (the law of the Roman Empire) as well as canon law (the law of the Roman Church), both of which theoretically claimed a universal scope of jurisdiction. Experts in both, such as Althusius and Leibniz, were, hence, called "doctors of both laws" [*doctores utriusque juris* = J.U.D.].

[89] Kelley, "*Vera Philosophia*."

2

The Medieval Law of Peoples

INTRODUCTION

The previous chapter investigated the doctrine of popular sovereignty emerging from the Glossatorial interpretations of the *lex regia* in the Middle Ages. The core of the dispute concerned the interpretive question whether, in conveying *imperium* to the Roman *princeps*, the people merely delegated their original sovereignty as a concessive and revocable grant or whether the people transferred their sovereignty completely and irrevocably as a legal act of alienation. Both sides of the dispute were vigorously defended, and the dispute shaped the later understanding of the *lex regia*, even in early modern legal thought.

What remains less clear, and in need of further investigation, however, is why medieval jurists would have invested so much intellectual energy interpreting the meaning of this *lex*. After all, the *lex regia*—if indeed it even existed—was only supposed to apply to the constitutional relationship between the Roman people and the Roman *princeps*. So why should such a Roman law matter in the post-Roman world of the European Middle Ages?

The short answer is that, from the jurists' perspective, theirs was not a "post-Roman world" at all. For the medieval jurists, the Roman Empire never really ceased to exist but continued, even to their day. This shared sense of Romanness, or *Romanitas*, permeated medieval thought, providing an encompassing identity, like the *Christianitas* of the Roman Church, universal in scope. It was an extraordinarily important idea in medieval social and political thought, if only for the implications for the interpretation and application of Roman law. It would mean, first of all, that there would still have to be, somewhere and somehow, a Roman *princeps*, even in the Middle Ages. It would mean that there would also have to be a Roman *populus*, still subject to that emperor. Above all, it would have to mean that Roman law—including especially the *lex regia*, the constitutional law by which the Roman *populus* authorizes and empowers the Roman *princeps*—was still, in principle, fully valid and active. In this way, the *lex regia* became, as J.P. Canning once put it, essential to the "fundamental constitutional law of Christendom."[1] It was not just a historical curiosity, an antiquated piece of Roman law. Insofar as the Roman law became

[1] Canning, *Political Thought of Baldus* 55.

part of a universal "common law" or *ius commune* in Latin Christendom, the *lex regia* was an essential part of this universal law as well, applicable in theory to all municipal and proto-national legal systems.[2]

The gradual reintroduction of Roman law into the Latin West reinforced this belief in a continuing *Romanitas* and, more important, a continuously valid system of Roman law. Yet, it also raised that fundamental problem of statutory interpretation which continues to plague jurists even in the modern era. How should jurists fix and understand the meaning of legal terms, such as *populus* and *princeps*, where the corresponding referents are, practically speaking, no longer in existence? Who can, for example, rightfully claim the title and the legal rights of a *princeps*? Who can be entitled to enact a *lex regia*? A legal-formalist answer, crafted within the legal rules and interpretive traditions of Roman law (as the Glossators had crafted), would pay no heed to such questions of correspondence to the social and political facts of medieval Europe. It would, indeed, be irrelevant to their primary task: what mattered to them was elucidating the *meaning* and the inner *coherence* of the legal rules and principles contained within the system of Roman law, as an autonomous domain of reasoning separated entirely from the external vicissitudes of social and political change.

But later medieval civilians, especially of the fourteenth century, who had studied the Roman law texts and began to contest the formalist interpretive traditions of the Glossators, inhabited a world where the fictive belief in a universal Roman Empire failed to map onto the political reality of a world where many different peoples and nations—*populi liberi* and *gentes*—French, English, Venetians, Milanese, Neapolitans, Sicilians, Germans, began to cultivate their own local indigenous sense of territorial independence, political authority, and legal custom.

Jurists could not ignore these changes without risking irrelevance for their own profession. Roman law—the sacred text of medieval priests of justice—had to become elastic in meaning, so as to bridge the growing gap and declining correspondence between Roman law and post-Roman fact. Roman law terms, such as *princeps*, had to mean something more than simply a Roman emperor, just as *populus* had to mean something more than simply the Roman people. Roman law had to become, in other words, not simply a law for the Romans, but a law for all peoples. In doing so, the constitutional principle of popular sovereignty embodied in the Roman *lex regia* was no longer seen to be simply the sole exceptional right of the Roman people but, potentially, the inheritance of all law-governed peoples. Just as the Roman people enacted a *lex regia* in Antiquity, so too could the French enact the equivalent of a French *lex regia*, just as the English could enact the equivalent of an English *lex regia*, or the Sicilians could enact the equivalent of a Sicilian *lex regia*.

[2] On the application of Roman law to local legal systems as a part of *ius commune*, see James Whitman, *The Legacy of Roman Law in the German Romantic Era* (Princeton: Princeton University Press, 1990) Ch. 1.

My goal in this chapter is to retrace this critical hermeneutic shift in later medieval legal thought. I begin with a discussion of the theory of *translatio imperii*, or "transfer of *imperium*," by which jurists attempted to explain the continuity and survival of the Roman Empire even into the Middle Ages. As I show, this doctrine established the principle that the medieval bearers of Roman *imperium*—the German "Holy Roman Emperors"—were entitled, according to Roman law, to a *de iure* universal sovereignty over the whole world and, thus, supreme even over kings and princes who lacked such a formal title. But such an imperial title to *de iure* universal sovereignty, a universal *imperium*, as I show, clashed with the *de facto* powers of kings, princes, and independent city republics, which did not, in practical terms, recognize the alleged superiority of the emperor and governed as if they were fully independent and territorially sovereign entities. The challenge, for jurists, was to reconcile this emerging gap between *de iure* and *de facto* sovereignty. Their strategy was to show that the Roman law establishing the *imperium* of the emperor—the *lex regia*—was not exclusive to the Romans, but merely one specific instance of a legal power to be found among all free peoples and nations. Popular sovereignty was, thus, not so much a privilege of Roman law, but an essential foundation of the law of all nations, a doctrine that would play a central role in the constitutional thought of the two most important civilian jurists of the later Middle Ages, Bartolus of Sassoferrato and his pupil, Baldus de Ubaldis, in what I shall call their theory of "peoplehood."

THE *TRANSLATIO IMPERII*: ROMAN *IMPERIUM* IN A POST-ROMAN WORLD

As we saw in the previous chapter, the *lex regia* played a very specific function in the legal thought of the Roman Empire. It was the legal act which, in theory, established the Roman Principate by a transfer of *imperium* from the Roman *populus* to the Roman *princeps*. Medieval legal historiography, in particular, had pinpointed the *lex regia* to the first century C.E., in the curiate *lex de imperio Vespasiani* which formally granted *imperium* to the Emperor Vespasian and his successors.

But there is more to the story, particularly after the fall of the Western Roman Empire in Late Antiquity. Once the *princeps* acquired the full *imperium*, it was, at least in theory, fully within his right to transfer that authority again to another party, as he saw fit—just as it was fully within the right of the *populus* to transfer that authority in the first place to the *princeps*. That is precisely what is thought to have happened in the fourth-century conveyance of *imperium* from the emperor to the Pope. This *translatio imperii*, or "transfer of authority," from *princeps* to *pontifex*, empowering the Church with the sovereign right to govern the Western Roman Empire under the authority of the Bishop of Rome, marked a critical moment in ecclesiastical history establishing the Papacy as a new kind of Caesar and transforming the Roman Empire into the prophesied Fourth Monarchy.[3] This legal act of *translatio*, known as

[3] Daniel 2:40.

the "Donation of Constantine" to Pope Sylvester (and recorded in a document shown, in the Renaissance, by Lorenzo Valla to be a forgery from the late eighth or early ninth century) invested the Pope, in theory, with the full temporal authority of the Roman *imperium*.[4] Because it turned the Pope into a *princeps*, the Donation of Constantine was, thus, in effect a "a new *lex regia*," by which the Roman Empire became Christ's empire and by which Christ's vicar on Earth became himself a Caesar.[5] According to this account, then, Roman *imperium* did not die out, but instead continued fully intact even after the historical decline of the Western Empire, with the Church as the caretaker of *imperium*.

There was a third stage in this sequence. This occurs when the Roman *imperium* was conferred upon the Frankish king, Charlemagne, in 800 by Pope Leo III, in effect making him a "holy" Roman emperor, theoretically continuing in an unbroken line of succession the imperial rule of the ancient Romans, first over the Carolingian empire and later, with the coronation of the German king, Otto I, in 962 over a new legal and political entity, a German *Reich*.[6] This new "Holy" Roman Empire became fundamental to the emerging constitution of medieval Christendom centered upon the joint rulership of Church and Empire, *sacerdotium* and *imperium*.

By this circuitous route in the Middle Ages, then, the Roman *lex regia* comes to play a foundational role in the shaping of medieval politics and law; indeed, the Roman people, in this account, hold a privileged position as the human agency or instrument through which God established the empire.[7] It was the trigger which set in motion this entire historical trajectory of Roman domination in the Christian world, "the necessary first stage in the process through which there was established Christendom's fundamental constitution."[8] What results, above all, from this sequence of *translationes imperii* (from *populus* to *princeps*, from *princeps* to *pontifex*, and finally from *pontifex* back to *princeps*) is the historical fiction of a continuous *Romanitas*, a shared Roman identity, lasting into medieval Latin Christendom and represented in the two principal "Roman" institutions with a supposedly universal jurisdiction over the world—the Roman Church and Empire.[9]

[4] Valla presented his case against the authenticity of the Donation in *De falso credita et ementita Constantini donatione declamatio* (1518).

[5] Canning, *Political Thought of Baldus* 59; *Ideas of Power in the Late Middle Ages* 148, 159–60.

[6] Loughlin, *Foundations of Public Law* 26–8 stresses the sacramental aspect of consecrating kings as "reinforc[ing] the official character of kingship."

[7] This was the explanation used to reconcile the *lex regia* with the Constitution *Deo Auctore*, in the *Code*, which locates the origin of the emperor's *imperium* not in the people, but in God. See also Accursius on the *Novels* 6, on *imperium*.

[8] Canning, *Political Thought of Baldus* 59.

[9] If the Roman Empire was indeed the prophesied Fourth (and final) Monarchy, it would be necessary to perpetuate this monarchy, in order to avoid the Apocalypse which was to follow its collapse.

This historical fiction of the *translatio imperii* was particularly important for legal thought in the High Middle Ages. Since, on this doctrine, the authority of the Roman Empire theoretically never ceased even after the decline of the Western Empire in Late Antiquity, it followed that the Roman *ius civile*, the civil law through which Rome was governed, remained fully valid in the post-Roman world of the European Middle Ages.[10] This mode of thought was critical when, in the eleventh-century, the texts forming the *Corpus Iuris Civilis* were discovered, bringing about what Paul Vinogradoff once famously called the "second life of Roman law."[11]

The discovery of Justinian's texts also helped to specify in much greater detail the imperial claims of the medieval emperors to universal authority over all other temporal rulers of Christendom. For this reason, medieval emperors were naturally interested in what Roman law had to say about the rights and powers of Roman emperors, or *principes*. No emperor was more invested in the civil law than the Hohenstaufen Emperor, Frederick I (Barbarossa), who recognized the civil law—as Gibbon would put it—as "a science most favourable to despotism" and as a potentially valuable tool for his ambitions of empire-building and consolidating German imperial authority, even over the wealthy communes of Northern Italy.[12] As we have already seen, the work of the early Glossators in the twelfth century, mining the Justinianic texts, uncovered ideas that defined and elevated the position of the medieval emperor as a Roman *princeps* who alone is "freed from the laws" [*legibus solutus*], invested by a popular *lex regia* with plenary lawmaking authority, and even "lord of all the world" [*dominus mundi*]. It was the work of these jurists who, for the first time in 1158 at the Diet of Roncaglia convoked by Frederick, enumerated the rights, powers, and prerogatives of the medieval emperor explicitly in the language of civil law.

These Glossators operated on the critical assumption that these imperial prerogatives were exclusive to the Roman *princeps*: only the *princeps* of Roman law, designating the legitimate bearer of Roman *imperium*, can legally hold them. But since, by the *translatio imperii*, the Roman *imperium* was thought to have continued in the rule of the German Holy Roman Emperor, the jurists concluded that the only person in all of Christendom legally entitled to the prerogatives of *princeps* was the medieval Holy Roman Emperor.

[10] Harold Berman, *Law and Revolution: The Formation of the Western Legal Tradition* (Cambridge: Harvard University Press, 1983) 122.

[11] Vinogradoff, *Roman Law in Medieval Europe* 13 and, more generally, Charles Radding and Antonio Ciaralli, *The Corpus Iuris Civilis in the Middle Ages: Manuscripts and Transmission from the Sixth Century to the Juristic Revival* (Leiden: Brill, 2007).

[12] Pennington, *Prince and the Law* 10, citing Gibbon. Skinner, citing the twelfth-century German chronicler, Otto of Freising, in *Foundations of Modern Political Thought* 1:4, points out that the Northern Italian communes were a "very garden of delights [which] surpass[ed] all other states of the world in riches and in power."

This line of reasoning inspired Frederick to consult the Bolognese doctors of law to specify the nature of his legal authority by virtue of his status as a *princeps*. Reflecting on the famous text of the *lex Rhodia* in the *Digest*, which describes the emperor as the "lord of the whole world [*orbis terrarum dominus*]," Frederick addressed the two most celebrated jurists of his day, Bulgarus and Martinus, in asking: "Am I the lord of the world?"[13] The crux of the ensuing debate, recorded initially in additions to Otto Morena's chronicle of Frederick and in Accursius' gloss on the *Code* [C.7.37.3], turned on the issue whether the emperor, by virtue of his jural status as *dominus* over the whole world, could also *ipso facto* claim *dominium* over particular parts [*res particulares*] of the world, meaning specifically the private property of his subjects or even whole kingdoms and cities subsumed under his supposedly universal jurisdiction.[14]

Bulgarus, hailed as the "golden mouth," acknowledged in his answer that the emperor may be *dominus* of the world in a narrowly technical sense, but absolutely denied that his universal *dominium* also entailed a particular *dominium* over the private property held by his subjects, including those of the Italian city-states.[15] But Martinus, favoring the emperor, ruled that universal *dominium* entails the particular *dominium* over all privately-held property as well [*dominus universalium, ita et sic particularium rerum*], thus providing a theory in which all lesser particular forms of *dominium* are nested within the universal *dominium* of the emperor.[16] For Martinus, the emperor was not only the ruler, but indeed, the owner of the whole world and everything in it—including the Italian states. And for this obsequious reply, the emperor awarded Martinus a horse, while Bulgarus received nothing, prompting his quip, "I lost a horse [*equum*] because I upheld equity [*aequum*], which is not equitable [*non fuit aequum*]."[17]

But even though Martinus won the horse, it was the dissenting opinion of Bulgarus, cited approvingly by generations of later jurists that prevailed throughout medieval legal thought.[18] Whether or not this dispute actually occurred, the substance of Bulgarus' position remained monumentally important because it prompted medieval jurists to specify more precisely the special nature of princely *dominium* and enabled a more sensible reading of the *Corpus Iuris Civilis*. For example, the *Code*, in a well known text known as the *Bene a Zenone*, suggests that "all things are thought to belong to the emperor" [C.7.37.3, *omnia principis esse intelligantur*] but Accursius' gloss on this text, narrowing the scope of princely *dominium*, clarified that the phrase, "all things" [*omnia*], is not a reference to the whole world, but merely refers to the public fisc [*fiscalia*] and the private patrimony [*patrimonialia*] of the princely ruler.[19] Moreover, the

[13] D.14.2.9. [14] Pennington, *Prince and the Law* 15; Fasolt, *Limits of History* 191.

[15] Stein, *Roman Law in European History* 47.

[16] Bartolus on the Constitution *Omnem*, §3 referencing D.14.29 and C.7.37.3.

[17] Pennington, *Prince and the Law* 16. [18] Post, *Studies in Medieval Legal Thought* 282.

[19] Magnus Ryan, in his chapter, "Political Thought" in *The Cambridge Companion to Roman Law*, ed. David Johnston (Cambridge: Cambridge University Press, 2015) 448, n.52, suggests, in commenting on this gloss, that Accursius introduces two distinct senses of *dominium* in medieval legal thought: *dominium* in the sense of "jurisdiction" and *dominium* in the sense of "property ownership." *Glossa Ordinaria* on C.7.37.3

argument for Bulgarus' position, supplied by Odofredus, is especially note-worthy in its direct appeal to the logic of property law: just as two people cannot simultaneously be *dominus* of the same thing, so too the emperor cannot simultaneously be the *dominus* of some object of property that is already owned privately by someone else.[20]

But there was an even more important implication following from this doctrine of the emperor's universal sovereignty over the world as *princeps*. If it is true that only the Holy Roman Emperor can be regarded as the sole *princeps* in Christendom, then it must also be true, for that very reason, that all other temporal kings, such as the King of France or the King of Sicily, cannot legally claim *imperium* for themselves, for to do so would be tantamount to *crimen laesae majestatis*, treason against the Imperial dignity.[21] In this way, the *princeps* enjoyed, at least initially, in the strict interpretation of the Glossators, a privileged legal position which no other king or temporal authority did. For as long as jurists continued to accept this strict interpretation, by which the *princeps* of Roman law referred exclusively to the Holy Roman Emperor, jurists could not licitly apply the Romanist doctrines of princely rule—such as the *princeps legibus solutus*—in crafting a general theory of kingship and princely power. As the Italian jurist, Guido of Suzarra, would write in an *addicio* to his gloss on the *Digest*, only the Roman Emperor can be *legibus solutus* because only he, and no other, is properly to be named the *princeps*.[22] It would be "heretical" [*haereticus*] to attribute that title to anyone else.[23]

But while this strict interpretation of Roman law may have crystallized the position of the emperor, it also complicated the status of temporal authorities such as kings, princes, and feudal lordships. If kings cannot be *principes*, then what are they really, in terms of the civil law? The Imperialist response, defending the legal rights and powers of the emperor, argued simply that all temporal kings, however powerful, were nevertheless to be regarded legally as inferior and subject to the *princeps*. It was a position that certainly drew strength from the gloss of Johannes Teutonicus that "the emperor is over all kings... and all nations are under him... He is the lord of the world... and no king may gain an exemption from his authority, because no prescription can run against him in this case."[24]

on "*Omnia*." The gloss cross-references D.43.8.2.4, which states that "For the property of the treasury is as it were the private property of the emperor" [*Res enim fiscales quasi propriae et privatae principis sunt*]. Cp. Kantorowicz's discussion of this "fiscal theology" (186) in *The King's Two Bodies: A Study in Mediaeval Political Theology* (Princeton: Princeton University Press, 1985) 179, n.275, where he also cites the important discussion of Baldus on C.10.1, §§11–13, where Kantorowicz observes Baldus' conclusion that by the *lex regia*, "ultimately the Roman people owned the fisc."

[20] Odofredus, *Lectura Super Codice* (Lyon, 1552) fol. 49 [on C.1.22.6, *Omnes cuiuscunque*].

[21] D.48.4.1.

[22] Pennington, *Prince and the Law* 94–5, citing Guido of Suzarra on D.1.3.31.

[23] Bartolus on D.49.15.24, on *Hostes*.

[24] Kenneth Pennington, "Law, Legislative Authority, and Theories of Government, 1150–1300," *Cambridge History of Medieval Political Thought*, ed. J.H. Burns (Cambridge: Cambridge University Press, 1988) 432, n.18, citing the gloss to the *Decretals* of Gregory IX.

From a legal point of view, the challenge for civilians was to describe the very real authority of temporal kings, such as the King of France or the King of Sicily, without relying on the civil law doctrines concerning the *imperium* of the *princeps*. The effort to fit this doctrine into the system of Roman law involved a good deal of legal casuistry, as may be seen in the writings of the French legist, Jacques de Révigny, whom we encountered in the previous chapter. Following the strict interpretation of the Imperialist position, Révigny argued that, if the emperor alone is *princeps*, then kings must, by implication, occupy some lesser office inferior to the *princeps*. Since only the *princeps* is "freed from the laws" [*legibus solutus*], even the most powerful king must somehow be regarded as "bound by the laws" [*legibus alligatus*].[25] It is true that a king does exercise authority. But because it is an authority that is defined, regulated, and bound by law, a king can only occupy, at most, something like the inferior Roman office of a *magistratus*, such as a *praeses provinciae*, who, likewise in civil law, is inferior to the *princeps* and merely exercises a delegated authority defined—and thus, limited—entirely by law.[26]

The problem with this Imperialist response is that the theory did not match the facts. It may certainly be true, *de iure*, that kings were subject to the *princeps*, as the Glossators' reading of the civil law suggests. But *de facto*, many kings, such as the King of France, did not recognize the superior authority of the *princeps* in temporal matters and governed just as if they were *principes* over their respective realms. So compelling was this observation that, by the late Middle Ages, the strict interpretation of the term, *princeps*, could no longer reasonably be defended, as jurists began to question and openly contest the view that *princeps* referred exclusively to the Holy Roman Emperor. Even kings were, in some sense, deserving of the Roman title of *princeps* and the rights, powers, and prerogatives that were attached to it.

REX IN REGNO SUO: THE FREE KING AS *PRINCEPS*

The ever-widening gap between the *de iure* universal sovereignty of the *princeps*, on the one hand, and the *de facto* territorial sovereignty of temporal kings forced upon jurists, particularly those arguing in defense of the territorial sovereignty of temporal kings, the necessity of crafting an alternative solution in civil law to explain the jural status of a temporal king vis-a-vis the emperor. On this alternative view, the emperor formally retained his legal title and prerogatives as *princeps*, a universal sovereign over the whole world.

[25] Pennington, *Prince and the Law* 105–6; on Révigny, 95–6.

[26] The interpretation is supported by the fact that independent kingdoms in Christendom, such as medieval France, were, under the Roman Empire, provinces such as Gaul, governed by a provincial governor, a *praeses* with legally defined rights and powers. Canning, at *Political Thought of Baldus* 126 in discussing the government of Italian cities, highlights the comparison of the *podestà* to a *praeses* with *merum imperium*.

But this titular retention was but a mere legal formalism, as the jurist, Albericus de Rosate (1290–1360), now clarified: "All kings are *de iure* subject to the empire."[27] Noteworthy in Rosate's analysis was the acknowledgement that the subjection of kings to the emperor was merely a formal, abstract construction of the civil law. Indeed, jurists like Rosate were very careful to point out that the inferior status of kings with respect to the emperor was valid only as a legal formalism: in practice kings might govern independently and freely, with the legal equivalent of a full sovereign authority over their respective kingdoms.

Kings who held a *de facto* sovereign authority, even if not *de iure* sovereignty, over their realms were generally designated independent, or "free," kings [*liberi reges*]. What made a king "free" or "unfree" depended entirely on whether or not they complied with an antecedent rule of recognition: does the king, as a matter of fact, recognize the superior authority of another in temporal matters? The criterion of non-recognition—established in *Per Venerabilem*, the famous decretal of Innocent III—was essential in answering this question concerning the relationship between emperors and kings.[28] Only such a "king in his own kingdom who recognizes no superior in temporal matters" could properly be a free and independent king.

This was the strategy of argument deployed crucially by medieval French jurists writing in defense of the jural independence of the French crown from the Empire, most notably the thirteenth-century Burgundian lawyer, Jean de Blanot, in a commentary on the *Institutes*. The King of France, Blanot argued, held a jurisdiction over his kingdom that, in theory, imposed a general obligation on everyone within the boundaries of his kingdom, including even those who claimed immunity from service to the king on feudal grounds.[29] Blanot characterized the king's jurisdiction in the Roman legal language of *imperium* and enabled him to conclude that the king was, at least within his kingdom, just the same as a *princeps*.[30] Blanot's contemporary, Pierre de Belleperche (d.1308), could, without contradiction, declare in his lectures on Justinian's *Code* that "everyone is subject to the emperor" [*omnia sunt subiecta imperatori*].[31] But for Belleperche, since the subjection is only a legal formality, and not a

[27] Albericus de Rosate, *Commentaria Super Digesto* (Venice, 1585; reprinted Torino, 1974) fol. 31r [on D.1.3.31], quoted in Pennington, *Prince and the Law* 95, n.74.

[28] Pennington, "Law, Legislative Authority, and Theories of Government" 432–3.

[29] As Ryan explains in "Political Thought" 435, the vassal of a tenant-in-chief (who held his benefice directly of the king as the latter's liege lord) did not owe homage or service to the king, since vassalage was fundamentally a personal relationship. But the jurisdictional authority that kings were now asserting was fundamentally different in character from feudal right, and so, even a lesser vassal who had no personal tie of duty to the king nevertheless was bound by the same sort of legal obligation that, in civil law, all subjects owed to a *princeps* with *imperium*.

[30] Pennington, *Prince and the Law* 96–7; Ryan, "Political Thought" 436. Among the studies cited are Robert Feenstra, "Jean de Blanot et la formule *Rex Franciae in Regno Suo Princeps Est*," *Études d'histoire du droit canonique dédiées à Gabrielle le Bras*, 2 Vols. (Paris, 1965) 2:890–91 and Calasso, *I Glossatori*, 110ff; 34ff.

[31] Walter Ullmann, however, describes this as the minority opinion in France in "Development of the Medieval Idea of Sovereignty" 7.

matter of fact, the Imperialist civilian doctrine of the emperor's *de iure* universal sovereignty over "the whole world" is fully compatible with the *de facto* territorial sovereignty of temporal kings over a specific "part" of the world, the kingdom or *patria*.[32]

This *de facto* argument opened a whole range of new legal possibilities in interpreting the rights and powers of kings in the juridical language of civil law. For, if it can be admitted that kings are *de facto* independent and free of the emperor, by the norm of non-recognition, then perhaps it can also be admitted that kings are, in some sense, legally equivalent to the *princeps* within the boundaries of their own kingdoms. Defenders of the jural independence of France eagerly explored this line of thought, which allowed even a free king, though legally subject only to the *de iure* universal sovereignty of the Holy Roman Emperor, nevertheless to be *de facto* entitled to the rights and powers of an emperor, so much so that, as a general principle, a free king might—as the jurist, Guilelmus Durandus (c.1236–1296), declared in the *Speculum Iudiciale*—be regarded as a *princeps in regno suo.*[33]

To be sure, jurists, such as Durandus, who were formulating this *de facto* argument were not claiming that a free king actually might be himself a Roman emperor, or even the direct successor or heir of the Roman emperor. It was, rather, a more subtle claim, simply that a "free king" with territorial authority had acquired the same status or right as a *princeps*. But since, in Christendom, there were numerous territorially-bound "free kings," it follows that there must correspondingly be numerous *principes*, all of whom were legally empowered with precisely the same *imperium* and other prerogatives defining the imperial authority. It was an interpretive principle formalized by Innocent IV—himself trained as a lawyer—which boldly asserted in civilian language that all free "kings have supreme and pure authority" [*reges . . . habent supremum et merum imperium*].[34] The implication, drawn by Guilelmus de Cuneo, is that, in theory, any monarchical ruler, such as the King of France, "who *de facto* does not recognize a superior" [*qui de facto non recognosca(n)t superiorem*] must be understood to have the "same" [*idem*] powers and prerogatives over his kingdom as the emperor does over the whole world.[35]

But perhaps the challenge to the strict interpretation of the Roman law *princeps* was made most forcefully by the radical jurists of the medieval Neapolitan school who, unlike their French counterparts, utterly rejected the very notion

[32] See also Fasolt, *Limits of History* 191–3 on Bartolus' argument on the difference between *dominium* over wholes and *dominium* over parts, in connection with D.6.1.1, on *Per hanc autem actionem*, §§1–2.

[33] Ullmann, "Development of the Medieval Idea of Sovereignty" 10, quoting Guilelmus Durandus, *Speculum Iudiciale* (Lyon, 1498–1500).

[34] Ullmann, "Development of the Medieval Idea of Sovereignty" 9, quoting the comment on the *Decretals* 2.22.15.

[35] Similarly, Guilelmus de Cuneo extends the point by saying, *idem in aliis regibus, qui de facto non recognoscant superiorem*. Cf. Guilelmus de Cuneo on D.1.11.1, quoted in J.P. Canning, "Law, Sovereignty and Corporation Theory, 1300–1450," *Cambridge History of Medieval Political Thought*, ed. J.H. Burns (Cambridge: Cambridge University Press, 1988) 467, n.47.

of the universal sovereignty, both *de facto* and *de iure*, of the emperor.[36] In disputing the emperor's alleged monopoly on *imperium*, the Neapolitan jurist, Andreas de Isernia (c.1220–1316), for example, declared that "free kings have just the same right as the Roman emperors."[37] It was a statement that was only made possible by demolishing the orthodox distinction between king and *princeps*, as Andrea's predecessor and fellow Neapolitan, Marinus de Caramanico (d.1288) argued in his commentary on the Emperor Frederick's legal code for Sicily, the *Liber Augustalis*, or the *Constitutiones Regni Siciliae*. As Marinus put it, the distinction between king and *princeps* is but a nominal distinction [*distincte in nomine*].[38] They are, rather, two different nominal species of the same genus of *princeps* and, therefore, can both lay a valid claim to the title of *princeps* and sovereignty for themselves. Like the French theorists, Marinus would assert that the King of Naples is *princeps in regno*.

Taken together, these doctrines ultimately had a devastating effect on the strict interpretation of the Roman law *princeps*, since all temporal kings could, in theory, call themselves "emperors" over their own kingdoms. As Kenneth Pennington has argued, "by the end of the fourteenth century, no academic jurist denied that a king had the same authority as the emperor."[39] The doctrine became a juridical commonplace and enabled the widespread application of Roman law across national legal traditions in developing what might be regarded as the beginnings of a distinctively medieval concept of sovereignty that was distinct from its Roman law origins. And this, in turn, was because of the growing recognition among later medieval jurists that "there existed in effect a plurality of territorially sovereign powers of which the emperor was but one."[40]

THE POPULAR CONSTITUTION OF ROYAL AUTHORITY: POPULAR SOVEREIGNTY UNDER THE *IUS GENTIUM*

For a jurist aiming to augment the powers and standing of temporal kings, the civil law was an indispensable tool. Yet, there was a price which had to be paid in order to use civil law arguments in these ways. For, as much as the

[36] These theories emerged in the context of the famous test case between Emperor Henry VII and Robert King of Naples brought by the anti-Imperialist jurists who defended Robert's claims of independence and immunity. Ullmann, "The Development of the Medieval Idea of Sovereignty"; Pennington, *Prince and the Law* Ch. 5; Kantorowicz, *King's Two Bodies*; Canning, "Law, Sovereignty and Corporation Theory, 1300–1450" 465–6.

[37] Andreas de Isernia, *In Usus Feudorum Commentaria* (Naples, 1671) fol. 304 [misprinted in this edition as "310"], §77 [on the *crimen laesae maiestatis*]; Ullmann, "Development of the Medieval Idea of Sovereignty" 22. The notion of *liberi reges* ["free and independent kings"] is further discussed by Marinus de Caramanico in the gloss on the *Liber Augstualis* where he defends the jural equivalence of *princeps* and kingship. *Liberi reges* appears also in a commentary of Lucas de Penna on C.11.51.1, cited in Woolf, *Bartolus* 108–9, n.1.

[38] Canning cites a passage from Marinus' *Super Libro Constitutionum* [*Proemium* 17] in Calasso, *I Glossatori* 199 to show his use of the *ius gentium* to make this point at 196.

[39] Pennington, *Prince and the Law* 105.

[40] Canning, *History of Medieval Political Thought* 125.

civil law attributed full *imperium* and prerogatives such as legal immunity to the *princeps*, it also imposed potential limitations or burdens on the *princeps* as well, and that is, fundamentally, because of the constitutionalist principle of the *digna vox* articulated in Justinian's *Code* that the authority of the *princeps* depended [*pendet*] entirely upon the "authority of the law" [*auctoritas iuris*]. This was indeed, as Accursius explains in the *Glossa Ordinaria*, the chief reason why the *princeps* was understood always to be limited or "bound by the laws" [*legibus alligatus*].

That law, to which the Emperors Theodosius and Valentinian traced their own authority as *principes* in the *Code*, was, according to Accursius, none other than the *lex imperii*, or "the *lex regia* which concerns the transfer of *imperium* from the people to the *princeps*."[41] But how does the *lex regia*, a legal act intended to release the *princeps* from the bond of legal obligation, bind or limit the *princeps* as well? We have already considered one answer in the previous chapter: the concession theory of Azo and Hugolinus, by which it was thought that the people merely "conceded" *imperium* to the *princeps*, who is constituted only to act as a delegate or agent of the people. As an agent holding authority only by concession, the *princeps* remains under an obligation to his principal, who theoretically retains the capacity to revoke his *imperium*. Even if there were no concession in the grant of *imperium* by *lex regia*, Accursius insists that "a democratic origin of power necessarily involves a constitutional limitation on it," a conclusion which Brian Tierney points out is "by no means self-evident."[42]

But these interpretations of the *lex regia*, as a limiting or binding device on the Roman emperors, raised a difficulty in assessing the authority of free kings, who also claimed to be like emperors within the boundaries of their own kingdoms. If the emperor were legally bound in this way by an antecedent *lex regia*, it might similarly be thought that any free king who claimed *imperium* over his own kingdom was also legally bound, in theory, by some anterior *lex regia*. This would similarly place a "free king" under a legal obligation, even as a debt, owed to his people, just as the Roman emperor was, under the *lex regia*, thought to be somehow legally obliged to the Roman people.[43] The question was this: Was royal authority, like *imperium*, also dependent upon something like a *lex regia*? Did kings derive their royal authority from a primitive grant of power from their people?

For at least two important reasons, civilian jurists initially exempted free kings from the binding force of the Roman *lex regia*. The first, as we have seen earlier, was that the *lex regia* was historically understood to be unique only to Roman civil law. Its singular function, on this view, was to establish the "universal imperial jurisdiction" of the medieval Church and Empire by activating

[41] C.6.23.3, and *Glossa Ordinaria* on C.1.14.4, cross-referencing Inst. 1.2.6 and C.1.17.1.

[42] Tierney, "The Prince Is Not Bound By the Laws" 392.

[43] Royal duties of justice framed the medieval view of a king as *debitor iustitiae*. See Kantorowicz, *King's Two Bodies* 163, n.223.

the first sequence in the theory of the *translatio imperii* through a permanent and irreversible alienation of authority from the Roman people to the Roman *princeps*.[44] But since this transfer had already occurred in Antiquity as a *translatio*, and not as a revocable *concessio* of sovereignty, the *lex regia* could have no "contemporary political relevance for the forms of government in kingdoms and independent cities."[45] The *lex regia* was, rather, just a mere historical artifact.

The second reason suggesting the independence of royal authority from the *lex regia* involves the conceptual incoherence of treating the *lex regia* as a general legal rule applicable outside the Roman imperial context, as a justificatory device or general "model for the origins of government and the relationship between rulers and ruled."[46] That is because the reference to "the people," or *populus*, as the origin of monarchical authority in Ulpian's account of the *lex regia*, concerns only the Roman people, not all peoples or all nations in general.[47] Strictly speaking, then, only the Roman *princeps* can be bound by the *lex regia*, whereas all "free" kings, such as the King of France, were fully independent of it. Indeed, even in the special case of the Holy Roman Emperor, as a *princeps*, it was not at all clear who the Roman people might be: "It could possibly be as wide as Christendom or as narrow as the inhabitants of the city of Rome."[48] Since most people in later medieval Europe did not obey or recognize the authority of the emperor, it would seem that the extent of the Roman people would actually have to be rather small.[49] Nor was it clear how, once a *princeps* has been legally constituted, the people might subsequently enforce their collective rights against their appointed agent, or even *in extremis* reactivate their residual dormant right to recover the *imperium* it had antecedently delegated to the *princeps* after centuries of imperial rule.

By contesting the legal validity of the *lex regia* in these ways, defenders of the independent authority of free kings were able to have their cake and eat it too. They could, on the one hand, appropriate fully the absolutist language of *imperium* in civil law while, on the other hand, conveniently discard the troublesome notion of popular sovereignty implied by the *lex regia*. The rejection of the *lex regia* consequently impressed upon such jurists the need for a different legal argument to explain the origins and foundation of temporal monarchical authority and, potentially, of all forms of constituted public authority coexisting alongside the emperor.

Yet, even though the Roman *lex regia* was eliminated in this way, not all jurists were prepared to reject the doctrine of popular sovereignty implied by it. Could there, in principle, be something like the *lex regia* undergirding the authority of free kings? Could there, for example, be the equivalent of a French *lex regia* undergirding the authority of the King of France, or an English *lex*

[44] Canning, *Political Thought of Baldus* 62.

[45] Canning, *Political Thought of Baldus* 62.

[46] Canning, *Political Thought of Baldus* 62.

[47] But see Canning's warning at *Political Thought of Baldus* 63, targeting the use of the *lex regia* by Ernst Kantorowicz, Ewarts Lewis, and Michael Wilks.

[48] Canning, *Political Thought of Baldus de Ubaldis* 56.

[49] Fasolt, *Limits of History* 169 and the discussion of Bartolus on D.49.15.24, §6.

regia undergirding the authority of the King of England? It was not entirely out of the realm of plausibility, but it would certainly require some degree of interpretive recalibration, as shown, for example, by Bracton in his gloss on the *lex regia*, where he seems to treat "the oath taken by the kings of England at their coronation in some ways analogous to the *lex regia* by which the Roman emperors at their accession had received the *imperium* and *potestas* of the people."[50] So too did Azo, in a *quaestio* concerning the authority of the King of France to surrender a vassal to another sovereign monarch, suggest that kings might legally be understood as having derived their authority from an anterior legal act of the people resembling the *lex regia*.[51] Nor was this line of reasoning restricted to civilians. The great canonist, Hostiensis (c.1200–1271), indicated that "if a king was emperor in his own kingdom, his power ought to reach him and be defined in scope by some such mechanism as the *lex regia*."[52]

But since, for reasons we have just seen, arguments from the Roman *lex regia* could not be directly marshaled in support of such a doctrine of popular sovereignty for non-Roman peoples, jurists speculating upon the popular foundations of monarchical authority had to look elsewhere, beyond the conventional boundaries of the civil law.[53] Ultimately, it was found not in the *ius civile*, but in the *ius gentium*, or the law of peoples, that body of law which, as the classical jurisconsult, Gaius, put it in his *Institutes*, was said to be what "natural reason [*naturalis ratio*] prescribed [*constituit*] to all men in common... [and] was observed by all peoples alike," whether Roman or not. This universal scope of the *ius gentium* differentiated it from the *ius civile* which consisted only of "those rules which a *civitas* [Roman or otherwise] enacts for its own members [and] are peculiar to itself."[54] Like "all peoples" [*omnes populi*], then, the Roman people were governed both by their own civil law—comprising "statutes, plebiscites, *senatusconsulta*, decrees of the emperors, and the authority of the jurists"—and by the law of nations.[55]

[50] Charles Howard McIlwain, *Constitutionalism Ancient and Modern* Ch. 4. McIlwain, relying on Selden's commentary in *Ad Fletam Dissertatio*, points out the grammatical sleight-of-hand, whereby Ulpian's phrase, *cum lege regia*, was not read as a causal conjunctive (indicated by the subjunctive, *conferat*), but as a simple preposition.

[51] Ryan, "Political Thought" 434 suggests that Azo's text "might even embody the first known use by a civilian of the *lex regia* outside the nexus of Roman people and Roman emperor to cover all monarchies."

[52] Ryan, "Political Thought" 444 and 451, n.92, citing Hostiensis, *Summa Aurea* (Venice, 1574) col. 1168 [§9].

[53] On the distinction between the *populus Romanus* and *populus alicuius loci*, see Pietro Costa, *Iurisdictio: Semantica del Potere Politico nella Pubblistica Medievale, 1100-1433* (Milan: Giuffrè, 1969) 243–7. Bartolus on D.49.15.24 distinguishes three categories: (1) enemies [*hostes*] of Rome; (2) the *populus Romanus*; and (3) all *populi extranei*. As Fasolt points out, the gloss on D.49.15.24 defines membership of the *populus Romanus* in terms of obedience to the Roman Empire [*accipe pro toto Imperio Romano*]. But since, in the fourteenth century, only very few would meet this criterion, Bartolus separates political obedience out from defining the boundaries of Roman peoplehood, so that even independent entities might still be considered part of the *populus Romanus*. What qualifies one for membership of the *populus Romanus*, for Bartolus, was recognition of the emperor's universal lordship over the world. This is what separates the *populus Romanus* from *populi extranei* who rejected the emperor's universal lordship, such as the Greeks, the Mongols, the Saracens, the Jews, the Turks, and the Indians. Fasolt, *Limits of History* 173.

[54] Gaius, *Institutes* 1.1.1; D.1.1.9; Inst. 1.2.1.

[55] D.1.1.7; Gaius, *Institutes* 1.1.2.

However, fixing the content of the *ius gentium* was a very tricky matter, partly because it could overlap almost indiscernibly with the *ius civile* on crucial points of law.[56] Slavery, for example, was certainly a central feature of the Roman law, essential to what Gaius called the *summa divisio* of the law of persons between free and slaves.[57] Yet, as Florentinus famously declares under the same rubric in the *Digest, De statu hominum*, slavery was not simply or exclusively an institution of the civil law, but more properly, "a decree of the law of nations [*constitutio iuris gentium*] through which one is subjected to the *dominium* of another contrary to nature."[58] So too were legal rules concerning property transactions such as simple delivery [*traditio*], occupation of *res nullius*, or creation of a *nova species* [*specificatio*], derived originally from the *ius gentium*, but recognized over time as valid rules of civil law once they were assimilated into Roman legal theory.[59] Indeed, as Rome's conquests brought new nations and peoples under its *imperium* and introduced the inevitable commingling between citizen and foreigner in practical legal matters, such as in commercial transactions, the line separating those legal rules properly belonging to the *ius civile*—or the even earlier *ius Quiritium*—from those belonging to the *ius gentium* was consequently blurred in Roman legal thought. Roman law, in this way, absorbed principles of the *ius gentium* and assimilated them to form a harmonious whole that did not rigorously distinguish between that law applicable only to Roman citizens and that law applicable both to Romans and non-Romans alike.

Where did the *lex regia*—or indeed, any rule or artifact of Roman public or constitutional law—fit into this analysis? As a legal act exclusively designated for the constitution of the Roman Principate, perhaps it should belong to the civil law of Rome. The difficulty, however, with treating the *lex regia* as exceptional to Rome is that the general principle of popular sovereignty and the popular constitution of princely authority expressed by it also belonged to the *ius gentium*, as the *Digest* indicated in a well-known reference to Hermogenian:

> As a consequence of this *ius gentium*, wars were introduced, nations differentiated, kingdoms founded, properties individuated, estate boundaries settled, buildings put up, and commerce established.[60]

While the civilians may technically be correct in their view that the *lex regia*, strictly speaking, was exclusive to the Roman legal tradition, the general principle of popular sovereignty embodied in the *lex regia*, as the means by which

[56] Kathleen Davis is thus right to stress that the category of *ius civile* "was and still is a self-conflicted category." *Periodization and Sovereignty* (Philadelphia: University of Pennsylvania Press, 2008) 40.

[57] D.1.5.3.

[58] D.1.5.4.1. Since slavery was considered a part of the *ius gentium*, so too was manumission, the legal act of releasing a slave from bondage and restoring liberty. D.1.1.4.

[59] D.41.2.1; Gaius, *Institutes* 2.66–9, 2.79.

[60] D.1.1.5. Accursius specifies in the gloss on D.1.1.5 that the phrase, *regna condita*, should be read as meaning kingdoms founded "by individual nations, which chose kings for themselves" [*a singulis gentibus quae sibi reges elegerunt*] which would include Rome, as a free people which selected their *principes* by the *lex regia*.

Roman monarchy was constituted, was understood to be common to all free nations, Roman or otherwise. Popular sovereignty, thus, might be seen, not as unique to the Roman legal tradition, but as an "operation of the *ius gentium* of which the [Roman] *lex regia* itself is but a specific expression."[61]

The upshot of this argument from the *ius gentium* had potentially radical implications for later medieval jurists, since it implied that every people or nation—not just those historically a part of the Roman Empire—had the latent capacity to enact the equivalent of a *lex regia* and so constitute—or even dissolve—their own system of public authority. Whether or not such a constitutive legal act of a free people should also be called a *lex regia* was a source of continuous technical debate, not to mention confusion for modern historians, who have often treated the term, *lex regia*, as a synonym for any popular grant of authority to another commissioned party. But that did not stop jurists such as Paul de Castro (c.1360–1441) from arguing that, by the *ius gentium*, a free people, or *populus liber*, held the sovereign right to constitute their own free kings [*liberi reges*] by a legal act functionally equivalent to the *lex regia* in Roman law. Paul, in particular, would even suggest that a people surrendering to another people—as in the case of Padua's submission to Venice—might legally be understood as a contemporary example of a *lex regia*, whereby the *communitas* of Padua "transferred all its *iurisdictio* and *imperium* to the *dominium* of the Venetians."[62]

But two problems emerged from this broader application of the *lex regia* doctrine of popular sovereignty as a general legal rule accessible not just to Romans, but to all nations under the *ius gentium*. One concerned the very concept of a "free people." The *Digest* classically defines a "free people," or *populus liber*, in terms of its relationship as an ally of the *populus Romanus*: it is a people "which is subjected to the power of no other people," yet may nevertheless be joined as clients or allies [*foederati*] on equal terms of friendship [*amicitia*].[63] It was, however, much less clear in the later medieval context, when the authority of the Empire was directly challenged, what counted as a "free people" entitled to create their own kings or make their own laws without an intermediary. Even if we knew who or what legally counted as a "free people," why would they ever want to part with the very popular sovereignty that made them "free" and legally sovereign in the first place?

The other problem concerns the *ius gentium* itself. Although the *ius gentium* recognizes popular sovereignty as a legitimate pathway toward the constitution of kings, it was not, by any means, the only pathway. Kingdoms could certainly be founded through a lawful war by right of conquest and acquisition, whereby the conqueror acquires the right of sovereignty over the vanquished and establishes justice in a new order.[64] Indeed, even Rome, in its founding

[61] Canning, *Political Thought of Baldus* 63.

[62] Ryan, "Political Thought" 445.

[63] D.49.15.7.1 and also the gloss on D.49.15.24 on *Vel praedones*, which cites D.49.15.7.

[64] Hermogenian at D.1.1.5 specifies that wars were introduced and acquired a legal status through the *ius gentium*. In the Middle Ages, wars resulting in the conquest of territory and establishing a new jurisdictional authority might even be understood as a kind of legal procedure, such as the ordeal.

myth, was thought to have been founded by Romulus through an original act of violence.[65] If the argument for undergirding the authority of independent monarchies was to be based on the *ius gentium*, it opened the very real possibility that perhaps monarchical authority was not based on popular consent or lawmaking at all, but, rather, on an original act of foreign domination and violence.

I shall deal with these two problems separately in turn.

POPULUS LIBER AND THE *CIVITAS*

In classical Roman law, the term, "free people" [*populus liber*], carried a technical meaning referring to the *foederati*, allies of the Roman people, though (prior to the Social War of the first century B.C.E.) not necessarily subject to their *maiestas*.[66] In classical law, the *liberi populi* or *gentes* referenced in the *Digest*, such as the Latins, were generally understood to be outside and beyond the scope of the Roman *imperium*. Such peoples were not Roman. There was no assumption that they were under any legal obligation to obey Rome or recognize Roman supremacy other than in those ways specified by an explicit pact. What made a people collectively "free," or *liber*, was the same attribute that, in private law, likewise made an individual free, and not a slave: They were "not subject to the power" [D.49.15.7.1: *subiectus potestati*], or "under the power" [D.1.6.1.1: *in potestate*] of another master, whether the mastery of another people or another person.[67]

The most important visible sign that a people was "free" and retained its popular independence was the capacity to make law [*potestas leges condendi*] for itself, a power which Gaius observes in the *ius gentium* to be inherent in all peoples:

> Now that law which each people has set up as a law unto itself [*quisque populus ipse sibi ius constituit*] is special to that particular *civitas* and is called *ius civile*, civil law, as being that *ius proprium* which is proper to the particular *civitas*.[68]

All lawmaking self-governing peoples are, by definition, free. In this respect, even the Roman people in the historical period after promulgation of the *lex Hortensia* (by which plebiscites "were to be deemed to have the force of statutes... [and] the same legal force"), but before the people's surrender of popular lawmaking power through the *lex regia*, was also free, just as any other

[65] Livy, *Ab Urbe Condita* 1.7.

[66] *Glossa Ordinaria* on D.49.15.7 on *Liberi* specifies that "free peoples" refer to "other men who have no truce [*treugas*] with us."

[67] Compare also Paul's explication of the word, *potestas*, at D.50.16.215.

[68] D.1.1.9. The *Digest* clarifies in D.1.1.6 that *ius proprium* might be treated as a narrower synonym for *ius civile*, so as to be distinguished from the *ius commune* that is universally binding on all persons, the *ius naturale* and *ius gentium*. As we will see in Ch. 3, the capacity to make law was essential to the legal definition of *iurisdictio*.

independent self-governing nation or people.[69] Rome was a *civitas*, and Romans were a *populus liber*, just like any other nation.

But perhaps the most noteworthy feature of Gaius' densely packed statement was the explicit conceptual connection he made between *populus* and *civitas*, such that the *ius civile* particular to [*proprium*] a *civitas* is shown to be equivalent in meaning to that law which a *populus* created, or "constituted" [*constituit*]. It was, indeed, a connection later to be exploited by Marinus, who, in citing this text by Gaius, opened the way to extend his earlier argument even further, so that sovereignty is not exclusive only to free kings and emperors, but also to "any people, of any municipality that is, or city, can make its own law . . . which municipal law is called the civil law, as if the specific law of that same city, as in D.1.1.9."[70]

In classical Ciceronian Latin, to be sure, the term, *civitas*, carried an important double-meaning, indicating both an independent city-state, as well as the citizenry [*cives*] of that city-state.[71] As Cicero would put it in the *Dream of Scipio*, a text of monumental importance for pre-humanist thought, all "public assemblies and gatherings of men united by right [*iure sociati*] . . . are called *civitates*."[72] This rich double-meaning of *civitas* had a direct impact on how the term, *populus liber*, could be interpreted in the legal thought of the medieval civilians—as both a unity and a plurality.

In the conventional usage of *Trecento* Italy, however, the term, *civitas*, had a more specific meaning and directly referred to the independent self-legislating city-republics or communes, as self-contained units or sites of political authority. These medieval communes were, in this respect, not all that different from Republican Rome before the *lex regia*, also an independent *civitas* that made its own civil law. From the perspective of the *ius gentium*, all such *civitates* held the status of a *populus liber*, an interpretation suggesting that perhaps these cities were actually *outside* the scope of the jurisdiction of the Holy Roman Emperor, just as any *foederatus* or *gens* was in Antiquity. This may have been a plausible analysis of the mutual relations between free and independent *civitates*, especially in the emerging horizontal foreign relations between cities shaping later

[69] D.1.2.2.8. See the previous chapter concerning the cross reference to this text in Accursius' gloss on the *lex regia* in D.1.4.1.

[70] Ryan, "Political Thought" 437, citing Marinus de Caramanico cited in Francesco Calasso, *I Glossatori e la Teoria della Sovranità*, 3rd ed. (Milan, Giuffrè, 1957) 180. On Marinus, see also Canning, *Political Thought of Baldus* 68–70; Pennington, *Prince and the Law* 103–5.

[71] Clifford Ando, "A Dwelling Beyond Violence: On the Uses and Disadvantages of History for Contemporary Republicans," *History of Political Thought* 31 (2010): 192, on the hypothesis of John of Viterbo in his *De regimine civitatum*, Ch. 2, that *civitas* originates from the phrase *(ci)tra (vi)m habi(tas)*.

[72] Cicero, *De Re Publica* VI, 13: *concilia coetusque hominum jure sociati . . . civitates appellantur*. This essential Ciceronian requirement that individuals are "united by right" or law also appears in the famous definition of the *res publica* as a *populus* at I, 39 (and similarly at III, 45): *populus autem non omnis hominum coetus quoquo modo congregatus, sed coetus multitudinis iuris consensu et utilitatis communione sociatus*. On the *Dream of Scipio*, see also Maurizio Viroli, *From Politics to Reason of State: The Acquisition and Transformation of the Language of Politics, 1250-1600* (Cambridge: Cambridge University Press, 1992).

medieval Italian politics, just as it was for the mutual relations in Antiquity between the Roman people and other free peoples.

But, in the medieval context, the juridical analysis was much more complicated because all cities of Christendom were legally understood to be within, not beyond, the universal jurisdiction of the Holy Roman Empire. As one influential jurist would put it, "all peoples and all kings [*omnes populi omnesque reges*] are subject to the temporal authority of the Empire, just as they are all under the spiritual authority of the Pope."[73] This was the conclusion, for example, of Glossators who treated Italian cities, not as free and independent peoples in their own right [*sui iuris*], but rather as holding a subject legal status, equivalent to that of a Roman *municipium* under the *imperium* of the *princeps*, just as free kings were thought to be equivalent to a Roman *praeses provinciae* similarly under the *imperium* of the *princeps*.[74] It seems then that, on the Glossators' analysis, the *civitates*, despite the fact of municipal self-legislation and self-government in local affairs, could not be fully independent of imperial authority, let alone a "free people," at least not in the juristic theory of civil law. They were, in theory, tied by obligation to obey the emperor as their imperial overlord.[75]

That being said, it nevertheless remained true that certain cities, as a matter of local practice, did make their own laws and govern their public affairs without seeking approval or authorization from a superior, an unavoidable fact that seems to have conflicted directly with the universal legislative sovereignty attributed in the *Code* exclusively to the emperor as "sole legislator" for the whole Empire. This gap between civil law and political fact presented an important difficulty for the jurists: how could a *civitas* legitimately hold an unlimited legislative power, even an *omnis* or *plena iurisdictio*, over its internal affairs (the essential mark of civic liberty) if, as the civil law clearly asserts, only the *princeps* is to be the true "sole legislator" in the Empire?

One early strategy for reconciling the *de facto* popular self-legislation in the Italian cities with the *de iure* legislative sovereignty of the Emperor was simply to diminish and explain away the legislative competence of these cities in various ways, using the interpretive tools already available in Roman law. A familiar explanation favored by the Glossators focused on the various sources of classical Roman law, such as the popular *lex*, the *senatusconsultum*, and magisterial

[73] Ullmann, "Development of the Medieval Idea of Sovereignty" 5, quoting Cynus de Pistoia on C.1.1.1.

[74] Woolf, *Bartolus* 113. The *municipium* was, in Roman Republican history, a city or town in Italy that was originally independent but subsequently brought under Roman control, in some cases, through the extension of the rights of citizenship. We should bear in mind Clifford Ando's reminder that extension of Roman citizenship was often an "instrument of domination" and "punitive." *Law, Language, and Empire* 87. Cp. *Glossa Ordinaria* on D.1.1.9 on *Suo proprio* how Accursius interpreted Gaius' phrase, *omnes populi*, as a term referring unambiguously, in his view, to *civitates* within the universal jurisdiction of the Empire. If a kingdom was equivalent to a *provincia*, the king must be equivalent to a magistrate, such as a *praeses provinciae*, which D.1.16 explicitly states holds no more than a delegated jurisdiction.

[75] On legislative activity at the sub-Imperial level of jurisdiction, see Kenneth Pennington, "The Birth of the *Ius Commune*: King Roger II's Legislation," *Rivista Internazionale de Diritto Comune* 17 (2006).

edicts. Among the sources identified in this context was custom, or *consuetudo*, which Julian defined as "the kind of law which is said to be established by use and wont."[76] The distinctive feature of custom was that, unlike a proper statute or edict, it was unwritten [*ius non scriptum*] and remained potentially a residual source of lawmaking power resting always with the people.[77] As Julian argues, the unwritten quality of custom does not detract at all from its being treated as equivalent to a written law with full "statutory force" [*pro lege*], and that is because the force of any law, whether written [*ius scriptum*] or unwritten [*ius non scriptum*], derives ultimately from the "will" [*voluntas*] or "judgment of the people" [*iudicium populi*], which can be expressed either formally by voting [*suffragio*] or, just as potently, by the "silent agreement" [*tacito consensu*] implied in the people's "very actions" [*factis*].[78]

This was a powerful statement, not only because it articulated the principle of popular sovereignty as directly justifying the validity of law, but also because it acknowledged the legislative capacity of cities to make valid law. Since cities were equivalently "free peoples" (in the sense of the *ius gentium*), it followed that cities could certainly legislate through custom just as any other people could, even while under the authority of the emperor. And that was precisely how the Glossator, Martinus (Gosia), treated city-made municipal statutes having the appearance of a proper written *lex*: They were nothing more than examples of "written custom" [*consuetudo scripta*], fully consistent with the supreme legislative authority of the *princeps* authorized by the *lex regia*.[79]

Another, more subtle strategy to combat the independence of cities, was to treat municipal legislative power merely as a limited local privilege which was the result of a concessive grant by the emperor. While *civitates* may have staked their claim to make new laws for themselves by the principle formally recognized in the *Digest* [D.1.1.9], the *Digest* itself, as an authoritative legal text for the Roman Empire, was, as the Glossators pointed out, ultimately a product of the emperor's own legislative will, as the *Code* indicates: "For we [emperors] very justly regard these works [comprising the *Corpus Iuris Civilis*] as ours, because all their weight has been derived from us."[80] Thus, a city can make a law, not by its own independent right derived from the *ius gentium*, but instead only because the emperor has allowed it. The legislative power of a city could, thus, really be no more than just a limited concessive grant authorized by sufferance of the emperor who, as one jurist put it, "can by a most trivial law revoke that law [D.1.1.9] and the statutes of the peoples."[81] Such a city might appear, at first glance, to be free, but as long as the emperor retained in reserve

[76] D.1.3.32. The *Digestum Vetus* has D.1.3.31. [77] Inst.1.2.9. [78] D.1.3.32.1.

[79] Canning, *Political Thought of Baldus* 96; Ryan, "Political Thought" 425 and 446, n.8, citing E. Cortese, *Il Problema della Sovranita nel Pensiero Giuridico Medioevale* (Rome, 1966) 96.

[80] C.1.17.1.6.

[81] Ryan, "Political Thought" 449, n.72, quoting Raynerius de Forlivio; cp., Canning, *Political Thought of Baldus* 109–10.

the legal right to withdraw that city's legislative power at any moment—or, to use a perhaps more familiar formulation in contemporary political philosophy, the "capacity to interere on an arbitrary basis"—it could not meet the legal standard required to be regarded a properly "free" or sovereign people.[82]

These were fairly common legal arguments among jurists clinging to the medieval ideology of universal Empire and the standard juridical treatment of a *civitas* as a kind of corporation, or *universitas*, with limited jurisdiction granted licitly only by imperial concession.[83] But, as Cecil Sidney Woolf once put it, "hard facts made it quite impossible to force... an independent city like Florence into that [position] of a mere Roman *municipium*," subject to the emperor's supposedly universal jurisdiction, just as it was difficult to place an independent monarchy such as France in the position of a mere Roman *provincia*.[84] What was needed, instead, was a recalibration in the interpretive legal science of civil law so as to accommodate, rather than ignore or try to explain away, the "hard fact" of civic independence and self-legislation as experienced in the political life of the medieval Italian communes.

THE COMMENTATORS: BARTOLUS AND BALDUS ON PEOPLEHOOD

The jurist who introduced this innovation in medieval jurisprudence, marking a clear departure from the traditional interpretive norms and conceptual assumptions of the Glossators, was the Perugian jurist, Bartolus of Sassoferrato (1313–1357), without doubt the most influential jurist of the later Middle Ages as the preeminent representative of the post-Glossatorial school of legal science known as the "Commentators." His extensive commentaries on the Roman law texts and applications of Roman law principles in the medieval context earned him a reputation as the indispensable authority on civil law even into the early modern period. As later civilians put it, "No one can be a good jurist unless one is a Bartolist jurist" [*Nemo bonus iurista nisi Bartolista*].

It was Bartolus who established as a fundamental norm of legal interpretation the principle that, "where the law and the facts collide, it is the law which must be brought into conformity with the facts," rather than the other

[82] Philip Pettit, *Republicanism: A Theory of Freedom and Government* (Oxford: Oxford University Press, 1997) 55.

[83] See, for example, *Bartolus* 134–35, who specifies the distinction between *merum et mixtum imperium* and mere *iurisdictio simplex*. The latter—a very legally limited right—is what cities have by concession from the emperor, just like any other *universitas*. Bartolus' innovation, however, is his concern for cities that acquire such jurisdiction by acquisitive prescription over time or even by usurpation. See also J.P. Canning, "The Corporation in the Political Thought of the Italian Jurists of the Thirteenth and Fourteenth Centuries," *History of Political Thought* 1 (1980), and Ryan, "Bartolus of Sassoferrato and the Free Cities" 76–7.

[84] Woolf, *Bartolus* 113.

way around, as the Glossators seemed to have done.[85] This new interpretive approach to Roman law, emancipated from textual fidelity to the Gloss, cleared an entirely new path for understanding the legal status of self-legislating cities in Italy in relation to the *imperium* of the *princeps*. What mattered above all else for Bartolus was the hard fact of independent civic legislation and self-government. Civil law, in his view, must be made to recognize this fact, and, for this reason, he rejected the tortuous legal casuistry of the Glossators, treating cities as mere dependents of the Roman *imperium*, like a corporation.

Instead, Bartolus reasoned that, since cities are entirely capable of popular self-government through the making of their own laws (not just "written customs"), by the consent of the people (whether tacit or express) and—crucially—without seeking authorization from any superior, it follows that cities must actually be independent of the emperor. Cities, in Bartolus' argument, were thus fully justified in viewing themselves as "free peoples," or *liberi populi*, as independent lawmaking cities outside the scope of imperial jurisdiction.[86] It was, as Canning once put it, a most "daring," construction of the law. By linking the medieval term, *civitas* (understood in medieval legal thought to mean a city *inside* and *subject to* the Empire, like a corporation), to the classical term, *populus liber* (understood in classical law to mean a people *outside* and *independent of* Roman control), Bartolus transformed the meaning of *civitas* itself, as an independent site of sovereign authority.[87]

What was revolutionary, however, even amounting to a landmark in the history of legal thought, were the implications that Bartolus drew from this treatment of the Italian cities and communes explicitly as "free peoples" in the civil law. One implication follows directly. If a free people—or, as he now feels justified in calling them, "free cities"—can make new laws independently and without authorization from a superior, it suggests that such a free people must *ipso facto* already be in possession of the highest degree of jurisdictional authority, what the medieval civilians—borrowing from the *Digest*—termed *merum imperium*.[88]

This analysis, however, presented another problem. According to the analysis of the Glossators, *merum imperium*, the highest and purest form of public

[85] Skinner, *Foundations of Modern Political Thought* 1:9, citing Woolf, *Bartolus* 6. See the text at Bartolus on C.7.45.13.

[86] Some key examples of Bartolus' connection of *populus liber* with *civitas* include his commentary on D.5.3.20, §2; 48.1.7, §14; C.11.31.3, §2. See also the useful summary in H.Y. Lee, *Political Representation in the Later Middle Ages: Marsilius in Context* (New York: Peter Lang, 2008) 77; cp. Ryan, "Political Thought" 400 and 449, n.70, citing Iacobus de Arena, *Commentarii in universum ius civile* on D.1.1.9.

[87] Canning, *Political Thought of Baldus* 96. It was a construction which seemed to justify popular legislation, and even popular revolution, in cities as a basic sovereign right of all free peoples in line with the *ius gentium*. See, for example, Magnus Ryan on Ricardus Malumbra's defense of the legal right of the Florentine *popolo*, under the *ius gentium*, to expel the Burdones faction and subsequently legislate anti-factional measures in 1293–95, "Political Thought" 400.

[88] D.2.1.3. Bartolus argues, as one sign of this *imperium*, is the capacity of a city to create citizens by law. See Julius Kirshner, "*Civitas Sibi Faciat Civem*: Bartolus of Sassoferrato's Doctrine on the Making of a Citizen," *Speculum* 48 (1973): 694–713. I discuss the *merum imperium* in greater detail in the next chapter.

power, could only be held by a *princeps* by right. On what grounds, then, can a city lay claim to hold an attribute that properly belongs to the emperor?

Bartolus took a cue from the earlier legal analysis of kings and emperors. A king, to recall from before, can have the attributes of a *princeps* simply by virtue of the fact that a king recognizes no superior *in temporalibus*. The fact of non-recognition is what makes a king the equivalent of a *princeps* over his realm and what entitles a king to the same sort of prerogatives and rights which the civil law attributes to a *princeps*.

Bartolus thought something similar might be said of a *civitas*, such as the Italian communes, which likewise, did not recognize a superior *in temporalibus*. To make his case, he gives the example of litigation and appellate jurisdiction within a city:

> If there is an appeal from the highest tribunal in the city, it will necessarily go to the city's superior. But supposing, as seems to be the case, that this city accepts and recognizes no superior? Then it must be its own superior [*sibi princeps*].[89]

Such a *civitas*, which, in fact, recognizes no superior *in temporalibus*—emperor or otherwise—has all the attributes constitutive of *merum imperium* such as immunity from *crimen laesae maiestatis* and the right to hold a fisc.[90] It is, then, for this reason that Bartolus feels fully justified in concluding with the statement that even a free and independent *civitas* can be treated as a *princeps* with a real authentic sovereignty over its temporal affairs: *civitas sibi princeps*, "The *civitas* is an emperor unto itself."[91]

This, as Woolf put it, was the "crowning step" in Bartolus' theory. Since, on Bartolus' analysis, the "free people" of the *civitas* have become the juridical equivalent of a *princeps* with full *imperium*, "it means that the *civitas* is now an independent sovereign state" in its own right, the essential constitutional form of which was invariably popular.[92] For Bartolus, it is always the people as a whole from which all public authority in a *civitas* derives, whether that authority is expressed and exercised institutionally through (as in the case of Rome) the government of princes, of senators, or through what Bartolus called the "government for the people" [*regimen ad populum*].[93]

[89] Ryan, "Bartolus of Sassoferrato and Free Cities" 77, n.40, quoting Bartolus on D.49.1.1. See also Bartolus on D.4.4.3 and 48.19.4.

[90] On fiscal rights as a sign of a free people, see Bartolus on D.5.3.30. See also Woolf, *Bartolus* 119–22.

[91] Ryan, "Bartolus of Sassoferrato and Free Cities" 79, offers an account explaining why this "double abstraction…of a city which is governed by its own disembodied *princeps*" was necessary to address not only questions of external sovereignty in the relations between cities, emperors, and popes, but especially of internal sovereignty and the nature of Italian popular politics.

[92] Woolf, *Bartolus* 160.

[93] In his political tract, *De Regimine Civitatis*, Bartolus explains that the *regimen ad populum* is most appropriate for a *civitas* of the "first grade of magnitude" such as early Rome at the promulgation of the *lex Hortensia* until the time, as Pomponius describes at D.1.2.2.9, when the Senate began to take a more active legislative role. But note also Bartolus' important distinction that "jurisdiction is with the people

But what is it about the people that it—rather than, say, the virtuous few or even one princely ruler—should collectively be the unique and exclusive source of public authority in a *civitas*? Interestingly, while Bartolus does not answer this question directly, it becomes one of the central points of focus organizing the thought of his pupil and most important successor in the school of the Commentators, Baldus de Ubaldis (1327–1400). While Baldus was, as Canning suggests, "no missionary for popular sovereignty," he nevertheless acknowledged the principle that the public powers of government [*regimen*]—including, above all, the power to make law without authorization or permission from another—are, by the *ius gentium*, "innate," "indigeneous," and "inherent" in all peoples, Roman or otherwise; indeed, such power "forms an integral part of a people's existence."[94]

The key to Baldus' explanation of this principle, as Canning has illustrated, was a skillful application of the law of corporation, or *universitas*, to the analysis of the *populus*.[95] What makes a *populus* so special for Baldus is that it exhibits precisely the same, even "mystical," features as a self-governing private corporation in civil law. It is, at once, a unity and a plurality.[96] Like a corporation, the *populus* is an abstract singular entity, capable of acting as if it were "one person."[97] Just as a corporation can own property, enter contracts, sue and be sued, incur debts and liabilities in the name of the whole *universitas*, so too can a *populus* act as one person in the name of the whole *civitas* such as in making law, pronouncing judgments, and waging war. To be sure, this notion of the legal personality of corporations developed in medieval canon law, above all, by Innocent IV, himself a jurist of great distinction in his own right.[98]

or multitude; but not that the whole multitude joined together should govern, but that a government entrusted to some people for a time." Bartolus, thus, shows a primitive understanding of the distinction between *popular sovereignty* and *popular government* (or "democracy") in which even a governing public council can be said to "represent the mind of the people" [*concilium representat mentem populi*], Bartolus on D.1.3.32 and C.10.32.2. I am grateful to Jonathan Robinson for providing his translation and edition of the *De Regimine Civitatis*, which are based on the edition of Diego Quaglioni, *Politica e Diritto nel Trecento Italiano: Il "De Tyranno" di Bartolo da Sassoferrato con l'edizione critica dei trattati "De Guelphis et Gebellinis," "De Regimine Civitatis" e "De Tyranno," Il Pensiero Politico* (Florence: Leo S. Olschki Editore, 1983).

94 Canning, *Political Thought of Baldus* 115, 105.

95 On the medieval legal analysis of corporation in general, see Pierre Michaud-Quantin, *Universitas: Expressions du Mouvement Communautaire dans le Moyen-âge Latin* (Paris, 1970).

96 Canning, "Corporation in the Political Thought of the Italian Jurists of the Thirteenth and Fourteenth Centuries" 9–32. On the people as a *corpus mysticum*, defined as *hominum collectio in unum corpus mysticum*, see Kantorowicz, *King's Two Bodies* 210 and also Baldus on C.9.2.3. For the Glossators' view, see *Glossa Ordinaria* on D.3.4.7.1 on "*Non debetur.*"

97 Canning, *Political Thought of Baldus* 189, quoting Baldus on C.6.26.2, which cross-references D.35.1.56 and 46.1.22.

98 Gierke famously attributed the theory of the legal personality of corporations to Innocent IV, but twentieth-century scholarship in medieval legal history has debunked this assertion. See, for example, Pierre Gillet, *La Personnalité Juridique en Droit Ecclésiastique Spécialement chez les Décretaistes et les Décrétalistes et dans le Code du Droit Canonique* (Malines, 1927) 163; Patrick William Duff, *Personality in Roman Private Law* (Cambridge: Cambridge University Press, 1938) 221–4; Tierney, *Foundations of the Conciliar Theory* 99–105.

But there is one crucial difference in Baldus' theory that deserves special attention. In the canonist theory, the personality and unity of the corporation was nothing but an empty legal fiction, a *persona ficta*. The legal capacity of a corporate body to act, even its very existence as a unitary legal entity, depended instead on some head, a representative agent or executive officer—variously titled *rector, procurator, actor*—empowered to act on the corporation's behalf by a concessive grant from some superior public authority (in modern corporate law of *ultra vires*, the "state" which grants and authorizes a corporation charter). In this respect, as Walter Ullmann observed, the juridical relationship between the corporation and its agent was often compared to that, in civil law, between the legally incapacitated minor or pupil and its appointed tutor or legal guardian who is said to "bear the personality" [*personam domini sustinet*] of a legally voiceless child.[99] Without the latter, the former was no person at all.

Baldus did not deny that the corporation was a legal person in the strictly legal sense that acts could be attributed to its name.[100] What he utterly rejected, however, was the suggestion that corporations, of all kinds, were nothing more than fictive creations or abstractions of law, existing only in language as a kind of heuristic device, contrivances of legal artifice. This was because all corporations, for Baldus, had a double aspect: Just as a corporation was a juridical unity, capable of acting as one legal person, it was just as much a plurality of humans, a composite body made up of the real individual members of the corporate body. These individual members, as Canning explains it, "are the physical expression of the abstract entity of the corporation which acts through the instrumentality of these members."[101] On Baldus' theory of corporations, there is no need for some externally instituted agent to "personify" the fictive personality of the corporation. It is, for Baldus, no fiction at all: The members themselves—when "rightly assembled" [*congregatur bene*]—are perfectly capable of acting for the whole corporation, not in their private individual capacities, but together as a "corporate person" [*persona universalis*] by the expression of the corporate will through their collective consent.[102]

What mattered, above all, for Baldus was the resulting balance of rights and powers in this analysis of corporation. Whereas, on the canonist theory, rights and powers ultimately had to accrue to the instituted head (such as a *rector*),

[99] Walter Ullmann, "Juristic Obstacles to the Emergence of the Concept of the State in the Middle Ages, *Annali di Storia del Diritto – Rassegna Internazionale, XII – XIII* (1968–9): 43–64. D.47.2.56.4. An analogy is also often drawn to the relationship between a *regnum* (or *respublica)* and *rex*, where the *rex* is said to be *tutor regni*.

[100] This is to differentiate the juridical discussion of the personality of corporations from philosophical discussions concerning the "realist" or "nominalist" metaphysics of groups, which jurists, such as Baldus' own student, Cardinal Francesco de Zabarella, viewed as "extreme Platonism" and entirely ancillary to legal questions. Tierney, *Foundations of the Conciliar Theory* 102.

[101] Canning, *Political Thought of Baldus* 188–9.

[102] Canning, *Political Thought of Baldus* 188, n.11, quoting Baldus on D.29.2.25.1, where the expression of the corporate will is achieved on some majoritarian principle.

just as, in the law of guardianship, rights and powers of the legally incapable pupil or minor were thought to accrue to the appointed tutor, Baldus resisted these conclusions, which ultimately would have disempowered the membership of the legally passive corporate body. For Baldus, the members comprising a corporate body retain their corporate legal rights and powers and are entitled to act upon them in the name of the corporation, even while certain of their powers may be delegated to some agent.

With this background analysis of corporations, Baldus is finally able to apply his findings to the political corporation of citizens in a *civitas*, the *populus*. Like other sorts of corporations, the *populus* also carries the double aspect of juridical unity and human plurality, described earlier.[103] On the one hand, the "people" is a "person," but only in the strictly legal sense that it is a unitary juridical entity, a "subject of rights distinct from its members."[104] Yet, on the other hand, the "people" is a corporate body, the membership of which is just the citizen-body. To be a citizen of a *civitas* is, by definition, to be a member of the corporation of the *populus*. The members of the citizen-body in a plenary assembly are fully capable of acting in the name of the corporate *populus* on all public matters, and, for this reason, the *populus* is rightly to be regarded as "the origin of governmental power and jurisdiction."[105] A *populus* is, in effect, a sovereign authority in its own right.

To be sure, this does not at all mean that the *populus* must assemble and govern at all times, like a direct democracy, just as a *princeps* need not personally attend to all matters of government at all times. Indeed, certain public functions of governing the *civitas* might be concessively delegated, as the people choose in determining the constitutional structure of the *civitas*, to lesser public bodies and magistrates to exercise and govern in place of the *populus*. It is a point which Baldus illustrated by reference to Pomponius' history of Rome. Just as the *populus Romanus* of Antiquity might govern its *civitas* directly, so too could it delegate certain public powers to the Senate and, later, even to the Decemvirate, Caesar's Dictatorship, and ultimately, by the *lex regia*, the Principate.[106]

What matters most here is the recognition that the *populus* remains sovereign over all organs and branches of its government in a *civitas*, however many and however powerful they may be, even while powers of government are actively exercised by way of concessive delegation. As Baldus puts it in a scholastic framing, the *populus* reserves a residual and potentially actionable right over such delegated authority *in habitu*, even while popular authority is exercised, *in actu*, through agents created and empowered by the *populus*.[107] In this

[103] Canning 190, *Political Thought of Baldus*, n.18, quoting Baldus on D.1.1.9. Cp. pp. 297–8.

[104] Canning, *Political Thought of Baldus* 191.

[105] Canning, *Political Thought of Baldus* 197.

[106] On this point, Baldus comments on Pomponius, D.1.2.2.9, cited at Canning, *Political Thought of Baldus* 199, n.52.

[107] The distinction between *actus* and *habitus* (or relatedly, *potentia*) is derived from Johannes Monachus. Canning, *Political Thought of Baldus* 203, n.74, points out that *habitus* appears also in Baldus' commentary on D.1.3.9, for which see Ch. 1.

way, the *populus* turns out not only to be the "*princeps* of its own citizens" but, most significantly, the rightful "owner," or *dominus*, of the authority loaned out for government agents to exercise on the people's behalf.[108]

In reconstructing Baldus' corporation theory of the *populus*, Canning had, in his influential study, concluded that Baldus crafted what might be regarded one of the first theories of the "state," as an entity to whom allegiance is owed and is distinct from both citizens, who are subjects as well as members of the state, and rulers, who govern the state.[109] But I would modify that conclusion, in the spirit of Canning's own recent critical reflection on whether terms such as "state" and "sovereignty" can be transparently employed in the analysis of concepts in a medieval writer like Baldus.[110]

What emerges in Baldus' system of thought is not simply a theory of the sovereign state, in a recognizably modern sense, but, more important, an interpretation that explicitly identifies "statehood" in associational and corporatist terms of "peoplehood." Baldus, thus, gives expression to an idea that will become central to early modern theorists of popular sovereignty—namely, that the form of state sovereignty can be nothing other than popular sovereignty, since the "state" just is the "people." This background serves to highlight one of the major misconceptions in contemporary understandings of sovereignty, which, without any compelling conceptual justification, tries to draw a sharp distinction between "state sovereignty" and "popular sovereignty." As can now be seen, and as we shall see in later chapters, they are, in fact, and should be understood to be two sides of the same coin.[111]

CONCLUSION

The later medieval civilians redefined the meaning and application of the legal term, "free people," so that even a self-legislating medieval city, though technically under the emperor's authority like a *universitas*, might nevertheless be considered free and independent, just as any nation or people under the *ius gentium*. This was an extraordinary achievement in the civil law tradition, because it marked a very clear departure from the near exclusive treatment of the *populus* as referring only to the historical "Roman people," as in the *lex regia*.

[108] Baldus on *Liber Extra* 1.2.8.10, quoted in Canning 203, n.72, and generally 203–6.

[109] Canning's target was originally Quentin Skinner, *Foundations* 2:352–8.

[110] Canning, *Ideas of Power* 147–57.

[111] For example, Nootens, *Popular Sovereignty in the West* Chs. 2, 4; Markku Suksi, *Bringing in the People: A Comparison of Constitutional Forms and the Practices of Referendum* (Dordrecht: Martinus Nijhoff Publishers, 1993) 122–3; Steven Curry, *Indigenous Sovereignty and the Democratic Project* (Burlington: Ashgate, 2004). Such studies violate one of the cardinal rules of proper social science, that is, to avoid the needless multiplication of entities in an explanation of a social phenomenon. The major problem, in my view, of these studies of sovereignty is not so much in the analysis of sovereignty, as such, but in the analysis of the *bearer* of sovereignty—"nation," "people," "state," "ruler," "community," "government."

Romans were merely one among many other free peoples in history, and so popular sovereignty was not exclusive to them. All free peoples could hold sovereignty over themselves. If it so chose, a people could transfer its *imperium* and *iurisdictio*, so as to subject itself to the authority of a prince, a king, or another people. But by that very freedom, a people could also retain its sovereignty in full, so that it might be collectively, a *princeps* over itself, with "just as much power over the people as the emperor has over the world."[112]

It is worth reminding ourselves, as I close this chapter, why I started on this investigation of the "free people" in the first place. To recall, jurists restricted the *lex regia* exclusively as an original constitutional act of the *populus Romanus* in constituting the authority of the Roman *princeps*. But they left open the question whether something functionally equivalent to the *lex regia* might, as a general principle from the *ius gentium*, undergird the authority of free kings, such as the King of France or the King of Sicily. Were these kings, like the Roman emperor, similarly tied in their holding of *imperium* to some anterior principle of popular sovereignty, as articulated in the juridical analysis of the *lex regia*? Or were they somehow exempt from it? The desire to craft a theory of princely authority using the materials of Roman law produced as synthesis of private and public law that would have far-reaching consequences for the theory of popular sovereignty.

[112] Bartolus on D.48.1.7, §14.

3

Roman Law and the Renaissance State: Dominium, *Jurisdiction, and the Humanist Theory of Princely Authority*

INTRODUCTION

In the gloss on the *lex regia*, Accursius observes Ulpian's report that the Roman people conferred "all their *imperium* and power" [*omne summ imperium et potestatem*] upon the emperor. As we have seen, it was allegedly by this popularly enacted *lex* that the Roman emperor originally derived the sole right to make and unmake law, and it was also by this *lex* that medieval jurists conjectured a general theory of popular sovereignty accessible to all peoples by the *ius gentium*, so that even non-Roman peoples could, in principle, exercise this constitutional power for themselves. What remains to be seen is how medieval jurists understood and interpreted the phrase, "*imperium* and power," a locution that remains far from clear and even more difficult to apply in a world where, as we have seen in the previous chapter, emperors, popes, kings, princes, feudalities, and even cities and autonomous corporate bodies of various kinds all claimed a legal right to assert *imperium* and power, often in competition and conflict with each other.

Accursius, evidently aware of these interpretive difficulties, and the multiplicity of meanings borne by these terms, explains that, for the purposes of legal science, the word, *imperium* in Ulpian's text should be understood properly as "*merum et mistum* [*sic, mistum=mixtum*]" *imperium*, while the word, "*potestatem*," should be understood as "*iurisdictionem*."[1] Thus, what the Roman people gave to their emperor by way of the *lex regia* was not some undifferentiated mass of power. On his reading, it was really a bundle of three discrete items: (1) *merum imperium*, (2) *mixtum imperium*, and (3) *iurisdictio*.[2]

For Accursius and his immediate readership, it was obvious what these three terms meant, and how they related to each other. But, for early modern scholars of Roman law who studied the *Digest* with the aid of Accursius' gloss,

[1] *Glossa Ordinaria* on D.1.4.1 on *Imperium* and *Potestatem*. Other Glossators, paraphrasing Ulpian's text, had sometimes used the word, *ius*, as well, such as Placentinus on C.8.52(53).2.

[2] D.1.21.1; 2.1.1; 2.1.3; C.3.13.

the meaning of these three terms was by no means self-evident.[3] Indeed, as the French jurist, Charles Loyseau (1564–1627), would put it, the task of explaining the meaning of these terms was "the most difficult point of all the Roman law without exception."[4] It was a task that would fill numerous scholarly volumes in the early modern literature on civil law specifically devoted to the topic, *de imperio et iurisdictione*.

Certainly, one strategy to determine the meaning of these three terms—*merum imperium*, *mixtum imperium*, and *iurisdictio*—might simply involve recovering the classical meaning of these terms, as they were used by Roman jurisconsults such as Ulpian, Papinian, or Paul. What should matter most, on this approach, is not what Accursius or any other medieval jurist thought these Roman terms meant, but rather, what Romans actually meant by these terms. As we shall see, this approach, amounting to a methodological "revolution" privileging classical usage above all else, increasingly became the favored strategy of legal hermeneutics and scholarship. It was championed especially in the sixteenth century by the "legal humanists," jurists who, influenced by the rise of classical humanism and techniques of philology, began to harbor suspicions about settled medieval understandings of classical textual sources and sought instead to reconstruct a more authentic interpretation.[5] In terms of methodology, these early modern legal humanists might be compared to modern "originalists": the authentic meaning of a legal text can be nothing other than its original meaning as understood within the mind or historical context of its author—whether that author happens to be a Gaius, a Gratian, or a Madison.

The problem with this historically oriented approach was that it treated the Roman law texts of Justinian as nothing more than artifacts of a dead classical civilization, trapped in a bygone Roman past. On this point, the contrast between the early modern legal humanists and their medieval predecessors, the *Accursiani* and *Bartolisti*, could not be sharper. Whereas the latter saw themselves as Romans, governed according to timeless principles based on Roman law, the former rejected the myth of *Romanitas* and stressed instead the unbridgeable gap between Roman Antiquity and post-Roman modernity. Rome was but a distant memory, an object properly to be studied with admiration and even reverence by classical scholars, rather than by practicing jurists.

[3] On the *mos Italicus*, see Donald Kelley, "Civil Science in the Renaissance: Jurisprudence Italian Style," *Historical Journal* 22 (1979): 777–94; Salvatore Riccobono, "*Mos Italicus* e *Mos Gallicus* nella Interpretazione del *Corpus Iuris Civilis*," *Acta Congressus Iuridici Internationalis VII Saeculo a Decretalibus Gregorii IX et XIV a Codice Iustiniano Promulgatis Romae*, ed. Pontificium Institutum Utriusque Iuris (Rome: Libraria Pontificii Instituti Utruisque Iuris, 1935).

[4] Charles Loyseau, *Les Oeuvres de Maistre Charles Loyseau* (Lyon, 1701) 36 [*Cinq Livres du Droit du Offices* 1.6, §28].

[5] On classical humanism and the rise of the legal humanists, see Skinner, *Foundations* 1:201–8; Kelley, *Foundations of Modern Historical Scholarship* Chs. 2 and 3; Julian Franklin, *Jean Bodin and the Sixteenth Century Revolution in the Methodology of Law and History* (New York: Columbia University Press, 1963).

The unavoidable consequence of the emerging modern humanist attitude was the unsettling realization that Justinian's law could have very little, if any, force or relevance in the early modern world. At best, Roman law could serve as a valuable source of raw data for classical scholars attempting to reconstruct a picture of classical Roman society. For others, who admired its elegance, clarity, and completeness, Roman law might even function as a model of a rational self-contained legal code, worthy of emulation by the nation-states, whether monarchies or republics, gradually beginning to assert their legal independence.[6] But by no stretch of the modern imagination could Roman law be treated as really anything more than that.

What would, then, be the point of elucidating the meaning of Latin terms like *imperium*, especially if there was no longer any *imperator* to claim or exercise it?[7] For some humanists, there could be no practical purpose, except as a vain academic exercise to explain what *imperium* may have once meant in an ancient culture. On this point, Loyseau observed the striking conclusion of Jacques Cujas (1522–1590), one of the greatest French humanist scholars of Roman law, derided by practicing jurists as nothing more than a mere grammarian: "The true meaning of these words—*merum imperium, mixtum imperium*, and *iurisdictio*—has been lost with the Roman state."[8] Applying the humanist analysis, Cujas rejected outright the medieval doctrine, "as very many have supposed" [*ut plerique opiniantur*], that there are three "branches" or "grades" of authority [*tres gradus*].[9]

But even if the "true meaning" of these words may have disappeared long ago with the fall of the Roman Empire, as Cujas, for example, insisted, it is also true that the same words themselves nevertheless remained vital to early modern legal and political thought, taking on a life—or perhaps "afterlife"—of their own. The legal humanists isolated two very distinct understandings of these legal words—how Roman jurists would have historically understood *merum imperium, mixtum imperium*, and *iurisdictio*, but also how medieval and early modern jurists understood them. Recognizing this semantic gap, their

[6] Stein, *Roman Law in European History* 86–101, and Wieacker, *History of Private Law in Europe*, for the modern reception of Roman law.

[7] Perhaps one of the most interesting and forceful arguments rejecting the Roman credentials of the German emperor was in the *Discursus Novus de Imperatore Romano-Germanico* by Hermann Conring (1606-1681). See Constantin Fasolt, "A Question of Right: Hermann Conring's *New Discourse on the Roman-German Emperor*," *Sixteenth Century Journal* 28 (1997), and the more complete study in *Limits of History*, locating the source of the problem in Bartolus.

[8] Loyseau, *Oeuvres* 36 [*Offices* 1.6, §28]. Loyseau is likely thinking of Cujas' discussion of *imperium* and *iurisdictio* in his *Observationes et Emendationes* (1598) 1029 [on D.2.1.3, Cap. 30], and also his *Solemnes Notae* (Frankfurt, 1598) 6–8 [on D.2.1.1; 3]. See also Chapter 5 concerning Bodin's relationship with Cujas in Toulouse.

[9] Cujas, *Observationes et Emendationes* 1029 [on D.2.1.3, Cap. 30]. Cp. Andrea Alciato 1:130 [*Commentaria* on D.2.1.3, §56] on the *tres gradus iurisdictionis*, which he identifies as *imperium merum, et mixtum, et minima iurisdictio*. Cujas rejects the equivalence drawn in the *Glossa Ordinaria* between *potestas* and *iurisdictio*, as if it were something entirely distinct from the two kinds of *imperium*. As he puts it, "there is no such thing" because "nothing is brought about by force without *imperium*," restating Paul's basic position of D.1.21.5.

main point was to stress that there was no necessary connection to be found between the two. Indeed, for an uncompromising "legal antiquarian" such as Cujas, any departure in meaning from classical usage could only be the result of textual corruption [*depravari*]—or worse, deliberate deception—which should be eliminated entirely.[10]

To be sure, not all jurists were as extreme as Cujas on this point. Acknowledging the multiplicity of significations carried even by a single Latin word of classical origin, such as *imperium*, some civilians recognized the need to distinguish classical denotations from the latter-day meanings affixed to it, even those based on textual corruptions.[11] As long as jurists acknowledged the separation between classical and post-classical usages, the texts of Roman law could potentially serve as useful vehicles for crafting a distinctive system of constitutional theory—a legal science that was Roman in appearance, but distinctively post-Roman in substance.

No set of terms in Roman law better exemplifies this linguistic transformation than *imperium* and *iurisdictio*, words that, in their classical Roman context, originally concerned matters of judicial process but became, especially in the later medieval context, foundational for what might be regarded as a general theory of public authority, garbed in the classical vocabulary of Roman law. My task in this chapter will be to investigate this transformation in medieval legal thought and examine how early modern jurists appropriated the Roman law vocabulary of *iurisdictio* and *imperium* to frame the conceptual analysis of sovereignty.

The chapter begins with an investigation of *iurisdictio*, as recorded in the *Digest* and the *Code*. *Iurisdictio*, as we shall see, was a very specific legal term in classical Roman law—specifically, the function of "declaring the law" [*ius dicens*]—performed by Roman magistrates, and fully delegable to agents appointed to act by mandate on their behalf. This classical Roman analysis of *iurisdictio* became foundational to the medieval theory of legal authority, developed by Azo, who treated the concept as a genus admitting multiple degrees or species of authority inclusive not only of the *imperium* held by emperors, kings, or inferior magistrates, but also of the feudal jurisdiction held by a lord, or *dominus*, over his fief.

Given this medieval background, I then turn to examine the humanist theory of "proper" jurisdiction [*iurisdictio propria*], crafted by French legal humanists of the sixteenth century, such as Alciato, Donellus, and Dumoulin, in reaction to the Azonian theory. The key to the humanist analysis was the restoration of a classical theory of *proprietas* to emphasize a distinction that

[10] Kelley, *Foundations of Modern Historical Scholarship* 112.

[11] The legal dictionary of Johann Kahl [*Calvinus*], *Lexicon Iuridicum*, identifies no less than eleven distinct senses of the word, *imperium*. Johann Kahl, *Lexicon Iuridicum Iuris Caesarei Simul et Canonici* (Genf, 1612) cols. 1280–2. The late medieval law dictionary, *Dictionarium Iuris tam Civili quam Canonici* (Venice, 1572), of Albericus de Rosate identifies eight distinct senses, while the *Repertorium Iuris Utriusque* of Giovanni Bertrachini (Nürnberg, c.1483) shows thirty-one entries.

would become vitally important in the modern theory of sovereignty—that is, the distinction between the legal "right" of sovereignty and the mere factual "use" or "exercise" of sovereignty. As we shall see, it is the humanists, relying on property law concepts, who introduce the notion that one's jurisdictional authority can, like an object of property, be loaned or delegated so that it may be "exercised" or "used" by other subordinate agents, such as magistrates. While the humanist theory is deployed to undermine claims of feudal or seigneurial rights of *dominium* over feudal jurisdiction, it also strengthens royalist claims in the private law language of *dominium* by presenting the right of sovereignty as akin to an absolute proprietary right of *dominium*.

IURISDICTIO AND *IMPERIUM* IN CIVIL LAW

Let us begin with *iurisdictio*. The word, *iurisdictio*, is itself derived from what was regarded to be the legal function of any person holding such authority in Roman law, "to declare what is law" [*ius dicere*]—that is, to grant a civil remedy in a dispute.[12] For Ulpian, the function of *iurisdictio* was broadly [*latissimum*] understood to be an "office" or "duty" [*officium*], which included, *inter alia*, the right to "grant possession of goods" [*bonorum possessionem dare*], "to assign guardians for unprotected wards" [*pupillis non habentibus tutores constituere*], and "to appoint judges to settle legal disputes" [*iudices litigantibus dare*]—it was perhaps, as Harold Berman once suggested, the "closest the Roman law of Justinian came to a definition of *iurisdictio*."[13]

But remarkably, such an important function in Roman law was not a uniquely *public* function for much of Roman legal history.[14] While the law granted jurisdiction officially to the public magistrates, such as the praetor, the proconsul, or *praesides provinciarum*, to be exercised personally and directly "by right of magistracy" [*iure magistratus*], such jurisdiction could nevertheless be delegated [*mandata*] by that same right of office so that it could be exercised indirectly on behalf of the magistrate through a "private judge," denominated in Roman law as *iudex*, or some other agent such as a legate.[15] The appointment of a private citizen to serve as judge and perform some jurisdictional function was essential to the delivery of justice in Roman law, because it enabled

[12] The legal humanist, Andrea Alciato, argues, as I shall show below, that *iurisdictio* is actually a gerund, or "verbal noun" [*nomen verbale*], derived from the verb, "to speak" or "to declare," *dicere*: It is not so much *iuris dictio*, as it is *ius dicens*. He is likely drawing this insight from Ulpian's phrasing at D.2.1.1, the "duty (or 'office') of declaring the law" [*ius dicentis officium*]. The phrase, "declaring-the-law" [*ius dicens*], carries a different active sense from "declaration of law" [*iuris-dictio*]. His purpose is to show that jurisdiction, of all sorts, implies an exercise or an action: It is a "doing," not a "thing." See also Varro, *Lingua Latina* 6.61, cited in Ando, *Law, Language, and Empire* 150–51, n.57; M. Lauria, "Iurisdictio," *Studi Bonfante* II (Milan, 1920) 492; Max Kaser, *Das Römische Zivilprozeßrecht* (München: Beck, 1966) 132. More generally, see Ernest Metzger, "An Outline of Roman Civil Procedure," *Roman Legal Tradition* 9 (2013): 1–30.

[13] D.2.1.1. Berman, *Law and Revolution* 290.

[14] Johnston, "The General Influence of Roman Institutions of State and Public Law" 93.

[15] D.1.21.1.

an efficient juridical division of labor in the Roman legal system. While the appointing magistrate had the task of narrowly crafting the legal question to be decided, the appointed judge would be responsible for answering that question based on the facts presented by the litigants. Indeed, litigation under the *legis actio* and formulary procedures used in the early Principate required the official *nominatio* of a private person to serve as *iudex*, to whom the power of judgment would temporarily and conditionally be delegated by the magistrate in the conduct of a trial. It became so routine that such "delegating" of jurisdiction was the first act required in the *incipit* of the formula initiating litigation, whereby the magistrate declares, "Let Titius be judge."[16]

Classical jurists envisioned this relationship between the appointing magistrate and the appointed private judge explicitly in terms of legal "mandate" [*mandatum*]—that is, as a kind of delegation of rights from one party to another who would then act on instructions. For Papinian, in particular, such a judge had absolutely "no competence of his own [*proprium nihil habet*], but exercise[d] [*utitur*] the jurisdiction belonging to the officer who gave him his mandate."[17] Thus, unlike the legally constituted magistrate who had discretion and independence in the exercise of public authority, the appointed judge was strictly temporary and limited in his exercise of jurisdiction.[18] Once the judge performed his judicial function, he immediately lost his jurisdiction and once again became a private person. Moreover, there were some things he was not empowered to do while holding jurisdiction. For example, private judges could not sub-delegate jurisdiction to others because, as Paul noted as a general rule, "one cannot delegate to another a jurisdiction which one holds by delegation."[19] Neither could appointed judges exercise coercive power, the *imperium*, to execute their judgments since, as Papinian observed, *iurisdictio* was narrowly construed to mean only the legal power to declare legal judgment in civil cases, but not the broader "pure" power of command and execution of legal judgment in criminal matters, which was called *merum imperium*, a power which was understood to be incapable of delegation and, thus, always remained with the magistrate.[20]

The private judge holding jurisdiction thus acted only in place of the magistrate [*is... fungetur vice eius qui mandavit*] and exercised only that share of jurisdictional authority explicitly delegated to him.[21] Since the jurisdictional authority of the judge was dependent on the grant conceded by the magistrate, the judge was said to hold his jurisdiction *alieno beneficio*—that is, solely by the permissive will or at the pleasure of the magistrate making the grant.[22]

[16] As can be seen in the quoted text above from D.2.1.1, the right to appoint judges is comprehended within the concept of jurisdiction. This delegation of jurisdiction to the private judge ended later in the Empire with the rise of the procedure known as *cognitio extra ordinem*.

[17] D.1.21.1.1. [18] C.3.4.1. [19] D.1.21.5. [20] D.1.21.1.1. [21] D.2.1.16, but cp. 2.1.17.

[22] D.1.16.6.1 indicates it is in the "free discretion" of the magistrate [*mandare... vel non mandare est in arbitrio proconsulis*] whether or not to delegate jurisdictional authority to another as well as the decision to "terminate" [*adimere*] a delegation.

Such delegated jurisdiction was fully revocable and often described in terms of "precarious tenure" [*precarium*], unlike the magistrate who held his office of magistracy "by his own right" [*suo iure*].[23]

The magistrate, therefore, was understood always to have a continuous *imperium* while in office, unlike the delegated judge who was said to have only a temporary *iurisdictio*. But there was an open legal question in Roman law whether the latter's delegated *iurisdictio* nevertheless entailed some minimal degree of coercive authority, or *imperium*, even if it did not rise to the level of the magistrate's *merum imperium* [*etiam imperium quod non est merum videtur mandari*]—that is, "the power of the sword" [*potestas gladii*] to inflict criminal and even capital penalties.[24] Was *iurisdictio* an inferior form of *imperium*, or not? The answer was complicated because, while the two were overlapping concepts, they did not map onto each other entirely.

Paul, for example, affirmed this interpretation, suggesting that there was, at least in theory, a species of *imperium* which "cohered" or was "attached to jurisdiction" [*iurisdictioni cohaeret*], and that it was only this minimal "modicum of coercive power" [*modica coercitione*] which is delegated to the "private judge" [*privato*].[25] *Imperium*, thus, was not a single unitary concept, but came in at least two basic forms for Paul. One was the simple judicial function of jurisdiction in civil matters which could be delegated to private judges at the magistrate's discretion. Because it was a power that could be held by both public magistrates and private persons, Ulpian described it as "mixed" [*imperium mixtum*].[26] The other, by contrast, was the coercive power of the sword to execute judgments in criminal matters. Such power [*potestas*] was regarded as the quintessence of magisterial authority and, thus, could never be delegated. For these reasons, Ulpian described it as "pure" [*imperium merum*].[27]

What must be emphasized, above all, is that *merum* and *mixtum imperium* in classical law were entirely unrelated to constitutional questions concerning the sovereignty or authority of the Roman *princeps*. The Romans already had another term for such a notion, *maius imperium*, so as to distinguish the authority of high magistrates and, later, the *princeps* from the *minor imperium* of lesser magistrates.[28] Indeed, nothing in the classical law of Justinian specifically linked *merum imperium* to the *princeps*. The only statements about *merum imperium* in the *Digest* (at D.1.21.1.1 and D.2.1.3) concerned, in a narrowly technical sense, the judicial function of magistrates in criminal jurisdiction—that is,

[23] D.2.1.5. The gloss on *Alieno Beneficio* has the phrase, *sua propria iurisdictio*.

[24] Ulpian explicitly defines *merum imperium* as the *potestas gladii* at D.2.1.3, to distinguish from lesser forms of authority, which he calls *mixtum imperium*. Papinian and Paul both agree that *merum imperium* cannot be delegated with jurisdiction.

[25] D.1.21.1.1, 1.21.5.1. [26] D.2.1.3. [27] D.2.1.3; cp. 50.16.215.

[28] E.g., D.1.16.8; 1.18.4, referring to the *maius imperium* of the *praeses* with his province, surpassed only by the *imperium* of the *princeps* himself. Victor Ehrenberg, "*Imperium Maius* in the Roman Republic," *American Journal of Philology* 74 (1953): 113–36; Hugh Last, "*Imperivm Maius*: A Note," *Journal of Roman Studies* 37 (1947): 157–64; E.S. Staveley, "The *Fasces* and *Imperium Maius*," *Historia: Zeitschrift für Alte Geschichte* 12 (1963): 458–84.

"the power of the sword to punish wicked men" [*gladii potestatem ad animadvertendum facinorosos homines*].[29]

To be sure, classical jurists certainly did connect *imperium*, as a general concept of authority and command, to the *princeps*—or, as he was also called, *imperator*—by virtue of the *lex de imperio* by which the *populus Romanus* was customarily said to have conveyed *imperium* to the emperor. And, as we have seen in Chapter 1, this was likely intended to legitimize retrospectively the imperial authority of the Principate by likening the emperor to Republican magistrates who similarly acquired their *maius imperium* by a *lex de imperio* from a comitial act of the assembled *populus*.[30] But there was no statement in the Justinanic texts of Roman law explicitly identifying *merum imperium* as an attribute specifically of the *princeps*; nor was there a statement in classical law connecting *merum imperium* to the *maius imperium*. Perhaps they may have argued that, because the *princeps* could be understood to be a kind of magistrate, insofar as he is constituted *lege de imperio*, just as any other Roman magistrate, *merum imperium* of the *princeps* is implied.[31] But that is not an argument of Roman constitutional theory explicitly made by any classical jurist.

IURISDICTIO IN MEDIEVAL LEGAL THOUGHT: AZO'S DOCTRINE

The characterization of *merum imperium* as a power specifically of the *princeps* was instead a latter-day interpretation introduced by medieval Glossators intending to specify and augment the legal powers of their *princeps*, the Germanic Holy Roman Emperor, using the resources of the, then, newly discovered Roman law. In order to see why the Roman law concepts of *iurisdictio* and *imperium* became central in framing the analysis of the authority of the *princeps*, we must turn, once again, to the legal thought of the medieval Glossators.

A famous, though apocryphal, story among medieval jurists—retold for centuries—traditionally accompanied the presentation of the problem.[32]

[29] D.2.1.3. John Richardson, "The Meaning of *Imperium* in the Last Century BC and the First AD," *The Roman Law Foundations of the Law of Nations: Alberico Gentili and the Justice of Empire*, ed. Benedict Kingsbury and Benjamin Straumann (Oxford: Oxford University Press, 2010).

[30] D.1.21.1.pr, however, discusses authority granted to magistrates not only by *lex*, but also by *senatusconsultum* and *constitutio principis*, broadening the legal devices to empower magistrates beyond the traditional legislative form of the *lex de imperio* in the Republic.

[31] That is precisely the suggestion made by medieval jurists, such as Belleperche and Bartolus. The latter treats the *imperium* of those whose sentences cannot be appealed as *maius*. See Jesus Vallejo, "Power Hierarchies in Medieval Juridical Thought: An Essay in Reinterpretation," *Ius Commune: Zeitschrift für Europäische Rechtsgeschichte* 19, ed. Dieter Simon and Michael Stolleis (Frankfurt am Main: Klostermann, 1992).

[32] Gilmore, *Argument from Roman Law* 17–20; Pennington, *Prince and the Law* 19–20. Early accounts of the story are to be found in Azo's *Summa Codicis* on C.3.13 and, again, in Odofredus on D.2.1.3 on *Imperium* in *Lectura Super Digesto Veteri* (Lyon, 1550) fol. 38. For more recent assessments, see, for example, Kinch Hoekstra, "Early Modern Absolutism and Constitutionalism," *Cardozo Law Review* 34 (2013); Ando, "Dwelling Beyond Violence" 197–98.

According to the story, the Holy Roman Emperor, Henry VI, summoned the leading jurists of the day, Azo Portius (whom I discussed earlier in Chapter 1) and Lothair of Cremona, to discuss the legal question whether he, in his capacity as a Roman *princeps*, was exclusively entitled to hold the *merum imperium* referenced in the Roman law texts. Lothair, answering first, affirmed this view, while rejecting the notion that lesser magistrates had any claim to *merum imperium*. At best, magistrates held the mere exercise of Imperial authority by a concessive grant, which should be described instead as an inferior "mixed" authority, or *mixtum imperium*.

Azo, by contrast, answered in the negative and denied that *merum imperium* was exclusive to the *princeps*. Even inferior magistrates were competent to hold *merum imperium*, as he explained in a well-known passage in his *Summa* on Justinian's *Code*:

> Can it be that this *merum imperium* belongs only to the emperor? They declare that he alone has it... But certainly even exalted magistrates [*sublimes magistratus*] have *merum imperium*, as it is to be observed in the *Digest* at [D.2.1.1] if the definition of law which we have declared is valid. For the governors of provinces [*praesides provinciarum*] have the right of the sword [*ius gladii*], as at [D.1.18.6.8; cp. *Glossa Ordinaria* on D.2.1.3 on *Potestatem*]. Yet, it is true also that municipal magistrates do not have such power, as discussed at [D.2.1.12]. I say, therefore, that full [*plena*] or the fullest [*plenissima*] jurisdiction belongs to the emperor alone, since by the *lex Hortensia* [= the *lex regia*] the people transferred [*transtulerit*] to him and in him all *imperium* and all power, as at [Inst. 1.2.6], so that only he can decree a common justice, as at [C.1.14.1], which the definition of jurisdiction suggested. For the text there says "the establishing of equity." I grant nevertheless that any magistrate can make a new law in his city [*in sua civitate*], as at [D.2.2.1]. And I say that even *merum imperium* belongs to other exalted authorities.[33]

In the end, the emperor favored Lothair who, for his obsequious reply, was awarded a horse, leading to Azo's famous quip that, "I lost a horse [*amiserim equum*], but this was not just [*aequum*]." But even though Lothair won the Emperor's horse, it was Azo's dicta that would become critical in the development of the medieval theory of *iurisdictio*.

Several important things are happening in Azo's text. First, and most obvious of all, is Azo's view, against Lothair, that *merum imperium* is non-exclusive. No emperor can monopolize it as an exclusive power for the simple reason that even the bare text of Roman law allows high or "exalted" [*sublimes*] magistrates to wield it lawfully. So there can be, on Azo's view, a coexistence of *mera imperia* in the medieval Empire—the *merum imperium* of the emperor and the

[33] Azo, *Summa Azonis, Locuples Iuris Civilis Thesaurus* (Venice, 1566) column 179 [Azo on C.3.13, §17]. The reference to the *lex regia* here is noteworthy and explains, in part, why the *Glossa Ordinaria* renders the phrase, *imperium et potestatem*, in the *Digest* as *merum imperium, mixtum imperium*, and *iurisdictio*. Pennington observes in *Prince and the Law* 19, n.48, that Azo's term, *sublimiores*, is an ambiguous designation. We do not know from this which specific magistrates actually have *merum imperium*. It is rather the principle of non-exclusivity that seems to matter most here.

merum imperium of magistrates. But there must be some way to differentiate between these authorities; emperors, after all, are not the same as magistrates.

Azo's strategy was to look somewhere else besides *merum imperium* to specify this differentiation, and he found this in the concept of *iurisdictio*.[34] Emperors and magistrates differed not so much in *merum imperium*; they differed, rather, in the *scope* of their jurisdiction. Whereas the emperor held what Azo regarded the *plenissima iurisdictio*, exclusive to the emperor by a plenary grant of the Roman people through the *lex regia* (thought here to be, as in the Gloss, the *lex Hortensia*), all other magistrates held, by contrast, what Azo called simply *minus plena iurisdictio*, literally, the "less-than-the-full jurisdiction" of the emperor.[35]

The key to Azo's reasoning relied on a new medieval analysis of *iurisdictio*, the significance of which, as John Perrin once argued, "cannot be overemphasized."[36] The Glossators redefined *iurisdictio* in such a way that it—and not *imperium*—became the conceptual cornerstone for medieval public law by encompassing within it all types of powers, including the coercive power of the sword, the *merum imperium*.[37] *Iurisdictio* became the genus, of which *merum imperium* was but a mere species.

This reinterpretation marked a radical departure from classical Roman law, opening the way for a distinctively new medieval theory of jurisdictional authority. Whereas Papinian and Ulpian saw *iurisdictio* simply as a delegable judicial function of magistrates, the Glossators saw it as a generic concept of power.[38] Irnerius, for example, in a gloss on D.2.1.3, defines *iurisdictio*, not so much in terms of the granting of legal remedies in civil disputes, but in general terms as the "power introduced with a view to the necessity of settling quarrels according to the law and of establishing equity."[39] Rogerius, likewise, treats *iurisdictio* as "the function imposed by the public authority, given the need of making and maintaining the law, and of establishing equity."[40]

Azo was following the new interpretive convention introduced by earlier Glossators when he similarly defined *iurisdictio* in his *Summa* as "the power introduced for the public arising from the necessity of making law, and of establishing equity," which, most influentially, would become the standard

[34] Costa, *Iurisdictio*; Francesco Calasso, "*Iurisdictio* nel Diritto Comune Classico," *Annali di Storia del Diritto* 9 (1965): 89–110.

[35] Azo, *Summa Azonis* column 177 [Azo on C.3.13, §2]. The term, *plenissima iurisdictio*, appears in D.1.16.7.2. The Glossator, Pillius, uses this language to describe the emperor's *iurisdictio* as *plena* in his *Summa de Ordine Iudiciorum*. See Brian Tierney, *Religion, Law, and the Growth of Constitutional Thought* (Cambridge: Cambridge University Press, 1982) 31, n.3.

[36] J.W. Perrin, "Azo, Roman Law, and Sovereign European States," *Studia Gratiana* 15 (1972) 93.

[37] This is because of Ulpian's statement in D.2.1.1 that the *officium* of jurisdiction was of the "widest extent" [*latissimum*].

[38] Jurisdiction would continue to be seen in this way, even as a synonym for sovereignty, until the seventeenth century. Tierney, *Religion, Law, and the Growth of Constitutional Thought* 30.

[39] Irnerius' text is quoted in Francesco Maiolo, *Medieval Sovereignty* (Delft: Eburon, 2007) 144–5.

[40] Maiolo, *Medieval Sovereignty* 145.

definition of the *iurisdictio* in Accursius' *Glossa Ordinaria*.[41] And this general definition, Azo explained, followed from the origin of the term from two key words in Latin, "*ditio* (which is power) and *ius*," confirming for him the core meaning of *iurisdictio* as any "lawful" or "rightful power" [*legitima potestas*] over something or someone.[42]

By this analysis, virtually anybody could have *iurisdictio*—and that was Azo's design. Certainly, emperors and magistrates each, respectively, held *iurisdictio: plenissima* and *minus plena*. But that only gives a very small glimpse of the widened jurisdictional and legal pluralism entailed by Azo's analysis. Just as the emperor can have *iurisdictio* over the whole world, so too could a king have *iurisdictio* over his kingdom and a magistrate over his *civitas*. Moving even further down the scale of jurisdictional authority, minor judges and officers could also, in theory, be said to have a share of *iurisdictio*, albeit to a lesser degree, in certain specified matters.[43] Even private persons can be said to have *iurisdictio*—fathers over their children, husbands over their wives, even tutors over their pupils. As a general principle, then, Azo allowed a perfect correspondence between the holder of *iurisdictio*, on the one hand, and the type of *iurisdictio* thought to be "proper" [*propria*] to—or belonging to—that holder, on the other. A father had his paternal species of *iurisdictio*; a magistrate had his magisterial species of *iurisdictio*; a king had his royal species of *iurisdictio*; an emperor had his *plenissima iurisdictio*—all coexisting alongside each other in a jurisdictional hierarchy of hierarchies.

Azo's analysis of *iurisdictio*, as a generic concept of authority inclusive of multiple degrees or grades [*gradus*] of jurisdictional authority such as *merum imperium*, became the standard view recorded prominently in Accursius' *Glossa Ordinaria* on the *Digest*: *Iurisdictio* is defined as a generic power, in precisely the same manner as Azo defined it in the *Summa*. But, unlike Azo, Accursius took a further step and specified these degrees of jurisdiction, using the conceptual resources already available in the *Digest*. For Accursius,

> There are four grades of *iurisdictio*. For some are *merum imperium*, others are *mixtum imperium*, others *coercitio modica*, and finally others remain in its own name and are simply called "*iurisdictio*."[44]

[41] Azo, *Summa Azonis* columns 176–7 [Azo on C.3.13, §1]. This is the identical text appearing in the *Glossa Ordinaria* on D.2.1.1 on *Potest*.

[42] Cp. Fasolt, *Limits of History* 275, n.75. Early modern legal humanists, such as Godefroy insisted that this etymology was false, pointing out the difference between *ditio* as an exercise of power and *ius dicere* as the declaring of law.

[43] This is to say nothing of the web of ecclesiastical jurisdictions that follow a similar analysis. See, for example, Durandus, *Tractatus de Iurisdictione Ecclesiastica*.

[44] *Glossa Ordinaria* on D.2.1.3 on *Mistum Est* [*sic*]. See also the useful discussion of Gilmore, *Argument from Roman Law* 30; Vallejo, "Power Hierarchies in Medieval Juristic Thought" 8–10. The confusing double-signification of *iurisdictio* in the Gloss and later treatments of jurisdiction is often clarified by distinguishing between "*iurisdictio* understood as a genus" [*iurisdictio in genere sumpta*] and "*iurisdictio* understood as a species" [*iurisdictio in specie sumpta*], or "simple *iurisdictio*" [*iurisdictio simplex*].

In this way, Accursius added some precision to the basic insight introduced by Azo. He organized all species and degrees of jurisdictional authority by four principal terms, derived from the Roman law texts on jurisdiction.[45] All forms of jurisdictional authority should, in theory, fit into one of these four degrees identified.

THE PROBLEM OF "PROPER" JURISDICTION: *IURISDICTIO* AND *DOMINIUM*

This analysis reflected the fragmentary layered structure of feudal society, and it is for this reason, as Gilmore observes, "the opinion of Azo should have prevailed [in later medieval legal thought]. His solution, by allowing *iurisdictio* to others than the emperor, was much more adaptable to the social system, namely feudalism, which the Postglossators [that is, the Commentators] were trying to rationalize."[46] Even those with jurisdictional authority over some territory, a city [*civitas*], an estate [*villa*], and even a castle [*castrum*], held an "ordinary" [*ordinaria*], rather than "delegated" [*delegata*], jurisdiction, just as a magistrate, that was unrestricted and general in scope [*universaliter*] over all matters [*in omnibus causis*] in his competence.[47] In this way, even feudal lords, or *domini*, of all ranks—dukes, barons, counts, and lesser feudal lords—were, in principle, incorporated into Azo's vision as fully legitimate bearers of an independent jurisdictional authority over their fiefs, much like a Roman provincial governor with an autonomous *plena iurisdictio* over his province that was surpassed in authority only by the *princeps*.

But there is a difficulty in Azo's suggestion of feudal, or "praedial," jurisdiction. Even though feudal jurisdiction is presented here as an *ordinary* jurisdiction, it still originates in an antecedent grant from some higher authority—more specifically, it is "granted by the *princeps*" [*datur a principe*]. What is the nature of this grant? One is tempted to say that this is simply a species of delegation—a feudal lord is, after all, in a subordinate position as a vassal owing allegiance to his king in exchange for the fief—or indeed, the "fee"—he receives in return for rendering service. Should this vassalic relation between the king and a feudal lord, originating out of a feudal grant "enfeoffing" a freeman, be treated as a case of delegation?

If the feudal lord actually were the recipient of a delegation from the king, the king would, in theory, have reserved in full certain rights over the granted fief. The lord would, on this view, be no better than a precarious tenant whose delegated jurisdiction is held at the king's pleasure. But that is precisely the conclusion Azo wants to avoid by his description of feudal jurisdiction as

[45] The chief sources are D.1.21.1.1, 1.21.5.1, 2.1.3.

[46] Gilmore, *Argument from Roman Law* 31.

[47] Azo, *Summa Azonis* column 177 [Azo on C.3.13, §3]. Cp. Durandus on the lord's delegation of *merum imperium* to the *civitas* or *castrum* in his *Speculum Iuris*, discussed at Gilmore, *Argument from Roman Law* 33.

ordinaria, rather than as *delegata* or *mandata*.[48] Properly speaking, a delegate, such as the private judge of Roman law, has no competence or independence of his own, as we have seen earlier; he is merely an instrument carrying out a strictly limited function on a mandate from his principal.[49] And because a delegate performs his function on another's mandate, he is said to hold it only by "another's pleasure" or permission or commission [D.2.1.5, *alieno beneficio*]. Unlike the holder of an ordinary jurisdiction, such as a magistrate who has a general jurisdictional authority over all matters in his competence "by his own right" [D.2.1.5, *suo iure*], the holder of a delegated jurisdiction has a precarious hold on a limited authority only over specially defined individual matters [*in singularibus causis*].

By denying that a feudal lord, or *dominus*, has a delegated jurisdiction, Azo necessarily situates feudal jurisdiction as equivalent in dignity and authority to the sort of ordinary jurisdiction held by the magistrate in civil law. Like a magistrate, a feudal *dominus* holds *iurisdictio*, not *alieno beneficio*, but *suo iure*. It is, in this way, a *iurisdictio* that is "proper" [*propria*] to, or belonging exclusively and rightfully to, its holder, rather than to some other party [*aliena*], as something shared in "common" [*communis*]. It would not be right, therefore, to treat the original grant of such *iurisdictio* from the *princeps* as a delegation. It must rather have been the result of some other type of transaction.

One crucial implication of this line of reasoning was the view that a fief, as well as the *iurisdictio* annexed to it, might actually be considered as private property rightfully belonging to a feudal *dominus*. Indeed, fiefs were customarily treated not only as vendible objects, but also as heritable objects, just as any other patrimonial good. For this reason, it was thought to be entirely within reason to treat feudal jurisdiction in the juridical language of *dominium*. A *dominus* had *dominium* over his fief and the bundle of jurisdictional rights attached to it.[50]

This conceptual connection between *iurisdictio* and *dominium*, prominent especially from the thirteenth century, became one of the hallmarks of feudal thought. Just as a feudal lord had a *iurisdictio* over his fief, so too did he have *dominium* over it. Indeed, "there was perfect symmetry between *dominium* and jurisdiction... In a fundamental sense, they were identical."[51] To have a proprietary right of "owning" feudal territory implied and entailed a corresponding juridictional right of "ruling" that territory, and vice versa.[52]

[48] On the "ordinary" and the *arbiter delegatus* in Bulgarus and Gratian, see Kenneth Pennington, "The Big Bang: Roman Law in the Early Twelfth Century," *Rivista Internazionale di Diritto Comune* 18 (2007): 43–70.

[49] Azo, *Summa* [Azo on C.3.13, No. 5], quoting Papinian's famous phrase, *nihil habet proprium*, from D.1.21.1.1. The Glossators' analysis of delegated jurisdiction is applied in similar terms to ecclesiastical jurisdictions in canon law. See, for example, Gulielmus Durandus, *Speculum Juris, De Judice Delegato*.

[50] On the medieval legal treatment of the fief, see more generally the *Liber Feudorum* which was one of the texts included in the Vulgate *Volumen Parvum* of Roman law texts.

[51] Fasolt, *Limits of History* 186, 187.

[52] Tierney, *Religion, Law, and the Growth of the Constitutional Thought* 30–2.

But what exactly was the nature of this feudal *dominium*? It is difficult to specify because, as Stephen Lahey once put it, *dominium* became a "portmanteau concept" in medieval legal and social thought, with importance not only in law, but also in theology and philosophy.[53] Like *iurisdictio*, the term, *dominium*, originates in classical Roman law, where it carried a very specific linguistic function in the law of property. *Dominium* indicated full and absolute legal ownership over some thing, or *res*.[54] It was, as W.W. Buckland once put it, "the ultimate right, that which has no right behind it... a *signoria*."[55] Because of the essential connection between the *dominus* and the thing that is owned by the *dominus*, *dominium* was understood in classical law fundamentally to be a relational concept. It implied an asymmetrical relationship of dependence and subjection which extended not only over tangible objects, such as land and movables, but even over other persons or animals, and even abstract notions, such as an inheritance, use-rights or a legally contracted obligation.[56] Indeed, in one infamous passage in the *Digest*, it was suggested that even the whole world [*orbis terrarum*] is regarded to be subject to *dominium*—namely, the *dominium* of the emperor, to whom "all things" [*omnia*] were said, in Justinian's *Code*, to belong.[57]

Such a system of legal relations revolving around *dominium* left very little room for ambiguity, because there could never be more than one *dominus* over

[53] Stephen Lahey, *Philosophy and Politics in the Thought of John Wyclif* (Cambridge: Cambridge University Press, 2003) 24. *Glossa Ordinaria* on C.7.37.3 [*Bene a Zenone*] on *Omnia Principis*, where Accursius explains that the emperor's *dominium* over "all things" [*omnia*] should be understood in the sense of jurisdiction and the duty of protection. Pennington, *Prince and the Law* 22–24; Canning, *Political Thought of Baldus* 82. The gloss cross-references D.43.8.2.4, which states that "For the property of the treasury is as it were the private property of the emperor" [*Res enim fiscales quasi propriae et privatae principis sunt*]. On *dominium* in medieval thought: Richard Tuck, *Natural Rights Theories* (Cambridge: Cambridge University Press, 1979) Ch. 1; Annabel Brett, *Liberty, Right and Nature* (New York: Cambridge University Press, 1997) Ch. 1.; Burns, *Lordship, Kingship and Empire* 19–25; Tierney, *Religion, Law, and the Growth of Constitutional Thought* 30, 32; Janet Coleman, "*Dominium* in Thirteenth and Fourteenth-Century Political Thought and Its Seventeenth-Century Heirs: John of Paris and Locke," *Political Studies* 33 (1985): 83–5; Janet Coleman, "Medieval Discussions of Property: *Ratio* and *Dominium* according to John of Paris and Marsilius of Padua," *History of Political Thought* 4 (1983): 209–28; Janet Coleman, "Using, Not Owning—Duties, Not Rights: The Consequences of Some Franciscan Perspectives on Politics," *Defenders and Critics of Franciscan Life: Essays in Honor of John V. Fleming*, ed. Michael Cusato and G. Geltner (Leiden: Brill, 2009); Alexander Lee, "Roman Law and Human Liberty: Marsilius of Padua on Property Rights," *Journal of the History of Ideas* 70 (2009): 23–44.

[54] D.1.8; Inst. 2.1-2.2; Gaius, *Institutes* 2.1–2.22, for classical *divisiones rerum*. Peter Birks, "The Roman Law Concept of *Dominium* and the Idea of Absolute Ownership," *Acta Juridica* 1 (1985). This "absolute" conception of Roman ownership is one of the key features distinguishing Roman law from English common law and other customary legal systems, where notions of the "better" or "relative" rights to property prevailed. Jolowicz, *Historical Introduction to the Study of Roman Law* 142–43.

[55] Buckland, *Textbook of Roman Law* 188.

[56] D.1.8.1.1. For the Glossators, even the "whole world" could potentially be subject to *dominium*, without also owning the individual "parts" of the world, a doctrine established by applying the principle of D.6.1.1 that one can have *dominium* over a whole without also having *dominium* over the parts that make up that whole, such as a flock of sheep.

[57] D.14.2.9 and C.7.37.3. Pennington, *Prince and the Law* Ch. 1.

one *res*—as an indivisible unit [*in solidum*]—at any one time.[58] As Constantin Fasolt usefully describes it:

> *Dominium* was like an atom of social and material relations. Either you had *dominium* over a thing or you did not. There was nothing in between. You could not share *dominium*...and you could not divide it into different components to be parceled out among different individuals.[59]

The classical Roman legal worldview was, thus, one divided between those with *dominium* and those without *dominium*. It was, one might say, a *binary concept* implying exclusivity. If one was found in civil law to have *dominium* over some thing, it implied correspondingly that all others must lack *dominium* over that very same thing. This principle of exclusivity applied even to those with a lesser legal interest in the property recognized under Roman law, such as possession, usufruct, or *emphyteusis*.[60] When compared with the absolute proprietary right of the *dominus*, even a possessory, usufructuary, or emphyteuticary must ultimately be regarded as juridically inferior because such persons lacked *dominium* and, by implication, had no available action by which to "vindicate" their right of property.[61]

Such an "absolutist" system of property ownership, constructed upon a binary understanding of *dominium*, distinguishing owners from non-owners, might have made sense for the social organization of the "peasant-proprietor" culture of early Rome, in which ideas of absolute *dominium* first emerged and were necessary for the survival of the family estate.[62] But for the Glossators of medieval Christendom, this Roman concept of *dominium* presented a fundamental problem in the analysis of feudal jurisdiction. As J.H. Burns once explained:

> The problem was that feudal relationships [between lords and vassals] did not allow for any such absolute and exclusive right as Roman *dominium* implied. The vassal or subtenant was regarded as having something more than mere usufruct or bare possession [of the fief]. He too was in his way a *dominus*, and

[58] D.13.6.5.15; 41.2.3.5. See also the glosses of Accursius and Odofredus on this doctrine in Thomas Rüfner, "The Roman Concept of Ownership and the Medieval Doctrine of *Dominium Utile*," *The Creation of the Ius Commune: From Casus to Regula*, ed. John Cairns and Paul Du Plessis (Edinburgh, 2010).

[59] Fasolt, *Limits of History* 185.

[60] D.41.2.1.3; 41.2.3.1; 41.2.12.1; 41.2.13.pr.; 50.16.115; C.2.12.10.

[61] Peter Garnsey, *Thinking About Property: From Antiquity to the Age of Revolution* (New York: Cambridge University Press, 2007) Ch. 7, especially 184–90, 195–203; Janet Coleman, "Property and Poverty," *Cambridge History of Medieval Political Thought, c. 350–c.1450*, ed. J.H. Burns (Cambridge: Cambridge University Press, 1988) 611–15. The Praetorian law protected possessory claims against *dominium*, through interdicts that recognized a form of legal ownership known as "bonitary ownership," giving the possessor a protection against the *dominus* by pleading an *exceptio rei venditae et traditae*. In some cases defined under the *Actio Publiciana*, a *dominus* could even be prosecuted for "stealing" property which was technically under his own *dominium* but had already been sold and delivered to another party. D.6.2.1, 6.2.7.6, and 6.2.13.

[62] Jolowicz, *Historical Introduction* 139. Henry Sumner Maine advanced the influential thesis that the family unit was the most important unit in ancient legal systems. *Ancient Law: Its Connection with the Early History of Society and its Relation to Modern Ideas* (London: John Murray, 1924) 270.

> to allow for this it was necessary to devise ways in which *dominium* itself could be divided.[63]

The chief difficulty concerned the proper legal classification of the feudal vassal—at once a *dominus* over his fief, but also subordinate, in theory, to the king, who had granted him his fief in the first place and remained, in some ways, also a *dominus* over the very same fief. This "division" of *dominium* seemed like a practical arrangement to accommodate *dominium* into the layered structure of feudal society. But the problem was that this feudal arrangement appeared to violate one of the cardinal rules of Roman law: it allowed two lords, or *duo domini in solidum*, over one and the same thing—in this case, the fief.[64]

Something had to give way: either the language of *dominium* had to be reconceptualized, or it had to be eliminated altogether from the analysis of feudal jurisdiction. The Glossators, faced with this dilemma, really had no choice but to opt for the former strategy. Presented with these multiple strata of feudal lordships, the Glossators recognized the urgent need to revise the classical Roman concept of *dominium* so as to accommodate within the scheme of Roman law the feudal institution of the vassal's tenure and authority over his fief. What a classical lawyer might simply describe as a long-term lease over land, such as *emphyteusis, superficies*, or *ager vectigalis*, now became a form of *dominium* attached to its own actionable right of recovery.[65] As Robert Feenstra explains:

> Although in principle a vassal held land only by virtue of his relationship with the lord, many vassals acted as though they were in fact owners. To the Glossators the question arose as to the correct Roman law niche to which the vassal's right to the land should be assigned. The answer—probably given for the first time by Pillius—was that he could indeed be regarded as a kind of owner: whereas the lord had *dominium directum*, the vassal had *dominium utile.* [66]

In this way, *dominium* was, just like *iurisdictio*, treated as a generic concept, admitting two basic species, the *dominium directum* of the lord and *dominium*

[63] Burns, *Lordship, Kingship and Empire* 18. Burns, in turn, cites Francis Oakley, *Political Thought of d'Ailly* 67–70. Tuck gives a similar explanation in *Natural Rights Theories* 17. See also Herbert Rowen, *The King's State: Proprietary Dynasticism in Early Modern France* (New Brunswick: Rutgers University Press, 1980) 9–10, 29.

[64] D.13.6.5.15. Cp. Pennington, *Prince and the Law* 113–14.

[65] E. Meynial, "Notes sur la Formation de la Théorie du Domaine Divise," *Mélanges Fitting*, 2 Vols. (Montpellier: Société Anonyme de l'Imprimerie Générale du Midi, 1907-8) 417–18, references D.6.3.1 on the recovery of public lands. Robert Feenstra, "*Dominium* and *ius in re aliena*: The Origins of a Civil Law Distinction," *New Perspectives in the Roman Law of Property: Essays for Barry Nicholas*, ed. Peter Birks (Oxford: Clarendon Press, 1989) 113, suggests another likely source was C.11.62.12.

[66] Feenstra, "*Dominium* and *Ius in Re Aliena*" 112–13. Feenstra, in turn, speculates that the Glossators may have derived the *dominium directum/dominium utile* distinction from C.11.62.12 which treats the *emphyteuticarius* as a sort of *dominus* who is entitled to an *actio utilis*, just as a *dominus* is entitled to an *actio directa*. See also Garnsey, *Thinking about Property* 200 who cites D.9.2.11.10, and Meynial, "Notes sur la Formation de la Théorie du Domaine Divise" 429–41.

utile of the vassal.[67] This division of *dominium*, what has traditionally been called the doctrine of "divided *dominium*" [*dominium divisum*] or "double *dominium*" [*dominium duplex*], became the standard medieval theory of *dominium*, and it helped explain why even a vassal, such as the King of Sicily, might nevertheless have, by reason of *dominium utile*, a superior or sovereign claim to his territory, superior even to that of his feudal lord.[68] No longer a binary concept, *dominium* became instead a *scalar* concept in medieval legal thought, implying both "conditional property... [and] parcellized sovereignty."[69]

But it was, once again, Bartolus who supplied the most complete and definitive analysis of divided *dominium*, offering a conceptual synthesis that treated it as "synonymous with *iurisdictio* and *imperium* in the public law sense."[70] Bartolus linked *dominium* explicitly with *iurisdictio*. There was, as he put it, a functional equivalence of meaning—or an *aequiparatio*—between the concepts of *iurisdictio* and *dominium* [*aequiparatio de iurisdictione ad dominium*], such that anybody with *iurisdictio*, in the sense that Ulpian, Papinian, and Paul describe in the *Digest*, could also be said to have *dominium* as well.[71] Thus, a magistrate with an *ordinaria iurisdictio* can be said to have *dominium*. So too could a vassal with *iurisdictio* in a fief similarly be said to have *dominium*—namely, a *dominium utile*. Even the emperor, who is said to have "fullest" [*plenissimam*] or "all jurisdiction" [*omnem iurisdictionem*] also can be said to have *dominium*, over the "whole world." In this way, for Bartolus, the two terms, *dominium* and *iurisdictio*, were identical, or perhaps two sides of the same coin, both expressing in common the notion of a legal right which "applied equally to private property and public power."[72]

[67] Vallejo, "Power Hierarchies in Medieval Juridical Thought" 22–23, n.48.

[68] Tuck, *Natural Rights Theories* 16. See also Helmut Coing, "Zur Eigentumslehre des Bartolus," *Zeitschrift für Savigny-Stiftung für Rechtsgeschichte* 70 (1953): 349–71; Robert Feenstra, "Les Origines du *Dominium Utile* Chez les Glossateurs," *Fata Iuris Romani* (Leiden, 1974): 215–59; Robert Feenstra, "Der Eigentumsbegriff bei Hugo Grotius im Licht Einiger Mittelalterlicher und Spätscholastischer Quellen," Okko Behrends, et al., *Festschrift für Franz Wieacker* (Göttingen, 1978): 209–34; Feenstra, "*Dominium* and *ius in re aliena*" 111–22; Wieacker, *History of Private Law in Europe* Ch. 5, especially 58–9; J.P. Lévy, *Histoire de la Proprieté* (Paris, 1972) 44–6. Marinus de Carimanico, *Prooemium in Constitutiones Regni Siciliae* in Calasso, *I Glossatori*.

[69] Anderson, *Lineages of the Absolutist State* 25.

[70] Bartolus on D.21.2.39.1; cp. Baldus on D.1.1.9, §3, and C.2.3.28. Garnsey, *Thinking about Property* 200, citing Coing, "Zur Eigentumslehre des Bartolus" 70 (1953): 365–6. Maiolo, *Medieval Sovereignty* 156.

[71] Bartolus of Sassoferrato, *Super Primam Digesti Veteris Partem* in *Commentaria Cum Adnotationibus Thomae Diplovatatii*, ed. Baptista de Tortiis (Venice, 1506), facsimile reprint ed. G. Polara, Vol. 1 (Rome, 1996) fol. 49, §15 [Bartolus on Dig. 2.1.1, under *Ius dicentis*]; Rosate, *Dictionarium Iuris*, under *Dominium*; Maiolo, *Medieval Sovereignty* 156; Fasolt, *Limits of History* 186; Woolf, *Bartolus* 155. On the method of "aequiparation," see Kantorowicz, *King's Two Bodies* 182.

[72] Bartolus on 2.1.1, §16, *Ius dicentis*; Fasolt, *Limits of History* 187, 198, where Fasolt suggests that *ius* is the concept that links *dominium* and *iurisdictio* together in one complete juridical system. Bartolus enumerates three basic types of *dominium: dominium directum, dominium utile*, and *quasi dominium*, which indicates the legal fiction of ownership recognized and protected under the *Actio Publiciana* in a person who is in the process of acquiring *dominium* through usucaption.

What made this construction possible was Bartolus' innovative doctrine that *dominium*—not as a property concept, but as a generic concept—may be inclusive, in the broadest possible terms, of any right over any kind of thing, and not simply in the narrow legalistic sense of ownership of private property.[73] While Bartolus certainly allowed there to be *dominium* not simply over tangible objects of private property in classical law, such as land, movables, or even notional or "incorporeal things" such as "the estate of a deceased person, a usufruct, and obligations however taken on," he expanded the scope of *dominium* to include every conceivable thing in the world—movables, persons, lands, whole kingdoms and cities—and even the whole world itself.[74]

Perhaps more important, however, was Bartolus' insistence that both *iurisdictio* and *dominium* were actionable legal rights or attributes attached to persons.[75]

> Just as therefore *dominium* coheres in the person of the *dominus*, nevertheless the *dominium* is over the thing [*in re*]. Likewise *iurisdictio* coheres to the office [*cohaeret officio*] and to the person of him who has the office [*personae eius qui habet officium*]. Nevertheless *iurisdictio* is over territory [*in territorio*], and thus it is not a quality of the territory [*qualitas territorii*] but instead a quality of the person [*personae*].[76]

Taken together, then, there was an exact correspondence between *iurisdictio* and *dominium*.[77] For every species and degree of *iurisdictio* there was, in theory, a corresponding form of *dominium*, both of which were held by one unique *dominus*. Indeed, an appropriate slogan for this Bartolist design might thus be, "One *dominus* for every thing in every relationship."[78]

To illustrate this basic principle, Bartolus gives the example of the emperor: "The emperor has all *iurisdictio*, as at D.1.4.1, and from this, he is said to be *dominus mundi*, as at D.14.2.9."[79] But the emperor was not the only one entitled to his own unique bundle of *iurisdictio* and *dominium*. Just as there were multiple species, degrees, or layers of *iurisdictio* and *dominium*, so too were there, correspondingly, multiple persons as bearers of such *iurisdictio* and *dominium*.[80] Thus, kings had their *iurisdictio* and *dominium* over their kingdoms. Feudal lords had their *iurisdictio* and *dominium* over their fiefs. Even

[73] Brett, *Liberty, Right and Nature* 22, citing Coing, "Zur Eigentumslehre des Bartolus" 349.

[74] Bartolus on D.6.1.1.2, *Per hanc actionem*; cp. Bartolus on C.10.1, §3, and Fasolt, *Limits of History* 190–98; Maiolo, *Medieval Sovereignty* 322.

[75] Bartolus is arguing against the doctrine, *iurisdictio cohaeret territorio*. On Bartolus' position, see Pietro Vaccari, "Utrum Iurisdictio Cohaeret Territorio: La Dottrina di Bartolo," *Bartolo da Sassoferrato* (Milan, 1962).

[76] Bartolus on D.2.1.1, *Ius Dicentis*.

[77] Fasolt, *Limits of History* 186. It is a suggestion made, but not followed through, by Vallejo, "Power Hierarchies in Medieval Juristic Thought" 22–23.

[78] Fasolt, *Limits of History* 197.

[79] Bartolus on D.2.1.1.

[80] Bartolus modifies Azo's definition of *iurisdictio* in one critical way, to specify that it is a power held by a "public person" [*publica persona*].

free cities had *iuridictio* and *dominium* over their territory. The result, then, was a complex hierarchy of powers, visually illustrated in the Bartolist "tree of jurisdictions," originally designed by the Bartolist jurist, Giasone de Maino, and which reappeared in the many early modern print editions of Bartolus' *Commentaria* on the *Digestum Vetus* (see Figure 3.1).[81]

Taken together, the result of Bartolus' analysis was one fully consistent with Azo's pluralist doctrine. Like Azo, Bartolus accepted that *merum imperium* was not the exclusive property of the supreme princely ruler. Rather, the different degrees of *imperium* belonged to the corresponding degree of "noble judge" who held his share of *iurisdictio*, as if by right of property.

The picture that emerged from Bartolus' influential analysis of *iurisdictio* was of a political and social world constituted by overlapping and sometimes intersecting layers of public authority and private rights. It was indeed a picture that faithfully represented the underlying social realities of feudalism, as Gilmore observes:

> This whole exposition by Bartolus of the grades of jurisdiction represents a careful attempt to explain fourteenth-century *dominium* in terms of the Roman law... Bartolus achieved a hierarchy of superiorities, wherein each superior had what might be called a property right in his power.[82]

The genius of Bartolus' system is that it allowed, in theory, for a peaceful coexistence among holders of *iurisdictio* and *dominium* all the way down. Authority was not to be monopolized by a single supreme princely ruler, but rather, held simultaneously by different members of the body politic. Thus, what we find at the conclusion of Bartolus' analysis, is an overlapping pluralism of authority at all grades and levels of the feudal hierarchy. By Bartolus' reasoning, a territorial control—whether by the emperor, a king, a lord, or some other *dominus*—entailed not only a right of *iurisdictio*, but also a right of *dominium*.

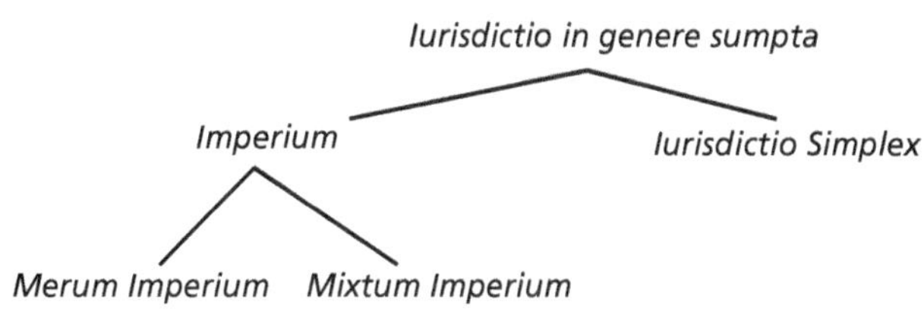

Tree of Jurisdictions

Figure 3.1

[81] This image appears in Bartolus' *Commentaria* on the *Digest* and, later, in Godefroy's edition of the *Corpus Iuris Civilis*. It follows Azo's basic analysis of *iurisdictio*, but it introduces an important categorical distinction between two different species of generic *iurisdictio—imperium* and (what he called) *iurisdictio simplex*.

[82] Gilmore, *Argument from Roman Law* 41–2.

In medieval public law, the two were inseparable. It was a doctrine that established the legal orthodoxy in matters of public law and state in the twilight of the Middle Ages.

THE HUMANIST THEORY OF *IURISDICTIO*: ALCIATO ON PROPERTY AND *IURISDICTIO PROPRIA*

By the sixteenth century, as feudalism began to crumble under its own weight in the shadows of the ascendant early modern state, Azo's pluralistic doctrine allowing multiple sites of *iurisdictio* within a single legal order ran against the current which favored the centralization of public authority in a single unitary source—above all, in a princely ruler with complete jurisdictional competence in his realm. Consequently, jurists began to question the validity of the Azonian position and reconsidered whether Lothair had, in fact, arrived at the proper reading of the civil law on *merum imperium*. Might Lothair, rather than Azo, have been correct in suggesting that *merum imperium* was the exclusive property and domain of the ruling *princeps*?

The first jurists to contest Azo, and take seriously Lothair's suggestion that *merum imperium* was the exclusive property of the supreme princely ruler, were the French legal humanists of the sixteenth century. Based primarily in the law faculties of the French universities, especially Bourges, the legal humanists occupy a critical position in the history of European law. Reacting to what they perceived to be the excessive interpretive license of the Bartolist jurisprudence which dominated late medieval Italian legal thought, the early modern French humanists demanded the restoration of a pristine text of the Roman *Corpus Iuris Civilis*, stripped of what they regarded to be medieval barbarisms. Using the philological tools of textual analysis developed and applied by humanists to other classical texts such as Cicero, as well as Scripture, the humanist jurists sought to reconstruct a more historically informed and context-sensitive understanding of the Roman law.[83] Above all, the humanists wanted to stress that, because Roman law was but the cultural product or artifact of the Roman Empire, the *Corpus Iuris Civilis* could not be regarded as the universal foundation for all legal systems. It was in vain, then, to call Roman law "written reason" and the "universal law," as medieval civilians had done.

There were numerous reasons why the legal humanists spent so much energy dismantling the doctrines of the Glossators and the Commentators. While some of these reasons were purely technical and academic, there were also substantive ideological reasons for the humanists' rejection of the medieval Vulgate Roman law. Some of the humanist complaints even expressed a bitter contempt for the allegedly backward medieval scholasticism of the lawyers, as the humanist Eguinaire Baron (1495–1550) once wrote:

[83] Donald Kelley, *Foundations of Modern Historical Scholarship*; Julian Franklin, *Jean Bodin and the Sixteenth Century Revolution in the Methodology of Law and History* (New York: Columbia University Press, 1963).

> When a dog has pissed somewhere there is no cur... that will not come to raise his leg and do likewise; so when Bartolus, Baldus, and such pettifoggers discuss a point in some passage, no matter how long or irrelevant, the whole pack of doctors will come to befoul the same passage with conclusions, conditions, reasons pro and con... and other apparatus.[84]

One of the humanists' most serious complaints concerned the treatment of *imperium* and *iurisdictio*. This was because Azo's doctrine was thought to have yielded what was, for the humanists, an unacceptably fragmented and multi-layered model of public authority, more appropriate for the feudal pluralism of the Middle Ages than for the centralized princely state being championed in the age of Machiavelli. For humanist jurists who favored subsuming local feudal jurisdictions under the supreme princely jurisdiction, Azo's teachings on *iurisdictio* bordered on heresy, because it allowed multiple bearers of *iurisdictio* simultaneously within a single legal order. The inevitable conflicts of authority resulting from such an arrangement could only undermine the legal supremacy of the princely ruler, which legal humanists tried to defend. Rejecting the Azonian tradition, then, the humanists speculated that perhaps Lothair had accurately captured the essential attribute of *merum imperium*, which was its exclusivity to the ruling *princeps*. By deliberately siding with Lothair, humanists had established the groundwork for the early modern expression of princely power in the juridical language of "property": they explained what it means for power to be legally "proper" [*propria*], or exclusive, to the *princeps*.

The first major critic of feudal jurisdiction in the sixteenth century was Andrea Alciato (1492–1550). Originally from Milan, Alciato probably deserves, more than any other jurist, the title of "founder" of legal humanism, or, as it was then described, the "French manner of teaching the law" [*mos gallicus docendi iuris*].[85] Not only was this because Alciato was a master technician of the humanist craft, but more importantly, because Alciato was directly responsible for training an entire generation of humanist jurists, during his tenure as Professor of Civil Law in the University of Bourges, the intellectual mecca of European legal humanism. So widespread was his impact on civil law that even his name became synonymous with the humanist school and the distinctive methodology it practiced: his followers were derisively called, *Alciatei*, by opponents of the humanist school.

[84] Donald Kelley, "The Rise of Legal History in the Renaissance," *History and Theory* 9 (1970): 180, quoting Eguinaire Baron reported in Noël du Fail, *Contes et discours d'Eutrapel, Oeuvres facétieuses* (Paris, 1874) 1:263.

[85] Legal historians generally have agreed that the title should be shared between Alciato, Guillaume Budé, and Ulrich Zasius. See, for example, Michael Monheit, "Guillaume Bude, Andrea Alciato, and Pierre de l'Estoile: Renaissance Interpreters of Roman Law," *Journal of the History of Ideas* 58 (1997): 21–40. Although legal humanism was identified with the "elegant" jurisprudence of early modern France, we should also remember its Italian origins in the humanist scholarship of Lorenzo Valla, Angelo Poliziano, Pietro Crinito, and Giulio Pomponio, all of whom had been early influences on Alciato's thought. Skinner, *Foundations* 1:203–4; Kelley, *Foundations of Modern Historical Scholarship* 39–50.

Alciato did not begin his intellectual life as a humanist. He was, in fact, trained in the Bartolist tradition and even studied for some time with Giasone del Maino at Pavia, whose fame among civil lawyers is due, among other accomplishments, to his illustration of the Bartolist "tree of jurisdictions." But it was his prodigious literary skill in classical languages, coupled with his unforgiving disdain for historical ignorance, that activated a period of critical consciousness-raising that led to his eventual break with the more traditional Bartolism of his Italian contemporaries. It was precisely this critical attitude that guided his rejection of the medieval view of autonomous feudal jurisdiction, independent of royal authority.

Alciato's starting point was the Roman law of jurisdiction itself, discussed at several places in the *Digest* and *Code* under the rubric, *De iurisdictione omnium iudicium*.[86] As we have seen earlier, Azo had suggested that *iurisdictio* ought to be understood, not so much as a specific judicial function of magistrates, but rather as a generic concept of power, inclusive of many degrees corresponding to the plural layers of feudal hierarchical authority. But for the humanist jurists of early modern France, Azo's doctrine was thought to have yielded an unacceptably fragmented and decentralized model of public authority, highly inappropriate for the sort of centralized princely state emerging in Renaissance France. For these jurists, who favored subsuming all lesser jurisdictions under one supreme princely jurisdiction, Azo's teaching on *imperium* bordered on heresy, because it allowed multiple bearers of *merum imperium* simultaneously within a single legal order. The inevitable conflicts of authority resulting from such an arrangement could only undermine the legal supremacy of the princely ruler, which reform-minded legal humanists tried to defend.

Rejecting the medieval Azonian tradition, then, the humanists speculated that perhaps Lothair had more accurately captured the essential attribute of *merum imperium*, which was its exclusivity to the ruling *princeps*. By siding with Lothair, the humanists had established the groundwork for the early modern expression of princely power in the Roman vocabulary of *imperium* and *iurisdictio*.

There is a great irony that the humanists would take up the substance of Lothair's position in this interpretive debate. For all their talk of restoring historical context-sensitivity to Roman law using the tools of philology, the humanist theory of jurisdiction actually perpetuated the ahistorical dogma that *merum imperium* was an attribute of the Roman *princeps*, a doctrine that has no surviving precedent in the Justinianic texts of classical Roman law.[87] And it was, above all, Alciato who crafted this humanist dogma.

Alciato offered his most influential statements on the question of public powers in two of his works on civil law, the *Paradoxa* and, later, more fully, in his humanist-inflected *Commentaria in Digesta*. His point of entry centered on the old medieval dispute between Azo and Lothair on the question of *iurisdictio*

[86] D.2.1, C.3.13. Also D.1.21.

[87] As we shall see later, Bodin criticizes the humanists on precisely this point.

and *merum imperium*, which he discusses in Book II of the *Paradoxa*. Like his medieval predecessors, Alciato acknowledged that *imperium* might be treated as an object of property, in the sense that it must belong to, or be "proper to" [*propria*], somebody. But to whom did it properly belong? The Azonian doctrine, it will be recalled, established a principle of non-exclusivity: *merum imperium* could belong to anybody who had the coercive power of the sword annexed to his jurisdiction. Both the *princeps* as well as the magistrate could therefore have *merum imperium* at the same time. Indeed, given the abusive venal practice of purchasing state offices, which became a critical source of royal revenue in early modern France, it is not surprising why so many would have concluded that magistrates actually owned the jurisdiction attached to their offices as objects of private property.[88]

But Alciato was unsatisfied with Azo's solution, not only because of its latent legal pluralism allowed multiple centers of jurisdictional authority within the realm, but, more importantly, because of its apparently simplistic understanding of the quality of "proper-ness," or rather, "exclusivity."[89] From Alciato's point of view, this was the root of the problem in all of the earlier medieval discussions treating *iurisdictio* in connection with *dominium*. Alciato thought the medieval jurists who participated in this debate merely stipulated who should be the legal bearer of *merum imperium*—and more generally, of *iurisdictio*—without clearly specifying what it would actually mean to treat a jurisdiction as one's own, *sua propria*. By leaving unsettled the question of what "ownership" over jurisdiction legally entailed, the Glossators actually left unanswered the most important question of all. Alciato's first task, thus, was to restore conceptual clarity and rigor in the legal analysis of property, even before addressing the more contentious legal issue of property ownership over jurisdictional authority at the heart of the notion of private jurisdiction and patrimonial hereditary offices.

The chief cause of difficulty was the feudal doctrine of divided *dominium*. To recall, in classical Roman law, *dominium* was an absolute indivisible binary concept—either one had *dominium* or one did not. Divided *dominium*, however, violated this binary logic, by dividing what was regarded classically to be indivisible. The humanists were not the first to observe the doctrine's departure from classical law. Even among some of the Glossators, divided *dominium* was treated with some suspicion. As Balduinus, one of Accursius' rivals in the Bolognese law faculty, and, later, Hostiensis, the canonist, both reportedly put it, the doctrine of divided *dominium* was but "a chimera," totally foreign to

88 J. Russell Major, *From Renaissance Monarchy to Absolute Monarchy: French Kings, Nobles and Estates* (Baltimore: Johns Hopkins University Press, 1994) Ch. 3, especially 104–6. Howell Lloyd, *The State, France, and the Sixteenth Century* (Boston: Allen and Unwin, 1983).

89 The quality of "proper-ness"—and not "property" in the modern usage—is what I would suggest here is suggested by Alciato's use of the word, *proprietas*. The relevant connection is between *proprius/a/um* and *proprietas*, not so much as property, but the quality of something being "proper" or "exclusive"—hence, "proper-ness" or "exclusivity." However, Alciato also uses the term, *proprietas*, in the more conventional sense of property ownership and, for this reason, often connects *proprietas* with *dominium*.

the system of Justinian.[90] The humanist jurist, Hermann Vultejus, would be even less charitable, calling the doctrine of *dominium divisum* "not consonant with the purity of jurisprudence...[but] seeped out of the faeces of the latter centuries."[91]

What was needed was a restoration of the classical theory of *dominium*, and it was this emerging neo-classical treatment of *dominium* which Alciato had championed. His purpose in doing so was to underscore one of the key distinctions in the Roman law of property which he felt the Glossators and Commentators had distorted and obscured beyond recognition—that is, the classical distinction between the full legal *right* of ownership in some object of property versus some lesser proprietary interest falling short of *dominium*, such as the mere factual use or exercise of that property. As Alciato pointed out, these two could be entirely decoupled from each other, so that one could be said to enjoy and make use of a property legally belonging to someone else. Such a person could not properly be said to have *dominium* (not even a *dominium utile*), but something else.

In classical law of the *Digest*, this category designating one's personal right "to use and enjoy the things of another without impairing their substance" was, as we have seen earlier, a "usufruct" [*ususfructus* = "the use of the fruits"] and was regarded a particular species of a class of "personal servitude," similar to the English easement.[92] In the private law framework of the *Corpus Iuris Civilis*, this right of usufruct functioned by imposing a "burden on property obliging the owner to allow someone else [i.e., the usufructuary] to use it for some purpose."[93] In so doing, a usufruct introduces a relationship between the usufructuary, who held only what jurists later called a limited "right in someone else's property" [*ius in re aliena*]—that is, the personal right of use and enjoyment—and the *dominus*, who is said to have retained the bare title of ownership [*nuda proprietas*—or simply *proprietas* or *ius proprietatis*] in the servient property.[94] Simply using or enjoying some object of property did not, by that fact alone, make one the *dominus* of that property, as the medieval theorists of divided *dominium* had argued.[95] For the *dominus*, the property remained "his

[90] Tuck, *Natural Rights Theories* 16; Meynial, "Notes sur la Formation de la Théorie du Domaine Divise," 425.

[91] Garnsey, *Thinking About Property* 201, quoting Vultejus on Inst. 2.1 (1598).

[92] D.7.1.1, 7.1.4, 41.2.52. Usufruct can be compared to other personal servitudes such as *usus*, which is literally "use" without the "fruits" or profits, and *habitatio*, which is a servitude connected to dwellings. It is a legal right in another person's property and, therefore, is regarded a *ius in re aliena*, to be distinguished from *dominium*, which indicates one's right to use and to dispose of one's own things [*ius utendi et abutendi re sua*]. However, the formulation, *ius in re aliena*, was a humanist innovation, which Robert Feenstra attributes chiefly to Donellus.

[93] Garnsey, *Thinking About Property* 186. D.7.1.13.7.

[94] Feenstra, "*Dominium* and *Ius in Re Aliena*" attributes the phrase, *ius in re aliena*, to Donellus.

[95] Alciato 1:153 on D.2.1.3, §108 observes that even the argument of *usucapio* or prescriptive acquisition—that long undisturbed usage and *bona fide* possession could "ripen" into full ownership—was invalid here since, as the *Digest* declared, "prescription of time does not run against the fisc" or, in the case of France, against the crown. D.41.3.18

own" [*res propria* or *res sua*]; for the *usufructuarius*, the property was regarded as "someone else's" [*res aliena*].

But despite the humanists' claim of fidelity to classical law, the description of the lesser usufructuary right, not as a *dominium utile*, but as limited right of use in someone else's property [*in re aliena*] was itself a post-classical interpolation not to be found in any of the classical sources. Nor was the notion original with Alciato. One early modern jurist exploring this notion was the German jurist, Joannes Apel (1486–1536), who exemplified the Protestant German humanist tradition pioneered by Philipp Melanchthon in the study of law.[96] In his study of *dominium* in his *Methodica dialectica ratio ad iurisprudentiam accommodata*, Apel observed that legal *dominium* could be subdivided. But unlike his predecessors, who subdivided *dominium* into *dominium directum* and *dominium utile*, Apel clarified that the proper subdivisions of *dominium* should rather be organized into the terms, *proprietas* [or more specifically as *nuda proprietas*] and *ususfructus*, both of which had classical antecedents in Justinian's texts. Even a *dominus* who surrendered use of his property to a usufructuary nevertheless retained a residual proprietary right to which use would revert [*ad proprietatem reverti*]; this was, indeed, the source of the proprietor's supremacy over the usufructuary.[97]

Alciato was familiar with this new analysis of property, as he used the exact same concepts of *nuda proprietas* [*id est, sine usufructu*], *ususfructus*, and *plena proprietas* to replace the older medieval system of divided *dominium*.[98] But while Alciato developed his own views on the humanist analysis of property in his commentary, he was not interested in the neo-classical theory of *dominium* simply for its own sake, but for its potential application to the analysis of the controversy whether magistrates might have some legal right akin to a property right in their jurisdictional authority, such that it could be described as "one's own" [*propria*], even by a *dominium utile*.[99] For Alciato, this new humanist analysis of property was critical because it explained not only why, as Lothair opined centuries before him, magistrates could never be regarded as having a true legal right to their jurisdictional authority as "their own" [*iurisdictio propria*], but also why Azo's position on the issue of *iurisdictio* was fundamentally untenable. By combining elements of the law of jurisdiction with the humanist neo-classical theory of property, Alciato was simultaneously able to deploy his full critique on the notion of private jurisdiction while also introducing an entirely new theory of princely authority.

Alciato began his critique by observing that, as a general rule, anybody who "uses" [*utitur*] someone else's property can be said to have the same sort of right that a usufructuary has in servient property. He has no "right of property" [*ius*

96 Berman, *Law and Revolution* 2:113 ff.

97 D.7.1.3.2.

98 Alciato 1:36 on D.1.21.1.1, §2; cp. Alciato on C.5.9.3.1a.

99 Indeed, Alciato's discussion of *proprietas* and *ususfructus* figures prominently in his commentary on D.1.21, the rubric concerning "delegated jurisdiction."

proprietatis]; rather, he has only a limited right like a usufruct. But now, Alciato takes the extraordinary step of applying this general rule from the law of property to the analysis of delegated jurisdiction, a connection with no real precedent in classical law. His point of entry is Papinian's statement in the *Digest* that a private judge who "uses" [*utitur*] a magistrate's *iurisdictio* "by delegation" [*mandata*] "has nothing of his own" [*proprium nihil habet*] in it.[100] He observes, in particular, that the appearance of the word, *utitur*, in Papinian's text signals that a magistrate's delegate—such as an appointed *iudex*—is directly comparable to a usufructuary or even a simple usuary in civil law [*veluti usuarius*] because, like a usuary, the delegate "has nothing of his own" [*sicut usuarius non habet proprium*] while he uses someone else's jurisdictional authority.[101] Because such authority is used while it "nevertheless is owed to someone else [*alicui debita*] under certain terms [*sub conditione*], it is said rather to be someone else's [*dicitur aliena*]," rather than one's own [*propria*].[102]

But what does it mean for something to be "one's own" [*proprius*]? He explains, again in general terms of property law:

> Something [*res*] is said to belong to somebody as "one's own" [*propria*]—which is more appropriately written as "one's own" [*sua*]—so long as no one else has another right [*aliquod ius*] in it [D.8.4.5].

Thus, anything to which one can claim an exclusive and absolute right can be said to be one's "own proper thing" [*res propria sua*] belonging to the *dominus*. This general principle helps to illuminate why a magistrate's delegate, such as a private judge, can never be said to have "his own" *iurisdictio*:

> For this reason the *iurisdictio* of a delegate is not said to be his own [*propria*], and that is because ordinary magistrates [*ordinarii*] already have a legal right [*ius*] in it. They can take away what they have delegated at their pleasure [*potest... ad libitum removere*].[103]

Alciato never contests the prevailing assumption that *iurisdictio* can be treated as a kind of *res*, capable of ownership by a claim of *proprietas* or use by usufruct. So much, thus, is uncontroversial with respect to delegates of ordinary magistrates, such as the private judge in the *legis actio*.

[100] D.1.21.1.1.

[101] On the distinction between usufructuary and usuary and *ususfructus* and *usus*, see Buckland, *Textbook of Roman Law* 273–4; D.7.8.1-2.

[102] Alciato 1:42 on D.1.21.1. Cp. 1:14, where Alciato writes, "Thenceforth we say the delegate is a debtor [*Inde dicimus delegatus debitor*]," to the one who delegated the authority in the first place. It should be noted here that, with respect to the Roman law theory of jurisdiction, *aliena* and *propria* were antonyms. Thus, if a jurisdiction is said to be *res aliena*, it cannot, by definition, also be a *res propria* to the one presently exercising it—and vice-versa. Otherwise, it would give rise to the paradox of a *res* being owned by multiple *domini* which the concept of *dominium* as exclusive and absolute does not allow. *Sub conditione* is a reference to C.11.31(30).2, concerning *administratio*, which Alciato cites again in the *Paradoxa* 2.6 in Alciato 4:38.

[103] Alciato 1:37 on D.1.21.1, §10.

But what about the ordinary magistrate himself who appoints such a private judge? Could he be said to have his *iurisdictio* as "his own" [*propria*]? Could he be said even to have his *imperium* (which was, to recall, a species of *iurisdictio*) as "his own"? It is difficult to say since even the *Digest* explicitly allows that magistrates hold their jurisdictional authority "by their own right" [*suo iure*] and refers to the Roman praetors as having "their own *imperium*" [*suo imperio*], invested with the coercive power of the sword to impose criminal penalties.[104] Indeed, it was on this basis that Azo and, later, the Bartolists ruled that magistrates did have their own *imperium* attached to their ordinary *iurisdictio*.

But Alciato was not prepared to enfranchise magistrates with such a robust right. Magistrates are, after all, intermediary subordinates, inferior to another superior, so someone else must in theory also have a residual legal right to the magistrate's *iurisdictio*. What Alciato says on this point is remarkable: "Even ordinary magistrates [*ordinarii*] do not hold *iurisdictio* as their own [*propria*]."[105] Indeed, the jurisdictional authority exercised by all magistrates (even the highest form of such magisterial authority, *merum imperium*) is always regarded as "someone else's thing" [*res aliena*], and it is, correspondingly, only by "another's grace" or "goodwill" or "pleasure" [*alieno beneficio*] that such authority is to be used.[106] But by no means could an ordinary magistrate, or *ordinarius*, have such authority *iure proprio*.[107]

Magistrates, then, were really no better off concerning their status than the appointed private judge in the classical setting of Roman litigation. Like the judge, the magistrate likewise held his jurisdictional authority by delegation and, therefore, only "exercised" or "used" [*utitur*] a right belonging to someone else. On this analysis, all magistrates, even those at the highest levels of authority, occupied the inferior legal position comparable to a usufructuary in civil law, but never that of a *dominus* with proprietary right precisely because magistrates merely exercised powers which they did not own.[108]

This direct comparison of the magistrate to the condition of the usufructuary led Alciato to give his own view on what it might mean for a magistrate to have "his own *iurisdictio*," in terms that closely mirrored the humanist pattern of property law separating the *proprietas* from the *ususfructus*. He explains that the term, *iurisdictio*, is a "verbal noun" or gerund [*nomen verbale*] and carried a confusing double-meaning [*duplex*] in the civil law, signifying either (1) the "right itself" [*ipsum ius*] of jurisdiction or (2) the mere "deed itself" [*ipsum factum*] (or elsewhere, the "use itself" [*ipse usus*]) of jurisdiction.[109] This analysis helps illuminate what, Alciato thinks, the Roman lawyers actually meant to say when they refer to magistrates holding the highest form of *iurisdictio*—that

[104] D.1.21.3. [105] Alciato 1:37 on D.1.21.1, §10.

[106] D.2.1.5. Alciato cites D.1.21.1 and Nov.15 as his evidence that *iurisdictio* is inclusive of both *merum* and *mixtum imperium*.

[107] Alciato 1:144 on D.2.1.3, §90. [108] Alciato 4:38 [*Paradoxa* 2.6, §3].

[109] Alciato 1:143-4 on D.2.1.3, §90; 4:38 [*Paradoxa* 2.6, §§4-5]. Gilmore, *Argument from Roman Law* 49–50. Cp. D.45.1.38.9 on *Habere*.

is, *merum imperium*: they mean *iurisdictio* specifically in the second sense, as a mere fact of use or exercise. Alciato, thus, writes that, "When *iurisdictio* is said to be 'one's own' [*suam iurisdictionem*] in the law, what is actually meant by 'one's own *iurisdictio*' [*sua iurisdictio*] is really one's own *exercise* [*sua exercitatio*] of it. The use [of *iurisdictio*] is what is one's own [*ipse usus est suus*] not the legal right of *iurisdictio* itself."[110] He specifies elsewhere as a general point that, whenever the law describes a magistrate "having" or "holding" jurisdictional authority as "his own," what jurists really mean to express is the mere "exercise" [*exercitatio*], "administration" [*administratio*] or "use" [*usus*] of that authority, not the "very right" to that authority itself [*ius ipsum*], like a *nuda proprietas*.[111]

But by positioning the magistrate as a kind of usufructuary without a true right of property in his jurisdictional authority, Alciato's argument raised another important question. If magistrates were, like usufructuaries, merely entitled to use jurisdictional authority without any right of their own, who *did* have such a full legal right over the *merum imperium* [*meri imperii ius ipsum*]? Who was, as Alciato put it, this "proprietary owner" [*proprietatis dominus*]?

For Alciato, there could only be one answer to that question, and that was the *princeps*, in whom the full legal proprietary right to all forms of *iurisdictio*—including the *merum imperium*—"remains" [*remanet in principe*] fully intact, even while it is delegated for others to exercise on his behalf.[112] Only the *princeps* could be said to have *iurisdictio* which was fully and exclusively *propria*, his own, and thus, only the *princeps* could be entitled to his *iurisdictio* "by full right of property" [*pleno iure proprietatis*].

With Alciato's exposition, it was possible to explain why princely rule must always be superior to that of all lesser magistrates. All powers of magistrates—even those of the highest officers of state as well as those with feudal jurisdictions—were fully derivative from a prior concessive grant of the *princeps*. Indeed, it was precisely for this reason that Alciato called the prince "the fountain, source, and constitutor of all magistrates" [*princeps est fons, et origo, et constitutor omnium magistratuum*].[113] Yet, at the same time, because such grants of power were always interpreted as concessive delegations, and never as full transfers or alienations, of power, it was possible to argue that all jurisdictional authority remained fully with the *princeps*, as the sole *dominus* over his realm to whom such authority could be called *propria*. To suggest otherwise was an illegal usurpation on princely right. There was, therefore, no independent right of magistracy: no magistrate could claim his office as an object of private property, separable from the prince. Instead, Alciato tells us, they must be seen merely to be "borrowing" a share of rights and powers belonging to the prince. And as the principal owner with a residual *nuda proprietas* in his delegated powers, it was within the right of the *princeps* to recover whatever powers he has lent away to his inferiors agents.

[110] Alciato 1:144 on D.2.1.3, §90.
[111] Alciato 1:145 on D.2.1.3, §92.
[112] Alciato 1:144 on D.2.1.3, §§90, 92.
[113] Alciato 1:143 on D.2.1.3, §88.

This analysis was significant in several ways. First of all, it provided a "new reason" [*nova ratio cur merum imperium in delegatum non transeat*] to explain why, as the classical jurists insisted, *merum imperium* could not be delegated by magistrates to others. Since magistrates were essentially usufructuaries, but not proper "owners of jurisdiction" [*domini iurisdictionis*], they were bound by the general principle governing all forms of delegated rights, that delegates may not sub-delegate or reassign their rights to another.[114] To do so would, in effect, not only be equivalent to an illicit act of alienation, exposing the delegate, in principle, to legal remedies for restitution from the original *dominus*. It would also generate an infinite regress, since it would allow a "subdelegate to delegate to another inferior *in infinitum*."[115]

But Alciato gives another explanation originating in the principle that certain forms of *imperium* can never be delegated. To recall, the *Digest* insists that, even if some minimal *imperium* "cohering" to *iurisdictio* may be delegated by the magistrate, *merum imperium* can never be delegated to a private judge.[116] But since Alciato has now elevated the *princeps* as the sole person entitled to *iurisdictio* as "his own," while all others merely use *iurisdictio* by *alieno beneficio*, the rules of delegation now are presumed to apply also in the agency relationship tethering magistrates to the *princeps*. Thus, Alciato declares that *merum imperium* is never delegated [*nunquam delegatur*] and that magistrates consequently never have *merum imperium*. But what is significant is the reason why the magistrate never has *merum imperium* as "his own": it would violate the classical Roman principle that the Glossators tried so hard to circumvent by the casuistic doctrine of double *dominium*—that is, *duo in solidum*, that there can only be one *dominus* in a given object of property at any one time.[117] Simply put, if the *princeps* is the *dominus* over all jurisdiction, it also means that no one else can claim *dominium*.

So, in the end, Alciato's theory of jurisdiction and princely authority is grounded in a technical notion originating in the law of property, such that all forms of public jurisdictional authority can be treated as an object of property belonging rightfully to the *princeps*. Taken together, Alciato's analysis represented "the first important statement which adapted the interpretation of *merum imperium* to the facts of state power."[118] Indeed, because of Alciato's

[114] Alciato 4:39 [*Paradoxa* 2.6, §§5-6]; 1:44 on D.1.21.1. Alciato does not seem to account for the conflicting statements of Ulpian and Paul, which allow a usufructuary to grant [*concedere*] usufructuary right to another, such as D.7.1.12.2 and 7.1.63. Nor does Alciato properly account for C.3.4.1 which allows that a judge with *sua iurisdictio* can delegate. Cf. Dumoulin 79, §57.

[115] Alciato 1:44 on D.1.21.1.

[116] D.1.21.1.1; 1.21.5.

[117] Alciato 1:143 on D.2.1.3, §88, citing D.1.18.6.8 and 13.6.5.15. Cp. 43.14.1.pr.

[118] Gilmore, *Argument from Roman Law* 49–50. I disagree strongly, however, with Gilmore's statement that Alciato also represented a critical "stage in the dissociation of government and private property which has been so fundamental to modern political thought." If anything, this analysis plainly shows that Alciato actually perpetuated the use of property concepts in early modern French public law, and this is precisely the reason why Bodin was to attack him so fiercely in his critique of humanist jurisprudence by denying that *merum imperium* belonged as property to magistrates or even to the *princeps*.

work, humanists were able to begin sounding the death-knell for the end of legal pluralism and private seigneurial justice, so central to medieval feudalism. Instead, they presented the groundwork for a vision of an early modern state, in which the machinery of legitimate violence and justice were placed exclusively in the hands of a supreme princely ruler. For reform-minded jurists, such as Alciato and his followers, such a vision of princely rule, championing royal justice over local injustice and abuses of power, was positively to be favored.

THE ALCIATEI ON JURISDICTION

Alciato's analysis of jurisdiction provided a fresh stimulus in French legal thought, especially among later jurists of the law faculty at Bourges. One of Alciato's most faithful followers in the humanist tradition was his pupil, François Le Douaren, or Duarenus, (1509–1559), Alciato's eventual successor in the chair of civil law in the University of Bourges and a torchbearer of the legal humanist school.[119] Duarenus occupied a central role in the humanist school by continuing to propagate the analysis crafted by his teacher. In his commentaries on the *Digest*, Duarenus restated Lothair's basic position that magistrates did not have the *merum imperium*. He conceded Azo's observation that, while magistrates can certainly hold the coercive power of the sword—the quintessence of *merum imperium*—he specified that magistrates never held such power rightfully as their own, like property belonging to them [*proprius*], but only by a special delegative grant of the law [*nisi lege specialiter delatam*], appointed to "use" or "exercise" *iurisdictio* as a usufructuary of public power.[120]

The point is illustrated with a discussion of Roman magistrates. Even the high magistrates of Rome such as the praetors and the provincial governors, whom Azo and his followers so often cited as examples of officials allegedly holding *merum imperium* with an ordinary jurisdiction, only did so by special concessive delegation, a point which Duarenus buttressed with the observation of Pomponius that, when the Roman magistracies were originally created, the magistrate did not automatically receive the power of the sword.[121] It was only by a separate permissive grant, in the form of a *lex de imperio*, that magistrates received the *imperium*, but it was by no means necessary that magistrates should have *imperium* simply by the creation of their offices. Duarenus, therefore, understood all powers of magistrates to be derivative, because they were derived through some prior concessive grant, whether from the emperor [*a principe*] or even from the people [*a populo*]. Because such powers

[119] Kelley, "Civil Science in the Renaissance: Jurisprudence in the French Manner" 264–6. See also the related entries in Michael Stolleis, ed., *Juristen: Ein Biographisches Lexikon von der Antike bis zum 20.Jahrhundert* (München: Beck, 1995).

[120] Duarenus 1:40, col. 1 on D.2.1, Cap.3; 1:43, col. 1 on D.2.1, Cap. 6.

[121] Duarenus 1:40, col. 1 on D.2.1, Cap. 3.

were delegated by grant, they could just as easily be revoked, thereby dispossessing the magistrate of his office and its powers. For just this reason, then, Duarenus described the jurisdiction of magistrates, following the letter, but not the spirit, of the *Digest*, as "delegated jurisdiction" [*iurisdictio mandata*], held not *suo iure*, but *alieno beneficio*.[122]

Duarenus argued, like Alciato, that the very word, "jurisdiction," originating from *ius dicens*, was itself an exercise-concept, and so, must be equivalent to the mere exercise of jurisdiction [*iurisdictionem exercere*].[123] Instead, full proprietary right in all jurisdictional powers of state must belong exclusively to the prince, who created and empowered all magistracies in the first place and could potentially also dissolve such magistracies as well.

Duarenus' analysis thus fully absorbed the Romanist concept of property that lay at the heart of the humanists' understanding of princely power. Here again, the influence of Alciato was palpable, first, by Duarenus' endorsement in the *Disputationum Anniversiorum* of the principle that there can never be "two owners" [*duo domini*] over the same object of property [*in solidum*] at any one time, but also by the axiom that public powers can be owned as objects of property.[124] Above all, he reaffirmed the classical legal idea that the bare juridical essence of property [*nuda proprietas*] was distinct and separable from the mere usufruct [*separata ab usufructu*] or exercise [*exercere*] of some thing, since even a usufructuary can use something legally belonging as property to someone else. True right of property, then, cannot be determined simply by one's use or exercise of some thing, but it must be grounded in something else. It was this property analysis which showed why a prince, who has delegated away the direct exercise of his powers to his magistrates, can nevertheless remain the supreme ruler over his realm with full property right in his powers. Magistrates merely "use" or "exercise" what still legally belongs by full right [*pleno iure*] to the prince.

In this way, Duarenus underscored the basic premise of the French humanist theory of jurisdiction—that the ruling prince is really like a *dominus* who alone has full legal right of property over all jurisdictions within his realm. But not content simply to describe the magistrate as a delegate or usufructuary, Duarenus took a further step in his analysis, observing that:

> Magistrates to whom jurisdiction is delegated act in the place of the one who delegated the jurisdiction to them in the first place, just as if he held his place [*veluti locum eius tenet*]. For this reason, the magistrate is said by Papinian to have nothing proper to themselves [citing the Gloss on D.1.21.1.1 on *Nihil proprium habet*]. Indeed, [the magistrate] is most similar to a *procurator* to whom a *dominus* has delegated the administration of his affairs [*similis procuratori, cui negotia gerenda mandavit*, a reference to D.3.3].[125]

[122] Duarenus 1:43, col. 1 on D.2.1, Cap. 7; D.1.21.1.1 and 2.1.5.

[123] Duarenus 1:38, col. 2 on D.2.1, Cap. 1.

[124] Duarenus 4:19, col. 2 [*Disputationum Anniversiorum* 1.17].

[125] Duarenus 1:43, col. 1 on D.2.1, Cap. 7.

The passage is remarkable not only for its direct comparison of a prince to a *dominus*, but even more especially, the comparison of a magistrate to a *procurator*, "one who transacts the business of another on a mandate from his principal."[126] The implication is that, as a representative or "place-holder" [*locumtenens*] for his princely *dominus*, every magistrate is limited in his rights and powers, in the same way that a *procurator* is.[127] For example, the magistrate, as *procurator*, can never worsen the position of his principal [D.3.3.49]; he can never alienate the principal's property [*res domini*] [D.3.3.63]; nor can he transact public business [*negotium publicum*] in the jurisdiction of the *civitatis actor* [D.3.3.74]; one cannot give to another a power which he does not rightfully possess as his own [D.50.17.54]. Only the prince, as *dominus*, has full right over such powers. Even if the princely *dominus* did not exercise his powers directly, but only indirectly by delegation, he nevertheless remained supreme just because of his residual right to reclaim and redistribute those powers as he wished.

Perhaps the most nuanced humanist treatment of *iurisdictio* came, however, from Duarenus' star pupil at Bourges, Hugues Doneau, or Donellus (1527–1591), who treated the topic at length in in his *Commentaria de Iure Civili*. Donellus was revered, as one of the leading 'systematizers' of the Roman law in the later sixteenth century.[128] Like other legal humanists, Donellus insisted upon restoring the classical meaning of the term, *iurisdictio*. Rejecting Azo's controversial etymology in the *Summa*, Donellus observes instead that *iurisdictio* functions as a generic 'word for power' [*potestatis verbum*], signifying the "power of examining and declaring a judgment concerning a matter [*potestas de re cognoscendi iudicandique*], conjoined with the power of carrying out what has been legally decided [*iudicati exsequendi potestate*]."[129] His definition is significant for requiring that *iurisdictio* be not simply understood as a power to judge [*iudicare*], but also a power to execute [*exsequi*] a public judgment.[130] It is the latter, "this power of coercing and carrying out" [*hanc coercendi et exsequendi potestatem*] or "the power of ordering and commanding" [*iubendi imperandique potestas*], which he specifically calls *imperium*.[131] Recalling Paul's doctrine in the *Digest* that there is no *iurisdictio* without even minimal coercion [*iurisdictio sine modica coercitione nulla est*], Donellus thought likewise that there is "no *iurisdictio* without *imperium*." It is indeed "necessary" [*necessario*] to treat *imperium* as being, in this way, "mixed" [*mistum*] with *iurisdictio*.[132]

126 D.3.3.1.pr.

127 The phrase, *locum tenere*, signifying the function of a "place-holder" acting on mandate, is likely to be referring to D.2.1.16 . It is the origin of the term, "lieutenant," as it is used in French legal texts of the period, including especially Bodin, to signify the function of government agents who act and stand in place of an absent sovereign.

128 Franklin, *Jean Bodin and the Sixteenth-Century Revolution in the Methodology of Law and History* 28.

129 Donellus 4:1087 [*Commentaria* 17.6, §5].

130 Donellus 4:1089 [*Commentaria* 17.6, §7] citing D.1.21.5.1.

131 Donellus 4:1089 [*Commentaria* 17.6, §7].

132 Donellus eliminates altogether the Bartolist category of *iurisdictio simplex*—i.e., a *iurisdictio* entirely detached from all *imperium*.

What is especially striking about Donellus' definition is that he brings the term back to its Roman origins in litigation. *Iurisdictio* is an attribute, above all, of judges overseeing trials, and all judges, whether public or private, are understood to have the power of *imperium* essential for enforcing their judgments "mixed" in with their *iurisdictio*. But not all judges had the same jurisdictional authority since, as Donellus observes from among the "crowd of interpreters" [*in vulgus interpretum*] of civil law, some judges who "preside over public *iurisdictio*" [*iurisdictioni publice praesunt*] held *iurisdictio* as legally constituted "ordinary" judges [*ordinarii*], while others who "are appointed judges by superiors" [*a superioribus iudices dati sunt*] held *iurisdictio* merely as their "delegates" [*delegati*].[133]

What concerned Donellus, however, was the difference between the *iurisdictio* of "ordinary judges" [*ordinarii*] and that of "delegated judges" [*delegati*]. The difference relied on the conceptual distinction between *res propria et sua* and *res aliena* introduced earlier by Alciato, such that, while *ordinarii* are said to hold *iurisdictio* as "their own" [*propria*] and "by their own right" [*suo iure*], *delegati* are said to hold it merely "by another's favor" [*alieno beneficio*].

Yet, while the analysis was clearly inspired by Alciato, Donellus nevertheless departed from Alciato in one very important way. To recall, Alciato insisted that only the *princeps* can be said to have *iurisdictio* as *propria*, while all others—even *ordinarii*—held *iurisdictio* by *alieno beneficio*, and "used" [*utitur*] such authority like a usufructuary. But Donellus, recognizing that concepts of *iurisdictio* and *imperium* had very little to do with the *princeps* in classical law, explained that the ones who actually held *iurisdictio* as "their own" and "by their own right" were magistrates, not emperors.[134] Indeed, he emphasizes that "no one has *iurisdictio* as their own, except magistrates" [*nulli igitur propriam habent, nisi magistratus*].[135] All others who have *iurisdictio* not as their own are, thus, necessarily understood to hold it *alieno beneficio*, as a trust or mandate.

This framework allows Donellus to establish several related points. The first is a critical analysis of the concept of delegation itself and the nature of the principal-agent relationship between ordinary magistrates and delegates to which it gives rise. Donellus explains, as a general principle, that "to delegate" [*mandare*] something does not mean "to transfer something to another" [*non est quidquam ad alium transferre*].[136] It means, rather simply, "to commit to his management and handling a matter which nevertheless remains our own" [*ei rem gerendam tractandamque committere ut nihilominus res nostra maneat*], as in the case of a *procurator* in Roman law who "transacts the business of another on a mandate from his principal."[137]

[133] Donellus 4:1094 [*Commentaria* 17.6, §12], citing uses of *delegati* elsewhere in the civil law, such as at C.3.1.5, 3.1.16, 5.7.1.1.

[134] Donellus 4:1099 [*Commentaria* 17.7, §4].

[135] Donellus 4:1111 [*Commentaria* 17.7, §13].

[136] Donellus 4:1119 [*Commentaria* 17.8, §3], cp. D.50.17.11, 50.17.54.

[137] D.3.3.1.

This is precisely how Donellus thinks the notion of delegated *iurisdictio* should be understood. In delegating *iurisdictio*, the magistrate is not "transferring" it, like a gift, such that the magistrate thereby loses all his legal rights of ownership to it. Instead, he is simply:

> Giving his *iurisdictio* to another to manage and handle it [*exercendam et exsequendam*], even though it nevertheless remains [the magistrate's]. Only the *use* and *exercise* [*usus tantum et exercitio*] of it is transferred [*transferatur*] to...[the one who stands] in place of the magistrate [*magistratus locum*], whom they generally call a "placeholder" [*locumtenentem*, or, literally, a "*lieutenant*"].[138]

In so doing, it is understood that the magistrate always "retains *iurisdictio* as his own [*iurisdictionem suam retinet*], and can therefore revoke it [from his delegate] whenever he wishes [*revocare potest cum vult*]."[139]

But Donellus makes an even stronger claim. While the magistrate could licitly delegate his *iurisdictio*, he could never "transfer" away his *iurisdictio*—"whether free of charge or for a price"—even if he wanted to do so.[140] In explaining his reasoning, Donellus remarkably does not reproduce Alciato's *nova ratio*, which we saw earlier in the *Paradoxa*. Alciato's view, to recall, was that, since magistrates were essentially usufructuaries, but not *domini*, they were bound by the legal rule prohibiting all usufructuaries from subdelegating or even alienating the servient property to someone else. Donellus, by contrast, explains that there are certain things which are simply inalienable, or non-transferable, such as certain attributes of one's character, so the analysis of usufructs is, for Donellus, entirely superfluous.

But what is especially remarkable in this entire discussion is that the *princeps* is, strictly speaking, not a part of Donellus' theory of delegated *iurisdictio* at all. The *princeps* plays instead an "extra-jurisdictional" background role in Donellus' constitutional theory, not so much by holding or wielding *iurisdictio*, but rather, by *creating* it.

This is what differentiates the *princeps* from the legally constituted magistrate, who is said to have been "created" by a legislative act of the *princeps* [*creatur a principe*]. This is important: creating a magistrate with *iurisdictio* is a fundamentally different act from delegating a *iurisdictio* one already has. Whereas legally constituted magistrates are entitled to do the latter, only one entity within a single constitutional order can perform the former, the legal creation of magistrates [*creatio magistratuum*].[141]

[138] Donellus 4:1119-20 [*Commentaria* 17.8, §3].

[139] Donellus 4: 1119-20 [*Commentaria* 17.8, §3]. Feenstra argues that "all the credit [for first making the distinction between *dominium* and *ius in re aliena*] should be given to Hugo Donellus." Feenstra, "*Dominium* and *Ius in Re Aliena*" 115. Like Alciato, he seems to be using the civil law action of the *dominus*' "right of revoking and recovering property for oneself" [*ius revocandae et sibi vindicandae rei*] away from another person with a lesser *ius in re aliena*, such as an *emphyteuticarius*, as a model for the ordinary magistrate's right of revoking the delegate's jurisdiction.

[140] Donellus 4:1117-19 [*Commentaria* 17.8, §2].

[141] Donellus 4:1105 [*Commentaria* 17.7, §9].

But it is not just the *princeps*—in the narrow legalistic sense of the Roman emperor—who holds this extra-jurisdictional power to create magistrates and distribute *iurisdictio* by law.[142] Indeed, anybody "who holds sovereign [*summa*] power, such as emperors, kings, and any other sort of leader [*alii principes*] with the same right, can create and constitute [*creare et constituere*] magistracies according to his *imperium*."[143]

This insight opens the way for Donellus' remarkable statement that this extra-jurisdictional power can be held not only by emperors and kings, but even by a whole people, or *populus*, which can play precisely the same constitutional role as a *princeps*—as the Roman people once did. His inspiration is clearly the *lex regia*, when he observes that this extra-jurisdictional power to create magistrates once "belonged to the Roman people before the emperors came to power"—that is, when they were a "free people" [*populus liber*].[144] Indeed, "the *princeps* could not create magistrates [*non . . . potest magistratus creare*] and decide on matters in judgment from any other cause until the power of the people has been transferred to him" [*potestate populi in eum translata*].[145] It is only "after the people have transferred [*transtulit*] all their *imperium* and *potestas* to the *princeps*, straightaway they ceased to have any of their own . . . [but] as soon as the people have a *princeps* to whom the highest power [*summa rerum*] is attached, the power of creating magistrates [*creandorum magistratuum potestas*] no longer belongs to the people, but to the *princeps*."[146]

Donellus, then, formulates not only the basis for a humanist theory of popular sovereignty, based once again on the Roman model of the *lex regia*, which implicitly treats popular sovereignty as a sort of constitutional "default" position from which authority can be delegated or even transferred to a king, a *princeps* or some other institutional intermediary. He accomplishes something far more important for early modern constitutional theory by identifying the content of such sovereign authority—that is, the legal power of "constituting" or "creating" magistrates empowered with *iurisdictio*. By segregating such a power from the ordinary constituted jurisdiction of magistrates, it is perhaps Donellus who establishes in the vocabulary of Roman law, for the first time (and centuries before Sieyès), that critical distinction in modern constitutional theory, the distinction between "constituent power" of the people and the "constituted power" of government.

[142] Observe the double-meaning of "magistrate." *Magistratus* is a "twofold word" [*verbum anceps*], which can mean either the "person" or the "office." He is perhaps arguing against the ambiguity in the Bartolist doctrine that *iurisdictio cohaeret officio, et personae eius qui habet officium*.

[143] Donellus 4:1105 [*Commentaria* 17.7, §9].

[144] Donellus 4:1106 [*Commenaria* 17.7, §10].

[145] Donellus 4:1106 [*Commentaria* 17.7, §10].

[146] Donellus 4:1106 [*Commentaria* 17.7, §11].

THE CRITIQUE OF "PROPER" JURISDICTION: DUMOULIN ON FEUDAL JURISDICTION

Perhaps the most important critique of the theory of "proper" jurisdiction came from Charles Dumoulin (1500–1566), whom his contemporaries hailed variously as "the prince of the jurisconsults," "the glory of all France," "the French Papinian," and "the ornament of all lawyers."[147] A product of the law faculty of Orléans, Dumoulin was most highly regarded by the jurists of his day for his grand project of identifying a reformed customary law of France by redacting and codifying the previously unwritten local customs of the French provinces, as collected in his chief work, the *Commentaria in Consuetudines Parienses*, "the first comprehensive and critical history of feudalism," originally published in 1539.[148] It was a project that necessarily required him to enter into the heated debates on the nature and scope of jurisdiction.

In the context of sixteenth-century France with its increasingly volatile royalist politics, Dumoulin's analysis of the Parisian customs could hardly have been seen as merely an innocent intellectual project of purely antiquarian interest.[149] Because the customs of Paris, described by one commentator as "the head of all customs of this kingdom and even all of the Low Countries" [*caput omnium huius regni et totius etiam Belgicae Galliae consuetudinum*], were fully inclusive of the rights and prerogatives of the French monarchy and the royal domain, his investigations of the Parisian customs necessarily involved a direct engagement with the most fundamental questions at issue in the debates concerning kingship and the scope of royal jurisdiction.[150] Despite its outward appearance as a scholarly work in legal historiography and the origins of French feudalism, Dumoulin's *Commentaria*, particularly its most innovative sections on feudal jurisdictions, *De Feudis*, must be read as one of the chief works of early modern French constitutional theory.

Dumoulin's position in the *Commentaria* was thoroughly royalist. As Quentin Skinner put it, Dumoulin was "the most systematic defender of royal supremacy" among the French legists, and his chief purpose in documenting and systematizing the various customs was to unify the fragmented jurisdictional entities of the French kingdom under a single unifying head, the King of France.[151] What Dumoulin ultimately desired to see was a juridically unitary

[147] Bodin, *Commonweale* 1.8, 108; G. Kelley, *Foundations of Modern Historical Scholarship* 190.

[148] Jean-Louis Thireau, *Charles Du Moulin, 1500–1566* (Geneva: Droz, 1980) 28; Kelley, *Foundations of Modern Historical Scholarship* 189.

[149] Kelley, "Civil Science in the Renaissance: Jurisprudence in the French Manner" 264; Donald Kelley, "De Origine Feudorum: The Beginnings of a Historical Problem," *Speculum* 39 (1964): 222–25; Davis, *Periodization and Sovereignty*.

[150] Kelley, *Foundations of Modern Historical Scholarship* 192. *Gallia Belgica* is a geographical term in Ptolemy's *Geography* referring to that part of Gaul under Caesar's rule between the Rhine, the Seine, and the "Brittanicus Oceanus." It was applied to the Low Countries as well as to Burgundian possessions. Alastair Duke, *Dissident Identities in the Early Modern Low Countries*, ed. Judith Pollmann and Andrew Spicer (Surrey: Ashgate, 2009) 29–30.

[151] Skinner, *Foundations* 2:261.

state with a uniform system of law, more authentically aligned with the historical customs and constitutional traditions of France.[152] Dumoulin envisioned such a state partly for the sake of administrative efficiency, when he asked:

> Who does not see that it would be more advantageous to the state if all lords [*domini*], whether secular or ecclesiastical, who hold by royal munificence and concession [*ex munificentia et concessione regia*] all kinds of *iurisdictio* [*iurisdictionem omnimodam*] in their lands and their *dominia* [*dominiis suis*], had instead only one grade of jurisdiction [*unum tantum iurisdictionis gradum*], which would be administered much better and more diligently [*diligentius administrandum*]?[153]

For Dumoulin, there was no question that a centralized legal order would have been far superior and, more important, more just than the feudal pluralism which governed France, and elsewhere.

But the real political issue concerned how it might be possible to empower the monarchy to assert such a supreme jurisdictional authority over the realm at all. Feudal rightsholders throughout France jealously guarding their local privileges in the form of seigneurial jurisdictions, and local particularistic privileges and immunities would never permit such a centralization of power. To realize his vision of the state, then, Dumoulin believed it was necessary to dismantle the vestigial fossilized remnants of feudal France. As long as these feudal *seigneurs* viewed themselves as independent, like mini-states, beyond the scope of royal control, the central assertion of royal authority remained practically impossible.

Dumoulin's strategy of reform targeting the independence of fiefs, thus, invoked the basic conceptual assumption of the humanist theory of jurisdiction, that France itself was an object of jurisdiction and *dominium*, a "great lordship" [*grand seigneurie*] over an indivisible and inalienable estate under the exclusive *dominium* and supreme jurisdiction of the King of France. In this way, Dumoulin's thought exemplified what Constantin Fasolt once described as "a constitutional theorem of the first order"—namely, that "in a world of lords, fiefs, and vassals, grants of jurisdiction and grants of land were the foundation of all order... [because] *dominium* and jurisdiction were by definition included in grants of territory."[154] Such a constitutional theorem had critical implications for Dumoulin's theory of kingship, since it positioned the king as a kind of *dominus* with a *plenissima iurisdictio* over the kingdom and all the lesser feudal jurisdictions attached to it.

But if the king is a *dominus*, then how should a lesser feudal lord be treated? What sort of legal claim does the *dominus* have over his fief? Does he merely exercise jurisdictional authority as a judge to hear and decide disputes arising among the inhabitants subject to that jurisdiction? Or does he actually "own" the fief, as an object of private property subject to legal *dominium*? Is

[152] William Farr Church, *Constitutional Thought in Sixteenth Century France: A Study in the Evolution of Ideas* (Cambridge: Harvard University Press, 1941) 190.

[153] Dumoulin 1:128 [*De Feudis*, §3, Gloss 3.10].

[154] Fasolt, *Limits of History* 197.

the *iurisdictio* "proper" to him? One prevailing theory was that inferior judges in the French judicial system, such as the *castellanus* [Fr. *châtellain*] or the *praepositus* [Fr. *prêvot*], actually had full legal ownership of the jurisdictional authority tied to the feudal benefice in their patrimony, such as a *castellum* [*châtellainie*]. Jurisdictional authority could, like the land or property to which it was attached, be treated as *res patrimonialis* and, therefore, vendible and inheritable, as any other object of private property.

Dumoulin fiercely contested this interpretation of feudal jurisdiction, which, he believed, illegitimately mixed concepts of public jurisdiction together with concepts of private property. As long as this proprietary understanding of jurisdiction remained in place, *iurisdictiones* would continue to be "sold like a hereditary flock of cattle or sheep…[so much so, that even] a peasant could buy the dignities and jurisdictions belonging [*sunt proprium*] to the patrimony of the seller."[155] Even worse, according to Dumoulin, private commercial transactions, involving feudal estates, such as the sale and purchase of castles and villas, tended to include also the sale and purchase of "*merum* and *mixtum imperium*, and every kind of *iurisdictio*" [*cum mero et mixto imperio, et omnimoda iurisdictione*] attached to those estates.[156] It was through this custom of the private acquisition of jurisdictional authority that Dumoulin felt legally constituted judges with higher appellate jurisdiction, such as the *baillis*, had been illegally "cheated of their own right" [*frustrando superiore iure suo*] to exercise proper jurisdictional authority.[157]

He therefore focused, like his humanist contemporaries, on the concept of the *iurisdictio* itself and investigated the seemingly aberrant institution of feudal or "seigneurial" jurisdiction in the French constitutional order, which straddled the divide between public and private law. What made feudal jurisdiction so problematic was that it was tied in with notions of property and ownership: the right of authority was inseparable from the right of property. But Dumoulin insisted that "*iurisdictio* can stand by itself, and can be separated, with its substance intact, from castles, estates, and other feudal properties."[158] And this, in turn, was because there was "nothing in common between proprietary ownership of estates and *iurisdictio* [*proprietas praediorum cum iurisdictione*]."[159]

It was, therefore, imperative to keep separate the notions of private ownership and public jurisdiction in the treatment of feudal estates. The difficulty in

[155] Dumoulin 1:81 [*De Feudis*, Gloss 5 on *Le Fief* §63].

[156] Dumoulin 1:80 [*De Feudis*, Gloss 5 on *Le Fief* §63]. Cp., the medieval dicta, *iurisdictio cohaeret territorio*, and its early modern transformation, such as in Annabel Brett, *Changes of State* (Princeton: Princeton University Press, 2011) 170.

[157] Dumoulin 1:78 [*De Feudis*, Gloss 5 on *Le Fief* §52].

[158] Dumoulin 1:77 [*De Feudis*, Gloss 5 on *Le Fief* §44]; cp. Bartolus on D.2.1.1, which stressed the distinction between jurisdiction over land and ownership over land.

[159] Dumoulin 1:77 [*De Feudis*, Gloss 5 on *Le Fief* §45], citing a discussion of a territorial dispute and use of D.50.16.239.8 and C.4.19.4 by the canonist, Oldradus de Ponte, *Consilia seu Responsa* (Venice, 1585) 88–9 [*Consilium* 176].

the case of feudal land is that ownership and jurisdiction may overlap and coincide, even though they are entirely separate legal concepts. Thus, any private person who acquired a feudal estate by some transaction, such as purchase, or by inheritance of patrimony did not *ipso facto* automatically acquire the jurisdictional authority that may have historically been attached to that fief.

One reason for this relies on Dumoulin's unshakeable belief that *iurisdictio* was, by its very nature, a public right and, thus, never to be treated as private property. He was absolutely clear on this point: "*iurisdictio* does not properly belong to one's patrimony, nor to the class of vendible goods; neither can it be treated as a patrimonial good... since it is a part of the public law."[160] Moreover, no private person can ever be said to "own" *iurisdictio* by a legal right of *dominium* because all forms of jurisdictional authority are, rather, "only entrusted or delegated [*solum committur seu mandatur*] for *exercise* and *administration* [*in exercitium et administrationem*], as in the concession of an office."[161] Even though a feudal estate might legally be sold and delivered to a private person, its holder can never actually alienate the *iurisdictio* attached to it by that same transaction. It is not his to give away, since all grants of *iurisdictio* are always "personal, not territorial" [*concessa personae, et non territorio*], and remain in the domain of the *dominus* who invested his vassal with the *iurisdictio*.[162]

By describing *iurisdictio* as a "delegated thing" [*concessa res*], Dumoulin shows that there is nothing unique about feudal or seigneurial jurisdiction that justifies treating it as somehow distinctive from the humanist analysis of magisterial *iurisdictio* in civil law. The holder of feudal jurisdiction could assert, at most, a limited inferior right in the use and exercise of the public authority attached to his fief, even though he may own the fief itself as property. On this point, Dumoulin closely followed Alciato. Citing Alciato's appropriation of Lothair's doctrine with approval, Dumoulin reasoned that "no magistrates have any right or ownership in their *iurisdictio* [*ius aut dominium in iurisdictione*]... they have only its exercise and administration" [*exercitium et administrationem tantum*].[163]

Dumoulin, therefore, accepts Alciato's conclusion that fiefholders are in the juridically inferior position of a usufructuary without any legal right to alienate, reassign, or subdelegate their *iurisdictio* to another. Just as a "usuary cannot constitute [*nequit constituere*] another usuary" in civil law, neither are inferior magistrates "able to constitute their own deputies or lieutenants" [*non possunt sibi constituere vicarios, vel locum tenentes*].[164] This is because no one holding *iurisdictio*—whether ordinary magistrates or feudal tenants—could be said to be "owners of their jurisdiction" [*domini iurisdictionis*], to do with as they please, but merely its "simple administrators" [*simplices administrantes*]

[160] Dumoulin 1:81 [*De Feudis*, Gloss 5 on *Le Fief* §64].

[161] Dumoulin 1:78 [*De Feudis*, Gloss 5 on *Le Fief* §48].

[162] Dumoulin 1:77 [*De Feudis*, Gloss 5 on *Le Fief* §46].

[163] Dumoulin 1:79 [*De Feudis*, Gloss 5 on *Le Fief* §57].

[164] Dumoulin 1:79 [*De Feudis*, Gloss 5 on *Le Fief* §58].

exercising a strictly limited authority only as agents acting on behalf of their principal.[165]

But if the jurisdictional authority exercised by feudal tenants is to be regarded as *res aliena*—"someone else's thing"—there must be, in principle, someone in the legal order who could rightfully treat such authority as *res propria*—"his own"—just as we have seen in Alciato's analysis. Dumoulin, following the humanist theory, gave his answer when he declared that all "right, ownership, and possession" [*omne ius, dominium, et possessio*] in jurisdictional authority must "belong to the *princeps*" [*residet penes principem*], as his property.[166] The *princeps*—here referring to the King of France—was thus, to be understood legally as the supreme *dominus* over all the authority of the realm.

In this way, Dumoulin performed the transformative task of "devitalizing" the vestigial remnants of the feudal system that framed the exercise of feudal jurisdiction in the early modern constitutional law of France.[167] To argue, as Dumoulin did, that the various grades and ranks of particularistic feudal jurisdictions in France originated ultimately in a permissive royal grant had a leveling effect on the pyramidal structure of feudal France. By denying the quasi-independence of feudal lords, Dumoulin had flattened the pluralistic system of feudal jurisdiction and *dominium* into a single undifferentiated grade of subjection under one sovereign *dominus*, the king, whose sovereignty was understood to be a supreme *dominium*.[168]

CONCLUSION

The stated goal of the legal humanists was to recover a pristine text of Roman law and to restore a historically sensitive understanding of civil law, as the Romans would have understood it. But Alciato, and the many jurists influenced by him, did no such thing when it came to the question of *iurisdictio* and *imperium*. While it is true that the humanist jurists of Bourges rejected the teachings of Azo, they nevertheless remained steadfastly within the medieval paradigm, and that is because, in their frenzy to distance themselves from Azo and the medieval barbarisms of the Glossators and Commentators, they simply adopted (perhaps by default) the view of Azo's nemesis, Lothair, whose own fidelity to the classical meaning of the text was questionable.[169] Like Lothair, early modern humanists attributed public legal authority, especially the *merum imperium*, exclusively to the *princeps*.

It is not difficult to see why French jurists of the sixteenth century would have found Lothair's doctrine, endowing the *princeps* with an exclusive right

[165] Dumoulin 1:79 [*De Feudis*, Gloss 5 on *Le Fief* §57], citing Baldus on the *Decretales*, X.1.29.41.

[166] Dumoulin 1:79 [*De Feudis*, Gloss 5 on *Le Fief* §57].

[167] Church, *Constitutional Thought* 181.

[168] Church, *Constitutional Thought* 194.

[169] The one major exception among the humanists was Cujas.

to the highest legal powers, especially attractive. France, at the beginning of the sixteenth century, was a polity that was deeply fragmented, divided by local loyalties and provincial identities, and plagued by a deep-seated legal pluralism, which separated the *pays du droit coutumier* in the North from the *pays du droit écrit* in the South. Such divisions were only exacerbated by the religious violence of the civil wars to explode later in the century.

The one central institution which could provide an elevated sense of "national" identity and unity amidst this chaos, as one body politic or *respublica*, was the monarchy, and it was this belief that fueled both French royalist ideology and early modern French "nationalism."[170] For jurists aiming for nothing short of wholesale national legal reform and the rationalization of law, such national unity, centered in a legally absolute monarchy, was essential for juridical unity. And it is, not surprisingly, for this reason that humanists, following the analysis of Lothair, arrived at the conclusion that the *princeps* of a kingdom such as France was exclusively entitled to the highest public powers constitutive of *merum imperium*, such as the power to make and unmake law. As the humanist Guillaume Budé would put it, the king was not only *legibus solutus* but "quasi-divine... a god among men and a law unto himself."[171]

But even if the humanist doctrine of royal authority may have drawn inspiration from Lothair's teachings on the *princeps*, their explicit and novel treatment of *iurisdictio* and *imperium* in the juridical language of property, as things exclusive or "proper" to the *princeps* and not to be shared with subordinate authorities, underscored the unavoidable commingling of private law concepts with public law concepts. This analysis was indicative of what might be regarded a background proprietary theory of authority, where public authority of all types—including those designated *merum imperium, mixtum imperium*, and *iurisdictio*—could potentially be "owned" in the sense that the legal right to such powers can be treated as being exclusive and conceptually separable from the mere use or exercise of such authority.[172] With the venality, or sale, of public offices, beginning especially with the institutionalization of the revenue-raising practice by François I in 1522, this attitude treating potentially all legal forms of public authority, including magisterial offices and feudal dignities, as private property—jurisdictions that were "proper" to its holder—would only become more engrained in the early modern mind.[173]

Humanists combatted this proprietary theory by marrying public law theory to private law theory. Since *imperium* is "proper" only to the *princeps*, subordinate magistrates could, at most, have authority merely as a usufructuary or administrator of some kind. Such authority, on this doctrine, did not really

[170] See, for example, Lawrence Bryant, "Making History: Ceremonial Texts, Royal Space, and Political Theory in the Sixteenth Century," *Changing Identities in Early Modern France*, ed. Michael Wolfe (Durham: Duke University Press, 1996).

[171] Church, *Constitutional Thought* 61, citing Budé's *Annotationes in Quatuor et Viginti Pandectarum Libros* (Basel, 1557) 67, on D.1.3.31.

[172] Loughlin, *Idea of Public Law* 76–7.

[173] Major, *From Renaissance to Absolute Monarchy* 104.

belong to them, but only to the *princeps* who granted such authority in the first place. There could, thus, be no private claim of proprietary right in a public office. As Loyseau, who tried to dismantle the confused notion of a legal right of "property in power" [*puissance en propriété*], would eventually put it in his treatise, *Du Droit des Offices*, subordinate authorities, such as magistracies or feudal seigneuries, have nothing more than "the mere exercise" [*le simple exercice*], "the use" [*l'usage*], or "the administration" [*l'administration*], but never the "true ownership" [*vraye proprieté*], of the public *imperium*.[174] Magisterial and feudal offices and powers, for Loyseau, were simply not the sorts of things that can be privately owned.

What is most revealing about Loyseau's statement is the reason why a subordinate can never properly own his power, and that is because it already belongs to someone else: it remains the property of the prince.[175] So, as much as humanist theories were designed to attack proprietary theories of public power, they were, as it turns out, fundamentally dependent on them.

These proprietary theories of public power, central to the constitutional thought of the later sixteenth century, will have consequences of monumental importance for the early modern doctrine of popular sovereignty, not only because they serve as a juridical model, derived from private law, which delineates the substance of sovereignty conceptualized as a claim of exclusive right over public powers of state.[176] It is also because they give rise to a new set of questions for constitutional theorists to consider. If sovereignty is comparable to a claim of an exclusive right over such powers as *imperium* and *iurisdictio*, who then should be entitled to hold such a legal right? Must it be always, and in all places, a *princeps* of some kind? Should such sovereign right even be held by one person, as if it were private property? Constitutional modernity begins in the concerted effort to address these concerns.

[174] Loyseau, *Oeuvres* 96 [*Offices* 2.1, §§8, 20].

[175] Loyseau, *Oeuvres* 96 [*Offices* 2.1, §20]. See Adrianna Bakos, *Images of Kingship in Early Modern France: Louis XI in Political Thought, 1560–1789* (London: Routledge, 1997) on Louis XI, the "spider king," as the embodiment of the tyrannical king.

[176] On the centrality of the proprietary theory in sixteenth century constitutional thought, see Rowen, *King's State* Ch. 2, and the more technical discussion of Ralph Giesey in *Juristic Basis of Dynastic Right to the French Throne* (Philadelphia: American Philosophical Society, 1961).

4

Popular Resistance and Popular Sovereignty: Roman Law and the Monarchomach Doctrine of Popular Sovereignty

INTRODUCTION

The humanist theories of "proper" jurisdiction—the idea that *iurisdictio* was "proper to" [*propria*] or belonged to some identifiable legal owner—emerged at a critical moment in French constitutional history, just as the monarchy began asserting a supreme or "sovereign" authority over all lesser jurisdictions within the realm. Like a Roman *princeps* who was said to be *legibus solutus*, the King of France was similarly thought to be unbound by law and custom and, for this very reason, absolute in his rights and powers like a *dominus* over his estate.[1] Some French royalist authors of the sixteenth century, such as Charles de Grassaille (1495–1582), even insisted that the King of France had acquired the same sort of universal authority once attributed to the emperor and the pope, hailing the French monarch as "king of kings" and "vicar of Christ."[2]

These theories coincided with the Reformation and questioned the legitimate scope of authority held by public authorities, such as the "Most Christian King of France." The toxic admixture of religious dissensus and political theory brought into new focus some of the foundational questions concerning the nature of political obligation. Are matters of faith comprehended under princely *imperium* and *iurisdictio*? Are subjects under obligation to obey an "impious" or "ungodly" prince who practices a "false" religion? Above all, could a king legitimately enforce, by his supreme public right of *imperium* and *iurisdictio*, a policy of religious uniformity?

The major Reformers, such as Luther, Melanchthon, and Calvin, investigated these topics at great length in a series of tracts that described the civil

[1] Geoffrey Butler, "Roman Law and the New Monarchy in France," *English Historical Review* 35 (1920): 55–62. On the notion that the king is a *dominus* with proprietary *dominium* in his public powers over the kingdom, see Church, *Constitutional Thought*; Rowen, *Proprietary Dynasticism*; Dick Pels, *Property and Power in Social Theory* (London: Routledge, 2002) Ch. 1. The argument continues in seventeenth century French legal thought, such as in the writings of Charles Loyseau and Jean de Baricave. Bakos, *Images of Kingship in Early Modern France* 110.

[2] Charles Grassaille, *Regalium Franciae* (Paris, 1545) 2.

authority of princes and magistrates as divinely sanctified and ordained solely for the purpose of securing the civil peace. The implication of this doctrine, however, is that any other use of civil authority beyond this divine warrant—including especially the enforcement of belief—is fundamentally illegitimate and undeserving of obedience. As Luther would famously put it in his 1523 tract, "On Secular Authority," any exercise of such authority beyond its properly ordained limit should properly be regarded as the act of a tyrant. Addressing the German princes of the Empire, he explains:

> I owe you obedience with my life and goods. Command me what lies within the limits of your authority, and I will obey. But if you command me to believe, or to surrender my books, I will not obey. For then you will have become a tyrant and overreached yourself, commanding where you have neither right or power.[3]

Most striking in Luther's classic statement is the likening of ungodliness to tyranny. In the Lutheran analysis, tyranny was to be understood more widely than in the classical Aristotelian or Ciceronian analysis of unjust rule, since even a prince governing justly or lawfully might yet still be a "tyrant" simply for practicing a "false" religion.[4]

These theories fixing the proper scope of civil authority had special resonance in sixteenth century France, where a sizable community of Protestants, or Huguenots, had emerged as a persecuted religious minority in a Catholic majority state that clung to the unifying belief in "one faith, one law, one king." In this context, the major constitutional question of later sixteenth century France concerned the appropriate position of the Catholic Valois monarchy and its government with respect to the increasing religious pluralism of the kingdom. Initially, a policy of religious toleration, formalized in the Edict of Saint-Germain on the initiative of the Queen Regent of France, Catherine de Medici, attempted to steer a moderate course, a middle way between the two opposing groups, not so much for reasons of faith, but rather, for reasons of state. But it was an unstable settlement that could not permanently defuse or contain the explosive elements of a religiously divided society, and ultimately gave way to a royal policy of enforcing a Catholic religious uniformity. The inevitable result was civil war, which began with the Massacre of Vassy in 1562 and escalated through a series of violent conflicts as the monarchy perceived the Huguenots, militarized under the leadership of the Admiral Gaspard de Coligny, as threats to church and state. These Wars of Religion culminated finally in the Massacre of St. Bartholomew in 1572, which originated with the assassination of Coligny and other members of the Huguenot leadership targeted by the monarchy, and exploded into mass violence resulting in the deaths of thousands of Huguenots in less than a month.

[3] Martin Luther, "On Secular Authority," *Luther and Calvin on Secular Authority*, ed. Harro Höpfl (Cambridge: Cambridge University Press, 1991) 29.

[4] Cp. Skinner, *Foundations* 2:16–17.

Needless to say, the experience of religious warfare and violence became among the most traumatic memories of sixteenth century Europe, irreversibly changing the perception of Catholic monarchy and the grounds of justifiable obedience due to such authority.[5] The memory of St. Bartholomew confirmed for the Huguenots the fragility of customary limitations binding a legitimate public authority within (what they saw as) its proper domain of securing civil peace and illustrated, more troublingly, just how easily a prince might overstep those customary boundaries to exercise an "ungodly," "impious," "irreligious," and—what was, for them, just the same—a "tyrannical" power beyond right. From the Huguenot perspective, then, the constitutional question is interpreted as the appropriate remedy for such "non-compliance." What is legally permissible to subjects, individually or collectively, when a prince fails to "comply" with, or observe, the limitations binding his public authority? May a subject directly enforce those limitations and ensure that a prince "complies"? May a subject forcefully depose or even kill a prince for failure to comply?[6]

This chapter concerns the reply of the two most important French Huguenot treatises that addressed these questions in meticulous detail in the immediate aftermath of the Massacre of St. Bartholomew—the *Francogallia* (first published 1573, and then re-published in significantly revised form in 1576 and 1586) of François Hotman (1524–1590) and the pseudonymous *Vindiciae Contra Tyrannos*, which first appeared in 1579 under the name Stephanus Junius Brutus, and is generally attributed to the Huguenot leader, Philippe du Plessis Mornay (1549–1623), but also to Hubert Languet (1518–1581)).[7] In the history of political thought, the *Francogallia* and the *Vindiciae Contra Tyrannos* have been widely regarded as founding documents of early modern constitutionalism. Harold Laski once regarded them as stepping-stones paving what he regarded as a "direct" path from the conciliarism of Constance to the Whig liberalism

[5] The Massacre would be chronicled prominently, for example, in later editions of Foxe's *Book of Martyrs*, playing an indispensable role in shaping the popular English consciousness of French Catholic treachery.

[6] Pierre Mesnard, *L'essor de la Philosophie Politique au XVIe Siècle* (Paris: J. Vrin, 1951); Robert Kingdon, *Myths about the St. Bartholomew's Day Massacres, 1572–1576* (Cambridge: Harvard University Press, 1988); Michael Walzer, *Revolution of the Saints: A Study in the Origins of Radical Politics* (Cambridge: Harvard University Press, 1965).

[7] For many years, authorship of the *Vindiciae* was a principal matter of scholarly debate, narrowing down the list of candidates to Philippe du Plessis Mornay and Hubert Languet. Skinner, *Foundations* 2:305, n.3; Figgis, *From Gerson to Grotius* 153; Julian Franklin, *Constitutionalism and Resistance* (New York: Pegasus, 1969) 138–40; E. Armstrong, "The Political Theory of the Huguenots," *English Historical Review* 9 (1889): 18–19; A. Waddington, "La France et les Protestants Allemands sous Charles IX et Henri III: Hubert Languet et Gaspard de Schomberg," *Révue Historique* 42 (1890): 243; Ernest Barker, "The Authorship of the *Vindiciae Contra Tyrannos*," *Cambridge Historical Journal* 3 (1930): 164–81; Georges Weill, *Les Théories sur le Pouvoir Royal en France pendant les Guerres de Religion* (New York: Burt Franklin, 1967) 109. More recent studies in this debate on authorship include M.N. Raitiere, "Hubert Languet's Authorship of the *Vindiciae Contra Tyrannos*," *Il Pensiero Politico* 13 (1981): 395–420; Derek Visser, "Junius: The Author of the *Vindiciae Contra Tyrannos*," *Tijdschrift voor Geschiedenis* 84 (1971): 510–25. I avoid entirely this debate on authorship, so I refer to the author of the *Vindiciae* as "Brutus."

of 1688. George Sabine considered the Huguenot theorists to be the authors of "the most significant chapter in political philosophy."[8] And Michael Walzer has interpreted Calvinist radicalism as a program deliberately designed to set aside the "legality and order" circumscribed by medieval structures of authority so as to introduce a new extralegal and extraordinary politics based on "permanent warfare."[9]

The single most important point these theorists shared in common with other Calvinists, such as John Knox and John Ponet, was the acknowledgement of a legal right—and, in some formulations, even a positive duty—of subjects to depose and remove tyrannical princes by force, a doctrine that earned these authors the title of *Monarchomach* (or king-killers), a label of derision coined in a 1600 treatise by William Barclay, a Franco-Scottish jurist whom John Locke once called "that Great Assertor of the Power and Sacredness of Kings" and "the great Champion of Absolute Monarchy."[10] And it is this doctrine of resistance to princely authority that would later be invoked to justify revolutionary politics far outside the context of the French Wars of Religion, such as the Dutch Revolt and the English Civil War.[11]

There is no question that Huguenot Monarchomach treatises should be understood as texts shaped by the religious violence they witnessed and barely escaped. But the suggestion that the Monarchomachs were merely religious ideologues advocating armed resistance and radical politics from the point of view of a persecuted religious minority misses what was perhaps the most important and enduring feature of their thought, that is, the juridical grammar of Roman law or, as Donald Kelley put it simply, the Monarchomachs' "incorrigible legal-mindedness," in explaining the legality of resistance to constituted public authority.[12] This is not surprising considering, especially, that the major authors of the Monarchomach tradition, such as Hotman,

[8] George Sabine, *A History of Political Theory* (New York: Henry Holt and Company, 1937) 372.

[9] Walzer, *Revolution of the Saints* 111–12.

[10] Resistance to unlawful kings becomes a positive duty owed to God in, for example, the formulation of the "double contract" in the *Vindiciae*, where both kings and peoples are duty-bound under obligations owed to the God. William Barclay, *De Regno et Regali Potestate Adversus Buchananum, Brutum, Boucherium, et Reliquos Monarchomachos, Libri Sex* (Paris: Chavdiere, 1600). Locke, *Two Treatises of Government* 419 [II.§232], 424 [II.§239]. Paul-Alexis Mellet, *Les Traités Monarchomaques: Confusion des Temps, Résistance Armée et Monarchie Parfaite, 1560-1600* (Geneva: Droz, 2007) 37–44. It should be observed that Barclay even thought Catholics, such as Jean Boucher, who favored armed resistance to the Protestant Henri IV should also be treated as a "Monarchomach." The term, thus, had no essential confessional content to it.

[11] J.H.M. Salmon, *The French Religious Wars in English Political Thought* (Oxford: Clarendon Press, 1959); Martin Van Gelderen, *The Political Thought of the Dutch Revolt, 1550–1590* (Cambridge: Cambridge University Press, 1992); Martin Van Gelderen, "Aristotelians, Monarchomachs, and Republicans: Sovereignty and *Respublica Mixta* in Dutch and German Political Thought, 1580–1650," *Republicanism*, Vol. 1, *Republicanism and Constitutionalism in Early Modern Europe* (Cambridge: Cambridge University Press, 2005).

[12] Donald Kelley, *François Hotman: A Revolutionary's Ordeal* (Princeton: Princeton University Press, 1973) 240. See also the criticism of Anne McLaren, "Rethinking Republicanism: *Vindiciae, Contra Tyrannos* in Context," *Historical Journal* 49 (2006): 31, and George Garnett's reply, "Law in the *Vindiciae, Contra Tyrannos*: A Vindication," *Historical Journal* 49 (2006): 877–91.

Mornay, Languet, and Beza, were educated and credentialed in civil law.[13] And yet, this also remains perhaps "the greatest weakness of scholarship on the Monarchomachs up to now: an almost total ignoring of the role of Roman law," as Ralph Giesey once suggested.[14] Arguments from Roman law were central to Monarchomach thought. It not only enabled the Monarchomachs to justify the legal permissibility of resistance. It gave them the conceptual tools to interpret *popular resistance* as a specific sign or expression of a more general constitutional theory of *popular sovereignty*.

But how was this notion of "popular sovereignty" expressed in the framework of Roman law by these Monarchomach authors? Quentin Skinner, who deserves the greatest credit for showing that the Monarchomachs turned to "Roman law traditions of radical constitutionalism," suggested that "the Huguenots began to make a systematic use of... Roman law theories of *imperium*" to "derive the right of resistance from a general theory of *imperium*."[15] Skinner, resuscitating arguments once made by Gierke and Carlyle, regarded the Monarchomach theory of popular resistance as a logical consequence of the Roman *lex regia*, by which the people merely delegated *imperium* to the king. Resistance, on this view, is to be interpreted as nothing other than a legally valid act of a *populus liber* recovering the sovereignty they had originally delegated to their king.

In this chapter, however, I want to go beyond this traditional analysis and investigate how Roman private law functioned as a critical source for the Monarchomachs, rather than follow the conventional account that was based on the theory of the *lex regia*. There is good reason for revising the conventional thesis in this way. The traditional thesis concerning the *lex regia* and the delegation of *imperium* by the people does not compare favorably with one of the key arguments developed in the Monarchomach treatises, which interprets popular sovereignty not so much in terms of the public law concept of *imperium*, but rather in terms of the private law concept of *dominium*.

Indeed, one of the central features of this polemical literature was the Monarchomach claim that only the people as a whole, not the king, can hold the legal status of a *dominus* over the rights and powers of the commonwealth.[16]

[13] Hotman, in particular, became a prominent scholar of Roman law in the humanist tradition, in his own right, producing studies such as the *Antitribonian*, critical of the use of Roman law as a legal authority in France and the authenticity of the Roman sources.

[14] Ralph Giesey, "The Monarchomach Triumvirs: Hotman, Beza and Mornay," *Bibliothèque d'Humanisme et Renaissance* 29 (1970): 52.

[15] Skinner, *Foundations* 2:321–22. This thesis has been expanded and restated most recently in Quentin Skinner, "Humanism, Scholasticism and Popular Sovereignty," and "From the State of the Princes to the Person of the State," *Visions of Politics*, Vol. 2, *Renaissance Virtues* (New York: Cambridge University Press, 2002). The thesis is challenged by Skinner, who considers the Monarchomach argument not so much to be innovative as imitative of medieval radical scholastic theory. However, Skinner is not the first to offer this observation. See for example, J.W. Allen, *A History of Political Thought in the Sixteenth Century*, 2nd ed. (London: Methuen, 1941) 313; Sabine, *History of Political Theory* 372.

[16] See, for example, the *Vindiciae*, in which Mornay speaks of the "corporation of the people" [*universitas populi*], the "whole people" [*populus universus*], and the people as the "true proprietor" of the commonwealth [*populus... vere proprietarius*]. Otto von Gierke, *Das Deutsche Genossenschaftsrecht*, 4 Vols. (Berlin: Weidmann,

The public authority held by kings and magistrates was, rather, only a temporary, limited, and conditional grant extended by the people as a delegation or concession of power, such that the constituted rulers in their official capacities—indeed, even the king—could only use, exercise, or administer public powers on behalf of the people as a whole, who collectively "owned" those powers and could, in principle, take back direct control of their "property," at their pleasure. Unlike the classical theory of *lex regia*, the people, in this Monarchomach account, never really alienated their sovereignty to kings as a full *translatio* because they retained their collective title of ownership, just as a landlord who leases or mortgages a fief to a tenant still retains the rights of ownership.

There is a vibrant anti-royalist agenda, aiming at what we might call a "republican constitutionalism," in this assertion of popular sovereignty.[17] By locating sovereignty in the people and identifying them, rather than kings, as the "co-owners" of the public powers of the commonwealth, these writers effectively stripped kings of their claim of an exclusive right of *dominium* over their kingdoms, a point of conventional wisdom in the humanist legal theories of the king's *sua propria iurisdictio* investigated in the previous chapter.[18] Instead, because the people were thought to hold a legal status as the sole corporate proprietors and owners of the commonwealth, all rights accrued completely to them, and never to kings.[19] Kings, according to the Monarchomachs, had no rights in the commonwealth to begin with: they were the inferiors or subordinates of the people.[20] And the Monarchomachs invoked various titles, such as "trustee," "pilot," "servant," "administrator," "minister," "executor," "guardian," "curator," "promissory," and "tutor," to elucidate just how kings were inferior to the people.[21] The people were not the subjects of royal power, but rather, the *sources* of royal power and the true authors of the law.

The chapter begins with a discussion of the doctrine that the people, rather than the king, hold the right of *dominium* over the public rights and powers of the commonwealth. The coherence of this doctrine, however, relied on the legal principle that even a people can be understood to be a legal person bearing

1913), especially Vol. 4. Gierke's thesis, however, has been criticized as being "vitiated…by ahistorical dogma." Harro Höpfl and Martyn Thompson, "The History of Contract as a Motif in Political Thought," *American Historical Review* 84 (1979): 919.

[17] I borrow the term "republican constitutionalism" from Benjamin Straumann, "The Roman Republic as a Constitutional Order from the Principate to the Renaissance," *Republics and the Classical Past, 1500–1800*, ed. W. Velema and A. Westseijn (Leiden: Brill, forthcoming).

[18] On this point, the following may be consulted. Ullmann, *Law and Politics in the Middle Ages*; Black, *Monarchy and Community*; Kantorowicz, *King's Two Bodies*; Ralph Giesey, *Juristic Basis of Dynastic Right to the French Throne*.

[19] *Vindiciae* 1579: 86.

[20] For an extensive discussion of Renaissance theories of French kingship, see Mellet, *Les Traités Monarchomaques* 364–400.

[21] Respectively, *Francogallia* 335; *Francogallia* 399 and *Vindiciae* 75; *Vindiciae* 74; *Vindiciae* 89; *Vindiciae* 104; *Vindiciae* 104; *Francogallia* 205, 399 and *Vindiciae* 104; *Vindiciae* 119; *Vindiciae* 130; *Francogallia* 205, 399; and *Vindiciae* 158.

actionable rights and obligations, much like a corporation. As we shall see, this enables the Monachomachs to frame the constitutional relationship between the people and their prince around corresponding relationships in private law such as that between a *dominus* and usufructuary, a pupil and tutor, and an owner and a possessor. These legal models provide the foundation for what I argue is one of the first early-modern theories of constituent power, locating the source of constitutional authority in the *populus*. I conclude with the Monarchomach argument for the "vindication" of popular sovereignty, which is constructed on the Roman law idea of the *vindicatio*, the Roman action for recovery of real property.

THE *UNIVERSITAS POPULI* AS *DOMINUS*

The Monarchomachs targeted the central axiom of the humanist theory, that kings had somehow acquired *dominium* over the kingdom just as if it were within their patrimony.[22] As we have seen in the previous chapter, the humanist theory was distinctive for commingling juridical concepts derived from Roman private law, such as *dominium*, with emerging doctrines of public law, such as *iurisdictio*. Indeed, humanist jurists such as Alciato and Dumoulin had no hesitation in judging offices, fiefs, and even whole kingdoms or commonwealths to be the sort of things that could be held as property by a *princeps*.

Certainly, one plausible strategy of argument, which the Monarchomachs could have taken in dismantling the royalist theory, might have simply involved segregating these concepts of private and public law entirely, in the manner once suggested by Seneca, so that "the king holds all things by his *imperium*, but individuals only hold them by right of *dominium*" [*omnia rex imperio possidet, singuli dominio*].[23] Indeed, early modern jurists who were focused on the project of crafting a modern system of public law were especially careful to keep doctrines of Roman private law outside the conceptual terrain of public law and constitutional theory.

But this was, remarkably, not the strategy that the Monarchomachs pursued. Instead of eliminating private law concepts from public law doctrine, they fortified that practice by retaining the Roman concept of *dominium* as central to their theory of popular sovereignty. While they vehemently argued that kings could "by no stretch of the imagination be considered proprietary lords [*dominus proprietarius*] of the fisc, kingdom, or royal patrimony [*fisci*,

[22] In the following discussion, I use "commonwealth" [*respublica*], "kingdom" [*regnum*], and "people" [variously, *populus* and *universitas*] interchangeably, in the same manner that the Monarchomachs did. For these early modern thinkers, they both signify the self-governing body politic or association that is governed under some sort of lawful rule. See also Hankins, "Exclusivist Republicanism and the Non-Monarchical Republic" and Eric Nelson, "Talmudical Commonwealthsmen and the Rise of Republican Exclusivism," *Historical Journal* 50 (2007): 809–35, on the flexible meaning of *respublica* prior to 1600, so that even a *regnum*, such as France, is to be understood as a kind of *respublica*. As we shall see later, some jurists, such as Althusius, simply equate *respublica* and *regnum*.

[23] Seneca, *De Beneficiis* 7.5.1.

patrimonii regalis]," they nevertheless were unwilling to eliminate the concept of legal *dominium* itself altogether from their analysis.[24] Someone else had to have *dominium* over those powers, if it was not to be the king.

That "someone," according to the Monarchomachs, was the people, explicitly conceptualized as a corporate entity, a *universitas*, in the same manner as the jurists of the medieval *ius commune*. By locating *dominium* in the *universitas* of the people rather than in the king, the Monarchomachs crafted a theory that began from precisely the opposite position, from the right of free peoples, rather than from that of kings. It was for this reason that only the people taken together as a whole [*ut universi*] were rightly to be regarded the sole "proprietary owner" [*dominus proprietarius*] of the powers attached to the "whole kingdom" [*universi regni*].[25] It was a strategic choice in argument that would have consequences of enormous importance for the early modern doctrine of popular sovereignty.

For the Monarchomachs, the immediate purpose of this analysis was to underscore the limited scope of royal power. A king could not treat his kingdom as if it were his property because ownership, in the sense of *dominium*, did not belong to the king at all. Rather, as Hotman writes, in wording reminiscent of Azo's and Accursius' glosses on the *lex regia*, "the ownership of that property remains with the people [*proprietas penes populum manet*]," which, by the law of property, implies that kings must always be under some sort of binding legal limitation.[26]

But simply relocating the source of *dominium* in the *populus* raised a host of other conceptual problems. Insofar as the *populus* was to be regarded as a bearer of the sovereign right of *dominium*, it presupposed that the *populus* must be treated specifically as a singular whole [*universi*], and not as an aggregate of individuals [*singuli*]. From the start, then, the Monarchomachs address the basic conceptual problem of popular sovereignty, namely, the dual identity of the *populus* as both a unity and a plurality. Recalling Azo's statement on the origins of *iurisdictio*, the Monarchomachs specified that it is always the *populus*, conceptualized as a whole [*universus*], that is properly to be regarded the bearer of *dominium*, not the mass of individuals [*singuli*] who make up that corporate body.[27] This move, in turn, was required by the very concept of legal *dominium* as an indivisible absolute right. Since the bearer of *dominium* can only be one and not many, it follows that the Monarchomach attribution of *dominium* to the people, if it is to be coherent, must likewise only be one and not many.

The analytical tool which allowed the Monarchomach jurists to conceptualize the *populus* in this way as both a unitary bearer of sovereign rights and as a plurality of individuals was the legal fiction of corporate personality, a concept

[24] *Vindiciae* 113, 119 [*Vindiciae* 1579: 137–8, 145]. Cp. Rowen, *The King's State* 38, and n.41.

[25] *Vindiciae* 124 [*Vindiciae* 1579: 150]. [26] *Francogallia* 254, 255.

[27] *Vindiciae* 78 [*Vindiciae* 1579: 89]; *Vindiciae* 156 [*Vindiciae* 1579: 194].

developed, as we have seen earlier, out of Roman and canon law by medieval jurists. One of the major innovations in medieval legal thought was the doctrine that a legal corporation [*universitas*] was a kind of abstract or fictive person [*persona ficta*], in the sense that it was the bearer of actionable legal rights and obligations separate from the individuals who made up that corporation.[28] A *universitas* could, thus, engage in legal actions as any private person, such as enter contracts, own, buy, and sell property, sue and be sued in its own name, all without tying, by the same transaction, individual members into the same obligation. Thus, as the *Digest* declares, "A debt to a corporate body [*universitati*] is not a debt to individuals [*singulis*] and a debt of a corporate body is not a debt of individuals."[29]

This corporatist frame of legal thought enabled jurists, beginning at the end of the twelfth century, to extend this analysis of fictive personality to all varieties of collective—or even "mystical"—bodies, including those designated classically in Roman law by such terms as *collegium, societas, civitas*, and *municipium*, as particular species of the generic *universitas*.[30] Of greatest significance for constitutional thought, however, was the explicit connection that jurists made between the *universitas* and the *populus*, so that the people too (broadly understood as a generic term) could be understood, by fiction, also to be a legal or corporate person.

But, despite similarities, the juristic personality of corporations was importantly different from that of individuals. Single individuals did not ordinarily need any intermediary in order to act with a unified will and voice since they were, by nature, one person.[31] They could simply present themselves at law; they needed no "representation." By contrast, the members of a corporation were, by nature, many persons, and consequently, had many wills and voices. Thus, in order to be counted legally as one person and to have actions attributed to it as a single entity, rather than as many persons, it would be necessary for the corporation of the people to be "represented" in the law, so that it "stands as if it were a single person."[32] A collection of individuals were, in this respect, comparable to legally incapacitated persons in civil law, such as underage minors. Just as a minor can express a legally valid will and act only through representation by a tutor or guardian, so too can a *universitas*, a

[28] But not all jurists accepted this distinction between the juristic personality of a whole corporation and the juristic personality of its individual members. Cp. *Glossa Ordinaria* on D.3.4.7 on *Non debetur*; cp. D.3.4.1, 5.1.76, 46.3.98.8, 45.1.83.5.

[29] D.3.4.7.1; 2.14.4; cp. *Vindiciae* 59–60. This explains, as Garnett points out, why the people are bound by covenant to the king only as a whole corporation [*universi*], but not necessarily as individuals [*singuli*].

[30] Skinner, *Visions of Politics* 2:14–15.

[31] As we see below, there were exceptions such as underage minors [*minores*], spendthrifts [*prodigi*], and madmen [*furiosi*] who could act only through intermediating agency of their guardians.

[32] *Vindiciae* 1579: 37, citing D.46.1.22, which suggests that even an "inheritance enjoys the function of a person [*personae vice fungitur*], like a municipality [*municipium*], a club [*decuria*], or a partnership [*societas*]."

populus, or even a *respublica* express a will and act only through the agency of another.[33]

The Monarchomachs readily absorbed this medieval corporatist background into their own explanation showing that a *populus* could certainly be a juristic person with *dominium*, but only as a fictive and represented person [*persona ficta et repraesentata*]. They often underlined this point by referring to the people as the "corporation of the people" [*universitas populi*] or simply as "the whole" [*universus*]. The *populus*, thus, was more than the many-headed hydra described by Horace which anti-democratic writers both in Antiquity and in the Renaissance feared—an image which Brutus must have had in mind in reciting the royalist objection to the people as "that monster... with countless heads."[34] The people could have, by law, a unified will and voice, just as any king could have, by nature, a unified will and voice.

But if the people could only be a *dominium*-bearing person by application of such a representational fiction, it followed that a people as a whole could only act legally in the same way as any legal corporation could act—that is, through the agency of some appointed intermediary or agent whose designated function was to represent and stand for the whole corporate body as a single person. The actions of the *populus* could legally only be realized through the actions of those who represent the *populus* as a person, roles which civil law denominated by such terms as *actor, procurator, administrator,* and *syndicus*.[35]

Who should be this intermediary agent representing the body politic of the people as one legal person? Medieval constitutional theory had traditionally suggested that this was the exclusive function of the princely ruler, to serve as the agent for the people—or, indeed, the head governing and giving voice to the body politic.[36] The Monarchomachs, however, proposed a different answer. Brutus explains in an important passage in the *Vindiciae*:

> When we speak of the whole people [*de universo populo*], we mean those who have received authority from the people—the *magistrates*, clearly, who are inferior to the king and chosen by the people, or constituted [*constitutos*] in some

[33] This is the so-called minority thesis based on C.2.54(53).4 and C.11.30.3. See Ullmann, "Juristic Obstacles" and Canning, *Political Thought of Baldus* 193–97.

[34] *Vindiciae* 45. Horace, *Epistolae* 1.1.76. It is a common image of the people conjured up by other Monarchomachs, such as George Buchanan in *A Dialogue on the Law of Kingship among the Scots* [*De Iure Regni apud Scotos Dialogus*] trans. Roger Mason and Martin Smith (Burlington: Ashgate, 2004) 55.

[35] Bartolus and Baldus famously avoided this doctrine by allowing that a corporation may act by itself independently of a representative agent. The Commentators extended this doctrine to the case of any *liber populus*, such that a "free people" such as a *civitas* may also act independently without some representative agent such as a *podesta* or other form of constituted ruler.

[36] See, for example, John Fortescue, *On the Laws and Governance of England*, ed. Shelley Lockwood (Cambridge: Cambridge University Press, 1997) 20 [*De Laudibus Legum Angliae*, Ch. 13], who cites Cicero's Scipio, by way of Augustine, to make the contrary point that "a community without a head is not by any means a body." See Church, *Constitutional Thought* 32–33, for the French context of the social organic analogy in Claude de Seyssel, and the classic discussion of this argument in Kantorowicz, *King's Two Bodies*.

other way... [as] partners in command and ephors of kings... [and who] represent the whole assembled people [*universum populi coetum repraesentant*].[37]

Hotman, similarly, viewed "the people" as represented properly through assembled estates or "orders" of the realm. This analysis of corporate peoplehood enabled the Monarchomachs to establish their basic thesis. Because a people can legally be represented as a person, a people can likewise be fully capable of asserting a legal right of *dominium*, even without kings. Indeed, kingship becomes entirely superfluous on this analysis and becomes, instead, a mere ornament to what becomes, in effect, a general theory of popular sovereignty, where even the most powerful monarchies are really subject to popular authority.

Of course, the Monarchomach's assertion of the people's *dominium* over the kingdom ran immediately into the problem of its obvious lack of fit with the facts of royal government in this age of princely rule. This was, indeed, one of the central criticisms of the Monarchomach argument. In what sense could the people as a whole [*ut universi*] actually be said to have proper rights of *dominium* over the *imperium* and *iurisdictio* of a kingdom, particularly when government and administration were in the control of monarchs? How could the Monarchomach theorists reconcile the *de facto* realities of royal government with the *de iure* argument for popular sovereignty, expressed in this civilian language of *dominium*?

To do this, the Monarchomach jurists turned again to Roman law and mined the Justinianic texts to specify in greater detail the unique juridical position of the king within the French constitution as a figure of public authority who, at once, lacked *dominium* over the kingdom, and yet exercised broad public powers over the realm. Civil law offered several key examples of such cases, which the Monarchomachs readily exploited in their discussion.

KING AS USUFRUCTUARY

One example was the usufructuary, discussed in Book VII of the *Digest*. As we have already seen, usufruct imposed a "burden on property obliging the owner to allow someone else [i.e., the usufructuary] to use it for some purpose."[38] In so doing, it introduces a relationship between the usufructuary, who may use and enjoy some property, and the *dominus*, who is said to have retained the bare title of ownership [*nuda proprietas*] in the servient property enjoyed by the usufructuary. But usufruct not only created a right to enjoy another person's property, it also activated a positive duty in the

[37] *Vindiciae* 46 [*Vindiciae* 1579: 46–7], with emphasis added. It is critical that Brutus only treats of magistrates "who have received authority from the people." Like Calvin, he is consciously distinguishing between magistrates who derive their authority by concessive delegation from the king, and "popular magistrates" such as the Ephors of Sparta, the Demarchs of Athens, and the Tribunes of Rome, where the source of delegated authority is the people.

[38] Garnsey, *Thinking About Property* 186. D.7.1.13.7.

usufructuary to maintain the value of the property granted for use. There were, thus, strict legal limits to what a usufructuary could do in his use and enjoyment. The usufructuary could not, for example, substantially alter the property in a way that would result in loss of value.[39] He was prohibited from "wrong use" and required to contain his enjoyment within the boundaries of "due moderation."[40] Nor could the usufructuary perform any action that would worsen the position or status of the real owner [*causam proprietatis*] during the usufruct.[41] The usufructuary is, moreover, fully liable to the owner for damages under the *Lex Aquilia* and remains vulnerable to possessory interdicts.[42] But above all, the usufructuary could not alienate the owner's property, since it could never be within the right of the usufructuary to authorize such a loss of the owner's rights without his consent.[43] Because of such limitations, usufructuary right was always regarded as inferior to the absolute right of the *dominus*.

The duty-imposing implications of the usufruct provided one of the key models that Monarchomachs exploited to elucidate the constitutional relationship between the king (who had no right of *dominium*) and the people (who did have *dominium*). Even though kings "used" and "exercised" the public powers of the kingdom and enjoyed the dignities and rights of the royal office, they did not "own" them and, therefore, had no *dominium* in them. In this respect, kings were like usufructuaries. Only the whole people [*populus universus*] held *dominium* over the civil powers of the commonwealth, as Hotman explains in the *Francogallia*, using the law of usufruct:

> The simple ownership [*nuda proprietas*] of this is that of the body of the people as a whole, or of the commonwealth [*penes universitatem populi, sive Rempublicam*], while the usufruct is the king's [*ususfructus autem penes Regem*].[44]

Since kings held a mere usufruct in their royal office and powers, they must be understood as being bound by the same sort of duties that the civil law imposes on usufructuaries. They can use, but they cannot abuse. They are required to exercise due moderation and to ensure that, in their tenure, they do not worsen the position of their *dominus*, the people. And they are prohibited, as French fundamental law forbids, from alienating the domain, as it is not for them to alienate without the consent of their *dominus*, the assembled estates representing the people.[45]

Yet, as important as the usufruct argument was for Hotman, it did not satisfy all Monarchomachs. In the *Vindiciae*, Brutus takes an even more demanding

[39] D.7.1.44. [40] D.7.1.15. [41] D.7.1.13.4. [42] D.7.1.13.2. [43] D.7.1.12.2.

[44] *Francogallia* 255. The seventeenth-century Tübingen Publicist jurist, Christopher Besold, appeals to this principle to articulate a German public law theory of double sovereignty. Christopher Besold, *Dissertatio Politica-Iuridica, de Maiestate in Genere* (Tübingen, 1625) 9.

[45] *Franogallia* 257; Garnett in *Vindiciae* 120, n.356 on the Edict of Moulins (1566) which codified the law regarding the royal domain.

position than Hotman by insisting that kings are not even to be regarded as the usufructuaries of the kingdom:

> Clearly [the king] is no sort of usufructuary. A usufructuary is able to give in pledge [*pignori dare potest*]; but... kings cannot mortgage the patrimony of the fisc. A usufructuary is able to give away fruits at will [*suo arbitrio*]. On the contrary, extensive grants on the part of the king are considered invalid, unnecessary expenses are revoked, and extravagances are curtailed. Whatever is diverted to anything other than public use is deemed to be stolen. The king is no less bound by the Cincian law than any private citizen amongst the Romans; and particularly in Gaul, no gifts are valid without the consent of what is called the *chambre des comptes*.[46]

Brutus' objection to the use of the usufruct model may stem, in part, from Paul's description of the usufruct in the *Digest* as a "fraction of ownership" [*pars dominii*], a statement which, Brutus fears, gives too much ground to power-hungry kings prescribing, even usurping, legal rights that rightfully belong to the people.[47] Since, for Brutus then, the comparison of kingship with usufruct was entirely improper, he suggests that a different model ought to be invoked to explain the position of the king:

> Kings are only administrators of the royal patrimony, not proprietors or usufructuaries [*reges patrimonii regii non proprietarios, non fructuarios, sed administratores tantum esse*]; and that since this is so, they are clearly still less able to bestow upon themselves the ownership, the use, or the fruits, either of anyone's private belongings, or of the public belongings of individual municipalities.[48]

Brutus, thus, is not satisfied simply with the denial of *dominium* by attribution of usufructuary right to the king. He requires something more demanding, an analysis that would establish the purpose or function of kings, not as "usufructuary" of the kingdom, but as a kind of "administrator."[49]

KING AS LEGAL GUARDIAN

Brutus developed this alternative argument through a radical reappropriation of what Walter Ullmann once called the "tutorial function" of princely authority—so called because it was derived from the Roman law of

[46] *Vindiciae* 124 [*Vindiciae* 1579: 150]. The *lex Cincia* was enacted in the tribunate of M. Cincius Alimentus (204 B.C.E.), mentioned by Cicero in *De Oratore* 2.71 under the title, *De Donis et Muneribus*. Among its provisions were limitations on the amount one could convey by gift, *inter vivos*, without a formal act of conveyance such as *mancipatio* or *in iure cessio*.

[47] D.7.1.4.

[48] *Vindiciae* 127 [*Vindiciae* 1579: 155].

[49] *Administratio* in civil law could be used in both private and public law contexts to mean the management of private affairs as well as the exercise of some public office. Thus, the *Digest* refers to "administrator of civil affairs" at D.3.4.10 or "administration of private affairs" at D.3.3.46.7. Brutus exploits this double-meaning but is recalling the earlier humanist analysis of magistrates as *administratores simplices* of the legal rights and powers belonging to another *dominus*.

guardianship, *De Tutelis*.[50] This compelling argument was designed to frame the constitutional relationship between the prince and the people by analogy with the juridical relationship between the guardian [*tutor* or *curator*] and the legally incapacitated ward [*pupillus*] in the civil law. Just as the guardian was to be merely an "administrator" of the ward's estate and his affairs, so too was the prince likewise thought to be an "administrator" of the people's estate and their affairs. As one commentator has put it, "it is the theme of tutorship within a corporative setting which justifies [the Monarchomach] constitutional theory."[51]

The force of this argument drew strength from the specific function of guardianship in the context of the Roman law of the family. In the *Digest*, Paul, citing Servius, defines guardianship as the "force and power [*vis ac potestas*] granted and allowed by the civil law over a free person, for the protection of one who, on account of his age, is unable to protect himself of his own accord."[52] At first glance, the relationship between the guardian and ward appears indistinct from other sorts of asymmetrical domestic relations of power within the Roman household, such as the relationship between the husband and the wife, the father and the child, and the master and the slave.[53] One is clearly in a position of advantage, while the other is in a position of disadvantage.

But this is not the case in legal guardianship, where the relationship between the guardian and ward is more ambiguous and even symbiotic in nature. What is exceptional in the definition of legal guardianship is that, even while the ward remains under the "tutorial" power [*in tutela*] and protection of the guardian during their minority or other period of legal incapacitation (such as being a madman—*furiosus*—or a spendthrift—*prodigus*), the ward is nevertheless legally regarded as a "free" person and always retains in full his right as an independent person who is *sui iuris*. Even while a ward is under the care of a guardian, he remains a *dominus*. Guardianship is, thus, fundamentally different from other sorts of domestic relations in which the subjected party is not said to be *sui iuris*, but rather, subject to someone else's authority [*alieni iuris*], such as slaves who are "under the power of their masters" [*in potestate . . . dominorum*], the wife who is under the power—or, literally, "in the hand" [*in manu*]—of the husband, and legitimate children who are "under paternal power" [*in potestate patria*].[54]

[50] Ullmann, *Law and Politics in the Middle Ages* 58, 92, 205; Walter Ullmann, *Carolingian Renaissance and the Idea of Kingship* (London: Methuen, 1969) 176ff; Ullmann, "Juristic Obstacles." See also Freegard, *Roman Law and Resistance Right*.

[51] Freegard, *Roman Law and Resistance Right* 66.

[52] D.26.1.1.pr.

[53] However, the husband's control of the dowry came with strings attached and, thus, became a model for princely rule, a model used by Hotman at *Francogallia* 257. The Neapolitan jurist, Lucas de Penna, for example described the *princeps* as "the husband married to the *respublica*" [*maritus reipublicae*] and, thus, restricted in how the *princeps* uses the public "dowry"—that is, the fisc. Lucas de Penna, *Lectura* (Lyon, 1529) fol. 184 [on C.11.58]. Cf. Kantorowicz, *King's Two Bodies* 214 and, more generally, Ullmann, *The Medieval Idea of Law*.

[54] D.1.6.1.1; 1.6.3. In the Roman law of intestate succession, the wife in a *manus* marriage is legally regarded as the "daughter" [*filiafamilias*] of the husband. Borkowski and du Plessis, *Textbook on Roman Law* 210.

Servius' definition explains why a "free" [*liber*] and "independent" [*sui iuris*] person would need a guardian—that is, age. In Roman law, even an orphaned minor or an underage child [*impuberes*] could legally hold the status and rights of a free and independent *dominus* over his household, a *paterfamilias*. An infant could, in civil law, be a head of household, so long as he was the eldest living male agnate in his family line of patrilineal descent.[55] The problem, of course, was that an underage minor could not possibly be expected to exercise power responsibly over the household by himself, even if he had the legal *right* to such power, and this is because he lacked the capacity and reason necessary for domestic government. There was no doubt that an underage *paterfamilias* was legally *dominus*, but he was a *dominus* who could not, for reasons of natural incapacity, exercise his *dominium*. He could only do so through another agent or intermediary, the guardian.

It was, thus, the function of the legal guardian to stand "in the place of the ward" [*loco domini*], while he was in a state of legal incapacitation, so as to exercise the ward's legal rights of *dominium* on his behalf. Among the most important of the guardian's duties was *administratio*—that is, the management of the ward's estate, or *res pupilli*. Since the ward could not legally act for himself, it was up to the guardian to act on his ward's behalf, particularly in relation to property transactions involving *res pupilli*. The guardian was legally empowered to act for his ward's benefit, as if he were the *dominus*. In this way, then, the guardian was said to "bear the person of the ward" [*personam domini sustinet*].[56]

However, the guardian himself could never be a *dominus* while serving in the tutorial capacity; he only stands as a representative "in place of the ward" [*domini loco*], as the ward's legal placeholder.[57] Nor could a guardian become *dominus* by usucaption or prescription on grounds of time; the ward's estate was, in this sense, "imprescriptible."[58] Whatever legal rights and powers a guardian exercised in his administration of a tutelage were thus not his own but those of his ward. And for this reason, the guardian operated under strict legal constraints, which exposed him to liability for potential maladministration of the estate.[59] For example, the law required a surety of the *tutor* before he entered into the tutorial office and administered the property.[60] The guardian could not alienate or embezzle the ward's property.[61] The guardian was also restricted from engaging in contracts that could potentially prejudice the

[55] D.1.6.4; 50.16.195.2. [56] D.47.2.56.4. [57] D.41.4.7.3.

[58] Cicero, *Letters to Atticus*, trans. E.O. Winstedt (New York: Macmillan, 1912) 1:17 [Letter 1.5].

[59] This point, as Canning once discussed in connection with Baldus, is what distinguishes the Monarchomachs' use of tutorial concepts from the minority thesis identified by Ullmann. Since the guardian is under obligation and potentially liable to the ward for wrongdoing, it is in fact the pupil or minor that is in the juridically stronger position.

[60] Inst.1.24; D.26.1.6.1; 46.6.1; 46.6.4; C.5.42.1, 5.42.3-5.

[61] D.26.10.3.5, which Brutus cites verbatim at *Vindiciae* 196–97, 207.

ward's future rights. He was even required, at the end of his tutorial tenure, to give an "accounting" of all the actions to determine whether his former ward, having now achieved the age of majority, might be entitled to a *restitutio in integrum* for any losses incurred.[62]

Because of the strict legal restrictions that civil law imposed on tutors and curators, guardianship was regarded an onerous burden—indeed, a whole body of Roman law [D.27.1 and C.5.62, *De excusationibus*] was devoted specifically to the "excuses" one could validly plead in order to avoid service as a guardian. Guardianship, thus, proved to be an especially appealing model to situate the constitutional relationship between the king and the people. As Brutus would put it, kingship, like guardianship, was merely "a function or procuratorship" but never "an inheritance or a property or a usufruct."[63] In this way, it provided yet another way for jurists to validate the king's legally limited exercise of public power, without also conceding *dominium* to him. The king could be understood to be a "tutor of the kingdom" [*tutor regni*] or "curator of the commonwealth" [*curator reipublicae*], who exercised public rights and powers that belonged rightfully to a people which, like the *pupillus* in civil law, nevertheless retained full legal *dominium* and status as free and independent, even while they are governed, *in tutela*, by kings. And just as a *tutor* in civil law is required to manage faithfully the ward's estate [*res pupilli*] during his administration of the tutelage, so too must a king faithfully manage the people's state [*respublica*].

By insisting that kings have duties of care in administering the *respublica*, like a *tutor* administering the *res pupilli*, and that kings are liable for any wrongdoing, Brutus is consciously connecting his analysis to an earlier tradition of the tutorial theory.[64] A true king must take on the role of a guardian, literally as the *curator reipublicae* with the duty of *administratio* over the *respublica*.[65] It is in this way, as Brutus concludes with a reference to the *Digest*, that kings "are held to be lords only so long as they take care of their wards, not unlike tutors."[66] As Brutus explains, "a true king is a *curator* of public affairs and an administrator of public resources, not a proprietary owner; and indeed he can no more alienate or squander the royal domain than the kingdom itself," just as a *curator* or *tutor* is similarly forbidden from alienating or squandering *rem pupilli*.[67] On this theory, then, the king is really just an elevated magistracy always subject to the *dominium* and "constant surveillance" of the people.[68]

[62] D.26.7.3.2; 27.3.1; 27.3.5; C.2.53(54).4.

[63] *Vindiciae* 125.

[64] Among the important sources of the tutorial theory include Accursius' gloss on C.2.53(54).4 on *Respublica* and *Solet*; 11.30.3; D.4.6.22.2, where *respublica* or *civitas* is legally equivalent to a pupil, a minor, or madman, all in need of guardianship and entitled to restitution in case of wrongdoing by the guardian. Cp. also Cicero, *De Officiis* 1.85.

[65] *Vindiciae* 1579: 144; *Vindiciae* 127.

[66] *Vindiciae* 127.

[67] *Vindiciae* 119 [*Vindiciae* 1579: 144].

[68] Skinner, *Foundations* 2:312.

KING AS POSSESSORY

In addition to arguments derived from the law of usufruct and the law of guardianship, the Monarchomach argument also appealed to the Roman law distinction between *dominium* and possession, a key distinction in the Roman law of property, as well as in earlier medieval scholastic disputes in the Church, as we have seen in earlier chapters.[69] According to this argument, kings held nothing more than a temporary possession, but not *dominium*, over the public powers and *iurisdictio* attached to the commonwealth. In this way, the Monarchomachs could certainly acknowledge the *imperium* which kings and magistrates exercised, but only as a mere possessory right. Like the subordinate who holds delegated *iurisdictio* by permissive grant, the *princeps* here is similarly thought to hold authority only by a permissive grant of the people. Hotman thus declares that royal rights attached to the royal office may certainly be at the disposal of kings, but never by a right of ownership: "[While] it is under his government, [it is] not in his domain [*imperio, non dominio . . . non proprietate*]."[70] It was a direct inversion of a principle previously expressed by the *Politique* Chancellor of France, Michel de l'Hôpital, who declared that kings have the right to tax because the wealth of their subjects belongs to them *imperio, non dominio et proprietate*.[71]

The argument drawn from the law of possession is crafted as a direct refutation of the prevailing theories of royal succession which, based on the Salic Law, treat the crown in the juridical terms of private patrimony.[72] As Brutus put it in the *Vindiciae*, kings are merely "put in possession of the kingdom [*in Regni possessionem mitti*], by the estates of the realm . . . who represent the corporation of the people [*universitate Populi*]," who, as the true sole proprietors, only delegate and lend temporarily to the king the royal powers over which the people retain their *dominium*.[73] Moreover, since they are thought to be in possession, kings can just as easily be dispossessed and removed from power, just as, in the law, a *dominus* can dispossess a tenant from his property.

Nevertheless, the Monarchomach strategy of argument was still vulnerable to one major legal objection from the civil law, inspired by the concept of prescriptive acquisition. Classical Roman law provided three principal methods for acquisition and transfer of property and the *dominium* attached to it among Roman citizens. Two of these methods of conveyance were *mancipatio* and *in iure cessio* and were formal, even ceremonial and collusive, in nature.[74] But the third civil method was prescription, or *usucapio*, literally, to "capture by use." Under the method of prescription, long, uninterrupted and continuous

[69] For a recent overview of the poverty debate, see Canning, *Ideas of Power* 109–10.

[70] Hotman, *Francogallia* 252, 253.

[71] Church, *Constitutional Thought* 166; Rowen, *King's State* 34, n.32.

[72] Giesey, *Juristic Basis of Dynastic Right*.

[73] *Vindiciae* 72–3 [*Vindiciae* 1579: 83–4].

[74] Gaius, *Institutes* I.119. These were sometimes called *imaginaria venditio*, or "imaginary sales." Jolowicz, *Historical Introduction* 145.

possession and use of some property would be sufficient to effect the civil transfer of lawful ownership from the civil *dominus* to the possessor—in classical law, two years in the case of immovables, and one year for movables.[75]

Of the various arguments available to them, royalists such as Bernard Du Haillan and Etienne Pasquier used this legal principle of prescription to argue for the validity of the king's title to the kingdom and to combat the suggestion that kings, especially those of the Capetian line, might somehow be usurpers without valid title.[76] Here, then, was a potentially fatal objection to the Monarchomach argument grounded in the Roman law. Even if kings and magistrates were merely temporary possessories of royal powers, as the Monarchomachs insisted, royalists could still yet claim *dominium* on historical grounds by showing that they "prescribed" it or "usucapted" to it by passage of time. Royalists could certainly argue, by taking a cue from Roman law, that the law of property mandates that long undisturbed possession activates prescription in favor of the civil possessory—in this case, the monarchy. On this royalist argument, then, the people had already lost any ancient rights in the commonwealth they might have had by some ancient or original popular constitution of an immemorial past.

But as compelling as this argument by prescriptive acquisition might have been, the Monarchomachs still had several strategies left open to them to handle this challenge, all of which drew support from civil remedies and legal exceptions to the rules concerning usucaption and prescription in the Roman law. One argument, articulated in the most complete form in the *Vindiciae*, developed the principle that prescription cannot prejudice the rights of the people.[77] In a lengthy section in the reply to the third *Quaestio*, Brutus argued that, even if long possession could transfer rights of ownership in the civil law, such an extraordinary transfer could never apply to kings and peoples.

It is no coincidence that French jurists in the sixteenth century, such as Dumoulin, used precisely the same idea of prescription and imprescriptable right to defend the validity of the king's rights and title to the throne. In his defense of the king's primogenitary rights, Dumoulin argued forcefully that a king's rights and title to the throne were fully *impraescriptibile* and were incapable of being prescribed [*non potest praescribi*] by private persons on grounds of long and undisturbed use.[78] Such regalian rights were set beyond the scope of ordinary rules of prescription and could not be transferred by the simple passage of time, as if it were like any ordinary object of property.[79] This was because they were part of what jurists regarded as an inalienable domain which

[75] XII Tables at Table 6.5; Gaius, *Institutes* 2.42–2.44; more generally, the titles C.7.33; D.41.3.

[76] On the *Researches* of these royalist legal historiographers, see Church, *Constitutional Thought* 84 and, more generally, Kelley, "Civil Science in the Renaissance."

[77] Allen, *History of Political Thought in the Sixteenth Century* 312; *Vindiciae* 1579, 103. More generally, see C.41.3.18 and D.7.33.1.

[78] Giesey, *Juristic Basis* 28.

[79] D.41.3.18.

was set beyond such temporal constraints ordinarily imposed on persons who were, as Kantorowicz states, "temporal beings ... within time." It was the centerpiece of medieval theories of kingship that, as Bracton argued, "no time runs against the king" [*nullum tempus currit contra regem*].[80] On this principle, even the passage of a great length of time could never prejudice royal rights.

Taken together, the suggestion that a whole *populus* might be a sort of extratemporal *universitas* which never dies, just like a king whose body politic also never dies, provided a powerful resource for the Monarchomachs who tried to refute the royalist argument from possession. The people were, in a sense, outside time and their corporate rights could not be subject to the ordinary rules of prescription that applied to natural persons who were within time. Thus, when he invokes the idea of prescription in the *Vindiciae*, Brutus' point is that prescription can operate only when there is a finite space of time in which prescription by long possession can be established.[81] But since the people, as a corporate person, are immortal and extratemporal in this way, perpetual like the water of a flowing river [*perennem fluvium fluxus*], time and temporality are made to be entirely irrelevant considerations.[82] The people's rights are, like them, immortal, imprescriptible, and inalienable, and not to be taken away by usurping princes simply on grounds of prescription.

The more important reply to the royalists' argument from prescription invoked the legal principle that possessories cannot prescribe stolen property, a basic principle of Roman law which can be traced to the XII Tables.[83] For usucaption or prescription to be valid, possession must at least be in good faith, *bonae fidei*. The basic thought here was that, because tyrannical kings had somehow knowingly "stolen" the rights to the commonwealth and had "usurped command by force and deception," they could not possibly claim to have rightful or just title to *dominium* over the kingdom by way of prescription.[84] Such kings were not legitimate rulers holding power *bona fide* but, in fact, "usurpers" of the people's power and "infringers" on their rights.[85] As Hotman thought,

[80] Kantorowicz, *King's Two Bodies* 164. Kantorowicz 171, stresses the need to sharpen this view distinguishing between the public and private capacities of the king.

[81] *Vindiciae* 90 [*Vindiciae* 1579: 104]. See also D.5.1.76, 46.3.98.8, 45.1.83.5.

[82] *Vindiciae* 90 [*Vindiciae* 1579: 104]. Cf. Aristotle, *Politics* III.3, 1276a. See also Kantorowicz on *aevum*, *aeternitas*, and *tempus* in *King's Two Bodies* Ch. 6.

[83] XII Tables at Table 6.5; Gaius, *Institutes* 2.45; D.41.3.4.6. In order for usucaption to be effected, the possessor had to meet what was called a *iustus titulus* requirement, a precondition designed to show that the possessor who was about to usucape had a just title to original acquisition of the thing possessed. Jolowicz, *Historical Introduction* 156. Here, the Monarchomachs, especially Hotman and Brutus, are claiming that tyrants are without title, *absque titulo*, and, in effect, robbers of the people's property [*Vindiciae* 1579: 171]. The legal remedies for theft in the Roman law directly become the normative principles of resistance. It is not simply recovery but also restitution.

[84] *Vindiciae* 140.

[85] This was a common form of political argument in Renaissance France, particularly in disputes concerning jurisdiction. For example, Dumoulin, who wrote his *Commentarii* to consolidate the rights and powers of the French Crown and its royal jurisdiction against the particularistic jurisdictions of nobles, called the seigneurs "usurpers" on the royal sovereignty. Gilmore, *Argument from Roman Law* 69.

kings had only a "bare and empty title."[86] Brutus was even blunter, simply calling them "tyrants without title" [*tyrannus absque titulo*] and thus "unjust possessors" [*iniustus possessor*] of sovereignty over the commonwealth.[87]

The normative content of this legal argument is thus structurally identical to the kind of historical principles involved in Robert Nozick's entitlement theory of justice in transfers. One cannot have a right to something that was taken from another unjustly, even with the passage of time, as the civilian rule normally allows. Thus, the prior historical injustice activates a claim of rectification, that is, "the rectification of injustice in holdings."[88] This was the normative logic of the Monarchomach's reply to the royalists. The people are "entitled" to rectify and remedy a historical injustice perpetrated by tyrannical kings. Tyrants had, in effect, stolen public rights and powers which were legally the property of the people.[89]

But, to execute this argument successfully, the Monarchomachs would have had the additional burden of showing that, in fact, kings did, as a matter of fact, usurp and steal those rights and powers which originally belonged to the people, and that the people were the originally true *dominus* of the commonwealth's powers. Simple normative or legal argument alone would not be sufficient to establish this point, but would need to be supplemented by an investigation of evidence in the historical record. It is for this reason, then, that constitutional argument becomes historical argument, in order to retrace the sequence of events by which French kings took illegal possession of the kingdom.

This was the principal polemical purpose of the constitutional history presented in Hotman's *Francogallia*, which traced the origins and development of the legal institutions of the French monarchy. In the *Francogallia*, a work which modern commentators describe as revisionist, "antiquarian," and a "very angry essay on the constitutional history of France," Hotman was especially concerned to emphasize the populist character of the original constitution of France.[90] The argument was clearly strategic and and designed to undermine the then-extant royalist claims to *dominium*. As Skinner notes, "if one could show that the constitution was originally populist in character, one might be able to insist that the same mechanisms of popular control ought to be maintained in operation at all times."[91]

[86] *Francogallia* 353.

[87] *Vindiciae* 140, 141 [*Vindiciae* 1579: 171, 172]. Brutus is relying on Bartolus' analysis of tyranny in his treatise, *De Tyranno*, which introduces the distinction between a tyrant on account of conduct [*exercitio*] and a tyrant by defect of title [*titulo*].

[88] Robert Nozick, *Anarchy, State and Utopia* (New York: Basic Books, 1974) 152.

[89] The reasoning here seems to follow the designation of public goods, including *respublica*, to be the property of the *populus Romanus* at D.50.16.15. This must be what Hotman had in mind at *Francogllia* 248, 249, when he recites the Roman definition of "public property" [*respublica*] as those things "which are common both by ownership and use of the state." D.3.4.1.1.

[90] Allen, *History of Political Thought in the Sixteenth Century* 309.

[91] Skinner, *Foundations* 2:310.

It is precisely this suggestion that motivates the "frequently tendentious and inaccurate" constitutional historiography of the *Francogallia*, which traces French kingship and the rules of succession in the Salic law to an ancient constitutional form of kingship that was based not on primogeniture and hereditary succession but, instead, on the popular election and constitution of kings.[92] Hotman argued that kings were always elected by the people until the late Middle Ages, a constitutional practice which he claimed to have traced back to the first meeting of the Gauls and Franks of late Antiquity to elect Childeric king of a united "Francogallia," by a "public council of the twin peoples" [*publico gemellae gentis concilio*].[93] Since time immemorial, free peoples established kingdoms not through hereditary succession, but through recurrent elections, where royal powers were "conferred by the people on someone who had a reputation for justice."[94]

The upshot of this presentation was to suggest that the modern practice of hereditary succession to the French crown under the Salic Law was, in fact, a relatively recent and a constitutionally illegitimate innovation lacking historical precedent in the ancient constitutional system of popular election. French dynastic patrimonialism was the exception, rather than the norm of an ancient constitutional democracy, the vestiges of which, the Monarchomachs pointed out, could be seen even in their day, in the constitutional practice embedded in the Aragonese coronation oath.[95]

The real villain, in Hotman's history, was Hugh Capet, "who had taken possession [*occupasset*] of the kingdom without any lawful hereditary claim."[96] For Hotman, the Capetians "laid it down that those who acquired [the crown] might retain them with the legal status of a patrimony and transfer them to their children and descendants with the rest of the inheritance," contrary

[92] Skinner, *Foundations* 2:318. Skinner discusses the criticism of the historical (in)accuracy of the *Francogallia* by Antoine Matharel, who, in his *Reply to François Hotman's Francogallia*, accused Hotman of "conveniently suppressing inconvenient evidence" to advance his theory of the ancient popular constitution.

[93] *Francogallia* 214–15. Even before the formation of Francogallia, Hotman noted that the Gallic and the Frankish peoples antecedently and independently had the custom of electing kings for themselves, *totius Gentis concilio communis* (*Francogallia* 149), a custom which was observed by classical authors such as Caesar and Tacitus. Cp. Skinner, *Foundations* 2:318, where he argues that Hotman subtly changes Sigebert's testimony that the Francogallic people "lifted" [*erigunt*] kings on their shields in order to read instead that the people "elected" [*eligunt*] kings. See, more generally, Richard Jackson, "Elective Kingship and *Consensus Populi* in Sixteenth Century France," *Journal of Modern History* 44 (1972): 155–71.

[94] *Francogallia* 154, 155.

[95] The Aragonese oath was often invoked by the Monarchomachs, including Hotman and Brutus, as an example of the elective and contractual nature of the constitutional relationship between king and people's assembly, the *Cortes*, binding the former to the latter. On the oath, see Ralph Giesey, *If Not, Not: The Oath of the Aragonese and the Legendary Laws of Sobrarbe* (Princeton: Princeton University Press, 1968). Hotman, *Francogallia* 306–9; *Vindiciae* 87, 136. Bodin quotes the text of the Aragonese oath in full in 1.8 of the *République*.

[96] *Francogallia* 376, 377. *Occupatio* was one of the *ius gentium* methods for conveyance of *dominium*, but it was not recognized within the Roman *ius civile*. Such an act of occupation and possession without right exemplified the Bartolist category of the tyrant without title, or defective title.

to the ancient practice of royal election by popular assembly.[97] Hotman had, thus, located in the early Capetian dynasty the moment of illegal usurpation that, in the Monarchomach view, had disqualified any subsequent royalist claim to *dominium* over the Francogallic state via prescription of the people's original sovereignty. In this way, the historical argument of the *Francogallia* was, in effect, a tacitly subversive criticism of early modern French dynastic politics in the sixteenth century and a call for a restoration of the ancient popular constitution, which, Hotman thought, was unjustly usurped by kings and corrupted by deceitful lawyers.[98] While Hotman's historicist analysis may seem to lack, as Skinner once observed, "the sort of revolutionary conclusions which the Huguenots were now committed to support" and even "an absolutely explicit attack on the behavior of the government," as displayed in the radicalized Huguenot pamphlet literature in the aftermath of St. Bartholomew, the radically populist implications of Hotman's legal argument would have been clear to any jurist.[99] A historical wrong entitled the people to assert—even "vindicate"—a legal right.

THE MONARCHOMACH THEORY OF CONSTITUENT POWER

Popular resistance was the logical consequence of the background juridical analysis of the people's collective *dominium*. It was the people of France—or rather, Francogallia—who really had the rightful title to *dominium*, whereas kings were merely temporary occupants, tenants, usufructuaries, or possessories appointed to exercise the people's rights and powers by a strict and fully revocable popular mandate. Because a *dominus* always retains the legal right of *dominium*, even while it is delegated, mandated, loaned, or entrusted, to another agent, as in these scenarios, it is fully within the right of the *dominus* to recover in full what it has conditionally given away.

But in order to explain and justify the coherence of this theory, the Monarchomachs had to give an account of the original concessive or delegative act by which authority was first entrusted to kings. In developing this theory of the original act of popular constitution, the Monarchomachs were perhaps the first to articulate a systematic statement of what, in modern

[97] *Francogallia* 410–12.

[98] Hotman called the lawyers of the Parlements "pettifoggers" whose power was almost like a royal power. *Francogallia* 497. In the sixteenth-century context, when the Estates were being called for the first time in about a century, Hotman took direct aim at the Parlements and the legal profession generally, calling them a "plague" which infected France, and usurpers of powers which rightfully belonged to the people assembled in their Estates. *Francogallia* 519.

[99] Skinner, *Foundations* 2:319, which seems to follow Allen, *History of Political Thought* 311. Skinner's presentation at 2:319–20 suggests that Hotman's analysis was entirely historical, lacking any radical or programmatic content, which had to be supplemented with a juridical analysis. But as we can see, Hotman's own historical argument was framed in order to flesh out a background juridical argument.

constitutional theory, has come to be known as the people's "constituent power," the authority-creative power of free peoples.[100]

The Monarchomach argument for this doctrine of popular constitution was actually quite simple in structure, as Brutus lays it out in *Quaestio* III of the *Vindiciae*.

1. "One who is constituted [*constituitur*] by another is held to be lesser."
2. "All kings were first constituted [*constitutos fuisse*] by the people."

∴ 3. "The whole people is more powerful [*potior*] than the king."[101]

They were convinced by the validity of the overall argument, but also recognized that the individual premises were controversial, especially among the royalist jurists. The Monarchomachs, therefore, needed to provide a closer analysis of each of the premises in order to defend their conclusion.

To begin with the second premise, the Monarchomachs had to establish that all kings were, as a matter of fact, "constituted" by peoples. Two related strategies of argument enabled them to achieve their goal. One was simply to demonstrate the conceptual incoherence of the alternative—namely, that peoples were somehow constituted by kings. Such a doctrine would require one to believe that, at some point in the distant past, the world must have been populated only by kings, but without peoples.

But how could it be possible, they ask, for there to be a king without a kingdom or a people? It would be just as incoherent as imagining a tutor without a pupil, a curator without a ward, a pilot without a ship, or a father without a family. Indeed, as Hotman observes, "all these [former] are appointed [*instituti sunt*] for the sake of the [latter], so the people are not found and procured for the sake of the king, but rather the king for the people."[102] The role and function of kingship, like tutors and guardians in civil law, are conceptually dependent on the people. It presupposed, according to the Monarchomachs, a people for a king to govern. Thus, Brutus, in mocking tone, summarily dismissed the idea of "a king without a people" [*Regem absque populo*] as simply "inconceivable."[103]

[100] The intellectual history of constituent power, thus, must be rewritten. It does not begin, as in the conventional wisdom, in the thought of the French Revolution. Sieyès is but the tail end of a long intellectual trajectory that begins in early modern legal thought.

[101] The premises in the Latin text are:

[1] *Vindiciae* 1579: 85: *Qui ab aliquot constituitur, eo minor habeatur; qui ab aliquot authoritatem accepit, suo authore inferior sit.*

[2] *Vindiciae* 1579: 82: *Reges omnes a Populo primum constitutos fuisse*; *Vindiciae* 1579: 77: *Dicimus iam, Populum Reges constituere, Regna tradere, electionem suo suffragio comprobare.*

∴ [3] *Vindiciae* 1579: *Populu[s] universu[s] Rege potior es[t].*

[102] *Francogallia* 398, 399, 401.

[103] *Vindiciae* 75; *Vindiciae* 1579: 87. Cp. *Vindiciae* 71; *Vindiciae* 1579: 82: *Nemo absque Populo regnare possit.* J.W. Allen, *History of Political Thought in the Sixteenth Century* 316, argues that this was a "commonplace" of medieval constitutional thought, locating sources of the idea in Aquinas and Ptolemy of Lucca.

Hotman, likewise, regarded the notion of a "king without a people [*populus sine Rege*]... as inconceivable as a pastor without a flock [*pastor sine grege*]."[104]

Having thus established the conceptual priority of the people, the Monarchomachs proceeded next to deploy their other strategy of argument, which was to establish the "temporal priority" [*prior tempore sit*] of the people as well.[105] In all states where kings now rule, they argue, the people must have antedated their ruling monarch. Framing the issue now as a sort of chicken-and-egg problem, the Monarchomachs insist that it is always the people who came first. This had enormous significance for the Monarchomachs' historical thought because it suggests that, in the distant past, the world must have been entirely without kings, having only peoples. The pre-political and pre-historical world of immemorial Antiquity was, for them, a democratic world. But since, in their day, the rule of kings and princes was now an established and unavoidable fact of political modernity, the Monarchomachs conjecture that there must have been some discrete point in history when peoples, by some popular act, created or "constituted" [*constituit*] kings over themselves.[106]

Historical investigation, though polemical and sometimes, as a result, distorted, became essential for Monarchomach constitutional theory. It marked one of the sources of the increasingly fashionable early modern focus on retrieving ancient constitutions and one source of inspiration for social-contract arguments concerning the pre-social condition of nature. Perhaps the most important source for Brutus in this respect was Scripture. Recounting the story of the Israelites' demand for a king, so as to be ruled "as all the other nations" [*ut caeterae gentes*], Brutus stressed the popular origins of the Israelite constitution, whereby the people of Israel—represented by the "elders of the people"– constituted and anointed Saul king over themselves.[107] But the popular constitution of kings was not unique to Israel, as Brutus continues: "Even amongst the heathens, kings are constituted by the people."[108] Citing Livy, he brings into his discussion the example of the second king of Rome, Numa Pompilius, upon whom royal authority was conferred by the "votes of the people" [*suffragiis Populi*] and the consent of the senate.[109] Hotman, similarly, cites

104 *Francogallia* 400, 401. Cp. *Francogallia* 206, 207, where Hotman regarded as "ridiculous" [*perabsurdum*] the suggestion that "a king named the people rather than that the people named a king.

105 *Vindiciae* 1579: 82.

106 Thus, Nimrod, the Biblical hunter-warrior who was the founder of Ninevah and regarded as the first king, was rejected as a mere tyrant. Genesis 10:8–12. But this is a very different interpretive position from someone like Bodin who viewed all states as having originated under the rule of some sort of conquering *dominus* like Nimrod. See *Commonweale* 200 [2.2].

107 *Vindiciae* 1579: 77–8. Brutus is citing Deuteronomy 17:14–15, which recites Moses' caution that the people will say, "Let me constitute a king over myself" [*Constituam Regem super me*]. On early modern discussions of the Israelite constitution and the idolatry of kingship, see Eric Nelson, *The Hebrew Republic* (Cambridge: Harvard University Press, 2010) Ch. 1.

108 *Vindiciae* 71.

109 Livy, *Ab Urbe Condita* 1.18. It also explains, for Brutus, why the Tarquins were properly to be regarded tyrants, "because [they were] created neither by the people nor by the senate, but held command by relying on force and power alone."

Tacitus' *Germania* as providing further evidence that all ancient kings "were created by suffrage only."[110]

Even national kingdoms of Western Christianity which appear to have long-established hereditary monarchies, such as England, Spain, and France, nevertheless adhere fully to this theory of popular constitution. For Hotman, "the kings of Francogallia were constituted [*constitutos fuisse*] by the authoritative decision and desire of the people [*populi . . . iudicio ac studio*] . . . rather than by any hereditary right [*hereditario iure*]."[111] Brutus takes an even more controversial stance along these lines in the *Vindiciae*, claiming that there is, in fact, no such thing as a hereditary king at all. All kings are, at some level, established by some antecedent act of popular constitution and election.[112] Part of the reason for this is the earlier analysis that the kingdom and the rights attached to the royal domain are not like private property which can be passed onto heirs, and thus cannot be claimed by any hereditary or patrimonial right. It is only by a corruption of reasoning, Brutus thinks, that people have come to interpret kingship in this way. Instead, what appears to be hereditary kingship is more properly to be described as "successive," allowing him to deflate the conventional distinction in early modern theories of kingship between "elective" monarchies (such as Poland, the Holy Roman Empire, and the Papacy) and "hereditary" monarchies (such as England, Spain, and France). The key feature of "successive" monarchy is that, like the elective varieties, kings are always subject to a popular act of investiture into the royal office. But whereas, in "elective" monarchies, the people select anew, at each interregnum, the individual who will be invested with royal power, "successive" monarchies function by requiring the people to select the dynastic line: The people "chooses the stem not the offshoot."[113] The point is that, in both elective and successive monarchies, kings are not born, but always made by the people. Each new king must still be constituted by a popular act of investiture into the royal office.

For the Monarchomachs, then, acts of popular constitution are to be regarded as a universal pattern undergirding every monarchy in history, and it is in this way that they regard the second premise to be true as a general constitutional principle.[114] But the second premise can only be compelling if it can be shown

[110] *Francogallia* 220, 221.

[111] *Francogallia* 231, 233.

[112] It should be noted that, in the *Vindiciae*, the popular act of constitution is always understood to coincide with the divine act of election. But, notwithstanding the divine element of the theory, it is clear that the human element is carried out always by the people.

[113] *Vindiciae* 74.

[114] Those who have not been so constituted by the people are not properly kings. Brutus gives the example of Turkey and Muscovy which are described to be "more robber bands than realms" *Vindiciae* 81 [*Vindiciae* 1579: 93–4]. The use of the Turks and Muscovites as the quintessential examples of lawless kingship is especially common in early modern thought. Bodin, for example, refers to them to exemplify his category of "seigneurial government," as opposed to "lawful government." See Daniel Lee, "Office Is a Thing Borrowed: Jean Bodin on Offices and Seigneurial Government," *Political Theory* 41 (2013): 409–41.

that there is some normative significance in the fact that the people historically constituted their kings. Thus, in order to establish the principle embodied in the first premise, Brutus is pressed to investigate the very meaning of the term itself, "to constitute" [*constituere*]. In civil law, the word functions as a generic term indicating the legal act whereby some special legal right or obligation is created, where none existed before. Often, this is expressed as the capacity of one to create or "constitute" some special legal condition, such as a rustic servitude [*constituere servitutem*] or a contract appointing a third party as surety to pay another's existing debt [*constitutum debiti alieni*].[115] It has special relevance for Roman public law as well: general legislation of the *princeps* is described as a decree, or "constitution" [as in the Antonine Constitution of 212 A.D.], and so, as Javolenus explains in *De verborum significatione*, *constituere* can mean the same as "to judge" [*censere*] or "to order" [*praecipere*] by means of some express decree or legal statement.[116]

But significantly, the term, *constituere*, is also associated with the act of appointing or creating a specially defined legal role of some kind. Thus, Ulpian is quoted in the *Digest* as defining the jurisdiction of civil magistrates as an *officium* which includes inter alia the capacity "to assign tutors" [*tutores constituere*]; elsewhere, he discusses legal agents or attorneys [*actores; procuratores*], who are similarly so "constituted" or appointed [*constitutus; constitui*].[117] Remarkably, medieval and early modern civilians invoked precisely this same language to frame the legal right of princes to create or constitute magistrates, such as Alciato, who, in his *Commentarii in Digesta*, described the *princeps* as "constitutor of all magistrates" [*constitutor omnium magistratuum*] and Dumoulin, who justified one's right "to constitute a magistrate" [*magistratum constituere*] as the direct "consequence of one's *dominium* over a jurisdiction" [*effectus dominii iurisdictionis*].[118]

It is this particular sense of *constituere* that Brutus must have had in mind when he observes that "such is the force of the word [*vis verbi*]: one who is constituted by another is held to be lesser; and one who receives his authority from another is inferior to his appointer."[119] Thus, a principal who "constitutes" an agent or *procurator*—such as when "masters [*domini*] are said to constitute their servants [*servi*], and kings their ministers"—is understood to be somehow superior over the agent he has created.[120]

Brutus illustrates this principle, again with numerous historical examples. Excavating Scripture, he observes that "Potiphar, the Egyptian, set Joseph

[115] D.8.3.26, 13.5.14.3. On the *constitutum debiti*, Reinhard Zimmerman, *The Law of Obligations: The Roman Foundations of the Civilian Tradition* (Oxford: Clarendon Press, 1996) 511–13. "Servitudes" were burdens imposed on one's property for the benefit of another party, similar to common law easements.

[116] D.50.16.111.

[117] D.2.1.1, 3.3.1.1, 3.4.10.

[118] Alciato 1:143 [*Commentaria* on D.2.1.3, §88]; Dumoulin 1:79 [Gloss 5 on *Le Fief* §57].

[119] *Vindiciae* 74 [*Vindiciae* 1579: 85].

[120] *Vindiciae* 74 [*Vindiciae* 1579: 85].

over his household; Nebuchadnezzar set [*constituit*] Daniel over the province of Babylon; and Darius set [*constituit*] one hundred and twenty governors over the kingdom," but, in doing so, each constitutor retained superiority over the constituted agent.[121] Moreover, the act of constituting need not be a personal act; even assembled bodies could corporately constitute legal authority in another, so that "he who accepts authority from any assembly is inferior to that assembly."[122] Invoking the conciliar doctrine that "an ecumenical synod was superior to the pope," Brutus expands it into a general principle of corporate representation to explain why a "chapter [*capitulum*] is [superior] to bishop [*episcopo*], corporation [*universitatem*] to agent [*actore*], court [*curiam*] to decurion [*decurione*]"—namely, because all the former bodies had constituted the latter person or role.[123]

The same principle operates in the popular constitution of kings, where the people is comparable legally to a *universitas* with the power of constituting officers for the corporation. Returning to the earlier example of ancient Israel, Brutus explains that, despite being "constituted [king] by grace of Israel [*Israelis gratia constituto*]...as a sort of public agent" [*quasi Actorem publicum*], the people of Israel, as a corporate body, nevertheless "was superior to Saul" [*Israel...Saule superior sit*].[124] Indeed, he writes, "the people constitutes the king, as a minister of the commonwealth [*ministrum Reipublicae*]."[125]

What remains to be explained is precisely *why* the king, as a constituted agent, is inferior to the people. As later critics of Monarchomach thought, such as William Barclay, pointed out, it does not necessarily follow that a constitutor must also be the superior of the constituted agent, since constitutional acts might be understood to be acts of alienation, as in some imperialist readings of the Roman *lex regia*.[126] To avoid this pitfall in the argument, the Monarchomachs carefully present constitutional acts in terms such that the constitutor is always understood to retain juridical superiority over the constituted party, as the agent.[127] Here, Roman law becomes essential to the

[121] *Vindiciae* 74 [*Vindiciae* 1579: 85]. Brutus, in turn, cites Genesis 39:4 [Vulgate: *praepositus*], Daniel 2:48 [Vulgate: *constituit*], and Daniel 6:1 [Vulgate: *constituit*].

[122] *Vindiciae* 47–8.

[123] *Vindiciae* 47 [*Vindiciae* 1579: 48] notes this is the first mention in the *Vindiciae* of the conciliar theory. Cp. D.2.4.10.4, 3.4.1.1 on representation of corporations by legal agents or syndics. More generally, on the uses of corporate representation in conciliar theory, Tierney, *Foundations of the Conciliar Theory*, Part II, §§2–3.

[124] *Vindiciae* 48 [*Vindiciae* 1579: 48]. Brutus' description of the king here as *actor publicus* is inspired by the model of municipal or corporate agents representing corporate bodies in legal actions, such as the *actor civitatis, actor universitatis*, or *syndicus* discussed in the *Digest* at D.3.3.74, 3.4.1.1, and 3.4.6.3.

[125] *Vindiciae* 74 [*Vindiciae* 1579: 85]. This redescription of the king as a *ministrum*—meaning also, an agent, a servant, even a waiter—is designed to buttress his later claim that he rules, as a minister, in concert with the other ministers, public officers, and peers of the realm. Brutus, thus, presents the king as a *primus inter pares* among other officers who are described not so much as the king's subordinates, but as "partners in royal command" [*regii imperii consortes*], at *Vindiciae* 77 [*Vindiciae* 1579: 89] and, even at one point, to be "in the place of brothers" [*fratrum loco habet*], at *Vindiciae* 144 [*Vindiciae* 1579: 175].

[126] Barclay, *De Regno et Regali Potestate* 401, cp. 268–9.

[127] To recall from Chapter 1, this was a suggestion made in passing by Accursius in the gloss on D.1.3.9.

explanation, such as in Brutus' analysis of the contract between king and people in terms of the Roman unilateral contract of *stipulatio*:

> The people made [*faciebat*] the king, not the king the people. So there is no doubt that the people stipulated, and the king promised; for the parts of stipulator are considered to be stronger in law [*in iure*]... The king promised absolutely, and the people conditionally: if he were to fail to fulfill his part, the people would be considered to be absolved from all obligation by that very right [*populus ipso iure omni obligatione solutus censeretur*].[128]

Here, the king is understood to be "constituted" as a promissory via a contract of *stipulatio* with the people. But since a *stipulatio* is, by definition, a unilateral contract where contractual obligations accrue only to the promissory, but never to the stipulator, the king is liable to legal action [*condictio*] for failure to "rule justly and according to the laws," whereas the people, as stipulator, retain the full legal right to compel the promissory to perform his obligation.[129] Elsewhere, Brutus invokes another model from the Roman law of obligations, the innominate contract of *precarium*—a revocable grant which the precarious tenant held only "by sufferance" or pleasure of the *dominus*—to drive home the same point.[130] To suggest here that kingship was constituted "as a sort of precarious grant" [*tanquam precariam possiderent*] had the same effect as the analysis of *stipulatio*: all legal rights accrued exclusively to the people who held the analogous position of the *dominus* [*loco domini*].[131]

The critical point in these legal models, however, concerns what the people may ultimately do to the kings who are placed under such obligations to their constitutor. Just as the people could constitute kings into their legally circumscribed role (such as usufructuary, tutor, curator, possessor, servant, promissory, precarious tenant), so too can they depose and remove them from those roles as well. This is fundamentally the reason why the people are regarded as juridically superior [*potior*] to the king. Kings owe their entire existence to the people, not simply because they "constituted" them, but also because they depend on the continuing approval and consent of the people for their lawful tenure in royal office.

128 *Vindiciae* 130–31 [*Vindiciae* 1579: 160]. Garnett observes that Brutus' attribution of a conditional obligation to the people does not quite fit the *stipulatio*, since stipulators do not promise anything. If the contract is a true *stipulatio*, the people do not owe the king anything, not even the conditional promise, as Brutus put it, "to obey faithfully so long as [the king] commanded justly." Only the king, as promissory, is under obligation.

129 *Vindiciae* 130. Double-obligation as surety in the original contract.

130 On the precarium, *De precario*, D.43.26. Garnett, in 16, n.14, suggests that Hotman's use of *precarium* in the analysis of feudal tenure in *De Feudis Commentatio Tripertita... Disputatio de Iure Feudali; Commentarium in Usus Feudorum; Dictionarium Verborum Feudalium* (Lyon, 1573) may have been a source for Brutus. Bodin similarly uses the *precarium* to distinguish between "officers" who enter a contract [*commodato*] with the sovereign for their office, and "commissioners" who are dependent upon the "sufferance" [*precario*] of the sovereign. See also pp. 212–15.

131 *Vindiciae* 1579: 86, 87. This formulation is different from the usage in classical law. The phrase, *loco domini*, is typically used to explain the position of the princely *tutor*, but here it is used to explain the position of the people.

The Monarchomach theory of popular constitution, thus, entails a perfect juridical *symmetry* between "constituting" and "de-constituting"; the right to perform one of these acts entailed a "symmetrical right" to perform the other. To suggest, therefore, that the people had created or constituted the king would have been extraordinary, since, on this analysis, it implied that the people who held the legal right to constitute or create kings also held a symmetrical right to depose kings as well, a point which Hotman concludes when he asserts that the people have both the power of "creating as well as of deposing the king" [*creando vel abdicando Rege*].[132] He explains:

> It is to be understood that, inasmuch as it was the right and power of the estates and the people to constitute and maintain [*constituendis retinendisve*] kings, so... the supreme power of deposing kings [*Regum abdicandorum summam potestatem*] was also that of the people.[133]

Brutus, in exactly the same way, argues for such a symmetry of constitutional rights, indicating that, since "it is not individuals [*singuli*] who constituted [*constituunt*] a prince, but all do so together as a whole [*universi*]," lawful resistance cannot, for that very reason, be an individual or private act, but only a solemn public act under the "command of all together" [*iussum universorum*].[134]

Taken together, the Monarchomachs used the Roman law to offer nothing short of "a theory of absolute popular control, not a mere theory about the possibility of restraining a king *in extremis*."[135] From afar, the argument appears simply to be a reincarnation of the concession theory of the *lex regia* articulated by Glossators such as Azo. Like those medieval concession theorists, the Monarchomachs accept that princely authority originates in the *populus*. They insist that the conveyance of authority was never a full alienation of popular sovereignty. And like their medieval predecessors, they argue that, because of the limited nature of the people's grant of authority, a princely ruler is always subject to removal, by force if necessary.

THE VINDICATION OF POPULAR SOVEREIGNTY

Yet, despite sharing a common legal heritage in the legacy of Roman law, the Monarchomachs remarkably avoided using the Roman *lex regia* in their analysis of popular sovereignty, as the medieval civilians had conventionally done.[136] Apart from a few perfunctory comments of antiquarian interest, Hotman and Brutus made no systematic effort to align their theory of popular

[132] *Francogallia* 332.

[133] *Francogallia* 234.

[134] *Vindiciae* 169 [*Vindiciae* 1579: 210]. He is speaking only of tyrants on account of conduct [*exercitio*] in this passage. Tyrants with defective title [*absque titulo*] may be resisted by individuals.

[135] Skinner, *Foundations* 2:313. This is why Hotman and Brutus are worlds apart from the theory of Jean de Terrevermeille who, as Giesey admits at *Juristic Basis* 16, was "in no way a partisan of popular sovereignty."

[136] Hotman's criticism of the validity of Roman law in France perhaps helps to explain why he refuses to treat the *lex regia* as a general principle: *Neque enim ex uno particulari recte de universis concluditur.* Hotman, *Francogallia* 414 ["A universal principle should not be concluded from one particular example"].

sovereignty with the Roman public law theory of the *lex regia*.[137] Instead, the Monarchomach argument for the legality of popular resistance was carefully presented as a body of technical legal arguments based in Roman private law, all of which accepted without question the supreme role of the *populus* as a *dominus* over the public rights and powers of France. Popular resistance could, thus, be very easily understood in civil law terms simply as a legal action by a *dominus* to recover what properly belongs to the people.

One such action which looms large in Monarchomach thought was the *vindicatio*, an action of general importance not only for the law of property, in which *vindicatio* functioned as a real action for recovery of property in someone else's possession, but also in the law of persons, as the *vindicatio in libertatem*, where it functioned as a form of manumission for free persons who were wrongly enslaved.[138] The Monarchomachs make use of both senses of the *vindicatio*. Insofar as a people governed under tyrannical kings can be said to be a free people wrongfully enslaved, the proper remedy to be sought must be some form of manumission that restores the enslaved people to its original liberty. This is certainly Hotman's point when he observes that the liberty of a free people such as Francogallia must be "vindicated" from potentially tyrannical authority.[139] It is also, as George Garnett has shown, what Brutus' argument from the Roman law action of the *vindicatio in libertatem* was supposed to demonstrate. So, a lawful act of popular resistance was really an act of popular liberation, "to vindicate [*vindicare*] the whole kingdom from tyranny [*a tyrannide*]."[140]

But what is less apparent, yet equally important, is the proprietary sense of *vindicatio* as an action for recovery. This action, "a very powerful action" described both as "power" [*potestas*] and as "right" [*ius*] in civil law, was central to the assertion of the right of the *dominus* in disputes over property "whether animate or inanimate, and in regard to land."[141] Its purpose was to determine, once and for all, who actually was the rightful *dominus* over the property in dispute, regardless of factual possession. Assertion of *vindicatio* could, thus, have the effect of dispossession, by which a *dominus* could lawfully recover property that is in the factual possession or use of another party.[142] Most important,

[137] Hotman, *Francogallia* 414–15 formulates the *lex regia* as: *lata lege Regia populum Imperatori omne suum imperium et potestatem concessisse* ["The *lex regia* being enacted, the [Roman] people conceded all its *imperium* and power to the Emperor]. *Vindiciae* 100, 131–2, 153.

[138] There was also in the law of persons a *vindicatio in ingenuitatem*, to restore one's personal status to that of a freeborn person, *ingenuus*. *Vindicta* also carried a more general sense of an act of vengeance for wrongdoing.

[139] *Francogallia* 214–15, 310–11.

[140] *Vindiciae* 153, 167, 168, 170 [*Vindiciae* 1579: 207–08, 210, 213]. The *vindicatio in libertatem* is mentioned explicitly at 101. See also Mary Nyquist, *Arbitrary Rule: Slavery, Tyranny and the Power of Life and Death* (Chicago: University of Chicago Press, 2013) 72–3.

[141] D.50.16.215, 42.1.63; 6.1.1.1.

[142] The Praetorian edict, however, later provided interdicts, such as the *unde vi* and the *uti possidetis*, designed to protect possessory claims, so as to avoid the costly "wagers of law" requiring a judge to determine *dominium*. John Anthony Crook, *Law and Life of Rome* (Ithaca: Cornell University Press, 1967) 146.

was its permanence. Once the question of title was formally adjudicated, there were very few limitations on the *dominus*.[143] He was, at least with respect to the property he has recovered, absolute in his right.

Here then is the point. If the people can be said to have *dominium* over the powers of the kingdom, then the *universitas populi* should also have the right to lay a claim [*vindicant*] against tyrannical kings who were in wrongful possession of power.[144] It is in this juridical language of vindication, as a show of ultimate and supreme right, that the Monarchomachs justified the legality of resistance. Brutus exemplified this argument from *vindicatio*, referencing it even in the title of his treatise. It explains why Brutus insisted repeatedly on identifying the people as "the owner of the commonwealth" [*dominus reipublicae*].[145] As *dominus*, the people permanently reserved the rights of ownership, even while the *respublica* was in the care and possession of kings.[146] Moreover, because the people was in the juridical position of the *dominus*, they could recover, by an action approximating the *vindicatio*, the powers of those who acted on the authority granted by the people, but especially those who acted contrary to the interests of the people who constituted them in the first place.

To be sure, the Monarchomach appropriation of the *vindicatio* was by no means a justification of mob violence as such. Nor was it a general justification of all private acts of resistance and disobedience.[147] Consistent with Pauline doctrine in Scripture, the Monarchomachs were careful to condemn such acts, precisely because they regarded them as seditious acts of private individuals [*privati* or *singuli*], not as legitimate constitutional acts of the whole people [*universi*].[148] Vindication of popular sovereignty, on the Monarchomach view, could only be attributable to the whole people, as a public act, because it is the people represented as a whole [*universi*], and not as an aggregate of individuals [*singuli*], that is properly *dominus* and, therefore, entitled to vindicate. Lawful resistance could, thus, only be activated through well-ordered and recognized procedures which represented and expressed the corporate will of the whole people, not simply through the actions of one individual or even a part or

[143] Jolowicz, *Historical Introduction* Ch. 10. Buckland, *Text-Book on Roman Law* 188–89, Andrew Borkowski and Paul du Plessis, *Textbook on Roman Law*, 3rd ed. (Oxford: Oxford University Press, 2005) 159–60.

[144] *Vindiciae* 159 [*Vindiciae* 1579: 211].

[145] *Vindiciae* 1579: 205.

[146] *Vindiciae* 167 [*Vindiciae* 1579: 208] gives the example of the Jews, who, by their resistance to the tyrant, Antiochus, "recovered possession of the kingdom . . . and vindicated [*vendicarint*] to themselves the royal dignity which belonged [*pertinebat*] to the tribe of Judah."

[147] As is well known, Brutus makes one exception for private acts of resistance, in the case of a "tyrant without title" at *Vindiciae* 150: "It is lawful for any private person [*privatus quislibet*] to oust this sort of tyrant, were he to force his way in." But such tyrants are not technically rulers to whom obedience is ever due. Thus, resistance in those cases is a justifiable act of self-defense, because one may repel force with force [*vim vi repellere licet*], as Bartolus suggests in his comment on D.43.16.3 in *De Guelphis et Gebellinis*, cited by Brutus at *Vindiciae* 157. On self-defense, see Kathleen Parrow, *From Defense to Resistance: Justification of Violence During the French Wars of Religion* (Philadelphia: American Philosophical Society, 1993).

[148] See above about symmetry of rights. Since it was the whole people (as represented in the estates and orders of the realm) that constituted the king originally, it must, by symmetry, only be the whole people that can remove the king. Often this point is discussed through the principle of D.50.17.35.

faction of the people. For the whole people to act legally, such as in a *vindicatio*, it must be done through constituted representatives or agents, just as a private corporation had to act through its properly constituted agent.

But the problem with this suggestion is that, in medieval legal thought, the king was supposed to be that agent or *actor*, who represented and acted for the whole corporate body of the people, as a *universitas populi*. Thus, there appears to be a difficulty in the argument, since it makes the king both the *agent*, as well as the *target*, of lawful resistance: it would implausibly require the king to resist himself. To circumvent this difficulty, Brutus specifies that, while the king is certainly the most important agent lawfully constituted by the people, he is not the only one.

He reminds his readers that all public officers of the realm as well as the nobility who assemble in the estates and orders of the realm are all to be considered agents duty-bound before God to represent the whole people. In this capacity, they are, as we have observed earlier, "partners in command" [*consortes imperii*] alongside the king. So, when the Monarchomachs speak of popular resistance through popularly constituted agents, as a public act of the people or *universitas populi*, they mean specifically the assembled officers and peers of the estates, in their official representative and "ephoral" capacity as intermediate agents between the king and the people.[149]

Thus, the simple Roman law model of the *dominus*, while compelling, was nevertheless incomplete, because it neglected to account for the unique intermediate juridical position of the estates and orders, as a third party. To account for this, Brutus introduced one final model from the civil law to elucidate the tripartite constitutional relationship between king–officer/estates–people, and explain how a king might be lawfully resisted and removed by an act of vindication.

This was the practice of co-tutorship in the Roman law guardianship. Earlier, we saw that the law of guardianship positioned the people to be like a *pupillus*, incapacitated by age from exercising their *dominium*, while the king was to be like a *tutor* or guardian, who was appointed legally to represent and "bear the person of the *domini*" [*personam domini sustinet*] and oversee the administration of the ward's estate [*rem pupilli administrat*].[150]

Suppose, however, that a guardian engages in criminal behavior during his administration of the estate—for example, by embezzling the ward's estate—or simply fails to carry out his duties, on account of "laziness, boorishness, inertia, or ineptitude."[151] What remedies for such maladministration would

[149] This is just another way of stating the Calvinist doctrine of ephoral resistance by "popular magistrates." Brutus sometimes portrays the role of the officers and estates as a kind of third-party judge or arbiter to enforce the contract between the king and the people. In this capacity, he calls public officers of the kingdom "judges and vindicators"—comparable to the Roman praetor—and "the vindicators and custodians of this covenant." *Vindiciae* 169, 179 [*Vindiciae* 1579: 211: *iudices et vindices*; 215: *Huius vero foederis seu pacti, regni officiarii vindices & custodes sunt*]. For Brutus' analysis of ephors, see *Vindiciae* 46, 80, 89, 131, and 166.

[150] D.47.2.56.4. [151] D.26.10.3.5, 26.10.3.18.

be available to the ward? In principle, the Roman law allowed the removal of such "untrustworthy guardians" by pleading an *actio tutelae*.[152] The difficulty with the *actio tutelae*, however, was that the *dominus* could only recover the lost property at the end of the tutelage, once a full accounting [*ratio*] of the guardian's administration has been concluded. The damage would have already been done.

Thus, in order to avoid this precarious situation and minimize the ward's exposure to injury during the tutelage, Roman law allowed for the appointment of multiple guardians, as co-tutors, to share in the administration of an estate, but also to keep all other tutors under constant mutual surveillance so as to ensure the overall protection of the ward's estate and interests. In this arrangement, primary day-to-day responsibility for administration would rest legally with an appointed principal tutor, whose actions would in turn be reviewed by the co-tutors.[153] But if any one of the tutors, including especially the principal tutor, proves to be untrustworthy [*suspectus*], the other co-tutors must sue to legally relieve him from his duties. If they do not do so, culpability is subsequently to be "imputed" [*imputatur*] to all co-tutors who are all made liable for inaction in restraining the offending tutor.[154] All co-tutors, thus, have a positive duty to have "untrustworthy" guardians "removed" [*remotus*].

It is this Roman law doctrine of co-tutorial responsibility which answered the need for a juristic model explaining the unique role of the estates of the realm. Officers and peers are jointly responsible with the king for sharing administration of the *respublica*, just as co-tutors are jointly responsible with the principal tutor for sharing administration of the *res pupilli*:

> Nobles should understand that they are called upon to share the burden as well as the honour, and that the commonwealth is assuredly committed and entrusted to the king as its supreme and principal tutor [*supremo eius ac praecipuo tutori*], but to them as co-tutors. Therefore, just as tutors—even honorary ones [*etiam honorarii*]—are granted as observers of the performance of the person who principally exercises the tutelage [*dati sunt, quasi observatores actus eius, qui tutelam praecipue gerit*], that they might regularly demand an account from him and take great care over how he comports himself [*qui rationem ab eo assidue exigant & sollicite current, qualiter conversetur*]; so the leading men are given to observe the king—who is deemed to be in the place of lord in so far as this is in the ward's interests.[155]

Moreover, because officers and nobles are legally in the position of co-tutors, they share co-tutorial responsibility for monitoring the actions of other officers of the realm, a point which he stresses by comparing them to joint promissory parties.[156] This introduces a very important shift in the argument for resistance since, as Brutus now argues, it is not only "lawful [for public officers and

[152] D.26.1.14.4. [153] D.26.7.3.2. [154] D.26.7.14.

[155] *Vindiciae* 158–59 [*Vindiciae* 1579: 197]. Freegard observes that Brutus' text is lifted verbatim straight from D.26.7.3.2 and 26.7.27.

[156] *Vindiciae* 166. Garnett cites C.4.2.5, D.45.2.18, 45.2.2, 45.2.3.1 on joint obligations.

peers]...to restrain a tyrant...but their office makes it incumbent on them to such a degree that, if they have not done so, they cannot be excused [*excusari*] in any way."[157] Inaction to prevent or stop tyranny makes them as fully and equally liable as the tyrannical king, as Brutus explains:

> Just as the deed of the tutor who is in charge is imputed to the co-tutors [*contutoribus imputatur*] if, when they should and could do so, they do not place him under suspicion, and also ensure that he is removed; and as this is assuredly the case if he does not keep them informed about his administration, if he does not faithfully perform his tutelage or charge, if he admits to deception, if he acts unbecomingly and perniciously towards his ward, if he appropriates some of his ward's possessions or is hostile to his ward; in short, if he is excessively boorish, dilatory, or incompetent, and so on; so also, the leading men are liable for the deeds of the prince if they do not abrogate or stand in the way of his tyranny, or do not make up for his inactivity by their own vigilance and diligence.[158]

Popular resistance as a vindication of popular *dominium* is, thus, to be mediated indirectly in this way through the human agency of the officers and peers of the realm, acting collectively in a co-tutorial capacity representing the *universitas populi*:

> For just as a ward cannot bring an action except by the agency of his tutor, even though the ward is in fact the real owner [*dominus vere*]...so the people cannot do so, except by the agency of those to whom it has transferred its authority and power [*in quos suam authoritatem & potestatem transtulit*], whether they be ordinary magistrates, or created extraordinarily in the public assembly [*in conventu publico extra ordinem creati*].[159]

This seems to suggest that, in practice, popular resistance was not really to be "popular" at all, but merely a "collegial power" of the estates.[160] We are led, then, to ask: "Must ephoral resistance always be a unanimous act, involving the participation of every public officer and peer of the realm?" The answer is, surprisingly, and notoriously, no, as Brutus spells out in the most radical

[157] *Vindiciae* 158 [*Vindiciae* 1579: 196]. *Excusari* is likely referring to the rubric on "excuses" of D.27.1 and C.5.62, discussing the various admissible "excuses" the prospective guardians may legally plead to avoid service. Brutus' point is that co-tutors cannot lawfully "excuse" themselves from their joint duty of removing untrustworthy tutors.

[158] *Vindiciae* 159 [*Vindiciae* 1579: 197–8]. Freegard again locates the close wording of this text in D.26.7.14, 26.10.3.18, quoted above, and 26.10.3.5.

[159] *Vindiciae* 169 [*Vindiciae* 1579: 210–11]. Notice, however, that Brutus now excludes the king as being among "those to whom [the people] has transferred its authority and power." Popular constitutional action is corporately to be mediated only through the estates. Note also the difference in the application of corporation theory between Baldus and Brutus. While both agree that the human agency through which a corporation acts need not be its appointed head or executive, as in the minority thesis, Brutus does not take the explicitly democratic turn that Baldus does, where the individual members of the corporation themselves may directly and collectively act for the corporation.

[160] Giesey, "The Monarchomach Triumvirs: Hotman, Beza, and Mornay" 51. This is because, as Garnett observes, "the author has as yet only advanced an argument for the 'collegial power' of the officers, based on their [collective] participation in the coronation ceremony." Garnett n.595 in *Vindiciae* 158.

pages of the *Vindiciae*, inspired by the Scriptural examples of Moses, Ehud, Jehu, and Deborah, extraordinarily commissioned by God to wipe out tyranny and avenge the injustices of kings.[161]

While it is true, under the corporation theory, that "anything which is done publicly is considered to have been done by all," public acts are, by definition, acts of a representational fiction.[162] It allows one to imagine a public actor to be something other than "the public" itself—an assembly of notables, orders and estates, a college of magistrates. What is most exceptional about Brutus is that he pushes this line of reasoning to the most extreme possible conclusion, suggesting that even a private person—"called extraordinarily" [*extra ordinem vocatus*] and "girded... with His [God's] sword" [*suo gladio. . .accingente*]—might, as an individual, also be a public person, even a champion of the people's liberty and sovereign rights, "raise[d] up [to be] *vindicator* [*vindice*] against tyranny from amongst private men."[163] Just as a representative body of magistrates or nobles may speak and act for the people, so too could a single individual in the most extraordinary circumstances.

CONCLUSION

Ralph Giesey once warned that, "To ignore or dismiss the Huguenot writers' use of Roman law is to affront their intelligence or their integrity."[164] Indeed, it is not, I think, an overstatement to say that the Monarchomach theory of popular sovereignty and the popular constitution of authority could not have taken the shape it did without the background of Roman law that supplied the basic conceptual material. The bottom line is that, without Roman law, there could not have been a Monarchomach theory. Given its centrality to the Monarchomach arguments for popular resistance and sovereignty, critical engagement with Roman legal thought was unavoidable among later detractors of Hotman and Brutus, such as William Barclay and Jean de Baricave, who produced critical refutations which incorporated careful discussions of the Roman law sources cited in the Monarchomach tracts.[165]

Having investigated the civilian background of the monarchomach theory and, in particular, their use of juridical concepts of property and exclusivity associated with the *dominium*, let me now conclude this chapter by way of stressing two related observations on the legacy of the Monarchomachs and their theory of popular sovereignty. The first general observation concerns the extent to which the French Monarchomach theory was appropriated by later

[161] *Vindiciae* 62. Brutus here relies on an important distinction in the *ius commune* theory of delegation between "ordinary constitution" and "extraordinary appointment" of subordinate authorities. Garnett reads this as a case of "extraordinary vocation," but there is a juridical element in public law that originates in both civil and canon law on delegated judges, continuing into later public law theory. See Chapters 5 and 6, on Bodin's use of the distinction in the theory of sovereignty.

[162] D.50.17.160. [163] *Vindiciae* 62, 171 [*Vindiciae* 1579: 68, 213].

[164] Giesey, "The Monarchomach Triumvirs" 53.

[165] Jean de Baricave, *La Defense de la Monarchie* (1614) 641–4.

thinkers to advance political causes, which were, in some cases, far removed from the immediate ideological context of the French Wars of Religion and the Huguenot struggle against the Catholic monarchy.[166] Recent historical scholarship has supplied us with numerous studies charting the various intellectual influences of Monarchomach thought in anti-royalist struggles across Europe, including the Dutch Revolt, the deposition of Queen Mary in Scotland, and, in the seventeenth century, the English Revolution.[167]

Perhaps most remarkable was the direct appropriation of the Monarchomach doctrine by Catholics who, in facing the possibility of a Huguenot king in France through the accession of Henri of Navarre at the extinction of the Valois line, exploited the doctrine of the deposition of heretical kings. Like the Huguenot Monarchomachs, these theorists of the French Catholic League, which included writers such as Jean Boucher, developed theoretical defenses for resistance largely mirroring the same sort of arguments found in the Monarchomach treatises.[168] In the case of Boucher's *De Iusta Abdicatione Henrici Tertii*, the argument was taken almost *verbatim* from the *Vindiciae* to defend the notion of resistance against the prospect of a heretical non-Catholic sovereign.[169] That such a set of doctrines as those articulated originally by Huguenot monarchomachs would eventually find its way into the hands of Catholic Leaguers testifies to the versatility as well as even the ideological ambiguity of popular sovereignty doctrine in this period of religious violence and constitutional crisis.

The reason for this remarkable versatility must be sought in the very idea of sovereignty itself, as deployed in the Monarchomach theories, and it is here that I wish to make a second and final observation. By framing the sovereignty of the people, as well as the people's constitutional relationship with the king and his government, in the juridical language of *dominium* and related private law concepts such as usufruct and guardianship, the Monarchomachs reveal themselves to be the direct heirs of the humanist analysis of jurisdictional authority. What makes the people "sovereign" or "supreme" over kings is their resolute belief that all public powers of the realm, even those of the monarch and the rights attached to the royal domain, are always "proper" and "exclusive" to the people as a whole, just as if they are, corporately, a *dominus*. Even

[166] Some excellent studies of this are J.H.M. Salmon, "The Legacy of Jean Bodin: Absolutism, Populism, or Constitutionalism?" *History of Political Thought* 17 (1996); Van Gelderen, *The Political Thought of the Dutch Revolt*; Van Gelderen, "Aristotelians, Monarchomachs and Republicanism: Sovereignty and *Respublica Mixta* in Dutch and German Political Thought."

[167] Skinner, *Foundations* 2:338ff, especially 344 concerning the phrase, *proprie pertinet*, in Buchanan's Monarchomach text, *De Iure Regni Apud Scotos*, indicating a relationship between popular possession and ultimate control of the Scottish crown.

[168] This is a central reason why Barclay has no hesitation in regarding the Catholic Ligeur writers such as Jean Boucher to be Monarchomachs as much as Brutus and Hotman. Catholic resistance theorists were to be condemned equally as Huguenot resistance theorists.

[169] Figgis, *From Gerson to Grotius* 159; J.H.M. Salmon, "Catholic Resistance Theory, Ultramontanism, and the Royalist Response, 1580-1620," *Cambridge History of Political Thought, 1450–1700*, ed. J.H. Burns and Mark Goldie (Cambridge: Cambridge University Press, 1991).

though a king may, within limits, exercise or use the people's powers, those powers nevertheless belong to the people, just as if it were their "property," at all times subject to the people's control and will.

This was, for the Monarchomachs, not to be a doctrine specific only to the case of one particular nation, such as France. Indeed, by meticulously applying the analysis to nations of both Antiquity and modernity, the Monarchomachs were very careful to stress what was perhaps their most important and lasting contribution to early modern thought, that popular sovereignty was to be a uniform, unchanging model of the source of public authority in all nations, a grand unified theory of sovereignty. The people *always* bear the proper and exclusive right of sovereignty. This is, of course, easily observable in republican polities such as Geneva, Venice, and the Dutch Low Countries, where popular sovereignty is reflected in the governing institutions constituted so as to embrace popular political participation. But even in nations, such as France and England, where monarchs govern with full authority, it is really the people, behind the scenes, that authorize such monarchies to rule, as an agent or deputy or even tutor, acting on behalf of the people. It is, as we shall see, a powerful source of inspiration for early modern theorists of anti-monarchical republicanism and radical constitutionalist thought. But it also becomes one of the key points undergirding the constitutional thought of the most important early modern theorist of sovereignty, Jean Bodin.

5

The Roman Law Foundations of Bodin's Early Doctrine of Sovereignty

INTRODUCTION

In a striking passage in his *Six Livres de la République*, Jean Bodin (c.1530–1596) delivered what was perhaps his most direct reply to the Monarchomach theory of popular resistance:

> They which have written of the dutie of magistrats, & other such like books, have deceived themselves, in maintaining that the power of the people is greater than the prince; a thing which oft times causeth the true subiects to reuolt from the obedience which they owe vnto their soueraigne prince, & ministreth matter of great toubles in Commonweals.[1]

The chief error in their reasoning, according to Bodin, was the assignment of the "ephoral" functions of surveillance and, *in extremis*, of the deposition of unlawful or tyrannical princes to magistrates, as a public charge attached to their capacity as representatives of the people. Citing the famous passage in Calvin's *Institutes*, which specified what appeared to be a public legal right of resistance to tyranny, actionable through "magistrats appointed for the defence of the people, and to restraine the insolencie of kings...[and] to resist and impeach their licentiousnesse and crueltie" such as the Demarchs of Athens, the Ephors of Sparta, and the Tribunes of Rome, Bodin explains that such ephoral resistance can only apply lawfully in "popular and Aristocratique states of Commonweales," where the highest public official of a state—even those bearing the title or cipher of "king" or "prince"—is nevertheless bound and limited by popular legislation.[2]

But in a "right Monarchie" such as France, where absolute sovereign authority resides in the king alone, no magistrate can ever have such a right, or even

[1] *Commonweale* 95 [1.8]; *République* 137–38; *De Republica* 89.

[2] *Commonweale* 224–25 [2.5]. John Calvin, "On Civil Government," in *Luther and Calvin: On Secular Authority*, ed. Harro Höpfl (Cambridge: Cambridge University Press, 1991) 82–3 [*Institutio Christianiae Religionis* IV, Ch. 20, §31]. As Richard Tuck observes, Bodin conveniently omits Calvin's statement that "in current circumstances, the authority exercised by the three estates in individual kingdoms when they hold their principal assemblies is of the same kind" [of authority as ephors, tribunes, and demarchs]. Calvin, "On Civil Government" 83. Tuck, *Sleeping Sovereign*.

duty, of resistance comprehended as part of his office, and that is precisely because the very source of all magisterial authority in France is the *princeps* himself, never the *populus*.[3] For a magistrate to resist the very source of his public right and authority would be an act of contradiction. Thus, any act of resistance to a sovereign authority, even to a wicked or tyrannical authority—whether by magistrates, or even directly by the people themselves—is "never lawfull" and to be condemned not only as an act performed without right, but as an act breaking the solemn bond of obligation all subjects in a monarchy owe to their sovereign prince, the duty of non-resistance.[4]

The overall coherence of Bodin's reply to the Monarchomach theory, as commentators have long observed, depended on a grand unified theory of sovereignty that permitted no legally enforceable limitation—whether by estates, magistrates, or subjects—on the prince's sovereign authority.[5] The very essence of sovereign authority, as Bodin would put it, is to be released, unbound, absolved, or "free from law" [*legibus soluta*].[6] Legally speaking, then, a sovereign prince owes nothing to his subjects: He is unreservedly free to exercise his sovereign authority however he wishes—even impiously or wickedly, if he so chooses. It is even his sovereign *right* to do so. Because a sovereign prince is free from all legal obligation, there can be no binding obligations for a subject to enforce or impose upon a sovereign. As a result, subjects are left with no legal grounds for an independent or residual right of resistance or contestation.[7] Whatever right they *do* have, such as the right of remonstrance

[3] The term, "right Monarchie" [*droit Monarchie*] or "royal" monarchy, has a technical meaning in Bodin's thought, to be distinguished from "lordly" or *seigneuriale* monarchy. Bodin discusses the difference in Book II of the *République*, which turns on whether monarchical authority is discharged through law or through the arbitrary will of the sovereign prince. See Lee, "Office Is a Thing Borrowed" 412–20.

[4] *Commonweale* 220, 225 [2.5]. This preexisting bond of obligation between sovereign and subject is what allows him to argue that foreign princes, who are under no such bond, are free to depose or kill another tyrannical prince.

[5] For example, Julian Franklin, "Sovereignty and the Mixed Constitution: Bodin and His Critics," *Cambridge History of Political Thought, 1450–1700*, ed. J.H. Burns and Mark Goldie (Cambridge: Cambridge University Press, 1991) 308–9. Franklin argues that the theory of sovereignty in the *République* is a "revision" from an earlier analysis in the *Methodus*, which, he argues, did imply certain limits. As I will argue in the following chapters, there is no evidence for such a shift. In this respect, Preston King and Richard Tuck are right to point out the continuity, rather than discontinuity, between the two works.

[6] *Commonweale* 14. Bodin uses the phrase *potestas legibus soluta* in the Latin *De Republica* in his famous definition of sovereignty at 78, 80, 82, 84 [1.8]. The source of this formulation in the Roman law maxim, *princeps legibus solutus*, is obvious.

[7] Of course, Bodin recognizes that subjects can, and do, resist by force. Bodin's point is simply to say that such an act of resistance is fundamentally an *illegal*—or perhaps, more accurately, an *extralegal*—act. There are several further points of nuance in Bodin's doctrine. Sovereigns may be free of *legal* obligation, but they are not free of other types of obligations, such as *moral* obligations (governed by natural law) and especially *contractual* obligations. As Julian Franklin rightly observes, violations of natural law are not enforceable by ordinary process of law. Contractual obligations, however, are of a different category altogether—and it is one reason why Bodin insists that "law" and "contract" are not the same thing. Both are obligation-creating devices, but contracts are, in Bodin's view, bilateral: they create obligations binding on all parties to a contract, including even sovereigns. No party to a contract, whether sovereign or not, may unilaterally exempt themselves from performance of contractual obligations, on Bodin's view.

in the Parlement, is nothing more than a mere privilege granted—so went the theory—by sufferance of the king.[8]

The *République* was, even by early modern standards, a monumental work. The first edition was over seven hundred pages and later expanded, partly in response to critics, to over one thousand pages in subsequent editions.[9] Yet, despite its vast scope on a wide range of topics, it was Bodin's reply to the Monarchomachs that became the focus of special attention, scrutinized both by royalists and radicals in the context of civil war. By justifying the legal impermissibility of resistance chiefly as a logical consequence of absolute sovereignty, Bodin positioned himself right in the crossfire of ideological conflict between the Huguenots and the French Catholic League.

It is not surprising, then, that Bodin's treatise became an instant target for criticism, which began almost immediately after its publication in 1576. Indeed, as early as 1577—only one year after the original publication of the *République*—the Genevan theologian, Simon Goulart, who oversaw an unauthorized publication of Bodin's treatise, would comment critically on what he saw as Bodin's deliberate misconstrual of the theory of magisterial authority in Calvin's *Institutes* to disempower subjects from the right of resistance.[10] Two years later, in 1579, a potentially more damaging criticism was deployed by Michel de La Serre who published the *Remonstrance au Roy*, actually charging Bodin with tacit Monarchomach sympathies in acknowledging the permissibility of foreign princes deposing tyrannical rulers.[11] Perhaps most remarkable is that, despite his personal and—as Ann Blair has persuasively shown—strategically calculated efforts to address these very criticisms, above all, in a pseudonymous reply to critics entitled the *Apologie de René Herpin pour la République de Jean Bodin* (originally in 1581, and then as an appendix to the 1583 revised edition of the *République*), Bodin's emphatic rejection of the legality of resistance to sovereign authority continues to shape the modern interpretation and understanding of his political theory in a way that treats him not only as an opponent of liberal rights and democratic constitutionalism but, most strikingly, as a prophet of precisely the sort of crude, lawless, arbitrary princely "absolutism" that he himself expressly rejected.[12]

[8] On the right of remonstrance, see Church, *Constitutional Thought* 136–50, on the view of remonstrances as potential limitations on French royal authority and the corresponding uses of the *lit de justice*.

[9] The Paris octavo edition ofJacqes du Puys, 1583, is regarded as the standard "text that scholars commonly cite." Julian Franklin, "Note on the Text," in his abridged Cambridge edition, *Jean Bodin: On Sovereignty* (Cambridge: Cambridge University Press, 1992) xxxvi.

[10] On Goulart, see Tuck, *Sleeping Sovereign* and Ann Blair, "Authorial Strategies in Jean Bodin," *The Reception of Bodin* (Leiden: Brill, 2013).

[11] Jean Bodin, *Apologie de René Herpin pour la République de Jean Bodin* (Paris, 1581) 4; Blair, "Authorial Strategies" 149.

[12] I have developed this argument in "Office Is a Thing Borrowed" and show Bodin's deep suspicion of *seigneurial* princes who, by definition, govern not according to law, but only according to arbitrary will, such as the Turks and Muscovites.

As I suggest below, however, this "absolutist" understanding of Bodin is now being scrutinized, such as in Loughlin, *Foundations of Public Law* 56–73, and Tuck, *Sleeping Sovereign*, Lecture 1. To be sure, it has not always been this way. Late nineteenth and early twentieth century scholarship on the history of political

But to view Bodin primarily—or even exclusively—as an anti-Monarchomach ideologue and royal absolutist is to misunderstand fundamentally the sheer breadth and systematic elegance of his thought. Pierre Bayle would regard him as one of early modern France's finest thinkers.[13] No modern scholar has done more to cement Bodin's reputation as the quintessential theorist of early modern absolutism and, by default, a sworn enemy of constitutionalism than Julian Franklin who, without reservation, denounced Bodin's doctrine of sovereignty as "a mistake," "a seductive but erroneous notion," and "a source of much confusion" in early modern political thought.[14] In a series of studies that has become something of an interpretive orthodoxy—most influentially in *Jean Bodin and the Rise of Absolutist Theory* (1973)—Franklin dissected Bodin's theory of sovereignty to show how, by denying any right of resistance or contestation as the Calvinists had argued, Bodin ensured that "a legal path was opened to autocracy."[15] Indeed, in Franklin's reading of Bodin, no doubt shaped by a distaste for the legal positivism in the tradition of John Austin, the elimination of all legally enforceable limitations on a prince's sovereign authority rendered the people of the political community virtually powerless.[16]

From this analysis, Franklin was able to conclude that Bodin's "idea of sovereignty is monarchical in connotation."[17] Sovereignty, he argues, can never belong to the whole political community or people precisely because the very idea of sovereignty "suggests the sway or dominion of one person over others,

thought often viewed him in precisely the opposite way, as a champion of the rule of law in the modern state, such as the classic study of Jean Moreau-Reibel, *J. Bodin et le Droit Public Comparé dans ses Rapports avec la Philosophie de l'Histoire* (Paris: Vrin, 1933). "The ideal of Bodin," Myron Piper Gilmore wrote in 1941, "was a constitutional ideal." Gilmore, *Argument from Roman Law* 109. And Ralph Giesey, in a brilliant article, demonstrated Bodin's "anti-absolutism" by a study of the juristic apparatus of medieval jurisprudence in "Medieval Jurisprudence in Bodin's Concept of Sovereignty," *Verhandlungen der Internationalen Bodin Tagung in München*, ed. Horst Denzer (München: C.H. Beck, 1973) 172. But, given the unrelenting criticism of sovereignty in modern legal and political thought by detractors of John Austin's legal positivism and, especially in the aftermath of World War II, by skeptics of the Westphalian international order, it was inevitable that Bodin's treatment of sovereignty as an "absolute power" would not escape scrutiny. One modern commentator has even regarded his work as the "apex of absolutist thought." Murray Rothbard, "Jean Bodin: Apex of Absolutist Thought in France," *An Austrian Perspective on the History of Economic Thought: Economic Thought Before Adam Smith*, Vol. 1 (Aldershot: E. Elgar, 1995). On the dating of the *Apologie*, Blair, "Authorial Strategies in Jean Bodin," 149.

[13] Pierre Bayle, *Dictionnaire Historique et Critique* (Rotterdam, 1720) 1:582, cited in John Brown, *The Methodus ad Facilem Historiarum Cognitionem of Jean Bodin: A Critical Study* (Washington: Catholic University Press, 1939) xi. Bodin's later writings on natural philosophy and religion would earn him the reputation of being an atheist and, indeed, the (dis)honor of having three of his books, including the *Methodus* and the *République*, listed on the *Index Librorum Prohibitorum*, the Vatican's official list of forbidden books. Paul Grendler, "Printing and Censorship," *Cambridge History of Renaissance Philosophy*, ed. C.B. Schmitt and Quentin Skinner (Cambridge: Cambridge University Press, 1988) 48.

[14] Julian Franklin, "Introduction," *Jean Bodin: On Sovereignty* (Cambridge: Cambridge University Press, 1992) xvii; Franklin, "Sovereignty and the Mixed Constitution" 298.

[15] Franklin, *Jean Bodin and the Rise of Absolutist Theory* 103.

[16] Charles Howard McIlwain, "Sovereignty," *Constitutionalism and the Changing World* (Cambridge: Cambridge University Press, 1939) 33.

[17] Franklin, *Jean Bodin and the Rise of Absolutist Theory* 26.

the first ruling and the others being ruled," a relationship that "does not obtain in any obvious or determinate sense" in a pure democracy.[18] In consequence, Franklin closes off entirely the possibility that Bodin might have allowed a doctrine of popular sovereignty.

The chief problem with this conclusion, however, is that it confuses *popular sovereignty* with *popular resistance*. This equation, as I hope to show, is a fundamental mistake. Sovereign acts of a constitutionally free and independent people need not be understood in terms of "resistance" at all, particularly since it assumes that the *target* of such resistance also has a better claim or title to sovereignty.[19] Bodin was—it is true—no friend to democracy, and he was certainly no Monarchomach radical agitating for resistance.[20] Yet, he was careful to observe that even democratic or "popular" states can be fully entitled to the right of sovereignty—what he variously designated in his own writings in Latin as *maiestas, summum imperium, summa potestas,* and *suverenitas*—just as much as a monarchical state. One does not need to be a democrat or Monarchomach to recognize the constitutional legitimacy of popular sovereignty as a valid form of sovereign authority, as Bodin quite clearly did. Indeed, the "popular form of state" [*status reipublicae popularis*] was one of three equally legitimate forms of state identified in Bodin's constitutional theory, alongside monarchy and aristocracy. It was, as he defined it, the state in which sovereignty was invested in the *populus*, a constitutional form which, he argued, could be observed in the history of states as diverse as Athens, Rome, Florence, and Geneva.[21]

What I hope to do then in this chapter, and the next, is to dismantle the interpretive orthodoxy that Bodin was fundamentally hostile to popular sovereignty. On the contrary, Bodin deserves to be properly recognized as perhaps the most important systematic early modern theorist of popular sovereignty, so much so, that the modern conceptual "shape" or "architecture" of popular sovereignty, as exemplified in the thought of modern political theorists such as Locke, Rousseau, and Sieyès, could not have taken the form it did without the foundational work pioneered in Bodin's comprehensive system of legal and political thought. It was Bodin who explained why a state that, at first glance, may appear to be manifestly undemocratic in form—such as Athens under

[18] Franklin, *Jean Bodin and the Rise of Absolutist Theory* 26. Franklin conveniently overlooks Bodin's response to precisely this sort of criticism of the conceptual coherence of popular sovereignty in *République* 99 [1.8], and again at 244 [2.7].

[19] The proper term, I argue, should not be "popular resistance," but rather what Philip Pettit has recently termed "popular control"—i.e., the control of a sovereign people over public institutions and agents. Pettit, *On the People's Terms* 160.

[20] Yet, it should also be noted that Bodin was a deputy in the Estates General of 1576 and favored enforcing limitations on the ability of the monarchy to alienate the domain, a policy that led to his fall from favor of the royal court and ended up costing him a royal appointment to a magistracy.

[21] Indeed, Bodin's classification of Geneva as a "popular state" was one of the chief "errors" in the *République* that Goulart hoped to rectify in the unauthorized Geneva edition of 1577. The problem with Franklin's reading is that he has no way to explain Bodin's quite extensive discussion of popular sovereignty as it operated in these sorts of states—above all, in the Roman Republic and the Roman Principate before Vespasian.

Pericles or the Roman Principate under Augustus—could nevertheless be constitutionally organized according to a doctrine of popular sovereignty.

Two points are essential in establishing the coherence of Bodin's doctrine of popular sovereignty. The first is his view that a "people" can, as a collective body, have the juridical position and status of a person, like a corporation, fully capable of performing legal—indeed, even sovereign—acts.[22] In this respect, Bodin was merely following an established traditon of legal thought originating in medieval jurisprudence. The second, and perhaps more important point, is Bodin's critical distinction between "sovereignty" and "government," a distinction that would become central to later political theorists, such as Hobbes, Pufendorf, and Rousseau, as Richard Tuck has recently shown.[23] What Bodin's theory allows is a sovereign people to delegate its sovereignty to legally constituted government agents to *exercise* sovereignty on their behalf while, at the same time, reserving the bare *right* of sovereignty to be reactivated only in extraordinary moments of crisis. In this way, Bodin tries to tame popular sovereignty by the constitutional means of lawful delegation.

In this chapter, I begin the analysis of Bodin's theory of delegated sovereignty as a preliminary to investigating his theory of delegated popular sovereignty, as it is presented in the *République* in Chapter 6. Bodin's treatment of these issues appears in his first major published work, the *Methodus ad Facilem Historiarum Cognitionem* of 1566, published a decade before the appearance of the *République*. The work deserves close attention not only because it presented a "detailed draft" of the constitutional theory of sovereignty that would appear in a more complete form in Bodin's later writings.[24] The *Methodus* displayed, in full view, the framework of Bodin's reasoning in the juridical language of legal science—that is, the Roman law—which Bodin had studied and, for a short time, taught at the University of Toulouse. It was, as Martin Loughlin has recently described it, a "prospectus for a new type of jurisprudence."[25] And as Myron Piper Gilmore once observed, "there can be no doubt that he [Bodin] first approached the problem of the organization of authority from an

[22] *De Republica* 92 [1.8], speaking of the *populus universus* and its unique capacity to enter and dissolve obligations. The marginal citation is to D.50.17.35, which establishes the principle that an obligation contracted by parties, whether *singuli* or *universi*, can only be dissolved by those parties. Cp. *République* 11–12 [1.2], which indicates Bodin's view that a "people" retains its identity through time, like Theseus' ship, and "never dies" so long as the sovereignty remains unchanged, citing D.7.1.56 on "perpetuity" and especially 5.1.76, establishing the continuity of identity and authority over time of such compound bodies as collegial courts, legions, and peoples, all of which are specific examples of "a thing being considered the same after its parts had been changed." The idea of the immortality of the people, who "never die," appears again at *Commonweale* 472 [4.3]. Franklin is simply incorrect when he says, in *Jean Bodin and the Rise of Absolutist Theory* 27, that Bodin has "no theoretical conception of a corporative or fictive" notion of sovereignty or of legal personality as in the law of corporations.

[23] See Tuck, *Sleeping Sovereign*. Here, again, Franklin is simply incorrect. He asserts that there is no conception of a constituent power of the people separable from the constituted power of the government in Bodin's thought. But that is precisely the idea that he has in mind when identifying the sovereign right of a people to constitute or create by law magistrates with ordinary jurisdiction in government.

[24] Brown, *The Methodus* xix.

[25] Loughlin, *Foundations of Public Law* 57.

examination of the Roman constitutional structure."[26] The *Methodus* provides the best evidence of this civilian background.

I proceed, then, as follows. I begin with a discussion of Bodin's early study of Roman law in order to establish more clearly the reasons for his initial engagement with questions of political and constitutional theory. As we shall see, it was by a circuitous route that Bodin came to deal with central questions about the constitutional theory of the state: through a debate on legal methodology with legal humanists. The historical and legal experience of the Romans as embodied in the *Corpus Iuris Civilis*, Bodin argued, could provide only limited guidance in achieving a truly universal science of law. But in order to realize such a legal science, Bodin had to expand the scope of his legal thought beyond the traditional domain of Roman law. It would be necessary to study in a rigorously comparative manner the laws of all historical states, not just the Romans. The *Methodus* dealt directly with practical problems of comparative law and historical methodology arising from such a grand project—including above all the unit of analysis, the state, or *respublica*. Rejecting the Aristotelian analysis of the state, adopted by Renaissance historians, Bodin offered a new analysis that identified its chief defining attribute as *summum imperium*. I offer a close analysis of this concept and illustrate how, despite his own protestations against the historical limitations of Roman law, Bodin's analysis was inseparably tied to the civilian tradition. Sovereignty, here functioning as a tool of historical analysis, turns out to be fundamentally a product of Roman legal science and paves the way for Bodin's distinctive understanding of the delegative relationship between the sovereign authority of the state and the subordinate government agents acting by mandate on its behalf.

UNIVERSAL HISTORY AND LEGAL SCIENCE

Bodin pursued a professional qualification in law—"an indispensable instrument," as one commentator has put it, "for hewing out an official career"—in one of the major centers of legal thought in early modern Europe, the University of Toulouse, to which he moved in around 1550, when he would have been about twenty years old. [27] In the mid-century, Toulouse had a vibrant intellectual and cultural life and hosted students and scholars not only from the south of France, but indeed, from across Europe. The university functioned as a French clearinghouse for Italian humanist philosophy, especially the Renaissance humanist Aristotelianism originating from Padua.[28]

Unlike the University of Bourges, the intellectual home of French legal humanism and its greatest advocate in France, Andrea Alciato, Toulouse remained a bastion of Bartolist legal science.[29] As we have seen, the Bartolist

[26] Gilmore, *Argument from Roman Law* 93–4.

[27] Brown, *The Methodus* 4.

[28] Brown, *The Methodus* 13.

[29] The law faculty of Toulouse was royalist and conservative in its outlook, supportive of the Valois monarchy's grand design for national centralization of royal authority. Allen, *History of Political Thought*

approach privileged the Roman law texts of the *Corpus Iuris Civilis* as the foundation for legal science, assimilable to all legal systems, whether Roman or not. Roman law was not simply the law of the Roman Empire; it was an essential component of the Western *ius commune*, common to all nations, just as the canon law was common to all of Western Christendom.

Bodin's legal training followed this conventional Bartolist curriculum, studying the commentaries on the various titles of civil law. But very quickly he seems to have developed a distaste for the conservative Italianate style of Romanist jurisprudence, which Toulouse had championed. As he would put it, Bartolism simply tried "to join together in a haphazard fashion limbs torn from the whole body of the law."[30] Reflecting later in his life upon his early legal education at Toulouse in the Second Preface to the French edition of the *République*, Bodin would ridicule "those princes of legal science—that is, Bartolus, Baldus, Alexander, Faber, Paulus, and Molinaeus, all outstanding figures—and virtually the whole order of judges and advocates" whom he thought "knew nothing, or very little."[31] The problem, as Bodin saw it, was that Bartolism tried to extract a universal science of law from the written code of one national legal tradition, that of the Romans. As Bodin would put it, Roman law was nothing more than "the legislation of one particular state"—indeed, a state that has ceased to exist for centuries.[32] On this point, the influence of the legal humanists was palpable. The Justinianic texts were cultural artifacts of a dead ancient civilization and, for this reason, should be read from a critical distance.[33]

It was for this reason that Bodin ridiculed the "absurdity of [jurists] attempting to establish principles of universal jurisprudence only from Roman law."[34] While he certainly admitted the technical superiority of Roman jurisprudence, he simply could not accept the medieval interpretive axiom that Roman law might be treated as a universally valid *ius commune*, commanding legal authority even over early modern France and functioning as the basis of a universal legal science.[35]

But as much Bodin resisted the Bartolist approach of the *mos Italicus*, like his legal humanist contemporaries, Bodin was unwilling to adopt the alternative, that is, the legal humanist methodology of the *mos Gallicus* in the manner of

in the Sixteenth Century 280; Brown, *The Methodus* 1–2. Church, *Constitutional Thought* 43, however, takes a more moderate position.

[30] *Methodus* 5.

[31] Translated and reproduced in abridged format by Kenneth McRae in his edition of the Knolles' edition of the *Commonweale* A71.

[32] *Method* 2.

[33] *Methodus* 7–8. Bodin was generally opposed to legal humanism. His target was most certainly Jacques Cujas who was equally critical, in turn, of Bodin's abuse of the civil law for the purposes of civil science.

[34] *Method* 2.

[35] *Commonweale* 108, where he criticizes Baldus "when hee writeth the Italians to bee bound to the Roman lawes." Cp. 17 [1.3], where he describes Justinian as a "blockish and unlearned Prince."

Alciato, Duarenus, and especially Cujas. As Bodin would put it elsewhere, the humanists were no better than "those who begin disputes in schoolboy fashion over words and trivial matters" interested more in "the quantities of syllables [than] in the scales of justice and equity."[36] His immediate target of criticism was perhaps Cujas, whom Bodin scorns as a mere "grammatical pest."[37] But it was a general indictment of the legal humanists who, as he put it, would "prefer to be regarded as grammarians rather than as jurisconsults; who assume a false reputation of knowledge and none of equity; who think that the state is served, judgments decided, and lawsuits settled by the quantities of syllables."[38]

What Bodin saw as absolutely necessary for legal science was an authentic synthesis of the legal methodological insights of Bartolism and legal humanism, yielding an approach that transcended traditional Roman legal science.[39] A single national legal tradition, even that of the Romans, was insufficient for legal science. This was to become the basic methodological axiom for Bodin's new legal science, "that no [single] national tradition could claim to represent humanity as a whole."[40] As Donald Kelley explains, "in general, [Bodin] assumed it was a fallacy to think that the experience of any single national group was sufficient for political philosophy."[41] To find a universal law shared in common by all nations, one must begin look beyond the legal history and institutions of Romans and study instead the laws of all nations. Jurists required a genuinely comparative approach with multiple and diverse sources of historical data.

It is for this reason that Bodin, early in his intellectual development, turns to the study of history, especially legal and institutional history, recognizing the importance of historical scholarship for a proper and complete jurisprudence. Bodin's first major published work, the *Methodus ad Facilem Historiarum Cognitionem* [Method for the Easy Understanding of Histories] of 1566, was the direct product of this early "historicist" stage of Bodin's intellectual development at Toulouse and reflected the general trend of French legal thought in this direction.[42] The *Methodus* was, as one commentator put it, the "syllabus of the New Jurisprudence."[43] It was Bodin's first formal attempt at moving beyond the narrow interpretive academic debates raging between Bartolists, favoring the *mos Italicus*, and legal humanists, favoring the *mos Gallicus*, while also transforming the historical insights of the *ars historica* into a general

[36] Bodin's second preface, reproduced in McRae's translation in *Commonweale* A71. [37] *Method* 8.

[38] *Method* 7–8. [39] Brown, *The Method* 37.

[40] Donald Kelley, "Development and Context of Bodin's Method," *Verhandlungen der Internationalen Bodin Tagung in München*, ed. Horst Denzer (München: C.H. Beck, 1973) 134.

[41] Kelley, "Development and Context" 133.

[42] Representatives of this approach include François Baudouin, *De Institutione Historiae Universae et eius cum Iurisprudentia Coniunctione Prologomena Libri II* (Paris, 1561) and Eguinaire Baron, *De Ratione Dicendi Discendique Iuris Civilis ad Studiosam Legum Inventutem Commonefactio* (1546).

[43] Brown, *The Methodus* 34.

scientific method that could potentially unlock the fundamental principles of "universal law."[44]

As a work of historical scholarship presented in the form of the intellectually fashionable early modern genre of universal histories, however, the *Methodus* was a highly unconventional work. It lacked the rhetorical elegance and literary style characteristic of the Italian *ars historica* such as Robortello, Patrizi, and Mascardi.[45] This was by design. For Bodin, the project of writing a universal history was distinct from (what he thought was) the simpler task of writing a national history or even a history of a single city.[46] Because it required the identification of universal historical patterns common to all nations, the project of a universal history was unavoidably a comparative project, requiring a proper comparative method in the historical study not simply of one nation, but the systematic or methodical study of numerous nations.

Bodin found it to be quite "remarkable that, among so many writers and in so learned an age, until now [1566] there has been no one who has compared famous histories of our forebears with each other and with the account of deeds done by the ancients."[47] For the historian setting out to write a universal history, the problem was not so much the shortage, but rather, the abundance as well as the variance in reliability and quality of historical sources.[48] The universal historian faces the unique difficulty of resolving basic problems of comparative method in historical scholarship, above all, determining how to prioritize and place in order each historical source for the larger project of extracting universal history out of the localized history of a particular nation. He, thus, warns his readers in the preamble of the *Methodus* that the most important preliminary task before him was to classify the existing historical raw data into more legible categories, a task which he undertook in the opening chapters of the *Methodus*.

Much of the material in these early chapters of the *Methodus* reads like a set of practical guidelines in sorting through historical narratives. Bodin, for example, devotes the second chapter of the *Methodus* to "the order of histories" [*de ordine historiarum*]. Likewise, the fourth chapter provides practical guidance on "the selection of historians," [*de historicorum delectu*] and guides his readers toward those most useful for composing a value-free history. He disregards writers such as Eginhard and Donato Acciajuoli, who are more appropriately classified as "orators" rather than proper historians because they "commemorate perpetually the praises and the virtues of a man, but do not mention his

[44] On historical methodology, see Marie-Dominique Couzinet, *Histoire et Méthode a la Renaissance: Une Lecture de la Methodus de Jean Bodin* (Paris: J.Vrin, 1996).

[45] Brown, *The Methodus* 52.

[46] The genre of such civic histories of Italian cities such as Florence would certainly include such historical texts as Bruni's *History of the Florentine People*, Machiavelli's *History of Florence*, and Guicciardini's *History of Florence*.

[47] *Methodus* 9.

[48] For a recent study on this theme, Ann Blair, *Too Much to Know: Managing Scholarly Information Before the Modern Age* (New Haven: Yale University Press, 2010).

vices."[49] He criticizes Livy and Polybius for their superstition and impiety.[50] On the other hand, he judges men "thoroughly experienced in public affairs" to be the most useful of historians.[51] Above all, he recommends the historical writings of authors with practical experience in warfare and statecraft such as Thucydides, Caesar, and Machiavelli.[52]

By organizing and evaluating historical sources in these ways, Bodin argued that it was possible "to establish an order and a manner of reading these [histories] and of judging carefully between them."[53] History, for Bodin, could not simply be a matter of recounting the natural chronological order [*ordo temporum, ordo naturalis*] of things but a constructed "artificial" order synthesized according to human reason [*ordo artificialis*].[54] By engaging systematically with the high volume of historical source material, he hoped to develop an art of reading history properly.

Bodin's thoroughgoing comparative approach to historical method reflected a deeper skepticism regarding the belief that the historical experience of one nation could plausibly be taken as representative of the experience of all nations. This skepticism was to become axiomatic for Bodin's new historical science, "that no [single] national tradition could claim to represent humanity as a whole" but had to be uncovered, decoded, and deciphered.[55] For the purpose of universal history, then, the historical experience of the nations of classical Antiquity, such as Rome, could not be privileged as being any more significant than that of any other nation, whether ancient or modern. Such an egalitarian and cosmopolitan outlook, anathema to the classical humanist, was axiomatic to Bodin's historical method.

All of these innovations in the practice of historical scholarship could have remained safely outside the domain of law and politics as a curious feature of early modern intellectual history and the historiography of chronology.[56] But it was because of Bodin's key insistence that "history for the most part deals with the state" [*in Rerumpublicarum statu*] that the project of universal history would have particularly compelling consequences for jurisprudence and the political theory of the state.[57] Indeed, for Bodin, and many of his contemporaries, the historical experience of a nation was expressed and embodied most clearly through its laws, customs, and legal institutions. Variations in the law, whether synchronically across different national traditions or diachronically across differents historical periods, were understood to be symptomatic of, and attributable to, more basic differences in historical experience. The study of law, thus, became the critical point of entry for the comparative study of

[49] *Methodus* 45. [50] *Methodus* 56–8. [51] *Methodus* 43. [52] *Methodus* 54–5.

[53] *Methodus* 16.

[54] Kelley, "Development and Context" 139–40. Cf. Kenneth McRae, "Ramist Tendencies in the Thought of Jean Bodin," *Journal of the History of Ideas* 16 (1955): 306–23.

[55] Kelley, "Development and Context"134.

[56] Anthony Grafton, *Cartographies of Time* (New York: Princeton Architectural Press, 2010).

[57] *Methodus* 150; *Method* 153.

history, by providing the historical raw data necessary for the historian to craft a genuinely universal history for all humanity transcending the local experiences and institutions of any one particular nation.

In this way, the project of universal history was, in Bodin's view, inseparable from legal scholarship. And just as historical scholarship would have to become comparative in approach, so too would jurisprudence. On this comparative approach to law, no single legal tradition or system could be treated more favorably than any other. To find a universal law common to all nations, one must begin first by methodically studying the laws of all nations.

None of the existing methods of legal scholarship and interpretation, however, whether French, Italian, or otherwise, offered a satisfactory starting point for such a comparative jurisprudence, and that was because sixteenth-century jurists continued to fetishize the Roman law as the *ius commune*. In reality, the Justinianic Roman law of the *Corpus Iuris Civilis* was really nothing more than the law of one nation, the Roman people. So, Bodin asked, why should Roman law artificially take precedence over other national legal traditions, such as the customary laws of France, especially in a world where the historical fiction of *translatio imperii* no longer held any credibility? There was no good reason why, in the search for universal history, Roman law should be privileged far above the legal traditions of other nations.

What Bodin sought to establish in the *Methodus* instead was an entirely new comparative approach in the study of law, one that moved beyond the traditional parameters of the Roman *ius civile* to a universal *ius omnium gentium*. The work was indeed not so much an "ad hoc selection of materials as practical requirements suggest, nor general reflections upon history as a supplement to legal education, but a systematic appraisal of law and legislation through a comparison and synthesis of all juridical experience."[58] Instead of focusing solely on Roman law and Roman institutions, Bodin relied instead upon a diverse array of historical sources, such as the laws of the Persians, Greeks, Egyptians, and Hebrews, in addition to Roman law.[59] He explains why in the epistle dedicatory to the *Methodus*: "The best part of the universal law lies hidden in history" [*In historia iuris universi pars optima latet*].[60] Only after uncovering and unmasking this universal law through a study of all available historical sources would it be possible to apply, as Bodin put it, "to the republic of the world the same analysis that has been made about one state."[61]

BODIN'S TURN TO POLITICAL THEORY: *DE STATU RERUMPUBLICARUM*

Bodin sought to provide "a general theory of law and legislation" of potentially universal scope, applicable across national and historical contexts.[62] The value of such a theory of law and state for the historian in need of a reliable

[58] Franklin, *Revolution* 69. [59] *Method* 3. [60] *Method* 8. [61] *Method* 116; cp. 168.

[62] Franklin, *Jean Bodin and the Sixteenth Century Revolution* 57.

comparative method would have been immediately apparent, and for this reason, it naturally formed one of the central topics in a treatise on historical method, occupying the sixth chapter on "the form of states" [*De statu rerumpublicarum*].[63]

But the significance of this chapter, the longest in the *Methodus*, extended far beyond the narrow academic concerns of historians, and that is because the chapter constituted a treatise in its own right, treating topics of central importance in legal and political theory, such as the rights of citizenship, sources of constitutional change, and, above all, the sovereignty of the state. Indeed, *De statu rerumpublicarum* was a treatise within a treatise and perhaps functioning even as a draft of major portions of the *République*.[64]

Bodin lays out the reasons for this explicit turn to the political theory of the state at the beginning of the chapter: "Since history for the most part deals with the state and with the changes taking place within it, to achieve an understanding of the subject we must explain briefly the origins, developed form [*status*], and ends of principalities [*imperiorum*], especially since there is nothing more fruitful and beneficial in all history."[65] This is an important methodological claim. It indicates that the state, not individual persons, should be understood as the proper subject of universal history. It naturally follows, for Bodin, that historians should have a clearer understanding of their subject. Historians need to know a bit of political theory, and it is for this reason that political theory takes a central place in the *Methodus*, in the service of history.

But what is there to be said about the state that hasn't already been said? Bodin asserts that "in so many centuries no one until now has explained what is the best kind of state [*optimus civitatis status*]."[66] And that is because this essential task of explaining the nature of the state has traditionally been taken up largely by historians and philosophers—in Bodin's view people entirely unqualified for such a task—when it should properly be reserved for experts in matters of law and state. Science—especially a comparative science of state—requires a decontested set of concepts and terms reflecting the essential properties of things in order to enable proper comparative analysis. Methodical

[63] Reynolds translates this title as, "the type of government in states," but this does not fully convey the significance of Bodin's use of the term, *status reipublicae*, which he distinguishes from *modus gubernandi*, or the structural continuity between the *Methodus* and his later work. In the *Commonweale*, Knolles translates the phrase as "the estate of the commonweale," which better captures Bodin's meaning indicating the constitutional form of a *respublica* which can be either a monarchy, an aristocracy, or a popular state.

[64] Richard Tuck, in *Sleeping Sovereign*, has suggested that the chapter may even have originated as a standalone critique of Book III of Aristotle's *Politics*.

[65] *Methodus* 150; *Method* 153.

[66] *Methodus* 150; *Method* 153. Bodin is usually careful to distinguish between *respublica* and *civitas*, but this is one rare instance where he elides the difference. He clarifies later that a *civitas* (which he defines in Ciceronian terms as determined by common laws and customs) can be a *respublica*, but a *respublica* is not necessarily the same as a *civitas*, since a *respublica* could conceivably be as diverse and complex as the Roman Empire which asserted *imperium* over many *gentes* and *civitates*.

comparison would otherwise be futile so long as opinions on the matter remained "so varied and divergent."[67]

Bodin, thus, proposed a definition of the state, or *respublica*, that he felt was appropriate for a comparative science of states, yet avoided the shortcomings of the alternatives proposed by classical historians and philosophers: "The state [*respublica*] is nothing other than a multitude of families and associations [*familiorum aut collegiorum… multitudo*] subjected under one and the same *imperium*."[68] As Bodin specifies, this definition was designed to be sufficiently flexible to apply in any historical context, whether ancient or modern. It applies equally:

> To villages, towns, cities, and principalities [*pertinet ad vicos, urbes, civitates, & principatus*] however scattered their lands may be . . . The concept is not conditioned by the size of the region or by its great expanse . . . [so that] Ragusa or Geneva, whose rule [*dominatus*] is comprised almost within its walls, ought to be called a state no less than the empire of the Tartars [*Tartarorum imperia*], which was bounded by the same limits as the course of the sun.[69]

But the definition was also designed to avoid the varieties of competing definitions of state that proceeded by fixing the essential attribute of statehood in some extraneous normative category of justice. What fundamentally made a state [*respublica*], for Bodin, was not so much a shared sense of law and justice, as Cicero once thought, since such an "absurd" requirement would then deny sovereign statehood to the Turkish Empire, a state marked fundamentally by its cultural and legal pluralism, yet united nevertheless by one common authority.[70] Instead, what made a state was its common subjection under one and the same *imperium*, an authority supreme over all others.

This attribute of supreme *imperium* alone was what made a state more than just a simple domestic or private association. Although he admits that the "true image of the state" [*Reipublicae veram imaginem*] is properly conceived in the likeness or form of the family and the *collegium*, there is a fundamental difference which sets apart the state as an association of a special kind. Unlike a family which was defined and united by the "domestic power" [*domestica potestate*] or "legitimate and limited *imperium* of the *paterfamilias*" [*patrisfamilias imperio legitimo ac moderato coniungantur*] or a corporate association which was defined and united by the "private *imperium*" [*imperio privato*] of its rector or procurator, the encompassing authority of the state, supreme or "sovereign" above the

[67] *Methodus* 159; *Method* 153.

[68] *Methodus* 155. It is essentially the same formulation that will appear in the *République*. Reynolds translates *imperium* as authority, but given the conceptual and linguistic difficulties presented by the term in Roman legal thought, I have chosen to leave the term in the Latin to stress the continuities with Roman law.

[69] *Methodus* 155; *Method* 158.

[70] Cicero, *De Re Publica* 6.13. *Methodus* 156 on the difference between *respublica* (which is defined by shared subjection to one common *imperium*), *civitas* (which is defined by one common *imperium* and shared law), and *urbs* (which is defined not only by *imperium* and law, but also the same walls), the last of which prompts a citation to Bartolus' commentary on D.50.16.2.pr on *Urbs*.

authority of any family or corporation within its jurisdiction, was distinctive both in its public nature and theoretically unlimited scope.[71]

Clearly, then, this concept of a supreme authority, a *summum imperium*, was the key concept that must be elucidated in the theory of the state. But Bodin also observes that it is less clear just what the concept of *imperium*, let alone *summum imperium*, entails. What actually is *imperium*? None of the classical authorities, according to Bodin, ever defined *summum imperium*, least of all Aristotle—"Bodin's favorite whipping-boy"—whose political theory was taken as the standard analysis on statehood by Renaissance historians.[72] Indeed, Bodin asserts that Aristotle entirely "overlooked" the concept of *summum imperium*.

The absence of a settled definition of the state's sovereign authority was detrimental not only for political theory and public law, but, indeed, also for the project of universal history. It presented, first of all, a problem in defining the constituent parts of the state, all of which were theoretically tied in subjection to the authority, or *imperium*, of the state. The concept of citizenship provides a useful illustration of this problem. "A citizen," Bodin writes, "is one who enjoys the common liberty and the protection of *imperium*."[73] Subjection to *imperium* was, for Bodin, the only necessary and sufficient requirement for citizenship. Fixing citizenship upon anything else, whether residence, political participation, shared ancestry, or some other criterion, was entirely irrelevant. Just as it was the *summum imperium* that united the various elements of the state and created a civic unity out of a natural plurality, so too was this the very same *imperium* that created citizens by subjecting free persons to its protection.

In offering this definition of citizenship, Bodin's target was, again, Aristotle. Bodin explained that Aristotle committed the error of trying to define citizenship in terms of its accidental, rather than essential, attributes and, consequently, led astray even his Renaissance humanist followers, such as Gasparo Contarini (1483–1542), Carolo Sigonio (d.1584), and Girolamo Garimberto (1506–1575), who tried in vain to apply Aristotle's concept of citizenship, appropriate only to the Athenian *polis*, to citizenship in other historical and national contexts, as he put it, *in errorem*.[74] Aristotle's mistake, according to Bodin, was a critical error of judgment, of trying to extract a universal out of a particular. He identified citizenship essentially with certain attributes of active political participation that were really only contingent and specific to democratic Athens "in the time of Pericles."[75] Athenian citizens just happened to participate actively in the public offices of the *polis*, but Aristotle's mistake was to

[71] *Methodus* 155. Bodin discusses the *paterfamilias* and family in *République* 1.3 and the association in *République* 3.7.

[72] Blair, "Authorial Strategies" 152.

[73] *Methodus* 155.

[74] *Methodus* 152. Gasparo Contarini, *De Magistratibus et Republica Venetorum Libri V* (Basel, 1547) 29–32; Carolus Sigonius, *De Republica Atheniensium Libri IV* (Bologna, 1564) 40; Girolamo Garimberto, *De Regimineti Publici de la Citta* (Venice, 1544) fol. xi. Bodin renews his complaint at *Methodus* 162.

[75] *Methodus* 152.

identify those practices of political participation as *the* defining feature of citizenship for all states, whether democratic or not, so that Aristotle can say that a citizen is nothing but "one who may share in the administration of justice, may hold office, or act in a deliberative capacity."[76]

In this respect, the Aristotelian theory of citizenship was, to Bodin, not a proper theory at all, and this because it dealt only with particulars, not with universals.[77] It failed to explain practices of citizenship in more general terms, far outside the classical context of the Athenian *polis*, the most important classical example of which, for Bodin, was the Roman Empire—let alone, early modern states.[78] It could not thus serve as the basis for a truly universal history or general civil science.

To illustrate his point, Bodin asks whether the classical Aristotelian analysis could make any sense of the notion of citizenship expressed in the Antonine Constitution, a noteworthy counterexample and test case to contrast with Aristotle. He asks: "What is to be done in the case of the Emperor Antonine, who in a proclamation ordered that all free men... should be Roman citizens?"[79] For Bodin, Aristotle's theory of citizenship in the *polis* cannot explain the civil status of Roman provincials following the universal grant of citizenship in the Antonine Constitution of 212 C.E. As he argues, if we were to follow Aristotle's analysis, free inhabitants of Roman provinces could be nothing more than "aliens because they had been denied popular rights... [i.e., they were] debarred from honors, judicial matters, and public counsels"—a result he described to be both "absurd and dangerous."[80] From an Aristotelian point of view, such free subjects held the unenviable and uncertain position of "exiles or strangers in their own cities [*in sua civitate exules aut peregrini*]," like members of the disenfranchised underclass in Athens.

But for Bodin, it should not matter one bit for ascertaining citizenship whether one is fully entitled to participate in the civil affairs of one's state, or whether one is fully disenfranchised from civil rights. The only essential criterion in identifying a citizen is shared subjection under one common authority [*esse sub unum & idem imperium subjecta*]. Indeed, if citizens of a state can be said to share anything at all together in common, it is only this fact of subjection and nothing else—not even the mutual sharing of common liberties, privileges or capacities for political participation—that generates a common civic

[76] *Methodus* 152, citing Aristotle, *Politics* III, 1, 1275b19 and 1275a23.

[77] *Methodus* 155.

[78] Bodin even suggests that Aristotle's theory cannot be applied even within the Athenian popular state because it does not count the invisible under-class population who were nevertheless inhabitants subject to the rule of the Athenian *polis*. *Methodus* 152.

[79] *Methodus* 152.

[80] *Methodus* 152. It was absurd because Aristotle's analysis allows one to be "partly citizens" [*partim cives*] and "partly foreigners" [*partim peregrinos*], *Methodus* 160. And it was dangerous, because harboring such a large domestic population of disenfranchised outsiders could function as "an excellent pretext for civil war," *Methodus* 152.

identity.[81] Such shared subjection to common *imperium* was alone what carves out a citizen-body out of nature, and, more important, it is what differentiates the citizen from the foreigner.[82]

BODIN ON *IMPERIUM*

The centrality of *imperium* to the understanding of the state and the boundaries of citizenship introduces the central theoretical issue of the *Methodus*: What actually is *imperium*? Following convention, Bodin treats it as a generic term for coercive legal authority.[83] But Bodin also observes that, in Roman law, *imperium* had a specific meaning signifying the coercive authority, not of sovereigns, but specifically of magistrates. To speak of the legal qualities of *imperium*, therefore, was really to speak of magisterial authority.

He begins by observing the many different degrees of magisterial *imperium* corresponding to the different ranks of magistrates. In the Roman context, *imperium* ranged from the simple power of arrest [*comprehensio*], which Bodin argued was a baseline threshold necessary to all forms of *imperium*, to higher degrees of *imperium*, such as the power of summons [*vocare*], the power of imposing various monetary penalties [*mulctam irrogare*], and the power of flogging [*potestas verberum*].[84] The upper limit [*extremum*] of magisterial *imperium* consisted ultimately in the capital power of the sword [*ius gladii*], what civilians long regarded as the quintessence of public authority, *merum imperium*.[85]

It was, in theory, possible for all degrees of *imperium* to be held by one person, although such "a state in which all *imperium* will be assigned to a magistrate" [*in qua magistratui omne imperium tribuetur*] would, as Bodin puts it, be a "rarity" [*raritas*] and "not well constituted" [*non... bene constituta*].[86] But

[81] Applying this analysis to the later Republic, Bodin flagrantly flouted the conventional understanding of the relationship between Rome and her allies, the *socii*, before the Social War of the first century B.C.E., arguing instead that the *lex Iulia de civitate*, the statute which extended civil rights—and, it was thought, Roman citizenship—to Latins and all *socii*, was an entirely superfluous act insofar as citizenship was concerned. All *socii* were, on Bodin's revisionist history, *already* Roman citizens of the same state [*respublica*], even though they lacked civil rights and were not of the same *civitas*. This was, in turn, precisely because they were all already under the Roman *imperium*. *Methodus* 157–59, 161.

[82] *Methodus* 161. [83] Cp., *Iuris Universi Distributio* 60 on *Imperium*.

[84] *Methodus* 167, citing Varro and Ulpian.

[85] All of these degrees of *imperium* were strongly reminiscent of the Bartolist tree of jurisdictions, and Bodin is perhaps trying to fit the Roman scheme into the French juridical distinctions between *haute, moyenne et basse justice*. On the equivalence of *merum imperium* and *ius gladii*, see D.1.16.6, 1.18.6.8, 1.21.1.1, 1.21.5, 2.1.3. Bodin distinguishes between the power of the sword [*ius gladii*] associated with the *merum imperium* from the power of life and death [*vitae ius ac necis*], which he associated with the *summum imperium*, at *Methodus* 167 and, for this very reason, was inaccessible to any ordinary magistrate. But *ius gladii* just was the power to impose capital penalties and, in the Empire, could be exercised by the *princeps* or, by delegation, by a magistrate. Bodin seems to be stressing the exclusivity of certain sovereign powers, but this text is unclear on how the distinction works.

[86] *Methodus* 166, 170. But he acknowledges that some modern states, such as the Turks, are governed "seigneurially" with full *imperium* being administered through the Grand Vizier, as well as Soderini's Florence.

given the complexities of public administration, it was unlikely and practically impossible for all such powers of state always to be monopolized in the hands of one person.[87] Thus, he acknowledges instead that *imperium* can, and even should, be distributed across the state and placed in many diverse hands of officials, ranging in rank and dignity from minor judges of the lowest feudal [*praediatoria*] jurisdiction, such as the deputy of a French *châtelain* [*castelli commissarios*], to the highest officials of the widest [*plenissima*] jurisdiction, such as a Roman proconsul.[88]

What united all these different species of *imperium* was the one essential quality they all shared in common: they were all commands emanating from the will of the commanding magistrate, backed by coercive force. For Bodin, anybody who lawfully held and exercised any of these degrees of *imperium* was *ipso facto* a "magistrate."[89] As he put it (referencing Cicero's description of the magistrate as *lex loquens*), the very "voice of the magistrate signifies *imperium* and power."[90] And that magisterial voice was to be expressed in the form of the *edictum magistratuum* which, like statutory *lex* in Roman law, carried coercive force binding all subjects within the magistrate's competence.[91] By their lawful exercise of *imperium*, magistrates had the duty of governing and policing the state; they were, indeed, as Bodin would later call them, citing Demosthenes, "the verie sinewes of the Commonweale."[92]

This connection of *imperium* to the legal status and function of Roman magistrates turned out to be quite useful for Bodin, as it helped sharpen and define not only what is (and what is not) *imperium*, but also what is (and what is not) a magistrate. Magistrates, as Bodin observed, performed various sorts of public functions, not all of which involved *imperium*. Some magisterial functions, of course, clearly did involve *imperium*, such as in the execution of capital

[87] Bodin viewed the centralization of *imperium* in one person—what he called a "sovereign magistrate" in the *République*—as symptomatic of primitive practices of government, prior to the invention of law, what he called "seigneurial" rule. While recognizing that, in extraordinary circumstances, a sovereign would be within its rights in choosing to suspend the government and commission a sort of dictator with extraordinary plenary powers, such a strategy of government would also be dangerous and should be avoided. Daniel Lee, "Office Is a Thing Borrowed: Jean Bodin on the Right of Offices and Seigneurial Government," *Political Theory* 41 (2013).

[88] *Methodus* 167, 168. The reference to "*plenissima jurisdictio*" is D.1.16.7.2, but perhaps Bodin also has Azo's commentary on C.3.13 also in mind. The term, "praeditoriall jurisdiction," appears again in Book III of the *République*.

[89] Bodin specifies, at *Methodus* 166, that a magistrate is *qui imperii publici partem habet*, to distinguish the public nature of their *imperium* from the private domestic *imperium patrium* of a *paterfamilias* and the *imperium herile* of a *dominus*. It is significant that magistrates hold *imperium* by law [*lege*]. The Roman dictator held *imperium*, but since the dictatorship was, according to Bodin, not technically an office legally defined with an ordinary charge, but a temporary "commission" [*curatio*], they were not properly magistrates.

[90] *Methodus* 166.

[91] The *edicta* of magistrates, forming the body of civil law known as the *ius honorarium*, are recognized as valid sources of law at D.1.2.2.10 and 1.2.2.12. In the Empire, it is attributed also to the *princeps* at D.1.4.1.1, who can use the *edictum* as a tool of Imperial legislation by decree.

[92] *Commonweale* 326 [3.5].

penalties. By contrast, other functions, such as those ceremonial or sacramental in nature, had nothing to do with *imperium*, even though they were public functions.

There remained, however, a distinct class of magisterial functions, where it was not clear whether they were authentic expressions of *imperium*. These included those public functions, collected together under the heading of *consilium*, such as giving counsel and participating in public deliberation, traditionally regarded in Aristotelian political science as essential to magisterial authority. These also included, more importantly, those judicial functions falling under the heading of *iurisdictio mandata* in Roman law. Here, Bodin refers to the private judges or arbiters in Roman procedure, to whom certain defined judicial functions were delegated by magistrates for the resolution of cases in civil law. It is true, he admits, that such private judges perform certain functions of public importance, such as the judicial function of deciding [*decernere*] and judging [*iudicare*] facts in specific cases presented before them. In this sense, private judges do exercise *iurisdictio*. But they do not, according to Bodin, hold *imperium*, which magistrates reserve when delegating *iurisdictio* in the appointment of private judges.

It is a mistake, then, to treat *iurisdictio* and *consilium* as equivalent to, or continuous with, *imperium*. In Bodin's view, this was ultimately the error of Aristotle who made no meaningful distinction between concepts of *imperium*, *iurisdictio*, and *consilium* in his definition of the magistrate. Because of this failure to distinguish, Bodin argues that earlier commentators often confused these different public functions of magistracy, and consequently treated them as all belonging to one undifferentiated category, such that the title of magistrate might be applied to persons who may perform functions of *iurisdictio* (like the lay private judge) or functions of *consilium* (like a counselor), yet lack *imperium*.[93]

The preceding analysis enables Bodin to identify magistrates in any state solely on the basis of whether or not they lawfully hold and exercise *imperium*. Thus, in the Roman context, consuls and provincial governors turn out to be magistrates, while senators and counselors sitting in deliberative or consultative bodies do not.[94] Likewise, praetors turn out to be magistrates, while private judges do not.

[93] Even more damaging, according to Bodin, were the humanist interpretations of the *grammatici*—Bodin singles out by name Festus, Carolo Sigonio, and Nicolas de Grouchy—who all attempted to apply the "rules" [*regulae*] of grammar, rather than rules of law [*regulae iuris*], to parse and uncover finer linguistic or verbal distinctions in words such as *potestas* and *imperium* signifying concepts of authority. *Methodus* 168, citing D.50.16.215 and 1.16.7 to show the incoherence of their views in civil law. It is noteworthy that Bodin singles out by name specific authors for criticism, even though elsewhere in the *Methodus*, Bodin discourages personal attacks of the living, as were Sigonio and de Grouchy when Bodin would have been writing the *Methodus*. See Blair, "Authorial Strategies" 151, n.39.

[94] For this reason, a public deliberative body such as the Roman Senate does not, in Bodin's view, have *imperium*, even though they generate resolutions, *senatusconsulta*, to be carried out by magistrates. Bodin restates this view of senatorial bodies in *République* 3.1; cp. *Commonweale* 273; Cp. *Methodus* 37.

But magistrates of all ranks, even the most powerful magistrates in a state, nevertheless occupied an undefined interstitial space between sovereignty and subjection. On the one hand, they were superior to ordinary citizens because of the *imperium* they lawfully held. They could command subjects by their public acts and *edicta*. Yet, on the other hand, magistrates, however great in magnitude their *imperium*, were nevertheless themselves subjects of yet a higher authority; indeed, such subjection was precisely what made them magistrates, and not sovereigns. Even the highest magistrates empowered with coercive *merum imperium* were, despite their power, uniformly tied under obligation to this higher *maius imperium*, which was preeminent over all magistrates with *imperium*, just as it was over any ordinary citizen without it. And this was, in turn, because even magistrates were bound and limited by that very law which created their office and invested them with *imperium* in the first place.

Bodin's findings on the magistrate played a critically important function by driving a sharp conceptual wedge, distinguishing the magistrate's ordinary *imperium* from the state's extraordinary *summum imperium*. All magistrates, by definition, held some degree of *imperium*, but because their tenure of office was defined and limited by law, magistrates themselves were tied by obligations to an even higher authority, the very source of law.[95] For this very reason, no magistrate could ever be regarded a sovereign, bearing and representing the supreme authority of state, the *summum imperium*. At most, magistrates could only be said to have—as Bodin put it—the government [*gubernatio*] or administration of the state's affairs [*Reipublicae administratio*], but never the *summum imperium*.[96]

Unlike magisterial *imperium*, then, *summum imperium*—what Bodin observes is called by the French as "sovereignty" [*suverenitas*]—was something quite unique and distinctively of its own kind, a *sui generis*.[97] To treat it, without differentation, as coextensive with the ordinary *imperium* of the magistrate would be a profound mistake. One way to draw this distinction was simply to stipulate the difference in functions between magistrates with ordinary *imperium* and sovereigns with *summum imperium*, on the reasoning that magistrates could not generally hold sovereign functions or exercise them by right. On this approach, *summum imperium* could never be defined simply in terms of

[95] Bodin's terminology is important. *Lex* and *edictum* both carry the force of a legal command, as Roman legal doctrine requires, and only one with *imperium* can issue them. But whereas the *edictum* belongs properly to the *imperium in magistratu*, the *lex* is exclusive to the *imperium in principe* [*sive populo*]. Both *lex* [rendered in French as *loi*] and *edictum* are to be distinguished from *ius* [rendered in French as *droit*], which does not carry any commanding force or obligation to obey. Bodin specifies in the *République* that legal limitations on magisterial *imperium* consist in the term of office, the legal requirements specifying how *imperium* may be exercised, what he calls the *legis actio*, and the manner in which a magistracy may be revoked.

[96] Bodin, *Methodus* 153. Bodin claims Aristotle, having failed to discern this distinction, never really discussed sovereignty, but only the magistrate's government and administration of the state. This crucial distinction is fleshed out in further detail in *République* II. *Methodus* 166.

[97] Bodin uses the term, *suverenitas* (rendered in the text in its accusative form), at *Methodus* 170.

the power of distributing rewards and punishments [*praemiorum ac poenarum potestate*], since even magistrates held such power by their *imperia*.[98]

Bodin's strategy of argument was thus framed as a search for the exceptional. We know what sort of things magistrates could do by their *imperium*. But we need to know what sort of things even the highest magistrates could *not* do by their *imperium*? These exceptional sovereign functions, constitutive of *summum imperium,* consisted of five essential elements: "Creating the highest magistrates and defining the office of each... making and unmaking laws... declaring war and peace... receiving final appeals from all magistrates... the power of life and death."[99] These sovereign functions were exceptional, in that they served a higher-order purpose in constituting the public authority of states. They chiefly concerned how magisterial *imperium* was to be constituted, organized, and regulated by law. Sovereignty was, in this sense, the *imperium* behind the *imperium*.[100] Given this, it followed for Bodin that *summum imperium* had to be regarded generally as exclusive and outside the scope of any particular magistrate's legal jurisdiction in a well-constituted [*republica bene constituta*] state. It was, as some might say, an "extraordinary" and extra-legal power.[101]

If sovereignty did not belong to magistrates, then to whom did it rightfully belong? Bodin explains that sovereignty in all states must be understood to "belong properly" [*propria esse*] only to a prince or a people, and never to a magistrate. This, and this alone, was to determine the true constitutional form of a state: "The form of state [*status reipublicae*] is determined by the bearer of *summum imperium*."[102] So, if *summum imperium* were held by one person, the state must be classified properly as a monarchy, even if the government and *administratio* were largely carried out by magistrates (as in the case of France or England). Likewise, if *summum imperium* were held corporately by the *optimati* or the *populus*, the state ought to be classified respectively as either an aristocracy or a democracy, even if the government and *administratio* of such states were carried out under the authority of a single appointed or elected official, such as the Doge of Venice (where Venice is understood to be an aristocracy)

[98] *Methodus* 170.

[99] *Methodus* 170. An abbreviated version of this list of sovereign rights appears in Chapter 3 of the *Methodus* 37 in the discussion of *disciplina civilis*, concerning *imperium, consilium*, and *executio*, as a domain separate from jurisprudence. The significance that Bodin attaches to the capacity to create magistrates underscores his civilian frame of thought, with the system of Roman magisterial authority functioning as his main point of reference. Gilmore, *Argument from Roman Law* 96–97.

[100] Bodin even admits that his original view was that *summum imperium* was to be defined as a "creative" or even perhaps constitutive power, in the "creation" or constitution of magistrates [*magistratuum creatione*] with *imperium*, *Methodus* 170. This magistrate-creative power was not original with Bodin, as Dumoulin likewise suggested that "the first effect of the ownership of the *imperium* was the ability to create a magistrate suitable for its exercise." Gilmore 96. Based on this, I have to disagree with Julian Franklin's claim that Bodin made no distinction between constituted and constitutive power as well as Franklin's conclusion following from this claim, that he was an absolutist.

[101] Kalyvas, *Democracy and the Politics of the Extraordinary*.

[102] *Methodus* 170–1 and 153: *status* [*Reipublicae*] *in summo imperio versatur*.

or the Roman *princeps* before Vespasian (where Rome is understood to be a democracy).[103] What Bodin absolutely did not allow was a fourth concept of the "mixed" state, wherein sovereign functions were disaggregated and distributed, so as to be held, even as property [*propria*], by different, mutually opposed members of the state.[104] This was not so much because of a normative concern, but a conceptual one. Dividing sovereignty would necessarily make the state unintelligible, since it is defined by common subjection to one united and supreme *imperium*.[105]

This analysis of *summum imperium* as indivisible and beyond the scope of a magistrate's *imperium* has led some commentators to think that perhaps the rights constitutive of sovereignty [*imperii summi ius*] were non-delegable, whereas ordinary magisterial *imperium* was delegable.[106] But this, I would argue, is a misconstrual of Bodin's position, for two reasons. First of all, he fully acknowledged that, on "extraordinary" occasions of "overwhelming necessity" [*nisi extra ordinem praemente necessitate*], the sovereign functions of *summum imperium* may indeed be granted to magistrates [*magistratibus tribuantur*] and even observed that this was a practice common not only in Antiquity but in modernity as well.[107] Of course, as a general principle of public policy, he advised against such institutional design as antagonistic to a well-constituted state, but he nevertheless left it as an open option for sovereigns to consider.

The more important reason, however, is that every major legal theorist in the civilian tradition, as we have seen in earlier chapters, approached and commented on the issue of high public authority—what they simply designated with the Romanist term, *merum imperium*—explicitly in terms of delegation and agency, even, and especially, among the French legal humanists of the sixteenth century, as we have already seen earlier in Chapter 3. Bodin, who framed his analysis in large part as a response to what he saw as the shortcomings of this new humanist jurisprudence of Alciato and Cujas, could not simply avoid what he felt were serious errors in judgment, and so he presents his position on whether sovereignty can be "delegated" to magistrates as a commentary on the old debate between Azo and Lothair on the concept of *merum imperium*.

[103] Richard Tuck points out that Bodin's probable source for the interpretation of Rome as a democracy, both in the Republic as well as the Principate, was Nicolas Grouchy in *De Comitiis*, the first comprehensive study on voting procedures in the Roman comitial assemblies of the *populus*.

[104] *Methodus* 177.

[105] The doctrine of the mixed constitution was, of course, a settled view of the balanced harmonious state in classical and medieval political philosophy, a continuous tradition of thought from Plato, Aristotle, Polybius, Cicero, Augustine, and Aquinas. At *Methodus* 176, Bodin criticizes Polybius, Dionysius of Halicarnassus, Cicero, Machiavelli, Contarini, Thomas More, Garimberto, Paul Manutius as representatives of this tradition.

[106] *Methodus* 176.

[107] He is likely hinting at what he will call "sovereign magistrates" in the *République*, where he cites the examples of the Turks and Muscovites who govern by extraordinary commissions of sovereign power to delegates.

BODIN ON AZO AND LOTHAIR

Bodin introduces the debate between Azo and Lothair on the *merum imperium* really as a dispute whether it is exclusive to the *princeps* alone [*an solius principis proprium sit*], or whether it is non-exclusive and, thus, accessible even by ordinary magistrates.[108] Bodin tells us several things about this debate. The exclusivity doctrine is (correctly) attributed to Lothair, while the non-exclusivity doctrine is attributed to Azo, and he notes that, while the Emperor Henry [VI] favored Lothair, "all other [jurists], except Alciato and Dumoulin, judged Azo's dicta to be the better view."[109]

But in recounting the history of this dispute, Bodin was merely expressing his frustration with earlier jurists in this debate. Part of the problem, in his diagnosis, was that the jurists focused their attention exclusively and narrowly on the concept of *merum imperium*, which, as Bodin rightly points out with a reference to the *Digest*, consisted only in the "power of the sword"—hardly an attribute unique to sovereignty since even magistrates, as he observes in the *Methodus*, held such power in Roman law.[110] As he pointed out earlier, *merum imperium* fell within the competence of the magistrate's jurisdiction; there was thus nothing distinctive or exclusive about such a power that it should be regarded uniquely indicative of *summum imperium*. Because they restricted their discussion to *merum imperium*, both Azo and Lothair (and their followers) failed to say anything about the sort of sovereign functions associated with the *summum imperium*, such as the right of "waging war, concluding peace, creating a magistrate, or of enacting law, or of distributing rewards and punishments."[111]

One point must be dispensed with immediately. Bodin fully acknowledges from the start that even these sovereign functions of *summum imperium* can also be "given by the *princeps* to a magistrate" [*imperium magistratui a principe datum*]—this is taken as given and is not really at issue.[112] Instead, the real issue seems to be whether the *imperium*, once granted to a magistrate, still remains the exclusive property of the *princeps* [*proprium principis*], or whether that *imperium* should be interpreted as having been "transferred" or "conveyed" [*transferatur*] to the magistrate so that it becomes instead his actual property.[113] The

[108] *Methodus* 171. Bodin's description of the *imperium* as something that can be *proprium*, or as something "proper" belonging to the *princeps* directly echoes the earlier humanist analysis of Alciato and Duarenus on *iurisdictio propria* of the *princeps*. Bodin is adopting the view that public authority can be treated as "property."

[109] *Methodus* 171.

[110] Bodin references Ulpian, but he is most likely thinking of D.2.1.3.

[111] *Methodus* 171.

[112] It is important to underscore this point because it marks a stark contrast with the influential interpretation of Franklin who, in viewing Bodin essentially as a disciple of Alciato's legal humanism, treated sovereign rights of *summum imperium* as incapable of delegation. This is simply incorrect: not only does Bodin explicitly separate himself from Alciato, by name, he allows that sovereign rights can be delegated to agents. The real issue, as I now argue, is *how* that delegation can properly occur: On what terms or conditions can a sovereign authority delegate the use and exercise of sovereign rights to a magistrate?

[113] *Methodus* 171.

dispute on sovereignty has become a kind of proprietary matter in Bodin's mind. Who has "ownership" of *summum imperium*? Is it the *princeps* who had the original right to grant it, or is it the magistrate who exercised it?

Most medieval jurists, as Bodin observed, followed Azo's non-exclusivity doctrine: The magistrate has a "proper" legal right to the *imperium* he is permitted to exercise as his own [*proprium*]. But Bodin also pointed out that more recent jurists—and here, he specifically names the legal humanist, Alciato, and the feudalist, Dumoulin—had begun to reconsider seriously and revive Lothair's exclusivity doctrine, in order to dismantle feudal jurisdiction and restore supreme princely authority over the jurisdictions attached to fiefs. According to this view, *imperium* remained exclusive to the *princeps*, even while it was exercised and in use by the magistrate.[114] We saw, in Chapter 3, that the legal humanists applied an essentially proprietary analysis in elucidating the relationship between the *princeps* and the magistrate: The *princeps* has a legal right of property, while the magistrate merely has the "use" or "exercise" of it.

Bodin found both of these traditions mired "in great obscurity" [*magna obscuritate*], and that is chiefly because the quasi-proprietary frame of reference used in these juridical debates failed to "define the question, but made it more ambiguous."[115] In Bodin's diagnosis, the chief problem is the failure to understand the proper role, function, and authority of the magistrate in a well-ordered state. Azo's dicta entitled the magistrate with something akin to a right of property in their *imperium*. By contrast, Lothair's (and the humanists') dicta "exploited [*usurpavit*] Papinian's rule" [*regulam Papiniani*, at D.1.21.1] and consequently treated the magistrate as a mere "servile" agent or deputy of the *princeps* entitled only to the "exercise" of authority [*publici iudicii exercitium*] by delegation, just like executors or administrators in legal proceedings who act by mandate on someone else's behalf.[116]

For Bodin, the reason why this debate lasted for as long as it did was the basic failure of civilians to recognize two distinct, but both essential, features of the magistrate's status and authority. On the one hand, he observed that the magistrate is fundamentally an artificial legal creation. His powers of *imperium* are defined and granted by the law [*lege tribuuntur*] and, for this reason, they "belong not so much to the magistrate personally, but to the very law itself."[117] Any official action undertaken by a magistrate, thus, is not properly a personal action of the magistrate, but an impersonal action of the

[114] In the *République*, he cites specifically Alciato's *Paradoxa* and Dumoulin's *Commentaria*. I discuss Bodin's reply to them in the next chapter.

[115] *Methodus* 172.

[116] Bodin's interpretation is further supported by Papinian's text which which the delegate "has nothing proper" or "of his own" [*nihil proprium habet*].

[117] *Methodus* 172. Since it is the sovereign who creates the law, the *imperium* of magistrates could ultimately be said to belong to the sovereign. Bodin perhaps is thinking here of the *leges de imperio* by which *imperium* was formally conferred upon Roman magistrates by the people assembled in *comitia*.

law—or more properly, of the author of the law—and, thus, he calls such action a *legis actio*.[118] In this respect, magistrates are merely conduits for the impartial expression and enforcement of the law.[119] And, insofar as magistrates act in strict compliance with the law, they are in the same subordinate or servile position as "private judges, arbiters, and delegates" [*privati iudices, aut arbitri iure dat, aut delegati*] in Roman litigation, holding and exercising someone else's power. They are merely agents, without *imperium*, appointed by a strict legal mandate to exercise some legal function properly belonging to the sovereign state.[120]

Yet, the magistrate also enjoys a wide degree of discretion and independence in ways that make him more than simply a slave to the strict letter of the law. That is because a true magistrate is empowered to do things not simply by the letter of the law, like a mindless drone, but also to do things for the sake of justice [*aequitate*] by virtue of his office or "duty" [*officium*], what Bodin calls *officium iudicis*. Indeed, by virtue of his office, a magistrate can exercise personal discretion and "decree and judge [*decernerent, iudicarent*] many things beyond the law, and indeed even sometimes contrary to the law"; so also can a magistrate, "by proposing edicts, emend, soften, moderate, or make the laws even more stringent by their own judgment."[121] These equitable functions, taken together, were constitutive of the magistrate's office and precisely what elevated the magistrate to a status of honor and dignity in the state, even making the magistrate "*nobile*."[122]

For Bodin, all true magistrates have, by his definition, legal powers of *imperium* granted and defined strictly by law [*legis actio*] as well as other implied powers derived from their offices [*officium iudicis*] endowing them with the discretion and independence to act freely to promote the public good. Bodin, of course, was certainly not the first or only theorist to point out this dual aspect

[118] In Roman law, *legis actio* indicated early Roman legal procedure in civil litigation, which separated initial formal proceedings before the magistrate [*in iure*] from the second stage before an appointed judge with jurisdiction delegated by the magistrate. Bodin ties this analysis to the Bartolist distinction between the *officium nobile* and the *officium mercenarium* of a judge in Roman law to suggest that the latter should not really be regarded as a proper office at all, but simply an instance of a "servile" or "slavish" [*servile*] process of law. *Methodus* 173. Brown observes that Bodin likely wrote a treatise, *De legis actionibus*, which, along with other treatises, such as the *De imperio et iurisdictione*, that are referenced obliquely in the *Methodus*, were written during his time at Toulouse and later destroyed, at Bodin's request. Cp. Bodin's entry on *legis actio* in *Iuris Universi Distributio* 58, where it is described as the *ipsius legis executio, vis, ac potestas*.

[119] Bodin's description of the strictures of *legis actio* sound almost republican, as he explains that the reason for defining and restricting a magistrate's freedom of action is to ensure that the "reputation, life, and finally the fortunes of citizens shall not depend upon the arbitrary will [*arbitrio*] of any man, but upon the will of the law itself."

[120] *Methodus* 173, where he also cites D.2.1.5. In the case of magistrates, their official actions are to be attributed to the state.

[121] *Methodus* 172; cp. *Iuris Universi Distributio* 78, on *Iudicis Officium*, citing D.1.1.7.pr; 48.19.21; 48.19.13.

[122] Bodin indicates that these functions correspond to what Bartolus on D.2.1.1 called the *officium iudicis nobile* to distinguish it from the *officium mercenarium* which, in Bodin's view, is not properly an office at all but a "servile" function.

of the magistrate.[123] But he was perhaps the first to use this duality to show in what ways the magistrate is tied or bound by obligation to the sovereign and in what ways the magistrate is free and unbound.

His answer was elegantly formed, though perhaps incomplete in the *Methodus*. Since magistrates receive their *imperium* only by law, they are legally restricted in how that authority is to be exercised.[124] Only with respect to *imperium* and official legal acts [*legis actiones*]—that is, everything that relates to the command functions—can magistrates be said to be in the subordinate position of a delegate, a commissioner, an agent, or deputy, even like a slave "constrained by the chains" [*vinculis constringerentur*] of law. This is why, in criminal proceedings in Roman law, even such a high-ranking official as the praetor can have no discretion and never "detract from the sternness or mildness of the law or add anything but must give sentence in a word, nay, rather in a letter, that is A., C., N.L. [*absolvo, condemno, non liquet*]."[125] Nor can magistrates sub-delegate or re-commit their delegated *imperium* to another party, for the same reason in civil law that one "who has a mandate cannot lend [*commodare*] that object to another as if it were a borrowed thing [*rem commodatam*], otherwise it would be regarded [as] theft" from the state which is, in a sense, the proper "owner" of all *imperium* within its boundaries.[126]

But if magistrates are slaves to the law in respect of their exercise of *imperium*, they otherwise enjoy independence and freedom of action with respect to the dignity and prerogatives in their office unrelated to *imperium*. Since these prerogatives are held "by their own right" [*suo iure*] or "by right of magistracy" [*iure magistratus*], it is solely within the discretion of the magistrate to decide whether or not they can be delegated or mandated to others.[127] Potentially, this analysis indicates that a seemingly infinite range of non-*imperium* public

[123] Donellus, for example, offers one of the clearest discussions of the magistrate as a legal concept signifying both the person and the office of magistracy. Bodin's discussion in the *Methodus* takes advantage of this linguistic ambiguity in the Latin word, *magistratus*, which, as Donellus put it, was a "double-pronged word" *verbum anceps*.

[124] It is significant that magistrates ordinarily receive *imperium* by law, rather than by an extraordinary commission, which, for Bodin, technically is not a legal act, but an extralegal act of a sovereign's arbitrary will. He makes this point more clearly in the *République* in distinguishing between ordinary and extraordinary grants of *imperium*, but an early version of this idea appears in *Methodus* 174, where he points to the example of Caesar who, by a one-time extralegal or "extraordinary commission" [*extra ordinem*], was given the sovereign right to declare war and conclude peace with Gaul, but only as a delegation of authority to be exercised strictly under the terms of Rome's mandate. Caesar's war powers were, thus, not a part of his office as a general, but merely a precarious grant [*precario*] fully revocable by the Roman people. He even clarifies that any such extraordinary precarious grant of *summum imperium* can never be regarded properly an office, but merely a *curatio*, the same term he uses in the Latin *De Republica* to indicate the polar opposite of office, the *commissaire*.

[125] *Methodus* 172, 174. This point is repeated in the *République* 3.5.

[126] *Methodus* 173, citing D.1.21.3 and 2.1.5; cp. *Iuris Universi Distributio* 40, defining the *commodatum* as *creditum ad tempus, ut idem reddatur*. The description of the magistrate's *imperium* as a *commodatum* appears in a different formulation in *De Republica* 263 [3.2], where he suggests that the office is a *res commodata*.

[127] *Suo iure* appears at *Methodus* 173, but refers ultimately to D.2.1.5. The related text of Papinian at D.1.21.1.pr mentions the *ius magistratus* to distinguish those things which a magistrate can lawfully "mandate" to another by virtue of his office.

functions, such as *consilium* and *iurisdictio*, under the broad heading of office—inclusive of all those functions that Bodin scrupulously separated from *imperium*—could theoretically be delegated to subordinates.

But not everybody who has *imperium* also has an office, just as not everybody who has an office necessarily also has *imperium*.[128] Bodin's most telling example illustrating this point in the *Methodus* is the Roman dictatorship, which was to be cited again more prominently in the *République*. Even though dictators monopolized all *imperium* for a very limited period of time and suspended ordinary magistrates during the dictatorship, Bodin refused to call the dictator a magistrate, and that was because his plenary *imperium*, unlike those of ordinary magistrates such as praetors and consuls, was granted only by an extra-legal or "extraordinary" [*extra ordinem*] act of state, which resulted not so much in an office, but a "commission" [*curatio*] with a date of expiry attached to it.

What makes a magistrate fundamentally different from a dictator is not so much the *imperium* they hold, but, rather, *how* they hold it—the "terms" upon which the sovereign grants authority to an agent. Because the dictator holds it as an extraordinary appointment, he serves only at the pleasure—or "by sufferance" [*precario*]—of the sovereign, and thus can be removed from his powers whenever the sovereign decides. But this is not the case with the magistrate, and that is because the magistrate holds *imperium* by ordinary appointment to a legally perpetual office that, in theory, continues even after the personal occupant of that office has "resigned" [*deponi*] it.[129] Bodin clarifies that the individuals who are appointed to a magistracy have certain legal rights by virtue of the office, which confer on them a non-trivial degree of independence. But this is not because magistrates "own" their office or the rights and privileges of office. Indeed, no individual private person can ever be said to have a magisterial office or honors [*nec magistratus, nec honores*] by "their own right" [*suo iure*]. Public office is simply not the sort of thing that can be treated as private or patrimonial property. Instead, the magistrates that are appointed to a magisterial office are rather more like those in civil law who hold someone else's property or money in deposit for safekeeping, "like a depositary or trustee" [*veluti depositos*], to be returned at some later date.[130] Only while they hold the office as a deposit entrusted to them by the public are magistrates rightfully entitled to do certain things by their office, that they otherwise would not be able to do.

[128] *Method* 168–69 specifies the need to distinguish proper magistrates with *imperium* from those who hold a mere office but with no *imperium*, such as "scribes, attendants, adjutants, public servants... [and] those who formerly were classed as slaves."

[129] *Methodus* 174. Bodin observes that "this word [*deponere*] disturbed Alciato." He is referring to Alciato, *Paradoxa* Book II, §§3–5, most likely in connection with Ulpian's comment at D.1.17.1 concerning the Prefect of Egypt "laying down *imperium*" [*deponit... imperium*].

[130] *Depositum*, comparable to the English bailment, is one of the four major "real contracts" or contracts *re* in the Roman law of obligations (the others being *mutuum*, *commodatum*, and *pignus*). The significance of this comparison is the bilateral structure of obligations in such contracts: both the depositer and depositary have obligations to each other. Cp. *Iuris Universi Distributio* 40, defining *depositum* as *creditum alterius obligationis causa contractum*.

Taken together, Bodin's analysis of the magistrate's authority and jurisdiction shows, without doubt, that sovereignty can certainly be delegated—whether by mandate, deposit, trust, extraordinary commission, or some other means. The real issue is determining how *imperium* can be delegated without also compromising the sovereign's full right of sovereignty. The answer depends entirely on just *how* such delegated authority—whether it is the *minimum imperium*, the *merum imperium*, or indeed, even the *summum imperium*—is given to another.

It is in the *Methodus* that Bodin gives the first indication that delegation of public authority to government agents is to be understood in terms of a legal or commercial transaction at civil law, a formulation that will become essential in the exposition of his doctrine of popular sovereignty in the *République*. A sovereign people may choose to delegate the exercise of their *imperium* by the constitution and appointment of magistrates in a permanent structure of offices—or "government." It is this fiduciary relationship of trust between sovereignty and the government of a state that is foundational not only to Bodin's theory, but it is also what gives popular sovereignty its distinctively recognizable shape within the modern constitutional tradition.

CONCLUSION

As a work of historical scholarship, Bodin's *Methodus* articulates his general message to historians: it is impossible to establish the true form of a historical state—whether ancient, such as Israel, Sparta, or Rome, or modern, such as Venice, France, or Germany—simply by looking at the structures and ordinary processes of government administered by its legally constituted magistrates and other "servile" public officers. What is instead necessary is the investigation of the sovereignty itself, the *imperium* behind the *imperium*. This is a task that historians, relying simply on accounts of public decisions, and the actions of magistrates, and even of public officials without *imperium* and writing without a proper theory of the state, had, in his view, failed to do. Political and legal theory played, at least in the *Methodus*, only a secondary and supporting role in the work of the comparative historian, as he synthesized a picture of universal law and history. Concepts of state, sovereignty, office, and magistracy were what made such comparative analysis possible.

This approach changes substantially, however, in the *République*, his most important work of political theory, where methodological questions of historical analysis are largely set aside, and the focus is fixed centrally upon crafting a general theory of state and sovereignty, as an intellectual task in its own right. It is in this transition away from history and toward theory that Bodin establishes the conceptual foundations of the modern doctrine of popular sovereignty.

6

Jean Bodin, Popular Sovereignty, and Constitutional Government

INTRODUCTION

Ten years separate the publication of the *Methodus* and the publication of the first French edition of the *Six Livres de la République*. It has often been suggested that, in the intervening decade, Bodin, who left behind his legal career in the Parlement to enter the service of the monarchy, underwent a radical transformation in his political thought, moving from a more moderate, even "constitutionalist," position on the question of the scope of state authority, informed by Roman constitutionalism, to a radical "absolutist" position advocating, in the face of civil war, a legally unrestricted notion of absolute sovereignty.[1] Consequently, it has become (certainly among legal and political theorists) commonplace to view Bodin's *République*, his most important text of legal and political theory, as little more than a precursor to Hobbes' *Leviathan* as a defense of an unbridled monarchical absolutism and rejoinder to Monarchomach theories of public resistance.[2]

Of the many points of conventional wisdom concerning Bodin's thought generated by this analysis, one has had a particularly lasting influence, and I would say, a devastating effect on the modern understanding of Bodin's legal and political theory. This is the notion that Bodin was not only an enemy of popular sovereignty and democracy, but—even more—that he denied even the very possibility of popular sovereignty as a coherent concept of rule.

My goal in this chapter is to challenge this view. As I hope to show, Bodin not only recognized the possibility of popular sovereignty in the *République*, especially in his analysis of sovereignty in classical republics where supreme constitutional authority was located in the *demos*, as in Athens, or the *populus*, as in the Roman Republic, but he was, in a fundamental way, perhaps the most

[1] Julian Franklin's influential explanation for this is the sudden outbreak of religious violence and acts of resistance after St. Bartholomew in 1572. *Jean Bodin and the Rise of Absolutist Theory* Ch. 3. But the suggestion that Bodin shifts from an earlier constitutionalism to a later absolutism has been challenged continuously, such as in King, *The Ideology of Order* and, more recently, in Richard Tuck, *Sleeping Sovereign*, who has suggested that the relationship between the *Methodus* and the *République* is comparable to that between Hobbes' *De Cive* and the *Leviathan*, as an unfolding and continual development of ideas.

[2] A recent example of such an interpretation is Eleftheriadis, "Law and Sovereignty" 535–69.

important and technically sophisticated early modern theorist of popular sovereignty as a general theory undergirding the constitutional foundations of modern states. This, of course, is certainly not to say that Bodin was a democratic theorist or, in any obvious sense, a champion of popular rule. On the contrary, Bodin, like Hobbes, saw the comparative advantages of monarchical over republican rule and remained deeply skeptical of the capacity of a sovereign people to exercise self-government in a stable and lawful manner. Indeed, a common theme in Bodin's theory is just how easily democracies are prone to degenerate into lawlessness.

Unlike early modern critics who saw democracy as one step away from full-blown anarchy, Bodin was exceptional in acknowledging the complexities and the particular challenges of constitutional politics organized in the "popular form of state"—or *status reipublicae popularis*—a fully legitimate, if perhaps misguided and suboptimal, constitutional form. Indeed, he recognized that some of the most important states of classical Antiquity, such as Athens, Sparta, Carthage, and, above all, Rome, were organized, at certain points in their constitutional histories, along the principle of popular sovereignty. And he further understood that popular sovereignty was not merely an artifact of ancient civilizations, but an unavoidable fact of modern politics, as he observed in the democratic politics of such early modern examples of popular sovereignty as the Florentine Republic and self-governing Swiss cantons such as Geneva, Grisons, and Uri. From the perspective of his political science in the *République*, then, the constitutional form of the popular state was an unavoidable fact, however much its enemies wished to deny its legitimacy and existence.

By accepting the existence of the popular state, Bodin takes up what he sees as one of the central tasks of his constitutional theory, which is to explain how a state, in which sovereignty is located in the *populus*, might best preserve its popular sovereignty and what sort of government might be most appropriate for such a state. As we shall see, Bodin's constitutional theory explores, in great depth, matters of central importance to the coherence of popular sovereignty as a viable constitutional doctrine, such as the proper understanding of the concept of "peoplehood," the varieties of constitutional design appropriate to such a sovereign *populus*, and whether the legal idea of popular sovereignty necessarily must entail some form of direct democracy. What emerges is not so much a blanket condemnation of popular rule, but a more nuanced theory of the institutional conditions under which popular sovereignty can be best preserved.

This chapter begins by exploring Bodin's analysis of sovereignty as "absolute power." As I show, with specific reference to his use of Roman law, Bodin understood sovereignty as necessary for the independence of a state, but this did not mean, however, that sovereignty was to be exercised in this way at all times. Instead, Bodin saw sovereignty as a legal right that could be expressed or exercised by delegation through agents or mandataries of government.

SOVEREIGNTY AS *POTESTAS LEGIBUS SOLUTA*

Bodin famously defines sovereignty in the First Book of his most important work of political and legal theory, the *Six Livres de la République*. There, in what is perhaps the most well-known sentence of the entire work, he defines sovereignty [Fr. *souveraineté*, L. *maiestas*] as "the most high, absolute, and perpetuall power over the citisens and subiects in a Commonweale."[3]

One way to understand the place of sovereignty in Bodin's mature system of thought is to consider its higher-order function in conceptualizing the "state" [Fr. *république*, L. *respublica*]. It is, as he argues in the earlier *Methodus*, the sort of power that must be assumed, in theory, to be necessary in order for a state to exist as a unitary and independent entity. In this way, sovereignty "carves" out the boundaries of an autonomous space in which political life can flourish. Sovereignty represents, in this way, "the autonomy of the political and is the foundational concept of modern public law."[4] This necessary connection between sovereignty and the state is indeed built into his very definition of the state, which he articulates in the very first sentence of the *République*: "A Commonweale [state, *république, respublica*] is a lawfull gouernment of many families, and of that which vnto them in common belongeth, with a puissant soueraigntie."[5]

To be sure, Bodin's doctrine concerning the necessity of a superior power to hold together, in common subjection, a collective association was not unique to the state. As he argues in the second chapter of Book I of the *République*, all associations—not just the state—were understood to be tied together by some common power. Families, for example, which Bodin treated as the basic unit of the state, was understood to be tied together by shared subjection to the paterfamilial power of the father.[6] So, too, were voluntary associative bodies such as corporations understood to be tied together by the power of its "attourney or agent" [*procuratorem, aut actorem*] who had the "right of punishing individual members" [*coercendi singulos ius habet*] of the corporate body.[7] In this respect, the state, as a body politic, was no exception to the rule. Collective bodies of

[3] *République* 122 [1.8]: *la puissance absolue & perpetuelle d'une Republique. De Republica* 78: *summa in cives ac subditos legibusque soluta potestas. Commonweale* 84. I use the Knolles translation for English texts, although I use the term "state" (instead of Knolles' "Commonweale") to translate *république* and *respublica*. In this respect, I follow the convention established in the Italian translation of Margherita Isnardi Parente and Diego Quaglioni (*lo stato*) and the German translation of Bernd Wimmer (*der Staat*).

[4] Loughlin, *Idea of Public Law* 72–3.

[5] *Commonweale* 1 [1.1], *République* 1: *République est un droit gouvernement de plusieurs mesnages, & de ce qui cur est commun, avec puissance souveraine; De Republica* 1: *Respublica est familiarum rerumque inter ipsas communium summa potestate ac ratione moderata multitudo.* Bodin refers again to this definition in the opening paragraph of Book I, Chapter 8, where he stresses again the essential necessity of sovereignty for the very existence of the state.

[6] *République* 10, *De Republica* 8, *Commonweale* 8 [1.2]; cp. *Methodus* 154, citing Ulpian on the meaning of *familia* at D.50.16.195.2 and 50.16.85. The same citation recurs at *République* 479 and *De Republica* 331 [3.7] to establish the principle that a *collegium* must have at least three members.

[7] *Commonweale* 365, *De Republica* 331 [3.7].

all sorts, whether public or private, could not be acephalous; they all required a ruling "head" of some kind to assert order over, and among, their members.

But for Bodin, what made the state unique was that it was, unlike all of these other bodies, fully independent. The state recognized no legal superior *in temporalibus* and was not bound by any legal obligation. Such political and juridical independence could only correspond to a power that was, as Bodin put it, "not limited either in power, charge or time certaine."[8] It was "absolute" in the technical sense that it was "absolved" of any such legal or temporal limitation or constraint. Bodin, thus, has no hesitation in formulating this doctrine in the traditional civilian manner: sovereignty is a power that is, as he puts it, *legibus soluta*.[9]

One consequence of this analysis is the modern interpretive suggestion that Bodin ought to be treated as the preeminent representative—indeed, even the "apex"—of "absolutist" thought, perhaps a precursor to later theorists of political absolutism, such as Filmer or Hobbes, or of legal positivism, such as Austin.[10] But there are several important reasons why we ought to contest the validity of such an interpretation.[11] The first is that Bodin's concept of "absolute power" (and by implication, sovereignty) plays a technically specific function in his legal theory. Indeed, for Bodin, "absolute power" had a specific meaning, deriving from its use in Roman law describing any extralegal authority, such as the authority of Pompey who was, by the *lex Gabinia*, "dispensed withall, and absolved from all the laws, [*omnibus legibus solutus*] ordinances, and customes of his Commonweale" for five years and, more important, the authority of the *princeps*, absolved or unbound by any legal constraint in perpetuity by the people's *lex regia*.[12] In civil law, such unrestricted power is illustrated in terms of strict adherence to procedures in executing certain legal actions or transactions, such as in the making of a will.[13] Whereas private persons were not ordinarily "absolved" of the obligation to enact a will according to the prescribed legal rules for doing so, only the *princeps* was "absolved" and understood to

[8] *Commonweale* 85 [1.8].

[9] *De Republica* 14 [1.3], 78 [1.8]. The margin of 82 treats of the topic of absolute power as *legibus soluta potestas*, stressing the juridical foundation of the concept, whereas *République* 128 has *puissance absolue*.

[10] Rothbard, "Jean Bodin: Apex of Absolutist Thought in France." There remains some considerable doubt among historians whether "absolutism" is even an accurate or useful category in the study of the political and intellectual history of early modern Europe, such as John Daly, "The Idea of Absolute Monarchy in Seventeenth Century England," *Historical Journal* 21 (1978): 227–50; Nicholas Henshall, *The Myth of Absolutism: Change and Continuity in Early Modern Monarchy* (London: Longman, 1992); and more recently, Cesare Cuttica and Glenn Burgess, ed., *Monarchism and Absolutism in Early Modern Europe* (London: Pickering and Chatto, 2011).

[11] Salmon, "Legacy of Jean Bodin" 500–22 explores some of these alternatives.

[12] *Commonweale* 90, *De Republica* 84 [1.8].

[13] *Glossa Ordinaria* on D.1.3.31 on *Princeps legibus* specifies that the emperor subjects himself to the law on testaments, *voluntate sua*. Accursius cites, in turn, Inst.2.17.8, reciting the rescripts of Severus and Antoninus that "though we are not bound by the laws [*legibus soluti sumus*], nevertheless we live [*legibus vivimus*] in accordance with the laws."

be "released" from that obligation. His "absolute power"—or perhaps equivalently, his "absolved power" [*potestas soluta*]—meant that he could make a will without having to adhere strictly to the letter of the law, so as to meet the legal requirements of will-making that others had to follow.

The point could be universalized and restated as a general lesson concerning all areas of law, not just about the law governing the making of wills. A sovereign with absolute power was, by definition, under no enforceable *legal* obligation to comply with the requirements of law.[14] But this did not therefore mean that all sovereigns were to be given license to govern as arbitrarily or lawlessly as they wished. Indeed, this civilian analysis of absolute power was always read in conjunction with the normative principle that, even though a *princeps* was technically "absolved" of legal limitations [*legibus solutus*], he should nevertheless always treat himself as "obliged" or "bound" by the laws [*legibus alligatus*].[15]

It is seldom remembered in the modern scholarship that Bodin was in fact a proponent of this nuanced understanding of "absolute power." We know this, first of all, because he explicitly distinguishes, as separate categories, between these two forms of *potestas publica* in the First Book of the *République*, separating sovereign power that is *legibus soluta* from the subordinate power that is *legibus imminuta*.[16]

It must be stressed, of course, that Bodin was certainly not the first to adopt this juridical analysis of absolute power. Indeed, as legal historians such as Brian Tierney and Kenneth Pennington have shown in various studies of the Glossators and Canonists, Bodin's view reflected what had become almost a commonplace in medieval legal thought concerning the relationship between kingship and the law. Even though a *princeps* may in theory have absolute power as an extralegal *potentia* or capacity in reserve, he should nevertheless govern within the law as if he did not.[17] Strictly speaking, a prince was not legally obliged or required to do so, but good counsel and policy made it practically a necessity.[18]

That Bodin was directly influenced by these medieval antecedents to the analysis of "absolute power" is clearly evident from examining the medieval

[14] This is because *lex* is formally defined as the command of the sovereign, a device which imposes legal obligation upon the subject. For a sovereign to be subject to a *lex* of its own making would be as incoherent, in Bodin's view, as a person being bound by an obligation to a promise made to himself. Bodin cites, almost verbatim, the principles of D.45.1.108.1 and 32.1.22.pr at *De Republica* 85 [1.8].

[15] To recall, the gloss on D.1.3.31 cites the contrary principle of the *lex Digna* at C.1.14.4, that even though a ruling *princeps* is technically *legibus solutus*, he ought nevertheless to conduct his rule so that he is *legibus alligatum*, "subject to the laws."

[16] *De Republica* 14 [1.3].

[17] Tierney, "The Prince Is Not Bound By The Laws"; Tierney, "Bracton on Government" 295–317; Pennington, *Prince and the Law*. Bodin cites C.1.14.4 at *De Republica* 97 [1.8].

[18] Stephen Holmes, *Passions and Constraints: On the Theory of Liberal Democracy* (Chicago: University of Chicago Press, 1995) 115, and Holmes, "Precommitment and the Paradox of Democracy" 214–15. This was because princes were bound by divine law and natural law, which no prince could violate, even by right of sovereignty.

authorities he cited as lending support for his own view.[19] Far from breaking radically from the medieval past and engineering an unprecedented and distinctively modern concept of absolute power, as some commentators have suggested, Bodin was actually quite careful to ensure that his doctrine of sovereignty was framed so as to be largely continuous and compatible with established medieval traditions of constitutional thought in the *ius commune*.[20]

This is not to say, of course, that Bodin's treatment of sovereignty in the *République* was entirely unoriginal or without innovation. What was original about Bodin's treatment was not so much in his definition and analysis of sovereignty as absolute power, as such, but rather, in his insistence that analytical and normative inquiries concerning absolute power must be treated separately, unlike medieval jurisprudence which often tended to conjoin them. This was a direct result of his systematic attempt to treat the concept according to the standards of proper science, which required, as a general methodological axiom, analytical domains of thought to be segregated strictly from the normative. Such a methodologically rigorous attitude was, Bodin recognized, essential for proper method in all sciences, but it was especially critical in legal science, where it was necessary, as Bodin put it, to demarcate the "essentiall and formall differences" in things.[21]

To this axiom, the analysis of absolute power was no exception. Bodin could, at once, investigate the concept of absolute power not only as a value-neutral concept of analytical political theory, but also as a proper object of normative inquiry. Though subtly understated, this dual approach is possibly one of the most important aspects of Bodin's theory of sovereignty. It is often overlooked in critical studies of Bodin, which indiscriminately commingle his analytical and normative treatments of absolute power as if they were one and the same.

But, by failing to distinguish between the analytical and the normative modes of Bodin's thought, many modern commentators have not only committed the "is/ought" fallacy of (mis)taking conceptual analysis for the normative, but they have also confounded the very distinction that Bodin insisted upon. Such a leap in logic has not only had the result of presenting Bodin's thought anachronistically in terms of a crude political "absolutism," totally alien to his system of thought, but it has also obscured one of Bodin's most important teachings concerning the sovereign powers of states. Just because sovereignty is formally "absolute" or limitless in the sense of being "absolved" or "free" of all legal and institutional constraints and obligations, it does not at

[19] Giesey, "Medieval Jurisprudence in Bodin's Concept of Sovereignty" observes that the major authorities cited by Bodin in *République* are Baldus, Bartolus, and Alexander Tartagnus, as well as the Canonists, Panormitanus and Felinus Sandaeus.

[20] Pennington, *Prince and the Law* 282–3. Some examples of this conventional view include Franklin, *Jean Bodin and the Rise of Absolutist Theory*; Mesnard, *L'essor de la Philosophie Politique au XVIe Siecle*; Allen, *A History of Political Thought in the Sixteenth Century*; Helmut Quaritsch, *Staat und Souveränität* (Frankfurt am Main: Athenäum, 1970).

[21] *Commonweale* 183 [2.1].

all follow that sovereignty *should* always be exercised or implemented in this way. On the contrary, as a normative matter, Bodin argues in fact for just the opposite.

SOVEREIGNTY AND GOVERNMENT: BODIN'S PRINCIPAL-AGENT ANALYSIS OF SOVEREIGNTY

Despite defining sovereignty as an "absolute power," Bodin nevertheless expressed great unease with the concept. On the one hand, he acknowledged the necessity of sovereignty for the very existence of the state. It is simply not possible to conceive of a state as an independent body without some unifying power that is, correspondingly, independent and free of any limitation or constraint. So he admits, as an axiom to his entire theory of the state, that every independent state in history—not only the great classical states such as Athens, Sparta, Rome, but also modern kingdoms, principalities, and republics such as France, Venice, and the Holy Roman Empire—must have some sovereign authority within their respective constitutions, tying its various parts together as one unit and allowing an autonomous space to be carved out for political life.

That having been said, Bodin was fundamentally concerned about *how* sovereignty was, in practice, to be exercised and implemented. The reason for his overwhelming concern reflected his keen awareness of the potential dangers of sovereignty, a concern he voices most clearly in connection with the sovereign power of legislation, the first "mark" of sovereignty. It is well known, for example, that, for Bodin, the free and unrestricted capacity to make and unmake law (in the sense of *lex*) is, no doubt, a formal legal right of sovereignty.[22] Yet, in Book IV of the *République*, Bodin also acknowledges what he sees as the dangers that are associated with the frequent exercise of such sovereign power and, thus, warns sovereign legislators of the many potential risks involved in exercising their sovereignty by introducing new laws. As he puts it, "there is nothing more difficult to handle, nor more doubtful in euent, nor more dangerous to mannage, than to bring in new decrees or lawes."[23] This is especially crucial with respect to constitutional or public law:

> To chaunge the laws which concerne the estate [*leges quae ad statum Reipublicae pertinent mutare*], is as daungerous, as to remoue the foundation or corner stones which vphold the whole weight or burthen of the buildings; in which doing, the whole fabrike is to be sore shaken, and beside the daunger of falling, receiueth more hurt by the shaking thereof, than it doth good by the new repairation, especially if it bee now become old and ruinous.[24]

[22] *Commonweale* 102–03 [1.8], is particularly critical of laws in Antiquity that were treated as if they were immutable. As he writes, "there is no law which is perpetuall."

[23] *Commonweale* 470 [4.3].

[24] *Commonweale* 470, *De Republica* 426 [4.3].

So, even though it is certainly a sovereign right to make whatever new legislation a sovereign wishes to make, there are nevertheless real dangers and risks associated with such choices, which should enter into the sovereign's decision-making calculus. With respect to legislation, then, Bodin's position is remarkably Burkean: sovereigns should only exercise their sovereignty through introducing any legal change in the least disruptive manner, "by little and little...and not violently all at once."[25] Indeed, as a rule, sovereigns ought to avoid as much as possible having to exercise their legislative authority directly.

But there is a general lesson that can also be taken from this. The more frequently, wantonly, or recklessly sovereignty is exercised, without proper deliberation or institutional restraint, the more the state risks exposing itself to potentially destructive forces. Indeed, the careless exercise of the state's absolute power can threaten the very existence of the state itself. It is indeed for this reason that Bodin strikingly advises sovereigns to avoid having to exercise their sovereignty. The central normative doctrine emerging from Bodin's theory of sovereignty was, thus, a principle of self-restraint. Being formally free and entitled to exercise sovereignty without restraint does not at all mean that one *should* exercise sovereignty in such a way and at all times.[26]

So the question is this: *How* should such sovereignty actually be exercised in the practical day-to-day task of governing and managing affairs of state? To address this question, Bodin introduced a distinction that would become critical not only for his theory of the sovereign state, but would also become one of his major contributions to modern constitutional thought and subsequently shape the thought of modern political theorists such as Hobbes, Pufendorf, and Rousseau—that is, the distinction between "the state of a commonwealth [*l'estat d'une République du gouvernement; status reipublicae*]...[and] the administration and government of the same" [*administration; gubernatio*].[27] By drawing

[25] *Commonweale* 471 [4.3].

[26] On this point in Bodin's thought, see Holmes, "Precommitment and the Paradox of Democracy" 214–15; Holmes, *Passions and Constraints* 115. On the question whether a sovereign legislator should actively introduce new legislation, especially on matters of state, Bodin indicates that such sovereign power should rarely be exercised, except in cases of "urgent necessitie." Bodin, *Commonweale* 470–71 [4.3]. See also Lee, "Office Is a Thing Borrowed" 416–20.

[27] *République* 272; *De Republica* 189; *Commonweale* 199 [2.2]. The word, "state," in this formulation, I argue, is being used in the sense of "form" or "condition"—as in the Ciceronian formulation *status reipublicae* or even the *optimus civitatis status*—and not so much in the substantive sense of the modern "nation-state," which is represented instead by the terms, *respublica* or *république*. Hobbes, for example, discusses the distinction between the "the right of *summum imperium*" [*summi imperii ius*] and the mere "exercise" [*exercitium*] in *De Cive* 1647: 213–14 (13, §1). At 214, Hobbes, following the legal humanist analysis, speaks of *summum imperium* held and administered either "by one's own proper right" or "by the right of another" [*sive proprio, sive alieno iure*]. Rousseau introduces the discussion in Book III of the *Social Contract*, especially in Ch. 1, which treats "government" as "merely the minister" of the sovereign authority, "an intermediate body established between subjects and sovereigns...charged with the execution of the laws and the maintenance of freedom." *The Social Contract*, ed. and trans. Victor Gourevitch (Cambridge: Cambridge University Press, 1997) 82–3. This trajectory is discussed in Loughlin, *Foundations of Public Law* 59, 76, 80, 108–17, as central to the autonomous category of the *droit publique*. This distinction is also the central organizing theme of Tuck's lectures on *The Sleeping Sovereign*.

this distinction, Bodin carved out a normative domain of analysis concerning *how* sovereignty ought to be exercised, separate from the conceptual task of explaining *what* sovereignty is.

One important theme that immediately emerges in Bodin's normative treatment of sovereignty in this way is that sovereignty is properly to be exercised, not directly, but *indirectly*, through delegation of powers to others—as "agents" of sovereignty. While it is certainly true that sovereignty could, by right, be exercised directly and immediately by the sovereign authority, it could just as well be exercised *indirectly* through an intermediary agent or mandatary, legally constituted with a share of public authority, as he explains in the case of monarchies:

> There is a great difference betwixt the State, and the government of the State: a rule in policy (to my knowledge) not before touched by any man: for the state may be in a monarchie [*Monarchie; reipublicae status regalis*], and yet the government nevertheless popular [*gouverné populairement*; *gubernatio popularis*]; if the king do distribute all places of command, magistracy, offices, and preferments indifferently unto all men, without regard of their nobility, wealth, or virtue. But if the prince shall give all command, honors, and offices unto the nobility only, or to the rich, or the valiant, or to the virtuous only, it shall be a royal monarchy, and that simple and pure, but yet tempered in manner of an aristocracy.[28]

The modes of government by which sovereignty is exercised are, as Bodin admits, potentially unlimited.[29] The difference in these modes depends entirely on *how* the sovereign authority assumes "an institutional form," so as to be exercised and expressed through the agency of others.[30]

Bodin's principal-agent approach was important for several reasons. It indicated, first of all, that a sovereign authority, whoever or whatever it was, was fully entitled, if it so chose, to exercise supreme power by delegating it in any way it pleased, so that it may be legally exercised through an agent or mandatary without, in any way, compromising the principal's right to sovereignty. Delegated sovereignty, in short, was fully compatible with absolute and indivisible sovereignty, just as granting the use, care, or management of one's

[28] *République* 272; *De Republica* 289; *Commonweale* 199 [2.2]. In Book VI, Bodin clarifies that "there bee few or rather no such monarchies indeed." *Commonweale* 786 [6.6].

[29] Bodin allows, as a minimum, no less than nine different possible forms of "government," and likely more. Each of the three basic forms of states (monarchy, aristocracy, and the popular state) can be governed in one of three ways, as Bodin indicates at *République* 273 [2.2] and 507 [4.1]; *Commonweale* 200 and 409. Monarchies can be governed in a "royal" or "lawful" [*legitime*] manner, a "seigneurial" manner, or a "tyrannical" manner. Aristocracies can be governed lawfully, seigneurially, or in a "factious" [*factieuse*] manner. Popular states can be governed lawfully, seigneurially, or in a "turbulent" manner, which Bodin, citing Cicero, calls "the greatest tyrannie of all." Cp. *Commonweale* 199 [2.2], 409 [4.1], 700 [6.4]. But Bodin allows more than just these nine principal forms of government, since in his discussion of "harmonic justice" in Book VI Bodin actually enjoins monarchies to delegate authority by constitutional law so as to "knit together" a "government so compound and mixed" of both aristocratic and popular elements. *Commonweale* 755 [6.6].

[30] Loughlin, *Foundations of Public Law* 186.

proprietary estate to another was still fully compatible with the owner retaining the right of property.[31]

That Bodin envisaged such a principal-agent analysis to model the corresponding relationship between the sovereign state and its government is indicated right at the beginning of his famous chapter on sovereignty in Book I of the *République*, where he tries to specify what is (and what is not) the essence of sovereign authority by introducing certain extreme threshold cases illustrating how even the state's "absolute power over citizens could certainly be given to one or many" without also compromising the principal's status as sovereign.[32]

By far, the best known example in Bodin's thought where the state's "absolute power...[is] granted...to one or many to manage their estate and entire gouernment" [*donne puissance absolute de manier l'estat & gouverner entierement; summam ac legibus solutam potestatem... dari*] was that of the Roman dictator, an example we have already seen briefly in the *Methodus*.[33] As he famously—and controversially—states, the Roman dictator could never properly be regarded as the bearer of sovereignty in Rome, despite his exercise of such extraordinary power, because his hold on that power always came with an expiry attached to the dictatorship.[34] For Bodin, there was no doubt or disagreement that dictators held a legally unlimited "absolute" power, but it was a power which was valid only "for a short period of time [*breve tempus*], and not in perpetuity."[35] So even though Roman dictators such as Cincinnatus (for fifteen days), Servilius (for eight days), and Mamercus (for one day), certainly may have held *supreme* or *absolute* power over Rome, it could hardly be a genuine *sovereign* power, precisely because it was temporally limited.[36] Nor was the dictator even a kind of "supreme magistrate" [*Magistrat souverain; summu(m) ... magistratu(m)*], such as the Roman Praetorian Prefect or the Merovingian French Mayors of the Palace, since dictatorial appointments were, in Bodin's view, extraordinary and precarious grants of power held during the sovereign's pleasure.[37] At most,

[31] Bodin invokes analogies of property relations in explaining delegated sovereignty in *De Republica* 80–01 [1.8] and cites especially D.2.1.6, 2.1.6, 41.2.3, in connection with his analysis of the relationship between the sovereign people of the Cnidiens and the Amymones, to whom *imperium* was entrusted as deposit [*depositum*].

[32] *Commonweale* 84 [1.8]; cp. *Commonweale* 767 [6.6].

[33] *République* 124; *De Republica* 80; *Commonweale* 86 [1.8].

[34] *République* 123 [1.8]. Bodin thus distances himself from those who did consider the dictator to hold sovereign authority, such as Pomponius' attribution of *summa potestas* to the dictator in the *Enchiridion* (D.1.2.2.18) and Renaissance writers such as Sir Thomas Elyot who, in the *Boke Named the Governour*, treated the dictator as "sovereign" and in possession of the "pristine authority and majesty of a king." See Tuck, *Sleeping Sovereign* Lecture I. Grotius would criticize Bodin on precisely this point at *War and Peace* 281–3 [1.3.11] suggesting instead that "the dictator, during the whole time of his office, exercised all the acts of civil government, with as much authority as the most absolute King." However, Pufendorf would later defend Bodin against Grotius' criticism, at Book VII, Ch. 6, §15 of *De Iure Naturae et Gentium*. These arguments against Bodin's position seem to anticipate Carl Schmitt's arguments against the impossibility of commissarial dictatorship as something distinct from sovereignty. I thank David Dyzenhaus for pointing out this linkage.

[35] *De Republica* 79 [1.8]. [36] *De Republica* 80 [1.8].

[37] Bodin makes a fundamental distinction between "commissioners" [*commissaires*] and "officers" [*officiers*], with the latter including all magistrates. The notion of "supreme magistrate" or "sovereign magistrate" is

the dictator could only be said to have absolute power delegated as a "simple commission," charged exclusively with the expeditious completion of certain defined tasks.[38]

While the dictatorship was perhaps the best known example to illustrate this point, it was by no means the only one. Using a variety of classical examples, such as the Roman Decemvirate, the Spartan Harmost, the Thessalonian Aesymnetes, the Maltese Archus, and the Athenian Archon, Bodin underscores his general point that the mere holding or exercising of absolute power does not, by itself, make one a sovereign, precisely because such power may be held as a temporary grant. Such persons of high authority, Bodin argues, never have sovereignty. They are, rather, merely agents appointed as temporary "depositaries of power" [*depositaires de la puissance; potestatem precariam*].[39]

Nor was the practice of delegating absolute power to agents merely an institutional practice restricted only to the tumultuous politics of classical states. Even modern states, as Bodin observed, granted absolute power to agents, especially in moments of constitutional emergency, such as in Florence in the time of Machiavelli [*populari potestate*], where such power was extraordinarily committed by the populace to the *Balia*, an emergency council of citizens convoked by a *parlamento* for major fiscal or institutional reforms.[40] National monarchies likewise governed by the grant of commissions of absolute power to subordinate bodies or agents, such as the Habsburg King of Spain who granted, on his sufferance, a plenary, though fully "revocable," absolute authority to senatorial bodies governing in his name over the conquered Duchy of Milan and the Kingdom of Naples.[41] Even in his native France, Bodin acknowledged that the king could exercise absolute power over the kingdom "by precarious commission" [*commission precaire; precario*] of such power to agents, such as

discussed at *République* 451–2 [3.6]. Bodin also gives here the example of Henry, Duke of Anjou, appointed as the *Prince de France* and *Lieutenant General* to King Charles IX, an example appearing prominently at *République* 127 [1.8].

[38] In *De Republica* 79–80 [1.8], "commission" is translated as *curator*, which is the Latin term used at *De Republica* 259 [3.2] for *commissaire*, and *commissarium*. It is noteworthy that Bodin indicates that a dictator extraordinarily appointed on simple commission can, nevertheless, discharge specific sovereign functions to be identified later in 1.10, such as "the making of warre" [*curatio belli gerendi*], "the reforming of the state" [*reipub(licae) constituendae*], and "the instituting of new officers" [*magistratuum creandorum*].

[39] *République* 124; *De Republica* 80. *Commonweale* 86 [1.8] has it as a "borrowed power." The French edition only has a crucial marginal citation to Ulpian at D.1.17.1, which discusses the Prefect of Egypt "lay[ing] down the *imperium*" [*deponit . . . imperium*], which was "given to him by law" [*lege . . . ei datum est*]. See p. 185, n.129 for Bodin's comment in the *Methodus* on Alciato's worry about Ulpian's statement to "lay down" authority and office.

[40] *De Republica* 79 [1.8]. Bodin again makes reference to the Florentine *Balia*, at *De Republica* 304–05 [3.3]. On the *Balia*, see John Najemy, *A History of Florence, 1200–1575* (Oxford: Blackwell, 2006) and Nicolai Rubinstein, *The Government of Florence under the Medici* (Oxford: Oxford University Press, 1997). I thank Mauricio Suchowlansky for this point. It is, as Bodin explains later, an institutional design strategy typical of what he calls *seigneurial* regimes, states that govern not through law, but by the arbitrary will of the sovereign authority, such as the Turkish Sultan, who entrusts absolute power as an extraordinary commission to the Grand Vizier.

[41] *République* 126; *De Republica* 81; *Commonweale* 87 [1.8].

"the Regents or Viceroyes of kingdoms" [*Regents des Royaumes; Regentes regni*] as was the Queen Regent Catherine de Medici during the minority of her son, Charles IX, and especially through the institutional device of Lieutenants-General of France, to which Bodin alluded, with some alarm, as an increasingly common and destabilizing practice in French constitutional politics of the sixteenth century:

> There was neuer greater power giuen to magistrat next vnto his prince, than that which was of late yeares graunted to Henrie of Fraunce, duke of Aniou, by king Charles the ninth his brother, for it was most great and perpetuall, without any exception of the regall power [*de regale*; *regalis potestate*]: yet for all that one cannot say that it was soueraigne [*souverain*; *summa*], inasmuch as he was called Leiutenant General for the king [*Lieutenant general pour le Roy*; *legatus sui principis*], *So long as it shall stand with our good pleasure*, ioyned vnto it in his letters patents: which wel declareth a power but during pleasure [*souffrances*; *precariu(m) imperium...significat*]. Which power of lieutenancie (as of all magistracies) ceaseth in the presence of the prince.[42]

The King of France, in Bodin's analysis, remains fully sovereign, even while power is exercised by other agents within the realm, whether they happen to be the legally constituted magistrates of Parlement or extraordinarily commissioned lieutenants serving at the king's pleasure.

All of these examples, whether of classical or modern origin, are however prefatory to the most important example, which Bodin very deliberately seems to have held back in order to complete his analysis of delegated sovereignty. This was the example of the *lex regia* of Roman law which, as he put it, epitomizes all the cases where a sovereign "people have given absolute power [to a man] so long as he liveth."[43] Without taking an interpretive position on the old medieval dispute as to whether or not the *lex regia* represented a full alienation of popular sovereignty to the *princeps*, Bodin charitably acknowledges that, even under the *lex regia*, the *princeps*—who, as Ulpian declares, is

[42] *Commonweale* 85, 87–8 [1.8]; *République* 123, 126–27; *De Republica* 79, 81–2. In addition to Henry, Duke of Anjou, Francis, Duke of Guise was also made Lieutenant General. The use of the term, *legatus*, to describe the juridical position of the Lieutenant General is particularly significant, and he does so frequently to indicate one way of understanding the relationship between sovereign and subordinate levels of authority. Bodin's marginal notation in this part of the text cites, inter alia, D.1.16.3 in the rubric on Roman legates to stress the point that, as agents of proconsuls, legates have no *iurisdictio* "as of right" [*nihil proprium habent*, cp. D.1.21.1.1] but only by "express mandate of the proconsul" [*a proconsule mandata*]. The principle that subordinate authority delegated to magistrates ceases "in the presence of the prince" also appears at *Commonweale* 170 [1.10], but it was not specific to monarchical states, but a general principle of sovereign authority in all its forms. Thus, at *Commonweale* 344 [3.6], "in Popular estates, the greatest magistrats as well as the least...laid down their mases and other tokens of honour before the people, and so standing, spake vnto the people sitting: showing, that in their presence they had no power at all to commaund." But it is also worth pointing out Bodin's worry about the suspension of magisterial power: "For the suspending of all magistrates in general, is a thing right dangerous, not only in Popular and Aristocratic estates, but even in a Monarchie also." *Commonweale* 281.

[43] *République* 127; *De Republica* 82; *Commonweale* 88 [1.8], citing D.1.4.1 with the verb, *contulit*. Bodin specifies later, following convention, that the *lex regia* is equivalent to the *lex de imperio Vespasiani*, and not the *lex Hortensia*.

legibus solutus—might nevertheless be said to be limited, precisely because he is an agent of the Roman people and, thus, limited by the residual relationship of agency between the Roman people (as principal) and the Roman *princeps* (as agent). This is, as he observes, only plausible if the original popular grant of authority by the *lex regia* is interpreted as a kind of concessive delegation, as in the concession theory of Azo and Accursius, so that a *princeps*, despite his absolute powers, can be regarded as nothing more than "a plaine [*simple*] officer, or leiutenant, regent, gouernour, or guerdon and keeper of another mans power" [*gardien, & bail de la puissance d'autruy*].[44]

In all of these examples, the main point that Bodin wanted to stress was the incompatibility of sovereignty and agency: all agents, however great their power was in magnitude, were always understood to be limited by their status as agents. For this reason alone, agents can never be sovereign.[45] This point is, of course, not difficult to see in cases where the agent holds a limited power, such as an inferior magistrate whose power is defined and bound [*imminuta*] by law.[46] Because such agents were limited in these ways, they could never be considered sovereign, which, by definition, was *legibus solutus*, legally unlimited.

But Bodin wants to make an even bolder and more controversial statement. Even those agents to whom a legally unlimited absolute power is granted—like the dictator, the *Balia*, the lieutenant general, and even the *princeps*—are also excluded from the right of sovereignty because their grasp on such extraordinary power is always temporary and tenuous. Even if such authority figures might technically be legally unlimited and absolute in their powers, "exempted from all laws" [*omnibus (legibus) solutus est*] during their tenure, they are nevertheless tied by an overriding bond of obligation that all agents, even the most powerful, always owe to their principals.[47] Their power comes with strings attached, tethering them to their respective sovereigns, whether they happen to be princes or peoples.

[44] *Commonweale* 88 [1.8]; *République* 127. Bodin uses the analogy of public power holders to a mere *gardien* or *bail* at 439 [3.5]. *De Republica* 82 shows Bodin to be more deliberate and careful in the use of his terms to describe the *princeps* as agent of the people, to be called *magistratus, aut curatoris, aut legati appellatione . . . aut procuratoris*, all of which correspond to specific roles defined in Roman (and canon) law.

[45] *République* 127 identifies three modes of agency-creation (1) *par commission*, (2) *par institution*, or (3) *par delegation*, each for either a defined term or in perpetuity. The Latin text at *De Republica* 82, however, identifies only two modes, (1) *curatio* and (2) *magistratus*, each of which can also be either temporally limited [*ad breue tempus*] or unlimited [*in perpetuum*].

[46] *De Republica* 14 [1.3] distinguishes two types of public power: public power that is "*legibus soluta* belonging to those who have the right of *summum imperium*" and public power that is "*legibus imminuta*" belonging to magistrates and other subordinate authorities. Cp. *République* 19 [1.3].

[47] *De Republica* 84 [1.8]. This passage in the Latin *De Republica* explains, at 85, that, even though the *princeps* Augustus was "exempted from all laws of his country in perpetuity" [*omnibus patriae legibus in perpetuo solutus sit*], he "nevertheless made himself subordinate to the whole people most often when making a direct appeal to the people" [*populo tamen vniuerso . . . inferiorem se simulans rogationes ad populum saepissime ferebat*], just as a Republican magistrate making a similar appeal to popular authority. This passage does not appear in the corresponding page of the French text, *République* 131.

The lesson here, then, was a simple, but centrally important, one for Bodin. No government agent, however powerful, could ever be said to be a sovereign because the very concept of delegated agency by some derivative or concessive act of mandate always implied some limit—otherwise, it wouldn't be delegation. As Bodin puts it, a sovereign "never giveth so much power vnto another, but that hee alwayes keepeth [*retienne; reservavit*] more vnto himselfe."[48] Since such delegated power is limited by the very terms or conditions under which power—even absolute power—is delegated, it cannot, by definition, be a sovereign power, but something inferior and subordinate.

THE JURIDICAL SOURCES OF BODIN'S PRINCIPAL-AGENT ANALYSIS OF SOVEREIGNTY: THE ROMAN LAW OF DELEGATED JURISDICTION

By summarily disqualifying all agents, however powerful, from sovereignty, Bodin considerably and controversially narrowed the field of candidates eligible to assert a right of sovereignty. He excluded, for example, the Holy Roman Emperor, the Doge of Venice, and the King of Poland from the category of sovereignty because they all held their regnal titles and authorities only by way of election, as "agents" of their electors who, in his view, should properly be regarded as the bearers of sovereignty. He likewise excluded any holder of a legally constituted permanent public office—even the most powerful magisterial office, such as the Roman consul or praetor—from sovereignty since such officers were always understood to exercise the public power attached to their office under fixed legal terms.

But despite specifying more precisely the criterion of sovereignty in terms of actionable rights, Bodin also made his task considerably more difficult in a way, and that was because the search for sovereignty, in Bodin's theory, could no longer rely simply on the actual exercise or simple possession of absolute power as the sole criterion for sovereignty, since even the holder of such a great power might nevertheless hold it as an agent. How could it be possible, then, to identify such a sovereign authority, which has, divested itself of sovereignty through delegation and "de-activated" itself into a state of constitutional hibernation or dormancy to become, as Richard Tuck has suggested, a "sleeping sovereign?" Conventional language cannot help in this task because what may appear to be a name or sign indicating sovereignty—such as a title of royal dignity, as in the case of the Holy Roman Emperor or the Doge of Venice—may, in fact, be nothing more than an empty [*inane*] title or "cipher."[49]

What was needed, instead, was a new science of sovereignty that circumvented both conventional language (especially those of classical historians) and traditional considerations of magnitude or exercise of power. For Bodin,

[48] *République* 123; *De Republica* 79; *Commonweale* 85 [1.8]. There is a marginal citation on this sentence in the French and Latin editions to the *Liber Sextus* VI 3.4.14.

[49] *De Republica* 79; *Commonweale* 85 [1.8]; cp. *De Republica* 82.

the focus had to be fixed entirely upon the "essentiall and formall" qualities of states, rather than upon mere "externall accidents," especially normative value-laden considerations, which are potentially "innumerable."[50] One of Bodin's most urgent tasks for his civil science of the state was to provide some guidance on how a principal-agent analysis might be conducted, so that it would be possible to "trace" and "uncover" the form of the true sovereign authority in any state, as the principal sovereign entity, which, by implication, was understood to be hidden behind all institutional forms legally constituted to govern the state, and to exercise public power in its place, while sovereignty is de-activated and laying dormant.

Of course, in the early modern context, before the rise of the modern social sciences, Bodin had limited analytical resources available to him to express the essentials of such a principal-agent analysis and the associated problems of principal-agent relations in law, economics, and public administration—what might be called today "agency slack," "information asymmetry," and "transaction costs."[51] What he *did* have available to him, however, was the legal science of civil law, and insofar as the civil law was chiefly concerned with relations between legal persons, it enabled him to approach the body of concepts and principles approximating modern principal-agent analyses, although framed in the juridical language of the *Corpus Iuris Civilis*. The point of entry into Bodin's thought concerning the delegated exercise of sovereignty by way of agency must, I argue, be through this juridical framework.

Bodin was, of course, not the first to frame the principal-agent analysis of sovereignty in terms of civil law. As we have already seen, in sixteenth-century jurisprudence, the legal humanists of Bourges, beginning above all with Alciato, crafted the enormously influential theory that the *princeps* of Roman law alone might be understood to be a principal or *dominus* with full right in their *imperium*, like the legal right of *nuda proprietas*, while magistrates were simple agents of the *princeps* who were granted limited *usus* or *exercitium* in the public *imperium* belonging rightfully to the *princeps*.

But Bodin was largely resistant to the humanist doctrine of delegation and agency, represented above all, in Bodin's view, by Alciato, Donellus, and Dumoulin. The main reason for his opposition might be traced to what he viewed as an unjustified argument in the humanist theory of delegated authority. They treated all agents of the state's sovereignty indifferently—from the highest magistrate to the lowest clerk—as if they were all in the same position

[50] *Commonweale* 183 [2.1]. In this respect, Bodin may be seen, therefore, as a progenitor of modern legal positivism and one of the first to stress what, in the modern social sciences, has been called the "fact-value distinction." Bodin's call for a value-free inquiry into sovereignty was intended largely as a critique of Aristotelian political science which, in his view, improperly combined the normative and the conceptual dimensions of analysis.

[51] Arthur Lupia, "Delegation of Power: Agency Theory," *International Encyclopedia of the Social and Behavioral Sciences* 5 (2001): 3375–7; Darren Hawkins, David Lake, Daniel Nielson, Michael Tierney, ed., *Delegation and Agency in International Organizations* (Cambridge: Cambridge University Press, 2006).

of inferiority and dependence with respect to the sovereign authority, just as any simple agent in civil law was with respect to a *dominus*.

To recall the humanist analysis, all magistrates in public law were understood to be legally indistinct in status from other legal agents in civil law, such as a *procurator*, an *administrator*, or a *usufructuarius*. This was the important innovation of Andrea Alciato who, in his *Paradoxa*, remarked that all legally constituted magistrates were not proper "owners" of their jurisdictional authority [*domini iurisdictionis*], but merely its usufructuaries. The unavoidable consequence of this humanist analysis was that a magistrate, even the highest magistrate of state, was legally incapacitated from acting in certain ways contrary to what is "proper" [*propria*] for an agent in civil law. For example, on the humanist theory, a magistrate was strictly prohibited from sub-delegating his authority to another agent, because they held their authority on a strict mandate. Such magistrates had, as we have already observed in Bodin's *Methodus*, "the *exercise* of public authority [*publici iudicii exercitium*], but were unable to delegate it again to others."[52]

But for Bodin, this humanist argument positioning all magistrates as simple agents without any proper right of their own was an absurdity, a "reason without appearance" [*raison sans apparence; absurdum*], on two important grounds.[53] It contradicted the bare text of Papinian's rule [D.1.21.1.pr] in Roman law that "magistrats may depute and commit...as they themselves please, of such things as they have by vertue of their office [*iure magistratus*], and which are proper to their estate." There was also an obvious mismatch between law and fact in the humanist theory which, if enacted, would have artificially and unjustifiably restricted magisterial authority in a way potentially damaging to the government and general welfare of the state.[54]

Bodin began with a point of fact: ordinary magistrates—Bodin has in mind permanent judges with ordinary jurisdiction—did actually have the right to appoint agents and to delegate some share of their authority to them.[55] This was the case not only in early modern France, but also in Roman legal procedure under the *legis actio* and formulary systems, where the first formal act in litigation was the *nominatio* of a private judge [*iudex* or *arbiter*] by the magistrate and delegation of jurisdiction to that agent. If magistrates were really nothing more than simple agents appointed to act on a strict mandate, as the humanist had opined, then it would follow, by that same logic, that magistrates cannot

[52] *Methodus* 171.

[53] *République* 441; *De Republica* 305; *Commonweale* 334 [3.5]. The marginal note in the French and Latin cite two royal decrees of Charles VII and Charles VIII concerning the constitution of the legally autonomous offices of *Lieutenans des Baillifs & Seneschaux* [*Praetorum legatos suo beneficio*]. Bodin is almost certainly taking this from Dumoulin who makes the original citation in *De Feudis* §58.

[54] *République* 441; *De Republica* 305–06; *Commonweale* 334 [3.5]. The French marginalia cites D.1.21.1 as well as 2.1.5 and 2.1.16.

[55] David Parker, "Sovereignty, Absolutism and the Function of the Law in Seventeenth-Century France," *Past and Present* 122 (1989): 36–74; Richard Bonney, "Bodin and the Development of the French Monarchy," *Transactions of the Royal Historical Society: Fifth Series* 40 (1990): 51.

re-commit that authority unto another agent, which was, Bodin thought, factually untrue.[56]

Even more troubling than this mismatch between law and fact was, for Bodin, the humanist argument explaining just *why* a magistrate could not sub-delegate.[57] Specifically, the humanists relied upon a haphazard commingling of private law and public law ideas, by treating magisterial *iurisdictio* as if it were an object of private property in the care of magistrates, acting as if they were "usufructuaries" or "usuaries" of servient property.[58] Since, on this view, magistrates were essentially usuaries, but not the proper "owners of jurisdiction" [*domini iurisdictionis*], they were thought to be bound by the general rule of equity that usuaries may not sub-delegate or reassign their rights of use onto another.[59] To do so would, in effect, be equivalent to an illicit act of alienation, exposing the usuary to liability and civil remedies for restitution litigated by the *dominus*. This analysis provided, as Alciato put it in his *Paradoxa*, the "new reason why *merum imperium* is non-transferable" [*nova ratio cur merum imperium in delegatum non transeat*].[60]

Since, on the humanist theory, public authority can be treated as validly subject to rules of property, it follows that rules prohibiting sub-delegation or reassignment should also be applicable in the case of delegated jurisdiction. Dumoulin, who approvingly cited Alciato's *Paradoxa* on this point, similarly reasoned that, just as a "usuary cannot constitute [*nequit constituere*] another usuary," neither were magistrates "able to constitute their own deputies or lieutenants" [*non possunt sibi constituere vicarios, vel locum tenentes*].[61] Ordinary magistrates were not "owners of jurisdiction" [*domini iurisdictionis*] but merely its agents, as "simple administrators."

Bodin, however, felt that this humanist application of private law was deeply problematic, and he accused, by name, Alciato and Dumoulin of introducing—"without reason"—rules of private law in the analysis of public office.[62] According to Bodin, both Alciato and Dumoulin (and their humanist disciples) were guilty of describing magistrates—such as the French bailiff and seneschal or the Roman *praetor*—"but as simple *usagers* or *occupiers*" [*usuarii*] of

[56] If the humanist analysis *were* true, a magistrate such as a praetor or provincial governor would have no right to delegate jurisdiction to a private judge or legate. But that is, as Bodin argues, clearly not how Roman procedure worked.

[57] Gilmore, *Argument from Roman Law* Ch. 2.

[58] Bodin, *République* 441 [3.5], accuses Dumoulin of comparing public magistrates to private-law *usagers* which, in the Latin *De Republica* 305, is called a *usuarius*. Cp. *Commonweale* 333 [3.5], magistrates as "mere executors and ministers" [to describe the *legis actio*]. Cp. *Methodus* 171: *executores & administratores.*

[59] Alciato 4:39 [*Paradoxa* 2.6], and also 1:44 on D.1.21.1. Alciato does not seem to account for the conflicting statements of Ulpian and Paul which allow a usufructuary to grant [*concedere*] usufructuary right to another, such as D.7.1.12.2 and 7.1.63.

[60] Alciato 4:39 [*Paradoxa* 2.6, §§5–6].

[61] Dumoulin 1:79 [*De Feudis*, Gloss 5 on *Le Fief* §57].

[62] *Commonweale* 334 [3.5]. Gilmore, *Argument from Roman Law* 104. Bodin's targeting of Alciato and Dumoulin is continuous with his earlier brief statement on this point in the *Methodus*, an important piece of evidence to show the trajectory and continuity of thought between these two works.

sovereign authority who lacked the power of "the appointing of their deputies" [*potestatem legatos constituendi*].[63] Bodin accuses Dumoulin, by name, for having "addeth the Pretors of cities, whom wee call Bailifes, and Seneschals, by the lawes of this realme, to have the power taken from them for the appointing of their deputies."[64] The problem with this application of the law of usufructs was not only that it opened the door to what Bodin saw as an unacceptable commingling of private law with public law. The more serious problem was that this would, in effect, bind magistrates to an artificial rule of private law with absolutely no validity in public law—namely, the rule that "he which hath a thing but only to use and occupy, cannot make any other *usager or occupier* but himself."[65]

BODIN'S CRITICISM OF THE HUMANIST THEORY OF DELEGATED AUTHORITY

The legal humanist theory, thus, became one of Bodin's chief targets of criticism in the *République*. As in the *Methodus*, Bodin was especially concerned to show that, while high public authority can certainly be delegated to magistrates and other subordinates, such delegation did not thereby reduce magistrates to the status of a mere manager or usuary of a property belonging to someone else, as in private law. The relationship, as Bodin wants to show, was fundamentally different, and he relied on a different Roman law source to make that argument.

As Bodin was well aware, even in his earlier work such as the *Methodus*, the origins of the humanist theory could actually be traced back to the medieval debate on *imperium* between the Glossators—Azo and Lothair—which he had already discussed in the *Methodus*. Bodin also knew that the humanists were responsible for deliberately reviving Lothair's doctrine, thereby unsettling a legal doctrine that had been long settled through centuries of medieval legal science. As he observed, "many since have [adopted] the opinion of Lothair, so that the question [concerning *imperium*] remaineth yet undecided."[66] It was, above all, Alciato who reformulated Lothair's doctrine using the civilian framework of agency to emphasize how even the most powerful magistrate or vassal was nevertheless inferior to his prince. In reviewing the history of this legal debate, Bodin viewed Lothair, Alciato, and Dumoulin together as representing one unified school of thought on the issue of magisterial authority, despite their separation over a period of several centuries—in opposition to the standard view of Azo, Accursius, and Bartolus.

[63] *République* 441; *De Republica* 305; *Commonweale* 334 [3.5]. This was factually untrue in the French case of bailiffs and seneschals who held appellate jurisdiction in the early modern French judiciary.

[64] *République* 441; *De Republica* 305; *Commonweale* 334 [3.5].

[65] *République* 441; *De Republica* 305; *Commonweale* 334 [3.5]; cp. D.7.1.63.

[66] *Commonweale* 327 [3.5].

As in the *Methodus*, Bodin renewed his complaint that neither side adequately explained this question of delegated public authority.[67] But the argument of the *République* is, in some important respects, richer and more conceptually sophisticated than in his earlier account. This was, Bodin thought, because they did not specify whether they intended their dicta on *imperium* to be a general theory of delegation applicable to all states, or a more narrowly crafted historical interpretation of delegated authority applicable only within the classical Roman context. Because of this failure to specify, Bodin thought the lawyers "entangled themselves, some mistaking the practise, and some the theorique" of the Roman state.[68]

If the intent had only been to describe Roman practice, Bodin declared that he could not conclusively judge which of the two had the better view. As he scornfully observed, "neither of them [i.e., Azo and Lothair] well knew Rome" and had "no insight into the estate or government of the Roman Commonweale."[69] On the one hand, Lothair might be said to have had the better view "if hee had spoken but of the auntient Pretors of Rome" during the Republic.[70] On the other hand, however, Azo might be said to have had the better view if the Emperor's question referred to the constitution of magistrates in the Principate where, as Bodin observed, the Roman Emperors granted a wide degree of discretionary power as *imperium* to the high magistrates such as the praetors, "the great Provost of Rome" [*praefecti urbi*], and the "presidents and governours of provinces" [*praesides provinciarum*], all of whom had the power to judge "according to their owne discretion" [*arbitrio suo*] and had "the power of the sword" [*gladii ius* = *merum imperium*] when the formulary procedure fell into disuse and was replaced by the *cognitio extra ordinem*.[71] Bodin's criticism

[67] It is not surprising that Bodin would be so deeply interested in the topic of magisterial *imperium* and *iurisdictio* in Roman law. Indeed, he devoted an entire treatise, *De imperio et iurisdictione*, specifically to this topic, almost certainly written during the early years of his intellectual development as a scholar of Roman law at Toulouse. We know this because, at various points in the *Methodus*, Bodin makes reference to his earlier work on civil law, *De imperio*, where he says he had discussed at length the debate between Azo and Lothair concerning the magistrate's *imperium* in that work. The *Iuris Universi Distributio* also devotes significant space to matters of legal process and, especially, the function or "duty" of the judge [*officium iudicis*]. For someone such as Bodin, so deeply committed to elucidating the foundations of modern public law, the dicta on magisterial authority in the *Digest* were the major points of entry. It is for this reason, then, that Bodin's earliest writings on the public authority of the state began as commentaries on civil law. See Chapter 5 on the *Methodus*.

[68] *Commonweale* 334 [3.5].

[69] *Commonweale* 327 [3.5].

[70] *Commonweale* 329 [3.5], 334 [3.5]. *République* 432 and *De Repulica* 300 explain that no magistrate in the early Roman Republic had the *ius gladii in cives*, the power of capital penalty over citizens. Bodin cites, in support of his observation of the early Roman Republican constitution, Books VII and X of Livy, *Ab Urbe Condita* and Cicero, *Pro Rabirio* and *In Catalinam*. As Bodin explains in *Commonweale* 293 [3.3], all delegations of ancient kings before the invention of law were all by way of commission, where "the prince's word, becke, and will, serv[ed] instead of all lawes, who both in time of peace and war, by commissions gave out charge to whome they pleased; and againe at their pleasure revoked the same." Citing Pomponius, Bodin argues, since the period of the Roman Monarchy fell chronologically prior to the XII Tables, early Roman officials were not properly magistrates but commissioners.

[71] *Commonweale* 330 [3.5]; *De Republica* 303. The important difference between the *legis actio* and the formulary procedures, on the one hand, and the *cognitio extra ordinem*, on the other, was that the latter

was that, depending on the specific period of Roman constitutional history, both Azo and Lothair were correct—and incorrect. We just cannot tell from the medieval sources alone.

But even if Azo and Lothair had intended to articulate a general theory of delegated state authority, applicable beyond the narrow classical Roman context, there still remained a more basic conceptual problem, in Bodin's view: the relationship between *princeps* and magistrate was framed exclusively in terms of private law categories, almost as if the *princeps*-magistrate relationship emerged out of a commercial transaction between two private parties in civil law. Both views articulated by Azo and Lothair were faulty, but for different reasons. He thought, on the one hand, that Azo treated magistrates as the actual legal "owners" in their magisterial authority, just as if the supreme *princeps* had "communicated" to them a right of property in their public powers by an act of alienation approximating a *donatio inter vivos*. On Azo's view, as we have seen, jurisdictional authority might be said to belong "properly" to the magistrate, just as, say, a plot of land belongs "properly" to its owner.

Lothair's view, was, in some respects, even worse, in Bodin's view. By denying magistrates any legal right to the public *imperium*, but limiting them merely to the simple "use" or "exercise" of such power, Lothair effectively reduced all magistrates to the inferior status of a personal agent or deputy, serving only at the pleasure of the supreme or sovereign authority.

What was wrong with Lothair's (and, thus, the humanists') treatment of magistrates as simple agents, according to Bodin? His chief complaint was a technical point: Lothair's doctrine was based on a sloppy reading of Roman law. As we saw previously in the *Methodus*, "Lothair exploited [*usurpavit*] Papinian's rule [D.1.21.1] by which magistrates are said to have, but are not able to delegate [*mandare*], the exercise of public judgment."[72] Lothair took an arcane rule of public law, articulated originally by Papinian, concerning the narrow topic of delegated magisterial authority, and (mis)applied it as a general rule concerning all forms of authority, including the relationship between the prince and his magistrate.

It will be recalled that, in the classical law of the *Digest*, a magistrate may, by mandate, delegate *iurisdictio* to a private judge. The jurist, Paul, even acknowledged that this delegated jurisdiction might be termed a species of *imperium*, so that it is fully reasonable to think that a magistrate may, by right of his office, delegate *imperium* to his agent. What the magistrate *cannot* do, however, was delegate *merum imperium*, the coercive power of the sword given exclusively to

dispensed with the use of lay judges. The magistrates were directly involved in all aspects of the trial. But it is not clear how much Bodin would have known about the *legis actio* procedure, considering that Gaius, the major modern source for the details of the procedure, was only rediscovered in the nineteenth century. It is possible that Bodin may have had in mind Pomponius at D.1.2.2.6 which treats the *legis actio* as any *actio legitima*, the basis of statute-regulated legal process originally developed under the XII Tables. I thank Clifford Ando for this suggestion.

[72] *Methodus* 171. See p. 182.

the magistrate by law. Lothair apparently took Papinian's analysis of principal-agent relations between the magistrate and judge in the context of civil litigation in Roman law as a general model to frame the principal-agent relation between a sovereign *princeps* and the magistrate. In doing so, he had assumed that the agency relationship between the *princeps* and all inferior magistrates could be treated as structurally homologous to the agency relationship between the magistrate and judge in Papinian's analysis in the *Digest*. One was a principal; the other an agent.

But, as Bodin argued, these were not homologous relationships. Certainly, an appointed private judge in the context of Roman litigation may be thought of as an "agent" of a Roman magistrate (as Papinian opined), just as a magistrate may be thought of as an "agent" of the *princeps* (as Lothair and Alciato opined). But judges and magistrates were agents in fundamentally different ways. Judges held authority only so long as the superior magistrate permitted it, but magistrates held authority independently as laid out impartially in the law. It would, thus, be wrong to treat both just as if they were the same as any agent in private law—such as a *procurator* or *actor*—appointed by strict mandate to carry out some task on behalf of his principal. Failure to keep these concepts of delegation and agency analytically distinct had produced errors in legal reasoning, as he complained in Book III of the *République*:

> Whereas the Romans had properly separated the "office of the Proconsuls Lieutenant" [*l'office du Lieutenant du Proconsul*], whom they called *Legatum* [*Legatum*, as in D.1.16: *De officio proconsulis et legati*] from the office of the Proconsull himselfe: and so of the deputie tearmed a "particular Commissioner" [*le deputé en titre de commissaire particulier*; *Iudicem datum*, as in the *Decretales* X.1.29, *De officio et potestate iudicis delegati*] from the Commissioner himself, and of him unto whome power was given by the magistrate to command, whome they called *eum cui mandata iurisdictio est* [as in D.1.21: *De officio eius cui mandata est iurisdictio*], the doctors [of law] have confounded all together under the name of "Delegats."[73]

[73] *République* 441; *De Republica* 306; *Commonweale* 334 [3.5]. Visually, Bodin's point might be represented as follows:

	D.1.16	X.1.29	D.1.21
Principal	Proconsul	*Ordinarius*	Magistrate
Agent	*Legatus*	*Iudex datus*	"He to whom *iurisdictio* is delegated" = Private Judge

Knolles' translation of this passage does not quite fully capture Bodin's meaning, which is better expressed in the Latin phrasing in the 1583 and 1586 texts. Bodin was referring to the rubric indicating the two texts in the *Digest* separating the original jurisdiction of the *proconsul* or the *praetor* from the delegated jurisdiction of the *legatus* or the *iudex*, as well as the canonist distinction in the rubric, *De officio et potestate iudicis delegati*, in the *Decretales*. His point seems to be that, despite the differences between delegates and sub-delegates, jurists have treated them uniformly under the generic and undifferentiated label of "delegate," as delegates under some sovereign authority.

Bodin, thus, lay the blame with Lothair and, by implication, his early modern humanist disciples, the "younger lawyers" who followed his dubious analysis of agency.[74]

To clarify: In Bodin's diagnosis, the fundamental problem was *not* that Lothair applied a principal-agent analysis to differentiate magisterial authority from the supreme or "sovereign" authority. Bodin, after all, did accept in principle that all magistrates were in some sense like agents when they exercise authority on behalf of the sovereign state. The real problem, according to Bodin, was that Lothair and the humanists assumed erroneously that *all* magistrates could be uniformly modeled by such a simplistic model of agency which treated all magistrates—even the highest magistrates such as the praetor—indifferently as equivalent to one's personal servants, deputies, lieutenants, or attorneys in civil law.[75] But in doing so, the humanists utterly failed to elucidate what Bodin thought was the unique quality of magistrates that made them different from simple agents in private law. Something more, he felt, was needed.

COMMISSIONS AND OFFICES: THE ROMAN LAW OF OBLIGATIONS IN BODIN'S THEORY OF CONSTITUTED MAGISTRATES

Bodin, thus, set out to remedy what he thought was not only a hopelessly simplistic position, but also an extreme position adopted by the humanist legal science. Indeed, the conditional exercise of sovereignty through delegated agency could actually be quite diverse in form. Whereas one might hold public power as a personal grant only at the pleasure [*arbitrio*] of the sovereign authority, another might hold public power by a formally promulgated statute [*lege*] constituting a permanent and impersonal office. The failure to detect this diversity in form, according to Bodin, was due entirely to the humanists' inability to draw the proper finer-grained distinctions in the *means* by which authority can be delegated unto others.

One can give authority, even supreme authority, to another party in one of two ways, either as a "pure donation" [*donatione pura*] with "no conditions"

[74] *Commonweale* 294; cp. 295 [3.3] and 334 [3.5]. Bodin probably also means the many Commentators, identified in the margin of *République* 441 and *De Republica* 306, whom he cites for criticism such as Bartolus, Baldus, Fulgosius, Alexander Imolensis, Paul Castro, Cynus da Pistoia, and Panormitanus. But it was not only jurists who committed this error in the analysis of delegated authority. Humanist historians were also guilty of it, for example Nicholas Grouchy and Carolus Sigonius who, as Bodin put it, failed in "having understood the difference betwixt an *office* and a *commission*" because they were "ignorant in the knowledge of matters of law and of state." *Commonweale* 283 [3.2]; *Methodus* 167–8, where he also faults Varro. See also C.J. Smith, *The Roman Clan: The Gens from Ancient Ideology to Modern Anthropology* 70; William McCuaig, *Carlo Sigonio: The Changing World of the Late Renaissance* (Princeton: Princeton University Press, 1989) 174–223.

[75] In the *Commonweale*, Knolles translates this term by the words "deputie" or "lieutenant," as at *Commowneale* 279 [3.2].

[*conditiones nullas, sine conditione*] attached or as a "conditional grant" that generates valid obligations.[76] The point was essential in the analysis of commercial transactions between private parties in civil law. As Bodin observed, classical legal science distinguished between a *donatio perfecta* which, once made, "does not attach to any subsequent conditions" [*condiciones postea non capit*] and other conditional transactions whereby the original donor retained certain residual rights in whatever is given to the donee.[77]

Bodin applied this analysis to the various sorts of grants a sovereign authority may choose to make in delegating public authority to a subordinate. Like any object of property, the state's powers could be framed explicitly in terms of the Roman juridical language of private commercial transactions: public power could be "given" by the state to others.[78] Insofar as this is true, the relevant question then to ask concerned the *terms* on which such power could be given. On the one hand, such power could be given freely as a *donatio perfecta*, without any conditions or restrictions, so that the state could have no residual right or claim to those powers, once they are given away. As Bodin observes, these are not, properly speaking, delegations at all but, in effect, full and irreversible alienations of authority given in perpetuity. Once completed, they cannot be undone or reversed; and for this reason, Bodin is very careful in cautioning states to avoid enacting these sorts of perpetually self-limiting acts, such as permanent grants of immunities and privileges.[79]

Such alienations, however, are to be distinguished from conditional grants of authority which, as he puts it, are nevertheless tied or "entwined" [*implexa*] by some "stipulation" [*causa*] or "condition" [*conditione*] binding the donee to some obligation owed to the original donor or principal of the delegated authority, the state. Again, Roman law was the legal authority cited by Bodin to illustrate and sharpen the underlying concept. A principal may give some share of authority to an agent, such as a "praetor who is exercising someone else's jurisdiction" [D.1.21.3]. But so too can that same praetor further "delegate jurisdiction" [*iurisdictionem mandare*] onto another agent appointed to then "act in place of the praetor who delegated it" [*fungetur vice eius qui mandavit*], and "not in his own right" [*non sua*].[80] What distinguishes all these cases of conditional grants from the other cases of alienations or donations is that, here, the donor "giving" authority to the donee, as his agent, nevertheless retains some residual right to the delegated authority, even while the agent is in temporary possession of it. The donor can always recover what he has given away.

[76] *De Republica* 82 [1.8]; cp. *Iuris Universi Distributio* 38, under the heading of *Gratuitum*, where Bodin distinguishes between *Donatio Pura, & Conditionalis; Iuris Universi Distributio* 52 on *Alienatio*.

[77] C.8.54(55).4.

[78] *De Republica* 82 [1.8]: *ut alteri omnia iura maiestatis sine conditione donaret, perinde ut si quis pura donatione rei suae dominium ac possessionem tradidisset.*

[79] Cp. *Commonweale* 91 [1.8]; 321 [3.4] on the dangers of the "derogatory" effect of privilege on sovereignty.

[80] D.2.1.16.

The basic distinction then is between *unconditional donations* of power and *conditional grants* of power. But Bodin did not stop his analysis here.[81] He was keenly aware that, within the latter category, conditional grants of authority were even further divisible, depending entirely on the sort of *conditions* that were attached to the grant from sovereign to agent.

On the one hand, a sovereign might grant public power to an agent as a temporary or provisional grant to be held only "by sufferance" at the pleasure of the sovereign and revocable at any time. Bodin had generally called agents of this kind a "commissioner" [*commissaire; curator*].[82] Such commissioned agents held, by definition, an "extraordinary charge" [Fr. *charge extraordinaire*; L. *extra ordinem*], which was unregulated by law [*sine lege*] and entirely provisional. It was made as a gratuitous grant of the principal's authority "which ceaseth by the death of him that granted the same, or by the revoking of the commission."[83] What distinguished this grant of commission was not so much the magnitude of power—after all, even the Roman dictator was regarded a commissioner with "absolute" power—but rather, the fact that a commissioner's power was fully dependent on the source of that power.[84] Indeed a commission could, at any time, be "arbitrarily revoked" at the pleasure of the sovereign [*arbitrio revocantur*] and "ceaseth at death."[85] It was for this reason then that Bodin thought all commissioners, even the most powerful commissioners, such as the Roman dictator or the Turkish vizier, were nevertheless "bound, and as it were, tied unto the very words of their commission, and especially where question is of the affairs of state."[86]

But extraordinary commissions were not the only sort of conditional grants a sovereign could make to a subordinate agent. Just as a sovereign can make conditional grants of public power so that the commissioned agent is bound by a *unilateral* obligation to the sovereign, so too can a sovereign make conditional grants that are doubly binding by creating a *bilateral* obligation which not only tied the agent to the sovereign, but more importantly, tied the sovereign to the agent. This latter form of conditional grant of power was denominated "office," and its incumbent the "officer" [*officier; officialis*].[87]

[81] If he did, his position would be indistinguishable from, say, Alciato who allows a conditional grant in the same manner as a usufruct, where the *dominus* retains a bare *nuda proprietas* over the servient estate.

[82] *République* 372; *De Republica* 259; *Commonweale* 278 [3.2]; cp. *Commonweale* 283.

[83] *De Republica* 259 [3.2].

[84] *De Republica* 262 [3.2]: *Dictatura quoque curatio fuit, non ordinaria potestas.* He invokes the same example of Aemylius Mamercus, the one-day dictator, cited at *République* 124. Recall Bodin's comment at *Methodus* 174: *Dictator qui non proprie magistratum, sed curationem gerebat,* which is the only comment in the *Methodus* that hints at the magisterial office/commission distinction of the *République*.

[85] *Commonweale* 283 [3.2]; *De Republica* 421; *Commonweale* 286.

[86] *Commonweale* 289 [3.2].

[87] *République* 372; *De Republica* 259 [3.2]. "Officer" is a generic category, of which "magistrate" is a species. The specification is necessary for Bodin since not all "officers" hold *imperium*, such as a "senator" who has a public advisory and deliberative function, but no *imperium*, as he explains in 3.1.

What crucially distinguished the officer from the commissioner was the nature of the "charge" by which each held and exercised their power by way of agency. Whereas agents appointed by commission held public authority as an "extraordinary charge," held only as a temporary personal grant at the pleasure of the sovereign, agents appointed to a proper office held what Bodin called an "ordinary charge" [*charge ordinaire*] made not by an extralegal sovereign act of will, but as an impersonal legislative act formally enacted through settled law [*limitee par edict; lege definitum*].[88] Just as any other statute, a public office must be constituted according to a publicly recognized process of legislation, a point that Bodin observes in the different processes used to appoint officers and commissioners.[89] This is what separated, in Bodin's analysis of Roman public law, proper officeholding magistrates, such as the consul and the praetor, whose offices were established by law and whose powers of *imperium* were conferred formally by *leges imperii*, from mere temporary commissioners with no office or permanence, such as the dictators, *quaestores parricidii*, and the *duumviri*.

Legal permanence and continuity were the essential features distinguishing an office from a commission. As Bodin put it, offices "continue for ever after they be once by edict erected," even after the sovereign authority which created such office by law has died or is no longer in office.[90] It is precisely for this reason that all officeholders enjoy an independence and autonomy in their offices that commissioners do not: "The power of an officer... is better authorized, and larger than a commissioner."[91] This independence and autonomy was indeed what Bodin, following Bartolus, considered to be the "noble" [*nobile*] quality of office and, by extension, of the incumbent officeholder.[92] Office implied certain legal rights to which the officeholder was entitled, but were inaccessible to all commissioners. By virtue of his office, a magistrate licitly could do certain things by "right of office" (which we have already seen has been described in Roman law as acting "by their own right" [*suo iure*] or, more specifically, "by right of magistracy" [*iure magistratus*]), which simple commissioners could not do, such as appoint agents and delegate powers to them by a mandate. Classical Roman law in the *Digest* (Papinian), as we have seen earlier, made special note of these legal "rights of magistrates" [*iura magistratus*], which made the humanist interpretation highly untenable.

Magistrates, thus, were not simple commissioned agents, as the humanists thought, comparable to the *iudices* or *arbitri* of Roman law, conceived as mere instruments without any discretion for the *legis actio*. They were, in a sense,

[88] *République* 372; *De Republica* 259; *Commonweale* 278 [3.2]. It is important to stress that, for Bodin, not all personal or private acts of a sovereign were necessarily public legislative acts.

[89] *Commonweale* 280–81 [3.2]. Such legally constituted offices can only be disestablished by a contrary act of formal legislation, and not simply by an arbitrary act of the sovereign.

[90] *Commonweale* 280 [3.2].

[91] *Commonweale* 289 [3.2].

[92] *Commonweale* 311 [3.4], 334 [3.5], and cp. *Methodus* 173.

also principals in their own right [*suo iure*] who had "integritie and discretion" in the scope of their jurisdiction. Bodin quite remarkably interpreted these rights of magistracy broadly, so that magisterial office, or what he called *officium iudicis*, even implied certain capacities empowering the magistrate to act for the sake of equity or even piety—sometimes even against the written law, as justice required.

Richard Bonney once identified this distinction between commission and office as one of the most original and enduring contributions in Bodin's constitutional thought.[93] Indeed, Carl Schmitt, writing in his treatise on *Dictatorship*, regarded this analysis as "an extraordinarily clear and detailed juridical foundation" for the analysis of dictatorship.[94] Bodin himself thought it to be critical to understanding his analysis of government, separating "seigneurial governments", where the sovereign authority is also the "owner [*dominus* or *seigneur*] of all things" in the state, from properly "lawful governments" where the sovereign authority, governing not by naked aribtrary will, but through law, can never have "the proprietie of the publike demains," and that "propertie of the crowne lands is not the princes," but instead, "belong[s] unto the commonweale."[95]

What is most important, however, is how Bodin tries to explain the nature of this difference between commissions and offices by an analogy with commercial transactions in civil law:

> An office is a thing borrowed [*vne chose empruntee; commodato*], which the owner cannot demaund againe before the time it was lent for bee expired: but a commission is a thing which one hath but by sufferance, [a]nd as it were by leave [*vne chose qu'on a par souffrance, & par forme de precaire; precario*], which the owner [*seigneur*] may againe demaund when he seeth good.[96]

The vocabulary invoked by Bodin in the Latin here is especially significant, and that is because *commodatum* and *precarium* were two types of legal obligations in Roman law. But there was an important difference between them that was critical for Bodin's argument in distinguishing between delegation of authority to officeholding magistrates and delegation of authority to commissioners.

The *precarium* was the exemplar of what jurists called a "unilateral obligation"—that is, an obligation where only one party has the right to demand performance of some action by another duty-bound party.[97] By describing

[93] Bonney, "Bodin and the Development of the French Monarchy" 43–61.

[94] Carl Schmitt, *Dictatorship: From the Origin of the Modern Concept of Sovereignty to Proletarian Class Struggle*, trans. Michael Hoelzl and Graham Ward (Cambridge: Polity, 2014) 25.

[95] *Commonweale* 130 [1.9]; 652 [6.2]. See also Lee, "Office Is a Thing Borrowed" for a fuller discussion on seigneurial governments.

[96] *République* 378; *De Republica* 263; *Commonweale* 282 [3.2]. The Latin text, which alone shows a marginal citation to D.2.1.6, formulates the passage as thus: *Ut autem planius magistratuum & curatorum disciplina intelligatur, his quidem precario, illos quasi commodato munere fungi putemus: precarium autem semper repetere licet; commodatum non item, sed tempore definito.*

[97] *Precarium* and *precaire* is translated as "sufferance" in Knolles; Franklin follows this convention. Cp. *Iuris Universi Distributio* 40, defining *precarium* as *creditum utendi causa domini arbitrio.*

extraordinary commissions as comparable to the unilateral obigation arising from a *precarium*, Bodin was actually saying a great deal about the sort of legal relationship he envisaged between the sovereign and the commissioner. Since, in a commission, all rights accrued entirely to the sovereign, the commissioner served only at the arbitrary pleasure of the sovereign who could arbitrarily revoke the commission at any time [*imperantis arbitrio revocari*], just as in a *precarium*, the owner could arbitrarily and rightfully revoke the grant away from his precarious tenant at any time.[98]

By contrast, the *commodatum*—the legal model of office—was an example of a "bilateral obligation," arising from a "real contract" [*obligatio re contracta*] involving generally the delivery [*traditio*] of some article of property to another party with the expectation of return at some later date. The distinctive feature of these bilateral obligations consisted in the juridical symmetry since rights and duties in these cases were reciprocally binding on both parties to the contract.[99]

The upshot was clear. If the magisterial office was, legally speaking, *res commodata*, then it must follow that the magistrate appointed to such an office, as well as the sovereign, who not only constituted the office but enabled the appointment of the officeholder, were *both* tied by a mutually binding bilateral obligation, and not just the magistrate. On the one hand, the magistrate is bound by his obligation to the sovereign, as a sort of "borrower" of the public office and its *imperium*, to exercise it in good faith as well as to lay down [*deponere*] and return the office to the sovereign upon completion of his legally specified term of office.[100] Yet, so too is the sovereign bound by an obligation to the magistrate, by a duty of non-interference. In a government where offices are constituted by law, the sovereign authority must not interfere in the affairs of the magistrate or remove the magistrate without cause.[101] So, while the sovereign authority may certainly be exempt from its own laws, *legibus solutus*, it is not exempt from its contractual obligations, especially where those obligations arise from legal grants of office to magistrates.

That Bodin understood the relationship between the sovereign authority and government offices in terms of bilateral obligations is supported further by his embrace of the whole range of bilateral real contracts in Roman law, not

[98] *De Republica* 262 [3.2]. [99] Cp. Gaius 3.137.

[100] Bodin uses the verb, *deponere*, in the corresponding passage of the *Methodus* where this argument is developed. He is referring to Ulpian at D.1.17.1, which he cites on multiple occasions in *République* 1.8. See Chapter 5 on his comment in the *Methodus* referring to Alciato's worry about Ulpian's notion of the "laying down" of an office.

[101] Bodin argues that, even though sovereigns may be exempt from their own laws, they are nevertheless bound by the laws of nature and of nations. One of those higher legal norms which are binding even on sovereigns is the general principle that contracts are binding: "The soveraigne prince is bound unto the contracts by hime made, bee it with his subiect, or with a straunger." The binding force of contracts is what prevents the sovereign from treating offices and officers arbitrarily: "For if a prince have once bestowed an honour or an office upon a man, it is deemed, that he may not without iust cause take it againe away from him" *Commonweale* 106 [1.8].

just the contract of *commodatum*, but also the contract of deposit [*depositum*] and the contract of security for a debt [*pignus*], all of which appear in one of the most famous passages in all of the *République*:

> [Supreme magistrates empowered with *summum imperium*] cannot, therefore, be called "sovereign princes" [*summi principes*] but rather are, for that period of time, merely the "guardians" [*custodes; depositaires, & gardes*] of the supreme power and *imperium*, until such time when the sovereign prince or people [*summus princeps populusve; au peuple ou au Prince*] might demand back [*reposcat; revoquer*] the entrusted [*depositum*] *imperium*, of which they are properly named the "possessors" [*possessores*] as well as the "owners" [*domini*]. They are, not unlike those individuals [in civil law] who gave [on the word, "gave"/*dederunt*, Bodin adds citations to D.41.3.33.4 and 41.2.18] their own things [*res suas*] to others by loan or by mortgage [*commodato, vel pignori*]. Such sovereign princes and peoples merely "entrusted" [*permiserunt*] their own [*suam*] *iurisdictio* or *imperium* for another's "enjoyment," either for a certain period of time, or for as long as the sovereign pleases [*precario; precaire*]. They do not however cease to be the lords as well as possessors [*arbitri ac possessores*] of their own [*suae*] power and *iurisdictio* [citation to D.2.1.5, 2.1.6].[102]

There is a general point worth stressing before proceeding further. Bodin's notion of "absolute" sovereignty is an absolution or release *only* from his own laws.[103] It is not, however, to be understood as a release from other sources of binding obligations, including, especially, those contracts a sovereign authority enters into voluntarily with subjects.[104] What this suggests is that the proper way of understanding the relationship between a sovereign authority and a

[102] This is my translation based on the Latin text of *De Republica* 79 [1.8], which most clearly shows the centrality of Roman law in this analysis. Neither the French text nor Knolles' English text properly convey the legal significance and technical meaning of the argument here. The citation to D.41.3.33.4, which is in the marginalia of the French and Latin texts by its incipit, *Qui pignori*, explains why the sovereign authority must be in the position not only of a *dominus* [Fr. *seigneur*], but also a *possessor* [Fr. *possesseur*] over any *imperium* or *iurisdictio* that is delegated to a subordinate party. *Depositum imperium* occurs again at *De Republica* 81. Cp. *Iuris Universi Distributio* 40, which treats obligations of *commodatum, depositum, pignus*, and *precarium* under the general heading of *creditum*.

[103] Note also Bodin's stipulative definition of "law" (*loi, lex*) to differentiate from "right" (*droit, ius*), but which in English, can also be "law." Cp. *Iuris Universi Distributio* 14 [*Ius Quid Sit*], 16 [*Lex Quid*]. The essence of law, as in the *Methodus*, is command. But Bodin specifies here that a law imposes a general obligation—all subjects, without differentiation, are bound to comply with the rule created through Bodinian legislation. Not all commands of a public authority are general in scope, such as magisterial edicts (which are legally binding, but still can be overridden in theory by sovereign legislation), and acts which impose a non-general obligation only on some subjects (which are not properly "laws" but, as Bodin calls it, "privileges").

[104] This is why it is so central for Bodin to distinguish between "law" and "contract." Both are obligation-creating devices. But only "contracts" create obligations that bind sovereigns in ways that laws do not. *République* 135; *De Republica* 87; *Commonweale* 93 [1.8]. The marginalia of the French and Latin text cites C.1.14.5 and, most notably, D.50.17.35, which establishes the principle that an obligation is to be dissolved [*dissolvitur*] by the same means through which it is contracted [*colligatum est*]. The Latin text alone has a further citation to D.2.14.58 which illustrates the principle in various sorts of bilateral Roman consensual contracts such as the *emptio-venditio* and the *locatio-conductio*.

subordinate magistrate in a legally constituted office of government is in terms of a contractual obligation, to which both parties are bound.

CONSTITUTIONAL CHOICES: GOVERNMENT OF MAGISTRATES OR GOVERNMENT OF COMMISSIONERS?

Bodin's analysis of sovereignty and government, and of offices and commissions, suggests a stark choice to be made between two very different options of constitutional design. A sovereign may, on the one hand, choose to govern by means of "commissioners," all directly subservient to the sovereign's "word, beck, and call," and holding their magisterial *imperium* at the sovereign's pleasure, or *arbitrium*. Bodin called this type of government "*seigneurial*" because it positioned the sovereign authority as a *seigneur* [= *dominus*] with respect to his commissioned agents who held subordinate authority "by sufferance" only.[105] It was the mode of government by which the earliest kings, such as the legendary hunter-king, Nimrod, governed, before the invention of law. And it was the mode of government in unfree states, such as among the Turks and Muscovites. By contrast, a sovereign may, on the other hand, choose to govern by means of legally constituted magistrates, by legally constituting or creating permanent public offices and investing officers occupying those offices with *imperium* to be exercised according to publicly known terms of office.

A sovereign authority is entirely free to establish whatever mode of government it pleases, whether a government of magistrates constituted by law, or a government of commissioners appointed by will, or some combination of both. But the issue of government was not entirely a neutral question of institutional design. Bodin was deeply concerned that the unrestrained or unregulated exercise of sovereign authority would, in the end, threaten the very stability and existence of the state itself.

What appeared to be a purely analytical question of civil science concerning institutional design quickly became, for Bodin, a normative question of political theory concerning how a state should properly be governed and how a state's public institutions should be designed and regulated. Insofar as it is accepted that states must be governed indirectly through the delegation and entrusting of state authority to state agents, the further question must be asked whether a state should be governed through magistrates with a legally defined office or through commissioners, whose dependence on the arbitrary will of the sovereign makes them no better than a mere *seigneur* or *dominus*?

Bodin's answer was unambiguous: It is, on balance, better to govern indirectly through law and through legally constituted magistrates. Bodin offers some strictly utilitarian reasons for this. Direct, unmediated exercises of sovereignty by the sovereign authority (whether a prince or a people) always has

[105] English translations have translated "seigneurial" variously as "lordly" (Knolles) and "despotic" (Tooley, Franklin). I prefer, however, to keep the French to stress the feudal-proprietary aspect of seigneurial rule whose agents are like agents of private law.

some sort of "transaction cost." The more it is so exercised, the more the state exposes itself to the risk of losing sovereignty altogether:

> If the [sovereign] prince or the [sovereign] people shall take upon themselves the authority of the senate, or the commands, offices, or jurisdictions of the magistrates, it is much to be feared, least that they [i.e., the sovereign] destitute of all help, shall at the length be spoiled of their own sovereign majesty also.[106]

Thus, in making the public choice to exercise sovereignty directly—for example, when designing new public institutions, declaring war, reforming laws, or creating new offices—the sovereign authority must strategically weigh these "transaction costs" and measure the calculated risks that must be endured in matters of state. This is why he states, as a general—although perhaps counterintuitive—principle of sovereignty, that "the less the power of the sovereignty is... the more it is assured."[107]

But Bodin's theory was further complicated by the fact that the sovereignty of a state could take one of three forms—monarchy, aristocracy, or popular sovereignty—depending on who, or what, is recognized as the exclusive and ultimate bearer of sovereign right within a state. So, for example, a state in which sovereignty is indivisibly and exclusively held by a king is to be classified as a monarchy, while a state in which sovereignty is held collectively by a group of optimates or nobles is to be classified as an aristocracy.

More importantly, Bodin insists that there can be no universal "one size fits all" formula for government that can be applied with equal success to monarchies, aristocracies, and popular states. Public institutions that may function best with a monarchy may not be appropriate, say, for a popular state. And that is because each form of sovereign state brings with it a unique set of problems that may be absent in other forms. To stress this point, Bodin introduces an analogy from medicine. Sovereign states are comparable, he argues, to different types of organic bodies, each with different sorts of diseases and ailments that are unique to each type. As Bodin puts it, "the first rule for the keeping and preserving of commonweales in their estates is well to know the nature of every comonweale, together with disases," so that the sovereign can prescribe the proper institutional remedies to cure those diseases that weaken sovereignty.[108] Government—the whole institutional structure by which public authority is exercised on behalf of the sovereign—functions, in this analogy, as medicine, introduced to cure or minimize those illnesses that may cause further harm to the body politic.

Sovereigns of all states, thus, confront this most basic of challenges in the constitution of government. Should the state be governed "seigneurially" or "lawfully"?

[106] *Commonweale* 518 [4.6]. This, as we shall see, is precisely what Bodin thought happened to the Roman Republic: The *populus Romanus*, beginning with the Gracchi, began to exercise its sovereignty in a more direct and seigneurial manner, directly intervening in high matters of state by the extraordinary appointment of popular "commissions"—especially Sulla, Pompey, Caesar—rather than by ordinary lawful magistrates.

[107] *Commonweale* 517 [4.6].

[108] *Commonweale* 469 [4.3].

Should the state constitute ordinary magistraterial officers or should it rely on commissioners? How large or small should government be? Who should be eligible, and ineligible, for positions of authority? What ought to be the procedures for appointment to such positions? Under what circumstances should the sovereign authority in the state interfere in the actions and decisions of its government?

THE PROBLEM OF POPULAR SOVEREIGNTY: GOVERNING THE POPULAR STATE

We now, finally, arrive at Bodin's theory of sovereignty in the "popular state," what he called *status reipublicae popularis* [*l'estat populaire*]. The popular state, as Bodin defines it, is that in which "all or most of the people together commandeth in soveraigntie over the rest altogether, and over everie one in particular."[109] Like the other two principal forms of state in his theory—that is, monarchy and aristocracy—the popular state has its own idiosyncracies, even ailments, that require an appropriate constitutional remedy.

But unlike monarchy and aristocracy, the popular state presents a unique conceptual difficulty, and that is because the vertical relation of sovereignty and subjection is obscured where the people holds sovereignty. In a monarchy, a king holds sovereignty over subjects, just as, in an aristocracy, the optimates collectively hold sovereignty over the common people.[110] But in a popular state, the people seem to play both roles of sovereign and subject; they hold sovereignty over themselves.

This presents a problem for Bodin, since he regards the notion of self-rule as incoherent. Just as one cannot bind oneself to promises or obligations, neither can a popular self be capable of self-binding. But he is unwilling to dismiss the validity of popular sovereignty outright. Instead, while acknowledging the criticism that one "cannot bind itselfe unto itselfe," Bodin offers a theory of the popular state that relies on a typical argument derived from medieval corporatist thought to get around this problem. There is, he argues, a need to distinguish between two concepts of the people—one, as a collective body that can be bound "all together" and another, as an aggregate of individuals who can each be bound "everie one in particular."[111] Given this distinction, he specifies that "the people in general is a certaine universall bodie, in power and nature divided from every man in particular."[112] Sovereignty—as an indivisible bundle of rights and powers—has to belong legally to one unitary party. So, in the case of popular sovereignty, the people, as bearer of sovereign authority, must be understood not as an aggregate or multitude of particular individuals, but

[109] *République* 332; *De Republica* 229; *Commonweale* 244 [2.7]. Both conditions of rule must hold.

[110] *République* 143, 255; *De Republica* 92; *Commonweale* 99 [1.8], 185 [2.1].

[111] *Commonweale* 99; *De Republica* 92 [1.8] renders the relevant terms as *populus universus* and *singuli*.

[112] *Commonweale* 99 [1.8]. The marginalia in the corresponding passage at *République* 143 and *De Republica* 92 again cites D.50.17.35, establishing the principle of symmetry that an obligation is to be dissolved [*dissolvitur*] by the same means through which it is contracted [*colligatum est*].

represented as one unitary entity, like a legal corporation, capable of owning and asserting actionable rights, of having oaths and acts attributed to it, and of being bound by obligations—just like a *princeps*.

Bodin is, thus, very clear that popular sovereignty is to be recognized as a fully legitimate and valid form of political rule in an independent state. There is no doubt in his mind that the popular state is a state and should be recognized as such, and he applies this label to numerous states organized around the principle of popular sovereignty, such as Athens, Sparta, Thebes, Florence, the Swiss cantons, and, above all, Republican Rome.

That having been said, however, it is well known that Bodin does not think much of the popular state, which, at one point, he compares to an immodest strumpet.[113] The principal ground for his criticism of popular sovereignty is in the natural instability of the people as a sovereign entity, a worry that is expressed most clearly in Book VI of the *République*. Even though a people can be thought of as one unitary entity, it is naturally a plurality. Its natural tendency is to decay or degenerate into a mass crowd or multitude [*turbum*] of private and conflicting interests, wills, and passions. Politically, he argues, such decay presents an existential threat to a popular state: "No tyrannie," he writes, "is so dangerous as that of a multitude."[114] And that is because a people, in possession of sovereignty, can very easily lose it: "Maiestie," as he put it, "doth perish and decay in a multitude."[115]

What accounts for this natural tendency of popular degeneration? The natural instability of popular sovereignty derives entirely, in Bodin's analysis, from what he calls the "true nature of the people"—the unchecked popular desire for "libertie without restraint of bit or bridle" and "to have all men equall," even contrary to the natural inequality prescribed by the law of nature.[116] One inevitable political consequence of this popular egalitarianism is the common sharing of sovereignty in the *populus*, not only by "judicious and wise men," but also by "furious, ignorant, and mad men."[117] It is therefore necessary in a popular state to institute measures, by some form of constitutional engineering, as "brakes" to slow the almost inevitable degeneration of a naturally "fickle and fanatical" people into a condition of "madness" or a "turbulent" mob or perhaps even a "beast with many heads, without jugement, or reason," and incapable of self-rule.[118]

[113] *Commonweale* 703–4 [6.4].

[114] *Commonweale* 700 [6.4], cp. 200 [2.2], where Bodin, citing Cicero calls it "the rage of the furious and turbulent people."

[115] *Commonweale* 703 [6.4]. Bodin's most important classical example illustrating this danger, at *Commonweale* 706 [6.4], was the rise of Pericles in classical Athens—as he put it, with a citation to Thucydides, the "very monarch" of Athens.

[116] *Commonweale* 250, [2.7], 701 [6.4]. Bodin's argument against democratic egalitarianism is framed here as a sort of "leveling-down" objection.

[117] *Commonweale* 708 [6.4]. Bodin's criticism of popular sovereignty in the language of justice, for enabling public authority to be placed in unworthy hands, draws heavily on Platonic sources. Cp. *Method* 268.

[118] *Commonweale* 424 [4.1], 409 [4.1], 199 [2.2].

Bodin's proposals for curing the ills of democracy were, in part, aimed at remedying, or at least containing, the capricious and fickle nature of the people by non-institutional means. Recognizing that a people can so easily be swayed by the force of the rhetorical trickery of "popular men" who can trap a state as "unto spiders webs," Bodin proposes, as a sort of counter-measure, some device to stabilize the naturally weak and inconsistent psychology of a people, so that they do not become like a fanatical or beastly madman in need of government by a tutor—or worse, in danger of enslavement by another power.[119] To soothe and calm this natural and latent ferocity of the people, Bodin suggests that perhaps even music or rhetoric could serve this function.[120]

But the more important proposals for protecting a sovereign people from itself were fundamentally institutional in nature, and concerned the question how a sovereign people should exercise its sovereignty. As a general principle, Bodin argued that states generally expose themselves to the most danger when sovereigns get *too* directly involved in politics—especially by "intermeddling" with the legislative and judicial powers of state.[121] This is, to be sure, the case not only for popular states, but indeed, also for monarchical and aristocratic states. Monarchies, for example, are exposed to the most risk of political instability where sovereign princes, governing "seigneurially," intervene too frequently in the political process. The safest strategy of constitutional design in a state, thus, is one of "de-politicizing" sovereignty to remove and de-activate the sovereign authority from the day-to-day tussle of politics and policy-making which properly ought to be delegated to legally constituted magistrates. In this respect, Bodin becomes one of the most important early theorists, arguing for the instrumental rationality of the constitutional strategy of precommitment and self-binding.[122] The interest of the state calls for a self-limitation on the exercise of sovereignty, in all its forms. Thus, Bodin argues, monarchs should govern through legally constituted magistrates with ordinary offices and defined powers, rather than extraordinary commissioners empowered with, and subject to, the potentially faulty arbitrary will of a prince.

The same lesson applies to popular states. Just as princely states should govern to minimize the need for sovereign intervention, popular states should likewise govern in such a way that popular sovereignty is voluntarily limited and regulated through institutional means, so as to minimize occasions when the people are required to intervene directly in matters of state and activate their popular sovereignty. This principle informs some of Bodin's views on

[119] *Commonweale* 701 [6.4].

[120] On music, *Commonweale* 456 [4.2], 530–31 [4.7]. On rhetoric, *Commonweale* 294 [3.3] and 706 [6.4], where Bodin acknowledges the power of "orators and pleaders" in the Athens of Demonsthenes. Bodin's populism is to be distinguished from the "ferocious populism" of Machiavelli, as in John McCormick, "Machiavellian Democracy: Controlling Elites with Ferocious Populism," *American Political Science Review* 95 (2001): 297–313.

[121] *Commonweale* 517.

[122] Holmes, "Precommitment and the Paradox of Democracy."

institutional design in popular states. For example, he cites the example of the Swiss cantons to show that most functions of government should be delegated to magistrates, so that the sovereign people play only a minimal role, with "nothing being almost left unto the people more than the choosing of their officers."[123] Observing the natural ambition of citizens nurtured in democracies, where offices are equally open to all citizens, Bodin advises that magistracies should be numerous and temporally limited, so as to allow a constant turnover to satisfy such ambition and prevent "an appetite or desire to some one or other ambitious citizen to aspire unto the sovereignty alone."[124] He even argues magistrates in a popular state should be allowed to be "at variance and discord among themselves."[125] And since reliable access to such public offices ensures constitutional stability, Bodin warns that "the laws and ordinances concerning the magistrate's time [in office in a popular state should] be not changed, neither their charge prorogued, if the necessity be not very great."[126]

But there is a potentially anti-democratic consequence to these prescriptions, since it suggests that a people who legally have the right to sovereignty nevertheless should, for reasons of state, voluntarily remove themselves from the task of public administration, of exercising functions of government. Instead, Bodin advises, popular states should "deposit," "lend," or "entrust" their popular sovereignty to legally constituted government officers empowered to exercise public authority on behalf of the people. What emerges, then, in Bodin's doctrine of popular sovereignty is not so much a theory of direct democracy, but one of *indirect* democracy: The people exercise their sovereignty through other government agents, intermediaries, or mandataries by an act of legal delegation.

Of course, as we have now seen, not all grants of public authority are the same. While some grants may be made on sufferance as extraordinary commissions, subject only to the arbitrary will of the sovereign, other grants of authority are made in the form of legally prescribed impersonal grants of office detached from the popular will. This basic difference accounts for the wide variations in the stability (or to use a more contemporary term, "institutional performance") of popular states throughout recorded history. While some popular states, such as the Roman Republic, Geneva, and the Swiss cantons, enjoyed a remarkable degree of political stability over time, others, such as Pericles' Athens, Soderini's Florence, and Caesar's Rome, suffered from civil disorder eventually resulting in the loss of popular sovereignty.

What accounts for the difference between the more successful and the less successful popular states? The answer, according to Bodin, was entirely due to the constitutional choices a sovereign people make in designing their government. The issue is this: How much of a role should the people actively play in

[123] *Commonweale* 518 [4.6].

[124] *Commonweale* 485–86 [4.4].

[125] *Commonweale* 497 [4.5].

[126] *Commonweale* 420–1 [4.1].

the governing institutions they create? When institutions are designed so as to "insulate" the people from political activity and, in a sense, "de-activate" what Bodin saw as the potentially self-destructive force of democratic politics, popular states become the most durable. Such states, in Bodin's view, have institutions that address the special needs and problems unique to popular states; such institutions function as devices to limit and regulate the potentially self-destructive force of unbridled popular sovereignty, a fate that has, in Bodin's view, brought the people in countless popular states such as Athens, Rome, and Florence to lose not only their popular liberties, but also their popular sovereignty.

THE ROMAN MODEL: POPULAR SOVEREIGNTY AND NON-POPULAR GOVERNMENT

As in so many other areas of his thought, the political experience of classical Rome provides Bodin with a point of reference to illustrate his analysis. For Bodin, Republican Rome was the exemplar of the popular state.[127] This democratic interpretation of Roman Republican politics, it is worth noting, was a highly unconventional view, running against the tide of the historically dominant mixed-constitution tradition of Polybius and Cicero that viewed the Roman constitution not as a "pure" form of state, such as a monarchy, aristocracy, or democracy, but as a "mixture" of all three, with monarchical power in the consulate, aristocratic power in the senate, and democratic power in the popular assemblies. The likely source for Bodin's democratic interpretation, according to Richard Tuck, was the historical scholarship of Nicholas de Grouchy, who, in his study, "On Roman Assemblies" [*De Comitiis Romanis*], had uncovered the voting procedures in Roman popular assemblies.[128]

But despite locating Roman sovereignty corporately in the *populus Romanus* as assembled in their *comitia*, Bodin nevertheless observed that Roman popular sovereignty was coupled with non-popular or non-democratic institutions of government. In this arrangement, most public tasks of government, within Italy and among the provinces, were legally administered by high-ranking magistrates with *imperium* together with the senate, a socially exclusive group composed mostly of patricians. For this reason, Bodin concludes that, even though Rome was technically a *popular* state, its government was *aristocratic*, and perhaps even a "harmonic" mixture of aristocratic and popular elements of government.[129] It was, moreover, a highly advantageous combination of

[127] This was before the *lex de imperio Vespasiani*, which Bodin, following the scholarship surrounding Rienzo's discovery, treated as the *lex regia* transferring sovereignty from the Roman *populus* to the Roman *princeps*. See Chapter 1.

[128] Tuck, "Hobbes and Democracy" 181–82. *Commonweale* 244 [2.7] on the curiae of Rome.

[129] *Commonweale* 785–76 [6.6] introduces Bodin's interpretation of Rome as a popular state coupled with a "harmonic government" of aristocratic and popular elements, possibly as a concession to mixed-constitution theorists of Rome. At 249, Bodin clarifies, in his constitutional history of Rome, that the *lex Canuleia* [permitting intermarriage between patricians and plebs] from 445 B.C.E. marks an important

sovereignty and government for the Romans, since it was precisely the non-democratic arrangement of Roman government in the magistrates and senate that accounted for Rome's longevity and conquests: "Rome never flourished more than in the popular estate," when most government was handled indirectly by the senate and magistrates.[130]

Of course, the Roman Republic did not always rely on the government of properly constituted magistrates and senates. In extraordinary moments of crisis or emergency, Rome suspended the ordinary government and placed plenary authority in a dictator for resolution of such crises. He observed more troubling patterns of government in the Late Republic, which revealed an unsettling willingness to innovate and do away with settled institutional patterns of government to satisfy immediate short-term plebeian interests. One important example was the tribunate of the Gracchi, whose populist actions aimed at enlarging the power of the plebs by expropriating public lands made the people "entirely rabbit" [rabid].[131] This was precisely the corruption of popular sovereignty that Bodin thought Roman Republican government was designed to protect against.

But, by far, the most important examples illustrating the violent decay of popular sovereignty were the extraordinary dictatorial commissions and civil wars in the last century of the Republic in the dictatorships of Sulla, Pompey, and Caesar—the inevitable consequences, in Bodin's view, of too much direct involvement by the people in matters of state.[132] On Bodin's analysis, no Roman dictator ever held sovereignty; it always remained with the Roman people even during the dictatorship, which Bodin characterized merely as a precarious grant on sufferance—that is, a "commission." But the difference in this critical period preceding the fall of the Republic was the irreparable damage that such repeated "commissionate government" was inflicting not only upon the ability of the senate and the magisterial order to govern Rome and her provinces, but also upon the institutional function of the Roman government as a check on the potentially self-destructive force of populism.[133]

The lesson Bodin takes away from the case of Rome is how the dismantling of well-settled government institutions and abrogation of public laws in popular states—as the sovereign people of Rome did by extraordinarily and even "seigneurially" assigning plenary authority to dictators—could very well result ultimately in the loss or forfeiture of popular sovereignty. This is precisely what happened with the perpetual dictatorship of Caesar and the

transformation in the evolution of Rome's aristocratic government to the more complex structure of the Late Republic.

[130] *Commonweale* 411 [4.1], 518 [4.6].

[131] *Commonweale* 517 [4.6].

[132] Technically, Pompey was never a dictator—but Bodin observes that he was granted absolute power by commission, since he was, by an extraordinary act, made consul without a colleague.

[133] Pomponius makes a brief reference to this decline in effective governance by the senate in explaining the rise of the Principate at D.1.2.2.11.

subsequent rise of the Principate.[134] No doubt, the people of Rome had an original right to their sovereignty, to be exercised as they please and by their mandate. Bodin's point, however, is more nuanced, that the exercise of such sovereign right comes with real dangers and costs attached, almost as an irresistible intoxicating effect on the bearer of sovereignty. It is almost as if sovereignty is a naturally addictive substance, the use of which, without proper restraint, invites its bearer (whether a prince or a people) to use it even more and to the point that it can cause irreversible harm.

Bodin's analysis of popular sovereignty lays the foundation of what some have called the modern "paradox of constitutionalism." A people with the full right of sovereignty nevertheless can only exercise it effectively through some non-popular indirect means, by delegation, mandate, agency to legally constituted magistrates—or to use a more modern formulation—by "representation."[135] It is a paradox that many commentators have associated with modern political theorists such as Sieyès. But the source of this paradox, I want to argue, is ultimately in Bodin who, despite his (undeserved) reputation as a royal absolutist, actually turns out, on this reading, to be perhaps the most important theorist of popular sovereignty. His is a model of an indirect and delegated popular sovereignty that serves as the guiding ideal in the constitutional thought of early modern civilians who concluded that sovereignty could only be popular in structure.

CONCLUSION

The aim of this chapter has been to present Jean Bodin as a theorist of popular sovereignty and to show how his particular version of popular sovereignty emerges from his background legal theory. The key to my analysis has been Bodin's treatment of delegated authority, designed to show that even a people with the full right of sovereignty, just like a monarch, is nevertheless fully entitled to exercise their public authority by way of delegation to government agents. One of the important consequences emerging from Bodin's theory is the segregation of popular sovereignty from democratic government. Indeed, for Bodin, popular sovereignty need not imply democracy, let alone direct democracy, as he tries to illustrate in his study of government in Rome and Geneva. On the contrary, popular sovereignty is understood to be most secure and most effective as a constitutional form where government is least democratic and insulated from the vicissitudes of democratic politics and mass decision making.

None of this, to recapitulate, is intended to suggest that Bodin should be regarded as a democratic theorist favoring democracy. Instead, the purpose

[134] Bodin applies the same analysis to Florence where, he argues, the popular conferral of extraordinary power on Soderini by commission was a proximate cause of the fall of the Republic.

[135] Loughlin and Walker, *Paradox of Constitutionalism*. Istvan Hont, "Permanent Crisis of a Divided Mankind: 'Contemporary Crisis of the Nation State' in Historical Perspective," *Political Studies* 42 (1994): 166–231.

here has been to highlight the many complex layers of Bodin's theory, which, despite his own personal misgivings about popular constitutions, acknowledges popular sovereignty as a valid constitutional form alongside monarchy and aristocracy. But by showing how popular states are to govern themselves, by some mode of delegation and legal constitution of government offices, Bodin perhaps inadvertently prepared the groundwork for what would become the standard theory of popular sovereignty in early modern constitutional thought, where the only legitimate source of public authority can be the *populus* and never a *princeps*.

7

Popular Sovereignty, Civil Association, and the Respublica: *Johannes Althusius and the German Publicists*

INTRODUCTION

In the *République*, Jean Bodin had established the conceptual framework and the terms by which political speculation and theory would, thereafter, be expressed, in the language of sovereignty, in early modern Europe. The political ideas of the leading theorists of the seventeenth century, such as Grotius, Hobbes, Pufendorf, Spinoza, Filmer, and Locke all echoed, albeit to varying degrees, the basic theoretical framework of the sovereign state first articulated by Bodin in the sixteenth century. Of course, given Bodin's own predilection for the monarchical form of state sovereignty, Bodin's theory was most actively used, as is well known, to promote royal absolutism across early modern Europe, and it securely established his modern reputation as an intellectual founder of French royal absolutism. But it is equally true, if often forgotten, that Bodin's doctrine of sovereignty was just as influential on the constitutional thought of the opponents of monarchy as well.[1]

The European-wide influence of Bodin's ideas is aptly captured by the oft-quoted observation in Gabriel Harvey's *Letter Book*: "You can not stepp into a schollars studye but (ten to one) you shall litely finde open...Bodin De Republica."[2] Royalists, in particular, were delighted to incorporate the basic principles of Bodin's theory of sovereignty and actively sought to integrate his ideas in support of the broader program of augmenting royal power. Bodin's theory was taken up especially by theorists such as Barclay, Blackwood, and Gregorius, who re-articulated the theory of royal sovereignty against the resistance theories of the Monarchomachs.[3]

[1] See, for example, Franklin, *John Locke and the Theory of Sovereignty*.

[2] Gabriel Harvey, *Letter-Book of Gabriel Harvey, A.D. 1573–1580*, ed. Edward John Long Scott (Westminster: Nichols and Sons, 1884) 79. Quoted in Salmon, *French Religious Wars in English Political Thought* 24.

[3] Barclay, *De Regno et Regali Potestate*; Adam Blackwood, *Adversus Georgii Buchanani Dialogus, De Iure Regni Apud Scotos, Pro Regibus Apologia* (Paris: A. Sittart, 1588); Pierre Grégoire, *De Republica Libri XXVI* (Lyon: Ioannes Baptista Buysson, 1609).

Still, it would be misleading to label Bodin a conventional royalist, for the same reason that it would be incorrect to call him a democrat or a populist. This was because Bodin's civil science of state was designed to be analytically exhaustive and fully capable of classifying and parsing the structure of all historically possible states—not simply monarchical ones, such as France, but even those that were non-monarchical in form, such as Rome, Venice, and Geneva. Because of this, Bodin's theory functioned, as J.H.M. Salmon once observed, as an "encyclopedia of political wisdom, and not as a source of controversial argument."[4] Indeed, one of Bodin's central aims, consistent with his broad identification with the thought of the other French *Politiques*, such as the French Chancellor, Michel l'Hôpital, was precisely to defuse potentially explosive argument about religious uniformity and the proper location of sovereignty within a state, whether in a prince, an aristocratic council of optimates, or the whole people, through a value-free civil science. He assiduously avoided taking sides in periodic debates on questions concerning the true, optimal, or most natural form of state. In a sense, he was, what Lars Vinx might describe, an adherent of "constitutional indifferentism" about the form of state sovereignty, and so, had to admit the notional plausibility of the three basic forms of state—monarchy, aristocracy, and democracy.[5] However, it must be said, this was hardly an innovative position, but a traditional way of approaching political science. As James Hankins noted, Bodin's usage of the term, *république* or *respublica*, did not really signal a particular kind of constitutional order but, rather, merely a generic polity or state, which could take a variety of possible forms—which is why Bodin, and later Hobbes, consistently refer to states as being governed under the power of "princes or peoples."[6]

While Bodin himself might have reasonably thought his civil science would securely have closed the matter, such constitutional indifferentism proved to be an act of remarkably poor political judgment, as it only intensified precisely the sort of controversial political argument about constitutional forms which Bodin had tried to extinguish. Indeed, Bodin's insistence on the irreducibly essential diversity of forms of sovereign states generated the widespread complaint that Bodin's political theory was in fact radically incomplete, by leaving open multiple forms of sovereignty. To be a fully complete theory, the critics argued, the theory must settle upon a single uniform theory of a state's sovereignty, so as to eradicate these open political possibilities. But whereas Bodin refused to venture into the realm of normative political argument by treating this question substantively in the *République*, the task of articulating such a uniform theory of state sovereignty fell upon Bodin's later critics and interlocutors, both within and outside France, who collectively generated a

[4] Salmon, *French Religious Wars in English Political Thought* 22; Glenn Burgess, *The Politics of the Ancient Constitution: An Introduction to English Political Thought, 1600–1642* (Houndsmills: Macmillan, 1992) 123–4.

[5] Vinx, "Constitutional Indifferentism and Republican Freedom" 809–37.

[6] Hankins, "Exclusivist Republicanism and the Non-Monarchical Republic."

vast critical literature in early modern political science and the newly emerging field of public law.

This chapter focuses on Bodin's critics in the German states of the Holy Roman Empire and, above all, the Calvinist jurist Johannes Althusius (1557–1638), who attempted to create such a uniform theory. The chapter begins with a discussion of the incompatibility between sovereignty and the constitutional structure of the Holy Roman Empire. Unlike France or England, early modern Germany was characterized by a deeply fragmented constitution, with *de facto* power held and exercised by the princely nobility and independent free cities of Germany. I show how, in this context, German jurists investigated the popular and, specifically, contractual nature of sovereignty, a thought pursued most systematically by Althusius. Althusius, as I argue, absorbed Bodin's teachings about the absolute and indivisible nature of sovereignty in his major work of constitutional thought, the *Politica Methodice Digesta*. Yet, Althusius differed from Bodin in one very important respect: he rejected Bodin's "constitutional indifferentism" concerning the form of sovereignty. For Althusius, sovereignty can only be popular in form, and that is because sovereignty emerges out of what he regarded as the essentially "consociational" nature of the state. Not everybody accepted Althusius' exacting position on the indivisibility of sovereignty, especially in such a complex constitutional form as the Empire, and so, the chapter considers the German theorists of the so-called doctrine of "double sovereignty," which divides sovereignty in the Empire into the "real sovereignty" [*maiestas realis*] of the community and the "personal sovereignty" [*maiestas personalis*] of the emperor. I conclude with a discussion of the influence of these German constitutional ideas on later theorists, most notably Grotius.

BODIN'S CRITICS

In announcing the demand for a uniform theory of state sovereignty, Bodin's critics re-opened precisely that theoretical debate which, Bodin thought, his theory had successfully avoided. That was the question concerning the "correct" or "true" form of the sovereign state, the *vera respublica*, a notion which Bodin thought was chimerical since it was theoretically irrelevant whether the sovereignty was located in one man, a few men, or the whole people. All three pure forms of state were equally valid forms of state from the perspective of the civil science. On a strict Bodinian theory, it should not matter where sovereignty was located, as long as there was a publicly recognized and settled constitutional norm assigning some point within it as the perpetual, indivisible, and absolute power. Indeed, for Bodin, it ultimately made no difference, as long as there was a clear chain of command radiating throughout the state from a single center headed by the *maiestas*-holding sovereign authority.

But Bodin's critics were quick to point out that his principled indifference to the question of form was precisely the problem with his theory and, indeed, the reason why, according to them, it was fundamentally incomplete. To be sure, they had good reasons to worry about the potential normative consequences of Bodin's constitutional indifferentism, particularly given his refusal to specify a single valid form of commonwealth. For one, his insistence on the logical necessity of three basic pure forms of state automatically excluded, as we have seen, a fourth possibility, the mixed form of state [*status reipublicae mixtus*], which had been regarded a valid constitutional form in classical political theory from Plato, Aristotle, Cicero and Polybius, to early modern writers such as Bruni, Machiavelli, and Contarini. Bodin's categorical denial of even the logical possibility, let alone the normative desirability, of the mixed constitutional state committed the supreme offense against those Renaissance writers now generally called "neo-Roman" republicans, who took very seriously the notion of the *respublica mixta* as an embodiment and expression of, to use a contemporary term of art, liberty as "non-domination."[7] Moreover, anti-royalist readers of the *République* felt that Bodin's tacit acceptance of monarchy as one possible legitimate form of state was normatively unacceptable. The later republican writers, who saw all forms of royal power as criminal usurpations of a primitive and original sovereignty belonging rightfully to a free people, could never see kings and princes as legitimately sovereign in their own right and, thus, it forced them to reject Bodin's theory.

But this broad criticism of Bodin was symptomatic of a more subtle and theoretically grounded disagreement with Bodin's method of argument. By rejecting Bodin's version of civil science and renewing the demand for what might be called a grand unified theory of the state, the critics were really attempting to force open a discussion on the core meaning of the state itself. The critics, in short, were renewing the demand for a theory of the *vera respublica*, the true state.[8]

While it is true that Bodin presented a stipulative definition of the state in the opening of the *République*, as "a lawful government of many families and of that which unto them in common belongeth, with a puissant sovereignty," that definition envisaged the concept of state in terms of an asymmetrical relationship of dependence and power between sovereign and subject. For Bodin, it was nothing but sovereignty that made the state a unitary entity, and nothing else.[9]

The problem with Bodin's analysis was that it contained an unexplained starting background assumption—that is, the unexplained prior presence of

[7] Quentin Skinner, *Liberty Before Liberalism* (Cambridge: Cambridge University Press, 1998); Pettit, *Republicanism*. On the mixed constitution, see more generally, Pocock, *Machiavellian Moment*; Hans Baron, *Crisis of the Early Italian Renaissance: Civic Humanism and Republican Liberty in an Age of Classicism and Tyranny* (Princeton: Princeton University Press, 1955).

[8] The search for the *vera res publica* proceeded in parallel to the early modern Neo-Aristotelian debate on the *optimus status rei publicae*, the best form of commonwealth, such as in the work of the Aristotelian Oxford philosopher, John Case. See the discussion in Richard Tuck, *Philosophy and Government, 1572–1651* (Cambridge: Cambridge University Press, 1993) 147–9.

[9] Skinner, "From the State of Princes to the Person of the State" 398–9.

a sovereign somehow already existing prior to the formation of the state. For a political theory, such as Bodin's, the notable absence of a broader theory explaining the source of sovereign power itself was deeply troubling and one of the chief weaknesses of his overall civil science.

To be sure, Bodin was meticulous in his analysis of the attributes of sovereignty, as outlined in the First Book of the *République*, where he carefully enumerated the true "marks" or *notae* of sovereignty. And, as a classically trained jurist, Bodin carefully distinguished between the various civilian-derived categories of *potestas*, such as the "the power of the husband over his wife, the power of the father over his children, the power of the lord over his slaves."[10]

Yet, perhaps because of his legal background, he notably did not engage openly with the more fundamental questions about the origins or sources of sovereign or civil power, which would command the attention of later generations of political philosophers in the modern natural rights tradition, such as Grotius, Hobbes, and Locke. As J.H.M. Salmon rightly observes, "Bodin refuses to dogmatize about the origins of authority."[11] Indeed, he may have had good personal reasons to avoid engaging with such questions.[12] Nevertheless, whatever the case, his foundational assumption of a sovereign power which existed prior to the state, remained one of the central intellectual puzzles of his whole political theory.

Because of this, Bodin's critics felt that he simply misunderstood the relationship between sovereignty and the state, and they regarded this assumption of a pre-existing sovereign power, anterior to the state, as an error of political reasoning. Whereas Bodin believed sovereign power to be a pre-existing unifying force that alone held a state together, like a father holding the subordinate members of a household together, his critics thought that the category of sovereignty itself had to be constructed and regarded as originating in some uniform manner.

Consequently, they reversed the relationship between sovereignty and the state. Following an older medieval pattern of argument, they argued that it was the state which produced sovereignty in the first place, not the other way around. Sovereign powers did not antedate states but, rather, it was the voluntary constitution of the state itself that activated its sovereignty and sovereign rights. Thus, to explain the origins of sovereignty, it would be necessary to offer a theory about what a state actually was, in the abstract, and ultimately to fix its definitive meaning in constitutional theory. That was the task of the new school of public law which began to emerge within the constitutional thought of the later sixteenth- and early seventeenth-century Empire.

[10] Bodin, *Commonweale* 14 [1.3]. [11] Salmon, *French Religious Wars* 48.

[12] Daniel Engster, "Jean Bodin, Skepticism and Absolute Sovereignty," *History of Political Thought* 17 (1996).

ALTHUSIUS' *POLITICA METHODICE DIGESTA*

The most important critical reply to Bodin originated not in France, but in Germany, in the 1603 *Politica Methodice Digesta* of the civilian jurist and Syndic of the City of Emden, Johannes Althusius, whom Carl Friedrich had once called "the most profound political thinker between Bodin and Hobbes" as well as "the political theorist of Calvinism par excellence."[13] The great nineteenth-century German legal historian, Otto von Gierke, had reserved for Althusius a special place in the history of political thought, regarding him as the author of the "first complete system of political theory which was wholly based on natural law."[14] Gierke indeed devoted a whole monograph to Althusius' political thought and recognized him as the architect of the standard model of the modern theory of social contract, involving both a *Gesellschaftsvertrag* as well as a *Herrschaftsvertrag*. It is, according to Gierke, Althusius who "first applied to the rights claimed for the people the precise concept of sovereignty presented in the state... *maiestas*."[15] But even in 1880, Gierke was fully aware that Althusius had been almost totally ignored in the political and historical scholarship of his day, observing that, "the name of Johannes Althusius is at the present time well-nigh forgotten."[16] Over a century later, there has been a resurgence of scholarly interest in Althusius, in no small measure due to the scholarly efforts of Gierke and Carl Friedrich. The wealth of new scholarship in the twentieth century and standard editions of the *Politica*, including those by Carl Friedrich and a translation by Frederick Carney, have secured Althusius' place in the history of early modern political thought.[17]

But even with the production of this modern scholarship, what has remained among the leading questions in the recent scholarship on Althusius concerns the place of his political thought with respect to the earlier sources already investigated in this study. Some have suggested that Althusius' thought should properly be framed as engaging with contractarian thought. Harro Höpfl and

[13] Carl Joachim Friedrich, "Introduction," *Politica Methodice Digesta of Johannes Althusius* (Cambridge: Harvard University Press, 1932) xv, xvii.

[14] Otto von Gierke, *Natural Law and the Theory of Society, 1500 to 1800*, 2 Vols., trans. Ernest Barker (Cambridge: Cambridge University Press, 1934) 1:37.

[15] Otto von Gierke, *The Development of Political Theory*, trans. Bernard Freyd (New York: Norton, 1939) 154.

[16] Gierke, *Development of Political Theory* 15.

[17] Gierke and Friedrich are perhaps most responsible for the resurgence of general scholarly interest in Althusius over the past 150 years. However, Althusius has been featured prominently in scholarship concerning German legal history, such as by Carlyle, Stintzing, Koschaker, and more recently Stolleis. In the twentieth century, there has been an even greater focus on the political and constitutional thought of Althusius, such as in Thomas Hueglin, *Early Modern Concepts for a Late Modern World: Althusius on Community and Federalism* (Waterloo: Wilfrid Laurier University Press, 1999); Bettina Koch, *Zur Dis-Kontinuität Mittelalterlichen Politischen Denkens in der Neuzeitlichen Politischen Theorie: Marsilius von Padua, Johannes Althusius und Thomas Hobbes im Vergleich* (Berlin: Duncker & Humblot, 2005). Johannes Althusius, *Politica Methodice Digesta*, ed. Carl Friedrich (Cambridge: Harvard University Press, 1932); Johannes Althusius, *Politics of Johannes Althusius*, trans. Frederick Carney (London: Eyre and Spottiswoode, 1965) and reprinted (Indianapolis: Liberty Fund, 1995). For English translations of the *Politica*, I have relied on the Carney translation.

Martyn Thompson, for example, have suggested that, "Althusius made the first attempt to bring contractual language explicitly derived from Huguenot and *Ligeur* sources and the scholastic's conceptions of civil society together into a self-consciously scholarly political theory."[18] Others have focused on Althusius' broader interest in isolating politics from law. Focusing on the Ramist style of argument and the deliberate focus on the category of *politica*, Quentin Skinner has regarded Althusius' work as significant for its quite modern claim to "emancipate" politics as a separate scientific discipline from the traditional intellectual domains of theology, jurisprudence, and ethics.[19] While there can be no doubt that Althusius' contributions to political theory can be measured in these terms, they reflect a deeper concern with the theory of sovereignty, expressed in his engagement and ultimate disagreement with the framework of thought presented by Bodin and the French legists who followed him.

Born in 1557 in Diedenshausen in the County of Wittgentstein-Berleburg, Althusius, a devout Calvinist, followed a course of study in Köln and Basel heavily influenced by Aristotelian philosophy and the *studia humanitatis*. He was made *iuris utriusque doctor* in 1586 at Basel with a dissertation, *De Successione ab Intestato*, concerning intestacy and the Roman law of succession, a topic of great importance in the 1580s among jurists such as Hotman, who were deeply concerned with royal succession and dynastic right. Soon after the awarding of his doctorate, Althusius was initially appointed Licentiatus, and later Professor of Law, at the Reformed Academy in Herborn, where he would build his academic career. Althusius' duties at Herborn included the delivery of lectures and the overseeing of disputations in philosophy and Roman law, including on the *Digest* and the *Institutes*. It was at Herborn that Althusius would write some of his most important works in scientific jurisprudence, including his influential civil-law textbook, *De Arte Iurisprudentiae Romanae, Methodice Digesta, Libri II* of 1586, the *Centuria Conclusionum de Pignoribus et Hypothecis* of 1591, the *Civilis Conversationis Libri Duo* of 1601, and of course the *Politica*. In this body of scholarship, Althusius would prove himself to be a ready disciple of the most innovative schools of Continental jurisprudence championed by such civilian masters as the French legist Donellus—whom Julian Franklin has called the master of the "systematizers" of Roman law—who likewise attempted to re-organize and systematize the *Corpus Iuris* according to proper method.[20]

[18] Höpfl and Thompson, "The History of Contract as a Motif in Political Thought" 935. As important as the contractarian language is in Althusius, we should heed Carl Friedrich's criticism of Gierke that the concept of contract is "distinctly minor" in Althusius' thought. "Introduction" to *Politica*, lxxxvii.

[19] Skinner, *Foundations* 2:341, n.1.

[20] On the new legal method and "systematizers" in the French School, see Franklin, *Jean Bodin and the Sixteenth-Century Revolution in the Methodology of Law and History* Ch. 2; Kelley, "Civil Science in the Renaissance: Jurisprudence in the French Manner"; Kelley, "Development and Context of Bodin's Method"; Donald Kelley, *The Human Measure: Social Thought in the Western Legal Tradition* (Cambridge: Harvard University Press, 1990) Ch. 11; Kelley, *Foundations of Modern Historical Scholarship*.

During Althusius' tenure there, Herborn Academy attracted an international student body from across Europe. But one prominent feeder of students to Herborn was the Calvinist City of Emden in the County of East Friesland, a region in the far northwestern corner of the Reich. Often called the "Geneva of the North," Emden became famous in early modern Europe not only as a refuge for Protestants, such as French Huguenots and English Puritans escaping religious persecution in their homelands, but also as the seat of what Carl Friedrich would later call "the Mother Church of Dutch orthodoxy."[21] Politically and legally, however, Emden was, unlike the independent Free Cities of the Reich, such as Ulm and Lübeck, fully dependent on the higher jurisdiction of the city's territorial lord, who was not Calvinist but Lutheran. Indeed, the City of Emden was a member of the territorial estate, the *Landtag*, under the feudal dominion of the princely lord. This status of dependence and subjection put Emden in a precarious condition in its dealings with its princely overlord and, more generally, in Imperial politics. The aspiration of the burghers of Emden was to achieve independence as enjoyed by the Imperial Free Cities. But to achieve this, it would be necessary for Emden to assert its rights in legal terms.

It was in these circumstances that the representatives of the City of Emden acknowledged the need for an outstanding legal mind sympathetic to Reformed orthodoxy to serve as its Syndic, or resident jurisconsult, in defending its political and legal independence against princely domination. Students from Emden who had studied at Herborn found their ideal candidate in Althusius whose formal exposition of political theory in the *Politica* coincided with the values and commitments of the community in Emden. Within a year of the publication of the *Politica*, the representatives of Emden invited Althusius to take up the post of Syndic, an office which he would hold until his death in 1638.

What had attracted the burghers of Emden to Althusius were not only his professional qualifications as an academic lawyer, his commitment to the Reformed faith, or even his experience in public affairs through his service in Herborn. What seemed to matter the most, above all, was Althusius' own substantive political philosophy and his personal identification with, and unreserved support for, the cause and the claims of the Estates in their continuing struggle against princely domination. Such a struggle was, of course, certainly not unique to Emden and East Friesland, but a general phenomenon of feudal government in the princely lands of the German *Reich*. And as we shall see later, one dominant school of German constitutional thought in the seventeenth century treated such constitutional struggles and negotiations between princes and their estates within the juridical framework of bilateral contracts, secured through the device of the *tractatus*, with sovereignty ultimately being divided and co-shared between the two parties.

But whereas the conventional analysis of constitutional arrangements in Germany distributed civil sovereignty across the prince and the estates—i.e.,

[21] On Emden, see Andrew Pettegree, *Emden and the Dutch Revolt: Exile and the Development of Reformed Protestantism* (Oxford: Oxford University Press, 1992).

the doctrine of double sovereignty, such that there were effectively two poles of civil power within a commonwealth, the *maiestas personalis* of the prince and the *maiestas realis* of the whole people—Althusius, by contrast, articulated a theory of the commonwealth that reserved the full undivided rights of sovereignty inalienably to the estates, as the sole representative body of the people. This was, as Althusius would argue, a universal and unalterable pattern of politics to be found in all states. The people, on this view, are always, without exception, to be regarded as the sovereign authority in a state, and their supremacy cannot be divided, alienated, or shared with any other body.

Most striking in Althusius' thought, however, is his close engagement with Bodin's concept of sovereignty to articulate this notion of the people's supremacy. It seems, in particular, that Althusius is directly attacking constitutional indifferentism. Althusius denies in the strongest terms possible that the discrete rights of sovereignty [*iura maiestatis*] can be held by a prince or an aristocratic council of optimates. Althusius' thesis posits instead that sovereignty, by its very nature, can only and exclusively be held with full right by the whole body of the people who constitute to and form a state. This is why he feels fully justified in regarding the state [*respublica*] as the people's property [*res populi*].[22]

In this way, as Martin Van Gelderen puts it, Althusius offers the "strongest German rejection of Bodin's theory of sovereignty."[23] The rights or "marks" of sovereignty can never be the property of kings or princes, or even of an aristocratic body of *optimati*. They remain inalienably with the people as a whole. In this sense, Carl Friedrich is right to say that Bodin is "the greatest opponent against whom the *Politica* is directed."[24]

Of course, in stressing the differences between Bodin and Althusius, it is important not to overlook the similarities between the two. In conceptualizing sovereignty as the indivisible supreme power of a state, Althusius was really no different from Bodin, and indeed he may even be regarded, as J.H.M. Salmon did, as one of Bodin's most important intellectual followers when he asserts in the *Politica* that the *potestas regni* "is always one power and never many."[25] On sovereignty, Althusius speaks with the voice of Bodin, when he declares:

> For it is the nature of the rights of sovereignty [*iura maiestatis*] that whoever has one of them is considered to have the others necessarily, for he cannot have the use of one of them unless the others are also granted to him. For they are connected and unitary.[26]

For this reason, as Friedrich suggests, "we may call Althusius a true Bodinian."[27]

[22] Althusius' appeal to the Ciceronian understanding of *respublica* as *res populi* is made explicit at *Politica* 88 [9, §4], where he cites Scipio's famous definition in Cicero, *De Re Publica*, through Augustine's discussion of the text in *City of God*.

[23] Van Gelderen, "Aristotelians, Monarchomachs, and Republicanism" 204; Salmon, "The Legacy of Jean Bodin."

[24] Friedrich, "Introduction" in *Politica* lix.

[25] *Politica* 91 [9, §18].

[26] *Politica* 406 [39, §18].

[27] Friedrich, Introduction lix.

The crucial area of difference between Bodin and Althusius, however, was the identity of the sovereign itself—i.e., who, or what body, had the legal right to sovereignty. Whereas Bodin's constitutional indifferentism left open the possibility of the sovereign being under the rightful control of either a monarchy, an aristocracy, or a democracy, Althusius was unyielding in his central constitutional doctrine that only the whole people of a realm can ever have the full right to sovereignty, and never a prince. Thus, Althusius complains that "Jean Bodin greatly errs in attributing absolute and all-encompassing power to the king."[28] Indeed, he explicitly condemns Bodin for his constitutional indifferentism whereby he failed to specify the origins and structure of sovereignty within a well-ordered commonwealth:

> By no means can the supreme power be attributed to a king or optimates, as Bodin most ardently endeavors to defend. Rather it is to be attributed rightfully only to the body of a universal association [*corpori universalis consociationis*], namely, to a commonwealth or realm [*reipublicae vel regno*], and as belonging to it. From this body, after God, every legitimate power flows to those we call kings or optimates.[29]

In Althusius' account, then, all sovereignty is by definition popular sovereignty, and all states are popular states, even those that are nominally governed by kings or princes.

If, however, the people are to be regarded corporately as the sovereign of the state, as Althusius requires, the theory of popular sovereignty offered by Althusius raises a number of related interpretive questions. First of all, if only the people can be the true sovereign, it becomes less clear what sort of role a prince could actually play, as it would seem his princely power would be non-sovereign, inferior and possibly even superfluous within a commonwealth in which the people are permanently sovereign. Since kings or princes can never, on Althusius' theory, hold sovereignty, it is thus necessary to reconceptualize the status of princes.

Of course, Althusius presented a variety of different modes of argument available to him, including the well-established language of contractual obligation which featured prominently in medieval scholastic political thought.[30] Not surprisingly, he suggests at some points that the prince and the people of the *respublica* might be likened to two free and equal parties entering into a contract and accepting mutual duties to each other [*obligatio mutua contracta*], a common medieval and early modern interpretation of royal coronation oaths.[31]

But the contractual theory in Althusius' theory of the *respublica* had only limited application, and instead a different set of legal metaphors were invoked, drawn from other areas of Roman law to explain the role of the prince, such

[28] *Politica* 148 [18, §69]. [29] *Politica* 92 [9, §22].

[30] Skinner, "Humanism, Scholasticism and Popular Sovereignty." See also Höpfl and Thompson, "The History of Contract as a Motif in Political Thought."

[31] *Politica* 165 [19, §29].

as the law of guardianship. As we have seen earlier with the Monarchomachs, guardianship was distinctive because it introduced an ambiguous juridical relationship between the relevant parties. Unlike contracts, such as the Roman *stipulatio* or the *emptio-venditio*, which in theory involve the exchange of rights and obligations between parties of equal standing, guardianship involves no such exchange at all. What is, above all, absolutely crucial in this analysis is that, in the civil law, the ward or minor in the protection of a tutor or curator must also be legally *sui iuris*, and independent, and, therefore, technically a *dominus*. As we have seen from the analysis of the medieval jurists, it was this detail that complicated the relationship between ward and guardian since, on the one hand, the ward as a free person *sui iuris* retains his rights of *dominium* in full even though, on the other hand, the guardian is empowered to exercise those rights and administer the ward's estate while the ward is under his protection.

Like his medieval predecessors, Althusius envisaged a similar sort of relationship between the prince and the *respublica* when he indicates that the people are "like a ward or a minor," while the prince is to be "like a guardian" for the protection of the people.[32] Such an application of concepts from Roman private law precludes any possibility of a dualist interpretation of the relationship between prince and *respublica*. By positioning the people to be like a ward in the protection of the prince as guardian or tutor, Althusius implies that the people retain their *dominium* and thereby reserve their rights, including the right to remove untrustworthy guardians, as provided in the *Digest*. It is a very carefully crafted argument designed simultaneously to endorse a normative theory of popular sovereignty, while also acknowledging the reality of princely government and its compatibility with popular rule.

The result of this mode of argument is that the prince is not *dominus reipublicae* but rather *curator reipublicae* or *tutor regni*, expressions common to later medieval political thought and, as we have already studied, revived in Monarchomach political theory, such as the *Vindiciae* which underscored the tutorial function of kingship. This subtle reduction of the princely office to a guardianship or curatorship in Althusius' political theory incapacitated princes from asserting rights, which, he argued, belonged inalienably and by full right to the people. The nature of their office of guardianship explicitly precluded princes from asserting any claim of sovereignty or ownership in the *respublica*, even by some mode of prescription. Instead, they were burdened by civil obligations or duties to the *respublica*, which was under the prince's protection and care. Thus, in a very revealing passage directed chiefly against the arch-nemesis of the Monarchomachs, William Barclay, Althusius writes:

> The king is constituted [*constituitur*] over affairs that belong to another, namely, over the affairs of the people and the universal association, the administration, direction, government, and care of which have been granted to him. He

[32] *Politica* 137 [18, §6]; [18, §§11–14].

> certainly is not constituted over the proprietary right [*ius proprietatis*] in these affairs. An example is that of a guardian or trustee who is constituted over the affairs of his ward or minor [*negotia sui pupilli minorisve*], or of a servant, minister, or overseer whom the proprietor [*dominus*] constitutes over his affairs, and who nevertheless does not for this reason have greater authority and power than the proprietor [*dominus*] who does the constituting. So the people or universal association constitutes the king over its affairs as director, governor, and trustee, but notwithstanding under itself.[33]

For Althusius, just as for the Monarchomachs, whatever powers the princes and lesser magistrates exercised in their administration and government of the *respublica* were ultimately derived from the people, by concessive delegation which could be recovered by the people, when necessary, just as a *dominus* in Roman law was legally entitled to recover his property under the management and care of an administrator. This is because the highest right always remains with the people: "The *populus* has retained [*retinuit*] to itself, under definite conditions, power and authority."[34] As Althusius explains, princes and lesser magistrates derive their powers from such a conditional grant or loan from the people in trust, so as to govern and administer the powers of the *respublica* on their behalf. But princes, he argues, are no more than mere trustees of popular rights. Princes are like representatives or *procuratores* in the sense that they "represent the whole people and their actions are considered to be actions of the community."[35]

We have already seen similar "tutorial" theories of princely government derived from civil law concepts of guardianship, especially in the *Vindiciae*, but there is one major difference in Althusius' system of thought. It is not in the exceptional case of constitutional emergency such as dynastic change, war, or in times of manifest tyranny that the people are to be regarded as the superior of the realm and convoked as a kind of court of final appeal to pass judgment on degenerate princes. For Althusius, sovereignty always remains with the whole people and is to be treated as inalienable or "incommunicable property" of the whole people.[36] This supreme power can never be alienated to anybody, not even to the supreme magistrate.

But, while sovereignty and the right of ownership [*ius proprietatis*] in the *respublica* could never be alienated, Althusius did certainly acknowledge that the public powers attached to the sovereignty could be temporarily and conditionally granted, or loaned out, to magistrates who represent the *respublica* and act as guardians, curators, or tutors with the obligation of governing and administering the rights and powers attached to the commonwealth, such as the ephors who hold the "rights of the sword" [*ius gladii*], but are nevertheless "elected and constituted by the consent of the entire people."[37] Althusius, like the Huguenot Monarchomachs, fully ruled out the possibility that magistrates might acquire princely *dominium* by prescription or usucaption. But Althusius

[33] *Politica* 152 [18, §93]. [34] *Politica* 152 [18, §§93–4]. [35] *Politica* 137 [18, §§10–11].
[36] *Politica* 154 [18, §104]. [37] *Politica* 137 [18, §7]; *Politica* 145 [18, §59].

went even further in underlining his commitment to popular sovereignty. Unlike the Monarchomachs who, as we have seen in a previous chapter, connected acts of popular sovereignty inseparably to acts of ephoral or magisterial resistance, Althusius regarded popular sovereignty to be a regular and normal feature of the constitutional order, and he made no secret of his normative expectation that the people, convoked together as an assembly, should routinely assert its sovereignty and the bundle of *iura maiestatis* attached to that supreme power.

Perhaps Althusius' most important example illustrating the assertion of popular sovereignty involved the law of royal succession and the constitution of the prince or, as he preferred, the "supreme magistrate." Here, Althusius' vision of the sovereignty of the people and the *respublica* is expressed remarkably in terms of proprietary right, which was almost certainly intended to target the proprietary theories of power and dynastic sovereignty which dominated French royalist thought of the late sixteenth century, especially Barclay and Gregorius. But whereas French theorists regarded the legal norm of primogeniture as settling the doctrine that the French throne is to be like "dynastic property," Althusius insists that the royal powers, which are held merely by way of possession or usufruct, "escheat" or revert to their owners, the people, once each prince relinquishes his tenure in office, whether by forfeiture or death.[38] It is thereafter in the power of the people to invest those powers in a new prince to act as guardian over the commonwealth:

> When the king dies, or is denied the regal throne by any legitimate means, these rights of the king . . . return to the people as to their proprietor [*regis iura ad populum redeunt, tanquam ad suum proprietarium*]. The people then reassigns them as it thinks wise for the good of the commonwealth.[39]

Althusius' position consequently is much more radical than conventional French and English theories of royal succession. If true, it transforms all forms of monarchical rule to elective kingships. For Althusius, each new prince does not enter into the princely office by a dynastic birthright or by right of blood, but solely by election and constitution by the whole people.

ALTHUSIAN PEOPLEHOOD: THE *CONSOCIATIO UNIVERSALIS SYMBIOTICA*

In our investigation of Althusius, we have largely followed, without deeper investigation, Althusius' background assumption that the people are to be the sovereign and ultimate source, and even the owner, of public power within the commonwealth. Such a claim of an inalienable popular sovereignty is obviously central to his view of the relationship between the prince and the people. But we must now explore in greater depth why Althusius arrived at such a

[38] *Politica* 153 [18, §103]. [39] *Politica* 153–54 [18, §§103–4].

notion and ask why, on Althusius' view, the bearers of civil sovereignty can only and exclusively be the whole body of the people.

Althusius' answer, in short, was that sovereignty, as a basic fact of social and political life in a well-ordered state, was created and activated by shared bonds of communal life and social activity. Princes cannot create sovereignty, only the whole people can. It follows, thus, for Althusius, that only the body of the people should be regarded as the owner of the supreme power which they collectively create and, indeed, own by their shared communal life together as a body. As Carl Friedrich puts it, sovereignty "springs from the living together."[40]

This was a starkly different picture from the formal juristic picture that is presented in Bodin's analysis of sovereignty, which, fundamentally, continued to reside in the abstract conceptual world of jurisprudence. Whereas Bodin merely assumed the prior existence of sovereignty without explaining its antecedent origins, Althusius took the latter to be one of his chief tasks in the *Politica*: to show how sovereignty takes shape in a well-ordered commonwealth. And he tried to accomplish this by investigating the natural foundations of civil association and the cultivation of a shared collective life, which, ultimately, must be regarded as activating the rights of sovereignty.

This task enabled Althusius to identify what he saw as the disciplinary boundary separating politics from law. Politics, Althusius thought, was essentially a science concerned with forming and sustaining associations, or *consociationes*, over time, so that men can fulfill their natural needs by living together and sharing a common life as a collective unit, as a body. The forming of such associations was, indeed, precisely what Althusius regarded to be the content of politics. As he stated in the opening words of the *Politica*:

> Politics is the art of associating men [*ars consociandi*] for the purpose of establishing, cultivating, and conserving social life among them . . . The subject matter of politics is therefore the association [*consociatio*], in which symbiotes pledge themselves to each other, by explicit or tacit agreement [*qua pacto expresso, vel tacito*], to mutual communication of whatever is useful and necessary for the harmonious exercise of social life.[41]

Taking the *consociatio* as the central unit of analysis, then, Althusius' political theory is ultimately a theory or science of groups or associations. Althusius insisted on the principle that an association can only form "by consent and agreement among the communicating citizens."[42] Citing Gregorius and ultimately Bodin as foils, Althusius utterly rejects the principle that an association can only be held together by the overarching power of an external sovereign or ruler. Althusius' fundamental point, instead, was that such a ruler is unnecessary and even incoherent, since it is only the free and voluntary consensual acts of individuals that brings an association into being and from which it derives its identity and right as a group.

[40] Friedrich, "Introduction" lxxv. [41] *Politica* 15 [1, §§1–2]. [42] *Politica* 18 [1, §§28–9].

But Althusius was not simply concerned to analyze just any association in his political theory. He did not care for men assembled without proper order or reason, which in his view amounted to nothing more than "a crowd, gathering, multitude, assemblage, throng or people."[43] Instead, Althusius was most interested in analyzing a particular species of association, what he called the "symbiotic association" [*consociatio symbiotica*]—i.e., the association or body of men united by *ius symbioticum* in which members are thought of as equals and "symbiotes," as mutually interdependent and organically interlinked participants bound together by common purposes, mutual obligations, and collective identity.[44] It is within such symbiotic associations, Althusius argues, that the natural, even biological, origin of civil sovereignty is properly to be located and should be treated as the starting point of a proper science of politics, divorced from theology, jurisprudence, and ethics.

Of course, Althusius acknowledges that, in social life, there are many different kinds of symbiotic associations, ranging from lesser "simple private associations" such as the family to more complex public corporate bodies such as cities and provinces. All such groups are thought to have a place in the Ramist-influenced hierarchical frame of Althusius' pluralist social ontology. In his view, the chief division in political science, from which all further subdivisions follow, was the division between private and public, and so, he organizes his methodical treatment of symbiotic associations, beginning with private associations and then turning to public associations. But despite this division, Althusius insists forcefully that politics pertains to both the private and public spheres, an especially crucial point of contrast with orthodox Aristotelian political science, which treats private associations such as the household as outside the sphere of politics and properly belonging to private household management [*oikonomia*].[45] For, as Althusius argues, "all symbiotic association and life is essentially, authentically, and generally political. But not every symbiotic association is public."[46] On Althusius' view, then, the family and private *collegia*, such as corporations, were all sites of political life.

So were, of course, public associations, which formed the core of Althusius' political theory. But public associations differed from private associations in the manner of their constitution. Unlike private associations, which were constituted by freely consenting individuals, public associations, according to Althusius' scheme, were constituted principally by other associations. Public associations were, in effect, associations of associations, or to use a more contemporary term of art, a social union of social unions.[47] Thus, Althusius writes,

[43] *Politica* 39 [5, §4]. [44] *Politica* 21 [2, §12].

[45] Aristotle, *Politics* I, but especially I.1, I.3 and I.8 [1256a1 et seq.] on the distinction between *oikonomia, chrematistike,* and the political life.

[46] Althusius, *Politica* 32 [3, §42].

[47] The reference here ["social union of social unions"] is to John Rawls, *A Theory of Justice*, Revised Edition (Cambridge: Harvard University Press, 1999) 456–64 [§79, "The Idea of Social Union"], and especially 462. What is interesting on this point is Rawls' debt to the German juristic tradition of social and political thought in articulating this vision of the well-ordered society, as one can see in his choice of textual

"public association [*consociatio publica*] exists when many private associations are linked together for the purpose of establishing an inclusive political order [*politeuma*]."[48] In this way, a corporatist and pluralist vision of public life begins to emerge in Althusius' analysis of civil association and, if we are to follow the interpretation of Friedrich, he sets the foundation for the "theory of a corporative state," one that mirrors not only the conditions of early modern German city states such as Emden but, indeed, the *ständische Verfassung* of the whole Romano-Germanic Empire.[49]

But, of all the forms of civil association studied in the *Politica*, the most significant was his treatment of the independent state or commonwealth, a category which he designated by a variety of classical terms, *respublica, regnum*, and, even at some places, the Bartolist signifier, *populus in unum corpus*—"the people assembled in one body."[50] This concept of state, like all lesser associations treated in his Ramist scheme, was interpreted as a species of *consociatio symbiotica*. But it was notably the highest form of such association and, thus, deserved a special title, the *consociatio universalis symbiotica*. This was because such a compound association was fully inclusive, in the sense that it included, and was constituted by, all lesser forms of association. As he explains, the members of the *consociatio universalis* "are not... individual men, families, or *collegia*, as in a private or a particular public association. Instead, members are many cities, provinces, and regions agreeing among themselves on a single body constituted by mutual union and communication."[51] It is in this organized association that "many cities and provinces obligate themselves to hold, organize, use, and defend, through their common energies and expenditures, the right of the realm [*ius regni*] in the mutual communication of things and services."[52]

It is just this form of civil association, the *consociatio universalis*, which Althusius regards to be "the polity in the fullest sense," a compound association of lesser associations "constituted partly from private, natural, necessary, and voluntary societies, partly from public societies."[53] Of greatest significance, however, is the special set of symbiotic rights, which only this, the highest, form of association can activate, and that is what he calls the *ius regni*, "the right of a major state or power... the universal power of ruling [*potestas imperandi universalis*... which recognizes no ally, nor superior or equal to itself. And this supreme right of universal jurisdiction is the form and substantial essence of sovereignty [*maiestatis*]."[54]

authorities, bringing him into engagement with Kant, Hegel, and Marx. Most notably, Rawls cites Wilhelm von Humboldt, *The Limits of State Action*, ed. J.W. Burrow (Cambridge: Cambridge University Press, 1969) as representative of a broader Germanic tradition of social thought that views shared communal life as essential to a well-ordered society governed by broadly acceptable principles of justice.

[48] *Politica* 38 [5, §1]; cp. *Politica* 39 [5, §10]. [49] Friedrich, "Introduction" lxxxvi, xix.

[50] *Politica* 88 [9, §§3–4]. [51] *Politica* 88 [9, 5]. [52] *Politica* 88 [9, §1]. [53] *Politica* 88 [9, §3].

[54] *Politica* 90 [9, 13].

Althusius' sovereignty, then, is a basic fact emerging from complex associational and social life. It is the natural product or consequence of "symbiotes" living together in associations in which members engage in mutual *communicatio* with each other.[55] But Althusius clearly was not content to leave his science of politics simply with a statement on the origins of sovereignty in associational life. Indeed, he pushes his analysis further and proceeds to bridge the fact-value divide with a normative theory of sovereignty.

Specifically, he explains that, not only are the rights which are constitutive of sovereignty in the state—i.e., the *iura maiestatis* or *iura regni*—activated or created by the people in their symbiosis or sharing of a common life, but such rights of sovereignty also belong to the people as an organized community, as a compound symbiotic association. These rights of the state [*regnum, respublica*] are properly to be regarded as the property of the whole people and, thus, are subject to the *dominium* and ownership of the people, and to no other. They are, to follow a Ciceronian maxim, *res populi*.[56]

As we have seen, this appeal to the proprietary theory of popular sovereignty was a commonplace in the Huguenot Monarchomach treatises such as the *Francogallia* and the *Vindiciae*. Just as the Monarchomachs targeted royalist legists, Althusius similarly targeted "the assertion of the absolutists [such as Bodin, Gregorius, and Barclay] who had proposed to consider the supreme power in the state a piece of property belonging to the prince . . . a flagrant violation of the Roman property concept."[57]

But if, as Althusius declares, sovereignty must be regarded as belonging exclusively and inalienably to the people, it raises again the fundamental question concerning how political theorists should properly conceptualize the people in a theory of popular sovereignty. For Althusius, "the people" can only be the whole community comprising all symbiotes or members actively cooperating and living together to form the *consociatio universalis*. The sovereign people appears only in those moments when all members, organized into their proper associations, jointly act and uniformly exercise their collective shared rights over the state. At the same time, however, Althusius also insists that the people must be regarded as acting just as if it were a juristic person with a unitary will. In asserting their rights of sovereignty, the people jointly act "as one body" and "as a representational and fictional person."[58] The people are, at once, the one and the many.

Nevertheless, popular sovereignty cannot be interpreted to imply that any particular member, faction, or subset of the civil association of the sovereign state, even a numerical majority, can claim full sovereignty. Citing the *Digest*, Althusius declares that the claim on sovereignty belongs exclusively to a separate entity, and that is the whole body of the people:

> This right of the realm [*ius regni*], or right of sovereignty [*ius maiestatis*], does not belong to individual members, but to all members joined together

[55] Friedrich, "Introduction" to *Politica* lx, lxvii.

[56] Cicero, *De Re Publica* 1.39, cited via Augustine's *City of God* 2.21.

[57] Friedrich, "Introduction" xlvi.

[58] *Politica* 42 [5, 27].

> and to the entire associated body of the realm . . . The right is said to be the property [*proprietas*] not of individual members, but of members jointly. Therefore, [D. 3.4.7.1] "what is owed to the whole *universitas* is not owed to individuals."[59]

Like a *universitas*, the whole people hold a corporate identity and set of corporate rights which are unique and irreducible to the members who constitute the civil association. One immediate implication of this doctrine is that sovereignty can never be alienated since, as Althusius notes, "when this right is taken away, sovereignty perishes."[60] By this chain of reasoning, it becomes clear why sovereignty can never be attributed to a king. Since sovereignty is directly constituted by the cooperative joint activity of living together and cultivating a common life, the removal of the conditions that enable such associational life in the first place must necessarily also eradicate the product of such collective activity, sovereignty.

Taken together, then, we can now see in full how Althusius solved the problem of constitutional indifferentism that was originally presented in Bodin's theory. Sovereignty cannot be attributed with equal validity to a monarchy, aristocracy, or a popular state, as Bodin allows in the *République*. Instead, sovereignty, by implication, can only be popular sovereignty because sovereignty, as a natural fact of social life, is derivative of symbiotic associational life that jointly forms the state in the first place. In short, without the anterior symbiotic association of individuals and groups, it is impossible to have sovereignty.

THE DOCTRINE OF DOUBLE SOVEREIGNTY: THE REICHSPUBLIZISTEN AND THE GERMAN SCHOOL OF PUBLIC LAW

So far I have investigated the critical reception of Bodin's theory of sovereignty and the state in the Holy Roman Empire, and I have focused particularly on the influential reply crafted in Althusius' *Politica*. The essence of Althusius' reply to Bodin involved the view that the only true form of sovereignty is popular sovereignty, a direct rejection of Bodin's thesis that the bearer of the rights of sovereignty can take the form of either a monarchy, an aristocracy [*optimati*], or a democracy [*popularis*]. As J.H.M. Salmon has rightly noted, "In the eyes of Althusius every state was a popular one in that the community was always the sovereign, whatever the form of government."[61] And this was because sovereignty, for Althusius, could only be the product of a set of one or more acts of free association by the people in the broader political community, which he set out to show with his complex political theory of consociational peoplehood.

[59] *Politica* 91 [9, §18], which includes Althusius' reference to D. 3.4.7.1.

[60] *Politica* 91 [9, §17].

[61] Salmon, "Legacy of Jean Bodin" 508.

While it is certainly true that Althusius' theory of politics was intended to offer a response to Bodin and other French absolutists, such as Gregorius and Barclay, it cannot be denied that the *Politica* was also designed to address one of the most contentious constitutional questions raging in early modern Germany. That concerned the constitutional form of the Holy Roman Empire, a topic of monumental importance to the German jurists, often collectively known as the *Reichspublizisten*, or Imperial Publicists.[62] As we can see in the example of Althusius, the German jurists actively sought to introduce concepts of sovereignty into the analysis of the constitutional politics of the Holy Roman Empire, the old *Reich*.

There were several closely related reasons for this interest in bringing the vocabulary of sovereignty into early modern German constitutional thought. Perhaps the first thing to observe is that Germany experienced a period of rapid legal transformation and renewal starting especially in the late fifteenth century. With the formal Reception of Roman law into the Empire in 1495 during the reign of the Emperor Maximilian I, early modern German jurists were involved in a broader project of legal reform, which involved, inter alia, the establishment of a court of final appeal for the whole Empire, the *Reichskammergericht*, and the official recognition of the learned law contained in the *Corpus Iuris Civilis* as the final and highest legal authority within the Empire, thereby displacing, or at least conflicting with, local customary law and other German legal sources such as the *Sachsenspiegel* practiced in lay *Schöffen* courts.[63] Needless to say, the reception had a transformative effect on German legal thought and practice, and indeed, it follows a long-observed pattern in European legal history whereby the introduction of Roman law has tended to coincide with the emergence of the modern nation-state.[64] In this case, the systematization of law in the early modern Empire, alongside the introduction of professional civilian, often Italian-educated, *iuris doctores*, gave expression to a broader desire for a more uniform and systematic legal science in Germany, a desire which manifested itself in a variety of ways: for example, the reform of municipal civil and criminal codes according to the systematic style and content of the Roman lawbooks in the Bavarian Reform of 1518 and in the Palatinate: and the replacement of lay judges with professional jurists.[65]

The aim was to unify and harmonize the German Empire from within, so that it would have the outward attributes or semblance of a unitary territorial state with a uniform system of public law. The problem, of course,

[62] On the *Reichspublizisten*, see Michael Stolleis, *Geschichte des Öffentlichen Rechts in Deutschland*, Vol. 1, *Reichspublizistik und Policeywissenschaft, 1600–1800* (München: C.H. Beck, 1988).

[63] Wieacker, *A History of Private Law in Europe* 71–155; Whitman, *Legacy of Roman Law in the German Romantic Era* Ch. 1; Stein, *Roman Law in European History* 88–94.

[64] Strauss, *Law, Resistance and the State* 73–4, 97–8.

[65] Strauss, *Law, Resistance and the State* Ch. 3; John Philip Dawson, *A History of Lay Judges* (Cambridge: Harvard University Press, 1960); Brundage, *Medieval Origins of the Legal Profession*; Sidney Bradshaw Fay, "The Roman Law and the German Peasant," *American Historical Review* 16 (1911): 234–54.

was that the Empire was not a unitary territorial state but, rather, a congeries of states. Indeed, despite historical and legal fictions, such as the *translatio imperii*, the Holy Roman Empire was, in practice, a deeply fragmented and internally decentralized polity that resembled more a confederation of autonomous principalities and free cities with overlapping and sometimes conflicting jurisdictions, rather than a single unitary state.[66] Indeed, this internal disarray in the Empire actually proved to be quite violent, especially in the early modern period, with constant feuding and private warfare among the German princely nobility.[67] Given the complexities of the Empire's internal constitutional arrangements, some theorists, such as Vincent Cabot, classified the Empire as a classic *respublica mixta*, or mixed state.[68] Samuel Pufendorf was even less generous who would later famously describe the post-Westphalian Empire not as a sovereign state at all, but as a "diseased state," an "irregular body," and even "like some mis-shapen monster" [*monstro simile*].[69]

Given these conditions, German jurists recognized that there was a critical need for the Empire to reform and position itself as an independent sovereign state like the other great early modern monarchies, such as France and England. It was in this context that the *Reichspublizisten* began engaging with civilian concepts of sovereignty and especially with the ideas of Bodin. But as soon as the Imperial jurists began to consider ways of applying Bodin's theories in the Germanic context, it became clear that there was a genuine interpretive puzzle as to whether concepts of sovereignty could even be applied to

[66] Hajo Holborn, *A History of Modern Germany*, Vol. 1, *The Reformation* (Princeton: Princeton University Press, 1982) 11–15. On the *translatio imperii*, see Lupold von Bebenburg [Lupoldus], *De Iuribus et Translatione Imperii* (Strasbourg, 1508); Lupold von Bebenburg, *Tractatus de Iuribus Regni et Imperii Romanorum* (Strasbourg, 1624); and especially the Frisian jurist, Hermann Conring, in the critical edition by Constantin Fasolt: Hermann Conring, *Hermann Conring's New Discourse on the Roman-German Emperor* [*Discursus Novus de Imperatore Romano-Germanico*], ed. and trans. Constantin Fasolt (Tempe: Arizona Center for Medieval and Renaissance Studies, 2005); and *De Origine Iuris Germanici* (1643), which has earned him the title as "the founder of historical jurisprudence in Germany." Otto Stobbe, *Geschichte der Deutschen Rechtsquellen*, 2 Vols. (Leipzig: Duncker & Humbolt, 1860–64) 2: 418–19.

[67] Hillary Zmora, *State and Nobility in Early Modern Germany: The Knightly Feud in Franconia, 1440–1567* (Cambridge: Cambridge University Press, 1997); Whitman, *Legacy of Roman Law in the German Romantic Era* 5–14.

[68] Vincent Cabot, *Variarum Iuris Publici et Privati Disputationum Libri Duo in Novus Thesaurus Iuris Civilis et Canonici*, ed. G. Meerman, Vol. 4 (The Hague, 1752) 623, cited by Julian Franklin, "Sovereignty and the Mixed Constitution: Bodin and His Critics," *Cambridge History of Political Thought, 1450–1700*, ed. J.H. Burns and Mark Goldie (Cambridge: Cambridge University Press, 1991) 309–10. Even German jurists, as we will see below, had entertained the possibility of treating the *Reich* as a mixed state, although Franklin has suggested that it might more accurately be called a "compound polyarchy." See, for example, Daniel Otto, "An Mixtus Detur Reipublicae Status?" in Dominicus Arumäeus, *Discursus Academici de Iure Publico*, 3 Vols. (Jena, 1620) [2:22], and Christopher Besold, "Dissertatio Singularis de Status Reipublicae Mixto," in *Dissertatio Politico-Iuridica de Majestate in Genere* (Strasbourg, 1625).

[69] Samuel Pufendorf, *On the Present State of Germany* [*De Statu Imperii*], ed. Michael Seidler (Indianapolis: Liberty Fund, 2007) 176 [6.9]. See Peter Wilson, "Still a Monstrosity? Some Reflections on Early Modern German Statehood," *Historical Journal* 49 (2006): 565–76; Peter Schröder, "The Constitution of the Holy Roman Empire after 1648: Samuel Pufendorf's Assessment in his *Monzambano*," *Historical Journal* 42 (1999): 961–83.

the Empire, where there was such an apparently unbridgeable gap between *de facto* and *de iure* sovereignty. Indeed, it was not at all clear that the Empire even possessed the characteristics of independent statehood. There was a question whether the Holy Roman Empire truly was a sovereign *respublica* or not.

Bodin's position on this question was well known, just as much as it was controversial. In his analysis of the Empire, he had concluded that it certainly was a sovereign *respublica* but specifically, a *respublica* of an aristocratic form, and not monarchical. Despite the official rule of the Emperor, Bodin argued that he could not be the bearer of civil sovereignty since the Emperor was elected into his office by the prince-electors, to whom the sovereignty theoretically reverts upon the Emperor's death or abdication. Because the power of election and appointment, for Bodin, was one of the clearest signs of sovereignty, and because the rights of sovereignty are *ex hypothesi* indivisible, it followed that the corporate body of the prince-electors, sitting as an electoral college, must in fact be the true sovereign of the Empire, and not the Emperor, who merely held *imperium* by appointment.[70]

This conclusion was, however, unacceptable to the *Reichspublizisten* who defended the sovereign rights of the Imperial Crown and continued to believe that the Holy Roman Emperor was a true sovereign, as much as the King of France. Bodin, they argued, was right to regard the Empire as a sovereign state, but wrong to say that it was an aristocracy. Indeed, as Julian Franklin has observed, "all the leading writers of the early 1600s [with a few notable exceptions] insisted that the German Emperor was a true monarch in some sense or another."[71] One of the leading examples of this monarchical view was the jurist, Theodor Dietrich Reinkingk who, as Peter Schröder, describes, "maintained the view—against Bodin, but employing his theory of sovereignty—that the Emperor was in possession of sovereignty within the Empire."[72] As Reinkingk steadfastly declares, in defiance of Bodin, whom he regards to be "ignorant" and "full of virulent hate" toward the Empire [*Bodinus, qui nescio qua odii virulentia inescatus*], the Emperor was in full ownership and control of those rights and powers which Bodin regarded as the "marks" of sovereignty [*iura maiestatis*], such as the right of creating or constituting magistrates [*ius creandorum Magistratuum*] and the right of declaring war and peace [*ius pacis et belli*].[73]

70 *Commonweale* 191 [2.1].

71 Franklin, "Sovereignty and the Mixed Constitution" 312. Two exceptions might include, of course, Althusius who regards the Empire as a popular state with sovereignty residing in the people, and Bogislaus Philipp von Chemnitz, one of the few German jurists who had agreed with Bodin's assessment that the Empire was really an aristocracy and not a monarchy. Bogislaus Philipp von Chemnitz ["Hippolytus a Lapide"], *Dissertatio de Ratione Status in Imperio Nostro Romano-Germanico* (1640) 247–56 [1.18]. Tuck, *Philosophy and Government* 127.

72 Schröder, "The Constitution of the Holy Roman Empire after 1648" 962. On Reinkingk, see the valuable study by Rudolf Hoke, *Die Reichsstaatsrechtslehre des Johannes Limnaeus: Ein Beitrag zur Geschichte der Deutschen Staatsrechtswissenschaft im 17.Jahrhundert* (Aalen: Scientia Verlag, 1968) 64–5, 155–6.

73 Theodor Dietrich Reinkingk, *Tractatus de Regimine Seculari et Ecclesiastico* (Frankfurt am Main, 1659) 55, 57 [1.2.2].

Similarly, the theologian, jurist, and philosopher, Bartholomaus Keckermann, a professor of Hebrew in Heidelberg, attempted to correct what he viewed as Bodin's inaccurate portrayal of the Imperial constitution as a pure aristocracy by stressing the Emperor's monarchical sovereignty over the German princely nobility. To be sure, Keckermann acknowledges that the Emperor is, to a certain degree, less absolute than the archetypal pure monarch exemplified by the French king and, thus, suggests that there are different degrees of monarchical rule. Keckermann explains in his *Systema Disciplinae Politicae*, that the Emperor, is undoubtedly sovereign, but of a more "tempered form" than, for example, the French Crown. It is, in some measure, like a "mixed" form of state in which the Emperor and the princely nobility act as co-equal partners in the ownership and exercise of sovereignty. However, Keckermann's understanding of the "tempered form" of state actually shows him really to be a careful follower of Bodin rather than a mixture theorist like Cabot since, in Keckermann's view, the form of state can be "tempered" by its mode of government and administration.[74] So, a state may be monarchical in form, even if that state is governed under a non-monarchical administration, as in the case of the Empire, where, as Keckermann argues, the Emperor is the monarchical sovereign, while the government of the Empire is administered through the nobility. Keckermann's reasoning is, thus, straightforwardly Bodinian by relying on the sovereignty-government distinction, with the only salient difference being the location of sovereignty in the Imperial Crown.

Perhaps the most influential defender of this monarchical interpretation of the Empire was Henning Arnisaeus, the professor of ethics and medicine at Frankfurt-am-an der Oder and at Helmstadt, and later, court physician to Christian IV, King of Denmark, in Copenhagen.[75] In the first part of his *De Iure Majestatis*, Arnisaeus treats "sovereignty in general" [*De maiestate in genere*] and focuses especially on the older Roman theories of the Emperor's universal lordship [*universale dominium Imperatoris*] to argue against what he views as the false Bodinian distinction between sovereign power (of the *Reichstag*), the rights of which [*iura maiestatis*] are inseparable [*non separari*], and mere titular sovereignty (of the Emperor).[76] Against this analysis, Arnisaeus declares that the Empire is a true monarchy, just as any other sovereign who is freed from the coercive force of the laws [*legibus solutus*] and "recognizes neither a superior nor an equal" [*nec superiorem potestatem, nec aequale agnoscere*].[77] It is a view that

[74] Franklin, "Sovereignty and the Mixed Constitution" 315, citing Bartholomaeus Keckermann, *Systema Disciplinae Politicae* (Hanover, 1608) 560 [2.4].

[75] Horst Dreitzel, *Protestantischer Aristotelismus und Absoluter Staat: Die "Politica" des Henning Arniseaus, ca. 1575–1636* (Wiesbaden: Franz Steiner Verlag, 1970). See also Stolleis, *Geschichte des Öffentlichen Rechts in Deutschland* Ch. 3 of Vol. 1.

[76] Henning Arnisaeus, *De Iure Maiestatis Libri Tres* (Frankfurt, 1610) 22 [Ch. 2], and 1 [Ch. 1]. Parts of this work are later translated into English by Sir John Eliot. See also Arnisaeus' *De Autoritate Principum in Populum Semper Inviolabili* (Frankfurt, 1612).

[77] Arnisaeus, *De Iure Maiestatis* 42 [Ch. 3].

he repeats later in his *Doctrina Politica*, where he suggests that the German Empire is properly to be conceived as a "pure monarchy" [*monarchia simplex*] where the Emperors "rule monarchically" [*Monarchice imperarint*].[78]

Yet, even while the *Reichspublizisten* interpreted the constitution of the Empire through the Bodinian framework of sovereignty, there were still many jurists who denied that the concept of sovereignty could even be applied at all to the circumstances of the Empire. For these others, it became immediately clear that the problem was not with the application of the concept of sovereignty, but instead, with the Bodinian concept of sovereignty itself, and, especially, Bodin's insistence that sovereignty must be regarded as indivisible and unitary in all states. The more critical among the German jurists insisted that the idea of sovereignty itself must be reconceptualized to fit the facts of Imperial government, rather than the other way around. In part, this was because the decentralized and fragmented structure of the Empire made it virtually impossible to locate, as Bodin's theory required, a unique singular site or locus of sovereignty. Given the multiple loci of power distributed and "mixed" across various political actors, the *Reichspublizisten* suggested that the Empire exemplifies a categorically distinct species of sovereignty, which, in their view, Bodin and his followers had failed to recognize and properly document.

That new species of sovereignty was what scholars have called the doctrine of "double sovereignty," typically signified in the Latin treatises as simply *maiestas duplex*, perhaps the most innovative contribution of early modern German jurists to the continuing Continental juristic debates on the concept of sovereignty. The concept was invented and first articulated systematically by the Marburg humanist, Hermann Kirchner, in his *Respublica* of 1608, what Julian Franklin has called the "*locus classicus* for the principle of double majesty."[79] Unlike Bodin who required sovereignty to be regarded as indivisible, Kirchner posited that all instances of sovereignty consist of two essential components, what he called the *maiestas realis* ["real sovereignty"] and the *maiestas personalis* ["personal sovereignty"]. All sovereign states, it was argued, must contain these two elements of full sovereignty.

But what is crucial to double sovereignty was the asymmetrical relationship between *maiestas realis* and *maiestas personalis*, with the former being regarded as superior to the latter. This was because the sovereign right of *maiestas realis* was not attached to any particular person or ruling party, but instead, was exclusively the property of the whole state, or *respublica*. Just as the *respublica* was, in the theory of the jurists, thought to be permanent, unchanging, and fixed, so too was the *maiestas realis* thought to be similarly permanent and immutable. By contrast, the sovereign rights of *maiestas personalis*, held personally by officers of the civil state, were constantly changing hands, and this

[78] Henning Arnisaeus, *Doctrina Politica* (Amsterdam, 1651) 190 [Ch. 8, *De mixta republica*].

[79] Hermann Kirchner, *Respublica* (Marburg, 1608). See also Franklin, "Sovereignty and the Mixed Constitution" 316. Cf. Althusius, *Politica* 93 [9, §§23–4].

was because such "personal" rights were derivative and dependent on the concessive and revocable grant of power made by the whole *respublica*.

The *Reichspublizist*, Matthias Bortius, for example, offers a very useful analysis of double sovereignty in the Empire, distinguishing between the *maiestas realis* and the *maiestas personalis*. The former, Bortius argues, belongs to no specific person or persons within the state, but rather, to the "very state itself" [*respublica ipsa*], or, as he writes elsewhere, "the whole state and, secondarily, the orders and estates of the Empire" [*tota Respublica et secundario ordines et status Regni*]. This "real sovereignty" is ultimately composed of a bundle of sovereign rights that Bortius brings under the broad label, *iura regni*, which include the right of the people to elect the Emperor (through the intermediary body of the *Reichstag*) and, more generally, to determine and constitute "the mode and the form of the government" [*modus et forma regiminis*].[80] They are rights pertaining to the whole *respublica* because they concern, above all, the establishment and preservation of the well-being of the state [*status reipublicae*].

By contrast, the *maiestas personalis* belongs specifically to the person of the *princeps* and his agents and is inclusive of all the *iura regia*—i.e., the *regalia maior et minora*—necessary for the government of the *respublica*. Bortius' key point, however, is that the Emperor's personal sovereignty is "limited" [*limitatus*] precisely because his personal *iura regia* are derived from a more primitive transfer of power originating from the people's "real sovereignty."[81] What begins to emerge, then, in Bortius' doctrine of double sovereignty is actually a surprisingly proto-Lockean theory of contract and revolution since the Emperor [*princeps*] is thought to be limited by the obligation created by *pacta expressa* to govern and care for the *respublica*. If the Emperor injures the *salus Reipublicae*, thereby violating the contract between the Emperor and the people, all obligations are dissolved [*dissolvitur obligatio*] and the people are empowered to resist and depose the *princeps*, since they are more powerful [*potior*] and the source of the Emperor's *maiestas personalis*.[82]

In the intellectual context of the German debates on sovereignty, the doctrine of double sovereignty was especially attractive since it offered a compromise, a middle way, between the polar extremes represented, on the one hand, by Althusius' populism and, on the other hand, by Arnisaeus' absolutism, shaped by Bodin. In this way, then, *maiestas duplex* offered a theory that better reflected and fitted the realities of the fragmented German state, with power shared and exercised jointly by the Emperor and the princely nobles of the estates of the Empire. Even more important, however, were the ideological

[80] Matthias Bortius, *De Natura Iurium Maiestatis et Regalium Explicatio* (Jena, 1614) [1.2].

[81] Bortius, *De Natura Iurium Maiestatis et Regalium* [1.30.5.9]

[82] Bortius, *De Natura Iurium Majestatis et Regalium* [1.30.7]: *contra quod remedium est, ut resistat populus et si opus, deponat eundem*. The suggestion of dissolution as relief or remedy and resistance to an "injury" [*iniuria*] committed against the people foreshadows the core of Locke's doctrine, but it also shows traces of the law of delicts and especially the Roman *Lex Aquilia* which includes, *inter alia*, the famous doctrine, D.9.2.4.pr: natural reason permits a person to defend himself against danger.

dimensions and contributions of the doctrine. Double sovereignty provided a new vocabulary for conducting the longstanding German debate on the power and status of the Emperor within the constitution of the Holy Roman Empire. By analyzing sovereignty along "real" and "personal" dimensions, the Publicists avoided having to identify, as Bodin required, a unique locus of sovereignty, but instead, could acknowledge that both the emperor and the Estates of the Empire participated in a share of the sovereignty, only different aspects of it.[83]

But the introduction of double sovereignty into early modern German political thought transformed the ideological nature of the debate, which, consequently, focused on the proper assignment of *maiestas realis* and *maiestas personalis*. Thus, what emerges in the German juristic literature of the early seventeenth century are attempts by the *Reichspublizisten* to present various constitutional interpretations of the structure of the Holy Roman Empire in terms of double sovereignty.

As Salmon points out, there were monarchical and aristocratic schools of interpretation concerning the *maiestas duplex*.[84] The leading defender of the monarchical interpretation of double sovereignty among the *Reichspublizisten* was Dominicus Arumäeus, founder of the Jena school of jurisprudence. In his *Discursus Academici de Iure Publico* of 1620, Arumäeus argues, like Reinkingk and Arnisaeus, that the Empire is a true monarchy. But since Arumäeus accepts that sovereignty is double, he is committed to specifying the Emperor's constituted authority as a *maiestas personalis*, and reserving the constituent power of *maiestas realis* to the Imperial Diet as representative of the whole Empire.[85] As Arumäeus explains, the *plenissima maiestas* remains in all *regna et respublicae*. Although it is true that the Emperor has his own personal *maiestas individua*, the crucial point is that the Emperor's powers and dignities are actually derived from a concessive grant from the whole *respublica* consisting of only *certas et definitas partes* of the Empire's full *maiestas*.[86] So, even though the Empire is monarchical in form, on Arumäeus' view, the Emperor's authority as a monarch is limited by the even greater constituting authority, or *maiestas realis*, of the whole Empire, or the *respublica*. In this way, he is able to deny the absolutist maxim that the Emperor is *legibus solutus*, but instead, acknowledge that "the supreme power ought to be circumscribed within legal limits."[87]

[83] One commentator, responding to Gierke's assessment, has regarded double sovereignty as, in some ways, the basis for modern theories of federalism, particularly in the analysis of *maiestas* found in German jurists such as J. Lampadius, *De Republica Romano-Germanica* (1634), B.C. Carpzov, *Commentarius in Legem Regiam Germanorum, sive Capitulationem Imperatorium* (1640), and Ludolph Hugo, *Dissertatio de Statu Regionum Germaniae et Regimine Principum Summae Imperii Rei Publicae Aemulo* (Helmstadt, 1661). Heinz Eulau, "Theories of Federalism under the Holy Roman Empire," *American Political Science Review* 35 (1941): 649–50.

[84] Salmon, "The Legacy of Jean Bodin" 509–10.

[85] Dominicus Arumäeus, *Discursus Academici de Iure Publico*, 3 Vols. (Jena, 1620).

[86] Arumäeus, *Discursus Academici de Iure Publico* [4.2].

[87] Arumäeus, *Discursus Academici de Iure Publico* [4.1]: *princeps legibus non solutus; summa potestas limitibus circumscribi debet.*

By contrast, Tobias von Pauermeister developed what Salmon regards an "aristocratic" interpretation of double sovereignty, in which he assigns the *maiestas personalis* not exclusively to the emperor, but jointly to a compound body comprised of both the Emperor and the estates of the Empire [*collegium civium reipublicae Romanae actu participum... in uno compendio repraesentivo*], while *maiestas realis* is reserved for the people of the *respublica*, as a whole [*omnes cives ut universi*]. In the *De Iurisdictione Imperii Romani* of 1608, a work Julian Franklin has called "one of the most acute and influential treatises of this period on German public law," Pauermeister's aristocratic interpretation of *maiestas personalis* indicates that such power is not literally "personal" in the sense of personal property, but rather, a bundle of powers and functions shared equally by the Emperor and the assembled Estates as active partners co-sharing in the duties of government.[88] Like Arumäeus, however, Pauermeister is in full agreement that *maiestas realis* must be reserved for the people of the *respublica*, who remain supreme and can choose either to reserve the *summa rerum* [*publicarum*] for themselves or to confer a limited share of their sovereignty "upon one or upon many" [*uni vel pluribus*].[89]

The aristocratic interpretation of double sovereignty that was championed by Pauermeister was later adopted by the Tübingen jurist, Christopher Besold, and his pupil, Johannes Limnaeus, who both expanded on Pauermeister's suggestion that powers of government, *maiestas personalis*, are shared between the Emperor and the princely nobility of the Empire. For Besold, *maiestas realis*, remains immovably in the *respublica* or the *populus*, even with the transfer of the people's shared powers to the Emperor by a *lex regia*. What is interesting in Besold's analysis is the Aristotelian suggestion that *maiestas realis* is the "efficient cause" of *maiestas personalis* which, in his view, explains the familiar doctrine that the royal domain [*domania regni*] and the rights of dignity [*iura dignitatis, regalia maiora et minora*] attached to the Emperor are inalienable and remain in the ownership of the whole people of the *respublica*.[90] Limnaeus explores further the notion of real sovereignty, describing it to be a power "adhering to the state."[91]

To be sure, in the broader context of German public law and constitutional thought, the doctrine of double sovereignty was rather short-lived, which, as Gierke observed, "finally vanished from the literature after the middle of the seventeenth century."[92] Nor was *maiestas duplex* terribly innovative in substance, at least. As Gierke argued, "*maiestas realis* is but a new name for the old popular sovereignty which is retained in principle," and double sovereignty

[88] Franklin, "Sovereignty and the Mixed Constitution" 323. Tobias von Pauermeister, *De Iurisdictione Imperii Romani* (1608) [1.3.10; 2.2; 2.11.18–20].

[89] Pauermeister, *De Iurisdictione Imperii Romani* [1.17.1].

[90] Besold, *Dissertatio Politica-Iuridica de Majestate in Genere* [1.1; 1.5; 2.10].

[91] Johannes Limnaeus, *Capitulationes Imperatorum et Regum Romanogermanorum cum Annotamentis* (Srasbourg, 1651) 532. Hoke, *Die Reichsstaatsrechtslehre des Johannes Limnaeus*.

[92] Gierke, *Development of Political Theory* 167.

merely gives a modern expression, in the language of sovereignty, to both mixed constitutionalism and the medieval theory of political dualism between the ruler and the ruled which early modern absolutists such as Bodin and, later, Hobbes sought to eliminate.[93] We are left to ask, then, what could be so significant or remarkable about the doctrine of double sovereignty.

The answer, I want to suggest, concerns the manner in which *maiestas duplex* was constructed and defended by the Publicists. Most remarkable in the analysis of *maiestas duplex* was its parasitic dependence upon one of the key conceptual distinctions to be found in Roman law, and that is the distinction in the law of actions, between "real" actions [*actio in rem*] and "personal" actions [*actio in personam*].[94] What the Publicists essentially accomplished was the superimposition of this distinction onto the concept of sovereignty so that, like the two categories of civil actions, "real" and "personal," sovereignty [*maiestas*] is similarly thought to be divisible into the corresponding civilian categories of real sovereignty and personal sovereignty. Application of private law in this manner is particularly instructive for what it can tell us about the German public lawyers' understanding of sovereignty and the *respublica*.

In Roman law, real actions were essentially suits concerning property and specifically the recovery of property classified as *res corporealis*. Central to a real action is the assertion of a claim, a *vindicatio*, that the particular object of property in question—i.e., the *res corporealis*—belongs to one party but is wrongfully in another party's possession. In the Middle Ages, the Glossators had expanded upon this notion of "vindicating" real property by the *actio in rem* to a more robust notion of a claim-right and, specifically, what the Bolognese jurist, Joannes Bassianus, had called a *ius ad rem*, the right of one person to an object of property [*res*] in the control or possession of another.[95] The notion of real sovereignty appears to reside within this constellation of private-law concepts, but with the important difference that the Publicists were less concerned with *dominium* over *res corporealis*, than with *dominium* over the *respublica*. Real sovereignty, for the German Publicists, was literally a real right, a *ius ad rem* in the same sense as Bassianus and Azo thought, but it was specifically a *ius ad rempublicam*, a proprietary claim to the state itself.

Personal actions, by contrast, were suits at civil law compelling those under an obligation, whether by contract or by wrongdoing, to perform what they are legally obliged to do. Unlike real actions, these were not about property ownership, but instead about personal obligations [*in personam*] and their enforcement. The Romans classically defined civil obligation as a "legal tie" or bond [*vinculum iuris*], so that persons under an obligation are said to be bound in some way, as when, for example, a person contracts to sell some of his property, he is legally obliged or bound to do so in fact.[96] The jurists even identified a kind of right, the *ius in personam* (distinct from the *ius in re* and the *ius ad rem*), empowering one person to compel another person under an obligation to

[93] Gierke, *Development of Political Theory* 165. Cp. Salmon, "The Legacy of Jean Bodin" 509.

[94] Gaius 4.2–4.5.

[95] Tuck, *Natural Rights Theories* 14.

[96] Inst. 3.13.pr. D.44.7.3.pr.

perform his duty. It is pretty clear that in crafting the notion of personal sovereignty, the German theorists imagined the position of the ruler with personal sovereignty similarly to be under a kind of *vinculum iuris*. But the obligation of the ruler with personal sovereignty is not tied to any particular person, but, rather, to the whole people and the state. Nor is it merely an obligation of *dare, facere, praestare, opertare*. The ruler's obligation was the most important of all, and that is the obligation to perform justice.

For the *Reichspublizisten*, the distinction between real sovereignty and personal sovereignty is rooted fundamentally in the Roman analysis of actions. We do not need to look far into this literature to find how this civilian framework of double sovereignty reintroduces a whole set of legal concepts we have already encountered previously. For example, the jurist, Daniel Berckringer, in elaborating on Kirchner's presentation of *maiestas duplex*, explains that *maiestas realis* and *maiestas personalis* correspond essentially to the civilian distinction between *dominium* and usufruct, since only the exercise, but not ownership, of the constitutive sovereign rights of the *respublica* is conferred by the constituting of a government with *maiestas personalis*.[97] It is an analysis repeated by Limnaeus, who regards the *maiestas personalis* to be a mere usufructuary right [*ius in re aliena*] of the Emperor, while *maiestas realis* is a full proprietary right of the state [*ius in re publica*] of *dominium* that resides immovably in the whole community of the *respublica*.[98] Similarly, Daniel Otto, another student of Arumäeus, offers an analysis of double sovereignty, appealing to concepts of *tutela*, or legal guardianship, in his treatment of *maiestas realis* as property under the *dominium* of the whole *respublica* and not, under any circumstances, of the emperor, whose limited and inferior *maiestas personalis* makes him merely *administrator... sed non proprietarius* and, therefore, incapable of *alienatio in detrimentum reipublicae* but is instead bound by his obligation to the people.[99]

But it is Pauermeister who links explicitly the new Germanic framework of *maiestas duplex* to the older medieval application of Romanist property concepts by highlighting a parallel construction found in the Glossators doctrine of *dominium divisum*, which we have examined in Chapter 3. The powers of *maiestas realis*, for him, remain inalienably in the body of the *respublica*, so much so, that he regards those powers as a *dominium verum et plenum*. By contrast, the *iura realia innominata* conceded and granted to the emperor and the Princes of the Empire can count as nothing more than *ususfructus*, which are

[97] Daniel Berckringer, *Institutiones Politicae sive de Republica* (Utrecht, 1662) [1.4.6–7]. Indeed, Berckringer even suggests that, following the law of obligations, that the emperor with *maiestas personalis*, always remains accountable to the *respublica* for "public wrongs" [*delicta publica*]. Berckringer's unpublished *Examen Elementorum Philosophicorum de Bono Cive* was thought to be a reply to Hobbes.

[98] Johannes Limnaeus, *Ius Publicum Imperii Romano-Germanici*, 2 Vols. (Strasbourg: Paul Ledertz, 1629–32) [1.10.14], where, among other authorities, he cites Mornay and Althusius.

[99] Daniel Otto in Arumäeus, Vol. 2 [14.17]: *Maiestas Regnantis maiestati Regni tanquam superiori obnoxia sit et obstringatur*, and also Otto [14.18–19].

always inferior to the full *dominium* of the *respublica* and subject to forfeiture and recovery by the people.[100]

Taken together, then, it is plainly obvious that, in the school of the German Imperial Publicists, the application of Roman private law to debates on sovereignty and public law breathed new life into an older idiom of constitutional thought that stressed the essential dualism or opposition between the rights of the ruler and of the ruled. What was critical, however, was the ultimate effect this doctrine of double sovereignty had on the existing debates on the nature of sovereignty and its popular foundations.

CONCLUSION

The aim of this chapter was to investigate the critical reception of Bodin's theory of sovereignty in the legal thought of the early modern Holy Roman Empire. In tracing the German critical reception of Bodin, I focused specifically on the thought of Althusius, who synthesized a theory of popular sovereignty based on the foundational premises presented by Bodin in the *République*, as well as the German *Reichspublizisten*, such as Arnisaeus, Besold, and Limnaeus, who modified the core elements of Bodin's theory to produce a distinctively Germanic doctrine of double sovereignty, or *duplex maiestas*, that more accurately fitted the fragmented conditions of the Holy Roman Empire.

Double sovereignty was a construction based on technical features of the Roman law of actions and it provided a useful conceptual tool to frame the constitutional politics of the early modern Empire. But the doctrine did not survive beyond the seventeenth century in Germany, in large part because of the triumph of territorial sovereignty and princely rule in the model of the *Obrigkeitsstaat* secured in the Westphalian settlement at the close of the Thirty Years' War.

This is not to say, however, that the doctrine of double sovereignty disappeared from early modern legal thought altogether. Even though the German Publicists, especially by the time of the modern "jusnaturalists" such as Pufendorf, Leibniz, and Thomasius, eventually discarded double sovereignty, jurists outside the German context of the Empire had accepted some of the key features of double sovereignty in the analysis of the constitutional state.[101] One notable example is Grotius who, in *De Iure Belli ac Pacis*, considers the question of the "bearer" of sovereignty within the state. As we shall see, Grotius plays a pivotol role in synthesizing Continental legal doctrines to create what becomes one of the most versatile notions of popular sovereignty in the emerging international order of the seventeenth century Europe.

[100] Gierke, *Development of Political Theory* 166 and note 133.

[101] Knud Haakonssen, *Natural Law and Moral Philosophy: From Grotius to the Scottish Enlightenment* (Cambridge: Cambridge University Press, 1996) Ch. 1. T.J. Hochstrasser, *Natural Law Theories in the Early Enlightenment* (Cambridge: Cambridge University Press, 2000).

8

Popular Liberty, Princely Government, and the Roman Law in Hugo Grotius' De Iure Belli ac Pacis

INTRODUCTION

Once hailed as "the miracle of Holland" by Henri IV of France, Hugo Grotius (1583–1645) is perhaps most remembered in the history of political thought for his pivotal role as one of the intellectual founders of modern international law, as set out in his chief work, *De Iure Belli ac Pacis*, first published in Paris in 1625.[1] What is perhaps remembered less often, however, is Grotius' rigorous engagement with the texts and ideas of classical Antiquity in designing his system of moral and political thought. As much recent scholarship has shown, Grotius carefully crafted his political and legal ideas using textual authorities of the Aristotelian and Stoic traditions to give content to his understanding of the natural reasons undergirding basic moral principles governing human society.[2]

Equally important, however, was Grotius' engagement with classical Roman law, an aspect of his thought which has commanded comparatively less attention in the recent scholarship and which, traditionally though wrongly, has been regarded as dispensable and substantially irrelevant.[3] Grotius, who was made an honorary doctor of civil law in the humanist law faculty of Orléans in 1598, relied on his civilian legal training throughout his career in the service of the state as Attorney General of Holland and Zeeland and as Pensionary of Rotterdam, and in the service of the Dutch East India Company, in which

[1] Charles Edwards, *Hugo Grotius, the Miracle of Holland* (Chicago: Nelson-Hall, 1981).

[2] Tuck, *Philosophy and Government* Ch. 5; Knud Haakonssen, "Hugo Grotius and the History of Political Thought," *Political Theory* 13 (1985): 239–65; Christopher Brooke, *Philosophic Pride: Stoicism and Political Thought from Lipsius to Rousseau* (Princeton: Princeton University Press, 2012) Ch. 2.

[3] The major exception is Benjamin Straumann, *Roman Law in the State of Nature* (Cambridge: Cambridge University Press, 2015); Benjamin Straumann, *Hugo Grotius und die Antike* (Baden-Baden: Nomos, 2007); Benjamin Straumann, "'Ancient Caesarian Lawyers' in a State of Nature: Roman Tradition and Natural Rights in Hugo Grotius' *De Iure Praedae*," *Political Theory* 34 (2006): 328–50; Benjamin Straumann, "Natural Rights and Roman Law in Hugo Grotius' *Theses LVI, De Iure Praedae* and *Defensio Capitis Quinti Maris Liberi*," *Property, Piracy and Punishment*, ed. Hans Blom (Leiden: Brill, 2009) 341–65.

capacity he would write the *Mare Liberum* as well as *De Iure Praedae*.[4] Roman law was additionally a central influence in his more formal and systematic legal theory, such as his *Inleidinge tot de Hollandsche Rechtsgeleerdheit* (1619–21, published in 1631), which combined Roman law with custom to produce one of the major early modern contributions to Roman-Dutch law.

But his application of Roman law extended beyond the technical arcana of jurisprudence. Like the many "Publicist" jurists of his age, such as Althusius, Limnaeus, and Conring, whom we have considered in the previous chapter, Grotius treated the *Corpus Iuris Civilis*, as well as the vast commentaries of the Glossators and the Bartolists, as a kind of "legal supermarket" supplying eclectic concepts and doctrines which could be used for the analysis of political and constitutional questions.[5] This wide application of Roman law is most readily visible in Grotius' use of civilian arguments in disputes arising in the imperial politics of his age, such as in the classification of the open seas as *res nullius*, making them ineligible, as he argues in *Mare Liberum*, for private acquisition by right of occupation [*titulo occupationis*] or by right of use [*titulo praescriptionis*].[6] Given his mastery of the civil law, it is not surprising to observe, as Peter Stein finds, that "what natural reason prescribed [for Grotius] often turned out to be what was set out or what could be inferred from Justinian's texts."[7]

Grotius' application of Roman law, however, was not exclusive to his international thought but extended deep into the core of what Annabel Brett has called his "civil philosophy," concerning such fundamental questions as the origins of the state, the constitutional structure of civil government, and the proper distribution of rights and powers between the people and their government.[8] In addressing these questions of political theory, Grotius owes a great intellectual debt to the juridical grammar and vocabulary of the Roman law, for, as we shall see, the substantive constitutional doctrines of civil government and public law in Grotius' thought, especially in *De Iure Belli ac Pacis*, were patterned in the mold of actionable rights and powers originating in Roman private law.

Nowhere was this application of Roman private law more controversial than in Grotius' analysis of the "free people" [*populus liber*], a concept of special resonance in Roman legal thought, as I argued in Chapter 2, and which functioned as the starting point for his own theory of popular sovereignty. Like his early modern contemporaries, Grotius appealed to the Roman legal notion of a "free person" to understand the attributes and the scope of popular

[4] Tuck, *Philosophy and Government* 154–69; see also more generally the biography by Henk Nellen, *Hugo de Groot: Een Leven in Strijd om de Vrede, 1583–1645* (Amsterdam: Balans Publishers, 2007).

[5] Stein, *Roman Law in European History* 2.

[6] Hugo Grotius, *Mare Liberum* published in the 1696 *De Iure Belli ac Pacis Libri Tres* (Frankfurt am Main, 1696) Ch. 7 and Ch. 9.

[7] Stein, *Roman Law in European History* 99.

[8] Annabel Brett, "Natural Right and Civil Community: The Civil Philosophy of Hugo Grotius," *Historical Journal* 45 (2002): 32.

liberty, especially in treating the controversial doctrine that a free people may voluntarily alienate their liberty and subject themselves to the domination of princely government, just as a free person in Roman law may similarly subject himself to the *dominium* of a master.

What distinguishes Grotius, however, was an overriding concern to reconcile the ideal of popular liberty, on the one hand, with the constitutional necessity of civil government, on the other. Indeed, Grotius offers a novel theory of liberty that is not opposed to the power of government, but, instead, is parasitic upon it. One surprising result of this analysis is the view that, in specially defined circumstances, a people may remain free and fully sovereign even while under the government of a prince. And it is precisely this strategy of argument, framed by the conceptual tools of Roman law that allows Grotius to avoid the republican criticism that would become central to the anti-monarchism of the seventeenth century.

The key to this analysis, I shall argue, is to be found in Grotius' technical understanding of Roman law, and it is my purpose in this chapter to retrace the steps of legal reasoning by which he arrives at this doctrine. I begin with an overview of the Roman law of persons and the juridical division in the *Corpus Iuris Civilis* between free persons and slaves. While this division has proven to be of special importance to the "neo-Roman" republican theory of liberty, I argue here that Grotius applies a unique meaning to the term, *libertas*, and connects it to the concept of power, or *potestas*: to be free is to have *potestatem in se*, a "power over oneself." I then proceed to show that Grotius envisaged the subject of such a free, self-regarding power to be not simply an individual, but also a whole people, a *civitas*, or—as he puts it—a *subiectum commune*. The purpose of this, I argue, is to situate a critically important legal analogy in Grotius' constitutional thought. Just as a "free man" [*liber homo*] can exercise his rights through another intermediary or agent while still remaining fully free and independent, so too can a "free people" [*populus liber*] be similarly governed. I show that Grotius' familiar contractarian argument about the origins of civil government critically invokes the Roman law on usufructs to model the corresponding constitutional relationship between a free people and its government, not as one of mastery and slavery, but as "ownership" and "usufructuary." Based on this investigation, I conclude the chapter with a number of observations on the place of Roman law not only in Grotius' thought but in the early modern theory of popular sovereignty.

LIBERTY AND SLAVERY IN THE ROMAN LAW

In his *Institutes*, the Roman jurist, Gaius, organized the principal divisions of Roman law into persons, things, and actions, a scheme which later featured prominently in the *Corpus Iuris Civilis*, under the rubric, *De statu hominum*.[9]

[9] Gaius 1.8; D.1.5.1.

Of these divisions, the law of persons, in particular, was of special interest to Grotius and other early modern jurists because it provided an elaborate classification of legal persons in terms of the legal rights and powers they held and the jural status of relationships they shared with others.

Perhaps the fundamental feature of the Roman law of persons was also its most controversial, and that was the critically important legal distinction drawn between "free persons" [*liberi*] and "slaves" [*servi*]. "All men," as Gaius explains, "are either free men or slaves," and it was from this basic distinction that all further classifications followed.[10]

The nature of this distinction was explained in several ways by the classical jurists, but perhaps the most useful explanation was to be found in Gaius' account. In his *Institutes*, Gaius explains that the distinction between liberty and slavery in the law of persons mapped onto a corresponding distinction between independent persons [*sui iuris*] and dependent persons [*alieni iuris*], respectively.[11] Persons of the latter category, persons *alieni iuris*, were said to be under the power of another [*in potestate*]. In classical law, the asymmetrical relationship of dependence and subjection experienced by those persons classified as *alieni iuris* included children under the patriarchal power of the father [*patria potestas*] and wives under the power of the husband [*manus*]. But perhaps the most important example of persons *alieni iuris* was the power of the master [*dominus*] over the slave [*in potestate domini*]. To be *alieni iuris* and *in potestate* was, therefore, to be in a state of subjection under the arbitrary will and power of a superior.

To be sure, the personal status of dependence, *alieni iuris*, to be in the power of another like a slave *in potestate domini*, was not a permanent or natural condition, but an artificial "decree" or "institution of the law of nations" [*constitutio iuris gentium*], just as the personal status of independence, *sui iuris*, was itself impermanent and carved out by law.[12] Both were, in fact, legally variable conditions. The classical jurists were at pains to emphasize this point in the law of persons. For example, as Modestinus observed, a person who is free and *sui iuris* may choose voluntarily to enter into the power of a father, by a process known as *adrogatio*, thereby reducing his status from civic independence to domestic dependence.[13] By the same token, the master who held the power of *dominium* over his slave could freely "manumit" or release the slave from his power. Similarly, the father with *patria potestas* could "emancipate" children under his power.[14] These *status permutationes* were, thus, relatively routine occurrences, which Roman law reflected.

These Roman ideas of liberty and slavery, and the corresponding notions of independence and dependence were crucial to the organization of classical Roman society, but their influence extended far beyond classical Antiquity.

[10] Gaius 1.9; D.1.5.3; Inst. 1.3. [11] D.1.6.1.

[12] Unlike Aristotle, the jurists acknowledged that slavery was contrary to nature. Inst. 1.3; D.1.5.4.1, 1.5.5.1.

[13] D.1.7.1; Inst. 1.11. [14] D.1.5.4 and Gaius 1.10, distinguish between *ingenui* and *libertini*.

Perhaps the most vital influence in post-classical thought may be located in the civilian influence on early modern republicanism and, in particular, the republican criticism of princely government. As historians of political thought such as Quentin Skinner have shown, the reception of Roman law fed directly into the formation of a distinctive "neo-Roman" anti-royalist republican ideology in sixteenth- and seventeenth-century political thought, exemplified by the writings of civic republicans such as Milton and Harrington, who uniformly invoked the Justinianic distinction between *libertas* and *servitus* under the rubric, *De statu hominum*, in the *Digest*.[15] For these early modern republicans, the Romanist framework of liberty and slavery provided the intellectual foundation to argue that liberty could only be fully realized in a state of popular self-government, where a people remain *sui iuris* and *non in potestate*, like the free person in Roman law.

The key to this neo-Roman analysis, as Skininer has explained, required the identification of princely rule with private *dominium*. For republicans, the government of a prince, even a benevolent prince, is tantamount to slavery in the classical legal sense, because the legal condition of the subject under such rule was identical to that of the slave under the private power of a master [*in potestate domini*]. He is, according to the republican, *in potestate* and *alieni iuris*. He lives under the power of a master with an arbitrary lawmaking will and consequently must be dependent upon the goodwill and permission of his master for his own well-being. What a secure republican liberty requires, therefore, is the absence of kings and princes, just as, in the Roman law, personal liberty requires the absence of the *dominus*. Only then can it be possible to claim the status of freedom as the Roman jurisconsults declared.

LIBERTY AS A *POTESTAS*

What is critical to observe is that Grotius, like these neo-Roman republicans, similarly appealed to this formulation in the Roman law of persons to craft a broader political theory concerning popular liberty and princely government. Like the republicans, Grotius constructed a political theory which took as its point of departure the division in jural status between liberty and slavery. Of course, whether Grotius himself should be identified as a civic republican because of this remains an open question.[16] But whatever the outcome of that interpretive debate, it is nevertheless clear that Grotius took this civilian

[15] Skinner, *Liberty before Liberalism*; Quentin Skinner, "John Milton and the Politics of Slavery," in *Visions of Politics*, Vol. 2 (Cambridge: Cambridge University Press, 2002); Quentin Skinner, "Classical Liberty, Renaissance Translation and the English Civil War," in *Visions of Politics*, Vol. 2, *Renaissance Virtues* (Cambridge: Cambridge University Press, 2002); Quentin Skinner, *Hobbes and Republican Liberty* (Cambridge: Cambridge University Press, 2008).

[16] Martin Van Gelderen defends a republican reading of Grotius in "From Domingo de Soto to Hugo Grotius: Theories of Monarchy and Civil Power in Spanish and Dutch Political Thought, 1555–1609," *Pensiero Politico* 32 (1999): 186–205, and "Aristotelians, Monarchomachs and Republicans: Sovereignty and *Respublica Mixta* in Dutch and German Political Thought."

analysis on personal status as the starting point for his own theory of popular sovereignty and constitutionalism, even if he did not necessarily follow the republicans in lockstep to their anti-royalist normative conclusions, as we shall see below.

Indeed, for Grotius, liberty was the natural starting point of man's social and political life. By declaring in *De Iure Praedae* that "God created man... free and *sui Iuris*," Grotius identified the condition of liberty as a kind of default position and as a natural state, from which men depart only by their voluntary acts of contract [*pactis*] and by the assumption of obligation, as Brett has observed.[17]

But what is remarkable is how Grotius uses Roman law to craft his understanding of liberty, especially in *De Iure Belli ac Pacis*, which was cast not simply in the classical Roman terms of "non-domination"—that is, to be ***non in potestate domini***—but also, significantly, in the medieval juristic terms of power [*potestas* or, more specifically, the *libera facultas*].[18] Florentinus had defined *libertas* classically in the *Digest* as a "natural power" [*naturalis facultas*], but for the classical jurists, this was conceptualized simply as an open-ended power of "doing what one pleases" within the bounds of law.[19] The critical difference in later post-classical jurists, including Grotius, was the deliberate connection drawn between liberty, on the one hand, and the more expansive notion of a subjective power [*potestas*], on the other hand.

In the classical law of Justinian, "power" embodied a number of intersecting meanings, as Paul is quoted in the title, *De verborum significatione*, of the *Digest*.[20] But, in Grotius' analysis, "power" had an added technical meaning that departed significantly from the *Digest* and followed, instead, the doctrine fixed by the Glossators. Most remarkable was the comparison of meaning drawn between power [*potestas*] and the notion of subjective right [*ius*], as an active power or capacity of a person to act justly—or to put it differently, to do or make justice. It is a definition suggested by scholastics such as Ockham who defined *ius* not, as the classical Roman jurists did, as the abstract quality of being "just and good" [*aequum ac bonum*], but rather as a "licit power" [*potestas licita*] attaching to the moral subject or agent empowered to realize and bring such a quality into the world.[21] It is an analysis that, in turn, influenced scholastic lawyers such as Johannes Monachus and was underlined by later neo-scholastic jurists such as Vitoria and Vàsquez, who similarly defined liberty in terms of a subjective *potestas*.

What distinguishes Grotius' own concept of liberty is precisely this scholastic notion of an active and subjective *potestas*, and this, I argue, is clear from the way he arrives at his own definition of liberty in *De Iure Belli ac Pacis*,

[17] Grotius, *Commentary on the Law of Prize and Booty* [*De Iure Praedae*], ed. Martine Julia van Ittersum (Indianapolis: Liberty Fund, 2006) 33, which cites Inst.1.1.3, Aristotle's *Politics* 6.1, C.4.35.21. On the influence of Vázquez and Suárez, see Brett "Natural Right and Civil Community" 38.

[18] Brett, *Liberty, Right and Nature* Chs. 4–6; Brett, "Natural Right and Civil Community" 41.

[19] D.1.5.4.pr. [20] D.50.16.215. [21] D.1.1.11.

by direct reference to the scholastic authorities. In commenting on the jurists' analysis of power, Grotius divided *potestas* into two classes. One type of power, Grotius argues, was to be distinguished in that it was directed "over others" [*potestas in alios*], a form of power which he simply identified with the various private legal powers already discussed in the *Corpus Iuris Civilis*. As we have already seen, these included the paterfamilial power of the father over children [*patria potestas*] and the power of a master over slaves [*dominium*].[22]

But in addition, Grotius suggested another secondary class of power—i.e., the power directed not over others, but over oneself [*potestas in se*].[23] This was a special category of *potestas* in Grotius' theory, to which he deliberately applied the term, "liberty" [*libertas*].[24] The free person, in the Grotian system, was one who directed an exclusive *potestas* over himself; that is indeed precisely what made him *sui iuris*. In this scheme, then, liberty was a particular type of power, but it was specifically a self-regarding or self-directed reflexive power, a novel suggestion in the theory of liberty. Unlike, for example, Hobbes who would regard considerations of power as fundamentally distinct from the concept of liberty, Grotius thought liberty itself was a particular species of power. Liberty did not eliminate power; it simply re-directed it, so that free persons were those who had exclusive power over themselves, and not over others.

This analysis of liberty in terms of subjective power and right evidently had wide, if critical, impact on the juristic thought of the seventeenth century. For example, in *De Iure Naturae et Gentium*, Pufendorf clearly follows Grotius by defining liberty as "a power over our own persons and actions."[25] On the other hand, the German jurist, Johannes Felden, criticized Grotius' analysis by pointing out that the civilians "never term liberty a *ius* in ourselves," a corruption of legal meaning which, Felden thought, must be attributed to Grotius alone.[26]

The criticism was, in part, motivated by a concern for the troubling consequences of this subjective conception of liberty, to which Grotius' analysis of liberty and *potestas* appears to have opened the door. In theory, a free person may act in such a way that he benefit himself, but, equally, he can also act in ways that may prejudice his own personal welfare, including suicide, which otherwise would be regarded as morally impermissible.[27] Of course, Grotius' most infamous statement of this view was the suggestion that a free person may fully and freely alienate the self-directed powers constitutive of his liberty and consequently put himself under the power of a master and become a slave,

[22] *De Iure Belli* 4 [1.1.5]. Cf. D.50.16.215.

[23] *De Iure Belli* 4 [1.1.5].

[24] Here Grotius cites D.1.5, Inst. 1.3.

[25] Samuel von Pufendorf, *De Iure Naturae et Gentium Libri Octo*, Vol. 1 (Oxford: Clarendon Press, 1934) 12 [1.1.19].

[26] Johannes Felden, *Annotata in Hug. Grotium. De Iure Belli et Pacis* (Amsterdam, 1653) 8–9. See also Andreas Blank, "Johannes Felden on Usucaption, Justice, and the Society of States," *Journal of the History of Ideas* 74 (2013): 403–23.

[27] *War and Peace* 2:943–7. Cf. D.48.21.3.pr; D.48.21.3.6.

just as a free and *sui iuris* person is at liberty, in the civil law, to subject himself to the power of a father, *patria potestas*, through *adrogatio*.[28]

In making this controversial claim, Grotius' purpose was certainly not to encourage free persons to submit themselves *in potestate domini*, under the power of masters. As Richard Tuck once put it, "interpretive charity" requires us to to "assume that all [rights] were not *in fact* renounced."[29] Rather, it was to acknowledge the legal permissibility of such self-prejudicial acts performed by free persons, especially when there are compelling reasons for a person to act in such a manner. It may be true that selling oneself into slavery might not be a desirable, well-considered, or even a morally proper act, but Grotius' point was that, despite these normative considerations, it would, nevertheless, be a free act and would be fully within the right and power of a free person.

LEGAL PERSONALITY AND POPULAR LIBERTY

This juristic model of the free person in Grotius' thought was central to the larger political theory that he sought to develop. The key to this connection between the individual free person and a free people was Grotius' working assumption that, insofar as legal rights and powers are concerned, a people may be considered to share the same status as an individual person. Of course, as we have seen in earlier chapters, this principle was hardly original with Grotius. The notion of a fictive juristic personality as a bearer of actionable rights was a foundational axiom of medieval jurisprudence, especially in the thought of the Italian Commentators.[30]

Building upon this tradition, Grotius had also accepted that a whole people could be considered a single person over time, even though the "separate and distant members" [*ex distantibus constat*] of the civil association were in constant flux, joining and leaving the association over time. Citing the *Digest*, Grotius explains that what makes the people a united civil body is that they are "united in name [*unique nomini subiectum est*]... as having one constitution [*spiritum unum*]."[31] As long as the "frame and constitution" [*ratio corporis*] of the civil body remained constant, the jural identity of the people would also remain constant, just as a single person, over time.[32] In this way, then, Grotius was able to declare that the civil state is "immortal" [*civitates esse immortales*] and a "unified and permanent body."[33]

[28] *De Iure Belli* 67–8 [1.3.8.1].

[29] Tuck, *Natural Rights Theories* 80 [emphasis in original].

[30] Canning, *The Political Thought of Baldus de Ubaldis*; J.P. Canning, "Ideas of the State in Thirteenth- and Fourteenth-Century Commentators on the Roman Law," *Transactions of the Royal Historical Society* (1983); Canning, "Law, Sovereignty and Corporation Theory."

[31] *De Iure Belli* 245 [2.9.3.1]; *War and Peace* 2:665–6, citing D.41.3.30.pr and 6.1.23.5. See also Brett "Natural Right and Civil Community" 45, 48–9.

[32] *De Iure Belli* 246 [2.9.4]; *War and Peace* 2:669.

[33] *De Iure Belli* 245 [2.9.3]; *De Iure Praedae* 36–7, citing D.41.3.30 and 5.1.76.

This move was crucial for Grotius because, if it could be shown that a free person in private law is empowered to act or exercise a certain right in some specified manner, then it could also be shown that a free people in public law is similarly empowered to act or exercise a corresponding collective or popular right, just as if it also were an individual person. This suggestion was more than simply an attempt at argument by analogy. Grotius took seriously the idea that even a state could be treated as a rights-bearing legal person. This was no doubt a central axiom for his broader project in *De Iure Belli ac Pacis* to elucidate the legitimate causes and laws of war, both private and public. As Grotius famously argues in connection with his discussion of *bellum publicum* and *bellum privatum*, the distinction between the rights of a private actor and those of a public actor is null, insofar as rights as such are concerned: both sorts of actors, for Grotius, could claim rights and seek remedies, as well as enter into contracts with other actors regulating the distribution and transfer of such rights.[34]

But this analysis extended beyond the laws of war and shaped even his views on the constitutional origins of the state and the scope of sovereignty. Since liberty was counted among the attributes of jural personality, Grotius was able to argue that it should, by parity of reason, apply to both the case of the individual person as well as the case of the whole polity bearing a shared legal personality. Thus, just as individual persons could enjoy liberty in the form of a personal liberty [*libertas personalis*], so could a whole people enjoy a similar liberty, in the form of a "civil" or "popular liberty" [*libertas civilis*].[35] In this way, then, the notion of popular liberty—the liberty of a whole people to exercise the rights and powers of self-government in the absence of foreign domination [*ius regendae reipublicae pro cive*]—was framed to parallel the notion of personal liberty in the law of persons.[36]

We might, at this point, reasonably expect Grotius to endorse the familiar civic republican conclusion that treats all forms of princely government as illegitimate and inconsistent with public liberty, just as the civilian doctors of law would insist that private *dominium* is similarly inconsistent with personal liberty. But that is, interestingly, not the position taken by Grotius. What we find in Grotius' constitutional thought is, rather, a more carefully nuanced view that accepts the notional possibility that a people can remain free and *sui iuris* even while in the government of princes. In this way, popular sovereignty remains fully valid, even while under princely government. The key to this analysis rests upon the principle that not all princes hold and exercise their power as a *dominus*.

[34] Straumann, "'Ancient Caesarian Lawyers' in a State of Nature" 340.

[35] *De Iure Belli* 77 [1.3.12.1]; *War and Peace* 1:285.

[36] *De Iure Belli* 489 [2.24.6.1].

POPULAR LIBERTY AND THE RIGHT OF GOVERNMENT

What we have attempted to establish is an account of how the Roman legal distinction between liberty and slavery provided Grotius with a vocabulary not simply for the analysis of the jural status held by private individuals, but also for the analysis of the jural status held collectively by the people of a state. As we have seen, Grotius invoked the Roman *libertas* from the *Corpus Iuris Civilis* as the starting point to model the civil independence and liberty of a free people. Drawing upon this civilian framework, he accepted that liberty necessarily excluded the dominion of a master [*dominum excludit*], a conception of liberty that has, in the recent theoretical scholarship, been called a concept of "non-domination."[37]

But, as we have seen, liberty for Grotius was not simply a condition of non-domination, but also necessitated an active power of self-government or self-determination [*potestas in se*]. This was because liberty was defined within the medieval juridical framework of subjective power, so that liberty was not simply the absence of domination, but also necessitated an active power, or *potestas*, over oneself. Since the subject in possession of liberty could validly be both an individual person as well as a whole people, it follows in Grotius' analysis that a free and *sui iuris* people must also be capable of exercising a power of self-government over themselves.

What requires further analysis, however, is what this popular power of self-government entails. Must the people, at all times, directly exercise this power of self-government in order to be free, or can they give up some share of power, without also compromising their popular liberty and status as an independent *sui iuris* state?

Perhaps the first thing to observe is that, for Grotius, it is a part of the liberty of a self-governing free people to decide who shall exercise this right of government [*ius regendi*], whether the people themselves or through some other agent.[38] This choice is indeed the essence of the independent constitution-making powers of a free people, what Peter Borschberg has called Grotius' "democratic constitutionalism."[39] For, as Grotius observes in the *De Iure Belli ac Pacis*, it is the right of a free people to determine for themselves "the form of government [*gubernationis formam*] they please," just as it is the legal right of a free person to choose which of the "several ways of living... he pleases."[40]

[37] *De Iure Belli* 77 [1.3.12.1]. Pettit, *Republicanism* Ch. 2, and Frank Lovett, *A General Theory of Domination and Justice* (Oxford: Oxford University Press, 2010). See also the criticism of Efraim Podoksik, "One Concept of Liberty: Towards Writing the History of a Political Concept," *Journal of the History of Ideas* 71 (2010): 219–40.

[38] The right to govern is expressed variously as *ius regendi, ius imperandi, ius regnandi, ius gubernandi*, and other similar forms, but the basic underlying concept remains the same. *De Iure Belli* 68 [1.3.8.1], 78 [1.3.12.3], 170 [2.4.10.2]; cp. *Commentarius in Theses XI* 214–5 [Thesis 1, §16].

[39] Peter Borschberg, *Hugo Grotius "Commentarius in Theses XI": An Early Treatise on Sovereignty, the Just War, and the Legitimacy of the Dutch Revolt* (New York: Peter Lang, 1994) 50; Peter Borschberg, "Grotius, the Social Contract and Political Resistance: A Study of the Unpublished *Theses LVI*" (2007) [IILJ working paper available at SSRN: http://ssrn.com/abstract=969250] 48–9.

[40] *De Iure Belli* 68 [1.3.8].

Such a right to "delegate these functions [of government] in whole or in part to specific persons" is an irrevocable natural right of a free people, as Grotius explains not only in the *De Iure Belli ac Pacis*, but also in the *Commentarius in Theses XI* (an early unpublished work) and the *Prolegomena* of *De Iure Praedae*.[41]

What remained an open question in Grotius' theory concerned the specific form of government that may result from such a free popular act of constitution-making. On the one hand, this could be understood to mean that a free people may collectively choose to constitute legally a popular form of self-government, so that the *populus* may reserve fully for themselves the sovereign right of governing [*ius regendi*] directly, without a princely or aristocratic intermediary. From his early writings on the Dutch Revolt, it is clear that this is how Grotius understood the constitution of the Dutch States, as well as other popular states in early modern Europe.[42]

But, on the other hand, the doctrine could also be understood to mean, as Grotius notoriously suggested, that a free people may voluntarily decide to surrender and freely alienate or cede their collective sovereign rights of self-government to another party and subsequently subject themselves to a status of dependence, *alieni iuris*, under princely government, a doctrine which would prompt Rousseau to characterize Grotius' political theory to be most "favorable to tyrants."[43] On this analysis, it is legally permissible, Grotius declares, for an independent sovereign people [*populo sui iuris*] to "deliver up themselves to any one or more persons, and transfer the right of governing them upon him or them, without reserving any share of that right to themselves."[44] Grotius explains this by reference to the Roman law governing such private legal acts of self-subjection as *adrogatio*, self-sale into slavery, or other legal acts resulting in a loss of jural status [*capitis deminutio*]. In short, it was within the rights of a civil body of free persons, just as it was within the rights of any free person under Roman law, to subject themselves by their own consent [*subiectio ex consensu*].[45]

At first glance, what results from Grotius' analysis is, as Richard Tuck puts it, a "Janus-faced" theory of popular sovereignty and constitutionalism that, at once, seems to speak "the language of both absolutism and liberty."[46] Grotius' seventeenth-century critics were less generous and took his doctrine that a

[41] *Commentarius in Theses XI* 256–57 [Thesis 7, §53], where Grotius cites Francisco de Vitoria, "Relection on Civil Power" [*De Potestate Civili*, §14], accessible in the volume, *Political Writings*, ed. Anthony Pagden and Jeremy Lawrance (Cambridge: Cambridge University Press, 1991) 30–02. Cp. *De Iure Praedae* 43 [Ch. 2], which invokes the Roman contract of mandate [*mandatus*].

[42] From *Commentarius ad Theses XI* and *De Antiquitate Reipublicae Batavicae*.

[43] Jean-Jacques Rousseau, *The Social Contract*, ed. Victor Gourevitch (Cambridge: Cambridge University Press, 1997) 42 [*Of the Social Contract* 2.4].

[44] *De Iure Belli* 68 [1.3.8]; cp. 198-99 [2.5.31].

[45] *De Iure Belli* 195 [2.5.26], where Grotius cites Inst.1.3.4. Cf. D.1.7, Inst. 1.16, D.4.5. On self sale, see Crook, *Law and Life of Rome* 60–1; W.W. Buckland, *The Roman Law of Slavery* (Cambridge: Cambridge University Press, 1908) 427.

[46] Tuck, *Natural Rights Theories* 79.

free people may voluntarily alienate their collective rights and freely "enslave" themselves under the dominion of princely government as compelling evidence for an endorsement of slavery. Johannes Felden, for example, complained that Grotius' admission of the legal permissibility of such a popular act of self-enslavement "destroys civil society, which is a community of free men [*coetus liberorum hominum*], and makes it an aggregation of slaves."[47] More recent commentators have continued to criticize Grotius on precisely these grounds.[48]

This is, of course, but a reductive simplification of Grotius' thought, which, I argue, is inadmissable on two grounds. First, the criticism mistakes the analytical for the normative. Far from endorsing the self-enslavement of a free people by their voluntary alienation of rights, Grotius' purpose was merely to comment neutrally on the scope of the constitution-making powers vested in a free people, without committing to any normative assessment of the constitutional choices that a free people may make.[49] Thus, even though the idea of voluntary alienation and self-enslavement may be morally repugnant, Grotius' broader point was to stress that such an act is nevertheless to be regarded as legally permissible from the perspective of a well-ordered civil philosophy. Grotius' position was, therefore, fundamentally at odds with later writers, such as the English theorist of parliamentary sovereignty, Henry Parker, who declared, "It is not just nor possible for any nation so to inslave it selfe, and to resigne its owne interest to the will of one Lord, as that Lord may destroy it without injury, and yet to have no right to preserve it selfe."[50]

Second, the criticism misleadingly portrays the constitutional choices to be made by a free people in Grotius' theory as nothing more than a stark dichotomous choice between slavery under princely absolutism or liberty in a state of popular self-government. This is, needless to say, a false choice because it omits a vast third category of states investigated by Grotius in which popular liberty can continue to flourish even while under legally constituted princely government. In this respect, Grotius arrives at a similar line of reasoning first articulated by Bodin on the government of popular states through nondemocratic means.[51]

Contrary to critics fearful of a condition of permanent slavery under princely absolutism, what Grotius actually offers is a more fine-grained analysis of the constitutional choices that a free people may make. What is critical in this analysis is that the popular act of constituting civil government does not always have to result in a state of full subjection, like slavery, and thus, a

[47] Felden, *Annotata* 35.

[48] Stephen Buckle, *Natural Law and the Theory of Property* (Oxford: Clarendon Press, 1991) 48–9.

[49] Tuck, *Natural Rights Theories* 78–80. Edward Keene, *Beyond the Anarchical Society* (Cambridge: Cambridge University Press, 2002) 42.

[50] Henry Parker, *Observations Upon Some of His Majesties Late Answers and Expresses* (London, 1642) 8. See also Skinner, "John Milton and the Politics of Slavery," in *Visions of Politics* 2: 296.

[51] See Chapter 6.

loss of liberty. Indeed, the analysis on slavery represents merely one extreme end-point on a full spectrum admitting numerous constitutional possibilities. There are, as Grotius argues, multiple degrees [*gradus*] of political subjection over a people, ranging from a "perfect and entire subjection" [*perfecta subiectio*] but also to lesser imperfect forms of political subjection.[52] Thus, for Grotius, it is simply not accurate to say that a free people must be limited to making a binary constitutional choice between either popular republican liberty or despotic princely slavery. Instead, there are many shades of grey in between these two constitutional forms where Grotius reconciled those two opposing ideals of popular rule and princely rule with each other.

The puzzle, of course, is to understand how he accomplished this task of political theory, and so, we may ask what kind of princely government can be made to be compatible with popular liberty. Part of the answer may be located in Grotius' treatment of the concept of sovereignty itself. The conventional juristic wisdom was articulated most notably in Bodin's influential treatment of sovereignty. But, as Grotius explains in his *Commentarius*, such sovereign rights—or, as he called them, *actus summae potestatis*—were fully divisible and could be distributed across multiple actors within the state, for example, between the people and the prince, as in his analysis of the Roman constitution.[53] Thus, a free people in full ownership of the rights of sovereignty—such as the power to tax, the power to create high officers of state, the power to create courts and appoint judges—not only may decide whether to alienate or retain those rights, but they may also specify *which* of those rights to alienate or retain.[54] In this way, then, a people can be said to remain free even while in the government of princes, as in a *respublica mixta* in which sovereignty is divided and shared between the people and the prince.

But Grotius' analysis did not end with this account of divided or mixed sovereignty. He pressed his analysis even further by inspecting more carefully the contractual nature of the original constitution-making act enabling the transfer of sovereignty from the people to the prince by something like a *lex regia*. The critical issue here concerned the "completeness" of that original transfer of rights: was it a complete and irrevocable alienation resulting in some form of absolutism, or was it an incomplete and reversible concession reserving a share of rights in the people?

The answer, for Grotius, was both. He accepted that a free people can voluntarily choose to make a limited concessive grant of power to a princely form of government, just as they also can freely choose to alienate their rights completely and irrevocably. In showing this, we are able to contest and revise the misleading suggestion, above, that Grotius' theory of popular alienation of

[52] *De Iure Belli* 199 [2.5.31].

[53] The term, *actus summae potestatis*, occurs in the unpublished *Commentarius in Theses XI* [Thesis 4] but Grotius also refers to sovereign rights as *actus* in *De Iure Belli*, such as at 312 [2.14.1.2, *actus regis*] and 83 [1.3.17].

[54] *Commentarius in Theses XI* 226–27 [Thesis 4, §25].

rights by contract must always be interpreted as a complete and irreversible act of voluntary subjection which necessarily resulted in enslavement to an absolutist princely *dominus*. If, as Grotius allows, the original contract constituting a government was a mere limited or concessive grant, fully and legally recoverable by the people, it cannot be proper, as Grotius' critics insist, to model the resulting relationship between the people and the prince according to the legal form of Roman slavery. If the people really were like slaves, *in potestate domini*, they would not have had access to such a remedy available to them in the first place.[55]

What Grotius required, therefore, was a more nuanced analysis that treated the relationship between the people and the princely government, not solely in the terms of slave and master [*servus, dominus*], but rather according to a different juridical model derived from Roman private law, such as guardianship [*tutela*], which allowed a people to remain fully free and *sui iuris*, even while in the government of a prince.[56] As we shall now see, Grotius found such a model in the Roman law governing the civilian relationship between the free rights-holding owner of property [*dominus*], on the one hand, and the usufructuary of property with limited rights of use or tenancy [*ususfructus*], on the other hand.

USUFRUCTUARY GOVERNMENT: *USUSFRUCTUS*

Grotius' argument likening princely government to *ususfructus*, rather than to *dominus*, was framed within the analysis of property which plays a central role in the argument of *De Iure Belli ac Pacis*. In Book I, Grotius reconstructs a critical distinction in the law of property, derived from Dumoulin's treatment of feudal jurisdiction in Title I of the *Commentarii in Consuetudines Parienses*.[57] Here, the distinction is drawn between two dimensions of analysis: that which concerns "the thing itself" [*de re*]—which was broadly inclusive of all forms of property, whether *res corporales* and *res incorporales*—and that which concerns the manner, or *modus*, of holding or enjoying the property in question [*de modo rei habendi*].[58] Following Dumoulin, Grotius observes that it is one thing to identify the *res* that is the object of property—which may range from private things, *res mancipi*, to public things, *respublica*—but it is another matter entirely to specify the degree of right by which one can lay a claim or interest in such property, whether private or public. This was because, for any given object of property, there were various degrees of strength by which one can claim a proprietary interest, and so, there is a second further dimension to be introduced concerning the *modus habendi*. One may have, on the one hand, the

[55] Since the people remain *sui iuris*, it is not possible in Roman law to be in the position of a slave, since one cannot legally be *sui iuris* and *alieni iuris* simultaneously.

[56] D.26.1 [*De tutelis*]; D.41.4.7.3.

[57] Grotius cites Dumoulin, whom Bodin hailed as "the ornament of all lawyers" in *Commonweale* 108, at *Commentarii in Consuetudines Parienses* [*Opera Omnia*] (Paris, 1681) [Title I, §2, gloss 4, 16–17].

[58] *De Iure Belli* 76 [1.3.11.1].

highest title or right to a *res* [*ius in re*] and one may hold and enjoy such *res* "by a full right of property" [*iure pleno proprietatis*], equivalent to *dominium*.[59] But so could one have, on the other hand, an inferior or lesser right which, though falling short of full proprietary right [*ius in re*], may nevertheless entitle the claimant to certain limited rights of use in property belonging to someone else [*ius in re aliena*]. Such lesser rights to property gave the illusion of ownership in an object of property, without actually counting as full legal ownership.

Certainly, one of the most important illustrations of such a lesser *ius in re aliena* was the personal right of usufruct [*ususfructus*], which, as we have seen, Paul defines in the *Digest* as the "right to use and enjoy the things of another without impairing their substance."[60] Like other lesser rights, usufruct was not ownership as such [*dominium*], but merely, as Paul put it, "a fraction of ownership" [*pars dominii*].[61] In the private law framework of the *Corpus Iuris Civilis*, this right of usufruct functioned as a "burden on property obliging the owner to allow someone else [i.e., the usufructuary] to use it for some purpose."[62]

What is remarkable about usufruct was that it created not only a right to enjoy another person's property, but also activated a positive duty in the usufructuary to maintain the value of the property granted for use. There were, thus, legal limits to what a usufructuary could do in his use and enjoyment of the property. The usufructuary could not, for example, substantially alter the property in a way that would result in loss of value.[63] Nor could the usufructuary perform any action that would worsen the position of the real owner [*causam proprietatis*].[64] But above all, the usufructuary could not alienate the owner's property, since it could never be within the right of the usufructuary to authorize such a loss of the owner's rights without his consent.[65] Because of such limitations, usufructuary right [*ius usufructuarii*] was always regarded to be inferior to proprietary right [*ius proprietatis*].

It was this distinction in the *modus habendi* between full proprietary rights and limited usufructuary rights in the *Corpus Iuris Civilis* that framed Grotius' analysis reconciling popular liberty with princely government. Applying this distinction to the analysis of princely government, Grotius identifies two species of princes—on the one hand, those princes "who possess the crown by a full right of property" [*pleno iure proprietatis*], and, on the other hand, those princes "who possess the crown by a usufructuary right" [*iure usufructuario*].[66] In the former, the ruling princes held a full right, and so, sovereignty is treated just as if it were the prince's private property.[67] In these sorts of princely governments, as Grotius observes, "crowns do not differ from other goods and chattels," so it is natural for Grotius to apply the rules of private property indifferently to the analysis of public power.[68] Because such "patrimonial" princes

[59] *De Iure Belli* 76 [1.3.11]; *War and Peace* 1:280. [60] D.7.1.1. [61] D.7.1.4.

[62] Garnsey, *Thinking About Property* 186. D.7.1.13.7. [63] D.7.1.44.

[64] D.7.1.13.4. [65] D.7.1.12.2. [66] *War and Peace* 1:280.

[67] *War and Peace* 1:300; cp. 1:140–1; *De Iure Belli* 65-66 [1.3.6].

[68] *War and Peace* 2:619; *De Iure Belli* 243 [2.7.25.1].

held the full right of property in the sovereign powers attached to the state, they held not simply rights of use [*ius utendi*] in those powers but also the full sovereign rights of disposal [*ius abutendi*] or of alienation [*ius aliendi*] which, as Grotius insists in his discussion, *De alienatione imperii*, were essential to the core idea of property, which must, by definition, include "a power of disposing of, or transferring, all or any part of their effects to other persons."[69] Citing Aristotle, he declares that "it is the definition of property to have in one's self the power of alienation."[70]

It follows, from this analysis of the full rights of property and its inclusion of the right of alienation, that a prince holding real sovereignty by a full right of property must also have the right to alienate that sovereignty, because if he did not have such right, that would be sufficient to show that the prince was not a true sovereign in the first place. Thus, Grotius observes:

> Now as it is in other things, so it is also in sovereignty, it may be alienated [*imperia alienari possunt*] by him who has a just title to it . . . by a king, if the crown be patrimonial [*si imperium in patrimonio*].[71]

Because of a patrimonial prince's rights of property in the rights of sovereignty, Grotius concludes that, "it may be in his power even to alienate it [the sovereignty over the state]."[72]

These princes with full proprietary rights, however, were to be differentiated from those other princes who "enjoy the sovereign power [*summum imperium*] by a usufructuary right [*iure ususfructuario*]."[73] Unlike patrimonial princes, these princes do not own their sovereign powers by right of property [*iure proprietatis*] but, like usufructuaries at civil law, may enjoy them under the conditions specified by the *dominus* from whom they receive the rights of sovereignty, as a *ius in re aliena*. That owner, of course, can be none other than the people who originally granted the prince a usufructuary right to sovereignty, not by popular alienation, but by concession or election [*per electionem conferebatur*].[74] The people, on this theory, remain sovereign and free, since they are voluntarily abstaining from exercising the right of self-government directly, and instead, purposely allowing an intermediary usufructuary to exercise those powers on their behalf. The nature of the usufructuary prince's grip on sovereign power is, thus, a "revocable right" [*ius revocabile*] and could be nothing more than what in Roman private law was classified as precarious tenure [*precarium*], an analysis that bears striking resemblance to Bodin's comparison of extraordinary commissions delegating public authority to the structure of a unilateral obligation.[75]

Princes with such limited rights of usufruct over their powers were designated usufructuary princes to signal their status as usufructuaries with rights

[69] *War and Peace* 2:566; *De Iure Belli* 200-1 [2.6.1.1].

[70] *War and Peace* 566, which cites Aristotle, *Rhetoric* 1.5 [1361a]; *De Iure Belli* 200–1 [2.6.1.1].

[71] *War and Peace* 2:568; *De Iure Belli* 201 [2.6.3].

[72] *War and Peace* 1:289; *De Iure Belli* 78–9 [1.3.12.2-3].

[73] *De Iure Belli* 76 [1.3.11.1]; cp. 93 [1.3.24]. *War and Peace* 1:280.

[74] *De Iure Belli* 223 [2.7.24]; 204 [2.6.10].

[75] *De Iure Belli* 77 [1.3.11.3]. On precarious tenures, see D.43.26.1–3.

extending only to the use and enjoyment of a power which they did not own, like a tenancy or easement. And because they held the limited rights of a usufructuary, Grotius is able to explain why princes of this type cannot perform certain public acts of sovereignty. Such princes cannot, for example, "alienate, either in whole or in part, the people's demain [*patrimonium populi*]... For they have no more than a usufructuary right [*ius fructuario*] to it."[76] While it may be true that a usufructuary prince has a right to use and exercise the instruments of civil power, the acts of a prince who "yet holds not his kingdom as his property" and whose "acts... as shall tend to an alienation, are void by the law of nature, because they relate to what is not his own."[77] Such an act of the usufructuary is "in itself void" [*actus... nullus est*].[78] This was entirely consistent with existing juridical authorities on the inalienability of sovereignty, such as Baldus and Oldradus, which Grotius had referenced directly to stress that such constitutional decisions must be made ultimately *a populo*, "by the people."[79]

But what is especially critical in this argument is the larger point that Grotius stresses. The usufructuary prince can exercise the right of government only as long as the people will allow him to do so, as their intermediary or agent. Where there is a conflict between the acts of the usufructuary prince and the interests of the people, it is always the latter which must prevail, and it is within the right of the people to dispossess the usufructuary prince of his powers and exert public right over princely government.[80]

CONCLUSION

Grotius' legally inflected discussion of the usufructuary prince and the nature of his regime is highly instructive, because it provides an indication of what he felt to be the essence of popular self-government and, therefore, of popular sovereignty. The chief requirement for such self-government is *not* that the people directly and at all times exercise the instruments of civil power, as in a direct democracy. That is, as Grotius concedes, neither practical nor necessary. Instead, what matters to Grotius is that the people remain, like an owner with *nuda proprietas*, in ultimate control of the rights and powers exercised by the prince because only then can the prince be regarded not as a *dominus*, but as a usufructuary: an intermediary or agent constituted to serve the public interest and not his own.[81]

[76] *De Iure Belli* 204 [2.6.11]; 79–80 [1.3.13.1]; *War and Peace* 2:575–6.

[77] *De Iure Belli* 312–13 [2.14.2.2]; *Rights of War and Peace* 2:804.

[78] *De Iure Belli* 112 [1.4.10].

[79] Grotius cites discussions of Baldus and Oldradus on the *Decretales*, X.2.24.33 [*Intellecto*], as well as Baldus' *consilium* 327, in the note to *De Iure Belli* 2.6.3. See also Peter Riesenberg, *The Inalienability of Sovereignty in Medieval Political Thought* (New York: Columbia University Press, 1955).

[80] *De Iure Belli* 112 [1.4.10].

[81] In this respect, I would say that Grotius, like Bodin, ought to be seen as the conceptual forebear of the the theory of popular control recently formulated by Pettit, *On the People's Terms* 160–79.

I think several related implications may be drawn from this analysis, and it is on these points that I want to conclude. The first thing to observe is that Grotius' theory of popular liberty does not demand a particular constitutional form of government, but rather, as we have seen, a certain relationship of rights in the polity. Unlike early modern civic republicans who insist that liberty is always incompatible with princely government, Grotius gives us a more nuanced picture of the kind of government that would be compatible with popular liberty. Indeed, for Grotius, it is immaterial to liberty whether civil power is exercised by one or by many or by some strategic combination of offices; what matters is how that power is exercised. So, even a princely government is compatible with popular liberty, as long as that prince acts in the constitutional role of a usufructuary, an administrator, or some other similar legally defined role that acknowledges the unconditional sovereign authority of the *populus*. This marks a significant departure from one of the longstanding assumptions of early modern republicanism: that popular liberty requires popular government. By denying the validity of such a special conceptual relationship, Grotius implicitly rejects the privileged position that democracy has enjoyed in the theory of liberty.

Yet, despite Grotius' interest in the notion of popular sovereignty and his acknowledgement of the free popular state as a valid form of government, it is also clear that Grotius did not attach any special normative priority to the notion of popular liberty in his systematic political thought, in the same way that, say, Machiavelli or Milton did. Indeed, as we have seen, Grotius approached the concept of popular liberty from a detached analytical frame of mind that, like other political theorists of his age such as Bodin, attempted only to catalogue the varieties of civic life without making any further normative commitment. This is perhaps why he so easily permits what so many others—above all, Rousseau—found to be impermissible, that a free people may, without reservation, voluntarily and completely alienate their public liberty and independence to a sovereign prince. The larger point here, it seems, is that the analysis of liberty does not lie in the realm of moral philosophy but in the realm of legal and civil philosophy, a distinction that is consistent from his early writings in *De Iure Praedae* to his more mature statements in *De Iure Belli ac Pacis*.

But finally, it is essential to stress the vehicle which made this analysis of liberty possible, and that was the Roman law. In this chapter, we have seen how Grotius invoked various aspects of the Roman law of persons, the law of property, and the law of obligations to craft a doctrine of popular liberty, which is distinct from those conceptions which today are conventionally labeled as theories of "non-domination" and "non-interference." Far from functioning as mere marginal Baroque ornamentation to the text, Grotius' critical reading of Roman law was essential to the substantive arguments on sovereignty and government deployed in *De Iure Belli ac Pacis*. It is indeed what connects him to that broader juristic pattern of thought that facilitated the introduction of a distinctively modern school of constitutionalism.

9

Popular Sovereignty and the Civil Law in Stuart Constitutional Thought

INTRODUCTION

In the *République*, Bodin attempted to apply his theory of sovereignty to England, just as he did to his own native France and the states of classical Antiquity. In addressing the constitutional question where sovereignty resided in the English constitution, Bodin declared without hesitation that "soueraigntie wholly without diuision belonged vnto the kings of England."[1] England, for Bodin, was to be regarded as a pure monarchy, just like France.

Such an unqualified assertion assigning an extralegal power "absolved of all laws" to the English monarchy made complete sense to Bodin, whose purpose was to locate one permanently fixed source of public authority exercised within a state. Indeed, because his analysis assigned absolute and perpetual power to the English monarchy, Bodin became (perhaps unwittingly) the champion and spokesperson for an emerging English theory of royal absolutism.[2] Especially after 1606, with the publication of Richard Knolles' translation, entitled *Six Bookes of a Commonweal*, which hastened the English reception of Continental theories of sovereignty, Bodin would quickly become one of the central authorities invoked by English royalists in the heat of constitutional debate in the Stuart monarchy.[3]

But, for some English readers of Bodin, this constitutional analysis was unacceptable, for the simple reason that the theory did not match the institutional

[1] *Commonweale* 98 [1.8].

[2] For example, Charles Merbury, *A Briefe Discourse of Royall Monarchie, as of the Best Common Weale* (London, 1581) 41. See, more generally, Johann Sommerville, *Royalists and Patriots: Politics and Ideology in England, 1603–1640*, 2nd edition (London: Longman, 1999) 41 and Glenn Burgess, *Absolute Monarchy and the Stuart Constitution* (New Haven: Yale University Press, 1996) 63–65; Glenn Burgess, "Bodin in the English Revolution," *The Reception of Bodin*, ed. Howell Lloyd (Leiden: Brill, 2013) 396–401.

[3] Robert Filmer, in particular, assimilated Bodin and his theory of sovereignty into the context of the English Civil War in "The Necessity of the Absolute Power of All Kings" [1648], reproduced in Johann Sommerville, ed., *Patriarcha and Other Writings* (Cambridge: Cambridge University Press, 1991). See also Burgess, *Absolute Monarchy and the Stuart Constitution* 63–64; George Mosse, *The Struggle for Sovereignty in England from the Reign of Queen Elizabeth to the Petition of Right* (East Lansing: Michigan State College Press, 1950). Debates on the Petition of Right, following the insertion of the phrase, "sovereign power," in the House of Lords, centered on the interpretation of sovereignty in the English constitutional context.

facts of English government.[4] As these critics observed, Bodin's theory could ill explain the vital role of the Parliament and courts in English legislation, which, if anything, would appear to "derogate" from, rather than reinforce, the king's chief right of sovereignty, the right to make and unmake law without the consent of any other.[5] Pointing to customary limitations on monarchical authority under English common law, English critics of the Bodinian theory argued that it was just not true, in point of fact, that English kings were (as Ulpian once described the extralegal condition of Roman emperors) *legibus soluti*, free to rule and legislate as they pleased without restriction. On the contrary, the history of English common law revealed a very different model of kingship in which monarchs were, over time, increasingly bound by law and custom. Because kings were so bound, later commentators raised the question whether there was even such a thing as sovereignty to be found in England. John Pym, remarking on the alarming attribution of sovereignty to the king, thought not.[6]

There was an added urgency, which nourished the hostility to Bodin's theory of sovereignty. Locating sovereignty exclusively in the monarchy would effectively invalidate one of the cardinal doctrines of English constitutional thought: that England's public institutions, including Parliament, exemplified the classical form of the "mixed constitution," where public authority was not to be "monopolized" by any one person or institutional actor, but dispersed and shared by many different actors.[7] Indeed, mixed constitutionalism had been so thoroughly entrenched in English constitutional thought since at least the time of Sir John Fortescue, that any departure from this constitutional norm was thought to be a dangerous innovation.

The concept of sovereignty represented perhaps the most dangerous innovation of all, in the eyes of English constitutional theorists and common lawyers. It is a puzzle, then, to see how early modern England, generally immune from the influence of civil law, would not only absorb the civilian theory of sovereignty but, even more, interpret that theory specifically to mean *popular* sovereignty.

[4] Burgess, "Bodin in the English Revolution" 401–5, citing especially William Prynne's *The Soveraigne Power of Parliaments and Kingdomes* (London: Michael Sparke, Senior, 1643) as an outstanding example. Burgess, *Absolute Monarchy and the Stuart Constitution* 78–9 gives another example of William Fulbecke who rejects Bodin's theory as inappropriate to England in *Pandectes of the Law of Nations* (London, 1602). A major point of disagreement between Bodin and Fulbecke concerns democracy, at *Pandectes* fols. 28–9, where he regards "democracie . . . to be no forme of a commonweale."

[5] Bodin actually anticipated these objections in his argument that parliamentary bodies and estates do not derogate from monarchical sovereignty. *Commonweale* 95 [1.8].

[6] Speech of John Pym in John Rushworth, *Historical Collections of Private Passages of State*, Vol. 1, (London: Tho. Newcomb for George Thomason, 1659) 568.

[7] Arihiro Fukuda, *Sovereignty and the Sword: Harrington, Hobbes, and Mixed Government in the English Civil Wars* (Oxford: Clarendon Press, 1997); Skinner, "Classical Liberty, Renaissance Translation and the English Civil War" 308–43; Corinne Comstock Weston and Janelle Greenberg, *Subjects and Sovereigns: The Grand Controversy over Legal Sovereignty in Stuart England* (Cambridge: Cambridge University Press, 1981); Corinne Comstock Weston, *English Constitutional Theory and the House of Lords, 1556–1832* (New York: Columbia University Press, 1965).

The goal of this chapter is to provide such an account of the origins of popular sovereignty ideas in Stuart England. As I show, Roman law theories of sovereignty surveyed in preceding chapters, such as the principle of the *lex regia* and the *legibus solutus*, played a critical role in explaining the operation of sovereignty in a custom-bound monarchy like England. I begin with the constitutional thought of the English civilians, English scholars and practitioners of Roman law such as Alberico Gentili and John Cowell, who were chiefly responsible for importing Continental ideas of sovereignty into English constitutional thought. By explicitly treating the English monarch as a *princeps* who is *legibus solutus*, the civilians polarized English constitutional discourse by forcing open a discussion on the origins of the sovereign's absolute powers as stemming from the primitive act of an originally sovereign people. It is in this context that writers, such as John Selden, broach the notion of an English *lex regia*, as a general constitutional principle applicable to all nations, not just the Romans. The chapter next considers the practical significance of these theories of popular sovereignty in the period of the English Civil War, in which opponents of the Stuart monarchy actively sought alternative theories of sovereignty. I consider the important doctrine of parliamentary sovereignty crafted by Henry Parker, but I also look especially to royalist critiques of these alternatives, from writers such as Dudley Digges, John Bramhall, and especially Robert Filmer, to show how Roman legal reasoning, especially the idea of "divestiture," is deployed in these debates. I conclude with a discussion of Thomas Hobbes, who I argue, deserves to be recognized as the preeminent English theorist of popular sovereignty for his treatment of sovereign peoplehood as being inseparably connected to sovereign statehood.

ROMAN LAW IN EARLY MODERN ENGLAND: THE ENGLISH CIVILIANS AND THE ENGLISH *PRINCEPS*

English common law, conceptualized as the cumulative product of historical experience and the "artificial reason" of judges deciding particular cases over time, projected an implicit hostility toward a Bodinian notion of legislative sovereignty. Law was not made but was, rather, to be found. Because it made no allowance for a legal-positivist legislative will capable of authoring law, common law simply could not provide the resources to realize what Stuart English royalists sought: an absolute monarchy organized around a concept of sovereignty. But Roman law, with its stylized language of sovereign authorities as *legibus soluti*, certainly could. And it is partly for this reason that early modern English jurists began turning in earnest to the *Corpus Iuris Civilis* and the innovations of early modern Continental legal science as an alternative model upon which English law might be reimagined and reformed.

It is often forgotten that Roman law made a considerable intellectual and social impact in England.[8] Beginning especially in the sixteenth century,

[8] Brian Levack, *The Civil Lawyers in England, 1603–1641: A Political Study* (Oxford: Clarendon Press, 1973); Charles Donahue, "The Civil Law in England," *Yale Law Journal* 84 (1974): 167–81; Daniel Coquillette, *The*

Roman law began to attract sustained intellectual interest from among the so-called "English civilians," English scholars and practitioners of Roman law. This was, in part, due to the foundation in 1540 by Henry VIII, of the two Regius Professorships in Civil Law in the English universities, which permitted Roman law to be taught as an approved area of study and examination at Oxford and Cambridge, not only as a counterweight to the juridical autonomy and power exercised by common lawyers and judges, but also as training for lawyers to practice in venues which more directly applied legal rules derived from Roman law, such as Doctors Commons, the High Court of Admiralty, the ecclesiastical Court of Arches, as well as in areas of international law.[9] But by and large, the English curriculum in civil law was not intended as preparation for legal practice. The universities, unlike the Inns of Court, "did not train students in court procedures and techniques."[10] Instead, the focus was "almost entirely theoretical" based on Justinian's *Institutes*, *Code*, and the *Digest* and intended "to cultivate the art of statesmanship."[11]

What was so special about Roman law that it should be so privileged in England? For English civilians, the intellectual value in studying such a "dead" law was analogous to that of studying a "dead" language. Classical languages in the humanist curriculum functioned as "an indispensable propaedeutic to the grasp of the liberal sciences."[12] Civil law, likewise, functioned in a similar way for the student of law, as a universal propaedeutic for the English study of legal and civil science. In this respect, Roman law was not simply an archaic body of legal rules, an artifact of some ancient civilization. It was, as Sir John Dodderidge once put it, "the ground of all law," and thus enjoyed a privileged status among all nations.[13] It was "an intellectual technique" providing "analytical clarity" and "the ability to consider English institutions from the outside."[14] Roman law was the key to understanding the science of right, and, for this reason, some even advocated the thorough integration of the civilian Commentators such as Bartolus and Baldus into university learning, to be read

Civilian Writers of Doctors' Commons, London: Three Centuries of Juristic Innovation in Comparative, Commercial and International Law (Berlin: Duncker & Humblot, 1988).

[9] The seventeenth-century University Statutes of Oxford, enacted during the Chancellorship of Archbishop Laud, detail the examination procedure for candidates for the degree of Doctor of Civil Law, which include *sex solemnes lectiones* on titles from the *Code* and the *Digest*. John Griffiths, *Statutes of the University of Oxford Codified in the Year 1636* (Oxford: Clarendon Press, 1888) 115–16 [*Pro Inceptore in Iure Civili*]. Levack, *Civil Lawyers in England* Ch. 1, especially 9ff, and Ch. 4. See also the useful study of G.D. Squibb, *Doctors' Commons: A History of the College of Advocates and Doctors of Law* (Oxford: Clarendon Press, 1977).

[10] Levack, *Civil Lawyers in England* 16.

[11] Levack, *Civil Lawyers in England* 16, 25; Mark Curtis, *Oxford and Cambridge in Transition, 1558–1642* (Oxford: Clarendon Press, 1959) 155.

[12] Quentin Skinner, *Reason and Rhetoric in the Philosophy of Hobbes* (Cambridge: Cambridge University Press, 1996) 22.

[13] Ken MacMillan, *Sovereignty and Possession in the New World: The Legal Foundations of Empire, 1576–1640* (Cambridge: Cambridge University Press, 2006) 27, citing BL Harley MS 5220, fol. 4_v.

[14] Burgess, *Politics of the Ancient Constitution* 122–3.

alongside Cicero and Plutarch.[15] In this vein, Francis Bacon, the philosopher and one-time Lord Chancellor of England, would remark that Roman civil law, like English common law, was "dictated verbatim by the same reason" shared by all nations and peoples.[16]

One major goal of the civilians was to diminish the perceived exceptionalism of English law and institutions, often seen as an aberration from other Western legal systems of the *ius commune*. Despite the appearance of incongruence, with its Law French vocabulary, adversarial court procedure, and legal rules, common law was—so the civilians thought—not all that different and could potentially be "translated" and reformed so as to be legible to outsiders. In this respect, Roman law functioned as a kind of primer for an early modern comparative jurisprudence, so as to align according to proper method the various areas of law such as property, contracts, and family law, and highlight both areas of convergence and divergence.[17]

There was additionally a constitutional dimension to this project in the case of public law, especially concerning the law of kingship. What legal role and powers did the King of England hold? What is most noteworthy about the English civilians concerned their direct application of Continental theories of sovereignty in answering this question, effectively enlarging royal powers beyond the traditional limitations imposed by common law.[18] In this respect, there was a seamless continuity between the political thought of the English civilians and Continental jurists, a continuity which can be traced to their shared intellectual tradition in the Roman law viewing the *princeps* as *legibus solutus*.[19] From the civilians' point of view, the English monarch became the equivalent of a Roman *princeps* with an *imperium* in his own right.

To describe the English king as a Roman *princeps* in this way was especially valuable to royalists because it carved out a conceptual space for extralegal

[15] William Fulbecke, *A Direction or Preparative to the Study of the Lawe* (London, 1600) fol. 26.

[16] Francis Bacon, "Maxims on Law," *The Works of Francis Bacon in Ten Volumes*, Vol. 4, *The Law Tracts* (London, 1803) 12, likely referencing D.1.1.9 and Inst.1.2.1. See also Burgess, *Absolute Monarchy and the Stuart Constitution* 86 and Burgess, *Politics of the Ancient Constitution* 125.

[17] John Cowell, *Institutiones Iuris Anglicani ad Methodum et Seriem Institutionum Imperialium Compositae et Digestae* (Cambridge, 1605); Richard Zouch, *Elementa Iurisprudentiae Definitionibus* (Oxford, 1636); William Fulbecke, *A Parallele or Conference of the Civill Law, the Canon Law, and the Common Law of This Realme of England* (London: Thomas Wight, 1601). Such comparative approaches to legal analysis became especially urgent with the need to manage differences between English law and Scottish law, which integrated elements of civil law, as Bacon observed in his law tracts, such as "A Preparation toward the Union of the Laws of England and Scotland" and "A Proposition to H.M. Compiling and Amendment of the Laws of England." Cp. Burgess, *Politics of the Ancient Constitution* 127.

[18] Some notable exceptions among the English civilians are the Cambridge historian, Isaac Dorislaus [in his lectures on classical history at Cambridge], Sir Henry Marten [in the debates on the Petition of Right], in Rushworth, *Historical Collections* 585, and Calibute Downing, *A Discourse of the State Ecclesiasticall of this Kingdome, in Relation to the Civill* (Oxford, 1632). See also Levack, *Civil Lawyers in England* Ch. 3; Burgess, *Politics of the Ancient Constitution* 123; Paul Kocher, "Francis Bacon and the Science of Jurisprudence," *Journal of the History of Ideas* 18 (1957): 3; Ronald Mellor, "Tacitus, Academic Politics, and Regicide in the Reign of Charles I: The Tragedy of Dr. Isaac Dorislaus," *International Journal of the Classical Tradition* 11 (2004): 153–93.

[19] But cp. Burgess, *Absolute Monarchy and the Stuart Constitution* 90; *Politics of the Ancient Constitution* 123.

powers which were, in principle, "absolute" and exclusive to the king. Common law doctrine, to be sure, acknowledged certain "extraordinary" powers that were, in principle, reserved to the monarch's discretion, designated under the "royal prerogative." But even these powers were traditionally circumscribed within customary constraints, such that, in practice, it was incongruent with the "absolute and perpetual" powers of sovereignty imagined by civilians such as a Baldus, a Rosate, or a Bodin. By treating English royal authority as a power, *legibus solutus*, civilians were able to expand the scope of the royal prerogative far beyond its traditional common-law bounds.[20]

A key example of this transition in English legal thought is to be found in the writings of Alberico Gentili (1552–1608), the Italian-born Regius Professor of Civil Law in Oxford, whom Levack had once called "the theoretical founder of absolutism in England."[21] Although perhaps more familiar to legal historians as the author of the *De Iure Belli*, a major influence on Grotius' own work on that topic, Gentili was one of the most outstanding civil lawyers in his own right in all of early modern Europe.[22] A critic of French legal humanism, Gentili insisted on treating Roman law as foundational to legal science, resulting in a prolific output of legal commentaries, particularly concerning the law of nations, the law of war, and legal issues arising from diplomacy.

Among those tracts was one which specifically treated the concept of royal authority "in a very Bodinian vein," the *Regales Disputationes Tres* of 1605, which Gentili dedicated to the new Stuart king, James I.[23] In the first *Disputatio*, concerning "the absolute power of the king" [*De potestate regis absoluta*], Gentili specified the essential quality required to make royal authority absolute and free: it must not be limited [*absque limitibus*], neither by any human nor by any legal bond [*neque hominem, neque legem*].[24] In presenting this analysis, Gentili was quick to highlight its origins in Roman legal science:

> The civil law says that the *princeps* is unbound by the laws [D.1.3.31] and that law is whatever pleases the *princeps* [D.1.4.1]. This law is not foreign, but Roman: It is indeed the most excellent [*praestantissima*] among the laws of men.[25]

In showing the classical heritage of the principle in Roman law, Gentili's purpose was to show that "absolute" authority was not an exclusively Roman

[20] Cp. Conrad Van Dijk, *John Gower and the Limits of the Law* (Cambridge: D.S. Brewer, 2013) 101–02, for medieval English interpretations of the *legibus solutus* that resisted absolutism. See also Nederman, *Lineages of European Political Thought* Ch. 6.

[21] Levack, *Civil Lawyers in England* 98, following Gezina van der Molen, *Alberico Gentili and the Development of International Law* (Amsterdam: H.J. Paris, 1937) 330–1.

[22] Benedict Kingsbury and Benjamin Straumann, ed., *The Roman Foundations of the Law of Nations: Alberico Gentili and the Justice of Empire* (Oxford: Oxford University Press, 2010).

[23] Benjamin Straumann, "The *Corpus Iuris* as a Source of Law between Sovereigns," Kingsbury and Straumann, *Roman Law Foundations of the Law of Nations* 104, n.9: Alain Wijffels, "Le Disputazioni di Alberico Gentili sul Diritto Pubblico," *Alberico Gentili: La Salvaguardia Dei Beni Culturali Nel Diritto Internazionale* (Milan: Giuffrè, 2008) 247–61.

[24] Alberico Gentili, *Regales Disputationes Tres* (London, 1605) 9.

[25] Gentili, *Regales Disputationes* 9.

notion, restricted only to those nations recognizing the civil law, but a universal one to be found in all independent states, including even in England.

To establish this point, Gentili observed, in the first place, that English legal theorists typically divided royal powers into two broad categories, so that "there is a double power [*potestatem duplicem*] to be found in the prince."[26] Taken by itself, there was nothing particularly unusual about this doctrine of double powers, which already became something of a commonplace in Stuart legal thought, actively debated and investigated by the most celebrated English legal thinkers, such as Bacon and Edward Coke.[27] Indeed, at least since the fifteenth century, common lawyers had been able to distinguish between the *potentia ordinata* of common law jurisdictions from the *potentia absoluta* of equity jurisdiction exercised in the Court of Chancery.[28] And, as Francis Oakley has shown, the distinction appeared repeatedly in the Tudor period, including in an outline of a *Treatise on the King's Prerogative*, left in manuscript form by Sir John Dodderidge.[29] It was, according to this conventional view, largely insulated from external influence and developed as a distinctively indigenous English legal phenomenon.

What *was* novel about Gentili's analysis, however, was his treatment of the crown's ordinary and extraordinary powers specifically in the terms of civil law, where ordinary power was said to be bound by the laws [*ordinariam adstrictam legibus*], while extraordinary power was said to be freed (or absolved) from the laws [*alteram extraordinariam legibus absolutam*].[30] Despite the common law view of the English crown as a limited monarchy, bound by the customary limitations imposed by the common law, Gentili insisted that, buried deep behind layers of customary practice, even English monarchs were invested with an "extraordinary and free power" [*extraordinaria et libera potestas*], which he specified, most controversially, was nothing other than "that which in England we signify by the name, Royal Prerogative."[31] So, despite appearances, English monarchs were not so different from other princely rulers who claimed an

[26] Gentili, *Regales Disputationes* 10.

[27] Francis Bacon, "A View of the Differences in Question Betwixt the King's Bench and the Council in the Marches," *The Letters and the Life of Francis Bacon*, Vol. 3 (London: Longmans, Green, Reader, and Dyer, 1868) 373. See also Harvey Wheeler, "The Constitutional Ideas of Francis Bacon," *Political Research Quarterly* 9 (1956): 928–30.

[28] Francis Oakley, "Jacobean Political Theology: The Absolute and Ordinary Powers of the King," *Journal of the History of Ideas* 29 (1968): 324, citing the Year Book of 1469, 9 Edward IV, Trin. 9. See also Pennington, *Prince and the Law* Ch. 2 on the canonistic origins of the distinction in Hostiensis' on Papal *potestas ordinata et absoluta*.

[29] Oakley, "Jacobean Political Theology" 325, citing *Treatise on the King's Prerogative*, Harley MS 5220, British Library, ff. 9v–10v. See, more generally, Margaret Atwood Judson, *Crisis of the Constitution: An Essay in Constitutional and Political Thought in England 1603–1645* (New Brunswick: Rutgers University Press, 1949) 25, 111. R.F.V. Heuston, *Essays in Constitutional Law* (London: Stevens, 1961) 61–2; Francis Wormuth, *Origins of Modern Constitutionalism* (New York: Harper, 1949) 34–9; Mosse, *Struggle for Sovereignty*.

[30] Gentili, *Regales Disputationes* 10, corresponding to the doctrines of C.1.14.4. and D.1.3.31.

[31] Gentili, *Regales Disputationes* 10.

extralegal *imperium*. Even in England, kings held absolute powers by virtue of their discretionary prerogative, which enabled them to exercise equity and even extraordinary jurisdiction and to make law, at least in principle, without consent of Parliament. The king's capacity to act on these prerogative powers "according to which he can take away another's right, however great, even without due process" [*sine caussa*] was, in Gentili's eyes, precisely what made the monarchy free and independent—that is, absolute.[32]

In this way, then, Gentili was among the first civilians to present a civilian account of how English royal authority was absolute—that is, *legibus solutus*. One important consequence of this analysis, in Gentili's mind, was that there was nothing exceptional about the English monarchy that made it any less "absolute" in its powers than, say, the French monarchy, as Fortescue once did in describing the English constitution as a *dominium regale et politicum*. Both were in theory "pure" monarchies, fully absolute and legally unrestricted in their sovereign authority over their respective realms. In this respect, Gentili's reasoning followed Bodin, thereby ensuring that "civil law spoke with the voice of Bodin" in England.[33]

This "absolutist" transformation of the meaning of the royal prerogative would be further developed concurrently by other English civilians, such as John Cowell (1554–1611), Gentili's counterpart in Cambridge as Regius Professor of Civil Law. Cowell offered a highly controversial definition of the *Prerogativa Regis* in his influential law dictionary, *The Interpreter*, a definition which would prompt James I, not to praise, but to admonish Cowell for attempting to define—and thereby limit—what was regarded as inherently indefinable and limitless, even sacrosanct and mystical.[34] For Cowell, the royal prerogative was "that especiall power, preeimennce, or priuiledge that the King hath in any kinde, ouer and aboue other persons, and aboue the ordinarie course of the common lawe, in the right of his crowne."[35]

What is crucial, in Cowell's definition, is the direct connection he tries to make between the English royal prerogative and the absolutist concept of sovereignty, in order to show that prerogative is in fact merely a particular instance of a more general category of sovereignty already present in the system of civil law:

> This word (*Praerogatiua*) is vsed by the Ciuilians in the same sense [C.10.41] . . . [as] that absolute heighth of power that the Ciuilians call *maiestatem, vel potestatem, vel ius imperii*.[36]

[32] Gentili, *Regales Disputationes* 10.

[33] Burgess, *Absolute Monarchy and the Stuart Constitution* 75.

[34] Levack, *Civil Lawyers in England* 98, citing S.B. Chrimes, "The Constitutional Ideas of Dr. John Cowell," *English Historical Review* 64 (1949): 473.

[35] John Cowell, "Prerogative of the King," *The Interpreter, or, Booke Containing the Signification of Words* (Cambridge, 1607) no page numbers.

[36] Cowell, "Prerogative of the King," *The Interpreter*.

This analysis led Cowell to arrive at exactly the same conclusion as Bodin on the proper classification of the English constitution, not so much as a limited or mixed monarchy, but as a pure absolute monarchy. Thus, in a passage of *The Interpreter* which might as well have been written by Bodin, Cowell can say, "I hold it incontrowlable, that the king of England is an absolute king," and even "aboue the Law by his absolute power."[37] It is for this reason that one commentator sees Cowell as marking off a new territory "outside the orthodox tradition of English constitutional thought."[38]

There was, however, a broader, more practical purpose driving the civilian project of envisioning the *Rex Anglorum* as the juridical equivalent of the Roman *princeps* that made it something more than simply an arcane academic exercise among university lawyers trying to harmonize English law with Roman law. Indeed, the model of the Roman law *princeps* offered a vision of legislative authority that was especially attractive to English jurists who, in the Stuart period, were strident in their criticism of the perceived backwardness and inefficiency of English common law, set beyond the reach of ordinary legislators.

In acknowledging the need to reform and "rationalize" English law, the immediate problem English jurists encountered concerned precisely how such a project of reform might proceed. To remake the law, they reasoned, it would first be necessary to unmake the law, especially those elements of the common law that would appear to be irrational or contrary to legal science. Who, if anybody, had such plenary legislative authority in early modern England, an authority that common law could not allow? At first glance, it seemed the answer must be nobody—least of all the king, who, if anything, was bound and restricted by the very same common law that needed to be reformed. Given the institutional complexities associated with how jurists believed common law developed over time, there could be no identifiable lawmaker in England—whether "Justinianic," "Bodinian" or "Austinian"—who held such a singular lawmaking will.

What the civilians offered to reform-minded English jurists was a clear alternative to this constitutional pluralism of "co-ordinate" estates acting as partners in legislation: plenary legislative *imperium* could be invested exclusively in the king, as if he were the English juridical equivalent of the Roman *princeps* who was *legibus solutus*. In this way, all valid law was, at least in principle, entirely reducible to "what pleases the prince" [*quod principi placuit*]. The king would stand, as Richard Zouch (c.1590–1661, Gentili's successor in the Regius Professorship) would put it in his *Elementa Iurisprudentiae*, in the exact phrasing of Justinian's *Code*, as the "ultimate author and interpreter of the law" [*conditor et interpres legis*] and champion of reform.[39]

37 Cowell, "Prerogative of the King" and "King," *The Interpreter*.

38 Sommerville, *Royalists and Patriots* 117.

39 Zouch, *Elementa Iurisprudentiae* 60–1, citing *inter alia* C.1.14.12 and D.1.4.1. See also Levack, *Civil Lawyers in England* 100–1.

THE ORIGINS OF ABSOLUTE POWER: AN ENGLISH *LEX REGIA*?

The civilian analysis of English kingship was vitally important for the emergence of royal absolutism. By positioning the English king as, by analogy, the Roman *princeps*, civilians could conclude that, in principle, the king was *legibus solutus*, absolved of the ordinary legal and institutional constraints of common law by prerogative powers that were exclusive to him. This shift in thought, as Glenn Burgess has argued, had major practical implications in the politics of Stuart England by "polarizing" English thought especially among the major institutional actors in English constitutional politics.[40]

One question following from this analysis concerns how the king came to be *legibus solutus* in the first place. The doctrine, *princeps legibus solutus*, was, after all, derived from Roman law, a legal system to which English jurists, as early as Fortescue, voiced hostility and against which they articulated what they saw as the exceptional qualities of common law. The suggestion that the king was "absolute," obviously attractive to early modern English absolutists, nevertheless presented an intellectual puzzle that demanded a solution: if the king were legally absolute, how was he so absolved in the first place?

The standard answer, offered not by jurists but by theologians and endorsed personally by James I, was framed in the political theology of "divine right" [*ius divinum*]: kings derived their absolute power exclusively from God and, thus, remained accountable in their exercise of such absolute power in civil and spiritual matters only to God, but never to any other human.[41] But divine right was never the only English theory crafted to explain the origins of royal power. Just as divine right royalists crafted a "descending theory" of power tracing royal authority to a divine source, positioning kings as agents ordained to exercise divine justice, so too did theorists critical of such royalism offer a contrary "ascending theory" of power, declaring that an abstract "people," not God, should be regarded the proper and exclusive source of all legitimate royal authority.[42] In early modern England, this doctrine of popular sovereignty was often treated derisively as the infiltration of a seditious Jesuit doctrine—indeed a "vast engine of *Popular Sedition*" (as Robert Filmer would put it)—most often associated with Jesuit theologians such as the Cardinal Robert Bellarmine, Francisco Suarez, as well as English Catholic theorists such as Robert Persons.[43]

[40] Burgess, *Absolute Monarchy and the Stuart Constitution* 78.

[41] The classic modern study remains John Neville Figgis, *The Divine Right of Kings* (Cambridge: Cambridge University Press, 1922). See also Glenn Burgess, "The Divine Right of Kings Reconsidered," *English Historical Review* 107 (1992): 837–61; Johann Sommerville, "Absolutism and Royalism," *Cambridge History of Political Thought, 1450-1700*, ed. J.H. Burns (Cambridge: Cambridge University Press, 1995).

[42] Morgan, *Inventing the People* Ch. 1. On "ascending" and "descending" theories, Ullmann, *Law and Politics in the Middle Ages*.

[43] Robert Filmer, *Patriarcha, or the Natural Power of Kings* (London: Walter Davis 1680) 4. See also Tuck, *Philosophy and Government* 260, and, more generally, Harro Höpfl, *Jesuit Political Thought: The Society of Jesus and the State, c. 1540–1630* (Cambridge: Cambridge University Press, 2004) Ch. 10.

What is most remarkable (and must be stressed) is that this Jesuit doctrine of popular sovereignty was manifestly an analysis derived directly from the Roman *lex regia*. Suarez, for example, appeals to the civil law at a crucial point in Book III of his treatise, *De Legibus ac Deo Legislatore*, where he takes up the important question of the origins of a prince's legislative power [*potestatem ferendi leges*]. Citing the *lex regia* in the *Digest*, he observes that, as a general legal rule, the community at large is always the valid source of such power: "The community transferred [such power] over to him" [*in illum transtulit communitas*].[44] Nor is this rule of popular sovereignty restricted only to the Roman people, or to those nations which observe civil law. It is, as Suarez writes, a universal legal rule written into the law of all nations and, therefore, a constitutional principle accessible to "all peoples" [*omnes populi*], and not exclusive to any particular nation [*gens*] or people [*populus*].[45] Romans and English alike have their own *leges regiae*. Most intriguing, however, is Suarez's treatment of popular sovereignty in terms of the Roman law of delegated jurisdiction, where the people's power is framed as a "delegable power" [*potestas delegabilis*] which can be transferred and committed to another, *suo arbitrio*, whether *simpliciter* or *conditionaliter*.[46] The implication is that, since delegates act only by a conditional trust owed to their principal who appointed originally them, any forfeiture can make the delegate, even a *princeps*, liable to removal or other some other punitive sanction.

Such Jesuit theories became immediate targets of suspicion in England, especially in the context of the Oath of Allegiance controversy, not only for suggesting the legitimacy of popular resistance, but also that of popular sovereignty.[47] If it is the Roman people who created the Roman *princeps* by a voluntary legal transfer of power, then it must, by legal analogy, be the English people who likewise created the English king by a similar legal transfer of power. The implication is that there must be something like an English *lex regia* still actively empowering the English monarchy. And this, in turn, is because of the interpretive principle that the Jesuits used in transforming the *lex regia* into a universal constitutional norm: what applies to the Romans must also apply to all peoples.

English theorists were, unsurprisingly, extremely wary of this suggestion of a native English *lex regia*, not least because of the potentially destabilizing

[44] Francisco Suarez, *Tractatvs de Legibvs, ac Deo Legislatore* (Lyon, 1613) 120 [3.2, §3]; 123 [3.4, §2], both citing D.1.4.1, 1.2.2.11. Suarez cites Aquinas' discussion on law in the first part of the Second Part of the *Summa*, at Question 90 [Article 1, Objection 3], which, in turn, also cites Ulpian at D.1.4.1. For Suarez, *communitas* is often used interchangeably with *populus* and, perhaps more remarkably, *respublica*.

[45] Suarez, *De Legibus* 120 [3.2, §3].

[46] Suarez, *De Legibus* 124 [3.3, §9], citing Bartolus on D.1.1.9; 125 [3.3, §9], citing D.1.21.1.

[47] Suarez addresses the Oath specifically in *Defensio Fidei Catholicae*, which applies resistance theory in the English context. English civilians were particularly keen to discredit Jesuit theories of popular resistance, such as Hayward, Sutcliffe, and Crompton. Levack, *Civil Lawyers in England* 104–13. See, in general, J.H.M. Salmon, "Catholic Resistance Theory, Ultramontanism, and the Royalist Response, 1580–620," *Cambridge History of Political Thought*, ed. J.H. Burns (Cambridge: Cambridge University Press, 1991).

consequences of popular sovereignty entailed by it, as they observed in the resistance theories developed by Continental jurists who appropriated the *lex regia* for explicitly anti-royalist purposes. If the king derived his absolute power from a prior concessive grant of the people, on the model of the *princeps*, then it opens at least the notional possibility that the people reserved a residual power in that original grant of power. For this reason, royalist commentators actively sought ways to exclude the *lex regia* from English constitutional thought.[48]

Opponents of popular sovereignty pursued several strategies to eliminate the possibility of an English *lex regia*. One influential line of argument synthesized principles derived from Roman law together with the perceived historical exceptionalism of England. If it were true that English kingship derived its absolute power in full from a prior voluntary act of the people, it should be possible, at least in principle, to locate some historical moment in time when the people of England collectively surrendered and conveyed their original *imperium* and right of self-government to a king, just as civilians often pointed to specific legislative acts of the Roman people in Roman history—such as the Republican *lex Hortensia* and the Imperial *lex de imperio Vespasiani* as indicative of a popular *lex regia*. But England, as opponents of popular sovereignty vociferously argued, followed a pattern of events dissimilar to the Roman experience, and that is precisely because English kingship, unlike the Roman Principate, was founded by an act of foreign *conquest*, not by popular *consent*. The popular sovereignty argument of the *lex regia*, thus, could not have any application in the specific case of England. It must be excluded.

The conquest in question was, of course, the eleventh-century Norman Conquest, the military invasion and occupation of medieval England by which the Duke of Normandy was said to have established a valid title to absolute kingly authority.[49] Though centuries removed from that pivotal event in English history, early modern English political and legal theorists recognized the continuing importance of assessing the Conquest for an understanding of the constitutional status of the early modern monarchy. For this reason, the Conquest loomed especially large in the English legal-historical consciousness, as a "constitutional moment" separating English history from an "immemorial" pre-history before England was ruled by kings.[50]

From a legal standpoint, any act of conquest (Norman, Roman, or otherwise) over a foreign land activated a fully valid right of government under the *ius gentium*. Parity of reason requires that the same argument should apply to the Norman Conquest, an act which likewise should have activated a valid title

[48] Sommerville, *Royalists and Patriots* 59.

[49] Johann Sommerville, "History and Theory: The Norman Conquest in Early Stuart Political Thought," *Political Studies* 34 (1986): 249–61.

[50] In his *Analecton Anglo-Britannicon*, John Selden describes the constitutional form of the pre-Roman Britons as not monarchical, but as *aristocratica reipublicae forma*. Tuck, *Philosophy and Government* 208.

and right of government under the *ius gentium*, just as it did for the Romans over the Gauls.

Here was the upshot: since the English monarchy owed its origins to an act of conquest, it follows that there could not possibly have been a popular act of consent involved in the original constitution of the monarchy. Conquest and consent were simply different and incompatible modes of establishing a monarch's valid title and right of government. English kingship, unlike (so they thought) the Roman Principate of Augustus or Vespasian, was founded by the shedding of blood, not by the voicing of popular consent. The conquest story was, thus, especially attractive to English royalists because it accomplished two tasks at once: It offered a legal justification, appealing to the authority of the *ius gentium*, indicating the origins and continuing validity of the king's absolute power, while avoiding entirely the unacceptably radical democratic consequences of the *lex regia* argument. In this way, Stuart legal theorists surgically removed and excluded the *lex regia* from England entirely, choosing instead to ground the legitimacy of English sovereignty on conquest.

A different strategy to exclude the *lex regia* capitalized on another point about legal recognition: Roman law, by itself, has no validity in England. This was an obvious point, but one that would have effectively served the purpose of excluding the popular sovereignty doctrine. The *lex regia* was, after all, of Roman origin, an alien legal culture in opposition to which the English legal mind was shaped. Excluding Roman law would *ipso facto* have to exclude the *lex regia*.

This was the strategy pursued by the English antiquarian, John Selden (1584–1654). In his *Ad Fletam Dissertatio*, Selden observes and tries to explain the anomalous presence of seemingly foreign legal texts in English common law sources, one of which was the *lex regia*. To a legal antiquarian like Selden, the *lex regia* presented a genuine interpretive puzzle: What would be the point of including it in English legal sources, like Bracton or *Fleta*?[51] As a starting point, Selden asserts unambiguously the common law view that "England was in [no] way subject to the [Roman] Empire or to the imperial [i.e., Roman] law."[52] Thus, the *lex regia*, as an artifact of classical Roman law, has no modern application in England. Indeed, any desperate attempt to revive the *lex regia* should be treated as nothing more than "mere flattery," whether in England or elsewhere.[53]

For this reason, he argues, "the civil law doctrine of sovereignty has no more force [in Germany, the 'Holy Roman Empire'], much less anywhere else," such as England.[54] As a strict matter of legal validity, Selden refuses to recognize the authority of this *lex* in modernity. His reply reflects the ongoing influence of legal humanism in his reasoning, when he explains that the civil law in England functions not so much as an authoritative source of valid law,

[51] Selden, *Ad Fletam* 39. [52] Selden, *Ad Fletam* 39. [53] Selden, *Ad Fletam* 41.

[54] Selden, *Ad Fletam* 41. Cp. Sir Arthur Duck's treatment on the authority of Roman law in England and Scotland in *De Usu et Authoritate Iuris Civilis Romanorum* (London, 1653) [2.8; 2.10].

but rather as an abstract, though alien, model of a legal system "grounded on reason," to which "recourse might be had" in two specific scenarios—"where [common] law lacked an express rule," or "where the two systems [i.e., civil and common law] agreed" so that "the matter in question might...be confirmed and elucidated by the civil law analogy."[55]

But he does not stop here. Even if a principle of Roman law, like the *lex regia*, may no longer command active authority, it is still possible in principle to examine the *lex* on the merits, as a scholarly interpretive exercise, just as the Glossators once tried to do as a matter of legal science. Selden, thus, does not hesitate to engage directly with the opinions of the medieval legists in trying to determine the proper original meaning of the *lex*. Like his medieval predecessors, Selden asks whether the popular sovereignty theory of the *lex* should be understood as a concession, or a full alienation, of Roman popular sovereignty to the *princeps*. Weighing the contrary positions carved out by Accursius, Odofredus, and Azo, the "correct interpretation" of the Roman *lex regia*, Selden declares, must be the alienation theory, a view he reaffirms in his treatise on *Titles of Honour*.[56] One reason for this conclusion concerns his objection to the concession theory defended by those commentators who "try to show that the transferrence or, as they prefer, the sharing of sovereignty was controlled by stipulations, expressed or implied" [*ex pactis ac conditionibus tacitis variatim conantur*].[57] Selden's objection is the objection of an antiquarian: there simply is no evidence of any such contractual arrangement limiting the *princeps*.

But perhaps the most important conclusion in Selden's commentary is that, even if the Roman *lex regia* may no longer command legal validity, the bare principle of popular sovereignty and princely legislative authority expressed in Ulpian's *lex* could certainly be recreated *de novo* variously "by diverse modern laws and customs" [*a legibus moribusque*]. Selden offers the modern example of the *De Capitulatione Caesarea seu Lege Regia Germanorum*, a treatise authored by the Saxon jurist, Benedict Carpzov (1595–1666) which sought the foundations of the Emperor's authority in a German *lex regia*.[58] So too did the French offer a powerful example of a reinvented *lex regia* in Hotman's *Francogallia*, which viewed the French monarchy, despite the rule of male primogeniture enshrined in the Salic Law, as an elective and limited kingship with full sovereignty remaining inalienably in the Francogallic people.[59]

[55] Selden, *Ad Fletam* 39. Cp. Whitman, *Legacy of Roman Law in the German Romantic Era* Ch. 1.

[56] Selden, *Ad Fletam* 39. Cp. John Selden, *Titles of Honour*, 2nd ed. (London: Printed by William Stansby for Richard Whitakers, 1631) 14: "Vlpian...calls that *Lex Regia*, which transferred the peoples power to the Emperor."

[57] Selden, *Ad Fletam* 41.

[58] Michael Randall, *The Gargantuan Polity: On the Individual and the Community in the French Renaissance* (Toronto: University of Toronto Press, 2008) 206.

[59] *Francogallia* 414–15 understands the Roman *lex regia* as a concessive act [*lege Regia populu*[*s*] *Imperatori omne suum imperium et potestatem concessi*[*t*]] and, on this model, interprets Merovingian and Carolingian kingship as a popular *constitutio*.

England was not in any way thought to be insulated from this reincarnation of the *lex regia*. If Germany, France, and other nations governed by kings could have their own *leges regiae*, then so too could England have its own authentic English *lex regia* patterned, at once, on a model of popular sovereignty coupled with princely government. The people of England could have, by an original constitutive act of popular sovereignty, created their kings by a transaction of power, almost as if it were a commercial exchange. Of course, there was no reason to think that the English *lex regia* had to look in any way similar to any other observable historical specimen of popular sovereignty, least of all the Roman *lex regia*.

Selden was not alone in this respect. In their academic study of Roman law, civilians were entirely willing to entertain, at least in principle, the logic of the popular sovereignty argument entailed by the *lex regia* as an abstract matter of constitutional theory. Indeed, when the discussion turned to the *lex regia*, English civilians approached it from a critical distance as an artifact of Roman Antiquity, a vestige of the Roman Empire with no authority over England, but potentially valid over other *gentes* and *populi liberi*. Just as early modern classical scholars could discuss and make sense of, say, Roman religion and sacral rites (as did Albericius Philosophus, Guillaume Du Choul, not to mention Machiavelli), so too, it was thought, could English civilians discuss and try to make sense of the Roman *lex regia*, without compromising their commitment to absolute monarchy.[60] In this respect, the scholarship of the English civilians was not all that different from the legal humanism of Dutch commentators on the *lex regia*. They were simply trying to make sense of an ancient *lex* on its own terms. But in doing so, English readers of Roman law were engaging directly with a substantive question of constitutional doctrine. How should we understand popular sovereignty?

Interpretive debate on the *lex regia* became, in this way, a kind of proxy for substantive disagreement on how best to understand popular sovereignty in a monarchical state. For many of the civilians, it was quite clear that the *lex regia* should properly be understood as an irrevocable alienation of popular sovereignty, as did the civilian Sir Arthur Duck (c.1580–1648) who described the *lex regia* as the device by which powers once held by the people *in Republica libera* were conveyed [*translatum*] irreversibly to the emperors.[61] Richard Zouch similarly declared that "the Roman people transferred all their authority and power [*omne suum imperium & potestatem contulit*] to the *princeps* by the *lex regia*, according to which not only subjects, but even magistrates are subject to him."[62] Even more remarkable was Sir John Hayward's *Reporte of a Discovrse*, which not only traced the origin of the Roman Principate to the Roman people who "by the law of Royalty transferred all their power," but also specified an Erastian twist that the *lex regia* transferred powers "as well as in religious as in

[60] Guy Stroumsa, *A New Science: The Discovery of Religion in the Age of Reason* (Cambridge: Harvard University Press, 2010) 151–2.

[61] Duck, *De Usu* fols. 14–15 [1.3].

[62] Zouch, *Elementa Iurisprudentiae* 101–2 [Part IV, §4].

civill affaires" to Augustus who thereby "annexed the greatest pontificate to the imperiall dignitie," and not simply those rights traditionally identified with civil sovereignty (and a sure sign that he saw Roman imperial authority as a model for English kings).[63] But not everybody accepted this interpretation, for example, the civilian, Isaac Dorislaus insisted in his 1627 lectures at Cambridge on a contractual interpretation of the *lex regia*, stressing the conditionality of princely rule.[64]

These attempts to make sense of the *lex regia* are revealing. They show that English theorists took seriously the notional possibility and structural coherence of popular sovereignty in the English constitution. They certainly did not have to take this stance. They could just as easily have taken the stance of antidemocratic skeptics who condemned popular self-rule as the many-headed monster of anarchy.[65] Even if the civilians were right to say that the Roman *lex regia* of Justinian had no authority whatsoever over England, it still left open the question whether there might, in principle, be some corresponding analogue to the *lex regia*, native to England though functionally equivalent to Ulpian's version. Could there be, in short, an English *lex regia*—some legal act whereby the people of England had "created" or "constituted" the king?

What is most important to stress is that, even though civilians introduce the analysis of this question only to reject it, the popular sovereignty theory of the *lex regia* takes on a life of its own in Stuart constitutional thought, as it is consciously appropriated by theorists who begin to realize during the constitutional crises of the Stuart monarchy that the most effective way to contest the king's sovereignty was not to deny sovereignty altogether, but, rather, to deny it only to the king.

THE ALTERNATIVES TO MONARCHICAL SOVEREIGNTY

Edmund Morgan had once memorably suggested that popular sovereignty had to be "invented" in the anti-monarchical setting of early modern English constitutional politics. It is not especially difficult to see why. If, as anti-monarchical theorists declared, the king was not properly sovereign, the burden by default fell upon those critics to explain just where sovereignty might be located. There needed to be a viable alternative to the civilians' influential notion of an English *princeps* who was *legibus solutus* and empowered by a *lex regia*.

This task became critically important in the tumultuous years leading up to, and during, the English Civil War, where a confluence of radical ideas advocating anti-clericalism, republicanism, and tyrannicide threatened the legitimacy

[63] John Hayward, *A Reporte of a Discovrse Concerning Svpreme Power in Affaires of Religion* (London: Imprinted by F[elix] K[ingston] for Iohn Hardie, 1606) 23–4.

[64] On Dorislaus, see Levack, *Civil Lawyers in England* 104–13, Mellor, "Tacitus, Academic Politics, and Regicide in the Reign of Charles I."

[65] Christopher Hill, "The Many-Headed Monster," *Change and Continuity in Seventeenth-Century England* (Cambridge: Harvard University Press, 1975).

of the king's exclusive right of sovereignty shaped in the civilian mold of the Roman imperial *princeps*.[66] Of course, one possible strategy, especially appealing to common lawyers, was simply to deny that there was even such a thing as sovereignty—popular, monarchical, or otherwise—to be found in the English constitution. Indeed, for writers wary of the doctrine, sovereignty had no place in England, as it did in the kingdoms, principalities, and republics of the Continent. England, on this view, was exceptional and unlike other nations. It was a sovereign state without a visible sovereign. Common lawyers, still clinging to the archaic "cult of the immemorial constitution," articulated this point most forcefully in attempting to explain the status of the common law as evidence of a legal order without a legislator.[67] As Thomas Wentworth would put it, the common "laws [of England] are not acquainted with sovereign power."[68]

Such sovereignty skepticism was, needless to say, an untenable strategy in contesting royal sovereignty. The reality was that sovereignty had already infected English constitutional and legal thought, in no small measure due to the gradual appropriation and application of the civilian analysis of an absolute *princeps* in re-imagining the authority of the English state. The result was an irreversible transformation of English constitutional discourse from one which categorically eschewed sovereignty to one which actively embraced it.

Nor was this embrace, it must be underlined, restricted to royalist partisans. As J.H.M. Salmon once observed, it became strategically advantageous, even "profitable to rationalize the contest for power in terms of sovereigns and sovereignty."[69] The question, for royalists and anti-royalists alike, was not really *whether* there was such a thing as sovereignty within the English state. This was increasingly taken as granted and treated as an axiom of constitutional theory shared across ideological lines. The question instead asked *who* the rightful holder of such sovereignty should be. If it was not to be the monarch, then English sovereignty had to belong to someone—or something—else.

Note the enormous implications of this line of reasoning. It suggested, first of all, that there was no necessary linkage to be found between kingship, as a constitutional form, and sovereignty. Although Bodin and his English royalist disciples regarded England as a pure monarchy, English sovereignty could theoretically be dissociated from monarchy and reconstituted into a strictly

[66] Landmark studies in this vast literature include Jeffrey Collins, *The Allegiance of Thomas Hobbes* (Oxford: Oxford University Press, 2007); Alan Cromartie, *The Constitutionalist Revolution: An Essay on the History of England, 1450–1642* (Cambridge: Cambridge University Press, 2006) Janelle Greenberg, *The Radical Face of the Ancient Constitution: St. Edward's 'Laws' in Early Modern Political Thought* (Cambridge: Cambridge University Press, 2001); Christopher Hill, *Intellectual Origins of the English Revolution* (Oxford: Clarendon Press, 1980); Christopher Hill, *The World Turned Upside Down: Radical Ideas During the English Revolution* (Harmondsworth: Penguin, 1984); Skinner, "John Milton and the Politics of Slavery"; David Wootton, "Leveller Democracy and the Puritan Revolution," *Cambridge History of Political Thought*, ed. J.H. Burns (Cambridge: Cambridge University Press, 1991).

[67] Salmon, *French Religious Wars in English Political Thought* 81.

[68] Speech of Sir Thomas Wentworth in Rushworth, *Historical Collections* 568–9.

[69] Salmon, *French Religious Wars in English Political Thought* 58; cp. 82.

non-monarchical form, so that, despite the outward appearance of a monarchy, the "true" or proper form of the English state might rather be some non-monarchical alternative—a republic, an aristocracy, or, perhaps most radical of all, a popular state, where sovereignty resided in the people or community at large. English sovereignty could therefore be disembodied or de-personalized, so that the bearer of sovereignty might be an impersonal or fictive collective entity, irreducible to any one person.

In this way, opponents of Stuart kingship treated sovereignty as a device essential, rather than antagonistic, to their project of contesting royal authority and radically re-envisioning the form of the English state, or "commonwealth," in some alternative constitutional form.[70] What that alternative should be, however, was less clear and remained open-ended. While anti-monarchical theorists might have been steadfastly united in their rejection of locating—indeed, embodying—sovereignty in one particular person, they were divided on just what the proper bearer of sovereignty in a non-monarchical England ought to be. Some had offered what we might regard as *institution-bound* theories of sovereignty—that is, theories which positioned sovereignty within constituted institutions with defined ordinary powers, jurisdiction, and functions. Others, by contrast, ventured into what we might label *extra-institutional* theories of sovereignty—that is, theories which situated the proper bearer of sovereignty outside existing and observable institutional forms.

As we will now see, both types of theories—institution-bound and extra-institutional—emerged in the voluminous anti-royalist literature in the years immediately preceding, and especially during, the English Civil War. And it is in this context that English popular sovereignty begins to take shape as a distinct theory of the constitutional foundations of the English state.

Those who first systematically and most creatively investigated the possibilities of non-monarchical forms of sovereignty were precisely those who felt increasingly disenfranchised under the Stuart regime of personal and arbitrary rule—that is, the Parliamentarians. With their experience suffering eroded Parliamentary privileges, arbitrary taxation policies, and prevented from assembling for eleven years during Charles' Personal Rule, the radical Parliamentarian writers produced the first institution-bound theories of a non-monarchical English sovereignty, situating sovereignty in what would become known as the Long Parliament—the doctrine of Parliamentary sovereignty.[71]

The classic statement of the doctrine was articulated in 1642 by Henry Parker (1604–52) in his *Observations upon some of his Majesties late Answers and*

[70] This has been typically been treated as a "republican" narrative. But as I suggest, the republican theory, often framed as hostile to the theory of sovereignty, openly exploited it in the anti-royalist effort.

[71] Classic modern statements of the doctrine include A.V. Dicey, *Introduction to the Study of the Law of the Constitution*, 3rd ed. (New York: Macmillan, 1889), Part I; Geoffrey Marshall, *Parliamentary Sovereignty and the Commonwealth* (Oxford: Clarendon Press, 1957). Recent reappraisals of the doctrine, particularly in light of challenges to the doctrine from EU and international law, include Jeffrey Goldsworthy, *The Sovereignty of Parliament: History and Philosophy* (Oxford: Clarendon Press, 2001); Pavlos Eleftheriadis, "Parliamentary Sovereignty and the Constitution," *Canadian Journal of Law and Jurisprudence* 22 (2009).

Expresses.[72] As the title of Parker's work indicates, the *Observations* (or "The Observator" as, Parker notes, it is "stiled at [royalist] Oxford") was crafted as both a reply and as a retrospective account of the official exchange between Crown and Parliament in the constitutional crisis on the eve of the Civil War.[73]

The theoretical issue at stake concerned the constitutional role of the Parliament vis-à-vis the monarchy. Parliament originally summarized its position in the *XIX Propositions*, which were presented to Charles I in June 1642, just weeks after the outbreak of violence at Hull. The *XIX Propositions* marked the beginning of a new official theory of Parliament and its constitutional status in relation to the monarchy. It declared, *inter alia*, that Parliament held a range of powers over royal acts, such as a power over the king's appointments to his Privy Council and of the Great Officers of State, requiring that all such appointments "shall be approved of by both Houses of Parliament," so as to compel the king to accept the public counsel and common consent of Parliament and not simply the private counsel of his ministers.[74] It further required that "all the Judges, and all the officers placed by approbation of both Houses of Parliament, may hold their places *quam diu bene se gesserint* [during good behavior]," intended to target the arbitrary removal of public officials.[75]

It was the Crown's reply to the *XIX Propositions* that provided the occasion for Parker's *Observations*. In *The King's Answer to the XIX Propositions*, issued on 18 June 1642, royal officials—specifically Viscount Falkland and Sir John Culpeper—vigorously denied the parliamentary sovereignty implied by the *XIX Propositions* and left no doubt that Parliament, and particularly the House of Commons, was "never intended for any share in government."[76] Indeed, they even suggested that the inclusion of the lesser estates of Parliament into the act of lawmaking and government would "undoubtedly intoxicate persons who were not born to it."[77]

Perhaps most problematic in the Crown's *Answer* was the theory it invoked to exclude Parliament from asserting sovereignty. Specifically, the *Answer* revived the mixed monarchy doctrine that envisaged the English state "moulded... out of a mixture of these [i.e., monarchy, aristocracy, democracy] as to give to this

[72] Salmon, *French Religious Wars in English Political Thought* 82. The best study on Henry Parker in the recent scholarship is Michael Mendle, *Henry Parker and the English Civil War: The Political Thought of the Public's "Privado"* (Cambridge: Cambridge University Press, 1995). This study updates and reconsiders commentary on Parker found in W.K. Jordan, *Men of Substance: A Study of the Thought of Two English Revolutionaries, Henry Parker and Henry Robinson* (Chicago: University of Chicago Press, 1942); Margaret Atwood Judson, "Henry Parker and the Theory of Parliamentary Sovereignty," Carl Wittke, ed., *Essays in Political Theory in Honor of Charles H. McIlwain* (New York, 1967) 138–67; Robert Zaller, "Henry Parker and the Regiment of True Government," *Proceedings of the American Philosophical Society* 135 (1991).

[73] Henry Parker, *Ius Populi, or A Discourse Wherein Clear Satisfaction Is Given As Well Concerning the Right of Subjects as the Right of Princes* (London, 1644).

[74] Proposition I, III. [75] Proposition XII.

[76] Charles I, "The King's Answer to the XIX Propositions, 18 June 1642," *The Stuart Constitution, 1603–1688*, 2nd ed., ed. J.P. Kenyon (Cambridge: Cambridge University Press, 1986) 19. See also Skinner, "Classical Liberty, Renaissance Translation and the English Civil War" 333.

[77] "King's Answer" 19.

kingdom...the conveniences of all three, without the inconveniences of any one."[78] Instead of declaring an absolute and undivided royal sovereignty over Parliament, the Crown reverted to an older idiom of constitutional thought by declaring that the laws of England were to be "jointly made by a king, by a house of peers, and by a House of Commons chosen by the people."[79]

Reversion to the older pattern of mixed monarchy was, as J.G.A. Pocock and Gordon Schochet put it, the "fatal move" in the royalist defense of the king's absolute sovereignty.[80] It failed to answer the fundamental problem of sovereignty—that is, locating with fixed certainty who actually was the lawmaking sovereign within the state. The *Answer* indicated multiply inconsistent possibilities, and it was this essential ambiguity in the *Answer* which opened the way for Parker to put forth not simply a counterproposal (which *The Observations* was) but, also, a positive theory and statement on the source and structure of English sovereignty.

"Power," Parker writes in the *Observations*, "is originally inherent in the People," and it is only by "the law of common consent" that such power can ever be conveyed and transferred, as if by a contractual transaction, from the people to another party.[81] Unlike all other institutions and offices of government whose share of civil power is derived by grant or concession from some prior source of authority, "the people" holds corporately "an underived majesty," which the people may in principle assume again *in extremis*.[82]

What is particularly innovative and even unsettling, however, is the subversive anti-royalist implication of Parker's view of popular sovereignty:

> Power is but secondary and derivative in Princes, the fountaine and efficient cause is the people, and from hence the inference is just, the King though he be *singulis Major*, yet he is *universis minor*, for if the people be the true efficient cause of power, it is a rule in nature, *quicquid efficit tale, est magis tale*.[83]

Power, on Parker's view, flows from the people to the prince, not the other way around. In crafting this theory, Parker makes no secret of his intellectual debt to the Continental jurists, particularly the Monarchomach principle, *maior singulis minor universis*, which was invoked and glossed earlier in the political argument of both the *Francogallia* and the *Vindiciae*, and later, in Althusius.[84] As it was for the Monarchomachs (and even earlier for Conciliarists and the civilian Glossators), the principle enables Parker to limit and reduce the princely

[78] "King's Answer" 18. [79] "King's Answer" 18.

[80] J.G.A. Pocock and Gordon Schochet, "Interregnum and Restoration," *The Varieties of British Political Thought, 1500–1800*, ed. J.G.A. Pocock (Cambridge: Cambridge University Press, 1996) 149.

[81] Parker, *Observations* 1. [82] Parker, *Observations* 15. Cf. *Observations* 2.

[83] Parker, *Observations* 2, applying an Aristotelian analysis of efficient causes in constitutional theory that was already explored by the German *Reichspublizisten* such as in Besoldus' theory of double sovereignty.

[84] Parker's intellectual debt to Bodin, Arnisaeus, and Grotius is clear in the *Observations*, but he did not explicitly cite his Continental sources until 1644 in the *Ius Populi*. Mendle, *Henry Parker and the English Civil War* 130–2; Salmon, *French Religious Wars in English Political Thought* 82–3; Tuck, *Natural Rights Theories* 146, n.8.

office to certain duties and functions, so that royal power is directed, as he writes, not for his own private benefit, but "meerly for the peoples benefit."[85]

But Parker takes a step beyond the Monarchomach argument and appeals to what he calls "a rule in nature": the doctrine that the cause or creator of something must be greater than the thing caused or created. Applying the general rule to the case at hand, Parker reasons that the people in fact had created the prince and, therefore, precisely because of the people's causal or constitutive role in the constitution of the prince's authority, must consequently be esteemed the greater of the two. Indeed, for Parker, the king "has his perpetuall dependence upon the People" and, for this reason, "cannot be sayd to have so unconditionate and high a proprietie in all our lives, liberties, and possessions."[86] His powers are merely "fiduciarie."[87]

Taken together, then, Parker raises no doubt in the *Observations* about his principled advocacy of popular sovereignty. But what about Parliament? What constitutional status does the Parliament have in this asymmetrical relationship between the prince and the people? More significantly, what is the relationship between the Parliament and the people in Parker's view? Parker's reply to these issues was less clear, though the ambiguity was likely deliberate. He notes that "Parliaments have the same efficient cause as monarchies"—the people—and this is consistent with the *magis tale* doctrine, that the constitutor [the people] must be greater than the constituted [Parliament].

On this point, however, he also adds a puzzling gloss on the doctrine in the case of Parliament: "For in the truth, the whole Kingdom is not so properly the Author as the essence itselfe of Parliaments."[88] In a similar vein, he writes elsewhere that "Parliament is neither one nor few, it is indeed the State it self."[89] And perhaps most revealing, in the *Ius Populi*, "The Parliament is indeed nothing else but the very people it self artificially congregated, or reduced by an orderly election and representation, into such a Senate or proportionable body."[90]

What is puzzling is that Parker equivocates on whether Parliament and the people are really distinct entities or whether they merely signify the same thing, the principal source of sovereignty in the English state. Was Parker's theory of peoplehood institution-bound or extra-institutional? The puzzle at least partially dissolves when we consider what Parker has to say on the powers and functions of Parliament. It is, first of all, the sole organ through which "publicke consent" is activated and expressed.[91] It "regulates" and gives an orderly form to the people, "the rude bulk of the universality," as a proper body politic, obviating the extreme need for irregular popular revolts and mass plebiscitary actions or assemblies.[92] Most important were the ways in which Parliament acts, by a representative fiction, as if it corporately were the people—through acts of judicature and acts of legislation. When Parliament speaks and acts, it is

[85] Parker, *Ius Populi* 1 and also 26; Cp. *Ius Populi* 2.

[86] Parker, *Ius Populi* 18; *Observations* 4.

[87] Parker, *Observations* 20.

[88] Parker, *Observations* 5.

[89] Parker, *Observations* 34.

[90] Parker, *Ius Populi* 18.

[91] Parker, *Observations* 13.

[92] Parker, *Ius Populi* 18.

not as "a meere convention of so many private men," but as the public itself.[93] Thus, when Parliament sits in judgment, it is not simply judgment rendered as a private court of peers, but the public judgment of the whole kingdom, sitting as a High Court with supreme jurisdiction over the realm. Similarly, when Parliament is convoked to give not only counsel [*ad concilium*] but consent [*ad consensum*], it is not simply as a passive assembly to give counsel "in such points as the King pleases to propose," but as the whole kingdom actively declaring law by a sovereign legislative act—with or without royal assent.[94] Parliament, then, just is "the people," and "parliamentary sovereignty" just is "popular sovereignty."

Parker's *Observations* has been interpreted variously as anti-royalist Parliamentarian propaganda, a statement of "bicameral parliamentary absolutism," and as a representative "neo-classical analysis of freedom and free commonwealths."[95] Whatever its functional purpose in the discursive context of civil war, one point that seems reasonably clear is that popular sovereignty appears only as an ill-fitting afterthought in Parker's defense of the Long Parliament, so as to elevate the intellectual credentials of his argument by linking Parliament with earlier theoretical defenses of popular sovereignty such as Buchanan, Brutus, and especially Bodin.

But it was an afterthought with monumental consequences. By locating the source of royal authority in an institutional-bound "people," as represented in Parliament, Parker actually succeeded in dampening the force of his own argument by introducing a critical distraction redirecting the course of English constitutional thought, one that required later commentators to take up explicitly the question of the viability of popular sovereignty in monarchical England.

The first prominent writer to take up Parker's theory of popular sovereignty on the merits as a target of substantive criticism was Dudley Digges (the younger, 1613–43), who wrote two direct responses to Parker, *An Answer to a Printed Booke* (1642) and *A Review of the Observations* (1643).[96] Digges' writings exemplified much of the royalist criticism of Parker on several key points and would model the strategy of royalist argument to become commonplace later in this period. He challenged, first of all, Parker's axiom that all public power was original and "inherent in the people." Recalling the divine right of kings, he insists that the source of all such power is always God, "the immediate donor of Regall power."[97] While Digges acknowledged that, in principle,

[93] Parker, *Observations* 7. [94] Parker, *Observations* 7.

[95] Mendle, *Henry Parker and the English Civil War* 48; Quentin Skinner, "Classical Liberty and the Coming of the English Civil War," *Republicanism: A Shared European Heritage*, Vol. 2, *The Values of Republicanism in Early Modern Europe*, ed. Martin Van Gelderen and Quentin Skinner (Cambridge: Cambridge University Press, 2002) 21.

[96] On Richard Tuck's reading of Digges primarily as a Seldenian Tew Circle natural rights theorist, see *Natural Rights Theories* 101–4.

[97] Dudley Digges, *An Answer to a Printed Book* (Oxford, 1642) 1, 4, and 8.

the people may play a secondary "instrumentall" role limited to the "choosing of one to beare the known Office," the office itself of kingship and of the rights and powers attached to it cannot be of human origin or constitution.[98] Otherwise, as Digges put it, the people would be endowed with an extraordinary "power *constitutive*" which, in effect, would reduce all royal authority to a mere "commissionary authority from the people," as an agent or deputy.[99] If the people *did* have such constitutive power, England would be nothing more than a "meere popular Republique" with sovereignty in "the body at large" like the "common-wealth of the *Venetians*, or of the *Hollanders*," as he thought, an absurd conclusion reducing kings to a "meer *non entia*."[100]

Even if, for argument's sake, the people *did* in fact hold such a "power constitutive," Digges rejected as incoherent and even ridiculous the corollary of popular constitutionalism, encapsulated in Parker's *efficit tale* doctrine. Creating something does not necessarily make one stronger than the thing created, a fallacy he illustrates by a simple example: "One that entreth into [another's] service, because he hath made him his master, shall conclude himselfe the better man, and challenge power over him. For *Quicquid efficit tale, est magis tale*."[101] To show that the royal powers of kings were but "secondary and derivative" effects of some original, anterior popular constitution did not by any means entail that the people were somehow superior to kings: anteriority does not entail superiority. What it shows, instead, is that the people "hath by solemne contract devested it selfe of that power, which was primarily in them."[102] In so doing, the people "emptied itselfe" of its original popular sovereignty and "parted" from it "without possibility of recalling it."[103]

Above all, because it was a voluntary divestiture of the people's original sovereignty, no people or nation could unilaterally "resume that authority... without manifest breach of divine ordinance and violation of publique faith."[104] To "endeavour a recovery" of such divested power would not only be contrary to law, but also to the duty of non-interference one has voluntarily assumed as a legal obligation by that very act of divestiture, just as "when I have given away my money, I cannot challenge it as due... because it would be to the injury of another."[105] To underline this principle, Digges appeals directly to the *Digest* to

[98] Dudley Digges, *A Review of the Observations Upon Some of His Majesties Late Answers and Expresses* (Oxford, 1643) 6. Digges is relying on a Jesuit trope in this distinction. Cp. Höpfl, *Jesuit Political Thought* 225.

[99] Digges, *Review* 4.

[100] Digges, *Review* 8, 20, 17.

[101] Digges, *Answer* 11.

[102] Digges, *Answer* 2.

[103] Digges, *Answer* 11, 12–13. Parker responds to this criticism by identifying cases where one party "invests the grantee without devesting the grantor," as in a property transaction involving "conveyance of lands." Parker, *Ius Populi* 17–18, which appeals to Aristotle's *utrique inesse* in the *Prior Analytics* [1.28: 44b1, 25–37]. Aristotle, *Complete Works of Aristotle*, ed. Jonathan Barnes, 2 Vols. (Princeton: Princeton University Press, 1984) 71.

[104] Digges, *Answer* 2; cp. 9, where valid divestiture is made "out of a probable feare of a harder usage," citing D.4.2.21. Cp. Tuck, *Natural Rights Theories* 104.

[105] Digges, *Answer* 8, 13.

elucidate what he called a "rule grounded on great equity": *Nemo potest mutare consilium suum in alterium injuriam*.[106]

Needless to say, this was, even in this context, an extreme position. One of the most basic principles in the law of obligations was symmetry: any obligation could be "dissolved" in precisely the same manner as it is originally "contracted."[107] Digges, aware of the principle, writes in the *Answer* that, concerning obligations, "it is most agreeable to reason, that the same power should by equall right, abrogate, as it did at first constitute."[108] But he pleads an exception in this special case of popular constitution. Divestiture of sovereignty activates a permanent obligation that can never subsequently be dissolved or abrogated.

Digges' critical reinterpretation of the original popular constitution of kings as an irreversible act of "divestiture" helped frame the anti-populist literature in the legal language of commercial transactions. John Bramhall (1594–1663), for example, the Anglican bishop who would later be known for his debate with Thomas Hobbes on liberty and necessity, writes in *The Serpent Salve* (1643) that the people "divested [them]selves of this [sovereign] power" which cannot be "resume[d] again at [their] pleasures."[109] And like Digges, Bramhall explains why divestiture can be the only sensible way to understand the original act of popular constitution. For otherwise, the king could not be "a true Possessor of Soveraigne Power, but a Keeper onely, as the Roman Dictator or an arbitrary Proctor for the People."[110] On this reasoning, England would be "no more a Monarchy but a Democracy" with only the name and superficial regalia of a king such as "the Prince of *Orange*" or the "old elective Kings of *Aragon*... [and] of *Polonia*."[111]

Probably one of the most intriguing theorists of popular divestiture following this pattern of thought was the Scottish bishop, John Maxwell (d.1647).[112] At first glance, Maxwell's treatise, the *Sacro-Sancta Regum Maiestas*, was "just another straw in the royalist wind."[113] One commentator has even suggested that portions of his text were copied straight out of Barclay's *De Regno*.[114] But that would misestimate the scope and originality of Maxwell's contribution, which attempted to "contextualize" and "sought to situate the new statists and their 'specious generall maximes' within the broadest flow of history," connecting Parker's doctrine of parliamentary sovereignty to medieval theorists such as John of Paris, Marsilius of Padua, William of Ockham, and Jean Gerson.[115]

106 D.50.17.75. 107 D.50.17.35. 108 Digges, *Answer* 12.

109 John Bramhall, *The Serpent Salve* (1643) 14; cp. 22–3.

110 Bramhall, *Serpent Salve* 21. Bramhall is using Bodin's analysis in *République* 1.8.

111 Brahmhall, *Serpent Salve* 18, 21, 23.

112 John Coffey, *Politics, Religion and the British Revolutions: The Mind of Samuel Rutherford* (Cambridge: Cambridge University Press, 2002).

113 Mendle, *Henry Parker* 123–24. 114 Salmon, *French Religious Wars* 91.

115 Mendle, *Henry Parker* 124; cp. John Maxwell, *Sacro-Sancta Regum Maiestas* (Oxford, 1644) 9, 14–15. As Maxwell writes at *Sancro-Sancta* 16, "I have insisted on this especially [so] that you may see that these tenets came not into the world with Luther and Calvin."

Like Digges, Maxwell finds that God, not the people, is the "proper efficient and constituent" source of all public power.[116] To speak otherwise "robbeth God and Christ of his glory."[117] But, supposing the people *did* have such original constituent power, he opined that the people's original "donation" of power necessarily "devests them totally of it," and any subsequent attempt by the people to recover or "resume" that power—"without the tacite or expresse consent" of the king—would be a "breach" of duty, even a sin akin to robbery from the king, the named beneficiary of such divestiture.[118] In this regard, Maxwell likens the popular constitution of princes to nothing more than a simple property transaction such as gift, sale, or any other method of conveyance effecting an "irrepealable" or "irrevocable" divestiture of right, "as when a man maketh over the right of his proper goods to another" such that the donor is "denuded of *ius proprietatis*."[119]

Maxwell's uncompromising insistence on this point about divestiture was designed to ensure that "the King's title [to sovereignty is] complete" and made entirely immune to populist claims, such as Parker's, that "Soveraigne power is habitually retained [i.e., *in habitu*] in the people" and, thus, "resumable" at any time.[120] What this shows for Maxwell is that anything short of a full divestiture could not really be regarded a proper "constitution" of royal authority, since any such constitution "dependeth ever from the liberty and free will of the constituent" [*pendet a voluntate constituentis*].[121] It is merely a precarious tenure, *durante bene placito*, no different from the discretionary terms of a subordinate appointee in the law, such as "a Viceroy or Judge."

To underline this crucial point, Maxwell appeals directly to the Roman law of obligations, where he invokes "a ruled Case in Law, *Nulla obligatio consistere potest, qua a voluntate promittentis statum accipit.*"[122] Maxwell's point, as in Roman law, is that any legal act where the constitutor or donor (whether of property or of sovereignty) is regarded as both "*giving a right, yet retaining it*" [*dans & retinens*], such as a lease, is an incomplete act precisely because it is revocable at will.[123]

Most remarkable of all, however, is Maxwell's application of this analysis on divestiture and constitution to the Roman *lex regia* as a model of sovereignty for all peoples and nations. The transfer of authority from the Roman people to the emperor is properly to be understood, according to Maxwell, not only as a constitutive act of the Roman people under its "Democraticall government,"

[116] Maxwell, *Sacro-Sancta* 81.

[117] Maxwell, *Sacro-Sancta* 112–3.

[118] Maxwell, *Sacro-Sancta* 131; 18.

[119] Maxwell, *Sacro-Sancta* 99.

[120] Maxwell, *Sacro-Sancta* 113; cp. 18, where the illegal act of "resuming" powers which have been divested is said to risk "disabling sovereignty" entirely and "loosen the sinewes of all society." Cp. Parker, *Observations* 15: "The people may resume its owne power to do itselfe right." Cp. Baldus on *in habitu* at p. 76.

[121] Maxwell, *Sacro-Sancta* 98.

[122] Maxwell, *Sacro-Sancta* 98, without citation, quotes D.45.1.108.1.

[123] Maxwell, *Sacro-Sancta* 131: "the donation devests them totally of it... except the King have it by way of loane, which to my thinking never any yet spoke."

but as a full and irrevocable divestiture to the *princeps*, so that no residual power remains, *in habitu*, in the Roman people:

> Jurists . . . did not imagine that the people transferring all their right upon the Prince, did habitually [i.e., *in habitu*] or in any case retaine it or any part of it, that in case of male-administration, they might supply, and in any exigent resume it . . . they [emperors] were totally and irrevocably invested with all power conceivable to be in the people.[124]

No less a civilian authority than Bartolus is invoked to underline this notion of divestiture in the *lex regia*: "Bartolus knew that not any power was reserved in any case or exigent to the people."[125] Maxwell extracts from this a general principle, which can apply even in an English *lex regia*: the people already gave up whatever powers they may have once had.

This strict royalist interpretation, viewing constitution as divestiture of popular sovereignty, no doubt anticipated the revival of the argument once made by the Monarchomach jurists that the people always reserve certain key rights, even while they legally constitute civil authorities such as kings and magistrates to exercise sovereignty on their behalf. One theorist to resuscitate this argument was the Scottish Churchman, Samuel Rutherford (c.1600–1661), who crafted a popular sovereignty theory in his *Lex, Rex* (1644) as a direct reply to Maxwell. Like his interlocutors, Rutherford begins with the thesis of popular sovereignty which locates the constitutive "power of Government . . . that is, of the power of making Governours and Kings" to be in "the community" as a whole.[126] Such power, Rutherford specifies, is entirely "free, voluntary, and active" and entitles a sovereign nation to a "perfect liberty to choose" their form of government, "either a *Monarchy* or a *Democracy*, or an *Aristocracy*."[127] What Rutherford does not allow however is divestiture: "No Communitie, without sin, hath power to alienate and give away this power."[128] The people are always presumed to "*reteine* . . . [*in*] *habitu*" their original sovereignty, not only in a democracy but even in a monarchical state where kings govern.[129]

So too did English Levellers, often regarded as exemplars of radical democratic populism in the Civil War period, insist on an interpretation of popular sovereignty that did not degenerate into simple divestiture or alienation, but reserved to "all people and all nations . . . liberty and power to alter and change their constitutions" at will.[130] This point became particularly important in legitimating their (failed) attempts to petition an increasingly recalcitrant

[124] Maxwell, *Sacro-Sancta* 100, citing D.1.4.1, though notably omitting Inst.1.2.6. Cp. p. 76.

[125] Maxwell, *Sacro-Sancta* 100, citing Bartolus on D.49.15.24, §4.

[126] Samuel Rutherford, *Lex, Rex* (London: Iohn Field, 1644) 50.

[127] Rutherford, *Lex, Rex* 50–01.

[128] Rutherford, *Lex, Rex* 59.

[129] Rutherford, *Lex, Rex* 59.

[130] John Clarke, "Extract from the Debates at the General Council of the Army, Putney" [1647], *The English Levellers*, ed. Andrew Sharp (Cambridge: Cambridge University Press, 1998) 128. On the Levellers as constitutional theorists, see Martin Loughlin, "The Constitutional Thought of the Levellers," *Current Legal Problems* 60 (2007). See also Rachel Foxley, *The Levellers: Radical Political Thought in the English Revolution* (Manchester: Manchester University Press, 2013).

Parliament to enact political and legal reforms. Sovereignty, Robert Overton and William Walwyn (two principal leaders of the Leveller movement) reminded their readers, belonged no more to kings than to members of Parliament, who were but mere "commissioners" and "agents" exercising a "betrusted" and "ever revocable" power. Rather, sovereignty always belongs to the "universality" of "freeborn people."[131] This is because the popular constitution of public authority is always by a "deputation" or "commission," understood to be held and exercised *ad bene placitum*, precisely what Maxwell had earlier denied.[132]

Most remarkably, even English republican theorists of this period, who are typically seen as hostile to the theory of sovereignty, viewing it as antithetical to liberty, and instead interested in the institutional design of republican government, nevertheless embraced popular sovereignty by implication: sovereignty occupied the core of the theoretical foundation of the republican vision of a commonwealth. There is perhaps no better representative of this implicit popular sovereignty at work than the English poet and republican polemicist, John Milton, writing as the official voice of the Commonwealth in defense of Regicide and of the constitutional change from monarchy to republic as a sovereign act of the English people. "The power of kings and magistrates," Milton explains, "is nothing else but what is only derivative, transferr'd, and committed to them in trust from the People... in whom the power yet remains fundamentally."[133] In Milton's view, then, no act of popular constitution can be a divestiture, as Digges, Maxwell, and other royalists maintain. The people hold it in reserve and can reactivate it at their collective pleasure.[134]

In consequence, kings are not so much "Lords and Masters" but mere "Deputies and Commissioners" with "intrusted power."[135] Tethered to the people's will in this way, kings as well as magistrates are seen to occupy precisely that grey area royalists sought to eliminate. Milton borrows from a classic Monarchomach line of argument framed in the language of Roman private law when he declares that a king should properly be understood as a "usufructuary" rather than as a *dominus*. Elsewhere, he says that kings have mere "possession," "use," and "enjoyment" of royal power, while the people collectively retain the right of "ownership," the *dominium*, in sovereignty.[136] In this

[131] Robert Overton with William Walwyn, "A Remonstrance of Many Thousand Citizens" [1646], and "An Agreement of the People" [1647], *The English Levellers*, ed. Andrew Sharp (Cambridge: Cambridge University Press, 1998) 33, 34, 95.

[132] Robert Overton, "An Arrow Against All Tyrants and Tyranny" [1646], *The English Levellers*, ed. Andrew Sharp (Cambridge: Cambridge University Press, 1998) 55, 56.

[133] John Milton, "Tenure of Kings and Magistrates," *Political Writings*, ed. Martin Dzelzainis (Cambridge: Cambridge University Press, 1991) 10.

[134] Cp. Algernon Sidney, *Discourses Concerning Government*, ed. Thomas West (Indianapolis: Liberty Fund, 1990) 21 [1,§6].

[135] Milton, *Tenure of Kings and Magistrates* 9.

[136] Milton, *Tenure of Kings and Magistrates* 11; *Pro Populo Anglicano* in Milton, *Political Writings* 180–81; 185. Milton cites the French legal humanist, Jacques-Auguste de Thou [*Thuanus*], *Historiarum Sui Temporais*

way, royal or magisterial authority should be seen as a "bond or covenant," even a "stipulation," attached to strict terms and conditions for use, violation of which would instantly allow "the people [to] be disingag'd" or released from their obligation to the king, just as "any void bargain or treaty."[137]

For Milton, this analysis was not exclusive to English monarchy, but something like a universal pattern to be observed in all states, whether governed by kings or magistrates. To illustrate this point, Milton—like his royalist contemporaries—turns once again to Rome as the classical model of a state governed, at various points in its history, by both kings and magistrates, while sovereignty remained with the Roman people as *dominus*. Whether during the Republic (when Rome was governed by magistrates constituted by *lex imperii*) or during the Principate (when Rome was governed by *principes* constituted by *lex regia*), the people always retained their sovereignty. This suggests that no legal act constituting Roman public authorities—least of all, the *lex regia*—could be a true divestiture of popular sovereignty in the way that royalists preferred to read the Roman sources.[138]

Milton's reading postulates instead a continuity of popular sovereignty throughout Roman constitutional history before and even after the Roman people's *lex regia* authorizing princely rule. Whatever powers the Roman people conferred upon the Republican magistrates prior to the *lex regia* had to be just the same powers given to the *princeps* after the *lex regia*.[139] This is Milton's strategy in reducing Roman emperors to the modest "tenure" of magistrates. There could be no fundamental difference of "tenure" between emperors and magistrates, since they all hold their powers of the people.

In view of these diverse appeals to popular sovereignty, it is critical to stress why popular sovereignty became so ubiquitous and unavoidable in the English Civil War period, such that royalists, republicans, and radicals alike could not afford to ignore the *lex regia* theory of the people as the anterior source of public authority. One way or another, all partisans had to confront it and, indeed, even welcomed it, and that is because popular sovereignty, postulating a primordial democracy from which all constitutional forms were subsequently derived, functioned as a "decontested" shared axiom in Stuart constitutional theory which could be exploited to promote divergent ideological ends and visions of political order.[140]

(Geneva, 1620) 3:186 in his common-place book to show that the king is the usufructuary, not the *dominus*, of the kingdom. Dzelzainis' note 41 at Milton, *Tenure of Kings and Magistrates* 11.

[137] Milton, *Tenure of Kings and Magistrates* 9–10, 25; *Pro Populo* 190.

[138] Milton, *Pro Populo* 180–81 only cites the concessive grant interpretation of Inst.1.2.6, but not Ulpian's account in D.1.4.1 cited by royalists.

[139] Milton, *Pro Populo* 184. Sidney makes a similar point at *Discourses* 70 [1,§20]. Cp. Ando, "Origins and Import of Republican Constitutionalism" 34.

[140] On "decontestation" of (essentially) contestable concepts, see Michael Freeden, *Ideologies and Political Theory: A Conceptual Approach* (Oxford: Oxford University Press, 1998) 76–7.

(RE)INVENTING THE PEOPLE

In these theoretical explorations of popular sovereignty, the background working assumption suggested that "the people" was a clearly identifiable party or entity, capable of holding and asserting sovereign rights and of binding itself under a legal obligation, such as a contract, bond, or stipulation of some type. But the theory also presented a different, and potentially more serious, problem that demanded special attention. Who, or what, actually was "the people" invoked in these theories of popular sovereignty? Who was included, and perhaps more important, who was excluded? Are peoples defined by shared ancestry, language, customs, or perhaps by some other criterion?

The ambiguities and difficulties attendant upon the definition of peoplehood are, of course, notorious in political theory and remain perhaps the central problem in contemporary democratic theory—the so-called "boundary problem."[141] In the case of early modern England, there were multiple dimensions to this boundary problem of peoplehood. One difficulty was that peoplehood in early modern English social thought was so often defined conventionally in terms of rigid class differences, such that "the people" signified, not so much a numerical aggregate of individuals in a given geographical territory, but instead the "commons," the "commonaltie," or the "common folk," corresponding to what Romans once designated the *plebs* or *vulgus*.[142] A similar pattern might also be observed in the ecclesiastical polity of the Anglican Church, which stressed the formal divide between the laity and the ordained priesthood or clergy, constituted not only to perform sacral rites and govern the Church body, but also to be represented by their "lords spiritual" as one of the principal estates of the realm.[143]

[141] Arash Abizadeh, "On the Demos and Its Kin: Nationalism, Democracy, and the Boundary Problem," *American Political Science Review* 106 (2012): 867–82; Robert Dahl, *After the Revolution? Authority in a Good Society* (New Haven: Yale University Press, 1970); Robert Dahl, *Democracy and Its Critics* (New Haven: Yale University Press, 1989); Paulina Ochoa Espejo, "People, Territory, and Legitimacy in Democratic States," *American Journal of Political Science* 58 (2014): 466–78; Robert Goodin, "Enfranchising All Affected Interests, and Its Alternatives," *Philosophy and Public Affairs* 25 (2007): 40–68; Sophia Näström, "The Legitimacy of the People," *Political Theory* 35 (2007): 624–58; David Owen, "Constituting the Polity, Constituting the Demos," *Ethics and Global Politics* 5 (2012): 129–52; Rogers Smith, *Stories of Peoplehood: The Politics and Morals of Political Membership* (Cambridge: Cambridge University Press, 2003); Sarah Song, "The Boundary Problem in Democratic Theory: Why the Demos Should Be Bounded By the State," *International Theory* 4 (2012); Marco Verschoor, "The Democratic Boundary Problem and Social Contract Theory," *European Journal of Political Theory* (online version 2015); Frederick Whelan, "Democratic Theory and the Boundary Problem," *Nomos 25: Liberal Democracy*, ed. J.Roland Pennock and John Chapman (New York: New York University Press, 1983).

[142] Robert Cawdrey's *A Table Alphabeticall* defines "communaltie" as "common people, or common-wealth." Robert Cawdrey, *The First English Dictionary, 1604: Robert Cawdrey's A Table Alphabeticall* (Oxford: Bodleian Library, 2007) 64. For a criticism of this forced similitude, see Robert Filmer, "The Free-Holders Grand Inquest," *Patriarcha and Other Writings*, ed. Johann Sommerville (Cambridge: Cambridge University Press, 1991) 115–16; cp. George Lawson, *Politica Sacra et Civilis*, ed. Conal Condren (Cambridge: Cambridge University Press, 1992) 23–4 [Ch.2, §§3–4]. On the phrase, *quas vulgus elegerit*, see Weston and Greenberg, *Subjects and Sovereigns* 79–80, concerning the king's "negative voice" in parliamentary legislation.

[143] The rubrics of the 1549 *Book of Common Prayer* rely on a strict division between "Clearkes" and "Priests," on the one hand, and "the People" on the other.

What essentially defined "the people" in these various corresponding models was their disenfranchised position, measured especially in terms of social and political exclusion. Exclusion from the offices, dignities, and titles of the governing elite defined the boundaries of peoplehood as a disempowered, passive, anonymous, subaltern mass. One implication of this analysis was that, by definition, not everybody could be included in this capacious category of "the people." Just as peoplehood was defined by exclusion, so too was the category of peoplehood itself exclusive. Peoplehood, in this specifically class-designated way, which pitted the many against the few, functioned as a partisan and even potentially agonistic category, characterized by an essentially anti-elitist, anti-establishment predisposition which viewed with suspicion institutional elites and hierarchies of all sorts—nobility, clergy, judiciary, and, of course, royalty—as foreign (indeed, "Norman") impositions upon an authentically native, popular—above all, English—identity.

What is most striking is that even the House of Commons itself—a body ostensibly assembled to represent the whole "commonaltie" or "universality" of the people, as Parker postulated—became, in this formulation, an object of suspicion as an anti-populist tool of elite manipulation and exclusion. Indeed, that is precisely how populist Puritan critics of the Long Parliament and Presbyterian policies, such as the Leveller, Robert Overton, saw Parliament: a "degenerate representative body" unworthy of "the people's trust," and necessitating an "appeal... over the heads of members of Parliament directly to the sovereign people."[144] On this view, popular sovereignty was understood to be a deliberately divisive and anti-establishment doctrine formulated not only to police the mutating boundaries defining peoplehood, but also to contest any political order that questions their supremacy. Attributing sovereignty to "the people" was indeed the battle cry of the disenfranchised to eliminate the inauthentic, foreign source of their shared disenfranchisement.

That populist battle cry, however, necessitated a wholesale revision of peoplehood, one that radicalized the concept from a passive condition to an active one, whereby the people acquired what, in the modern social sciences, is generally labeled *agency*—that is, the capacity to act independently and to make choices freely in unison as an identifiable singular agent. In this way, by attributing a collective agency to people, popular sovereignty suddenly became something more than simply the rhetorical trope of opposition or resistance of a disenfranchised class to an existing institutional order. It became, by itself, the foundation for a viable, though radically populist, constitutional norm.

There is, of course, nothing new or unique about the idea of popular agency. Classical Greek writers, for example, were fully accustomed to speaking of the

[144] Loughlin, "Constitutional Thought of the Levellers" 10, citing Overton, "An Appeal from the Degenerate Representative Body, the Commons of England Assembled at Westminster, to the Body Represented, the Free People in General" [1647], *Leveller Manifestoes of the Puritan Revolution*, ed. Don Wolfe (New York: T. Nelson and Sons, 1944) 163.

demos as an agent with a collective will, free to act as one unit.[145] So too were medieval jurists, such as Baldus, drawing on the law of corporations, prepared to assign agency to the people in a free *civitas*.[146] Even a political theorist such as Machiavelli emerges, in one recent influential reading, as a champion of a "ferocious populism" empowering the *popolo* as a single actor with both institutional and extra-institutional tools to monitor and control political elites.[147] What was novel for the English writers here was the growing recognition of the discontinuity between two distinctive concepts of peoplehood which began to come into clearer relief in English social thought—one which explicitly acknowledged the agency of peoplehood, the other which denied it.

I need to stress this point. Too often popular sovereignty is thought of as a uniform concept, signifying a single phenomenon—sometimes in contrast to monarchical or royal sovereignty, other times in contrast to what commentators have, without sufficient precision in my view, termed "state sovereignty."[148] What we find instead is that invocations of "the people" and their sovereignty masked deep conceptual instabilities in the populist rhetoric of early modern England, yielding at least two further, broadly inconsistent, ways of envisioning popular sovereignty—one based on a non-agential conception of peoplehood, the other based on an agential conception.

Let us explore each of these conceptions in turn. Suppose, on the one hand, that "the people" have no agency, but, instead, should be understood as a passive, anonymous mass or multitude of individuals, as scattered and disconnected atoms. As such, it cannot *do* anything or claim responsibility over any action, let alone exercise sovereignty directly. This non-agential conception of peoplehood became especially attractive to critics of popular sovereignty, for whom the word, "people," designated nothing more than an uncoordinated, formless multitude, a mass, a crowd, a throng, a heap, even a mob, incapable of any organized, let alone rational, collective action.[149] One writer could not see the notion of the people as anything other than a "gross heape," a "heavy dull body," even a "monster."[150] To speak of popular rule was, for such critics, to speak of no rule at all. It was, as Dudley Digges put it, "meere Chaos."[151]

[145] For example, Josiah Ober, *Mass and Elite in Democratic Athens: Rhetoric, Ideology, and the Power of the People* (Princeton: Princeton University Press, 1989).

[146] On Baldus' treatment of the *populus*, see Canning, "Corporation in the Political Thought of the Italian Jurists of the Thirteenth and Fourteenth Centuries" 10–14. See Chapter 2.

[147] John McCormick, *Machiavellian Democracy* (Cambridge: Cambridge University Press, 2011); McCormick, *Machiavellian Democracy* 297–313.

[148] See, for example, Chapter 2 of Noontens, *Popular Sovereignty in the West*, which tries to position "popular sovereignty" against "ruler sovereignty" and "state sovereignty." Cp. with the example of Hegel who was able to detect the subtle connections between state sovereignty and popular sovereignty, in *Philosophy of Right* §279.

[149] On the problem of inconsistency in collection action, see Philip Pettit's treatment of the discursive dilemma, "Deliberative Democracy and the Discursive Dilemma," *Philosophical Issues* 11 (2001): 268–99.

[150] Morgan, *Inventing the People* 75–76, citing William Sedgwick.

[151] Digges, *Review* 9.

But denying popular *agency* to the masses at large was not the same as denying popular *interest*, and even the boldest critics of popular sovereignty were minimally willing to acknowledge that the people may nevertheless have common interests, even though they may lack (as critics thought) a common—indeed, a general—will. That was, in fact, central to their argument for monarchical government, which, they argued, can better serve popular interests than democratic or republican government. Often the point is made, in early modern thought, with reference to the Roman law metaphor of tutorial guardianship over a pupil (that is, an underage *paterfamilias*) that just as a pupil or minor cannot legally act or do anything except through his legally constituted tutors or curators, neither can the people, act or do anything, except through those appointed to govern them.[152]

This subtle shift of focus to popular "interest" is significant, in several ways. It tacitly reconceptualizes the people, not so much as an agent or actor, but rather, as a passive, even helpless, *beneficiary*. Lacking agency, the people cannot act. But others can, in ways that potentially accrue to the people's collective benefit. In this way, satisfaction of the people's interests provides, in principle, a metric to measure political legitimacy, by assessing (as one theorist has put it) whether an existing political order "tracks" the people's "common avowable interests."[153]

Here is the interpretive puzzle. How could such a non-agential, interest-based, conception of peoplehood as the passive beneficiary of others' actions ever be regarded as popular sovereignty? Some might deny it outright. But it is worth stressing that some have tried to carve out a notion of popular sovereignty even in this interest-based, non-agential conception of peoplehood. The trick is to consider not so much the ideal case, where interests are satisfied and properly "tracked," but rather the non-ideal case, where interests fail to be so. In this respect, non-agential "popular sovereignty" simply denotes that corrective remedy, activated in the margins to reform or recalibrate the political order so that public institutions are made, once again, to track in congruence with the people's interests.

Popular sovereignty, on this non-agential conception, figures as a reactive, even extraordinary or radical, if momentary, act of opposition, resistance, or contestation, disrupting an otherwise self-regulating, interest-tracking device. The crucial point is that, in these non-agential models, popular sovereignty translates into not so much an act performed *by* the people (after all, the people have no capacity to do anything), but instead, an act performed *for* the people, by some popular champion or even "invigilator"—whether that champion happens to be a tribune, a demarch, an ephor, or a protector.

152 *Leviathan* 2:248-9 [Ch.16, ¶10].

153 Philip Pettit, *A Theory of Freedom: From the Psychology to the Politics of Agency* (Oxford: Oxford University Press, 2001) 159.

This non-agential popular sovereignty is to be contrasted with agential popular sovereignty, where "the people" is more than a passive beneficiary, but instead, understood explicitly to be an agent, acting in its own (sovereign) right. But here, a different problem now emerges in this agential model, chief of which was a Parmenidean puzzle. How can the many become one and act as one unit? One solution, of course, might be some scheme of representation; another might be some plebiscitary scheme involving majoritarian voting. But whatever scheme or decision-making rule is adopted to solve this puzzle, the lingering worry is that agential popular sovereignty cannot truly be "popular," and that is because devices used to generate collective agency will ultimately have an exclusionary, anti-populist effect. Popular sovereignty, on this criticism, becomes really nothing more than the *de facto* sovereignty of unstable democratic majorities or, in the case of representation, an insulated oligarchy of representative agents or proxies—Parliament, Council, Army, Protector, or some other body claiming not only to speak and act for the people, but even more, to *be* the people.

This is, incidentally, a worry most often associated with modern defenses of democracy, perhaps most famously in Rousseau's formulation of the general will in *The Social Contract*, which voices a deep-seated suspicion of schemes endowing a people with agency. And it has shaped generations of modern democratic theorists who, following Rousseau's lead, have insisted that genuine popular sovereignty must be understood to be, at some basic level, a direct, unmediated, even "plebiscitary" or—as one commentator has recently put it—"plenary" democracy.[154]

But, as I now want to show, such a demanding, impossibly idealistic, interpretation of agential popular sovereignty was originally articulated not by the doctrine's defenders as an archetype to be approximated, but rather, by its sworn enemies, who introduced it really as a debating point, an *argumentum ad absurdum*, to pour scorn on the very idea of the whole people acting in unison as one sovereign entity, *legibus solutus*, formed by a convergence of individual wills. What modern democracy, thus, takes as a regulative ideal to be imitated began really as an anti-populist exercise designed to show the folly of agential popular sovereignty, when taken to its logical conclusion.

The one English theorist who exemplifies this cynically "democratic" turn was Robert Filmer (1588–1653). Remembered chiefly as the foil for John Locke's *First Treatise of Government* for his patriarchical theory of government, Filmer is perhaps the first to offer a systematic, though critical, analysis of agential peoplehood, which he is able to do precisely because he observes, with the sharpest clarity, the inescapably semantic ambiguity of peoplehood. In this way, I argue that we can view Filmer as a theorist of a radically democratic

[154] Jeffrey Green, *The Eyes of the People: Democracy in an Age of Spectatorship* (Oxford: Oxford University Press, 2009) Ch. 4; Philip Pettit, *On the People's Terms: A Republican Theory and Model of Democracy* (Cambridge: Cambridge University Press, 2012) Ch. 4.

understanding of popular sovereignty, not because he endorses it, but precisely because of his critical distance from it.

Filmer's point of entry was via a critical examination of Philip Hunton's *A Treatise of Monarchie* (1643), a moderate work in the early years of the Civil War, which was once described as carving out a middle ground between Parker's theory of parliamentary sovereignty and the absolute monarchy of the royalists by advocating a "mixed" or "limited" monarchy of the sort suggested in the *King's Answer to the XIX Propositions*.[155] Filmer, however, summarily dismisses Hunton's theory, which he felt was nothing more than a recipe for anarchy, a sentiment signaled in the title of his formal reply to Hunton, *The Anarchy of a Limited or Mixed Monarchy* (1648).

One of the key features of Hunton's *Treatise* was his analysis of the popular origins of kingship, both in general and in the specific case of the English monarchy.[156] Hunton explains that "originally Power is in the People," and it is only by a "publick Fundamental Oath, Contract and Agreement" that such popular sovereignty is "conveyed"—or even "devested," as the case may be—to princes.[157] In theory, the people may do this by a collective act of self-binding, by imposing upon its collective self the bond of obligation to a newly constituted monarch by the people's voluntary surrender of its sovereign rights.

Filmer raises his objection here. What exactly is this collective self called "the people"? Filmer's approach in the *Anarchy* is deliberate and careful. He observes the semantic instability of the word, "people," noting that "this, as many other words hath different accept[at]ions, being sometimes taken in a larger, other whiles in a stricter sense."[158] In one sense, the people might signify "the whole multitude of mankind, but figuratively and synecdochecally" it might otherwise signify "the major part of a multitude, or sometimes the better or the richer, or the wiser," and even particular nations, "Regions or Countries."[159] Filmer's point was that there was no one right way to define and think about peoplehood, let alone popular sovereignty. It functions instead as, what might be called, an "essentially contested concept," yielding multiply inconsistent interpretations of popular sovereignty.[160]

Filmer's refusal to indicate a normatively proper way to conceptualize peoplehood is crucial for his broader critique of popular sovereignty. The semantic indeterminacy allows him to argue two critical points simultaneously: (a) that popular sovereignty is practically infeasible, and (b) that what most commentators think is popular sovereignty is not truly "popular" at all, but instead,

155 Nigel Smith, *Literature and Revolution in England, 1640–1660* (New Haven: Yale University Press, 1994) 98.

156 In the English case, Hunton argues that it was a free pre-Conquest people of England, a *populus liber.*

157 Philip Hunton, *A Treatise of Monarchie* [1643] (London: E. Smith, 1689) 3, 13.

158 Robert Filmer, *Anarchy of a Limited or Mixed Monarchy* ([London], 1648) 8. Cp. Sommerville's edition of the text in *Patriarcha and Other Writings* 140.

159 Filmer, *Anarchy* 8–9.

160 W.B. Gallie, "Essentially Contested Concepts," *Proceedings of the Aristotelian Society* 56 (1956): 167–98.

some form of oligarchy which, in effect, excludes broad sectors of the population from enjoying sovereignty.[161] His argument for the first point relies on a strictly aggregative conception of peoplehood, so that the will or judgment of a "people" requires the consent of each individual member of the popular body to be counted. His criticism, in effect, becomes a practical one. It is unreasonable to expect every individual to participate in every sovereign act of the people since there will always be absences: "One man is sick, another is lame, a third is aged."[162] Even more problematic for Filmer is the discontinuity of popular agency over time entailed by his strict agential conception: "Mankind is like the sea, ever ebbing or flowing, every minute one is borne, another dies, those that are the people this minute, are not the people the next minute, in every instant and point of time there is a variation."[163]

Given the practical impossibility of ever gathering the whole people as a plenary sovereign assembly, Filmer turns instead to consider devices to assign agency, by some fiction, through representative or majoritarian voting, as second-best alternatives to a universal direct democracy. Remarkably, his criticism strikes a familiar Rousseauian tone. Any such device can never be truly popular (and therefore legitimate) because its net effect is fundamentally exclusionary. What may seem to be an act of popular sovereignty really is nothing more than a partial act of a sovereign majority (in principle, even an oligarchy, or some powerful individual).

Filmer's principal worry is the position of the losing minority in such a voting situation. Why should such an excluded minority ever feel bound to comply and identify with the decision of a sovereign majority? His answer is stunning, but entirely consistent: they shouldn't. Indeed, no amount of casuistry can hide the ugly fact that dissenting minorities, by definition, have not consented. They are bound, in a "most unjust" fashion, to the majority against their will.[164]

What becomes clear is that the underlying principle of agential popular sovereignty for Filmer can be none other than unanimous consent. Anything short of unanimity cannot properly be agential popular sovereignty precisely because of its exclusionary effect. This is especially problematic in any majoritarian decision-making procedure, in which a decision carried by a majority is understood to represent a decision of the whole. So that there is no doubt, Filmer insists that, if there is even one lone dissenter in a voting situation, it cannot properly be an act of the whole, but merely that of a super-majority.[165] He illustrates this point in a *lex-regia*-type situation:

> If it were lawfull for particular parts of the world by consent to chuse their Kings, neverthelesse, their elections would bind none to subjection but only such as consented; for the *major part* never binds, but where men at first either agree to be so bound, or, where a higher power so commands.[166]

[161] Robert Filmer, *Observations upon Aristotles Politiques Touching Forms of Government* (London, 1652) 3.

[162] Filmer, *Anarchy* 10.

[163] Filmer, *Anarchy* 10; cp. *Observations* 23.

[164] Filmer, *Anarchy* 10.

[165] Filmer, *Observations upon Aristotles Politiques* 22.

[166] Filmer, *Anarchy* 9.

So, there is, for Filmer, a basic conceptual fallacy in imagining a majority to stand for a whole people, unless, by some prior act, all participants in the voting situation have explicitly agreed to such a decision rule in advance. Filmer's point is that we cannot simply assume *ex ante* the validity or rationality of majority rule; the rule itself has to be validated by everyone to be subjected to it.

Given this, Filmer unmasks the façade of popular sovereignty in England, targeting first the application of the *lex regia* theory that suggests that the people of England had independently created or elected their kings. It is not the "whole people" or even the "major part" of the nation assembled in "any *collective* or *representative* body" that participates in the constitution and election of a king, but merely an oligarchy of "the Nobility...[or] Great men" that make such choices.[167] The upshot is that, since most individuals are excluded from that action, it can hardly be called a sovereign act of the whole people: "The people taken in what notion, or sense soever, either *diffusively, collectively*, or *representatively*, have not, nor cannot exercise any right or power of their own by nature either in chusing or in regulating Kings."[168] In the same vein, Filmer attacks the populist suggestion that the House of Commons should be seen not only as representing the people, but as the people itself. As he points out, the Commons, insofar as they are a representative body, "onely represent a part of the lower or inferior part of the body of the People which are Freeholders worth 40s. by the year, and the Commons or Free-men of Cities and Burroughs, or the *major part* of them."[169] Again, his worry is not about concerns of proportionality or such, but exclusion. How can the Commons claim to represent the people when so many are excluded and disenfranchised—that is, the "*vulgus*, the *vulgar*, the *rude multitude* (which hath the Epethite of *ignobile vulgus*)...*common people*?"[170]

Filmer's critical analysis of peoplehood, however, takes on greatest significance when he considers the Roman Republic as the archetypal early modern constitutional model of popular sovereignty. For Filmer, Rome was "never truly popular."[171] Despite the "greatest shew of popularity," Rome was fundamentally anti-populist in character, for several reasons. One concerned simply the extraordinary scope of authority held by magistrates, especially the consuls, whose "Kingly powers," insulated from the vicissitudes of popular politics, made Rome, even before the *lex regia*, "an apparent kinde of *Monarchy*."[172] So too did dictatorships, though sanctioned by popular legislation, provide "the royallest evidence" that Rome was by no means a popular state but a state ruled under "an absolute King."[173] Even lesser magistrates, such as the "Pretors

[167] Filmer, *Anarchy* 11. [168] Filmer, *Anarchy* 14.

[169] Filmer, *Anarchy* 14. The 1647 *Agreement of the People*, at §1, explicitly envisages "the people of England" as an electorate "indifferently proportioned according to the number of inhabitants...[of] counties, cities and boroughs."

[170] Robert Filmer, *The Free-Holders Grand Inquest Touching Our Soveraigne Lord the King and His Parliament* (London, 1648) 46; cp. Sommerville's edition in *Patriarcha and Other Writings* 115–16.

[171] Filmer, *Observations* 22. [172] Filmer, *Observations* 20. [173] Filmer, *Observations* 20.

and Censors...did in many things exercise an arbitrary or legislative power" removed from popular consent.[174]

More important to Filmer's criticism, however, were the major plenary assemblies of the *populus Romanus*, the *comitia*, which effectively excluded large swaths of the Roman populace, free and slave, from having any part, let alone a "major part," to play in Roman politics, an observation supported by the Roman legal category of disenfranchised citizenship, *civitas sine suffragio*.[175] Filmer sharpens his point with a discussion about Roman voting procedure in popular assemblies. Instead of voting by head, "the true popular way," votes are cast by collegial units, such as *centuria* and *curia*, always with the wealthiest orders entitled to cast their votes first.[176] In no way can such bodies claim to be popular sovereigns, even "if but one man be excluded."[177]

Most remarkable in Filmer's extensive critical discussion of Roman popular sovereignty, however, is his target: Bodin. Filmer is commonly thought to be an uncritical English disciple of Bodin in applying the theory of monarchical sovereignty to the English context. But here, he explicitly singles out Bodin as the preeminent theorist of agential popular sovereignty, which he sees in the controversial interpretation of the Roman Republic as *status reipublicae popularis*. Bodin, Filmer argues, relies on a crude majoritarianism that reduces the sovereign *populus* to the will of a bare majority of voting tribes or units.[178] In doing so, it is Bodin who commits the error of mistaking part of the people for the whole, reinforcing Filmer's thesis that, in popular states, it is never the whole people who take part in the exercise of sovereignty. Someone, it seems, must always be excluded from sovereignty.

THE AMBIGUITIES OF POPULAR SOVEREIGNTY: HOBBESIAN PEOPLEHOOD

For the various critics and defenders of popular sovereignty during the Civil War period, there was no obvious reason why these contrasting conceptions of peoplehood should have to be joined together in one unified theory. As Filmer's critique had shown, it was much more profitable and strategically advantageous to reinforce these semantic differences because it exposed the supposed incoherence of popular sovereignty as a foundational constitutional doctrine. This does not mean, however, that English theorists did not try in earnest to synthesize a unified theory of popular sovereignty, one which acknowledged the dual identity of the people both as *singuli* and as *universi*. By far the most important was the political philosopher, Thomas Hobbes, and it is with Hobbes, clearly the most important English heir to the theory of popular sovereignty standardized by Bodin, that I want to close this chapter.

174 Filmer, *Observations* 33.

175 Filmer, *Observations* 24.

176 Filmer, *Observations* 25–6.

177 Filmer, *Observations* 22.

178 Filmer's discussion at *Observations* 22 suggests he had *Commonweale* [2.7] in mind.

At first glance, it might appear that "popular sovereignty" exemplifies what Hobbes derided as "absurd" or "insignificant" speech, as meaningless as "incorporeal substance."[179] How could the "people," an ambiguous notion, possibly be the unambiguous bearer of an indivisible sovereignty?[180] Like his contemporaries, Hobbes recognized that the problem of peoplehood was inescapably semantic, as he would famously observe early in his own investigation of the concept of the people. Indeed, the "grammatically singular" word, "people," as Hobbes observed first in *De Corpore Politico* (1640) and would later reexamine in *De Cive* (1642), "hath a double signification."[181] It could mean, on the one hand, nothing more than simply "a Number of Men" or "disorganized crowd [*multitudo*], to which no *action* or *right* may be attributed."[182] But, as Hobbes also observed, the "people" could mean something more than simply an "aggregate" or "multitude" of individual wills; it could signify a unity in its own right, a "Person Civil" [*persona civilis*] as Hobbes would put it in *De Corpore Politico,* "in the Will whereof, is included and involved the Will of every one in particular."[183] The people, so represented as such a "person," could in principle have a singular unitary will, with the agency required to act independently just as any private person, since "it is endowed with a will, and can therefore perform voluntary actions, such as command, make laws, acquire and transfer a right."[184]

Given the discrepancy in meaning, it was Hobbes who insisted, so as to eliminate any hint of inconsistency or equivocation in his civil science, that "a distinction must...be made" between two conceptions of peoplehood:

> Whenever we say that a People or a number [of men] is willing, commanding or doing something, we mean a commonwealth [*civitas*] which is commanding, willing and acting through the will of one man or through the wills of several men who are in agreement...But whenever something is said to be done by a number of men, great or small, without the will of that man or meeting, it means that it was done by a people as subjects, that is by many individual citizens.[185]

One counts as a sovereign act of state, the other a disorganized, chaotic tumult of a multitude of men. The distinction was critically important, above all, in

[179] *Leviathan* 2:60 [4, ¶21].

[180] On the indivisibility of sovereignty, Hobbes cites "*Bodin*, lib.2. cap.1.*De Repub.*" in *De Corpore Politico* 167 [II,8,§7].

[181] *De Corpore Politico* 86 [II,2,§11]; *De Cive* 76 [6,§1].

[182] *De Corpore Politico* 86–7 [2,§11]; *De Cive* 94 [7,§5].

[183] *De Corpore Politico* 87 [2,§11]. The *persona civilis* is what Hobbes calls the *civitas*, "commonwealth" or state at *De Cive* 73 [5,§9]. But here he links that term to the "people," in a way that he generally does not in *Leviathan*, indicating that there is an important equivalence in Hobbes' system of thought between "commonwealth" (*civitas*) = "people". One exception is at *Leviathan* 2:440, where Hobbes refers to the *lex regia* but chooses to render "people" in the Latin with *civitas*.

[184] *De Cive* 76–7 [6,§1].

[185] *De Cive* 77 [6,§1]. Hobbes singles out the common failure to make a "clear enough distinction between a *people* and a *crowd*" as "detrimental" to civil peace, *De Cive* 137 [12,§8].

voicing Hobbes' own skepticism on the English adoption of Monarchomach resistance theories, most especially in Parker's controversial dictum that "the King though he be *singulis Major*, yet he is *universis minor*."[186] Hobbes' worry concerns Parker's use of the term, *universus* to indicate the people represented in Parliament. Since the king is, on Parker's theory, "subordinate" to the whole people, the people may at their pleasure, as a valid act of popular sovereignty, resist and remove their king.

But "the speech," Hobbes writes, "is absurd."[187] The people cannot act as one unit, or "one person," unless there is prior universal agreement, or covenant, or some rule or convention so to do, whereby actions of a sovereign representative, whether of a prince or even an "Assembly of the people" [*Coetus Popularis*], are understood by all to stand for everyone else.[188] For this reason, Hobbes makes the startling proclamation that, in a monarchy like England, only "the *King* is the *people*," just as, in a democracy like Athens, only the *demos* is the people.[189] Because of this, it is an abuse of speech to say, that in "some great rebellion [against a sovereign prince] the *people* of the commonwealth has taken up arms . . . it is only true of those [individuals] who have actually taken up arms or are in league with them."[190]

One of Hobbes' great theoretical achievements, among his many, was his insistence on establishing a connection between these two, seemingly disparate, ways of thinking about peoplehood, producing what might be regarded as a grand unified theory of peoplehood. In this respect, it is entirely proper to treat Hobbes as the preeminent English theorist of popular sovereignty, but only if we are willing to see the "people," as Hobbes required, represented as a kind of "person"—specifically, the "person civil" described in *De Corpore Politico* and *De Cive*.[191] In this way, the sovereignty of the people, for Hobbes, is equivalent to the sovereignty of the "person civil"—that is, the *civitas* or state.[192]

To make sense of this equivalence, consider first "*Soveraignty*" [*Is qui summam habet Potestatem*] itself, what Hobbes called the "Artificiall *Soul*" of the commonwealth.[193] Sovereignty, Hobbes suggests, is unnatural. It can only be activated and exercised artificially through some form of representation, as Hobbes explains in one of the most reverberant passages of his masterwork, *Leviathan*:

> A Multitude of men, are made *One* Person, when they are by one man, or one Person, Represented . . . For it is the *Unity* of the Representer, not the *Unity* of

[186] Parker, *Observations* 2.
[187] *Leviathan* 2:280 [18, ¶18].

[188] *Leviathan* 2:280, 281 [18, ¶18].
[189] *De Cive* 137 [12,§8]; *De Corpore Politico* 79 [II,2,§2].

[190] *De Cive* 76 [6,§1]; cp. *De Corpore Politico* 87–8 [II,2,§11].

[191] *Leviathan* refers to the *persona civitatis* at 2:414 [26, ¶2].

[192] On the technical meaning of representation by fiction in Hobbes' theory of personality, see Quentin Skinner, "Hobbes and the Purely Artificial Person of the State," *Visions of Politics*, Vol. 3, *Hobbes and Civil Science* (Cambridge: Cambridge University Press, 2002); David Runciman, "What Kind of Person is Hobbes's State? A Reply to Quentin Skinner," *Journal of Political Philosophy* 8 (2000): 268–78.

[193] *Leviathan* 2:16, 17 [*Introduction*].

> the Represented, that maketh the Person *One*. And it is the Representer that beareth the Person.[194]

Hobbes specifies that a commonwealth is just such an artificial person, and the one who "carryeth this Person, is called SOVERAIGNE," through whose words and actions are represented the words and actions of each individual citizen of that commonwealth.[195] It is this sovereign actor—whether a monarch, a council of state, or a democratic assembly of citizens—which enables a multitude of unconnected individuals to be united to become just as if they were an agent, one person with one united will—a *civitas*, a state, country, a commonwealth, a people.

Hobbes famously calls this representation, but the representation involved here is not so much mimetic, but actively imaginative as in drama and liturgy, involving "man's natural power to form representations through…imagination and artifice," so that even a formless multitude can be recognized as one person.[196] It is the device by which something that does not naturally have a will or a voice (a multitude) can be seen as having one (a commonwealth).[197] Once the agency—or indeed—"personality" of the people has been established in this way, it becomes possible for Hobbes to treat popular sovereignty as an intelligible and precise, if pedantic, doctrine concerning the sovereignty of independent states. All states, whatever their form of government, always adhere by implication to the principle of popular sovereignty at some fundamental level, and that is because all sovereign states, *civitates*, are complex bodies—"bodies politic"—composed of a multitude of citizens.[198] They are, at once, the one and the many.

Whether Hobbesian popular sovereignty should be understood as a *democratic* theory, however, remains unsettled. It is a question that has recently generated considerable scholarly attention.[199] But the answer really depends on what counts as "democratic" or "democraticall" and whether we are willing

[194] *Leviathan* 2:248 [16, ¶13].

[195] *Leviathan* 2:262 [17, ¶14]; cp. *De Cive* 73 [5,§9], which specifies that "commonwealth" is a species of the genus "civil person," other species of which include "companies of merchants" and other corporations and "associations" subordinate to the commonwealth.

[196] Mónica Brito Vieira, *Elements of Representation* (Leiden: Brill, 2009) 5.

[197] *Leviathan* 2:248, 249 [16, ¶9]. Hobbes employs civil law analogies such as guardianship to elucidate this form of representation. See Daniel Lee, "Hobbes and the Civil Law: The Use of Roman Law in Hobbes's Civil Science," *Hobbes and the Law*, ed. David Dyzenhaus and Thomas Poole (Cambridge: Cambridge University Press, 2012) 223–7.

[198] In rendering the state or "commonwealth" by the Latin *civitas*, Hobbes is actively exploiting the equivocal double-meaning of *civitas* for both "city" and "citizen-body."

[199] Most notably, Richard Tuck, "Hobbes and Democracy" and Kinch Hoekstra, "A Lion in the House: Hobbes and Democracy," *Rethinking the Foundations of Modern Political Thought*, ed. Annabel Brett, James Tully, Holly Hamilton-Bleakley (Cambridge: Cambridge University Press, 2006); Murray Forsyth, "Thomas Hobbes and the Constituent Power of the People," *Political Studies* 29 (1981): 191–203. I am grateful to Richard Tuck for sharing an early version of the manuscript for his chapter on Hobbes in the forthcoming published version of his Seeley Lectures, *The Sleeping Sovereign: The Invention of Modern Democracy* (Cambridge: Cambridge University Press, forthcoming 2016).

to entertain any meaningful analytical distinction between *democratic* government, on the one hand, and *popular* sovereignty, on the other. I think there definitely is, and Hobbes elucidates this distinction when he shows how a sovereign people, a *civitas*, can govern itself either democratically or undemocratically.

What makes a Hobbesian democracy essentially different from a monarchy is in the constitutional choice a sovereign people makes concerning how its sovereignty is to be exercised—that is, in how it chooses to represent and govern itself. Of course, a people can, if it so chooses, authorize its sovereignty to be exercised through demonstrably undemocratic forms—even through the will of one man, a monarch, who is authorized to bear the civil personality of the people as a *civitas*. But as Hobbes also consistently argues in tones reminiscent of Bodin, such sovereignty can just as validly be exercised through the collective democratic will of "many men," determined by voting in a sovereign plenary assembly, variously rendered by Hobbes as *concilium, coetus popularis, populus*, or *demos*, acting just as a monarch does in a monarchy, in the exclusively sovereign capacity representing the whole *civitas*.

But Hobbesian democracies, unlike monarchies, are exceptional in one key respect: They involve two distinct entities, both asserting, at once, competing claims to be "the people":

(1) The people as *civitas* or *respublica* signifying the commonwealth or body politic of all citizens united together as one absolute and independent civil person;
(2) The people as *concilium, coetus, populus*, or *demos*, signifying the assembly of many men representing, through their collective actions, the civil personality of the *civitas*, (1).[200]

It is far too easy and common, Hobbes thinks, to confuse (1) and (2) with each other, or even to conflate them in ordinary speech. In most cases, it is proper to keep them distinct.

But he does admit that there is at least one special case where there is a perfect identity and no need for any fiction of representation, and that is when the first *civitas* was founded in human history: "When men have met to erect a commonwealth, they are, almost by the very fact [*paene eo ipso*] that they have met, a Democracy."[201] This primitive or "original" *civitas* is perhaps direct democracy in the purest and most literal possible sense. It is "an assembly of all the citizens [*concilium omnium civium*] so that each of them has the right to vote and can participate in debating issues if he so wishes."[202] Based on this, Hobbes

[200] Thus, Hobbes himself relies on a crucial equivocation of meaning on peoplehood even in his own analysis of democracy. But the equivocation begins to dissolve when we investigate the classical vocabulary to specify the different concepts of peoplehood and statehood.

[201] *De Cive* 94 [7,§5]; *De Cive* 1647: 124. The "almost" [*paene*] is crucial: Hobbes does not actually want to admit that all states begin as democracies.

[202] *De Cive* 91 [7,§1]; *De Cive* 1647: 119.

suggests, most clearly in *De Corpore* and *De Cive*, that democracy must be, by implication, the ultimate "origin" of the first state.[203]

This does not mean, of course, that states remain democratic forever, much less that Hobbes favors democracy. On the contrary, Hobbes' purpose, throughout his major theoretical texts, is to show how transitory, fragile, even inconvenient and dangerous democracy really is as a stable form of government, simply by pointing to its many practical procedural difficulties.[204] As a practical measure, then, "the *People* must devolve [*concedant*] at least the exercise of sovereign power [*usum summi imperii*] on some *one* man or *one* assembly [*alicui homini uni, vel concilio uni*]" temporarily. For these reasons, democratic government turns out to be a sham. Most people very rarely get to govern except indirectly.

Because of these inevitably oligarchical tendencies, genuine democratic government can never last and almost always transforms into a *de facto*—if not also *de iure*—aristocracy or monarchy.[205] But this does not necessarily mean the people therefore lose their sovereignty, for two separate reasons. One is a technical Bodinian point about sovereignty that Hobbes has apparently adopted. The people may simply loan the use of sovereignty temporarily to government agents. Referencing a familiar argument modeled on the Roman law of property, Hobbes explains that it is perfectly compatible for "*sovereign power* [*summum imperium*] (like *Ownership* [*dominium*]) [to] remain with the people [*in populo*], [even while] only its *use* or *exercise* [*usus*... *sive exercitium*] was enjoyed" by government agents who wield authority "as a *usufructuary*" [*ut usufructuario*].[206] Adopting a critical distinction from humanist civil lawyers such as Alciato and Donellus, Hobbes insisted on distinguishing between the *right* of sovereignty [*summi imperii ius*] and its *exercise* [*exercitium*], which he illustrates in precisely the same manner as Bodin and, to some extent, Grotius.[207] Like Bodin, Hobbes viewed the Roman Republican constitution as illustrating popular sovereignty, though coupled with undemocratic forms of "Administration" where the exercise of sovereignty was ordinarily delegated to the Senate, a "Counsel Aristocratical."[208] But mere administration, use, or exercise of sovereignty does not compromise the people's sovereignty because

[203] *De Cive* 91 [7,§1]; cp. *De Corpore Politico* 77–78, 81 [II,2,§1, §6]. *Leviathan* 2:264 noticably omits this sequence beginning with democracy, but traces of the original democracy remain in ¶¶1–2 of Ch. 18, where Hobbes enumerates the rights of sovereignty "conferred by the consent of the People assembled."

[204] *De Cive* 94 [7,§5].

[205] Hoekstra, "A Lion in the House" 203; Kinch Hoekstra, "The *De Facto* Turn in Hobbes' Political Philosophy," *Leviathan After 350 Years*, ed. Tom Sorell, Luc Foisneau (Oxford: Oxford University Press, 2004).

[206] *De Cive* 98–9 [7,§16]; *De Cive* 1647: 135–36; cp. *De Corpore Politico* 80 [II,2,§5]. *De Cive* 99, *De Cive* (1647) 137 refers to *populus* as *dominus civium*.

[207] *De Cive* 142, 143 [13,§1]; *De Cive* 1647: 213, 214. Hobbes invokes the distinction of D.2.1.5 between powers held and exercised *proprio* and *alieno iure*.

[208] *De Corpore Politico* 73 [II,1,§17].

they "can, if it shall see fit, deprive [officers] of [their] office [*administratio*]."[209] That is precisely why the Roman dictator who "had for a time the exercise of the whole Soveraignty" was nothing more than a "minister of the people."[210]

There is however another reason why, for Hobbes, popular sovereignty remains permanently fixed, even in the extreme undemocratic Hobbesian case where a people decide to transfer [*tradere*] away not simply the exercise or use of sovereignty, but even its full right of sovereignty [*ius suum... summum imperium*] unconditionally [*simpliciter*] to an absolute monarch.[211] That is because even under an absolute monarch, like the Roman *princeps* or the King of England, the people remain, "personated" as a *civitas*, in the actions of the *princeps*. So represented, it is this people-*civitas* to which the official acts of a *princeps* or king are to be attributed, and, as Hobbes suggests elsewhere, it is this civil body of the *civitas* who, like a *dominus* in civil law, is to be identified as the true legal "Owner," of acts performed by its personator or agent, whether that happens to be a monarch or not.[212]

While Hobbes, and his many modern commentators, have rightfully stressed the unity, personality, and sovereignty of the *civitas*, as an "absolute and independent" person, we need to remember that the *civitas* remains, at the same time, a citizen-body, a people assembled.[213] Sovereignty belongs as much, and even more, to them as it does to their representative. By linking statehood, peoplehood, and the *civitas* altogether in this way, Hobbes has established an equivalence of profound importance between two concepts that far too often are treated as separate in modern theoretical treatments of sovereignty: "popular" sovereignty and "state" sovereignty. It is by this equivalence that popular sovereignty takes on a new importance. It is no longer just one among many competing interpretations of sovereignty; it has become, instead, the only proper way to understand sovereignty.

209 *De Corpore Politico* 73 [II,1,§17]; *De Cive* 99 [7,§16]. 210 *De Cive* 99 [7,§16].

211 *De Cive* 1647: 128 [7,§11]; 133 [7,§15].

212 *Leviathan* 2:244 [16, ¶4]; cp. *De Cive* 73 equating *summa potestas, summum imperium*, with *dominium*.

213 *Leviathan* 2:348 [22, ¶2].

Conclusion

This book was conceived with four broad aims in mind. In this conclusion, I would like to review those aims in brief. The first aim, generally, has been to show the supreme importance of Roman law and the civilian tradition in reconstructing the intellectual history of sovereignty. Sovereignty, as a concept central to the modern understanding of statehood, simply could not have taken the shape that it did without the analytical precision that the *ius civile* historically provided for the concept's most important theorists. In this study, we have seen how Roman law concepts such as *imperium* and *iurisdictio, dominium* and possession, usufructs and servitudes, personality and agency, legal guardianship, and obligations generated by sale, lease, and mandate supplied early modern constitutional theorists with the tools to articulate some of the chief features of modern sovereignty, such as its absolute quality, its indivisibility, its perpetuity, and its immunity from the operation of ordinary law.

A second, more specific aim of this book has been to show how Roman law was exploited to craft what many theorists, such as Hotman, Brutus, Althusius, and Grotius, regarded as the only proper way to understand the operation of sovereignty in a state, that is, as popular sovereignty. In part, the civil law itself promoted this interpretive proclivity, especially among medieval jurists, with the example of the Roman *lex regia* referenced in the texts of the *Corpus Iuris Civilis*. Roman constitutional history helped to make popular sovereignty something like a basic constitutional theorem of state in all its forms, a notion that partisans of democracy and monarchy alike could, in principle, both share.

It was this ideological versatility of popular sovereignty that allowed its incorporation into very different theoretical traditions. We investigated, for example, the radical Monarchomach theorists, for whom the need for a doctrine of popular sovereignty was driven by a principled opposition to monarchy and expressed as part of a broader political effort to legitimize acts of resistance. But we also investigated, at the same time, theorists such as Bodin and Hobbes who, despite rejecting the legitimacy of resistance, nevertheless recognized and accepted the inner coherence of popular sovereignty as a foundational doctrine explaining the derivative nature of the state's authority.

In this respect, it is indeed remarkable that popular sovereignty can be seen to move along such opposing ideological trajectories. Some modern commentators, observing this ideologically Janus-faced nature of popular sovereignty, have preferred to speak of the doctrine as radically open-ended and incomplete. But what I hope the book has successfully demonstrated is that it is entirely unnecessary to view popular sovereignty strictly in terms of ideological trajectories. In a sense, the higher-order function of popular sovereignty might be said to be pre-ideological or even anti-ideological. Its purpose, in the minds of its theorists, was to serve a different end, as a decontested, standard *constitutive* theory of authority by giving a uniform account of those conditions that make possible a conceptual space for the ideological conflicts that animate politics.

Demonstrating this function of popular sovereignty as a constitutive theory of political authority was the third major aim of this book. In highlighting this constitutive function, I feel there are two points particularly worth emphasizing. The first is the use of Roman law, especially areas of private law such as property and obligations, in explaining not only what it meant legally to "create" or "constitute" a subordinate authority, as sovereignty theorists often did when they spoke of the people's public power to "constitute a magistrate" [*magistratum constituere*] or any government agent, but in also explaining the subsequent balance of rights and obligations in any popular act of constitution. In this respect, the detailed treatment and expropriation of the Roman law of jurisdiction by theorists of popular sovereignty played an especially critical role in providing a model to explain how a sovereign people can, just like a Roman magistrate with authority held *suo iure*, delegate or entrust its sovereignty to an agent. The second is a historical point. What is often termed the people's "constituent" or "constitutive" power, as a power distinct from the "constituted" power of government organs and agencies, is typically thought to be a modern innovation, originating especially in the French Revolution. But what I hope the book has shown is that the idea of the people's constitutive power has a long pre-history, stretching many centuries before Sieyès would ever ask the question, "What is the Third Estate?" While this book has not attempted to explore this pre-history in detail, it has, at least, given sufficient cause to warrant a renewed investigation into the origins of constitive power in medieval and early modern civilian legal thought.

But perhaps the most important and, in my view, the most difficult aim of the book concerns the concept of the people itself. One of the background themes running throughout these chapters has been the contrast between popular sovereignty and democracy. Very often, the two are treated as if they are synonymous. But one imperative that I think emerges clearly, especially in the juridical analysis of popular sovereignty, is the need to separate the two notions, particularly since a people may, if it so chooses under the doctrine of sovereignty, freely bind itself under undemocratic institutional forms. To be blunt, popular sovereignty has nothing essentially to do with democracy. This general lesson, as we have seen, was most often illustrated by the example of the Roman Republican constitution. Even though the sovereign Roman people may have exercised their sovereignty by constituting magistrates and, extraordinarily, appointing dictators, they nevertheless retained their sovereignty, in the same way that a landlord retains ownership in property that is temporarily leased to a tenant. The point might be generalized as a doctrine concerning the fundamental constitutional of all sovereign states, whatever their form of government.

Popular sovereignty, thus, takes on a certain priority, essential to all states, whatever their accidental and contingent features. Whether democratic or autocratic, monarchical or republican, liberal or authoritarian, Marxist or fascist, all states are constituted as a people or, as some of our authors have preferred to call it, as a body politic, a political community, a commonwealth. We are left, however, with an important question, which concerns the fourth and final broad aim of the book. Who is "the people" that is to be regarded "sovereign"? The theorists examined in this book have given us no shortage of possible images of peoplehood—as helpless pupils in need of tutorial guidance, as fictive corporations with a unitary will and agency, even as a vulgar and furious multitude that needs to be tamed. What unites the various interpretations of popular sovereignty in this book as part of one tradition of constitutional thought is an unshakable belief that the people, however scornfully they may be described, nevertheless all remain bearers of unassailable rights which always remain active and actionable not only against each other, but also against their government, whatever its form.

It is, in my view, this notion of sovereign peoples as collective bearers of rights that deserves to be recovered and revitalized. Peoples, just as much as individual persons, have rights to self-determination, to govern themselves as they please, to determine their collective destinies, political or otherwise. This principle takes on special resonance in the state-centric world which emerged at the beginning of the seventeenth century with the rise of Westphalian statehood and the emergence of an international legal order governing its constitutive parts, sovereign nations and free peoples, *gentes* and *liberi populi*. In this context, popular sovereignty becomes the standard starting point among theorists of state, public law, and international law as diverse as Locke, Vattel, Pufendorf, Rousseau, and Kant.

But as this Westphalian order of self-determining sovereign peoples now begins to decay in our own day, there is an immediate urgency in reminding ourselves of the demands that popular sovereignty makes, demands which often seem to be at odds with competing ambitions, such as the noble aspiration for global justice. Every people has the right to determine how it is to be governed, and no one else—whether a foreign power, a prince, a court, a faction, a party, an elite, even the "international community"—has any contrary right sufficient to override or intervene upon this fundamental indefeasible sovereign right of free peoples. Whether we should still be willing to meet that demand is a question that I am not entitled to answer, but I hope this book has succeeded at least in showing ways that the fulfillment of such demand can be more than a form of organized hypocrisy, as has been suggested, but rather, a goal worthy to be realized in its own right.

Bibliography

Roman law sources

Codex Iustinianus. Ed. Paul Krueger. Berlin: Weidmann, 1954.

Codicis. Ed. Denis Godefroy. Lyon, 1604.

Digesta Iustiniani. Ed. Theodor Mommsen and Paul Krueger. Berlin: Weidmann, 1870.

The Digest of Justinian. 4 Vols. Trans. Alan Watson. Philadelphia: University of Pennsylvania Press, 1985.

Digestum Novum seu Pandectarum Iuris Civilis. Ed. Denis Godefroy. Lyon, 1604.

Digestum Vetus seu Pandectarum Iuris Civilis. Ed Denis Godefroy. Lyon, 1604.

Infortiatum seu Pandectarum Iuris Civilis. Ed. Denis Godefroy. Lyon, 1604.

The Institutes of Gaius. Ed. Francis de Zulueta. Oxford: Clarendon Press, 1953.

The Institutes of Justinian. Ed. J.B. Moyle. Oxford: Oxford University Press, 1913.

Institutionum sive Primorum Totius Iurisprudentiae Elementorum. Ed. Denis Godefroy. Lyon, 1604.

The Twelve Tables. In *Ancient Roman Statutes*. Ed. Allan Chester Johnson et al. Austin: University of Texas Press, 1961.

Volumen Legum Parvum. Ed. Denis Godefroy. Lyon, 1604.

Sources

Abizadeh, Arash. "On the Demos and Its Kin: Nationalism, Democracy, and the Boundary Problem." *American Political Science Review* 106 (2012): 867–82.

Ackerman, Bruce. *We the People*. 2 Vols. Cambridge: Belknap Press of Harvard University, 1993.

"An Agreement of the People" [1647]. In *The English Levellers*. Ed. Andrew Sharp. Cambridge: Cambridge University Press, 1998.

Alciato, Andrea. *Commentaria in Digesta seu Pandectas Iuris Civilis*. In *Opera Omnia*. 4 Vols. Basel: Thomas Guarinus, 1582.

Allen, J.W. *A History of Political Thought in the Sixteenth Century*. 2nd ed. London: Methuen, 1941.

Althusius, Johannes. *Politica Methodice Digesta*. Ed. Carl Friedrich. Cambridge: Harvard University Press, 1932.

Althusius, Johannes. *Politics of Johannes Althusius*. Trans. Frederick Carney. Indianapolis: Liberty Fund, 1995.

Amar, Akhil. "Consent of the Governed: Constitutional Amendment Outside Article V." *Columbia Law Review* 94 (1994): 457–508.

Anderson, Perry. *Lineages of the Absolutist State*. London: Verso, 1979.

Ando, Clifford. "A Dwelling Beyond Violence: On the Uses and Disadvantages of History for Contemporary Republicans." *History of Political Thought* 31 (2010): 183–220.

Ando, Clifford. "From Republic to Empire." In *The Oxford Handbook of Social Relations in the Roman World*. Ed. Michael Peachin. Oxford: Oxford University Press, 2011.

Ando, Clifford. *Law, Language, and Empire in the Roman Tradition*. Philadelphia: University of Pennsylvania Press, 2011.

Ando, Clifford. "The Origins and Import of Republican Constitutionalism." *Cardozo Law Review* 34 (2013): 917–35.

Aristotle. *The Complete Works of Aristotle*. 2 Vols. Ed. Jonathan Barnes. Princeton: Princeton University Press, 1984.

Armstrong, E. "The Political Theory of the Huguenots." *English Historical Review* 9 (1889): 13–40.

Arnisaeus, Henning. *De Iure Maiestatis Libri Tres*. Frankfurt, 1610.

Arnisaeus, Henning. *De Autoritate Principum in Populum Semper Inviolabili*. Frankfurt, 1612.

Arnisaeus, Henning. *Doctrina Politica*. Amsterdam, 1651.

Arumäus, Dominicus. *Discursus Academici de Iure Publico*. 3 Vols. Jena, 1620.

Azo [Azo Portius]. *Summa Azonis*. Lyon, 1557. [Reprinted Frankfurt am Main, 1968]

Azo [Azo Portius]. *Summa Azonis, Locuples Iuris Civilis Thesaurus*. Venice, 1566.

Azo [Azo Portius]. *Lectura Azonis et Magni Apparatus ad Singulas Leges Duodecim Librorum Codicis Iustiniani*. Paris, 1581.

Bacon, Francis. "Maxims on Law." In *The Works of Francis Bacon in Ten Volumes*. Vol. 4. London: J. Johnson, 1803.

Bacon, Francis. "A View of the Differences in Question Betwixt the King's Bench and the Council in the Marches." In *The Letters and the Life of Francis Bacon*. Vol. 3. London: Longmans, Green, Reader, and Dyer, 1868.

Badouin, François. *De Institutione Historiae Universae et Eius Cum Iurisprudentia Coniunctione Prologomena Libri II*. Paris, 1561.

Bakos, Adrianna. *Images of Kingship in Early Modern France: Louis XI in Political Thought, 1560-1789*. London: Routledge, 1997.

Baldus de Ubaldis. *Commentaria*. 9 Vols. Venice, 1577.

Barber, Nick. *The Constitutional State*. Oxford: Oxford University Press, 2011.

Barclay, William. *De Regno et Regali Potestate Adversus Buchananum, Brutum, Boucherium, et Reliquos Monarchomachos, Libri Sex*. Paris: Chavdiere, 1600.

Baricave, Jean de. *La Defense de la Monarchie*. Toulouse, 1614.

Barker, Ernest. "The Authorship of the *Vindiciae Contra Tyrannos*." *Cambridge Historical Journal* 3 (1930): 164–81.

Baron, Eguinaire. *De Ratione Dicendi Discendique Iuris Civilis ad Studiosam Legum Inventutem Commonefactio.* 1546.

Baron, Hans. *Crisis of the Early Italian Renaissance: Civic Humanism and Republican Liberty in an Age of Classicism and Tyranny.* Princeton: Princeton University Press, 1955.

Bartolus of Sassoferrato. *Commentaria cum Adnotationibus Thomae Diplovatii.* Ed. Baptista de Tortiis. Venice, 1506. [Facsimile reprint Ed. G. Polara, Rome 1996]

Bartolus of Sassoferrato. *Opera Quae Extant Opera.* 10 Vols. Venice, 1590.

Bartolus of Sassoferrato. *De Regimine Civitatis.* In *Politica d Diritto nel Trecento Italiano.* Ed. Diego Quaglioni. Florence: Leo S. Olschki Editore, 1983.

Bayle, Pierre. *Dictionnaire Historique et Critique.* Rotterdam, 1720.

Bebenburg, Lupold von. *De Iuribus et Translatione Imperii.* Strasbourg, 1508.

Bebenburg, Lupold von. *Tractatus de Iuribus Regni et Imperii Romanorum.* Strasbourg, 1624.

Bellamy, Richard. *Political Constitutionalism: A Republican Defence of the Constitutionality of Democracy.* Cambridge: Cambridge University Press, 2007.

Bellomo, Manlio. *Common Legal Past of Europe, 1000–1800.* Trans. Lydia Cochrane. Washington: Catholic University of America Press, 1995.

Berckringer, Daniel. *Institutiones Politicae sive de Republica.* Utrecht, 1662.

Berman, Harold. *Law and Revolution: The Formation of the Western Legal Tradition.* Cambridge: Harvard University Press, 1983.

Bertrachini, Giovanni. *Repertorium Iuris Utriusque.* Nürnberg, c.1483.

Besold, Christopher. *Dissertatio Politica-Iuridica, de Maiestate in Genere.* Tübingen, 1625.

Bickel, Alexander. *The Least Dangerous Branch: The Supreme Court at the Bar of Politics.* New Haven: Yale University Press, 1986.

Bickerton, Christopher, et al., ed. *Politics without Sovereignty: A Critique of International Relations.* London: UCL Press, 2007.

Birks, Peter. "The Roman Law Concept of *Dominium* and the Idea of Absolute Ownership." *Acta Juridica* 1 (1985): 1–37.

Black, Antony. *Monarchy and Community: Political Ideas in the Later Conciliar Controversy, 1430–1450.* Cambridge: Cambridge University Press, 1970.

Blackwood, Adam. *Adversus Georgii Buchanani Dialogus, De Iure Regni Apud Scotos, Pro Regibus Apologia.* Paris: A. Sittart, 1588.

Blair, Ann. "Authorial Strategies in Jean Bodin." In *The Reception of Bodin.* Ed. Howell Lloyd. Leiden: Brill, 2013.

Blair, Ann. *Too Much to Know: Managing Scholarly Information Before the Modern Age.* New Haven: Yale University Press, 2010.

Blank, Andreas. "Johannes Felden on Usucaption, Justice, and the Society of States." *Journal of the History of Ideas* 74 (2013): 403–23.

Bodin, Jean. *Methodus ad Facilem Historiarum Cognitionem.* Paris, 1566.

Bodin, Jean. *Ivris Vniversi Distribvtio.* Paris [*Lvtetia*]: Jacques Du Puys, 1578.

Bodin, Jean. *Apologie de René Herpin pour la République de Jean Bodin*. Paris, 1581.

Bodin, Jean. *Six Livres de la République*. Paris: Jacques Du Puys, 1583.

Bodin, Jean. *De Republica Lbri VI*. Paris: Jacques Du Puys, 1586.

Bodin, Jean. *Six Bookes of a Commonweale*. Trans. Richard Knolles. London: G. Bishop, 1606.

Bodin, Jean. *Method for the Easy Comprehension of History*. Trans. Beatrice Reynolds. New York: Norton, 1945.

Bodin, Jean. *Exposé du Droit Universel [Iuris Universi Distributio]*. Ed. Lucien Jerphagnon, Simone Goyard-Fabre, and René-Marie Rampelberg. Paris: Presses Universitaires de France, 1985.

Bonney, Richard. "Bodin and the Development of the French Monarchy." *Transactions of the Royal Historical Society: Fifth Series*. 40 (1990): 43–61.

Borkowski, Andrew and Paul Du Plessis. *Textbook on Roman Law*. 3rd ed. Oxford: Oxford University Press, 2005.

Borschberg, Peter. "Grotius, the Social Contract and Political Resistance: A Study of the Unpublished Theses LVI." 2007 [IILJ working paper available at SSRN: http://ssrn.com/abstract=969250].

Bortius, Matthias. *De Natura Iurium Maiestatis et Regalium Explicatio*. Jena, 1614.

Bramhall, John. *The Serpent Salve, or, a Remedie for the Biting of an Aspe*. 1643.

Brett, Annabel. *Liberty, Right and Nature*. New York: Cambridge University Press, 1997.

Brett, Annabel. "Natural Right and Civil Community: The Civil Philosophy of Hugo Grotius." *Historical Journal* 45 (2002): 31–51.

Brett, Annabel. *Changes of State: Nature and the Limits of the City in Early Modern Natural Law*. Princeton: Princeton University Press, 2011.

Brito Vieira, Mónica. *Elements of Representation*. Leiden: Brill, 2009.

Brooke, Christopher. *Philosophic Pride: Stoicism and Political Thought from Lipsius to Rousseau*. Princeton: Princeton University Press, 2012.

Brown, John. *The Methodus ad Facilem Historiarum Cognitionem of Jean Bodin: A Critical Study*. Washington: Catholic University of America Press, 1939.

Brundage, James. *Medieval Origins of the Legal Profession: Canonists, Civilians, and Courts*. Chicago: University of Chicago Press, 2008.

Brunt, P.A. "Lex de Imperio Vespasiani." *Journal of Roman Studies* 67 (1977): 95–116.

[Brutus, Stephanus Junius]. *Vindiciae Contra Tyrannos*. Edinburgh [Basel], 1579.

[Brutus, Stephanus Junius]. *Vindiciae Contra Tyrannos*. Ed. George Garnett. Cambridge: Cambridge University Press, 1994.

Bryant, Lawrence. "Making History: Ceremonial Texts, Royal Space, and Political Theory in the Sixteenth Century." *Changing Identities in Early Modern France*. Ed. Michael Wolfe. Durham: Duke University Press, 1996.

Buchanan, George. *A Dialogue on the Law of Kingship among the Scots*. Trans. Roger Mason and Martin Smith. Burlington: Ashgate, 2004.

Buckland, W.W. *The Roman Law of Slavery*. Cambridge: Cambridge University Press, 1908.

Buckland, W.W. *A Textbook of Roman Law from Augustus to Justinian*. 3rd ed. Cambridge: Cambridge University Press, 1963.

Buckle, Stephen. *Natural Law and the Theory of Property*. Oxford: Clarendon Press, 1991.

Budé, Guillaume. *Annotationes in Quatuor et Viginti Pandectarum Libros*. Basel, 1557.

Burgess, Glenn. *Absolute Monarchy and the Stuart Monarchy*. New Haven: Yale University Press, 1996.

Burgess, Glenn. "The Divine Right of Kings Reconsidered." *English Historical Review* 107 (1992): 837–61.

Burgess, Glenn. *The Politics of the Ancient Constitution: an Introduction to English Political Thought, 1600–1642*. Houndsmills: Macmillan, 1992.

Burgess, Glenn. "Bodin in the English Revolution." In *The Reception of Bodin*. Ed. Howell Lloyd. Leiden: Brill, 2013.

Burns, J.H. *Lordship, Kingship and Empire: The Idea of Monarchy, 1400–1525*. Oxford: Oxford University Press, 1992.

Butler, Geoffrey. "Roman Law and the New Monarchy in France." *English Historical Review* 35 (1920): 55–62.

Cabot, Vincent. *Variarum Iuris Publici et Privati Disputationum Libri Duo in Novus Thesaurus Iuris Civilis et Canonici*. Ed. G. Meerman. Vol. 4. The Hague, 1752.

Calasso, Francesco. *I Glossatori e la Teoria della Sovranità*. 2nd ed. Milan: Giuffrè, 1951.

Calasso, Francesco. *I Glossatori e la Teoria della Sovranità*. 3rd ed. Milan: Giuffrè, 1957.

Calasso, Francesco. "*Iurisdictio* nel Diritto Comune Classico." *Annali di Storia del Diritto* 9 (1965): 89–110.

Calvin, John. "On Civil Government." In *Luther and Calvin: On Secular Authority*. Ed. Harro Höpfl. Cambridge: Cambridge University Press, 1991.

Canning, J.P. "The Corporation in the Political Thought of the Italian Jurists of the Thirteenth and Fourteenth Centuries." *History of Political Thought* 1 (1980): 9–32.

Canning, J.P. "Ideas of State in Thirteenth- and Fourteenth-Century Commentators on the Roman Law." *Transactions of the Royal Historical Society* 33 (1983): 1–27.

Canning, J.P. *Political Thought of Baldus de Ubaldis*. Cambridge: Cambridge University Press, 1987.

Canning, J.P. "Law, Sovereignty and Corporation Theory, 1300–1450." In *Cambridge History of Medieval Political Thought*. Ed. J.H. Burns. Cambridge: Cambridge University Press, 1988.

Canning, J.P. *A History of Medieval Political Thought*. London: Routledge, 2005.

Canning, J.P. *Ideas of Power in the Late Middle Ages, 1296–1417*. Cambridge: Cambridge University Press, 2014.

Canovan, Margaret. *The People*. Cambridge: Polity, 2005.

Carlyle, R.W. and A.J. Carlyle. *History of Mediaeval Political Theory in the West*. 6 vols. London: Blackwood and Sons, 1903–38.

Cawdrey, Robert. *The First English Dictionary, 1604: Robert Cawdrey's A Table Alphabeticall*. Oxford: Bodleian Library, 2007.

Charles I. "The King's Answer to the XIX Propositions, 18 June 1642." In *The Stuart Constitution, 1603–1688.* 2nd ed. Ed. J.P. Kenyon. Cambridge: Cambridge University Press, 1986.

Chemerinsky, Erwin. "In Defense of Judicial Review: The Perils of Popular Constitutionalism," *University of Illinois Law Review* (2004): 673–90.

Chemnitz, Bogislus Philipp von ["Hippolytus a Lapide"]. *Dissertatio de Ratione Status in Imperio Nostro Romano-Germanico.* 1640.

Chrimes, S.B. "The Constitutional Ideas of Dr. John Cowell." *English Historical Review* 64 (1949): 461–87.

Church, William Farr. *Constitutional Thought in Sixteenth Century France: A Study in the Evolution of Ideas.* Cambridge: Harvard University Press, 1941.

Cicero. *Letters to Atticus.* Trans. E.O. Winstedt New York: Macmillan, 1912.

Cicero. *De Officiis.* Loeb Classical Library. Trans. Walter Miller. Cambridge: Harvard University Press, 1913.

Cicero. *De Re Publica, De Legibus.* Loeb Classical Library. Trans. Clinton Walker Keyes. Cambridge: Harvard University Press, 1928.

Clarke, John. "Extracts from the Debates at the General Council of the Army, Putney." In *The English Levellers.* Ed. Andrew Sharp. Cambridge: Cambridge University Press, 1998.

Coffey, John. *Politics, Religion and the British Revolutions: The Mind of Samuel Rutherford.* Cambridge: Cambridge University Press, 2002.

Coing, Helmut. "Zur Eigentumslehre des Bartolus." *Zeitschrift für Savigny-Stiftung für Rechtsgeschichte* 70 (1953): 349–71.

Coleman, Janet. "Medieval Discussions of Property: *Ratio* and *Dominium* according to John of Paris and Marsilius of Padua." *History of Political Thought* 4 (1983): 209–28.

Coleman, Janet. "*Dominium* in Thirteenth and Fourteenth-Century Political Thought and Its Seventeenth-Century Heirs: John of Paris and Locke." *Political Studies* 33 (1985): 73–100.

Coleman, Janet. "Property and Poverty." In *Cambridge History of Medieval Political Thought, c.350–c.1450.* Ed. J.H. Burns. Cambridge: Cambridge University Press, 1988.

Coleman, Janet. "Using, Not Owning–Duties, Not Rights: The Consequences of Some Franciscan Perspectives on Politics." In *Defenders and Critics of Franciscan Life: Essays in Honor of John V. Fleming.* Ed. Michael Cusato and G. Geltner. Leiden: Brill, 2009.

Collins, Amanda. *Greater than Emperor: Cola di Rienzo and the World of Fourteenth-Century Rome.* Ann Arbor: University of Michigan Press, 2002.

Collins, Jeffrey. *The Allegiance of Thomas Hobbes.* Oxford: Oxford University Press, 2007.

Colon-Rios, Joel. "The Legitimacy of the Juridical: Constituent Power, Democracy, and the Limits of Constitutional Reform." *Osgoode Hall Law Journal* 48 (2010): 199–245.

Conring, Hermann. *Hermann Conring's New Discourse on the Roman-German Emperor.* Ed. and trans. Constantin Fasolt. Tempe: Arizone Center for Medieval and Renaissance Studies, 2005.

Contarini, Gasparo. *De Magistratibus et Republica Venetorum Libri V.* Basel, 1547.

Coquillette, Daniel. *The Civilian Writers of Doctors' Commons, London: Three Centuries of Juristic Innovation in Comparative, Commercial and International Law.* Berlin: Duncker & Humboldt, 1988.

Cortese, Ennio. *La Norma Giuridica.* 2 Vols. Milan: Giuffrè, 1962.

Cortese, Ennio. *Il Problema della Sovranità nel Pensiero Giuridico Medioevale.* Rome, 1966.

Costa, Pietro. *Iurisdictio: Semantica del Potere Politico nella Pubblistica Medievale, 1100–1433.* Milan: Giuffrè, 1969.

Couzinet, Marie-Dominique. *Histoire et Méthode a la Renaissance: Une Lecture de la Methodus de Jean Bodin.* Paris: J.Vrin, 1996.

Cowell, John. *The Interpreter, or, Booke Containing the Signification of Words.* Cambridge, 1607.

Cowell, John. *Institutiones Iuris Anglicani ad Methodum et Seriem Institutionum Imperialium Compositae et Digestae.* Oxford, 1636.

Cromartie, Alan. *The Constitutionalist Revolution: An Essay on the History of England, 1450–1642.* Cambridge: Cambridge University Press, 2006.

Crook, John Anthony. *Law and Life of Rome.* Ithaca: Cornell University Press, 1967.

Cujas, Jacques. *Observationes et Emendationes Libri XXIV.* Köln, 1598.

Cujas, Jacques. *Solemnes Notae.* Frankfurt, 1598.

Curry, Steven. *Indigenous Sovereignty and the Democratic Project.* Burlington: Ashgate, 2004.

Curtis, Mark. *Oxford and Cambridge in Transition, 1558–1642.* Oxford: Clarendon Press, 1959.

Cuttica, Cesare and Glenn Burgess. Eds. *Monarchism and Absolutism in Early Modern Europe.* London: Pickering and Chatto, 2011.

D'Addio, Mario. *L'Idea del Contratto Sociale dai Sofisti all Riforma e il De Principatu di Mario Salamonio.* Milan: Giuffrè, 1954.

Dahl, Robert. *After the Revolution? Authority in a Good Society.* New Haven: Yale University Press, 1970.

Dahl, Robert. *Democracy and Its Critics.* New Haven: Yale University Press, 1989.

Daly, John. "The Idea of Absolute Monarchy in Seventeenth Century England." *Historical Journal* 21 (1978): 227–50.

Davis, Kathleen. *Periodization and Sovereignty.* Philadelphia: University of Pennsylvania Press, 2008.

Dawson, John Philip. *A History of Lay Judges.* Cambridge: Harvard University Press, 1960.

De Maistre, Joseph. "Study on Sovereignty." In *The Generative Principle of Political Constitutions: Studies on Sovereignty, Religion, and Enlightenment.* Ed. and trans. Jack Lively. Piscataway, Transaction Publishers, 2012.

Dicey, Albert Venn. *Introduction to the Study of the Law of the Constitution*. 3rd ed. New York: Macmillan, 1889.

Digges, Dudley. *An Answer to a Printed Book*. Oxford, 1642.

Digges, Dudley. *A Review of the Observations Upon Some of His Majesties Late Answers and Expresses*. Oxford, 1643.

Dobner, Petra and Martin Loughlin. Ed. *The Twilight of Constitutionalism?* Oxford: Oxford University Press, 2010.

Donahue, Charles. "The Civil Law in England." *Yale Law Journal* 84 (1974): 167–81.

Doneau, Hugues [Donellus]. *Opera Omnia*. 12 Vols. Rome: J. Salviucci, 1828.

Downing, Calibute. *A Discourse of the State Ecclesiasticall of this Kingdome, in Relation to the Civill*. Oxford, 1632.

Dreitzel, Horst. *Protestantischer Aristotelismus und Absoluter Staat: Die 'Politica' des Henning Arnisaeus, ca. 1575–1636*. Wiesbaden: Franz Steiner Verlag, 1970.

Du Fail, Noël. *Oeuvres Facétieuses*. 2 Vols. Paris: P. Daffis, 1874.

Duck, Arthur. *De Usu et Authoritate Iuris Civilis Romanorum*. London, 1653.

Duff, Patrick William. *Personality in Roman Private Law*. Cambridge: Cambridge University Press, 1938.

Duke, Alastair. *Dissident Identities in the Early Modern Low Countries*. Ed. Judith Pollmann and Andrew Spicer. Surrey: Ashgate, 2009.

Dumoulin, Charles. *Omnia Quae Extant Opera*. 5 Vols. Paris: Damian Foucault, 1681.

Durandus, Guilelmus. *Speculum Iudiciale*. Lyon, 1498–1500.

Dyzenhaus, David. "Constitutionalism in an Old Key: Legality and Constituent Power." *Global Constitutionalism* 1 (2012): 229–60.

Edwards, Charles. *Hugo Grotius, the Miracle of Holland*. Chicago: Nelson-Hall, 1981.

Ehrenberg, Victor. "Imperium Maius in the Roman Republic." *American Journal of Philology* 74 (1953): 113–36.

Eisgruber, Christopher. *Constitutional Self-Government*. Cambridge: Harvard University Press, 2001.

Eleftheriadis, Pavlos. "Parliamentary Sovereignty and the Constitution." *Canadian Journal of Law and Jurisprudence* 22 (2009): 1–24.

Eleftheriadis, Pavlos. "Law and Sovereignty." *Law and Philosophy* 29 (2010): 535–69.

Elster, Jon. *Ulysses Unbound: Studies in Rationality, Precommitment, and Constraints*. Cambridge: Cambridge University Press, 2000.

Ely, John Hart. *Democracy and Distrust: A Theory of Judicial Review*. Cambridge: Harvard University Press, 1981.

Engster, Daniel. "Jean Bodin, Skepticism and Absolute Sovereignty." *History of Political Thought* 17 (1996): 469–99.

Esmein, Adhemar. "La maxime *princeps legibus solutus est* dans l'ancien droit public français." In *Essays in Legal History*. Ed. Paul Vinogradoff. Oxford: Oxford University Press, 1913.

Eulau, Heinz. "Theories of Federalism under the Holy Roman Empire." *American Political Science Review* 35 (1941): 643–64.

Fasolt, Constantin. "A Question of Right: Hermann Conring's *New Discourse on the Roman-German Emperor.*" *Sixteenth Century Journal* 28 (1997): 739–58.

Fasolt, Constantin. *The Limits of History*. Chicago: University of Chicago Press, 2004.

Fay, Sidney Bradshaw. "The Roman Law and the German Peasant." *American Historical Review* 16 (1911): 234–54.

Feenstra, Robert. *Studies of Political Thought from Gerson to Grotius*. Cambridge: Cambridge University Press, 1907.

Feenstra, Robert. "Jean de Blanot et la formule *rex Franciae in regno suo princeps est.*" In *Études d'histoire du droit canonique dédiées à Gabrielle le Bras*. Ed. Gabriel le Bras. 2 vols. Paris: Sirey, 1965.

Feenstra, Robert. "Les Origines du *Dominium Utile* Chez les Glossateurs." In *Fata Iuris Romani*. Ed. Robert Feenstra. Leiden: Presse Universitaire de Leyde, 1974.

Feenstra, Robert. "Der Eigentumsbegriff bei Hugo Grotius im Licht Einiger Mittelalterlicher und Spätscholasticher Quellen." In *Festschrift für Franz Wiacker*. Ed. Okko Behrends, et al. Göttingen, 1978.

Feenstra, Robert. "*Dominium* and *Ius in Re Aliena*: The Origins of a Civil Law Distinction." In *New Perspectives in the Roman Law of Property: Essays for Barry Nicholas*. Ed. Peter Birks. Oxford: Clarendon Press, 1989.

Felden, Johannes. *Annotata in Hug. Grotium De Iure Belli ac Pacis*. Amsterdam, 1653.

Figgis, John Neville. *The Divine Right of Kings*. Cambridge: Cambridge University Press, 1922.

Filmer, Robert. *The Anarchy of a Limited or Mixed Monarchy*. London, 1648.

Filmer, Robert. *The Free-Holders Grant Inquest Touching Our Soveraigne Lord the King and His Parliament*. London, 1648.

Filmer, Robert. *Observations upon Aristotles Politiques Touching Forms of Government*. London, 1652.

Filmer, Robert. *Patriarcha, or the Natural Power of Kings*. London: Walter Davis, 1680.

Filmer, Robert. *The Anarchy of a Limited or Mixed Monarchy*. In *Patriarcha and Other Writings*. Ed. Johann Sommerville. Cambridge: Cambridge University Press, 1991.

Filmer, Robert. *The Free-Holders Grand Inquest*. In *Patriarcha and Other Writings*. Ed. Johann Sommerville. Cambridge: Cambridge University Press, 1991.

Filmer, Robert. *The Necessity of the Absolute Power of All Kings*. In *Patriarcha and Other Writings*. Ed. Johann Sommerville. Cambridge: Cambridge University Press, 1991.

Filmer, Robert. *Observations upon Aristotles Politiques*. In *Patriarcha and Other Writings*. Ed. Johann Sommerville. Cambridge: Cambridge University Press, 1991.

Forsyth, Murray. "Thomas Hobbes and the Constituent Power of the People." *Political Studies* 29 (1981): 191–203.

Fortescue, John. *On the Laws and Governance of England*. Ed. Shelley Lockwood. Cambridge: Cambridge University Press, 1997.

Foxley, Rachel. *The Levellers: Radical Political Thought in the English Revolution*. Manchester: Manchester University Press, 2013.

Franklin, Julian. Ed. *Jean Bodin and the Sixteenth Century Revolution in the Methodology of Law and History*. New York: Columbia University Press, 1963.

Franklin, Julian. Ed. *Constitutionalism and Resistance in the Sixteenth Century: Three Treatises by Hotman, Beza, and Mornay*. New York: Pegasus, 1969.

Franklin, Julian. Ed. *John Locke and the Theory of Sovereignty: Mixed Monarchy and the Right of Resistance in the Political Thought of the English Revolution*. Cambridge: Cambridge University Press, 1981.

Franklin, Julian. Ed. "Sovereignty and the Mixed Constitution: Bodin and His Critics." In *Cambridge History of Political Thought, 1450–1700*. Ed. J.H. Burns and Mark Goldie. Cambridge: Cambridge University Press, 1991.

Franklin, Julian. Ed. "Note on the Text." In *Jean Bodin: On Sovereignty*. Ed. Julian Franklin. Cambridge: Cambridge University Press, 1992.

Freeden, Michael. *Ideologies and Political Theory: A Conceptual Approach*. Oxford: Oxford University Press, 1998.

Freegard, William. *Roman Law and Resistance Right: A Study of Question Three of the Vindiciae Contra Tyrannos*. Ph.D. Dissertation, University of Iowa, 1971.

Friedrich, Carl Joachim. "Introduction." In *Political Methodice Digesta of Johannes Althusius*. Cambridge: Harvard University Press, 1932.

Fritz, Christian. *American Sovereigns: The People and America's Constitutionalist Tradition*. Cambridge: Cambridge University Press, 2008.

Fukuda, Arihiro. *Sovereignty and the Sword: Harrington, Hobbes, and Mixed Government in the English Civil Wars*. Oxford: Clarendon Press, 1997.

Fulbecke, William. *A Direction or Preparative to the Study of the Lawe*. London, 1600.

Fulbecke, William. *A Parallele or Conference of the Civill Law, the Canon Law, and the Common Law of This Realme of England*. London: Thomas Wight, 1601.

Fulbecke, William. *Pandectes of the Law of Nations*. London, 1602.

Gallie, W.B. "Essentially Contested Concepts." *Proceedings of the Aristotelian Society* 56 (1956): 167–98.

Garimberto, Girolamo. *De Regimineti Publici de la Citta*. Venice, 1544.

Garnett, George. "Law in the *Vindiciae*: A Vindication." *Historical Journal* 49 (2006): 877–91.

Garnsey, Peter. *Thinking About Property: From Antiquity to the Age of Revolution*. Cambridge: Cambridge University Press, 2007.

Gentili, Alberico. *Regales Disputationes Tres*. London, 1605.

Gibbon, Edward. *The History of the Decline and Fall of the Roman Empire*. Ed. J.B. Bury. Cambridge: Cambridge University Press, 1898. [Reprinted 2013]

Gierke, Otto von. *Political Theories of the Middle Ages*. Trans. F.W. Maitland. Cambridge: Cambridge University Press, 1900.

Gierke, Otto von. *Das Deutsche Genossenschaftsrecht*. 4 Vols. Berlin: Weidmann, 1913.

Gierke, Otto von. *The Development of Political Theory*. Trans. Bernard Freyd. New York: W.W. Norton, 1934.

Gierke, Otto von. *Natural Law and the Theory of Society, 1500 to 1800*. 2 Vols. Trans. Ernest Barker. Cambridge: Cambridge University Press, 1934.

Giesey, Ralph. *The Juristic Basis of Dynastic Right to the French Throne*. Philadelphia: American Philosophical Society, 1961.

Giesey, Ralph. *If Not, Not: The Oath of the Aragonese and the Legendary Laws of Sobrarbe.* Princeton: Princeton University Press, 1968.

Giesey, Ralph. "The Monarchomach Triumvirs: Hotman, Beza and Mornay." *Bibliothèque d'Humanisme et Renaissance* 29 (1970): 41–56.

Giesey, Ralph. "Medieval Jurisprudence in Bodin's Concept of Sovereignty." In *Verhandlungen der Internationalen Bodin Tagung in München.* Ed. Horst Denzer. München: Beck, 1973.

Gillet, Pierre. *La Personnalité Juridique en Droit Ecclésiastique Spécialement chez les Décretaistes et les Décrétalistes et dans le Code du Droit Canonique.* Malines, 1927.

Gilmore, Myron Piper. *Argument from Roman Law in Political Thought, 1200–1600.* Cambridge: Harvard University Press, 1942.

Goldsworthy, Jeffrey. *The Sovereignty of Parliament: History and Philosophy.* Oxford: Clarendon Press, 2001.

Goodin, Robert. "Enfranchsing All Affected Interests, and Its Alternatives." *Philosophy and Public Affairs* 25 (2007): 40–68.

Grafton, Anthony. *Cartographies of Time.* New York: Princeton Architectural Press, 2010.

Grassaille, Charles. *Regalium Franciae.* Paris, 1545.

Gratian. *Decretum Gratiani.* Lyon, 1545.

Green, Georgina. *The Majesty of the People: Popular Sovereignty and the Role of the Writer in the 1790s.* Oxford: Oxford University Press, 2014.

Green, Jeffrey. *The Eyes of the People: Democracy in an Age of Spectatorship.* Oxford: Oxford University Press, 2009.

Greenberg, Janelle. *The Radical Face of the Ancient Constitution: St. Edward's "Laws" in Early Modern Political Thought.* Cambridge: Cambridge University Press, 2001.

Grégoire, Pierre. *De Republica Libri XXVI.* Lyon: Ioannes Baptista Buysson, 1609.

Gregorovius, Ferdinand. *History of the City of Rome in the Middle Ages.* Trans. Annie Hamilton. Cambridge: Cambridge University Press, 1898. [Reprinted 2010]

Gregory IX. *Decretales Gregorii Papae IX.* Paris, 1601.

Grendler, Paul. "Printing and Censorship." In *Cambridge History of Renaissance Philosophy.* Ed. C.B. Schmitt and Quentin Skinner. Cambridge: Cambridge University Press, 1988.

Griffiths, John. *Statutes of the University of Oxford Codified in the Year 1636.* Oxford: Clarendon Press, 1888.

Grotius, Hugo. *De Ivre Belli ac Pacis Libri Tres.* Paris: Nicolaus Buon, 1625.

Grotius, Hugo. *Mare Liberum.* In *De Iure Belli ac Pacis Libri Tres.* Frankfurt am Main, 1696.

Grotius, Hugo. *Commentarius in Theses XI: An Early Treatise on Sovereignty, the Just War, and the Legitimacy of the Dutch Revolt.* Ed. Peter Borschberg. New York: Peter Lang, 1994.

Grotius, Hugo. *The Rights of War and Peace.* Ed. Richard Tuck. Indianapolis: Liberty Fund, 2005.

Grotius, Hugo. *Commentary on the Law of Prize and Booty [De Iure Praedae]*. Ed. Martine Julia van Ittersum. Indianapolis: Liberty Fund, 2006.

Haakonssen, Knud. "Hugo Grotius and the History of Political Thought." *Political Theory* 13 (1985): 239–65.

Haakonssen, Knud. *Natural Law and Moral Philosophy: From Grotius to the Scottish Enlightenment*. Cambridge: Cambridge University Press, 1996.

Hamburger, Philip. *Law and Judicial Duty*. Cambridge: Harvard University Press, 2009.

Hankins, James. "Exclusivist Republicanism and the Non-Monarchical Republic." *Political Theory* 38 (2010): 452–84.

Harvey, Gabriel. *Letter-Book of Gabriel Harvey, A.D. 1573-1580*. Ed. Edward John Long Scott. Westminster: Nichols and Sons, 1884.

Hawkins, Darren, et al., ed. *Delegation and Agency in International Organizations*. Cambridge: Cambridge University Press, 2006.

Hayward, John. *A Reporte of a Discovrse Concerning Svpreme Power in Affaires of Religion*. London: Imprinted by F[elix] K[ingston] for Iohn Hardie, 1606.

Henshall, Nicholas. *The Myth of Absolutism: Change and Continuity in Early Modern Monarchy*. London: Longman, 1992.

Heuston, R.F.V. *Essays in Constitutional Law*. London: Stevens, 1961.

Hill, Christopher. "The Many-Headed Monster." In *Change and Continuity in Seventeenth-Century England*. Cambridge: Harvard University Press, 1975.

Hill, Christopher. *Intellectual Origins of the English Revolution*. Oxford: Clarendon Press, 1980.

Hill, Christopher. *The World Turned Upside Down: Radical Ideas During the English Revolution*. Harmondsworth: Penguin, 1984.

Hobbes, Thomas. *Elementa Philosophica de Cive*. Amsterdam: Elzevir, 1647.

Hobbes, Thomas. *De Corpore Politico: Or the Elements of Law, Moral & Politick*. London: Printed for J. Martin and J. Ridley, 1650.

Hobbes, Thomas. *On the Citizen*. Ed. Richard Tuck and Michael Silverthorne. Cambridge: Cambridge University Press, 1998.

Hobbes, Thomas. *Leviathan*. 3 Vols. Ed. Noel Malcolm. Oxford: Clarendon Press, 2012.

Hochstrasser, T.J. *Natural Law Theories in the Early Enlightenment*. Cambridge: Cambridge University Press, 2000.

Hoekstra, Kinch. "The De Facto Turn in Hobbes' Political Philosophy." In *Leviathan After 350 Years*. Ed. Tom Sorell and Luc Foisneau. Oxford: Oxford University Press, 2004.

Hoekstra, Kinch. "A Lion in the House: Hobbes and Democracy." In *Rethinking the Foundations of Modern Political Thought*. Ed. Annabel Brett et al. Cambridge: Cambridge University Press, 2006.

Hoekstra, Kinch. "Early Modern Absolutism and Constitutionalism." *Cardozo Law Review* 34 (2013): 1079–98.

Hoke, Rudolf. *Die Reichsstaatsrechtslehre des Johannes Limnaeus: Ein Beitrag zur Geschichte der Deutschen Staatsrechtswissenschaft im 17.Jahrhundert*. Aalen: Scientia Verlag, 1968.

Holborn, Hajo. *A History of Modern Germany*. Vol. 1. *The Reformation*. Princeton: Princeton University Press, 1982.

Holland, Ben. "The Moral Person of the State: Emer de Vattel and the Foundations of International Legal Order." *History of European Ideas* 37 (2011): 438–45.

Holland, Ben. "Sovereignty as *Dominium*? Reconstructing the Constructivist Roman Law Thesis." *International Studies Quarterly* 54 (2010): 449–80.

Holland, Ben. "Natural Law and the Theory of International Society: Otto von Gierke and the Three Traditions of International Theory." *Journal of International Political Theory* 8 (2012): 48–73.

Holmes, Stephen. "Precommitment and the Paradox of Democracy." In *Constitutionalism and Democracy*. Ed. Jon Elster and Rune Slagstad. Cambridge: Cambridge University Press, 1988.

Holmes, Stephen. *Passions and Constraints: On the Theory of Liberal Democracy*. Chicago: University of Chicago, 1995.

Honig, Bonnie. *Emergency Politics: Paradox, Law, Democracy*. Princeton: Princeton University Press, 2009.

Hont, Istvan. "Permanent Crisis of a Divided Mankind: Contemporary Crisis of the Nation State in Historical Perspective." *Political Studies* 42 (1994): 166–231.

Höpfl, Harro and Martyn Thompson. "The History of Contract as a Motif in Political Thought." *American Historical Review* 84 (1979): 919–44.

Höpfl, Harro. *Jesuit Political Thought: The Society of Jesus and the State, c.1540–1630*. Cambridge: Cambridge University Press, 2004.

Hotman, François. *De Feudis Commentatio Tripertita*. Lyon, 1573.

Hotman, François. *Francogallia*. Ed. Ralph Giesey. Trans. J.H.M. Salmon. Cambridge: Cambridge University Press, 1972.

Hueglin, Thomas. *Early Modern Concepts for a Late Modern World: Althusius on Community and Federalism*. Waterloo: Wilfrid Laurier University Press, 1999.

Humboldt, Wilhelm von. *The Limits of State Action*. Ed. J.W. Burrow. Cambridge: Cambridge University Press, 1969.

Hunton, Philip. *A Treatise of Monarchie*. London: E. Smith, 1689.

Isernia, Andrea. *In Usus Feudorum Commentaria*. Naples, 1671.

Jackson, Richard. "Elective Kingship and *Consensus Populi* in Sixteenth Century France." *Journal of Modern History* 44 (1972): 155–71.

Jolowicz, H.F. and Barry Nicholas. *Historical Introduction to the Study of Roman Law*. 3rd ed. Cambridge: Cambridge University Press, 1972.

Johnston, David. "The General Influence of Roman Institutions of State and Public Law." In *The Civilian Tradition and Scots Law: Aberdeen Quincentenary Essays*. Ed. D.L. Carey Miller and R. Zimmermann. Berlin: Duncker & Humblot, 1997.

Jordan, W.K. *Men of Substance: A Study of the Thought of Two English Revolutionaries, Henry Parker and Henry Robinson*. Chicago: University of Chicago Press, 1942.

Judson, Margaret Atwood. *Crisis of the Constitution: An Essay in Constitutional and Political Thought in England 1603–1645*. New Brunswick: Rutgers University Press, 1949.

Judson, Margaret Atwood. "Henry Parker and the Theory of Parliamentary Sovereignty." In *Essays in Political Theory in Honor of Charles H. McIlwain*. Ed. Carl Wittke. New York, 1967.

Kahl, Johann. *Lexicon Iuridicum Iuris Caesarei Simul et Canonici*. Genf, 1612.

Kalyvas, Andreas. "Popular Sovereignty, Democracy, and the Constituent Power." *Constellations* 12 (2005): 223–44.

Kalyvas, Andreas. *Democracy and the Politics of the Extraordinary*. Cambridge: Cambridge University Press, 2009.

Kantorowicz, Ernst. *The King's Two Bodies: A Study in Mediaeval Political Theology*. Princeton: Princeton University Press, 1998.

Kantorowicz, Hermann and W.W. Buckland. Ed. *Studies in the Glossators of the Roman Law*. Cambridge: Cambridge University Press, 1938.

Kaser, Max. *Das Römische Zivilprozeßrecht*. München: Beck, 1966.

Keene, Edward. *Beyond the Anarchical Society*. Cambridge: Cambridge University Press, 2002.

Kelley, Donald. "*De Origine Feudorum*: The Beginnings of a Historical Problem." *Speculum* 39 (1964): 207–28.

Kelley, Donald. *Foundations of Modern Historical Scholarship: Language, Law, and History in the French Renaissance*. New York: Columbia University Press, 1970.

Kelley, Donald. "The Rise of Legal History in the Renaissance." *History and Theory* 9 (1970): 174–94.

Kelley, Donald. "Development and Context of Bodin's Method." In *Verhandlungen der Internationalen Bodin Tagung in München*. Ed. Horst Denzer. München: C.H. Beck, 1973.

Kelley, Donald. *François Hotman: A Revolutionary's Ordeal*. Princeton: Princeton University Press, 1973.

Kelley, Donald. "*Vera Philosophia*: The Philosophical Significance of Renaissance Jurisprudence." *Journal of the History of Philosophy* 14 (1976): 267–79.

Kelley, Donald. "Civil Science in the Renaissance: Jurisprudence Italian Style." *Historical Journal* 22 (1979): 777–94.

Kelley, Donald. "Civil Science in the Renaissance: Jurisprudence in the France Manner." *History of European Ideas* 2 (1981): 261–76.

Kelley, Donald. *The Human Measure: Social Thought in the Western Legal Tradition*. Cambridge: Harvard University Press, 1990.

Keohane, Robert, Stephen Macedo, Andrew Moravcsik. "Democracy-Enhancing Multilateralism." *International Organization* 63 (2009): 1–31.

Kern, Fritz. *Kingship and Law in the Middle Ages*. Trans. S.B. Chrimes. Oxford: Blackwell, 1939.

King, Preston. *The Ideology of Order: A Comparative Analysis of Jean Bodin and Thomas Hobbes*. London: Allen and Unwin, 1974.

Kingdon, Robert. *Myths About the St. Bartholomew's Day Massacres, 1572–1576*. Cambridge: Harvard University Press, 1988.

Kingsbury, Benedict and Benjamin Straumann, eds. *The Roman Foundations of the Law of Nations: Alberico Gentili and the Justice of Empire*. Oxford: Oxford University Press, 2010.

Kirchner, Hermann. *Respublica*. Marburg, 1608.

Kirshner, Julius. "*Civitas Sibi Faciat Civem*: Bartolus of Sassoferrato's Doctrine on the Making of a Citizen." *Speculum* 48 (1973): 694–713.

Koch, Bettina. *Zur Dis-Kontinuität Mittelalterlichen Politischen Denkens in der Neuzeitlichen Politischen Theorie: Marsilius von Padua, Johannes Althusius und Thomas Hobbes im Vergleich*. Berlin: Duncker & Humblot, 2005.

Kocher, Paul. "Francis Bacon and the Science of Jurisprudence." *Journal of the History of Ideas* 18 (1957): 3–26.

Koeppler, H. "Frederick Barbarossa and the Schools of Bologna." *English Historical Review* 54 (1939): 577–607.

Kramer, Kramer. *The People Themselves: Popular Constitutionalism and Judicial Review*. New York: Oxford University Press, 2005.

Krasner, Stephen. *Sovereignty: Organized Hypocrisy*. Princeton: Princeton University Press, 1999.

Kratochwil, Friedrich. "Of Systems, Boundaries, and Territoriality: An Inquiry in the Formation of the State System." *World Politics* 39 (1986): 27–52.

Kratochwil, Friedrich. "Sovereignty as *Dominium*: Is There a Right of Humanitarian Intervention?" *Beyond Westphalia? State Sovereignty and International Intervention*. Ed. Gene Lyons and Michael Mastanduno. Baltimore: Johns Hopkins University Press, 1995.

Krisch, Nico. *Beyond Constitutionalism*. Oxford: Oxford University Press, 2012.

Kuhn, Thomas. *The Structure of Scientific Revolutions*. Chicago: University of Chicago Press, 1962.

La Douaren, François [Duarenus]. *Francisci Duareni Opera Omnia*. 4 Vols. Lucca: typis J.Rochii, 1765.

Lahey, Stephen. *Philosophy and Politics in the Thought of John Wyclif*. Cambridge: Cambridge University Press, 2003.

Laski, Harold. "Political Theory in the Later Middle Ages." In *Cambridge Medieval History*. Ed. C.W. Previté-Orton and Z.N. Brooke. Cambridge: Cambridge University Press, 1936.

Last, Hugh. "Imperium Maivs: A Note." *Journal of Roman Studies* 37 (1947): 157–64.

Lauria, M. "Iurisdictio." *Studi Bonfante II*. Milan, 1920.

Lawson, George. *Politica Sacra et Civilis*. Ed. Conal Condren. Cambridge: Cambridge University Press, 1992.

Lee, Alexander. "Roman Law and Human Liberty: Marsilius of Padua on Property Rights." *Journal of the History of Ideas* 70 (2009): 23–44.

Lee, Daniel. "Hobbes and the Civil Law: The Use of Roman Law in Hobbes's Civil Science." In *Hobbes and the Law*. Ed. David Dyzenhaus and Thomas Poole. Cambridge: Cambridge University Press, 2012.

Lee, Daniel. "Office Is a Thing Borrowed: Jean Bodin on Offices and Seigneurial Government." *Political Theory* 41 (2013): 409–41.

Lee, H.Y. *Political Representation in the Later Middle Ages: Marsilius in Context*. New York: Peter Lang, 2008.

Leibniz, Gottfried Wilhelm. "Caesarinus Fürstenerius: De Suprematu Principum Germaniae." In *Political Writings*. Ed. Patrick Riley. Cambridge: Cambridge University Press, 1988.

Lesaffer, Randall. "Argument from Roman Law in Current International Law: Occupation and Acquisitive Prescription." *European Journal of International Law* 16 (2005): 25–58.

Lévy, J.P. *Histoire de la Proprieté*. Paris, 1972.

Lewis, Ewarts. *Medieval Political Ideas*. New York: A.A. Knopf, 1954.

Limnaeus, Johannes. *Ius Publicum Imperii Romano-Germanici*. 2 Vols. Strasbourg: Paul Ledertz, 1629–32.

Limnaeus, Johannes. *Capitulationes Imperatorum et Regum Romanogermanorum cum Annotamentis*. Strasbourg, 1651.

Levack, Brian. *Civil Lawyers in England, 1603–1641: A Political Study*. Oxford: Clarendon Press, 1973.

Livy. *The History of Rome* [*Ab Urbe Condita*]. Loeb Classical Library. Trans. B.O. Foster. Cambridge: Harvard University Press, 1919.

Lloyd, Howell. *The State, France, and the Sixteenth Century*. Boston: Allen and Unwin, 1983.

Loader, W.R. "Pompey's Command Under the *Lex Gabinia*." *The Classical Review* 54 (1940): 134–36.

Locke, John. *Two Treatises of Government*. Ed. Peter Laslett. Cambridge: Cambridge University Press, 1988.

Loewenstein, Karl. *The Governance of Rome*. The Hague: Martinus Nijhoff, 1973.

Lomonaco, Fabrizio. *New Studies on Lex Regia: Right, Philology, and Fides Historica in Holland between the 17th and 18th Centuries*. New York: Peter Lang, 2011.

Lovett, Frank. *A General Theory of Domination and Justice*. Oxford: Oxford University Press, 2010.

Loughlin, Martin. "The Constitutional Thought of the Levellers." *Current Legal Problems* 60 (2007): 1–39.

Loughlin, Martin. *Foundations of Public Law*. Oxford: Oxford University Press, 2010.

Loughlin, Martin. "What Is Constitutionalisation?" In *The Twilight of Constitutionalism?* Ed. Petra Dobner and Martin Loughlin. Oxford: Oxford University Press, 2010.

Loughlin, Martin. "The Concept of Constituent Power," *European Journal of Political Theory* 13 (2014): 218–37.

Loughlin, Martin and Neil Walker. Ed. *The Paradox of Constitutionalism: Constituent Power and Constitutional Form*. Oxford: Oxford University Press, 2008.

Loyseau, Charles. *Cinq Livres du Droit du Offices*. In *Les Oeuvres de Maistre Charles Loyseau*. Lyon, 1701.

Lucrezi, Francesco. *Leges Super Principem*. Naples: Jovene, 1982.

Lupel, Adam. *Globalization and Popular Sovereignty: Democracy's Transational Dilemma*. Oxford: Routledge, 2009.

Lupia, Arthur. "Delegation of Power: Agency Theory." *International Encyclopedia of the Social and Behavioral Sciences* 5 (2001): 3375–77.

Luther, Martin. "On Secular Authority." In *Luther and Calvin on Secular Authority*. Ed. Harro Höpfl. Cambridge: Cambridge University Press, 1991.

MacMillan, Ken. *Sovereignty and Possession in the New World: The Legal Foundations of Empire, 1576–1640*. Cambridge: Cambridge University Press, 2006.

Maine, Henry Sumner. *Ancient Law: Its Connection with the Early History of Society and Its Relation to Modern Ideas*. London: John Murray, 1924.

Maiolo, Francesco. *Medieval Sovereignty*. Delft: Eburon, 2007.

Major, J. Russell. *From Renaissance Monarchy to Absolute Monarchy: French Kings, Nobles and Estates*. Baltimore: Johns Hopkins University Press, 1994.

Marshall, Geoffrey. *Parliamentary Sovereignty and the Commonwealth*. Oxford: Clarendon Press, 1957.

Martel, James. "Can There Be Politics Without Sovereignty: Arendt, Derrida and the Question of Sovereign Inevitability." *Law, Culture, and the Humanities* 6 (2010): 153–66.

Maxwell, John. *Sacro-Sancta Regum Maiestas*. Oxford, 1644.

McCormick, John. "Machiavellian Democracy: Controlling Elites with Ferocious Populism." *American Political Science Review* 95 (2001): 297–313.

McCormick, John. *Machiavellian Democracy*. Cambridge: Cambridge University Press, 2011.

McCuaig, William. *Carlo Sigonio: The Changing World of the Late Renaissance*. Princeton: Princeton University Press, 1989.

McIlwain, Charles Howard. "Sovereignty." In *Constitutionalism and the Changing World*. Cambridge: Cambridge University Press, 1939.

McIlwain, Charles Howard. *Constitutionalism Ancient and Modern*. Ithaca: Cornell University Press, 1947.

McLaren, Anne. "Rethinking Republicanism: *Vindiciae, Contra Tyrannos* in Context." *Historical Journal* 49 (2006): 23–52.

McRae, Kenneth. "Ramist Tendencies in the Thought of Jean Bodin." *Journal of the History of Ideas* 16 (1955): 306–23.

Mellet, Paul-Alexis. *Les Traités Monarchomaques: Confusion des Temps, Résistance Armée et Monarchie Parfaite, 1560–1600*. Geneva: Droz, 2007.

Mellor, Ronald. "Tacitus, Academic Politics, and Regicide in the Reign of Charles I: The Tragedy of Dr. Isaac Dorislaus." *International Journal of the Classical Tradition* 11 (2004): 153–93.

Mendle, Michael. *Henry Parker and the English Civil War: The Political Thought of the Public's "Privado."* Cambridge: Cambridge University Press, 1995.

Merbury, Charles. *A Briefe Discourse of Royall Monarchie, as of the Best Common Weale.* London, 1581.

Mesnard, Pierre. *L'essor de la Philosophie Politique au XVIe Siècle.* Paris: J. Vrin, 1951.

Metzger, Ernest. "An Outline of Roman Civil Procedure." *Roman Legal Tradition* 9 (2013): 1–30.

Meynial, E. "Notes sur la Formation de la Théorie du Domaine Divise." In *Mélanges Fitting.* Ed. Herman Fitting. 2 Vols. Montpellier: Société Anonyme de l'Imprimerie Générale du Midi, 1907–8.

Michaeud-Quantin, Pierre. *Universitas: Expressions du Mouvement Communautaire dans le Moyen-âge Latin.* Paris, 1970.

Michelman, Frank. "Constitutional Authorship by the People." *Notre Dame Law Review* 74 (1999): 1605–30.

Millar, Fergus. *The Roman Republic in Political Thought.* Hanover: University Press of New England, 2002.

Miller, Joshua. "The Ghostly Body Politic: The Federalist Papers and Popular Sovereignty." *Political Theory* 16 (1988): 99–119.

Milton, John. *A Defence of the People of England* [*Pro Populo Anglicano*]. In *Political Writings.* Ed Martin Dzelzainis. Cambridge: Cambridge University Press, 1991.

Milton, John. *The Tenure of Kings and Magistrates.* In *Political Writings.* Ed Martin Dzelzainis. Cambridge: Cambridge University Press, 1991.

Mommsen, Theodor. *Römisches Staatsrecht.* Vol. 2. 3rd ed. Leipzig: S. Hirzel, 1887.

Monheit, Michael. "Guillaume Budé, Andrea Alciato, and Pierre de l'Estoile: Renaissance Interpreters of Roman Law." *Journal of the History of Ideas* 58 (1997): 21–40.

Moreau-Reibel, Jean. *J. Bodin et le Droit Public Comparé dans ses Rapports avec la Philosophie de l'Histoire.* Paris: Vrin, 1933.

Morgan, Edmund. *Inventing the People: The Rise of Popular Sovereignty in England and America.* New York: W.W. Norton, 1989.

Mosse, George. *The Struggle for Sovereignty in England, from the Reign of Queen Elizabeth to the Petition of Right.* East Lansing: Michigan State College Press, 1950.

Musto, Ronald. *Apocalypse in Rome: Cola di Rienzo and the Politics of the New Age* Berkeley: University of California Press, 2003.

Najemy, John. *A History of Florence, 1200–1575.* Oxford: Blackwell, 2006.

Näström, Sophia. "The Legitimacy of the People." *Political Theory* 35 (2007): 624–58.

Nederman, Cary. *The Lineages of European Political Thought.* Washington: Catholic University of America Press, 2009.

Nellen, Henk. *Hugo de Groot: Een Leven in Strijd om de Vrede, 1583–1645.* Amsterdam: Balans Publishers, 2007.

Nelson, Eric. "Talmudical Commonwealthsmen and the Rise of Republican Exclusivism." *Historical Journal* 50 (2007): 809–35.

Nelson, Eric. *The Hebrew Republic.* Cambridge: Harvard University Press, 2010.

Nootens, Geneviève. *Popular Sovereignty in the West: Polities, Contention, and Ideas*. London: Routledge, 2013.

Nozick, Robert. *Anarchy, State and Utopia*. New York: Basic Books, 1974.

Nyquist, Mary. *Arbitrary Rule: Slavery, Tyranny and the Power of Life and Death*. Chicago: University of Chicago Press, 2013.

Oakley, Francis. "On the Road from Constance to 1688: The Political Thought of John Major and George Buchanan." *Journal of British Studies* 1 (1962): 1–31.

Oakley, Francis. *The Political Thought of Pierre d'Ailly: The Voluntarist Tradition*. New Haven: Yale University Press, 1964.

Oakley, Francis. "Jacobean Political Theology: The Absolute and Ordinary Powers of the King." *Journal of the History of Ideas* 29 (1968): 323–46.

Ober, Josiah. *Mass and Elite in Democratic Athens: Rhetoric, Ideology, and the Power of the People*. Princeton: Princeton University Press, 1989.

Ochoa Espejo, Paulina. *Time of Popular Sovereignty: Process and the Democratic State*. University Park: Pennsylvania State University Press, 2011.

Ochoa Espejo, Paulina. "People, Territory, and Legitimacy in Democratic States." *American Journal of Political Science* 58 (2014): 466–78.

O'Donnell, G.A. "Delegative Democracy." *Journal of Democracy* 5 (1994): 55–69.

Odofredus. *Lectura Super Digesto Veteri*. Lyon, 1550.

Odofredus. *Lectura Super Codice*. Lyon, 1552.

Otto, Daniel. "An Mixtus Detur Reipublicae Status?" In Arumäus, Dominicus. *Discursus Academici de Iure Publico*. 3 Vols. Jena, 1620.

Overton, Robert. "An Appeal from the Degenerate Representative Body, the Commons of England Assembled at Westminster, to the Body Represented, the Free People in General." In *Leveller Manifestoes of the Puritan Revolution*. Ed. Don Wolfe. New York: T. Nelson and Sons, 1944.

Overton, Robert. "An Arrow Against All Tyrants and Tyranny." In *The English Levellers*. Ed. Andrew Sharp. Cambridge: Cambridge University Press, 1998.

Overton, Robert and William Walwyn. "A Remonstrance of Many Thousand Citizens." In *The English Levellers*. Ed. Andrew Sharp. Cambridge: Cambridge University Press, 1998.

Owen, David. "Constituting the Polity, Constituting the Demos." *Ethics and Global Politics* 5 (2012): 129–52.

Parker, David. "Sovereignty, Absolutism and the Function of the Law in Seventeenth-Century France." *Past and Present* 122 (1989): 36–74.

Parker, Henry. *Observations Upon Some of His Majesties Late Answers and Expresses*. London, 1642.

Parker, Henry. *Ius Populi, or A Discourse Wherein Clear Satisfaction Is Given As Well Concerning the Right of Subjects As the Right of Princes*. London, 1644.

Parrow, Kathleen. *From Defense to Resistance: Justification of Violence During the French Wars of Religion*. Philadelphia: American Philosophical Society, 1993.

Pauermeister, Tobias von. *De Iurisdictione Imperii Romani*. 1608.

Pedersen, Olaf. *The First Universities: Studium Generale and the Origins of University Education in Europe*. Cambridge: Cambridge University Press, 1997.

Pels, Dick. *Property and Power in Social Theory*. London: Routledge, 2002.

Penna, Lucas de. *Lectura*. Lyon, 1529.

Pennington, Kenneth. "Law, Legislative Authority, and Theories of Government, 1150-1300." In *Cambridge History of Medieval Political Thought*. Ed. J.H. Burns. Cambridge: Cambridge University Press, 1988.

Pennington, Kenneth. *The Prince and the Law, 1200-1600: Sovereignty and Rights in the Western Legal Tradition*. Berkeley: University of California Press, 1993.

Pennington, Kenneth. "The Birth of the *Ius Commune*: King Roger II's Legislation." *Rivista Internazionale de Diritto Commune* 17 (2006): 1–40.

Pennington, Kenneth. "The Big Bang: Roman Law in the Early Twelfth Century." *Rivista Internazionale di Diritto Comune* 18 (2007): 43–70.

Perrin, J.W. "Azo, Roman Law, and Sovereign European States." *Studia Gratiana* 15 (1972): 89-101.

Pettegree, Andrew. *Emden and the Dutch Revolt: Exile and the Development of Reformed Protestantism*. Oxford: Oxford University Press, 1992.

Pettit, Philip. *Republicanism: A Theory of Freedom and Government*. Oxford: Oxford University Press, 1997.

Pettit, Philip. "Deliberative Democracy and the Discursive Dilemma." *Philosophical Issues* 11 (2001): 268–99.

Pettit, Philip. *A Theory of Freedom: From the Psychology to the Politics of Agency*. Oxford: Oxford University Press, 2001.

Pettit, Philip. *On the People's Terms: A Republican Theory and Model of Democracy*. Cambridge: Cambridge University Press, 2012.

Pocock, J.G.A. *The Machiavellian Moment*. Princeton: Princeton University Press, 1975.

Pocock, J.G.A. and Gordon Schochet. "Interregnum and Restoration." In *The Varieties of British Politicl Thought, 1500–1800*. Ed. J.G.A. Pocock. Cambridge: Cambridge University Press, 1996.

Podoksik, Efraim. "One Concept of Liberty: Towards Writing the History of a Political Concept." *Journal of the History of Ideas* 71 (2010): 219–40.

Ponte, Oldradus de. *Consilia seu Responsa*. Venice, 1585.

Post, Gaines. "A Romano-Canonical Maxim, *Quod Omnes Tangit*, in Bracton." *Traditio* 4 (1946): 197–251.

Post, Gaines. *Studies in Medieval Legal Thought: Public Law and the State, 1100–1322*. Princeton: Princeton University Press, 1964.

Prynne, William. *The Soveraigne Power of Parliaments and Kingdomes*. London: Michael Sparke, Senior, 1643.

Pufendorf, Samuel. *De Iure Naturae et Gentium Libri Octo*. Oxford: Clarendon Press, 1934.

Pufendorf, Samuel. *On the Present State of Germany*. Ed. Michael Seidler. Indianapolis: Liberty Fund, 2007.

Putterman, Ethan. *Rousseau, Law and the Sovereignty of the People.* Cambridge: Cambridge University Press, 2010.

Quaritsch, Helmut. *Staat und Souveränität.* Frankfurt am Main: Athenäum, 1970.

Rabkin, Jeremy. *Law Without Nations: Why Constitutional Government Requires Sovereign States.* Princeton: Princeton University Press, 2005.

Radding, Charles and Antonio Ciaralli. *The Corpus Iuris Civilis in the Middle Ages: Manuscripts and Transmission from the Sixth Century to the Juristic Revival.* Leiden: Brill, 2007.

Raitiere, M.N. "Hubert Languet's Authorship of the *Vindiciae Contra Tyrannos.*" *Il Pensiero Politico* 13 (1981): 395–420.

Randall, Michael. *The Gargantuan Polity: On the Individual and the Community in the French Renaissance.* Toronto: University of Toronto Press, 2008.

Rawls, John. *Political Liberalism.* New York: Columbia University Press, 1993.

Rawls, John. *A Theory of Justice.* Rev. ed. Cambridge: Harvard University Press, 1999.

Reinkingk, Theodor Dietrich. *Tractatus de Regimine Seculari et Ecclesiastico.* Frankfurt am Main, 1659.

Révigny, Jacques de. *Lectura Super Codice.* Paris, 1519.

Riccobono, Salvator. "Mos Italicus e Mos Gallicus nella Interpretazione del Corpus Iuris Civilis." In *Acta Congressus Iuridici Internationalis VII Saeculo a Decretalibus Gregorii IX et XIV a Codice Iustiniano Promulgatis Romae.* Ed. Pontificium Institutum Utriusque Iuris. Rome: Libraria Pontificii Instituti Utriusque Iuris, 1935.

Riccobono, Salvator. *Fontes Iuris Romani Antejustiniani.* 3 Vols. Florence: Barbera, 1941.

Richardson, John. "The Meaning of Imperium in the Last Century BC and the First AD." In *The Roman Law Foundations of the Law of Nations: Alberico Gentili and the Justice of Empire.* Ed. Benedict Kingsbury and Benjamin Straumann. Oxford: Oxford University Press, 2010.

Rienzo, Cola di. In *The Revolution of Cola di Rienzo.* Ed. Mario Emilio Cosenza, Ronald Musto, 3rd ed. New York: Italica Press, 1996.

Riesenberg, Peter. *The Inalienability of Sovereignty in Medieval Political Thought.* New York: Columbia University Press, 1955.

Rosate, Albericus de. *Dictionarium Iuris tam Civili quam Canonici.* Venice, 1572.

Rosate, Albericus de. *Commentaria Super Digesto.* Venice, 1585. [Reprinted Torino, 1974]

Rothbard, Murray. "Jean Bodin: Apex of Absolutist Thought in France." *An Austrian Perspective on the History of Economic Thought: Economic Thought Before Adam Smith.* Vol. 1. Aldershot: E. Elgar, 1995.

Rousseau, Jean-Jacques. *The Social Contract.* Ed. Victor Gourevitch. Cambridge: Cambridge University Press, 1997.

Rowen, Herbert. *The King's State: Proprietary Dynasticism in Early Modern France.* New Brunswick: Rutgers University Press, 1980.

Rubenfeld, Jed. *Freedom and Time: A Theory of Constitutional Self-Government.* New Haven: Yale University Press, 2001.

Rubinstein, Nicolai. *The Government of Florence under the Medici*. Oxford: Oxford University Press, 1997.

Rüfner, Thomas. "The Roman Concept of Ownership and the Medieval Doctrine of *Dominium Utile*." *The Creation of the Ius Commune: From Casus to Regula*. Ed. John Cairns and Paul Du Plessis. Edinburgh: Edinburgh University Press, 2010.

Ruggie, John Gerard. "Territoriality and Beyond: Problematizing Modernity in International Relations." *International Organization* 47 (1993): 139–74.

Runciman, David. "What Kind of Person Is Hobbes's State? A Reply to Quentin Skinner." *Journal of Political Philosophy* 8 (2000): 268–78.

Runciman, David. *Pluralism and the Personality of the State*. Cambridge: Cambridge University Press, 2005.

Rushworth, John. *Historical Collections of Private Passages of State*. Vol. 1. London: Tho. Newcomb for George Thomason, 1659.

Rutherford, Samuel. *Lex, Rex*. London: Iohn Field, 1644.

Ryan, Magnus. "Bartolus of Sassoferrato and the Free Cities." *Transactions of the Royal Historical Society*. Sixth Series 10 (2000): 65–89.

Ryan, Magnus. "Political Thought." In *Cambridge Companion to Roman Law*. Ed. David Johnston. Cambridge: Cambridge University Press, 2015.

Sabine, George. *A History of Political Theory*. New York: Henry Holt and Company, 1937.

Salamonius, Mario. *De Principatu Libri VI*. Paris: Du Val, 1578.

Salmon, J.H.M. *French Religious Wars in English Political Thought*. Oxford: Clarendon Press, 1959.

Salmon, J.H.M. "An Alternative Theory of Popular Resistance: Buchanan, Rossaeus, and Locke." In *Renaissance and Revolt*. Cambridge: Cambridge University Press, 1987.

Salmon, J.H.M. "Catholic Resistance Theory, Ultramontanism, and the Royalist Response, 1580-1620." In *Cambridge History of Political Thought, 1450–1700*. Ed. J.H. Burns and Mark Goldie. Cambridge: Cambridge University Press, 1991.

Salmon, J.H.M. "The Legacy of Jean Bodin: Absolutism, Populism, or Constitutionalism?" *History of Political Thought* 17 (1996): 500–22.

Savigny, Friedrich Karl von. *Geschichte des Römisches Rechts im Mittelalter*. Heidelberg: Mohr, 1834.

Schmitt, Carl. *Dictatorship: From the Origin of the Modern Concept of Sovereignty to Proletarian Class Struggle*. Trans. Michael Hoelzl and Graham Ward. Cambridge: Polity, 2014.

Schröder, Peter. "The Constitution of the Holy Roman Empire After 1648: Samuel Pufendorf's Assessment in his *Monzambano*." *Historical Journal* 42 (1999): 961–83.

Schulz, Fritz. "Bracton on Kingship." *English Historical Review* 60 (1945): 136–76.

Searle, John. *Speech Acts*. Cambridge: Cambridge University Press, 1969.

Searle, John. *The Construction of Social Reality*. New York: Free Press, 1995.

Selden, John. *Ioannis Seldeni ad Fletam Dissertatio* [*Ad Fletam*]. Ed. David Ogg. Cambridge: Cambridge University Press, 1925.

Selden, John. *Titles of Honour.* 2nd Ed. London: Printed by William Stansby for Richard Whitakers, 1631.

Seneca. *Moral Essays.* Vol. 3. *De Beneficiis.* Loeb Classical Library. Trans. John Basore. Cambridge: Harvard University Press, 1935.

Sheehan, James. "The Problem of Sovereignty in European History." *American Historical Review* 111 (2006): 1–15.

Sidney, Algernon. *Discourses Concerning Government.* Ed. Thomas West. Indianapolis: Liberty Fund, 1990.

Sigonius, Carolus. *De Republica Atheniensium Libri IV.* Bologna, 1564.

Skinner, Quentin. *Foundations of Modern Political Thought*, 2 Vols. Cambridge: Cambridge University Press, 1978.

Skinner, Quentin. *Reason and Rhetoric in the Philosophy of Hobbes.* Cambridge: Cambridge University Press, 1996.

Skinner, Quentin. *Liberty Before Liberalism.* Cambridge: Cambridge University Press, 1998.

Skinner, Quentin. "Classical Liberty and the Coming of the English Civil War." In *Republicanism: A Shared European Heritage.* Vol. 2. Ed. Martin Van Gelderen and Quentin Skinner. Cambridge: Cambridge University Press, 2002.

Skinner, Quentin. "Classical Liberty, Renaissance Translation and the English Civil War." In *Visions of Politics.* Vol. 2. Cambridge: Cambridge University Press, 2002.

Skinner, Quentin. "From the State of Princes to the Person of the State." In *Vision of Politics.* Vol. 2. Cambridge, Cambridge University Press, 2002.

Skinner, Quentin. "Hobbes and the Purely Artificial Person of the State." In *Visions of Politics.* Vol. 3. *Hobbes and Civil Science.* Cambridge: Cambridge University Press, 2002.

Skinner, Quentin. "Humanism, Scholasticism, and Popular Sovereignty." In *Visions of Politics.* Vol. 2. Cambridge: Cambridge University Press, 2002.

Skinner, Quentin. "John Milton and the Politics of Slavery." In *Visions of Politics.* Vol. 2. Cambridge: Cambridge University Press, 2002.

Skinner, Quentin. "The Rediscovery of Republican Values." In *Visions of Politics.* Vol. 2. Cambridge: Cambridge University Press, 2002.

Skinner, Quentin. *Hobbes and Republican Liberty.* Cambridge: Cambridge University Press, 2008.

Skinner, Quentin. "A Genealogy of the Modern State." *Proceedings of the British Academy* 162 (2009) 325–70.

Smith, C.J. *The Roman Clan: The Gens from Ancient Ideology to Modern Anthropology.* Cambridge: Cambridge University Press, 2006.

Smith, Nigel. *Literature and Revolution in England, 1640–1660.* New Haven: Yale University Press, 1994.

Smith, Rogers. *Stories of Peoplehood: The Politics and Morals of Political Membership.* Cambridge: Cambridge University Press, 2003.

Sommerville, Johann. "History and Theory: The Norman Conquest in Early Stuart Political Thought." *Political Studies* 34 (1986): 249–61.

Sommerville, Johann. "Absolutism and Royalism." In *Cambridge History of Political Thought, 1450–1700*. Ed. J.H. Burns. Cambridge: Cambridge University Press, 1995.

Sommerville, Johann. *Royalists and Patriots: Politics and Ideology in England, 1603-1640*. 2nd ed. London: Longman, 1999.

Song, Sarah. "The Boundary Problem in Democratic Theory: Why the Demos Should Be Bounded By the State." *International Theory* 4 (2012): 39–68.

Squibb, G.D. *Doctors' Commons: A History of the College of Advocates and Doctors of Law*. Oxford: Clarendon Press, 1977.

Staveley, E.S. "The Fasces and Imperium Maius." *Historia: Zeitschrift für Alte Geschichte* 12 (1963): 458–84.

Stein, Peter. *Roman Law in European History*. New York: Cambridge University Press, 1999.

Stobbe, Otto. *Geschichte der Deutschen Rechtsquellen*. 2 Vols. Leipzig: Duncker & Humblot, 1860–64.

Stolleis, Michael. *Geschichte des Öffentlichen Rechts in Deutschland*. Vol. 1. *Reichspublizistik und Policeywissenschaft, 1600–1800*. München: C.H.Beck, 1988.

Stolleis, Michael, ed. *Juristen: Ein Biographisches Lexikon von der Antike bis zum 20. Johrhundert*. München: Beck, 1995.

Straumann, Benjamin. "Ancient Caesarian Lawyers in a State of Nature: Roman Tradition and Natural Rights in Hugo Grotius" *De Iure Praedae*.' *Political Theory* 34 (2006): 328–50.

Straumann, Benjamin. *Hugo Grotius und die Antike*. Baden-Baden: Nomos, 2007.

Straumann, Benjamin. "Natural Rights and Roman Law in Hugo Grotius' *Theses LVI, De Jure Praedae* and *Defensio Capitis Quinti Maris Liberi*." In *Property, Piracy and Punishment*. Ed. Hans Blom. Leiden: Brill, 2009.

Straumann, Benjamin. "The *Corpus Juris* as a Source of Law between Sovereigns." In *The Roman Foundations of the Law of Nations*. Ed. Benedict Kingsbury and Benjamin Straumann. Oxford: Oxford University Press, 2010.

Straumann, Benjamin. *Roman Law in the State of Nature*. Cambridge: Cambridge University Press, 2015.

Straumann, Benjamin. *Crisis and Constitutionalism: Roman Political Thought from the Fall of the Republic to the Age of Revolution*. Oxford: Oxford University Press, 2016.

Straumann, Benjamin. "The Roman Republic as a Constitutional Order from the Principate to the Renaissance," In *Republics and the Classical Past, 1500–1800*. Ed. W. Velema and A. Westseijn Leiden: Brill, forthcoming.

Strauss, Gerald. *Law, Resistance and the State: The Opposition to Roman Law in Reformation Germany*. Princeton: Princeton University Press, 1986.

Strayer, John. *On the Medieval Origins of the Modern State*. Princeton: Princeton University Press, 1972.

Stroumsa, Guy. *A New Science: The Discovery of Religion in the Age of Reason*. Cambridge: Harvard University Press, 2010.

Suarez, Francisco. *Tractatvs de Legibvs, ac Deo Legislatore*. Lyon, 1613.

Suksi, Markku. *Bringing in the People: A Comparison of Constitutional Forms and the Practices of Referendum*. Dordrecht: Martinus Nijhoff Publishers, 1993.

Thireau, Jean-Louis. *Charles Du Moulin, 1500–1566*. Geneva: Droz, 1980.

Tierney, Brian. *Foundations of the Conciliarist Theory: The Contribution of the Medieval Canonists from Gratian to the Great Schism*. Cambridge: Cambridge University Press, 1955.

Tierney, Brian. "Bracton on Government." *Speculum* 38 (1963): 295–317.

Tierney, Brian. "The Prince Is Not Bound by the Laws: Accursius and the Origins of the Modern State." *Comparative Studies in Society and History* 5 (1963): 378–400.

Tierney, Brian. *Religion, Law, and the Growth of Constitutional Thought, 1150–1650*, Cambridge: Cambridge University Press, 1982.

Tilly, Charles. "Reflections on the History of European Statemaking." In *Formation of National States in Western Europe*. Ed. Charles Tilly. Princeton: Princeton University Press, 1975.

Tuck, Richard. "Hobbes and Democracy." In *Rethinking the Foundations of Modern Political Thought*. Ed. Annabel Brett et al. Cambridge: Cambridge University Press, 2006.

Tuck, Richard. *Natural Rights Theories: Their Origin and Development*. Cambridge: Cambridge University Press, 1979.

Tuck, Richard. *Philosophy and Government, 1572–1651*. Cambridge: Cambridge University Press, 1993.

Tuck, Richard. *The Sleeping Sovereign: The Invention of Modern Democracy*. Cambridge: Cambridge University Press, 2016.

Tushnet, Mark. "Popular Constitutionalism as Political Law." *Chicago-Kent Law Review* 81 (2006): 991–1006.

Ullmann, Walter. *The Medieval Idea of Law as Represented by Lucas De Penna: A Study in Fourteenth-Century Legal Scholarship*. London: Methuen, 1946.

Ullmann, Walter. "The Development of the Medieval Idea of Sovereignty." *English Historical Review* 64 (1949): 1–33.

Ullmann, Walter. *The Growth of Papal Government in the Middle Ages*. London: Methuen, 1962.

Ullmann, Walter. "Juristic Obstacles to the Emergence of the Concept of the State in the Middle Ages." *Annali di Storia del Diritto – Rassegna Internazionale, XII–XIII* (1968–9): 43–64.

Ullmann, Walter. *Carolingian Renaissance and the Idea of Kingship*. London: Methuen, 1969.

Ullmann, Walter. *Law and Politics in the Middle Ages*. Ithaca: Cornell University Press, 1975.

Vaccari, Pietro. "Utrum Iurisdictio Cohaeret Territorio: La Dottrina di Bartolo." *Bartolo da Sassoferrato*. Milan, 1962.

Vallejo, Jesus. "Power Hierarchies in Medieval Juridical Thought: An Essay in Reinterpretation." In *Ius Commune: Zeitschrift für Europäische Rechtsgeschichte 19*. Ed. Dieter Simon and Michael Stolleis. Frankfurt am Main: Klostermann, 1992.

Van der Molen, Gezina. *Alberico Gentili and the Development of International Law.* Amsterdam: H.J. Paris, 1937.

Van Dijk, Conrad. *John Gower and the Limits of the Law.* Cambridge: D.S. Brewer, 2013.

Van Gelderen, Martin. *The Political Thought of the Dutch Revolt, 1550–1590.* Cambridge: Cambridge University Press, 1992.

Van Gelderen, Martin. "From Domingo de Soto to Hugo Grotius: Theories of Monarchy and Civil Power in Spanish and Dutch Political Thought, 1555–1609." *Pensiero Politico* 32 (1999): 186–205.

Van Gelderen, Martin. "Aristotelians, Monarchomachs, and Republicans: Sovereignty and *Respublica Mixta* in Dutch and German Political Thought, 1580–1650." In *Republicanism: Republicanism and Constitutionalism in Early Modern Europe.* Vol. 1. Cambridge: Cambridge University Press, 2005.

Veen, Theo. "Interpretations of Inst.1.2.6, D.1.4.1, and D.1.3.31: Huber's Historical, Juridical and Political-Theoretical Reflections on the *Lex Regia.*" *Tijdschrift voor Rechtsgeschiedenis* 53 (1985): 357–77.

Verschoor, Marco. "The Democratic Boundary Problem and Social Contract Theory." *European Journal of Political Theory.* Online version, 2015.

Vico, Giambattista. *Universal Right.* Trans. Pinton, Giorgio and Margaret Diehl. Amsterdam: Rodopi, 2000.

Vinogradoff, Paul. *Roman Law in Medieval Europe.* Oxford: Clarendon Press, 1929.

Vinx, Lars. "Constitutional Indifferentism and Republican Freedom." *Political Theory* 38 (2010): 809–37.

Vinx, Lars. "The Incoherence of Strong Popular Sovereignty." *International Journal of Constitutional Law* 11 (2013): 101–24.

Viroli, Maurizio. *From Politics to Reason of State: The Acquisition and Transformation of the Language of Politics, 1250–1600.* Cambridge: Cambridge University Press, 1992.

Visser, Derek. "Junius: The Author of the *Vindiciae Contra Tyrannos.*" *Tijdschrift voor Geschiedenis* 84 (1971): 510–25.

Vitoria, Francisco de. "Relection on Civil Power" [*De potestate civili*]. In *Political Writings.* Ed. Anthony Pagden and Jeremy Lawrence. Cambridge: Cambridge University Press, 1991.

Waddington, A. "La France et les Protestants Allemands sous Charles IX et Henri III: Hubert Languet et Gaspard de Schomberg." *Révue Historique* 42 (1890): 241–77.

Waldron, Jeremy. *Law and Disagreement.* Oxford: Oxford University Press, 1999.

Waldron, Jeremy. "Constitutionalism – A Skeptical View." In *Contemporary Debates in Political Philosophy.* Ed. Thomas Christiano and John Christman. Malden, MA: Wiley-Blackwell, 2009.

Walker, Neil. *Sovereignty in Transition.* Oxford: Hart, 2003.

Walzer, Michael. *Revolution of the Saints: A Study in the Origins of Radical Politics.* Cambridge: Harvard University Press, 1965.

Watson, Alan. "Roman Private Law and the *Leges Regiae.*" In *Legal Origins and Legal Change.* London: Hambledon Press, 1991.

Weill, Georges. *Les Théories sur le Pouvoir Royal en France Pendant les Guerres de Religion*. New York: Burt Franklin, 1967.

Weinert, Matthew. *Democratic Sovereignty: Authority, Legitimacy, and State in a Globalizing Age*. New York: UCL Press, 2007.

Weston, Corinne Comstock. *English Constitutional Theory and the House of Lords, 1556–1832*. New York: Columbia University Press, 1965.

Weston, Corinne Comstock and Janelle Greenberg. *Subjects and Sovereigns: The Grand Controversy over Legal Sovereignty in Stuart England*. Cambridge: Cambridge University Press, 1981.

Wheeler, Harvey. "The Constitutional Ideas of Francis Bacon." *Political Research Quarterly* 9 (1956): 927–36.

Whelan, Frederick. "Democratic Theory and the Boundary Problem." *Nomos 25: Liberal Democracy*. Ed. J. Roland Pennock and John Chapman. New York: New York University Press, 1983.

Whitman, James. *The Legacy of Roman Law in the German Romantic Era*. Princeton: Princeton University Press, 1990.

Wieacker, Franz. *A History of Private Law in Europe*. Trans. Tony Weir. Oxford: Clarendon Press, 1995.

Wijffels, Alain. "Le Disputazioni di Alberico Gentili sul Diritto Pubblico." *Alberico Gentili: La Salvaguardia Dei Beni Culturali Nel Diritto Internazionale*. Milan: Giuffrè, 2008.

Wilentz, Sean. *The Rise of American Democracy: Jefferson to Lincoln*. New York: W.W. Norton, 2006.

Wilks, Michael. *The Problem of Sovereignty in the Later Middle Ages*. Cambridge: Cambridge University Press, 1963.

Wilson, Peter. "Still a Monstrosity? Some Reflections on Early Modern German Statehood." *Historical Journal* 49 (2006): 565–76.

Woolf, C.N.S. *Bartolus of Sassoferrato: His Position in the History of Medieval Political Thought*. Cambridge: Cambridge University Press, 1913.

Wootton, David. "Leveller Democracy and the Puritan Revolution." In *Cambridge History of Political Thought*. Ed. J.H. Burns and Mark Goldie. Cambridge: Cambridge University Press, 1991.

Wormuth, Francis. *Origins of Modern Constitutionalism*. New York: Harper, 1949.

Zaller, Robert. "Henry Parker and the Regiment of True Government." *Proceedings of the American Philosophical Society* 135 (1991): 255–85.

Zimmermann, Reinhard. "Foreword" to Franz Wieacker, *A History of Private Law in Europe*. Trans. Tony Weir. Oxford: Clarendon Press, 1995.

Zimmermann, Reinhard. *The Law of Obligations: The Roman Foundations of the Civilian Tradition*. Oxford: Clarendon Press, 1996.

Zmora, Hillary. *State and Nobility in Early Modern Germany: The Knightly Feud in Franconia, 1440–1567*. Cambridge: Cambridge University Press, 1997.

Zouch, Richard. *Elementa Iurisprudentiae Definitionibus*. Oxford: Lichfield, 1636.

Index